THE PRACTICAL WOODWORKER

A COMPLETE GUIDE TO THE ART
AND PRACTICE OF WOODWORKING

Written and Illustrated by Experts

and Edited by

BERNARD E. JONES

Editor of "Work," "The Amateur Mechanic," etc.

VOLUME I

Copyright © 2013 Read Books Ltd.
This book is copyright and may not be
reproduced or copied in any way without
the express permission of the publisher in writing

British Library Cataloguing-in-Publication Data
A catalogue record for this book is available from the
British Library

Woodworking

Woodworking is the process of making items from wood. Along with stone, mud and animal parts, wood was one of the first materials worked by early humans. There are incredibly early examples of woodwork, evidenced in Mousterian stone tools used by Neanderthal man, which demonstrate our affinity with the wooden medium. In fact, the very development of civilisation is linked to the advancement of increasingly greater degrees of skill in working with these materials.

Examples of Bronze Age wood-carving include tree trunks worked into coffins from northern Germany and Denmark and wooden folding-chairs. The site of Fellbach-Schmieden in Germany has provided fine examples of wooden animal statues from the Iron Age. Woodworking is depicted in many ancient Egyptian drawings, and a considerable amount of ancient Egyptian furniture (such as stools, chairs, tables, beds, chests) has been preserved in tombs. The inner coffins found in the tombs were also made of wood. The metal used by the Egyptians for woodworking tools was originally copper and eventually, after 2000 BC, bronze - as ironworking was unknown until much later. Historically, woodworkers relied upon the woods native to their region, until transportation and trade innovations made more exotic woods available to the craftsman.

Today, often as a contemporary artistic and 'craft' medium, wood is used both in traditional and modern styles; an excellent material for delicate as well as forceful artworks. Wood is used in forms of sculpture, trade, and decoration including chip carving, wood burning, and marquetry, offering a fascination, beauty, and complexity in the grain that often shows even when the medium is painted. It is in some ways easier to shape than harder substances, but an artist or craftsman must develop specific skills to carve it properly. 'Wood carving' is really an entire genre itself, and involves cutting wood generally with a knife in one hand, or a chisel by two hands - or, with one hand on a chisel and one hand on a mallet. The phrase may also refer to the finished product, from individual sculptures to hand-worked mouldings composing part of a tracery.

The making of sculpture in wood has been extremely widely practiced but survives much less well than the other main materials such as stone and bronze, as it is vulnerable to decay, insect damage, and fire. It therefore forms an important hidden element in the arts and crafts history of many cultures. Outdoor wood sculptures do not last long in most parts of the world, so we have little idea how the totem pole tradition developed. Many of the most important sculptures of China and Japan in particular are in wood, and the great majority of African sculptures and that of Oceania also use this medium. There are various forms of carving which can be utilised; 'chip carving' (a style of carving in which knives or chisels are used to remove small chips of the material), 'relief carving' (where figures are carved in a flat panel of wood), 'Scandinavian flat-plane' (where figures are carved in large flat planes, created primarily using a carving knife - and rarely rounded or sanded afterwards) and 'whittling' (simply carving shapes using just a knife). Each of these techniques will need slightly varying tools, but broadly speaking, a specialised 'carving knife' is essential, alongside a 'gouge' (a tool with a curved cutting edge used in a variety of forms and sizes for carving hollows, rounds and sweeping curves), a 'chisel' and a 'coping saw' (a small saw, used to cut off chunks of wood at once).

Wood turning is another common form of woodworking, used to create wooden objects on a lathe. Woodturning differs from most other forms of woodworking in that the wood is moving while a stationary tool is used to cut and shape it. There are two distinct methods of turning wood: 'spindle turning' and 'bowl' or 'faceplate turning'. Their key difference is in the orientation of the wood grain, relative to the axis of the lathe. This variation in orientation changes the tools and techniques used. In spindle turning, the grain runs lengthways along the lathe bed, as if a log was mounted in the lathe. Grain is thus always perpendicular to the direction of rotation under the tool. In bowl turning, the grain runs at right angles to the axis, as if a plank were mounted across the chuck. When a bowl blank rotates, the angle that the grain makes with the cutting tool continually changes between the easy cuts of lengthways and downwards across the grain to two places per rotation where the tool is cutting across the grain and even upwards across it. This varying grain angle limits some of the tools that may be used and requires additional skill in order to cope with it.

The origin of woodturning dates to around 1300 BC when the Egyptians first developed a two-person lathe. One person would turn the wood with a rope while the other used a sharp tool to cut shapes in the wood. The Romans improved the Egyptian design with the addition of a turning bow. Early bow lathes were also developed and used in Germany, France and Britain. In the Middle Ages a pedal replaced hand-operated turning, freeing both the craftsman's hands to hold the woodturning tools. The pedal was usually connected to a pole, often a straight-grained sapling. The system today is called the 'spring pole' lathe. Alternatively, a two-person lathe, called a 'great lathe', allowed a piece to turn continuously (like today's power lathes). A master would cut the wood while an apprentice turned the crank.

As an interesting aside, the term 'bodger' stems from pole lathe turners who used to make chair legs and spindles. A bodger would typically purchase all the trees on a plot of land, set up camp on the plot, and then fell the trees and turn the wood. The spindles and legs that were produced were sold in bulk, for pence per dozen. The bodger's job was considered unfinished because he only made component parts. The term now describes a person who leaves a job unfinished, or does it badly. This could not be more different from perceptions of modern carpentry; a highly skilled trade in which work involves the construction of buildings, ships, timber bridges and concrete framework. The word 'carpenter' is the English rendering of the Old French word *carpentier* (later, *charpentier*) which is derived from the Latin *carpentrius;* '(maker) of a carriage.' Carpenters traditionally worked with natural wood and did the rougher work such as framing, but today many other materials are also used and sometimes the finer trades of cabinet-making and furniture building are considered carpentry.

As is evident from this brief historical and practical overview of woodwork, it is an incredibly varied and exciting genre of arts and crafts; an ancient tradition still relevant in the modern day. Woodworkers range from hobbyists, individuals operating from the home environment, to artisan professionals with specialist workshops, and eventually large-scale factory operations. We hope the reader is inspired by this book to create some woodwork of their own.

CONTENTS

	PAGE
LIST OF THE CHIEF CONTRIBUTORS	vii
THE SCOPE AND OBJECT OF THIS WORK (9 *Illustrations*)	1
THE WORKSHOP AND ITS EQUIPMENT (53 *Illustrations*)	9
TOOLS FOR MEASURING AND MARKING (88 *Illustrations*)	27
SAWS AND SAWING (77 *Illustrations*)	46
HAMMERS AND MALLETS (8 *Illustrations*)	63
CHISELS AND GOUGES (26 *Illustrations*)	66
GRINDING AND SHARPENING TOOLS (32 *Illustrations*)	73
THE PLANE (68 *Illustrations*)	84
PLANING (83 *Illustrations*)	100
THE SCRAPER (21 *Illustrations*)	109
TIMBER : ITS GROWTH AND PROPERTIES (14 *Illustrations*)	114
GLUE AND GLUING (15 *Illustrations*)	135
NAILING, SCREWING AND BOLTING (59 *Illustrations*)	142
CHAMFERING, BEVELLING AND ROUNDING (28 *Illustrations*)	158
REBATING (17 *Illustrations*)	165
GROOVING, PLOUGHING AND TONGUEING (11 *Illustrations*)	171
SHOOTING AND MITRE CUTTING (33 *Illustrations*)	177
TIMBER : CONVERSION AND SEASONING (21 *Illustrations*)	185
RASPS, FILES AND GLASSPAPER (14 *Illustrations*)	195
MAKING MOULDINGS (14 *Illustrations*)	200
THE STANLEY "FIFTY-FIVE" PLANE (83 *Illustrations*)	204
HALVED, LAPPED, NOTCHED AND HOUSED JOINTS (52 *Illustrations*)	218
EDGE AND ANGLE JOINTS (48 *Illustrations*)	230

CONTENTS

	PAGE
DOWELLED JOINTS (35 *Illustrations*)	239
MORTISE AND TENON JOINTS (95 *Illustrations*)	247
SCARFING AND OTHER JOINTS (33 *Illustrations*)	265
MITRE JOINTS (5 *Illustrations*)	272
PLAIN DOVETAIL JOINTS (30 *Illustrations*)	274
LAP AND SECRET DOVETAIL JOINTS (29 *Illustrations*)	281
LEDGES AND CLAMPS (9 *Illustrations*)	288
BORING TOOLS AND THEIR USES (77 *Illustrations*)	291
A FEW ELEMENTARY EXAMPLES (51 *Illustrations*)	308
BOX AND PACKING CASE CONSTRUCTION (11 *Illustrations*)	320
DRAWING AND OTHER BOARDS (32 *Illustrations*)	326
PLAIN TABLES (43 *Illustrations*)	337
DOMESTIC WOODWARE (103 *Illustrations*)	349
DOMESTIC RACKS (28 *Illustrations*)	371
PIGEON COTE AND RABBIT HUTCHES (44 *Illustrations*)	379
DOG KENNELS (18 *Illustrations*)	392
BEEHIVE AND FITTINGS (25 *Illustrations*)	399
STEPS AND LADDERS (40 *Illustrations*)	407

List of the Chief Contributors

H. ALEXANDER	Machine Woodworking
I. ATKINSON	Toys, etc.
A.M.	Upholstery
W. A. C. BALL	Examples
J. D. BATES	Metal Fittings
R. V. BOUGHTON	Drawing
G. S. BOULGER	Woods and Timber
JOHN BOVINGDON	Veneering and Examples
R. S. BOWERS	Examples
C. W. D. BOXALL	Equipment, Examples, etc.
SYDNEY CAMM	Aeroplane Woodworking
A. CLAYDON	Examples, etc.
T. W. CORKHILL	Joint Making, Construction, etc
J. L. DEVONSHIRE	Examples
G. ELDRIDGE	Examples
H. E. V. GILLHAM	Examples
P. R. GREEN	Examples
R. GREENHALGH	Tools, Processes, etc.
T. HOLT	Joint Making
W. J. HORNER	Turning, Pattern Making, etc.
H. JARVIS	Joint Making, etc.
F. W. LOASBY	Billiard-table Making
R. H. LOMAS	Barrow Making
W. J. MOSELEY	Wood Finishing
G. F. RHEAD	Inlaying, etc.
W. S. ROGERS	Picture Framing, etc.
C. F. SHACKLETON	Examples
G. STRETHILL-SMITH	Examples
C. S. TAYLOR	Upholstery, etc.
H. TURNER	Wood Carving
C. E. A. WYATT	Examples

THE
PRACTICAL WOODWORKER

The Scope and Object of this Work

"THE PRACTICAL WOODWORKER" is believed to be the most comprehensive and exhaustive book yet published on practical woodworking. And yet it does not attempt to give every detail of every aspect of woodwork, because only a library of books could do that. But it does attempt so to instruct the reader as to make it possible for any person, even for one who has never even seen a plane or driven a nail, to be able from this book alone to make any ordinary piece of woodwork by sound craftsman-like methods. The book assumes scarcely

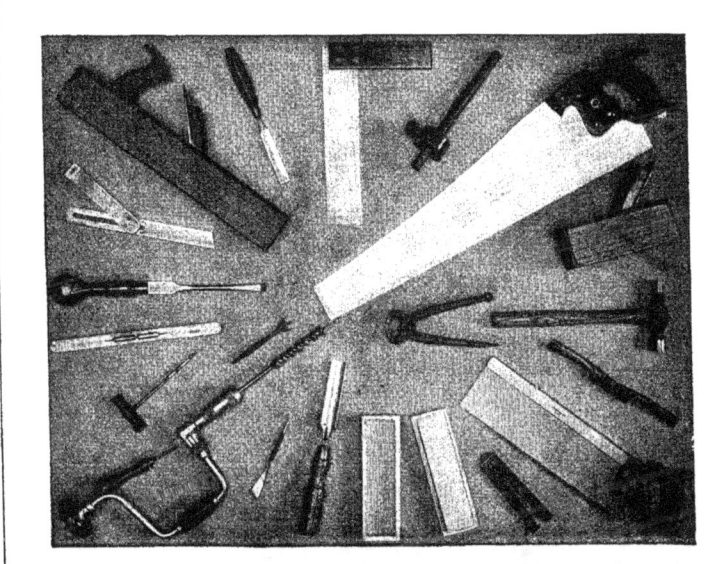

A Group of the Woodworker's Essential Tools

THE PRACTICAL WOODWORKER

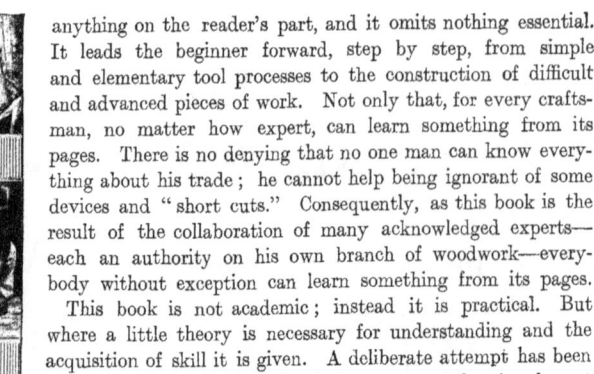

anything on the reader's part, and it omits nothing essential. It leads the beginner forward, step by step, from simple and elementary tool processes to the construction of difficult and advanced pieces of work. Not only that, for every craftsman, no matter how expert, can learn something from its pages. There is no denying that no one man can know everything about his trade; he cannot help being ignorant of some devices and "short cuts." Consequently, as this book is the result of the collaboration of many acknowledged experts—each an authority on his own branch of woodwork—everybody without exception can learn something from its pages.

This book is not academic; instead it is practical. But where a little theory is necessary for understanding and the acquisition of skill it is given. A deliberate attempt has been made to present in crisp, simple language and by the clearest of photographs and working drawings the essentials of skilled woodworking.

Little can be done in woodworking without a bench. If desired, a bench can be converted from an old table. Among the benches described throughout the book are some with racks, vices, bench stops, drawers, etc. Many craftsmen build a timber workshop to work in. Various types of workshops are shown in working drawings, and full instructions on their erection are given; and to make the workshop complete, grindstones, nail boxes, glue pots, steam-bending apparatus, saw stools and other workshop appliances and fittings are described in a later chapter. Instruments for marking and setting out are fully described and illustrated.

The reader will at once note that this book develops the subject progressively. The woodworker must understand and know how to select and purchase his tools; much money can easily be wasted in buying unsuitable or faulty ones. The uses and necessity of tools and the faults to be looked for and latest improvements to be obtained in them are therefore

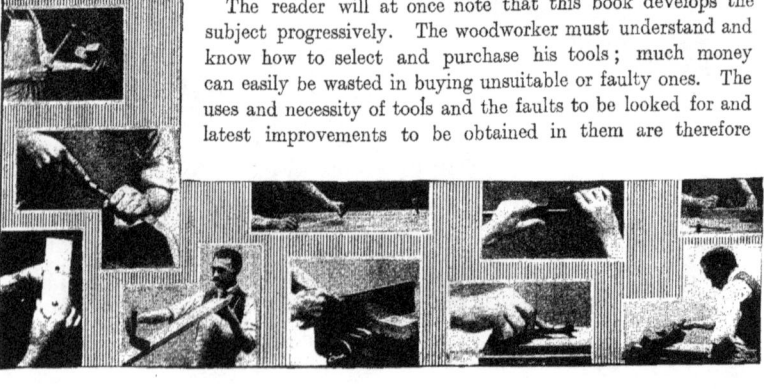

THE SCOPE AND OBJECT OF THIS WORK

explained and illustrated. Freak tools and amateur combination tools are not usually welcomed by the craftsman; but where a new tool or an improvement of an old one is on the market it is discussed, and, if thought an advantage, it is recommended. Many new tools may appear at first sight to be excellent contrivances, but after prolonged trial they are found not to be so useful as they look; on the other hand, it must be confessed that workmen are often slow in adopting new tools that undoubtedly make for quicker, easier or better work. Many really good tools in use in America are seldom, if ever, seen in Great Britain, and a number of these will be referred to, as in many cases they could be adopted with advantage.

Tools are treated very fully in this book, but the reader will remember that most jobs require only a quarter of the number described, and the amateur or apprentice need get only a few of them to begin with; his kit can be added to as his skill increases or as more difficult or specialised jobs come his way.

A formidable obstacle to the amateur or apprentice is the getting of his tools into good order and the keeping of them in perfect working condition. Edge tools, as chisels and planes, are not in good order when purchased new, and have to be sharpened and adjusted. Even skilled workmen often fight shy of sharpening their own saws. The upkeep, adjustment, sharpening, and grinding of every kind of woodworking tool is gone into thoroughly in this book with the determination to make every operation easy of attainment even by the novice. There is much truth in the saying "a workman is known by his tools," and sharp, correctly adjusted tools are not only necessary for the performance of good work, but they make work a pleasure instead of a harassing drudgery.

After understanding the shapes and uses of tools and

A Group of Examples which will be shown in detail in later pages

THE SCOPE AND OBJECT OF THIS WORK

after buying a few, the next thing is to learn how to hold and use them—a subject that provides a *motif* for the illustrations on pages 2 and 3. Tool operations and processes of woodworking are demonstrated clearly by many scores of photographs showing expert craftsmen at work. These photographs (for which see many later pages) are especial features of the book, and no trouble has been spared in producing them to make them "tell their story" in a way that cannot be misunderstood. These "how-to-do-it" pictures are, it is believed, unique in their thoroughness, clearness and detail, and they have been especially taken and posed for by the Editor and his Assistants.

The next step in woodworking is obviously the making of joints. Scores of these, from all branches of woodwork, are illustrated in complete detail and practical information given on making them. Dovetailing, in particular, is dealt with simply and exhaustively. Proficiency in this branch of woodworking is the hall-mark of the skilled craftsman, and that proficiency will be easily gained by anyone who carefully follows the lucid explanations presented later in the book and quietly practises the advice given him.

Before any piece of work is begun it has usually to be designed (by drawing out on paper), and later, for workshop use, the drawing has to be set out, full size, or, at any rate, to a large scale, on boards. These two processes are dealt with in a chapter on drawing for woodworkers. Setting-out is

A Typical Woodworking Shop

an indispensable process in modern woodworking; it gives speed and helps to accuracy and the avoidance of mistakes.

Jacobean Bureau

And it is a subject that can be simply explained, being merely a workshop adaptation of ordinary projection.

We now come to the construction of the actual woodwork examples, many of which are illustrated on a very small scale on pages 4 and 7. Some of these, as seats, steps, simple doors, tables, etc., are easily made, and do not require very accurate work or the use of many tools. Others, as bookcases, writing desks, sideboards, etc., require more care and skill, but one and all can be made, from sawing the timber to applying the polish, by anyone who will follow the instructions given in this book. And these examples will not be made anyhow, but with the best finish and by the best methods known to the skilled workman if the reader will but do as he is taught.

The book touches on every aspect of woodworking, but some sections have advisably not been treated as fully as others; furniture making, being perhaps the most useful section to the average woodworker, has been made the subject of hundreds of examples, whereas sections like foundry pattern making and aeroplane woodwork are briefer, although adequate, in their treatment. A glance at the table of contents will show the wide scope of the book.

Special attention is given to the fixing of locks, hinges and other metal fittings, many of which require much skill in their fitting and adjusting and call for the use of special tools.

Moulding, mitre cutting, picture framing, gluing, tool making and toy making are explained. Timber—its

Loose-seat-Armchair in Hepplewhite Style

varieties, measurement, defects, characteristics, stock sizes and purchasing—is fully described with a view to enabling

A further Group of Examples which will be shown in detail in later pages

the reader to select the best timber for any job and to purchase and use it economically.

In large workshops woodworking machines are much used at the present time, but notwithstanding this fact every good craftsman requires to know how to use the hand tools. Though machines will plane and saw and mortise, the workman still often does these operations by hand even in a machine shop, and his skill as a craftsman depends mostly on an expert knowledge of the processes dealt with in this book. But to show the relation of machine work to hand work and to make this treatise complete for the professional woodworker a chapter on wood-working machines is included towards the end of the book.

In order to make the book complete and enable the reader to carry his work through from the beginning right to the finished article, chapters are included on inlaying, carving, turning, upholstering, fuming, polishing, painting, enamelling, varnishing, etc.

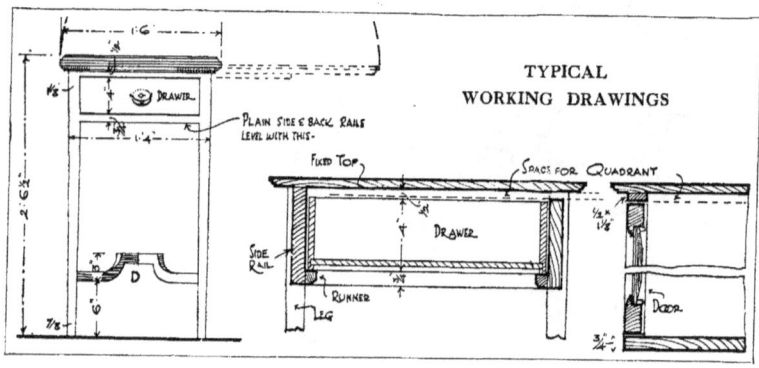

TYPICAL WORKING DRAWINGS

The Workshop and its Equipment

Arrangement of Small Workshop.— The workshop at home is generally a spare room, maybe a surplus bedroom or a room in the basement, but failing the necessary accommodation in the house, a small shed is often erected, as will be described on later pages.

A general view of a room equipped as a small workshop is presented by Fig. 1. The two windows shown help to make a well-lighted and ideal workshop. Fig. 2 is a plan of a similar room measuring about 12 ft. by 9 ft.

In cases where it would be more desirable and convenient to have a workshop erected in wood the same plan would serve, the wall thickness, of course, being less, and the dimensions of the workshop being modified to suit requirements. A specially built workshop could have a skylight.

Fig. 1.—Typical Small Workshop

Lighting the Workshop.—Windows facing north or east are usually preferred, but where this scheme is rigidly carried out to the exclusion of other windows the workshop is very cheerless, and such a system should therefore be avoided when possible. Where a workshop has skylights, these should be fitted with blinds so that the direct rays of the sun may be kept off the work or the operator. Artificial lighting may be by electricity, gas, acetylene, or oil, the first-named being the best and the last the worst. The light should be so arranged that the worker faces the light more or less, and therefore does not cast a shadow on his work.

BENCHES

Suitable Timber.—A common form of bench is shown in Figs. 3 to 9, and for general purposes is best constructed of red or white deal throughout. The advantage of a soft wood top is that, although more readily damaged than one of hardwood, it can be easily trued up providing that it is sufficiently thick for the purpose. The type of bench shown is designed for heavier and perhaps rougher work than those about to be described. The benches, shown by Figs. 10 to 24 should preferably be built of hardwood with the exception of the wellboard which may be of deal. Suitable hardwoods are beech and sycamore and even birch. The legs, rails and other parts of the frame may also be of hardwood, although good red or white deal would be found quite suitable both in strength and durability for these parts. If hardwood is used, some of the scantlings

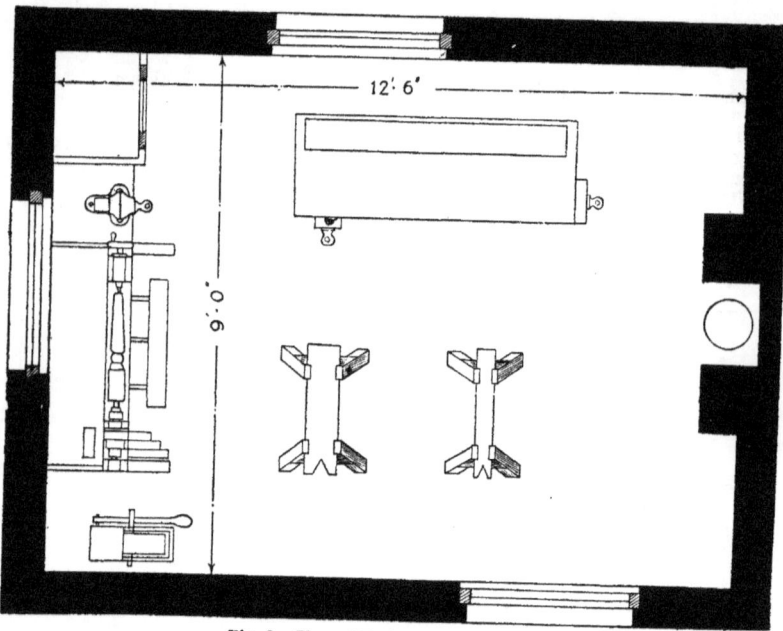

Fig. 2.—Plan of Typical Small Workshop

Fig. 3

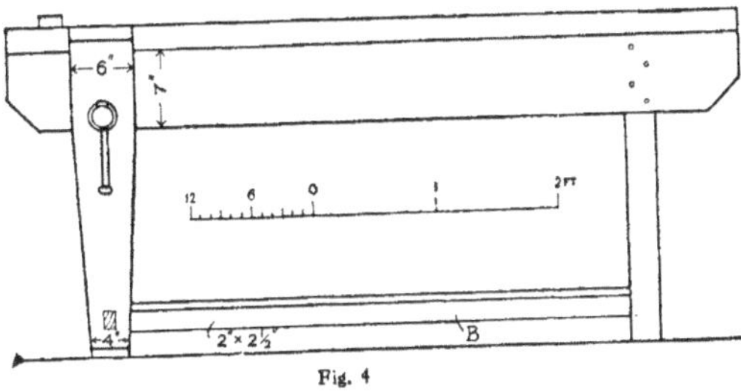

Fig. 4

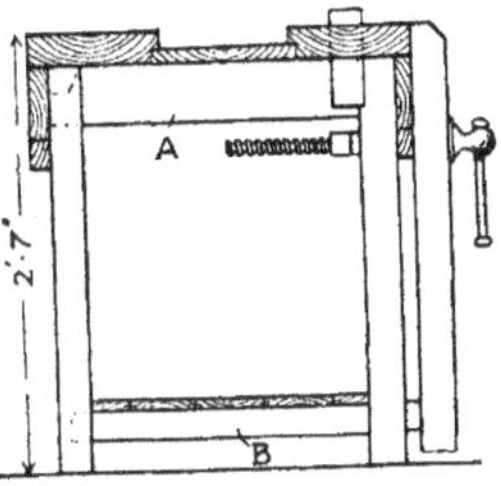

Fig. 6

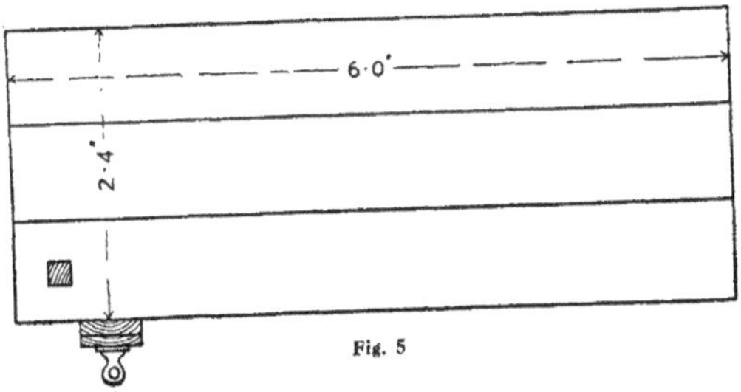

Fig. 5

Figs. 3 to 6.—Perspective View and Elevations and Plan of a Common Type of Bench — Trough-top Bench with Leg Vice

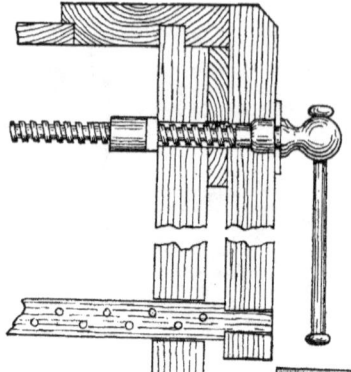

Fig. 7.—Method of Fitting Iron Bench Screw

platform (*see* Figs. 3 to 9, already referred to) is fitted with the " Dolly " form of vice, a leg vice of which the cheek is vertical and has a steel screw with box and runner below with pinholes and iron pin for adjustment. The top is formed of two 9 in. by 2 in. deal boards, the lower inner edges of which are rebated to receive a board 11 in. by 1 in. which forms the well or trough. Three of the legs are made of 3 in. by 2½ in. stuff, but the leg to which the vice is attached is stouter—4 in. by 2½ in. It is very important that this leg should have a tenon at the upper end fitting into a mortise made in the underside of the top, as illustrated in Fig. 8, so that when work could be less in size than those shown in the illustration.

A Common Type of Bench.—The common form of bench provided with a

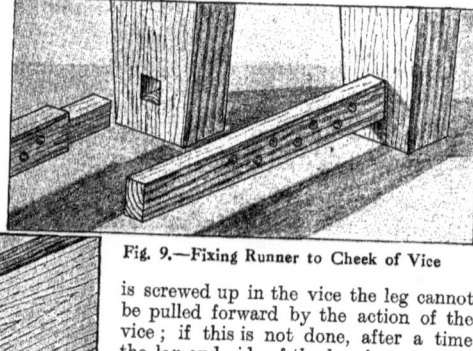

Fig. 9.—Fixing Runner to Cheek of Vice

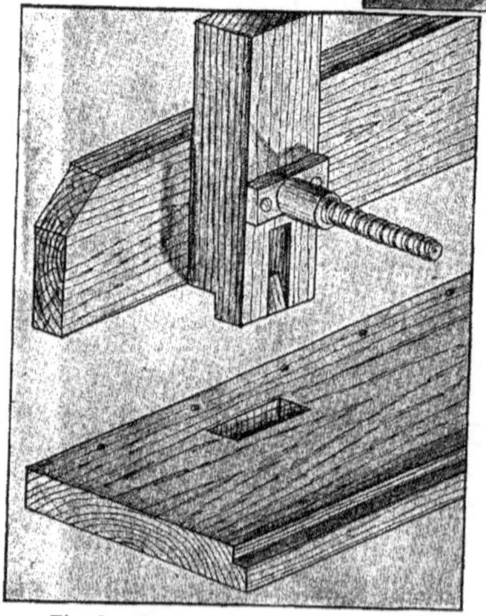

is screwed up in the vice the leg cannot be pulled forward by the action of the vice; if this is not done, after a time the leg and side of the bench are gradually forced forward, even when the top is strongly screwed to the side, so causing the latter to split. The top ends of the legs should be mortised and haunched as shown in Fig. 8 to receive the bearers (A, Fig. 6). The lower ends of the legs should be connected to the rails by ordinary stub-mortise and tenon joints, and the platform should be made of ¾ in. grooved and tongued boarding, machine-prepared floor-boarding being suitable for this purpose. The construction of the bottom of the runner and cheek will be clearly understood from Fig. 9. An enlarged sectional detail of the arrangement for fitting and connecting the iron screw is given by Fig. 7 on this page.

Fig. 8.—Construction of Top of Leg

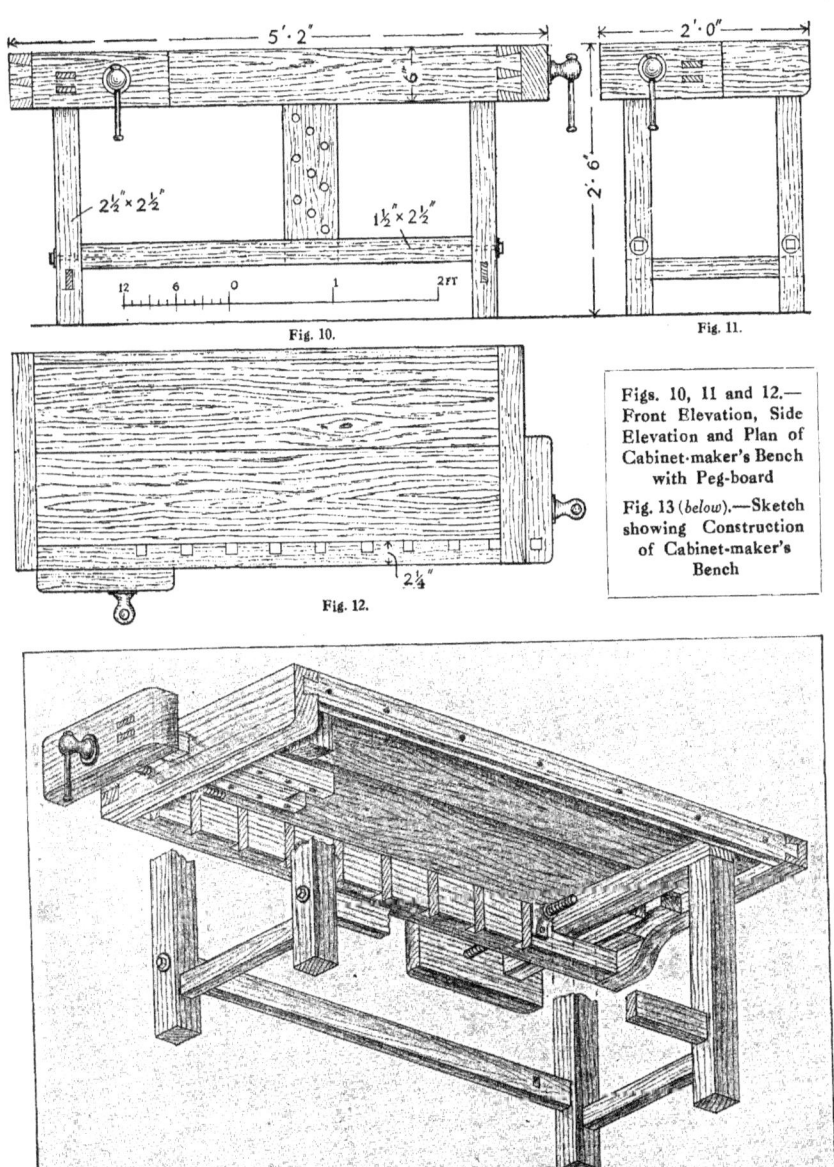

Fig. 10.

Fig. 11.

Fig. 12.

Figs. 10, 11 and 12.—Front Elevation, Side Elevation and Plan of Cabinet-maker's Bench with Peg-board

Fig. 13 (*below*).—Sketch showing Construction of Cabinet-maker's Bench

Fig. 13.

Fig. 14.—Sketch of Cabinet-maker's Bench with Tool Drawer

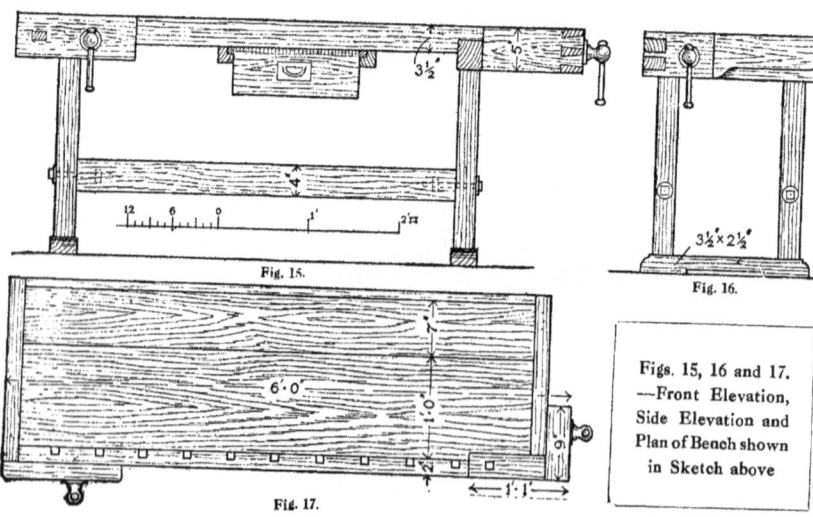

Figs. 15, 16 and 17.—Front Elevation, Side Elevation and Plan of Bench shown in Sketch above

THE WORKSHOP AND ITS EQUIPMENT

Cabinet-maker's Bench.—One form of cabinet-maker's bench is illustrated by Figs. 10 to 13. The top is constructed as follows: The two end pieces and the front cheek (which has the slots made in it for the stop) are dovetailed together at the angles, as shown in Figs. 10 to 13. The back piece is 1 in. thick and is lap-dovetailed into the end pieces, as shown at Fig. 13. The planing board and wellboard of the top are rebated together and their ends tongued into grooves made in the end pieces. The front cheek, after being notched for the stops, is glued and screwed to the planing board. The cross rails are connected to the legs by stubmortise and tenon joints and fixed wedged. If desired, as an alternative arrangement, the tenons could go right through and be pinned. The longitudinal rails have short stub tenons and are additionally secured by a bolt and nut, the latter being inserted in a mortise made in the rail, as clearly shown in Fig. 10. This method makes a very sound job, but, if desired, the old method of making a long tenon pass through the mortise and securing with a key wedge may be adopted.

A peg board for holding long pieces of timber for planing is shown fixed to the front of the bench (see Fig. 10). When a long piece of board is screwed up in the vice at one end, the other end is liable to drop when the pressure of the plane is applied, and to keep this end up a peg is put in one of the holes shown and the board rested on it. A number of holes are necessary to accommodate various widths of work.

Another example of a cabinet-maker's bench is shown in Figs. 14 to 18. It is fitted with an end vice for cramping up and holding work. The construction is generally similar to the preceding bench, but different in one or two details. The peg board is omitted, but a drawer for tools is shown. On the sides of the drawer are screwed small fillets which slide in grooved runners screwed to the underside of the bench. The legs are supported on base pieces which also act as end rails.

Portable Bench.—Figs. 19 to 23 are

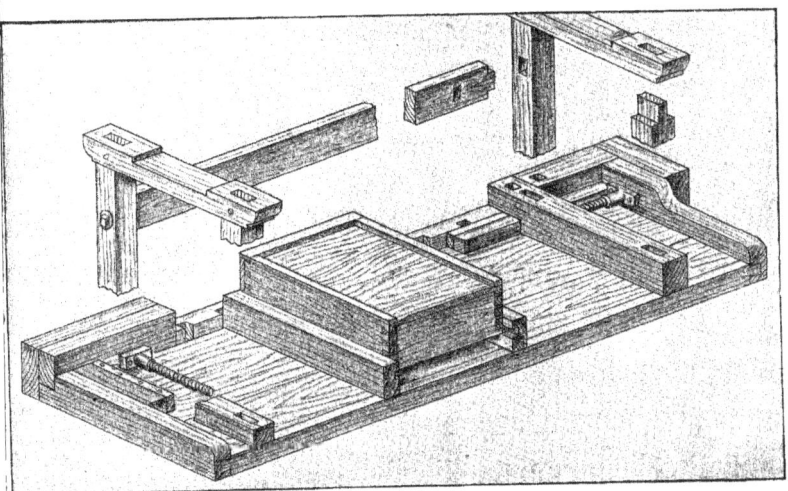

Fig. 18.—Sketch showing Construction of the Bench illustrated on preceding page

illustrations of a small portable bench which will be found very suitable where the available. The top consists of a planing or working board and a well. Sizes for general purposes are figured on the illustrations. Two ledgers are screwed to the underside of the top, and to these the top rails of the leg framings are attached with strong 3-in. butt hinges. The drawings clearly show the construction of the leg framing. A block of wood is screwed to the top; this has a hole bored through it, as have also the upper ends of the struts, and thus three parts can be held firmly together by a bolt and nut, a wing or butterfly nut

Fig. 19.—Sketch of Portable Bench

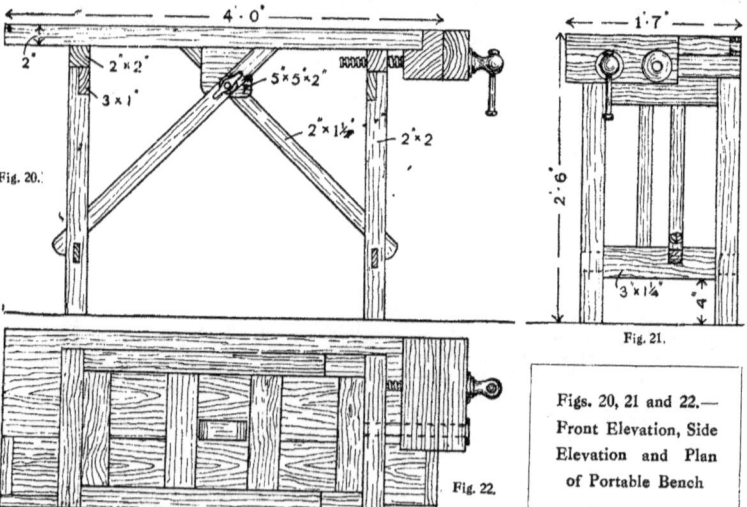

Fig. 22.

Figs. 20, 21 and 22.—Front Elevation, Side Elevation and Plan of Portable Bench

use of a bench is only occasionally required and a proper workshop is not available, being the most convenient. The lower ends of the struts are notched over the

THE WORKSHOP AND ITS EQUIPMENT

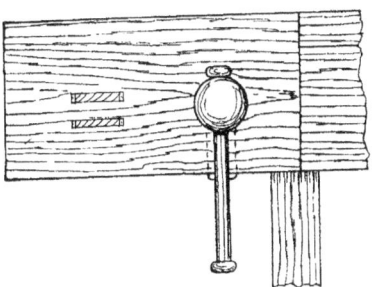
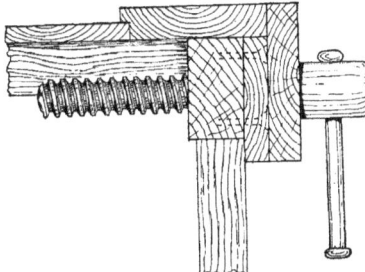

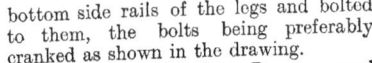

Figs. 24, 25 and 26.—Front Elevation, Vertical Section and Plan Looking Up, showing Method of Fitting a Wooden Vice. (See Fig. 27.)

bottom side rails of the legs and bolted to them, the bolts being preferably cranked as shown in the drawing.

Bench Fitted with Drawer and Cupboard.—The bench, shown by Fig. 28, is an extremely handy form, provided with three drawers and a cupboard. One or two of the drawers can be fitted up to hold chisels, gouges, bits and other of the smaller tools. The bottom drawer can be made to contain hollows, rounds, bead planes, metal planes and other of the small planes.—The cupboard can be fitted with shelves, so as to accommodate jack plane, trying plane, saws and other of the larger tools.

If the bench is made a fair size, say

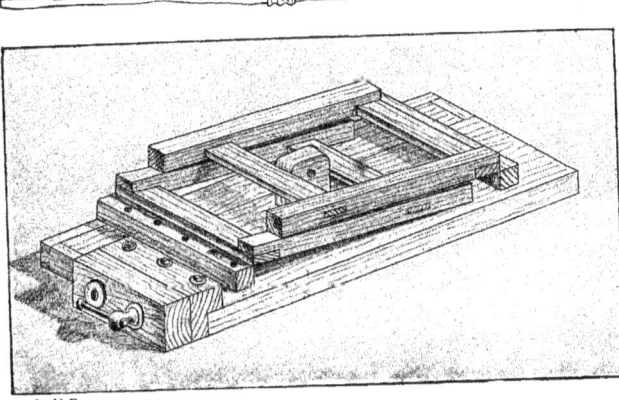

Fig. 23.—View of Underside of Portable Bench, showing Legs Folded Up. (For details, see preceding page)

about 5 ft. 6 in. long and 2 ft. 3 in. wide, it will contain all the tools for ordinary woodworker. The vice can be fixed to the underside of the top with two or three bolts and wing nuts, and consequently can be quickly detached.

Bench Vices.—The vice illustrated by Figs. 24 to 27 represents one constructed almost entirely of wood, the screw and nut usually being made of beechwood. The cheek and runner are best made of some kind of hardwood, all the other parts being of red and white deal. Formerly the

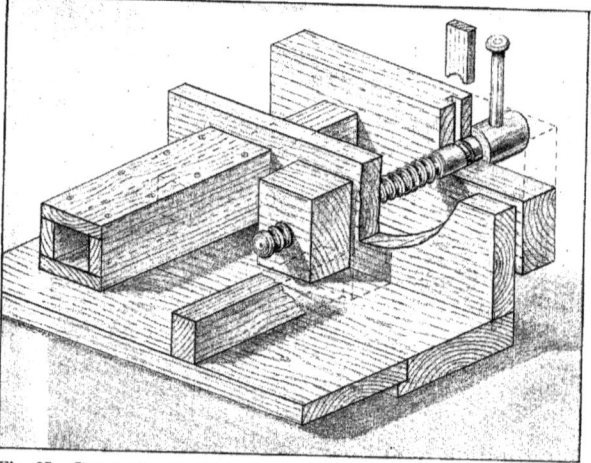

Fig. 27.—Sketch showing Method of Fitting Wooden Vice. (*See Figs.* 24 to 26)

requirements, without any tool chest, cupboard, or outside rack being necessary. This bench will be found especially useful and suitable for anyone who has not a proper workshop and has to make use of a room which, during part of the day, has to be employed for other purposes. By using a simple iron stop that can be screwed level with the top and a small iron vice as illustrated it is possible for the bench to form a piece of furniture when not in use by the wooden screw type of vice was more used than any other, but it has been super-

Fig. 28.—Sketch of Bench Fitted with Drawers and Cupboard

THE WORKSHOP AND ITS EQUIPMENT

seded since the introduction of metal screws and nuts (or boxes). The drawings fully and clearly show the construction. The sizes of the parts vary, of course, according to requirements. The screw and cheek are held together by means of a hardwood key which is inserted in a mortise made from the bottom edge of the cheek. The end of the key is hollowed so as to fit into the groove turned in the shank of the screw; this is shown in Fig. 27.

Fig. 29.—Vice with Steel Screw and Wooden Jaws

back of the cheek, holes being made to receive the bolt heads so that they sink a little below the surface. These are indicated at Fig. 30. The block is fixed to the top of the bench by three coach bolts. Bolts and nuts can be used, in which case the heads are sunk ⅜ in. below the surface of the top and pieces of wood fitted in the holes, glued and planed off flush with the top surface. This vice, if carefully made, will be found to work parallel, because of the strong connection be-

Fig. 30.—Detail of Vice (looking from Back)

The vice illustrated by Figs. 29 and 30 is an improvement on the one above described and illustrated. It is provided with a steel screw and nut and a runner is formed of a piece of strong ¾-in. to 1⅜-in. gas pipe or steam tubing, screwed at one end so as to fix ¦ into a 3-in. or 4-in. iron flange, in which four to six holes have been drilled and countersunk to receive stout screws. The flange may be more firmly fixed to the cheek by using range screws (or bolts) and securing with a nut at the

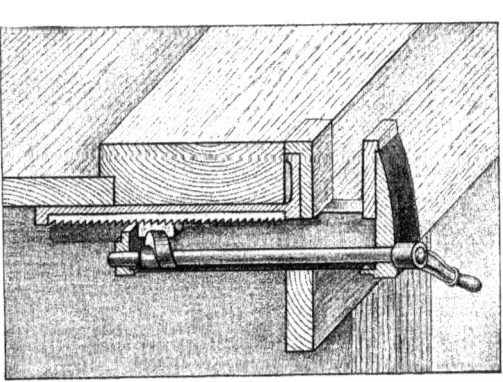

Fig. 31.—Instantaneous-grip Vice

tween the runner and cheek. It is quite suitable for either a side vice or end vice.

THE PRACTICAL WOODWORKER

Instantaneous-grip Vice.—Fig. 31 shows a type of instantaneous-grip vice which has been much used for many years. It is very strong and serviceable, although much more expensive than home-constructed vices. The action is as follows: Upon raising the handle, the bar and screw cam is turned; the diameter of the latter gradually decreasing causes the semi-nut (which has a rack on its upper side) to lower and disengage from the long rack, whereupon the front jaw slide can

illustrations in later chapters show a different type of instantaneous-grip vice.

Fig. 33.—Improvised Vice for Small Work

Other Kinds of Vices.—For curved work a vice whose jaws stand above the level of the bench top is very useful, as shown in Fig. 32; it is made with two long cheeks and a runner at the bottom with holes and pins for adjustment, the

Fig. 32.—Useful Vice for Curved Work

be drawn out the desired distance; the work is then placed in position and the jaw pushed close to it. When the handle is pressed down, the cam raises the semi-nut in contact with the rack; and the further movement of the handle forces the jaw to the work by the screw action of the cam. The top edges of the jaw are kept below the surface of the planing plank about 1 in., this allowing of both of the jaws being lined with hardwood, which is secured to them by screws. This wood lining prevents the edges of the tools being damaged by coming into contact with the metal. Photographic

Fig. 34.—Cleat for Holding Boards whilst Planing, etc.

inner cheek being screwed to the side of the bench.

THE WORKSHOP AND ITS EQUIPMENT

Fig. 33 shows an improvised form of vice which will be found useful for holding small work and when planing the edges for the cheek to rest upon, and a piece of iron screwed on each side of the cheek will prevent the cheek from slipping side-

Fig. 35.—Clamp for Use on Table

Fig. 36.—Underside of Clamp

of boards and for similar operations. A long iron bolt is forged into a hook form at its head end as shown. A hole is bored through the cheek of the vice large enough for the shank of the bolt to work in freely. The side of the bench and leg are bored

ways. For tightening the work a hardwood wedge is driven between the vice cheek and the forked nut head. The bottom of the cheek can be adjusted by

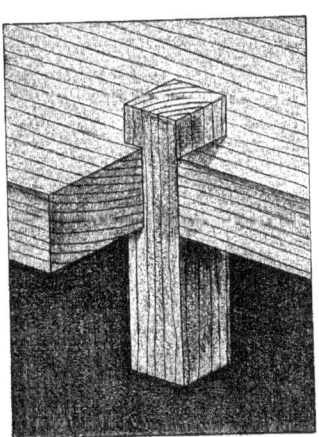

Fig. 37.—Ordinary Bench Stop

Fig. 38.—Wedge Bench Stop

so that the bolt passes through and is fastened at the back of the leg with a nut. A block is fastened to the leg of the bench

pieces of wood varying in width. Several wedges of different size will be found useful for different thicknesses of work.

22 THE PRACTICAL WOODWORKER

Figs. 39 and 40.—Vertical Section and Front Elevation of Adjustable Bench Stop. (*See Fig. 41 at foot of page*)

sunk so that it can be firmly secured to the board with a couple of stout screws. The board may be fixed to the table top by four hardwood buttons or clips and bolts with wing nuts, one of which is shown in Fig. 36.

Bench Stops.—The simplest form of bench stop is made by screwing a thin strip to the bench top as shown in Fig. 34. This form is especially useful when planing short wide boards, such as panels, etc.

Fig. 37 shows a simple form of stop which has probably been used more than any other kind. It is generally made from a piece of hardwood about 2 in. sq. fitting tightly into a mortise made through the top of the bench. To prevent splitting the top, care should be taken to make the breadth of the mortise the same as the stop. The two sides of the mortise having the end grain

Fig. 34 shows a cleat, which is a triangular-shaped piece of wood, screwed to the top edge of the bench; it will be found very useful for holding boards, etc., the edges of which are to be planed. This arrangement will hold the work fast as long as there

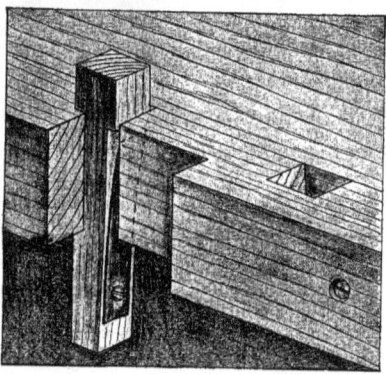

Fig. 42.—Spring Stop

is a pressure forward, but any back pressure will, of course, directly loosen the work.

In cases where it is not desirable or convenient to set up an ordinary bench and it is only required to do light work on a table, and without injury to it, the contrivance shown by Figs. 35 and 36 will be found convenient. A board about 9 in. wide and 2 in. thick and long enough to project about 3 in. at each end over the table top is required; a piece the same length and about 4 in. wide and 1½ in. thick is nailed or screwed to the board as indicated in the illustrations. Before fixing the edge piece, a strong G-cramp should be passed through a mortise made in it, the lower end of the cramp being fitted into a recess made in the underside of the planing board so that the surface of the metal is a little below that of the board. The lower end of the cramp should have been previously drilled and counter-

Fig. 41.—Sketch showing Adjustable Bench Stop

THE WORKSHOP AND ITS EQUIPMENT

Fig. 43.—Metal Stop

should fit tightly to the stop. The adjustment is made by simply striking the stop upwards or downwards with a mallet.

Fig. 38 is an improvement on the last-mentioned kind of stop. It is formed of a pair of wedges; to keep them together and allow them to slide, a slot is made in the front portion so that the shank of a round-headed screw can work freely in it, the screw holding firmly in the back wedge. A washer, as shown, will prevent the head of the screw from catching in the slot.

An adjustable stop that has proved most satisfactory for general use is shown by Figs. 39, 40 and 41. A slot is made in the side of the bench, so that a ½-in. bolt can work freely in it, the bolt passing through a block and the stop which have been bored to receive it. A wing nut (with a washer at the back) is fitted to the screwed end of the bolt.

Fig. 42 is a sectional view of a spring stop. This kind is largely used by cabinet-makers, and especially for benches with end vices, as by using two stops of this kind a piece of work can be firmly held between them and flat on the top of the bench. When holding work in this manner one stop is put in the bench top and the other in the end vice. The two stops are placed the proper distance apart and when the end screw is tightened the work is gripped between them.

Fig. 43 shows a cheap and effective form of metal stop. The view is given partly in section so as to show how the stop is fitted and fixed to the top of the bench. The stop piece, shown open and inclined, is raised or lowered by means of a screwdriver inserted in the head of the large screw. The general action will be clearly understood from the illustration.

Another good form of a metal adjustable stop, known as Morrill's pattern, is shown by Fig. 44. The view is given partly in section so as to show the fitting of the stop to the bench top, ready for screwing. The illustration clearly shows the construction of the stop.

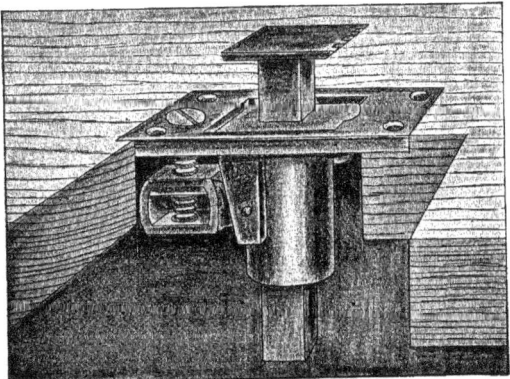

Fig. 44.—Metal Stop : Morrill's Pattern

THE PRACTICAL WOODWORKER

The disadvantages of metal stops are that they are liable to get choked with sawdust and chips of wood, and, secondly, tools are often driven against them and their edges damaged.

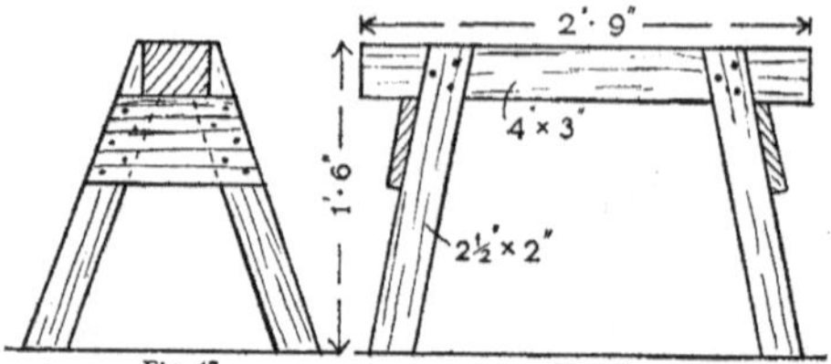

Figs. 45 and 46.—Front and End Elevations of Sawing Stool

SAWING AND OTHER STOOLS

Figs. 45 to 48 illustrate the ordinary strong form of stool which is very useful for sawing upon and for a great variety of other purposes. It is generally made of scantling, the legs being from 2 in. by 2 in. to 3 in. by 3 in. and the top 3 in. by 2 in. to 4 in. by 3 in. The legs should incline both ways as shown.

The upper ends of the legs of the stool should be cut as shown and the edges of the sides notched out to receive the legs, these being nailed or screwed to the top. Fig. 48 fully shows this construction.

The bracing piece at each end should be cut to fit and then nailed or screwed to the legs. The bottom ends of the legs should be scribed ("scribing" will be described in detail later), and then sawn to fit the floor. For general purposes red

Fig. 48.—Method of Fixing Legs of Sawing Stool

Fig. 47.—Sketch of Sawing Stool

or white deal will be found a quite suitable material for stools.

Fig. 49 shows a somewhat similar stool but having a much broader top in which a holdfast or other form of cramp can be fixed (*see also* Fig. 1 on an earlier page). This cramp will allow of broad material being held and more conveniently sawn off, and will also be found serviceable for many other purposes.

Mortising Stools.—The making of small mortises can usually be done at the bench, but when a number of mortises of large size have to be made through material 3 in. to 5 in. wide they are more conveniently and quickly worked by using a mortising-stool, the ordinary kind of which is shown by Fig. 50. As will be seen, the edges of the legs run up and

THE WORKSHOP AND ITS EQUIPMENT

project above the bed, forming "horns," and work placed on the bed between these can be held firmly if desired by pushing in a wedge, hand-tight, between the work and the horns. The size of the stool and sizes of materials will vary according to requirements. The legs may be from 2 in. to 3 in. thick and 7 in. to 11 in. wide; the bed may be 3 in. to 4 in. thick and 4 in. to 7 in. broad. The length may vary from 3 ft. to 5 ft.; height to top of bed about 1 ft. 6 in.

Stool for Small Work.—Fig. 51 shows a light and handy form of stool suitable for small work. It can be made of boarding ¾ in. to 1¼ in. thick and 6 in. to 9 in. wide. To make it rigid, a block is fixed in each inner angle, also two struts, as clearly shown in the illustration.

Fig. 49.—Sawing Stool with Wide Top

Fig. 50.—A Type of Mortising Stool

Fig. 51.—Handy Stool for Small Work

TIMBER RACKS

Fig. 52 shows a useful form of timber rack. It is made with vertical standards, from 3 in. by 3 in. to 4 in. by 3 in., mortised or bored to receive bearers, which may be pieces of round iron or old gas or steam piping (as shown in the upper part of Fig. 52), 1 in. to 1⅛ in. in diameter; or they may be of timber, 2 in. by 4 in. or 3 in. by 4 in., with tenons fitting into mortises as illustrated.

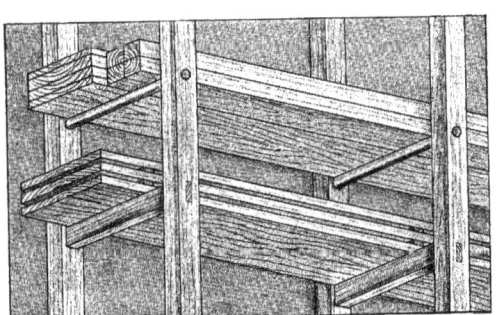

Fig. 52.—Timber Rack

26 THE PRACTICAL WOODWORKER

Fig. 53 shows a much handier, and at the same time stronger, kind of rack. Holes are cut into the brickwork about and plastering with cement. It will be obvious that timber can be more quickly stacked or removed with this form of rack than with others.

Timber is better if stacked with small strips of wood (called "skids") between the layers, as shown in the bottom part of Fig. 52, thus allowing the air to circulate all round the timber and enabling it to season better.

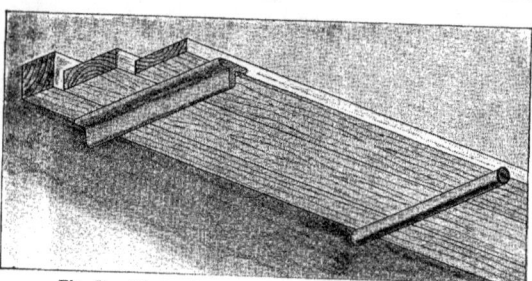

Fig. 53.—Timber Rack consisting of Metal Cantilevers

3 ft. to 4 ft. apart and 4½ in. to 6 in. deep; pieces of T-iron, H-iron, or strong piping are inserted and held firmly in the wall by wedging it with pieces of tile or slate,

Sometimes boards are stacked edgeways, in which case the rack may consist of a horizontal bar with vertical strips fixed to it, the boards lying in the slots between the strips.

Tools for Measuring and Marking

RULES

THE common type of rule used by woodworkers is the four-fold "two-foot," of which two varieties are shown: Fig. 3, a cheap type; Fig. 4, with brass edge plates to the joints and also with bevelled tenths, etc., of an inch are seldom used. Measurements in rough carpentry are considered accurate enough if given in eighths, but very often the phrases "bare eighth" or "full eighth" are used when the measurement is slightly under or

Fig. 1.—Transferring Measurement from Rule

Fig. 2.—Accurate Measuring with Bevelled-edge Rule

edges. Figs. 5 and 7 show rules with slides for measuring board thicknesses, taking the depth of rebates, etc.

Woodwork measurements in subdivisions of an inch are given in eighths; twelfths, above the division. Thus, if two carpenters were working together, one cutting whilst the other was fixing the work, one would observe to the other that he wanted a piece of wood, say, "2 ft. 6⅜ in. bare." In cabinet work, finer measurements are required, and they are commonly given to the nearest sixteenth, "bare" or "full" if necessary.

The ordinary sub-divisions of each inch in a four-fold rule are therefore eighths, but in some rules other divisions and scales are given, particularly in bevel-edged rules as Fig. 4. The pivot joints of good-class rules are often divided into degrees so that the legs of the rule can be set at any angle, rules being commonly used to do the work of adjustable bevels. (*See* Fig. 9.)

The bevel-edged portions of the rule are not only useful because of the scales on them but also because the bevel leads to greater accuracy by bringing the divisions of the rule nearer the surface to be marked, as illustrated in Figs. 1 and 2. Of course, the non-bevelled rule can be turned on its edge for accurate marking, as in Fig. 11.

A few years ago the two-fold "two-foot" (Figs. 7 or 9) was largely used,

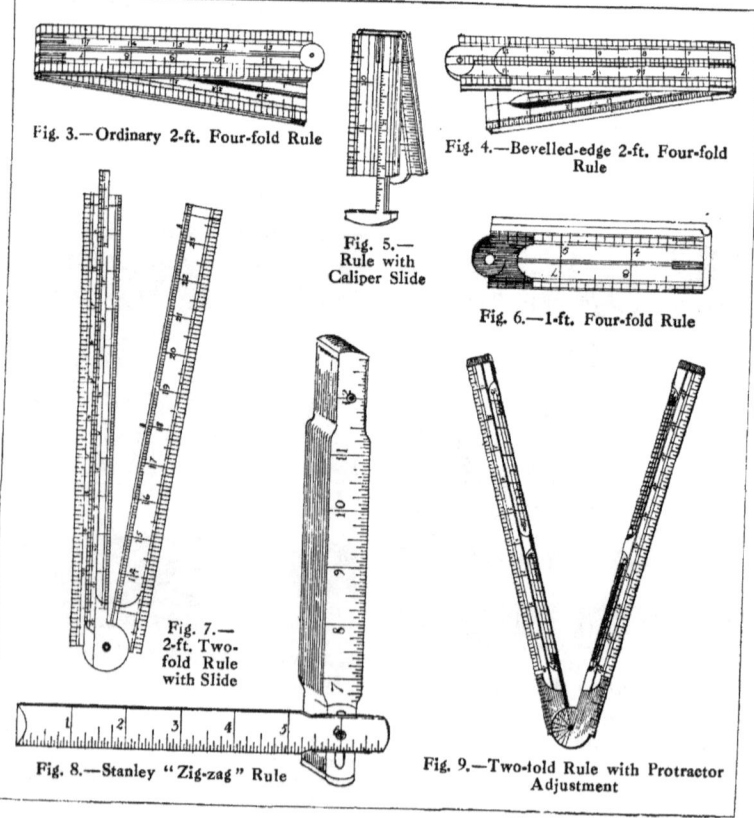

Fig. 3.—Ordinary 2-ft. Four-fold Rule

Fig. 4.—Bevelled-edge 2-ft. Four-fold Rule

Fig. 5.—Rule with Caliper Slide

Fig. 6.—1-ft. Four-fold Rule

Fig. 7.—2-ft. Two-fold Rule with Slide

Fig. 8.—Stanley "Zig-zag" Rule

Fig. 9.—Two-fold Rule with Protractor Adjustment

TOOLS FOR MEASURING AND MARKING

but is now practically out of date owing to being clumsy for carrying about; however, it is convenient for bench work. On the whole, the ordinary four-fold "two-foot" with square edges is mostly used, and is found accurate enough for almost every purpose. Four-fold "three foots" or "four-foots" are preferred by some woodworkers. On the other hand, four-fold "one-foot" rules are shown in Figs. 5 and 6, the latter having a slide for obtaining the thickness of boards, etc.; Fig. 8 shows a Stanley "Zigzag" rule. Other types of rules are occasionally met with, some having slides for calculating or drawing geometrical figures, but these are not of much use.

Using the Rule.—Of course, there is little difficulty in using a rule, but one or two workshop hints will prove useful. There are two ways of measuring a length — roughly and accurately. In the rough method the rule is taken in one hand and stepped along the surface to be measured, say a board, the termination of the rule on the board being judged at each step by the eye, or marked by a rub with the brass end of the rule. Fig. 10 shows the more accurate method, the length of the rule being ticked off on the surface of the board and the process repeated until the end of the board is reached.

The thickness of a board is measured

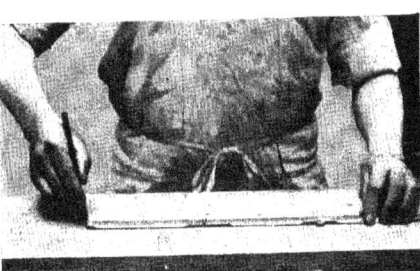

Fig. 10.—Measuring-off a Board for Length

Fig. 11.—Accurate Measuring with Rule on Edge

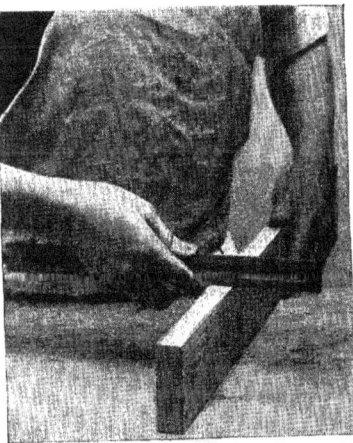

Fig. 12.—Measuring Thickness of Board

as in Fig. 12. This method is better than using the end of the rule, as the corners get worn. The rule shown in Fig. 5 is also useful for getting the thickness of the boards, the method of using it being obvious. The slide rule in Fig. 7 is useful for obtaining the depth of grooves, etc.

Fig. 13 shows a simple method of dividing the width of a board into two or more equal parts. Suppose a board 7 in. wide is to be sawn into three strips. Lay the rule in a slanting direction across the board and so that, say, figures 2 and 11 coincide with the edges of the board. Mark the board at figures 5 and 8; the board will thus be divided equally into three parts. Lines parallel to the edges are then drawn as shown in Fig. 14.

Other methods of measuring and drawing parallel lines will be given later.

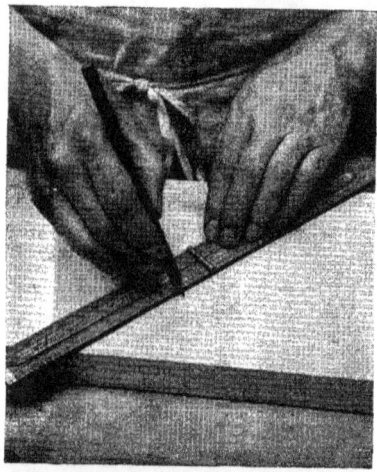

Fig. 13.—Dividing Board into Three Widths

Fig. 14.—Lining-down with Rule and Pencil

Fig. 15.—Taking Width of Recess with Pinch-rod—Two Laths, one sliding on the other

TOOLS FOR MEASURING AND MARKING

STRAIGHTEDGES

Straightedges are used in woodworking for testing and marking. They are of various sizes, a useful size for small jobs being about 3 ft. long, 2½ in. wide, and ¼ in. thick. Fig. 17 shows a typical example.

A straightedge may be tested for accuracy in three ways: (1) Hold another straightedge against it. (2) Place the straightedge on a flat surface and draw a line (see Fig. 18); turn the straightedge over and compare the edge with the line, then, if they coincide, the straightedge is accurate. (3) Spy down the edge of the straightedge (Fig. 16). Note that a good straightedge should be straight "both" ways: (a) the flat surface should be straight and (b) the edge should be straight.

Fig. 16.—Sighting Straightedge for Accuracy

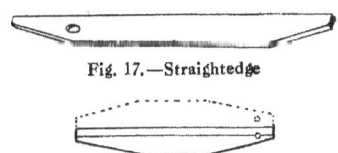

Fig. 17.—Straightedge

Fig. 18.—Testing Straightedge Geometrically

PENCILS

Any ordinary pencil is suitable for woodwork. "Carpenters' pencils," which were largely used a few years ago, are oval in section and last longer than the ordinary type, but they are clumsy and do not assist accurate work.

Pencils are made in various degrees of hardness and those by good makers have the degree of hardness printed on them. The degrees vary in good makes from 6B to 6H—the more B's there are the softer the pencil and the more H's the harder. The degrees are thus:—BB, B, HB, H, HH—Of late years a new degree F has been manufactured and is between HB and H. For general work F is the best—H being a little too hard and HB a little too soft. Of course any one of these three degrees is near enough for ordinary use.

Fig. 19 shows the ordinary method of sharpening the pencil, the length of the point being about an inch; if too long, the lead is apt to break and if too short or dumpy inaccurate work is likely to result. A chisel is more useful than a pocket-knife for sharpening pencils.

Sometimes the pencil is sharpened to a chisel point as Fig. 20; this will last longer and give fine lines, but is not so convenient to use, and cannot be conveniently used for writing.

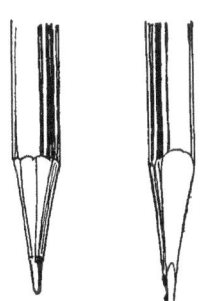

Fig. 21. Reel for Chalk Line

Figs. 19 and 20.—Shapes of Pencil Points

CHALK LINES

A chalk line is sometimes found very useful for marking long lengths. A cotton line is the best as it holds the chalk-dust better. A reel, as shown in Fig. 21, is often used to hold the line.

The line is chalked by fastening one end (or getting someone to hold it) and rubbing the line with a piece of chalk. To use the line (*see* Fig. 22) fasten one end at the correct point and pull the other end until the line is taut; then, as near the middle of the line as possible, pull the line a few inches away from the surface and let it go. A straight chalk line will thus be flicked on the surface. For use on white wood, a "chalk line" may be charged with black lead.

In Fig. 22 a short line is shown being marked in order to illustrate the method clearly.

PINCH ROD

Fig. 15 shows the method of obtaining the width of an opening by using a "pinch rod." The latter consists of two laths (or rules) which are held so that they touch each side of the opening and are then gripped together.

Fig. 22.—Chalk Line in Use

MARKING KNIVES AND AWLS

For bench work, and any work demanding accuracy, a marking knife is preferable to a pencil. Fig. 23 shows a usual type, one end being chisel shaped and the other pointed, the latter for ordinary marking, and the former for cutting into the surface of the wood a little, as in tenoning and dovetailing. Fig. 24 shows a marking knife with a handle which can be gripped better and is more convenient to use, while Fig. 25 shows a handled marking awl.

Fig. 23 represents the type in general use and is good enough for all practical purposes.

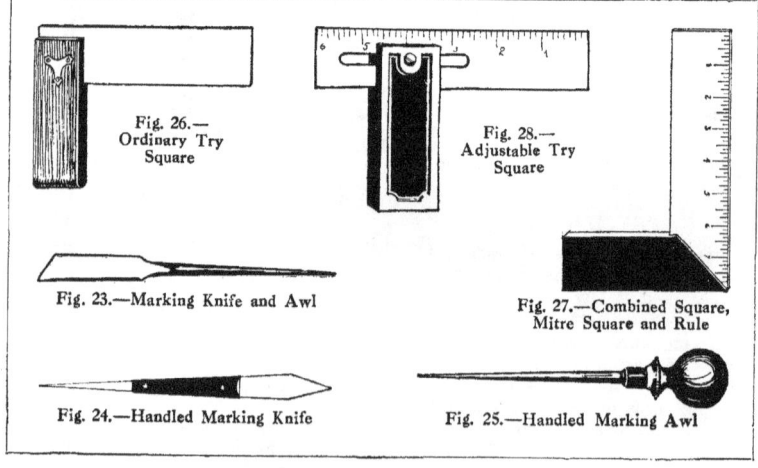

Fig. 26.—Ordinary Try Square

Fig. 28.—Adjustable Try Square

Fig. 23.—Marking Knife and Awl

Fig. 27.—Combined Square, Mitre Square and Rule

Fig. 24.—Handled Marking Knife

Fig. 25.—Handled Marking Awl

TOOLS FOR MEASURING AND MARKING

SQUARES

The most commonly used square in woodworking is the type shown in Fig. 26

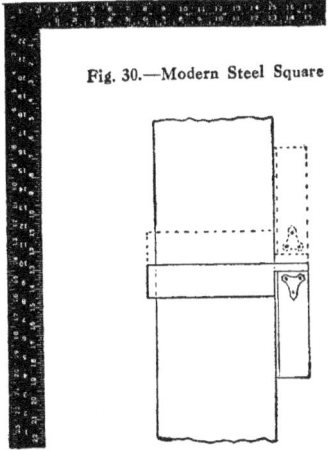

Fig. 30.—Modern Steel Square

Fig. 29.—Testing Try Square

with the blade 6 in. long, the blade being of steel and the stock usually of ebony lined with brass on the inside face to prevent wearing. This square is made in various sizes, the 12 in. being largely used.

Fig. 27 shows a mitre square and rule combined; this square can be used for lines at 90° or 45°. An adjustable try square is shown in Fig. 28.

Steel squares (Fig. 30) are nowadays used largely by woodworkers, but chiefly on roof work and to a lesser degree in staircasing. Fig. 31 shows how this square is used for getting the length of a rafter when the span and rise are given. In the illustration the span would be 16 ft. and the rise 6 ft., and the length of the rafter the distance between the points on the legs of the square, or 10 ft. If a fence were now screwed on the square lineable with A C, the square would be suitable for marking the top and bottom bevels for the rafters (see Fig. 33 and 34).

Ellis's patent steel square (Fig. 32) has a metal adjustable fence and other improvements.

Crenelated squares are useful for setting-out work, particularly carpentry. They have a series of notches in the blade, as illustrated clearly in Fig. 35. A pencil or marker is placed in a crenelation (or notch) and the square glided along the timber, thus making a mark parallel to the edge of the timber.

Wooden squares of a larger size than the metal type are often very useful for squaring frames, etc. A handy size for a square of this type is with the blade about 2 ft. long. The illustration (Fig. 36) shows the square with blade and stock pulled apart to show the joint. They are usually made of baywood (mahogany).

A square may be tested for accuracy as in Fig. 29. Select a board having a straight edge and, holding the stock firmly

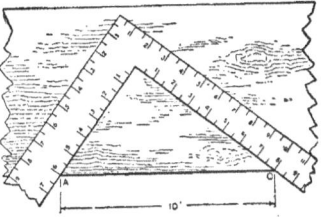

Fig. 31.—Obtaining Length of Rafter with Steel Square

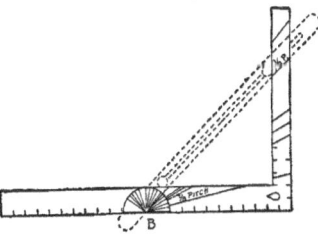

Fig. 32.—Ellis Steel Square

against the edge of the board, draw a line across the board; turn the square over and if the edge of the square coincides with this line then the square is

3—N E.

accurate. If not, draw another line, and the amount of inaccuracy will be half the angle between the two lines. In the case of a wooden square that has been accidentally knocked inaccurate, the top edge of the blade may be "shot" with the trying-plane until correct, when, of course, the under edge must not be used because that will remain out of square. When a metal square gets out of truth (with dropping on the ground usually) the best remedy is to buy a new one.

Another method of testing squares,

Fig. 33.—Adjusting Gauge of Steel Square

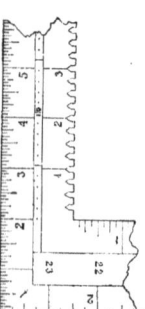

Fig. 35.—Crenelated Steel Square

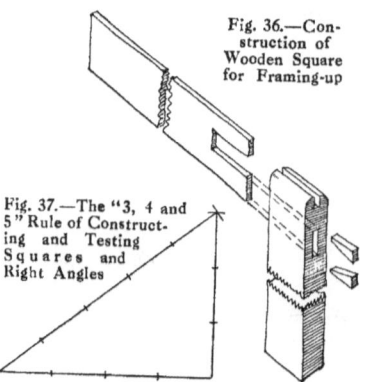

Fig. 36.—Construction of Wooden Square for Framing-up

Fig. 37.—The "3, 4 and 5" Rule of Constructing and Testing Squares and Right Angles

Fig. 34.—Marking Rafter Bevels with Steel Square

TOOLS FOR MEASURING AND MARKING

or of drawing square angles, is by means of the "3, 4 and 5 rule" (Fig. 37). Set off four units (inches, feet, or any other unit) along the line; strike off three units from one end to intersect five units set off from the other end. A triangle is equal to the square of the hypotenuse," that is, $3^2 + 4^2 = 5^2$. This rule is very useful for large angles.

Figs. 38 and 39 show the method of using the square for marking lines on timber. The chief point to be watched is that

Fig. 38.—First Position in Using Try Square

Fig. 40.—Testing Square Edges with Try Square

Fig. 39.—Second Position in Using Try Square

Fig. 41.—Using Adjustable Bevel

thus obtained with sides in the proportion of 3 : 4 : 5. This must be a right-angled triangle because "the squares of two sides of a right-angle triangle must be the stock of the try-square should be kept tightly against the edge of the timber.

In testing a piece of timber for squareness the try-square is held as Fig. 40.

Keep the stock tightly against the flat side of the timber—do not use the stock against the edge. Hold the timber towards bench. Apply the square at intervals of about 1 foot, or glide the square along the timber.

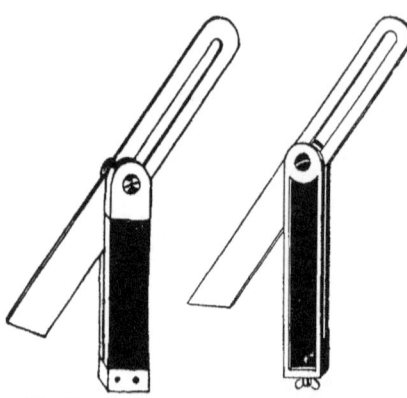

Fig. 42.—Ordinary Adjustable Bevel

Fig. 43.—Bevel with Double-wing Nut

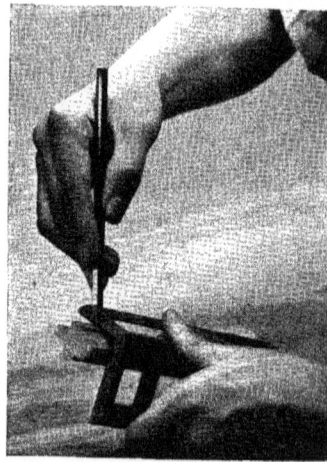

Fig. 45.—Using Square Template on Glazing Bar when Use of Try Square is Inconvenient

Fig. 46.—Mitre Template

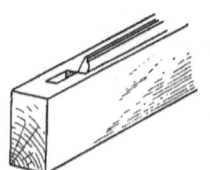

Fig. 47.—Using Mitre Template in Paring a Mitre

Fig. 48.—Mitre in Joint-making for which Mitre Template is used

Fig. 44.—Bevel with Single-wing Nut for Tightening

wards the light, as shown, for small work; in this way the smallest inaccuracy can be seen. When testing large pieces of timber one end can be rested on the

BEVELS

Bevels are necessary for marking and testing angles that are not right angles.

TOOLS FOR MEASURING AND MARKING

The ordinary type of bevel is shown in Fig. 42, the blade being slotted so that its length can be adjusted for various purposes and also so that the blade will shut into the stock when not in use.

The blade is secured in the required position by tightening the screw with a screwdriver. The method of adjusting correct the bevel is screwed up tightly. Fig. 43 shows a wing nut for tightening up, the nut being at the end of the stock. Fig. 44 shows a bevel with a single-wing nut instead of the usual screw.

For rough work a bevel may be dispensed with and the rule used instead; the rule is very handy and quickly set,

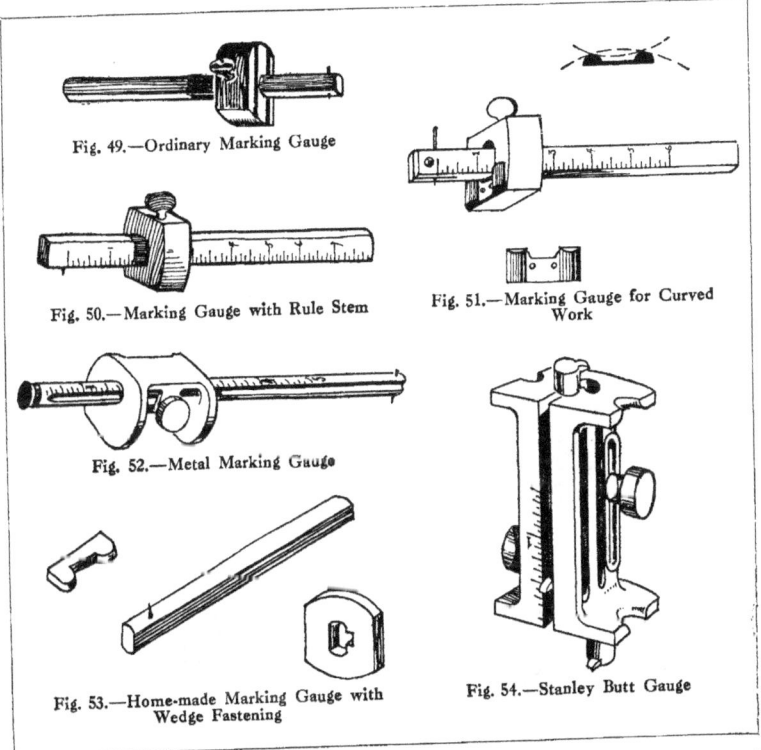

Fig. 49.—Ordinary Marking Gauge

Fig. 50.—Marking Gauge with Rule Stem

Fig. 51.—Marking Gauge for Curved Work

Fig. 52.—Metal Marking Gauge

Fig. 53.—Home-made Marking Gauge with Wedge Fastening

Fig. 54.—Stanley Butt Gauge

the bevel is first to set it to the correct angle; then tighten the screw and compare with the desired angle. It will usually be found that the bevel has altered a little in screwing up. The blade should therefore be tapped gently on the bench and the bevel again compared with the angle desired. When but is easily knocked out of the correct angle and is therefore unsuitable where accuracy is required.

TEMPLATES

A template in woodworking can mean either a pattern (say, of thin wood or paper) or a tool-guiding appliance used in marking or cutting angles. The latter kind of template includes the "mitre template" and the "square template."

Fig. 46 shows the ordinary brass mitre template which is used for mitreing and scribing joints, while Fig. 47 shows it in use. Care should be taken not to chisel too much off the joint—beginners have a tendency to do this. Take a little off at a time and gently tap the template backwards. But even at the finish leave the joint a little full here because this is the most noticeable part of the joint and it will easily crush up a little. Remember you can always take a little more off but you cannot put a little more on. Fig. 48 shows part of a mitred-and-tenoned joint showing where the end of the moulding has been cut with the aid of the mitre template.

Templates are also made in wood, but brass is better, as the chisel is bound to slip a little into the wood template occasionally, and thus destroy its accuracy.

Square templates are chiefly used for joiners, but it is not essential for most woodworkers. Fig. 45 shows the square template being used to square a line round a moulded sash bar.

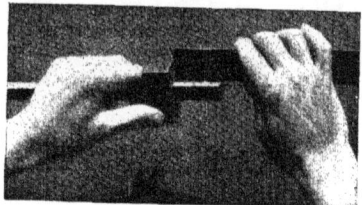

Fig. 55.—Setting Marking Gauge

Templates are used for dovetailing, etc., and mitre blocks and boxes are also forms of mitre templates; all these will be dealt with in later chapters.

GAUGES

Marking Gauges.—Gauges are used for marking parallel lines. The simplest

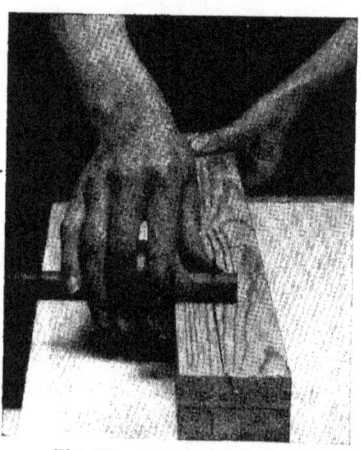

Figs. 56 and 57.—Holding and Using Marking Gauge: Note Disposition of Fingers

marking as in the case of window bars or other pieces of wood where it is awkward to use a square. It is a useful tool type is the marking gauge, varieties of which are shown in Figs. 49 to 54. The ordinary workshop type (Fig. 49) consists

TOOLS FOR MEASURING AND MARKING

of four parts: stem, head, fastening screw, and marker. The stem and head are usually of beech and the screw of

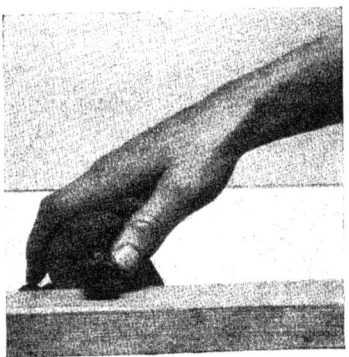

Fig. 58.—First Position of Marking Gauge: Arrow shows Direction of Stroke

boxwood. Various methods of fastening the head to the stem are in use (see Fig. 53 for another method) but the screw is the best. The marker is simply a pointed bit of steel.

In setting the gauge it is taken in the left hand (Fig. 55), the screw loosened, and the head adjusted to the correct distance from the point by using the rule as shown. After the screw is tightened the gauge should again be tested; it will probably have moved a little in tightening, when, if so, the head can be shifted a slight amount by tapping the end of the stem on the bench.

It is very often desired to gauge a line down the centre of a board. The obvious method is to measure the board, divide by two, and set the gauge; this takes too long and is not so accurate as from the description it would seem to be. Instead, guess half the width of the board, set the gauge accordingly and mark the distance from each side; two points near the centre of the board will thus be obtained and the gauge is then set accurately mid-way between them.

The method of holding the gauge is shown in Figs. 56 and 57. Hold it in the right hand with the thumb near the top of the stem, the first finger on the head, and the rest of the fingers on the stem. The chief thing to bear in mind is that the head of the gauge must be pressed continually against the edge of the timber from which you are gauging. Do not let the marker dig deeply into the wood; this is avoided by giving the gauge a slight rotary movement as shown in Figs. 58 and 59. At the beginning of the stroke the stem should be touching the wood at its far corner; as the gauge is pushed forward the point should be gradually pressed down into the wood, as shown in Fig. 59.

Fig. 50 shows a gauge with a scale on the stem. This is occasionally an advantage, but for good work simply setting the head to this scale is not accurate enough.

Fig. 51 shows a gauge with a metal plate attached to the face of the head; this enables the gauge to be used for either concave or convex work, as shown in the small sketch. Note also that this gauge has a small screw in the stem for adjusting the marking point.

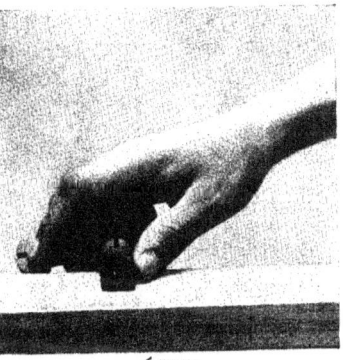

Fig. 59.—Final Position of Marking Gauge

A metal marking gauge is shown in Fig. 52; this has a point marker at one end and a roller marker at the other,

The latter makes a fine mark, and is useful across the grain and in knotty timber.

A home-made gauge is shown in Fig. 53, and in this a wedge is used for fastening, the wedge being made of such shape and size that it cannot fall out when the gauge is put together.

The "Stanley Butt Gauge" shown in Fig. 54 is a special type used chiefly in America for fitting butt hinges. The gauge has two bars; one bar has two points on it, one for gauging the edge of the door and the other for gauging the door casing, in which second case the end of the gauge head is used as a guide. The marking point on the other bar is used for gauging the thickness of the hinge. This gauge may be carried conveniently in the pocket.

Cutting Gauges.—This type of gauge (Fig. 62) is similar to a marking gauge except that it has a cutter instead of a marker. It is especially suitable for dovetailing, where it is an advantage to cut into the wood a little. Thin wood may be cut into strips, or small rebates may be made with a cutting gauge in first-class condition. The cutter is usually held in the stem by a small wedge.

Fig. 61 shows a combined marking, cutting, and pencil gauge. The last named is very useful for chamfering, because if an ordinary marking gauge were used the marks would be left on the timber after the chamfers were made.

Mortise Gauges.—A mortise gauge (Fig. 63) is similar to a marking gauge, but it has two points for marking two lines simultaneously. This, of course, saves much time when marking mortise and tenon joints. One point is attached to the stem as in a marking gauge and the other point is attached to a slide that works in the stem, and is adjusted by a screw at the bottom of the stem. Either a thumb screw or a flush screw is used, it being preferable to have the screw flush with the bottom of the stem (Fig. 63), as a projecting screw is liable to get out of order. Fig. 66 shows an inferior type of mortise gauge in which the slide is actuated by simply pulling or pushing it to the desired position; this is more difficult to set accurately than the preceding types.

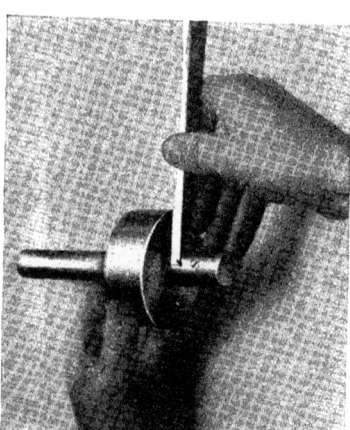

Fig. 60.—Setting Mortise Gauge to Width of Chisel

Fig. 60 shows how the mortise gauge is held when setting for mortising. The two points are adjusted to the correct distance apart by holding the mortising chisel against them. The head is then screwed up at the correct distance from them. In marking a mortise in the centre of a piece of timber the points should be set to the width of the chisel, the head "loosely tightened" as near the required position as can be guessed, and the points pricked into the timber from each side. Finally the gauge is adjusted by tapping slightly on the bench, and the screw in the head is then tightened up.

COMPASSES, DIVIDERS AND TRAMMELS

Compasses and Dividers.—The "compasses" used in woodworking are really dividers. Fig. 67 shows the usual shape and Fig. 68 illustrates a pattern with sensitive adjustment.

Fig. 61.—Combined Marking and Cutting Gauge

Fig. 62.—Ordinary Cutting Gauge

Fig. 63.—An Ordinary Type of Mortise Gauge: Flush Screw at End of Stem

Fig. 64.—Mortise Gauge with Projecting Wing Nut

Fig. 65.—Square-stock Mortise Gauge with Projecting Screw

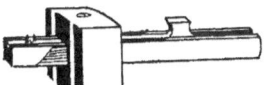

Fig. 66.—Mortise Gauge without Fine Adjustment

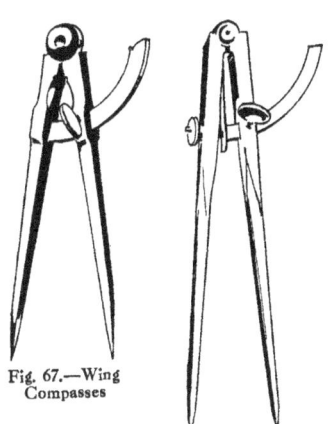

Fig. 67.—Wing Compasses

Fig. 68.—Wing Compasses with Sensitive Adjustment

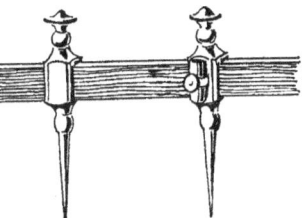

Fig. 69.—Trammel Points attached to Lath

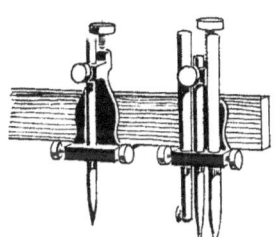

Fig. 70.—Stanley Adjustable Trammel Points

Compasses are used for drawing circles and other geometrical work, but the most common use to which they are put in practical work is scribing. Fig. 71 shows a piece of skirting that has to be fitted to an uneven floor. The skirting board is loosely nailed into position (or otherwise temporarily held) and the compasses vertical scribing distance constant, it is better to rest the wing on the floor when using; if this is done and the compasses kept vertical a mark will be made on the board at a constant distance from the floor. The skirting is then chopped or planed to this line, when it will be found to fit the uneven surface of the floor accurately.

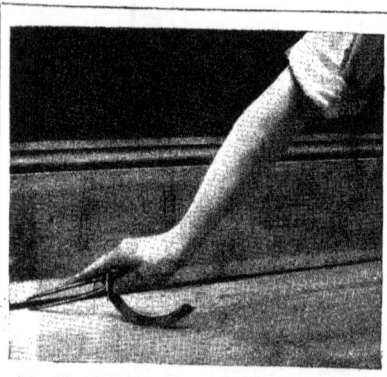

Fig. 71.—Scribing Skirting Board to Floor

Fig. 74.—Wait's Attachments Forming a Trammel

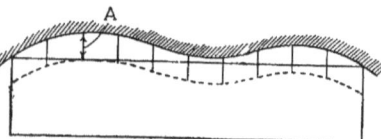

Fig. 72.—Scribing by the Spiling Method

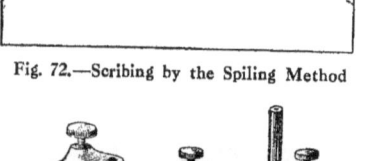

Fig. 73.—Wait's Rule Attachments

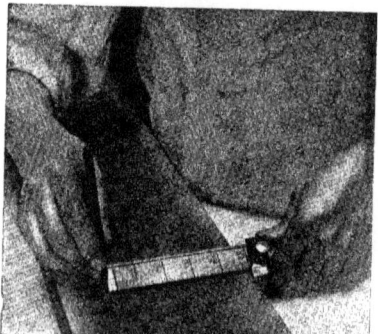

Fig. 75.—Wait's Attachment in Use for Lining-up a Board (attachment should be in close contact with edge of board)

set to the greatest width of the gap between the floor and the board. The compasses are then drawn along with one point on the floor while the other marks the board. In order to keep the

This method of scribing is used in numerous cases where linings, framings, plinths, etc., have to be fitted to uneven surfaces. Care should always be taken that the compasses should be set and held

TOOLS FOR MEASURING AND MARKING

in the precise direction that the board has to be moved up to fit into its final position; this is more clear in Fig. 72. Sometimes the compasses are dispensed with and parallel lines are drawn; along each of these parallel lines the scribing distance A (Fig. 72) is set. A freehand line through the points thus obtained will show the wood that must be removed. This method is sometimes called "spiling," a small strip of wood the length of A being used.

Trammel points are used for drawing large circles. A pair of these are shown in Fig. 69; they need only be screwed to a strip of wood at the correct distance apart. Fig. 70 shows a pair of Stanley trammel points; both points are ad-

Fig. 80.—Using Spirit Level with Side Openings above Operator's Head

justable for height, and one end has a pencil and a roller marker as well as a trammel point. A trammel for drawing ellipses will be dealt with later.

Wait's rule attachments (Fig. 73) are useful for drawing circles and parallel lines. Fig. 73 (A) is for use on a rule

Fig. 76.—Ordinary Spirit Level

Fig. 78.—Spirit-level Tubes: Correct and Incorrect Settings

Fig. 77.—Spirit Level with Side Openings

Fig. 79.—Section through Spirit Level

as a gauge; it is shown in use at Fig. 75. (B) Fig. 73 is attached to the rule and forms a centre point; (C) Fig. 73 is to hold a pencil. The last two attachments are shown in use in Fig. 74; a bradawl often replaces the small point shown at B (Fig. 73).

SPIRIT LEVELS, PLUMBS, ETC.

Spirit Levels are used for testing horizontals. When purchasing a spirit level avoid getting a fancy or flimsy article. The chief points of a good level are: (a) it should be as long as possible without being inconvenient; (b) it should be strongly made; (c) it should have a quick bubble. The reasons for these three points should be obvious; the longer the level the more accurate the work; it should be strongly made to withstand occasional knocks—a metal plate along the bottom is an advantage; a slow bubble is not as accurate and takes longer to use than a quick bubble.

Fig. 76 shows a cheap level; its chief fault is that it has no openings in the side so that the bubble can be seen when the level is held high up. This seems a slight matter, but in practice it is a great inconvenience not to be able to use the level at the height of the eyes or even above the head. Fig. 77 shows a better type with side openings.

A section of the level showing the tube in position is shown in Fig. 79. The tube is of glass and is nearly filled with methylated spirits. The bubble is the amount the tube is *short of being full;*

this means that when the tube is tilted the spirit runs to the bottom and the *bubble runs to the top.* Beginners have difficulty in accounting for the latter phenomenon, but if it is not understood a level cannot be used quickly and satisfactorily.

Sometimes the tube gets broken, but it can easily be replaced with a little tube. Press the tube gently into the plaster until the bubble comes to rest exactly in the centre. Note that the tube is slightly curved in length, and take care to fix it with the round or convex side upwards. When the tube seems to be correctly placed, mark round the level with a pencil on to the board; reverse the position of the level, keeping

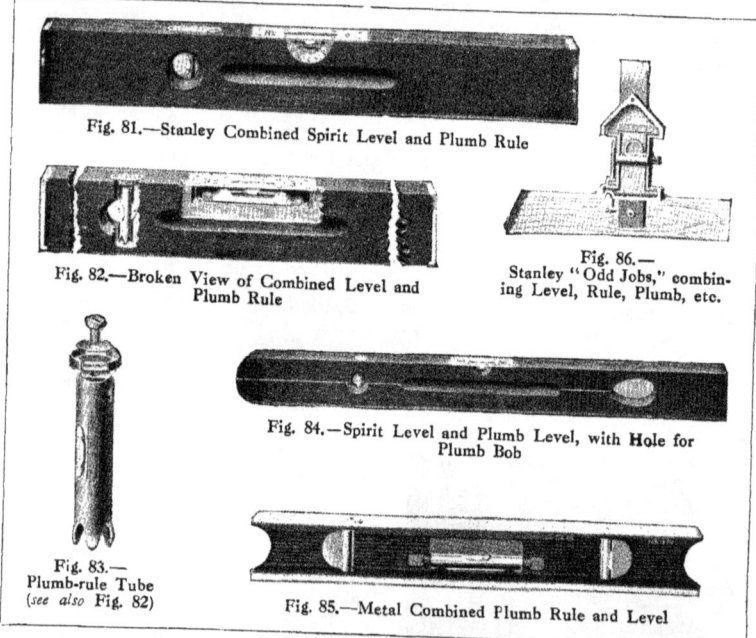

Fig. 81.—Stanley Combined Spirit Level and Plumb Rule

Fig. 82.—Broken View of Combined Level and Plumb Rule

Fig. 86.—Stanley "Odd Jobs," combining Level, Rule, Plumb, etc.

Fig. 84.—Spirit Level and Plumb Level, with Hole for Plumb Bob

Fig. 83.—Plumb-rule Tube (*see also* Fig. 82)

Fig. 85.—Metal Combined Plumb Rule and Level

care. Tubes (Fig. 78) can be bought separately from local dealers.

In fixing a new tube proceed as follows: Set a piece of smooth wood level on the bench or in the vice, testing it by means of a level of proved accuracy. Unscrew the plate off the top of the level to be repaired and scrape away the plaster-of-paris in which the broken tube was embedded. Mix some fresh plaster-of-paris with water and put a little in the groove (chiefly at the ends) that holds the to the pencil lines. Place the top plate in position and see whether the bubble is correct with it. If everything is all right let the plaster set a minute or two and then screw the top plate down.

In using the level greater accuracy is obtained if it is used on the top of a parallel straightedge, particularly if the surface to be levelled is rough or not straight.

The Stanley Company manufactures numerous patterns of spirit levels; for

TOOLS FOR MEASURING AND MARKING

example, Fig. 81 shows a combined spirit level and plumb rule, the small vertical tube being used for "plumbing" vertical work. Fig. 82 is a broken view of this rule showing how the levels are fixed in position. Both level and plumb tubes are made so that they can be ad-

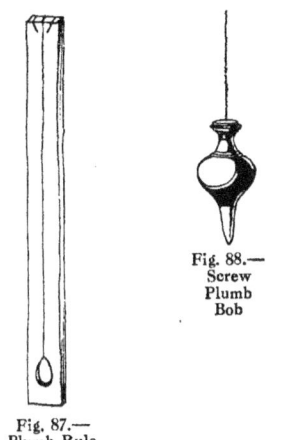

Fig. 88.—
Screw
Plumb
Bob

Fig. 87.—
Plumb Rule

justed; notice the small springs under the level tube, which can be screwed down at each end and any slight inaccuracy that arises in the level thus corrected. The vertical tube (shown enlarged in Fig. 83) is adjusted by means of the set-screw and the slotted cup. Notice the slight convex curve on the tube glass.

A level with plumb level and hole for a plumb bob is shown by Fig. 84, and a metal combined plumb rule and level by Fig. 85. Stanley fittings for use with levels include level sights for levelling at a distance and pitch adjusters for setting surfaces to any desired inclination. The Stanley "Odd Jobs" tool No. 1, illustrated in Fig. 86, combines level, rule, plumb, gauge, etc.

A Plumb Rule and Bob can easily be made. Fig. 87 shows a common design. A convenient size is 3 ft. 6 in. by 3 in. by $\frac{5}{8}$ in. Three saw cuts are made in the top for fastening the string. Lines are gauged down the centre of the rule and a hole formed near the bottom for the bob to swing into. A bob may be made by casting one in a sand mould and then boring a fine hole through it for the string. Turned lead bobs can be bought. Fig. 88 shows an iron or brass bob with the top to screw off so that the string can be threaded through it and the top screwed on again. They are neater in appearance than lead bobs.

"Plumb up" means vertical or pointing to the centre of the earth; "level" means tangential to the earth's surface, and therefore, at any point, a plumb line is at right angles to a level line.

In a later chapter detailed instructions on making a spirit level will be given.

Saws and Sawing

The Cross-cut Saw.—Hand saws may be divided into two classes, cross-cut saws and rip saws. As the names imply, the cross-cut saw is for cutting across, and the rip saw for cutting or ripping, with or along, the grain.

A cross-cut saw is shown in Fig. 1. The blade is of steel and varies in thickness, diminishing towards the end and the back, while the usual length is 26 in. A tapered blade is lighter, easier to handle, and clears itself in the saw kerf. The thickness varies, as shown by the numbers in Fig. 3, the smaller the number the thicker being the blade at that part; "E" means easy or bare and "T" tight or full.

Usually the back of the saw is straight (see Fig. 2), but the skew-back shape as in Fig. 1 is very common.

The shape of the teeth is shown at Figs. 7 to 9. Such a tooth-shape has been found to be of the best proportions for biting into the wood and yet sawing smoothly. The shape shown in Fig. 5 would cause the saw to stick and jump, and would make the sawing difficult and dangerous. On the other hand, the shape shown in Fig. 6 would not bite enough. Fig. 4 shows a mean between the two.

If the saw simply consisted of a blade with teeth stamped out as shown in Fig. 7 the saw could hardly be used at all, because (a) the "point" of each tooth would be an *edge* and therefore would not cut the fibres easily, and (b) the saw "kerf" (the cut made by the saw) would be so narrow that the saw blade would "bind" or rub on its sides.

If the teeth are filed on the slope they will appear as in Fig. 8. *Points* are thus formed on the teeth instead of *edges*, thus enabling the saw to cut better. If, next, the teeth are pressed alternately to one side and then to the other, as in the plan Fig. 9, the teeth will be wider at the cutting points than the thickness of the saw. A wide saw kerf will thus be made, through which the saw blade can pass easily to and fro. This bending of the teeth is known as "setting" the saw.

If any hard metal point (a nail) is dragged across a piece of timber a scratch results. Each tooth of a saw is like a sharp nail; see Fig. 12, which shows a piece of wood with a row of nails knocked into it and bent alternately to each side to demonstrate the "set" of a saw. It is obvious that if the nail points are sharp and if this instrument is dragged backwards and forwards across a piece of wood it will ultimately make a groove, or possibly cut the timber in two. In some such way the saw acts. Fig. 13 is an enlarged section of the saw kerf showing how the points of the teeth scratch their way through the wood while the other parts of the teeth remove the centre portion of the kerf. The amount of "set" on the saw determines the amount of clearance. More set is required for soft woods than for hard woods, and more for wet woods than for dry woods. A saw for use on wet soft wood should therefore have considerable set.

SAWS AND SAWING

Cross-cut hand-saw teeth are usually about six to the inch. The hardened and tempered steel blade of the saw should admit of being bent so that the tail nearly touches the handle, and of springing back straight so that there is no buckle in the saw. Any buckling of the blade may be easily seen by looking along the edge of the teeth.

The saw handle should be of a good shape for gripping firmly and easily, and should be attached to the blade by saw screws. If the blade ever becomes loose these screws should be tightened up with a brace and a forked bit (see Fig. 38 on a later page).

Using Cross-cut Saws.—The most difficult part in sawing is starting the saw. Guide the saw by putting the thumb against it as in Figs. 10 and 11. Take two or three up strokes to get a start. If you try to start by a down stroke there will be a danger of the saw jumping and damaging the work or cutting your finger. This method of starting the saw is applicable to all varieties of saws. Some workers guide the saw with the knuckle instead of the thumb.

Beware of two mistakes in sawing: (a) using short strokes, (b) pressing on the saw. Use as long strokes as possible; do not saw too quickly; do not press on the saw, but rather let it work by its own weight. If the saw is forced, it will require harder work and will be more difficult to guide. Simply pull the saw slowly backwards and push it slowly forwards in long strokes. This is the easiest method, and the safer, more accurate, and quicker in the long run.

Fig. 15 shows the method of sawing the end off a board—the latter resting on sawing stools, etc. The waste piece of board is supported by the left hand to prevent it from splitting a piece off the board. As the board is being cut this " short end " should be held in such a way that the kerf is widened, thus assisting the saw and preventing it from binding.

Sometimes a long board has to be cross

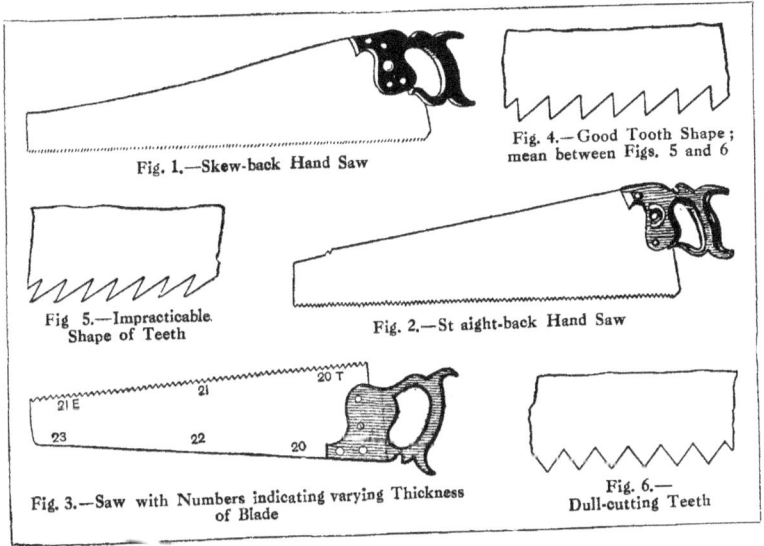

Fig. 1.—Skew-back Hand Saw

Fig. 4.—Good Tooth Shape; mean between Figs. 5 and 6

Fig 5.—Impracticable Shape of Teeth

Fig. 2.—Straight-back Hand Saw

Fig. 3.—Saw with Numbers indicating varying Thickness of Blade

Fig. 6.—Dull-cutting Teeth

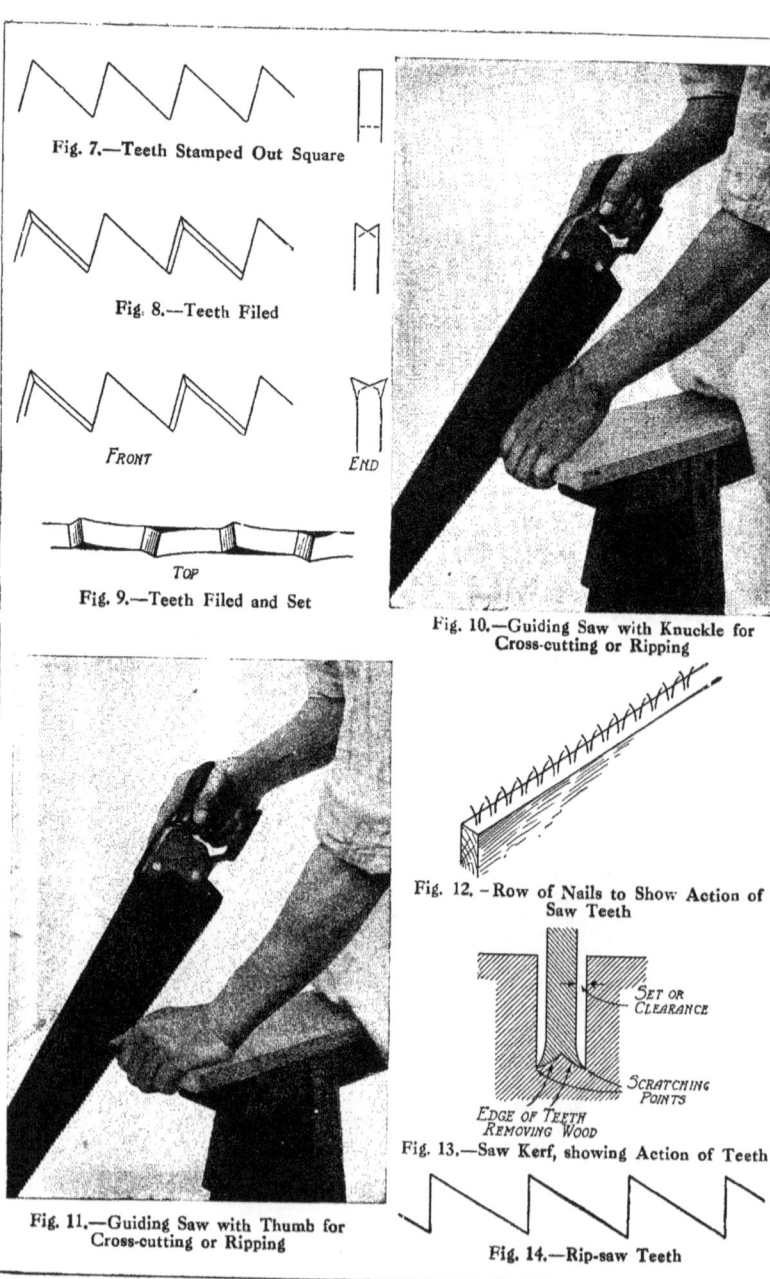

Fig. 7.—Teeth Stamped Out Square

Fig. 8.—Teeth Filed

Front   End

Top
Fig. 9.—Teeth Filed and Set

Fig. 10.—Guiding Saw with Knuckle for Cross-cutting or Ripping

Fig. 11.—Guiding Saw with Thumb for Cross-cutting or Ripping

Fig. 12.—Row of Nails to Show Action of Saw Teeth

Fig. 13.—Saw Kerf, showing Action of Teeth

Fig. 14.—Rip-saw Teeth

Fig. 15.—Method of Sawing End off Board to Prevent Splitting

Fig. 16.—Testing Squareness of Cutting

Fig 17.—Cross-cutting Long Board near Middle

Fig. 18.—Sawing End off Long Board: Only one Trestle available

cut in the middle (Fig. 17). In this case it is better if someone holds the work at one side of the saw. Notice that if the assistant drops the board slightly or lets it move towards the worker, the saw kerf will partly close and the saw will bind.

Fig. 18 shows the method of sawing the end off a long board when only one sawing stool is available.

The Rip Saw.—This saw is for cutting in the direction of the grain. Of course, a cross-cut saw can do this, but a rip

Using Rip Saw.—Three methods of using the rip saw are shown in Figs. 23 25 and 26. Fig. 23 shows the usual method; follow the same instructions as for cross-cutting. Fig. 25 shows a method of rip sawing favoured by cabinet-makers chiefly. Fig. 26 shows the method of ripping a piece of wood held in the vice; this method is, of course, only suitable for short lengths. Figs. 20 and 24 show two common faults.

Fig. 19.—Front View showing Saw Blade and Elbow in Same Plane

Fig. 20.—Defective Sawing: Saw Too Upright

saw does it more rapidly, as the teeth are especially designed for cutting with the grain. The shape of the teeth is shown in Fig. 14, the front of the tooth being vertical. There are usually four teeth to the inch, and the length (28 in.) is greater than that of the cross-cut. Otherwise the general appearance of the two is much the same.

Owing to the use of machinery, rip saws are now little used and the average craftsman does not possess one, the cross-cut being employed for all kinds of rough sawing.

The Panel Saw.—This saw has come more and more into use of late years, owing largely to the introduction of machinery and machine sawing for large stuff. It is the most useful all-round saw that a woodworker possesses. It can be used for cross-cutting, ripping, tenoning, and most other purposes. If a man can only afford one saw, this is the saw to get. Though it cannot be said to be as quick as a rip saw for ripping big stuff, or as a cross-cut saw for cross-cutting, or as handy as a tenon saw for small work, it will do the work of all three

Fig. 21.—First Position of Saw when Starting

Fig. 22.—End of First Up-stroke

Fig. 23.—Correct Slope for Saw

Fig. 24.—A Common Defect: Using Saw at too little slope

and leave the cut finer than the "rip" or the "cross-cut." Its length is usually 22 in., with teeth about the same size as those of the tenon saw.

Tenon Saws.—This saw (Fig. 27) gets its name from the fact that it is largely used for sawing tenons, for which purpose it is especially suitable owing to its length, size of its teeth, thinness of blade, etc. Along the top edge of the blade is a strip (called the "back") of grooved steel or brass into which the blade fits; this gives strength and rigidity to the thin blade, thus enabling greater accuracy in sawing to be obtained. The tenon saw is often known as a "back" saw for obvious reasons.

Using the Tenon Saw.—This saw is used chiefly for bench work. In sawing, a bench hook is often used for holding the timber. The bench hook may be cut out of the solid (Fig. 32) or made by nailing two small blocks on a strip of wood about 10 in. long; see Fig. 33. When sawing, the bench hook is hooked against the front of the bench and the timber to be sawn is pressed against the top block of the hook with the left hand and firmly held (see Fig. 37). A piece of timber insecurely held when sawing means time wasted, inaccurate work, buckled saws, and possibly cut fingers.

Fig. 34 shows a wider type of bench hook. Owing to the top piece stopping off short, there is less likelihood of mutilating the bench with the saw.

In using the tenon saw, one or two up strokes should first be made. Start sawing with the saw inclined at about 30 degrees (Fig. 35) and during sawing gradually bring the handle down until the saw is level and the strokes are level (Fig. 36).

Tenon saws are 12 in. to 18 in. in length, the usual size in use being a 14 in. The number of teeth to the inch is about ten.

Adjustable "back" or tenon saws are occasionally met with; see Fig. 31. Both the top and bottom edges of the blade have teeth, and the steel rib can be adjusted anywhere down the blade, thus adapting the saw for any depth of cut. These saws do not seem to have

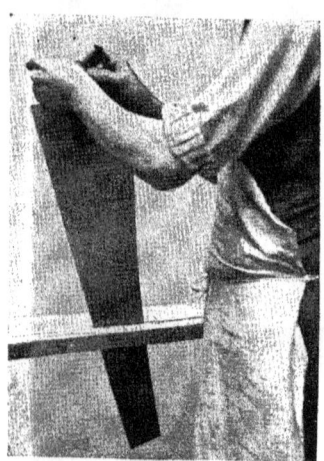

Fig. 25.—Method of Ripping largely used by Cabinet-makers

Fig. 26.—Ripping Short Length in Vice

SAWS AND SAWING

"caught on," and the trained craftsmen seldom possesses one.

Dovetail saws (Fig. 28) are similar in shape to a tenon saw but smaller—10 in. is the usual size—and with finer teeth, about 12 to the inch. Usually, as shown, the handle is not closed; the shape of the handle and the size are the only features

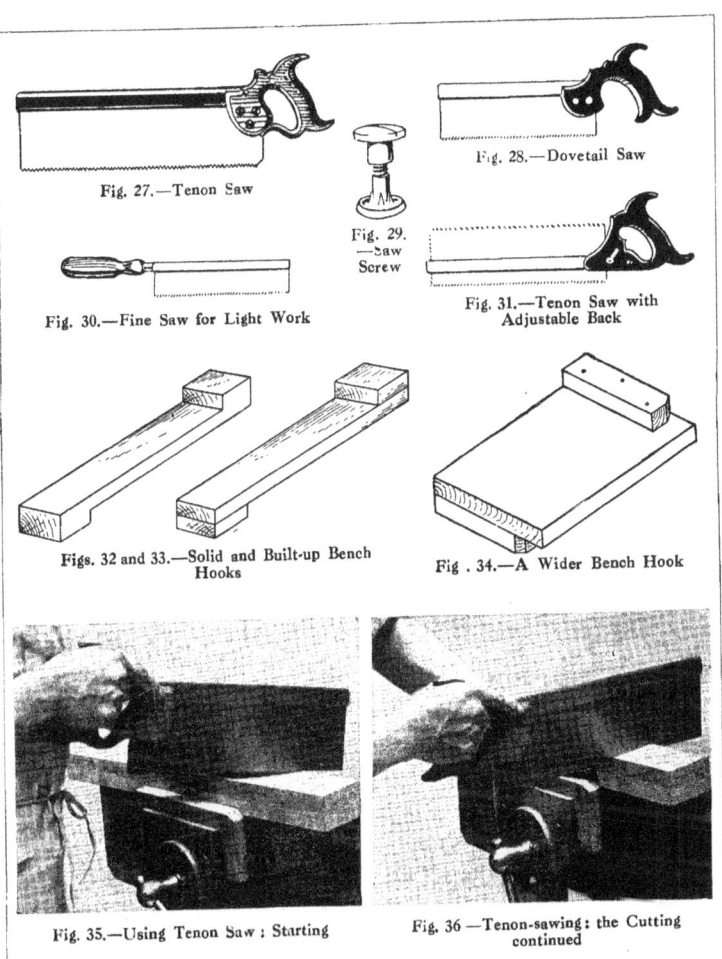

Fig. 27.—Tenon Saw

Fig. 28.—Dovetail Saw

Fig. 29.—Saw Screw

Fig. 30.—Fine Saw for Light Work

Fig. 31.—Tenon Saw with Adjustable Back

Figs. 32 and 33.—Solid and Built-up Bench Hooks

Fig. 34.—A Wider Bench Hook

Fig. 35.—Using Tenon Saw: Starting

Fig. 36.—Tenon-sawing: the Cutting continued

that distinguish it from a tenon saw. As the name implies, a dovetail saw is used chiefly for cutting dovetails and for other small work.

Fig. 37.—Using Bench Hook for Sawing

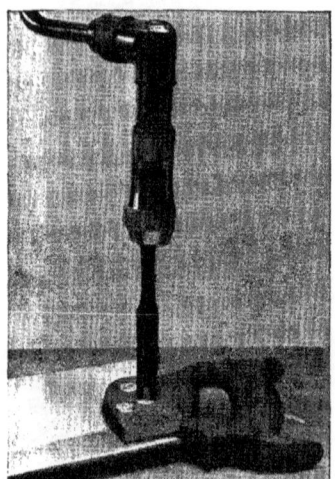

Fig. 38.—Tightening Saw Screw with Brace and Forked Bit

The handles of all the foregoing types of saws are fastened to the blades by saw screws. If the handle becomes a little loose it can be remedied by tightening these screws. Some of these screws have to be tightened by means of a forked brace-bit (see Fig. 38). A better type of saw screw that can be tightened with an ordinary screwdriver is shown in Fig. 29.

A small hardwood-handled light brass-backed saw is shown in Fig. 30. It is suitable for small work, such as cutting beading.

The Bow Saw.—This tool is not so largely used as formerly owing to the use of band saws; it is used for cutting shaped work by hand. The saw (Fig. 39) may be bought, or can be readily made as given in the details in Fig. 41.

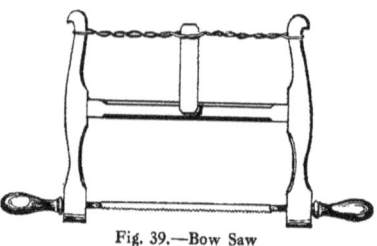

Fig. 39.—Bow Saw

Fig. 41 shows a form of bow saw which has stood the test of everyday workshop use for fifty years, and is still as useful as ever. By redrawing the squares shown at the left-hand side the worker should easily get the correct shape for the arms. The bow saw frame is made of beech, the arms being of 1⅛-in. thick stuff at the handles, tapering to ⅝ in. full at the top ends, all sharp edges being rounded off. The centre bar is of ¾-in. square stuff. The right-hand centre-bar joint is shown in section to explain clearly how the pivoting joint is formed. The bar shoulders, instead of being cut square, are rounded as at A to suit the corresponding hollows, which are cut out right across the inner sides of the arms; also, the bar tenons are merely stump-tenons ⅜ in. or so long, rounded from the extreme ends to the shoulders as at B, and they are made a working fit for the shallow sockets in

SAWS AND SAWING

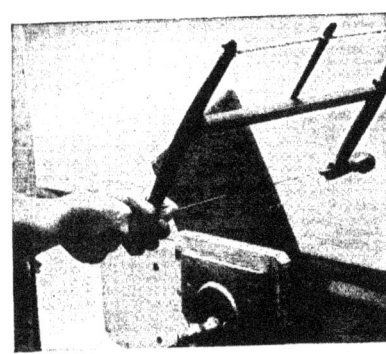

Fig. 40.—Using Bow Saw

Bow-saw handles and blades can be obtained separately from tool dealers. The saw when in use is stretched tightly by means of the tourniquet arrangement; if the blade is not stretched when in use it easily breaks, besides being difficult to saw with. The blade should be slackened when not in use.

Fig. 40 shows the bow saw in use. If a closed pattern (like a keyhole) has to be cut out in a piece of timber the blade has to be unfastened, inserted through the starting hole bored in the timber, and again fastened. This is troublesome, and therefore a keyhole saw (Figs. 42 and 44) or a compass saw (Fig. 43) is often used. The former is often

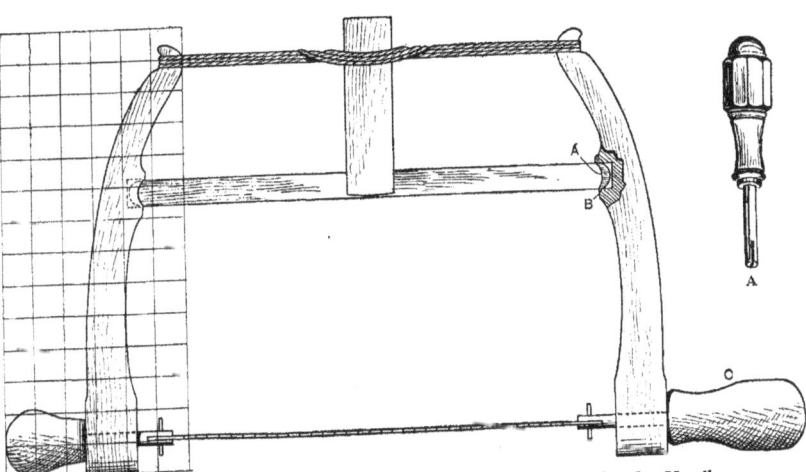

Fig. 41.—Details of Home-made Bow Saw; A, Alternative Design for Handle

which they work. The bar joint thus made forms a knuckle joint facilitating the saw tension, and also permits much latitude in using saws of varying lengths.

To give good control over the saw, the handle is made rather short and stumpy looking, shaped something like C, and the clip holes are bored right through and the ends riveted over iron end washers.

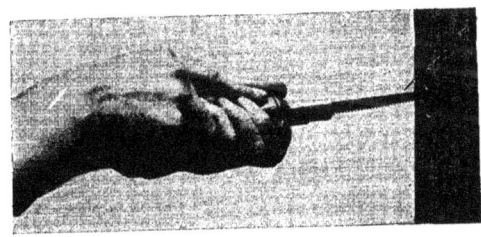

Fig. 42.—Using Keyhole Saw

called a pad saw—the handle being called a pad and being sometimes adapted to take a variety of tools; the blade fits into the handle when not in use.

A patent iron-handle pad saw is shown in Fig. 46; the wide end of the blade is shaped for use as a screwdriver.

Sometimes the compass-saw handle is made with an adjustable handle so that various blades for different classes of work may be used. A compass saw with three blades—one for sawing metal—is shown in Fig. 45.

The use of fretwork saws will be ex-

Saws become dull chiefly by sawing gritty timber, "catching" nails, etc. A dull saw on examination will show a speck of white on each tooth "point," whereas a tooth in good condition should have a sharp point.

Saw Setting.—The saw may or may not require setting. If it saws easily, making a wide saw kerf, it will not require that treatment. The saw may be set after being sharpened, but the other way is the more usual.

A saw may be set in a number of ways. The average workman uses a saw-set,

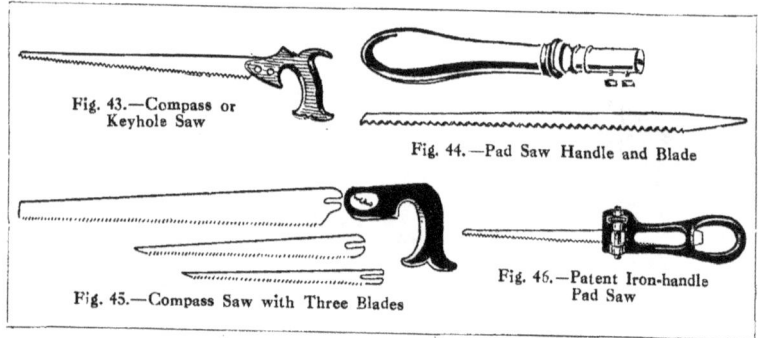

Fig. 43.—Compass or Keyhole Saw

Fig. 44.—Pad Saw Handle and Blade

Fig. 45.—Compass Saw with Three Blades

Fig. 46.—Patent Iron-handle Pad Saw

plained when an example of fretting is given in a much later chapter.

SETTING AND SHARPENING SAWS

Most tool dealers set and sharpen saws at a small cost, and many woodworkers prefer to send their saws to them rather than themselves tackle a job which is regarded as difficult. Some workers sharpen their own saws four or five times until, owing to lack of skill, the teeth have become uneven, and the saws have then to be sent to the saw expert. Saw sharpening is not really difficult, and the following instructions, which apply to most kinds of saws, should enable anyone to sharpen saws easily and efficiently.

the simplest type of which is shown in Fig. 47 and consists of a handled piece of steel containing a number of slots or notches, which are of various sizes to suit different thicknesses of saws. A slot is fitted over a tooth and the saw-set handle pressed downwards until it is judged that the tooth has been bent enough; that is, until it has been given enough set. This process is repeated with every alternate tooth on one side of the saw (see Fig. 51). The remaining teeth are then set from the other side.

In this method of setting the operator can only guess that each tooth has an equal amount of set. Some saw-sets of this type are therefore provided with a gauge (Fig. 48), which is so adjusted that when the tooth is bent sufficiently the gauge touches the side of the saw

SAWS AND SAWING

blade. In this way each tooth is given the same amount of set.

Plunger saw-sets are now largely used

iron block and hitting the teeth with a hammer is the oldest and most rapid method, though it is only recommended

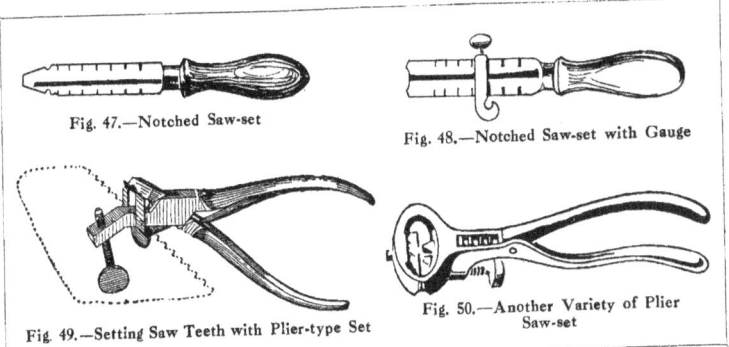

Fig. 47.—Notched Saw-set

Fig. 48.—Notched Saw-set with Gauge

Fig. 49.—Setting Saw Teeth with Plier-type Set

Fig. 50.—Another Variety of Plier Saw-set

(see Fig. 50). On pressing the handles together the plunger is pressed against the tooth; when the handles are released the plunger springs back. The saw-set can be adjusted for various sizes of teeth by turning the revolving disc, which is numbered for different sizes of saws. There are numerous variations of this

for use by the expert or for one who has a lot of saw setting to do. The average woodworker seldom uses this method. Fig. 53 illustrates the block and Fig. 54 the special saw-setting hammer. The iron block is about 7 in. or 8 in. long, with the top edges bevelled off as in the illustration. The bevelled edges should

Fig. 51.—Using Notched Saw-set

Fig. 52.—Using Plier Saw-set

type of saw-set, Figs. 49 and 52 showing two varieties in use.

Setting saws by placing them on an

be of different slopes so that they will do for different sizes of teeth. The saw is then held flat on the block with the teeth projecting over the bevel and each alternate tooth struck with the hammer. The saw is then turned over and the process repeated. The bevel edge with the most slope and the largest end of the hammer should be used for big teeth.

at different angles; B is a steel wedge, and C is a casting to hold the block and wedge. Fig. 56 shows the saw-set in use.

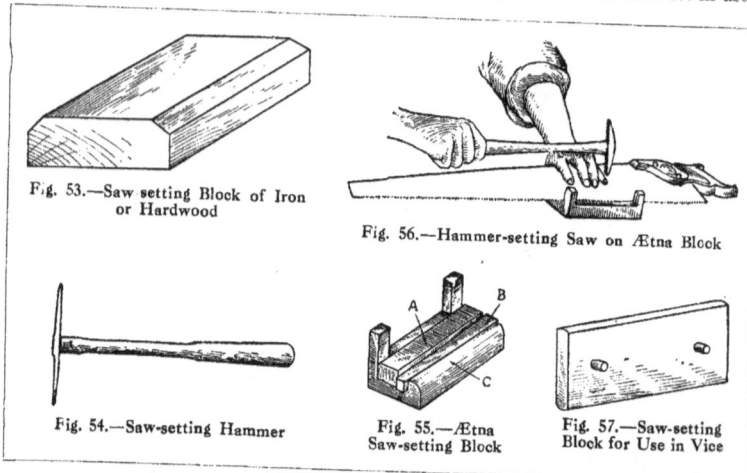

Fig. 53.—Saw setting Block of Iron or Hardwood

Fig. 56.—Hammer-setting Saw on Ætna Block

Fig. 54.—Saw-setting Hammer

Fig. 55.—Ætna Saw-setting Block

Fig. 57.—Saw-setting Block for Use in Vice

A block of iron, about 5 in. long, with a rounded top edge, as Fig. 57, is sometimes used fixed in the vice, the pins in the side preventing the block being

Fig. 58.—Setting Saw Teeth with Hammer and Punch

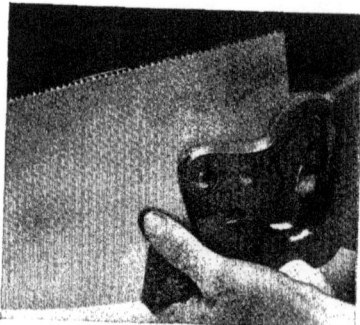

Fig. 59.—Needle Gliding between Points of Properly Set Teeth of Saw

A saw-set of the above type, called the Ætna, is illustrated in Fig. 55, in which A is a steel block with the edges bevelled

knocked down in the vice by the hammering.

A method of setting saws on the above

SAWS AND SAWING

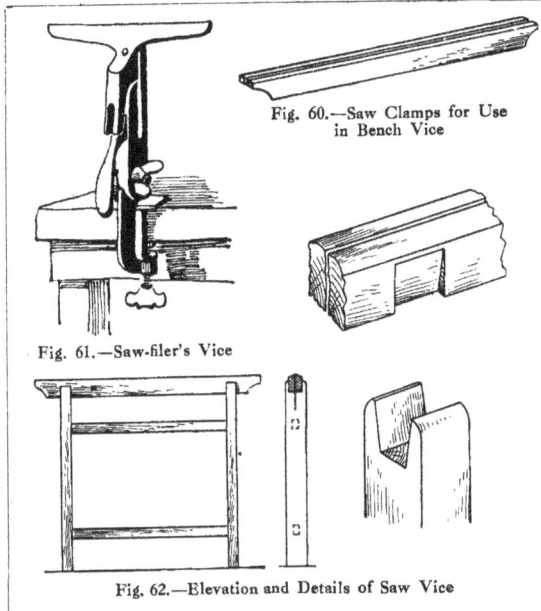

Fig. 60.—Saw Clamps for Use in Bench Vice

Fig. 61.—Saw-filer's Vice

Fig. 62.—Elevation and Details of Saw Vice

about 2 in. by 1 in. in section (*see* Fig. 60). The saw blade is placed between these two strips and the whole tightened up in a vice. The saw should not project more than about ½ in., or the teeth will spring or "give" when filing, but when using the saw-set of the plunger type the teeth must project more to accommodate the saw-set. Fig. 61 shows another type of saw vice.

The ordinary woodworker's bench vice is rather low for saw sharpening. A more convenient type of saw clamp of suitable height is shown in Fig. 62; the clamp pieces fit into tapered slots in the top of the stand, and when driven into position with a few taps from a hammer bind the saw blade tightly between them.

On sighting along the teeth of a dull

lines is to use a piece of *hardwood*, as Fig. 58. Place the saw on it, and hit each tooth with a nail punch and hammer. Each tooth will be bent a little—varying with the strength of the blow—but the hardwood will prevent the teeth being bent too far or getting broken. This method is very convenient when the workman has not a saw-set to hand or for the amateur worker who does not wish to go to the expense of buying one. A hardwood block similar in shape to Fig. 53 could be used.

When an ordinary hand saw has been properly set it will allow a needle to glide down the teeth as shown in Fig. 59 (which is reproduced from a straight, untouched photograph).

Sharpening Saws.—In order to hold the saw whilst sharpening, various devices are used, the simplest consisting of two pieces of wood the length of the saw and

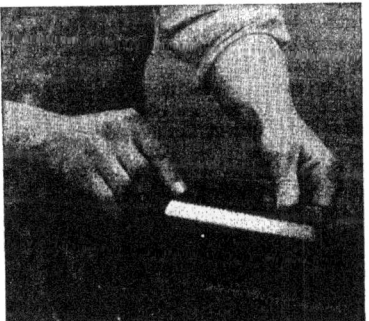

Fig. 63.—Topping Saw Teeth with Flat File

or badly sharpened saw it will be seen that the teeth are not in a straight line, but they are uneven. Therefore the first step in sharpening is to straighten—

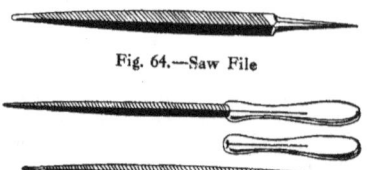

Fig. 64.—Saw File

Fig. 65.—Double-ended Saw File

or reduce to an even slightly convex curve—the line of the teeth, and this is done by running a file (preferably a flat one) over the points of the teeth. It is convenient to fit a flat file in a groove cut in a piece of wood, and then if this wooden guide is held against the side of the blade, the file will be kept level and the points of the teeth consequently filed more accurately, or a large file may be used without mounting it, as in Fig. 63.

A three-cornered or triangular file, incorrectly known sometimes as a "three-square" file (Fig. 64), is required for the actual sharpening. Such files are made in various sizes, a 4½ in. file being suitable for hand saws and a 3½ in. for tenon saws. A double-ended saw file (Fig. 65) is very convenient and the one generally favoured. An 8 in. file is a convenient size; though rather large for panel and tenon saws, it may be used to sharpen them as well as the hand saw.

The section of the file is an equilateral triangle, and the *size* of the file will not alter the *angles* of the file, which are 60° in every case.

Begin sharpening at the handle end of the saw. The file is held level but pointing towards the handle end of the saw. (Some saw sharpeners advise that the file should be inclined a little, about 15 degrees, but this does not matter much, and it gives the teeth an uneven appearance.) The position to hold the file may be determined by laying it between the teeth so that it will file the teeth and yet preserve the former shape. The position of the file is shown in Figs. 66 and 67.

File down into each alternate gap between the teeth until the white specks (denoting dullness) on the teeth points to the left of the file are *nearly* removed. The file should only be used on the forward strokes. Two or three strokes of the file will be required for each tooth.

The tooth to the left of the file is the one that is being sharpened, but, of course, the side of the tooth to the right will also be filed a little. It is for this reason that the white specks on the teeth do not need to be entirely removed whilst doing the first side of the saw; they will be entirely removed when filing from the other side.

Sometimes, when a workman is in a hurry, he does not bother to set the saw or to run the "flatting" file over the teeth points, but simply gives each gap one or two strokes of the file. This is a quick method, and an equal amount is taken from each tooth.

When the saw has been filed from one side, it is turned round and filed from

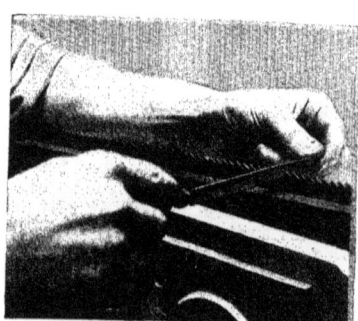

Fig. 66.—Filing Saw Teeth

the other; taking care that the file again points towards the handle end of the saw.

If the file were held at right angles to the saw blade the gap between the teeth would be exactly 60°, but by pointing the file towards the handle this angle

SAWS AND SAWING

is increased to about 64°. A good angle for the front (leading edge) of the teeth of a cross-cut saw is about 75°. The teeth angles will thus be as shown in Fig. 68.

The front edges of the rip-saw teeth are at about 90° to the edge (87° is shown in the diagram). The angle between the teeth will be about 62°, thus giving the shape as in Fig. 69.

The teeth of the rip saw are filed in the same manner as for a cross-cut saw,

Fig. 67.—Plan showing Angle of Saw File

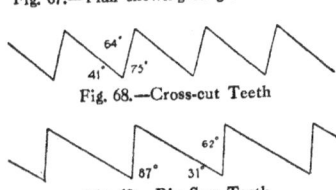

Fig. 68.—Cross-cut Teeth

Fig. 69.—Rip Saw Teeth

but the file is not pointed so much towards the handle (from 3° to 5° out of square is about right), whilst for a cross cut, tenon, or panel saw the file should be pointed about 20° to 30° out of square. The more the file is held out of square the finer will be the point and the keener the cutting, but the teeth will be weaker and more quickly dulled. Some experts contend that for rip saws the file should be held at 90° to the blade, each tooth then acting as a small chisel; but as the grain of timber is always more or less curved it is better generally to point the file towards the handle as before stated. For saws that are used mostly for cross-cutting soft wood a fine sharp tooth that will easily cut its way through soft fibres is desired, and this is obtained by holding the file more obliquely to the saw blade, say about 60° (30° out of square). For hardwood the teeth are better if less acute, and the file is held at about 70°

to 75° to the face of the saw (15° to 20° out of square)

Panel, tenon, dovetail, and compass saws are sharpened as for a cross-cut saw, but it is desirable to use a little

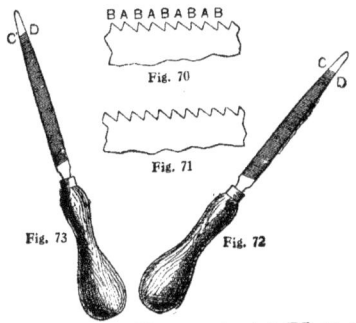

Figs. 70 to 73.—Diagrams showing Effects of Varying the Angle at which Saw File is Held

finer file. Pad saws are made with the blade tapering quickly towards the back edge, and therefore do not require setting.

If the above instructions are followed, no difficulty should be experienced in sharpening all the ordinary types of saws, but the beginner often finds that the teeth after being filed are not even and regular. Let it be assumed that the teeth, after filing, are similar to those shown in Fig. 70, while, properly filed, the angles should be alike, as in Fig 71. Teeth A (Fig. 70) are supposed to be filed with their points towards the filer and teeth B away from the filer. The file in the first place is held at an angle similar to that shown by Fig 72, and in the second place at that shown by Fig. 73. The greater pressure in each case is on the angle c, which tends to widen the roots of the teeth A, as the filing also tends towards the points of these teeth both in the face and back filing. With such filing the teeth on one range will (as will be seen) have a faster cut than on the other range, and if such filing is continued, eventually every alternate tooth will be filed out, or the saw gets into such a condition that it will be useless. The aim should be to hold the file at correct angles in each case and to avoid undue pressure with the thumb at the angles c (Figs. 72 and 73), for it will be clearly seen that the teeth A get most of the filing unless this is guarded against. Ease the pressure at the angle c, and increase it a little at D, so that the faces of the teeth (in each case) get their due amount of filing.

Accurate Sawing: Waste Caused by the Saw Kerf.—If a piece of wood exactly 6 inches long is sawn into halves exactly in the centre it might be thought that two 3 in. pieces would result. A little reflection will make obvious that each piece will be 3 in. long *less half the thickness of a saw kerf*. This does not matter on rough work but for good joinery, cabinet work, etc., if any joint has a gap the size of half a saw cut it is a bad job.

so that *half the line is left on the piece that is wanted*. This will conduce to accuracy. Remember that a few extra seconds spent on accurate sawing will save minutes of fitting and planing afterwards. Get into the habit of cutting a piece exactly right length the first time.

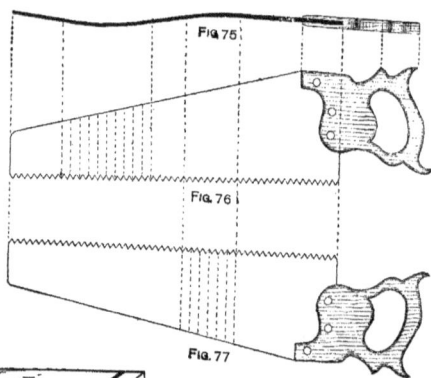

Figs. 75 to 77.—Top, Front and Back of Buckled Handsaw

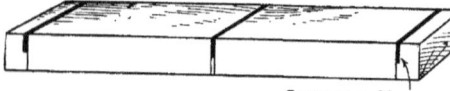

Fig. 74.—Sawing in the Waste

Suppose two pieces of wood exactly 1 ft. long each had to be cut out of a piece 2 ft. 6 in. long. First look to see if the ends of the piece are good or shaky, and square a line over one end to avoid any defects. Measure 1 ft. from the squared line and square another line; square another line over about a "bare eighth" (the thickness of the saw kerf) from this line. From the last line measure 1 ft. and square another line over the timber. If now the ends are sawn off with the saw kerfs in the waste wood and the centre sawn between the two lines the resulting pieces will be exactly 6 in. long (*see* Fig. 74).

It is clear from the above that the saw kerf should be in the waste wood, or the piece of timber wanted will be a little short. A good rule, when the timber is marked with pencil, is to try to saw

Buckled Saws.—The blade of a saw often gets buckled—that is, permanently bent—particularly when the teeth have little set and the tool is used on wet timber. Fig. 75 shows the plan of a buckled saw, Fig. 76 the front side, and Fig. 77 the back side. The curvature or buckle can be hammered out of the saw. A joiner's hammer with a slightly round face should be used so that the blade will not be marked. Saw experts use special hammers. The blade of the saw should be laid, hollow side down, on a block of iron, and the convex side hammered as shown in Figs. 75 and 76. The dotted lines show where the blades should be hammered. The saw shown will have to be hammered on both sides as indicated. In general it is better to have a buckled saw put right by an expert, as it is necessary to know beforehand the effect of every blow of the hammer.

Hammers and Mallets

THE best type of hammer for general woodworking is shown in Fig. 1 and is known as a Warrington hammer. This is the kind generally used by cabinetmakers and joiners. Some, however, prefer the London pattern (Fig. 1A). Various sizes may be obtained, but size 2 or size 3 is usual for bench work.

The head is made of cast steel; the of ash; sometimes beech is used, but it is not as suitable as ash, being more brittle. Ash is tougher and more elastic, and better able to withstand sudden jars than beech. The shape of the shaft varies somewhat according to the taste of each woodworker, and also with the kind of hammer, but the shaft shown in Fig. 1 is a favourite pattern.

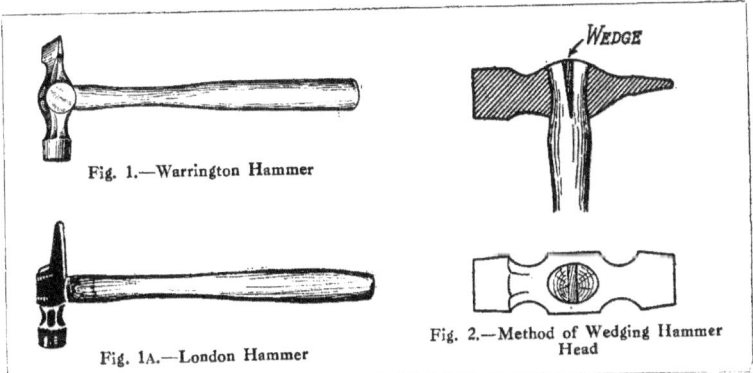

Fig. 1.—Warrington Hammer

Fig. 1A.—London Hammer

Fig. 2.—Method of Wedging Hammer Head

"face" should be slightly convex so that the timber is not easily marked when the hammer hits the surface. The thin end of the head is known as the "pene," and is useful for starting small nails held between finger and thumb, or for driving nails in grooves or other restricted places.

The handle or shaft is usually made It is usual nowadays to buy the hammer complete with shaft. If the shaft gets broken a ready-made one can be bought or one can easily be made. The shaft is fitted into the head and a saw cut made in the shaft to receive a wedge. This saw cut is better if made across the head (as Fig. 2); this wedges the shaft in the direction in which it has a tendency to work loose—the head has little tendency to work loose sideways. Iron wedges

Fig. 3.—Claw Hammer

are often used instead of wood, but on the whole they offer little if any advantage. When they get rusty they often become loose and may then fall out.

When the head works slightly loose it is generally due to the wood shrinking, and may be remedied by putting the hammer in water for an hour or so. This is obviously only a temporary remedy, as when the wood again shrinks the head will again become loose, and a better method is to put in a slightly larger wedge.

The claw hammer shown in Fig. 3 is largely used by carpenters, and is useful

Fig. 4.—Avoiding Hammer Marks

for pulling out nails. It is the favourite American hammer. Other hammers are often used, such as upholsterers',

veneerers' or saw-setting hammers, but these will be described later.

Little can be said about using a

Fig. 5.—Mallet

hammer; it is mostly a matter of practice, but two common faults with beginners are that the hammer is held too near the head and held too stiffly. Hold the shaft as near the end as convenient, and, when striking, do not press or push the hammer but let it drop on the nail with a smart rap. Use the force at the beginning of the blow and then let the head drop. This hint is given because beginners often seem to pull back a little as the hammer hits the nails, etc.; they rob the blow of part of its power besides causing harder work for themselves.

In using the hammer on finished work or anything that must not be "hammer marked" a small piece of wood—a hammering piece—is used between the hammer and the work (see Fig. 4).

A mallet (Fig. 5) might be described as a wooden-headed hammer. It is used where a hammer would injure the tools, etc. It should be used with all chisels, gauges, etc., as a hammer would soon split the handles.

The mallet may be made of beech or ash. Those bought ready-made are usually of beech, but it is preferable to have the handle of ash. The hole in the head is made tapered—bigger on the wide part; the handle is also tapered and passed through the hole in the head until it tightens in the hole. Being fastened in this way, the head does not easily work loose, as in striking the tendency is for the handle to be pulled farther through the head and thus tightened more securely.

The "hitting faces" of the mallet are bevelled so as to get a straight hit at the chisel, etc.; see Fig. 6, which demonstrates

HAMMERS AND MALLETS

that the faces should taper towards the point about which the mallet is swung when using.

Pincers are used for pulling out nails, etc. They vary in shape and size. A 7 in. pair of the Lancashire type (*see* Fig. 7) will be found suitable. Various methods of using and the mechanical principles of the pincers will be dealt with in the chapter on nailing and screwing. Another common pattern of pincers is shown in Fig. 8.

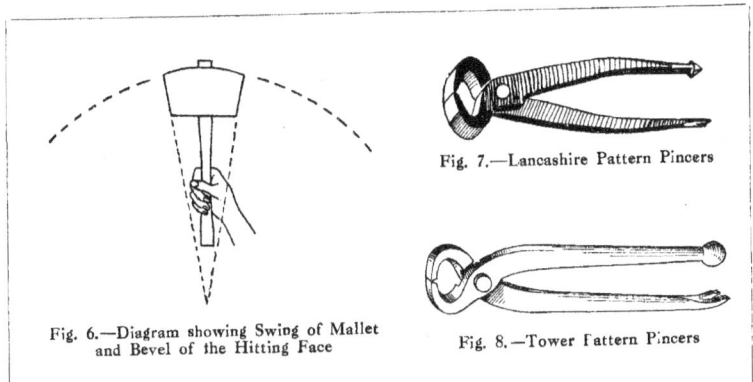

Fig. 6.—Diagram showing Swing of Mallet and Bevel of the Hitting Face

Fig. 7.—Lancashire Pattern Pincers

Fig. 8.—Tower Pattern Pincers

Chisels and Gouges

There are three chief types of chisels used by the woodworker: (1) firmer chisels, (2) paring chisels, (3) mortise chisels.

The firmer chisel (Fig. 1) is the most common type as it can be used in addition for either mortising or paring. The other is a "tang" which fits into the handle. The length of blade is about 5 in., and the chisels may be bought in different widths: from $\frac{1}{16}$ in. to $\frac{1}{2}$ in. rising by sixteenths; from $\frac{1}{2}$ in. to 1 in. rising in eights; from 1 in. to 2 in. rising in quarters.

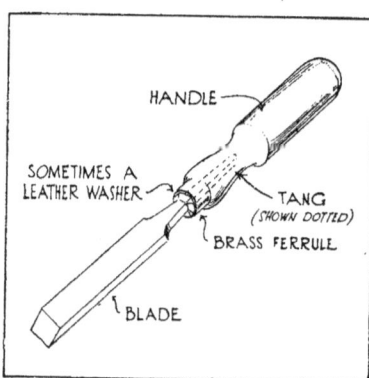

Fig. 1.—Firmer Chisel and Names of Parts

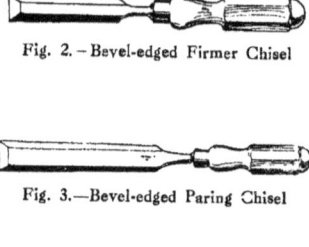

Fig. 2.—Bevel-edged Firmer Chisel

Fig. 3.—Bevel-edged Paring Chisel

Fig. 4.—Paring Chisel

handle is preferably of ash and, to prevent splitting, should have a brass ferrule as shown. As a further precaution against the handle splitting, a leather washer is often inserted between the edge of the handle and the shoulder of the "tang."

The blade is of cast steel and is ground and sharpened at one end, while at the

The chisel blade is often built up of two kinds of steel. Hard steel is necessary for the cutting edge, but if all the blade were made of this steel it would be difficult to grind. The blade, therefore, consists mostly of softer metal except at the cutting edge and is consequently tougher and less liable to snap.

CHISELS AND GOUGES

The two kinds of steel can be easily seen on examining a bright chisel or even more clearly on looking at a plane iron. (See Fig. 5.)

The edge of a chisel has two bevels— a grinding angle and a setting or sharpening angle. When bought a chisel is simply ground and has to be sharpened by Fig. 1, but it is not suitable for heavy work or mortising. It is of the same length and may be obtained in the same widths as firmer chisels.

Two types of paring chisels are shown in Figs. 3 and 4, one having bevelled edges. These chisels are thinner than firmer chisels and the blade is about

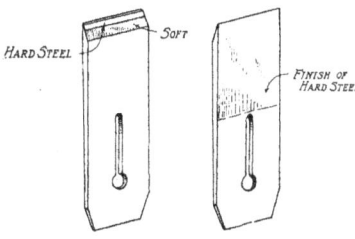

Fig. 5.—Front and Back of Plane Iron showing the Built-up Blade

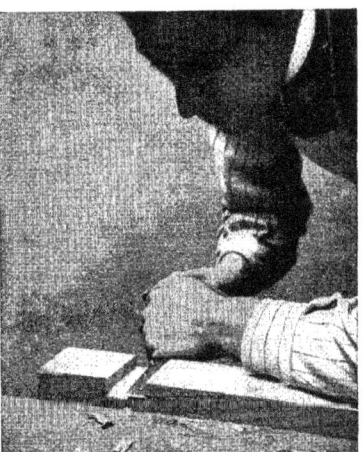

Fig. 7A.—Chiselling Slot: Incorrect Method. Note the Piece Splintered off the Back by Chiselling Through

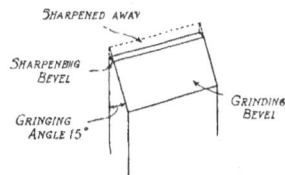

Fig. 6.—Chisel Blade, showing Grinding and Sharpening Angles

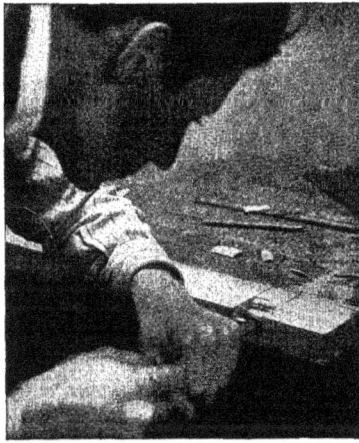

Fig. 7.—Chiselling Slot: Correct Method

before using; in sharpening, this bevel is not kept flat on the oilstone with the result that the sharpening angle is formed (see Fig. 6).

A bevelled-edge firmer chisel is shown in Fig. 2. It is generally used for paring, for which it is more suitable than that shown

twice the length. These long paring chisels are not much used by the average woodworker, being chiefly used by pattern makers. The firmer bevelled-edged chisel is suitable for paring, in fact, this chisel is sometimes called a paring chisel.

Using Firmer and Paring Chisel.— Fig. 7 shows the method of holding the chisel when chiselling a slot in a piece of wood, the sides of the slot having first been sawn down with the tenon saw. The slot should be chiselled from both sides; if the slot is chiselled straight through from one side there is a liability of breaking off the corner or edge of the slot at the other side as Fig. 7A. It is better to chisel half way through and take off a little amount at each cut until the right depth is reached. Then turn the wood round and finish from the other side.

If the timber is for a big and rough job the slot may be chiselled by laying the wood on the bench and using the mallet

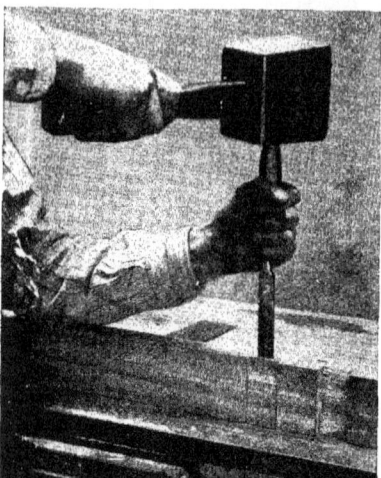

Fig. 8.—Using Mallet when Making Slot in Large Work

Fig. 10.—Chiselling Corner: Correct Method

Fig. 9.—Chiselling Small Corner

and chisel as Fig. 8. In paring in the direction of the length of a piece of wood always try to chisel with the grain. If the wood were chiselled in the other direction the chisel would dig in and tend to split the wood. An example of this is when chiselling a corner. This may be done by laying the wood flat on the bench and chiselling vertically as Fig. 10. Care should be taken to work inwards towards the end of the wood. If the end is chiselled by working outwards towards the edge of the wood a split is likely to occur as in Fig. 10A.

CHISELS AND GOUGES

Where the corner is smaller than the chisel the above precaution is not necessary and the chisel is held as shown in Fig. 9.

If the corner is very large it is better to fix the wood in the vice and pare the corner horizontally (more or less); care should be taken to pare in the direction from the edge to the end of the wood, otherwise there is a tendency to split off a portion of the corner (see Fig. 11).

When paring the end of a piece of wood it is easier to take off a little at a time as in Fig. 12.

In using chisels always try to keep

Fig. 11.—Paring Corner Horizontally

Fig. 10A.—Chiselling Corner: Incorrect Method. Note the Split

both hands behind the edge of the chisel and thus avoid accidents.

Mortising Chisel.—This type of chisel is not so much used in workshops as formerly owing to the employment of mortising machines. Though a firmer chisel is not so good for mortising it will perform the work satisfactorily. Two types of mortise chisels are shown by Figs. 13 to 14A, the second being of the socket type. It will be seen that these chisels are much stronger than firmer or paring chisels.

Fig. 15 shows a mortise chisel in use.

In cutting a mortise hole, start at the centre of the mortise and work towards the end of the hole. Hold the chisel upright and drive into the mortise as far as convenient but so that the chisel does not stick; repeat this in steps

Fig. 12.—Take Off a Little Only at Each Cut

backwards of about $\frac{1}{8}$ in. until the end of the hole is reached. For the last cut do not put the chisel quite on the line (the limit of the mortise) but a trifle nearer the centre of the mortise to allow for the chisel "drifting" a little as it is forced down. When this is done, start again from the centre of the hole and work

Removal of waste wood should only be done if strictly necessary, as usually it is a waste of time, besides tending to make

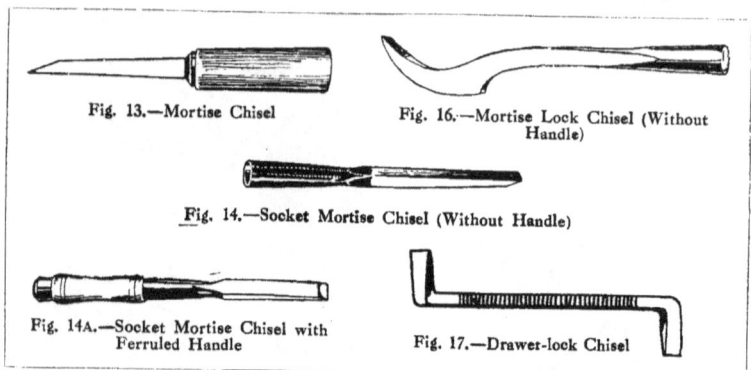

Fig. 13.—Mortise Chisel

Fig. 16.—Mortise Lock Chisel (Without Handle)

Fig. 14.—Socket Mortise Chisel (Without Handle)

Fig. 14A.—Socket Mortise Chisel with Ferruled Handle

Fig. 17.—Drawer-lock Chisel

towards the other end. Just before getting to the end of the hole some of the waste wood may be prised out with the

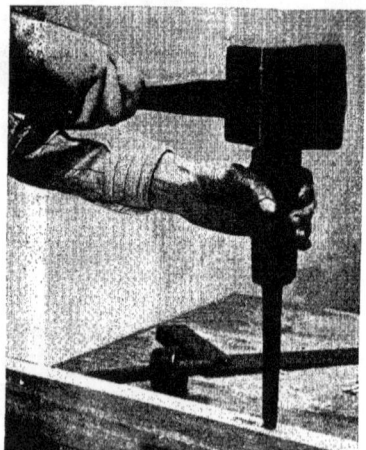

Fig. 15.—Using Mortising Chisel

chisel. Do not prise with the chisel off the end of the mortise or the corners or edges of the work will be spoiled.

a poor job of the mortise. The woodworker should have in his mind that a mortising machine only works with an up-and-down motion, and the closer the hand method to this the better.

When the wood has been mortised from one side, turn it over and complete from the other. Usually it will be better to hold the wood in the vice, particularly when working from the second side, as the core (waste wood) can be more easily removed. If the wood is too big to go in the vice raise it on two pieces of wood on the bench.

Sometimes a piece of wood (called a "drift") is used for driving out the waste wood from the mortise after using the chisel, but it is mostly used in machine mortising.

If a firmer chisel is used for mortising care should be taken not to break it; this readily happens when the chisel has been driven into the wood and the operator presses on it sideways to loosen it.

Some other Chisels.—Coachmakers' chisels are long, thick firmer chisels suitable for rough work and mortising. One of these chisels, about $\frac{1}{2}$ in. wide, is convenient for use in fitting mortise locks, but there is a special mortise lock chisel (*see* Fig. 16).

CHISELS AND GOUGES

A drawer-lock chisel is shown in Fig. 17. Its cranked shape makes it suitable for cutting the bolt hole for a drawer, it being difficult to use an ordinary chisel for that purpose.

A pocket chisel has a thin blade and is used mostly by joiners, chiefly for cutting the fronts of the weight pockets in vertically sliding windows.

GOUGES

A gouge (Fig. 18) may be roughly described as a chisel of circular curve. There are two chief varieties: inside ground and outside ground (Fig. 18). Fig. 19 shows a paring gouge inside ground. The inside ground type is usually the more convenient to use and the more difficult

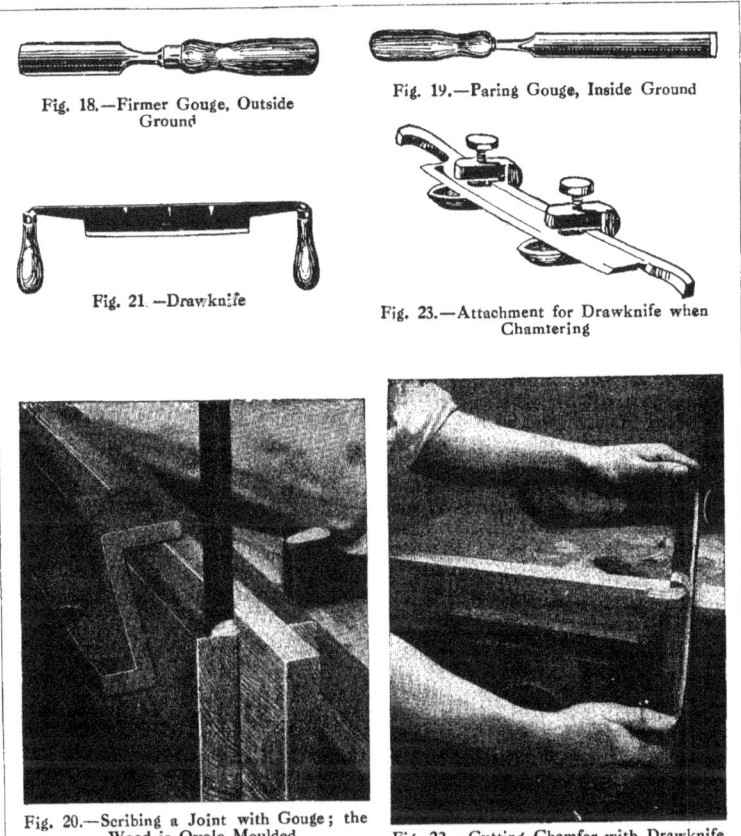

Fig. 18.—Firmer Gouge, Outside Ground

Fig. 19.—Paring Gouge, Inside Ground

Fig. 21.—Drawknife

Fig. 23.—Attachment for Drawknife when Chamfering

Fig. 20.—Scribing a Joint with Gouge; the Wood is Ovolo Moulded

Fig. 22.—Cutting Chamfer with Drawknife

to grind and sharpen. For the grinding an emery wheel is required. The use of an inside-ground gouge for scribing a joint is shown in Fig. 20.

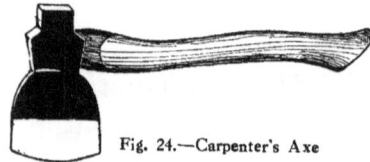

Fig. 24.—Carpenter's Axe

There are firmer gouges and paring gouges made in various widths from $\frac{1}{8}$ in. to $\frac{1}{2}$ in. They are also made in various curves in each size, that is, each size can be obtained in about six sweeps, from very flat, hardly differing from a chisel, to a very quick curve.

The Drawknife.—This tool (Fig. 21) is not so much used as formerly owing to the introduction of machinery, but it is still useful for many jobs such as chamfering. Fig. 22 shows it being used for the latter purpose, and Fig. 23 shows a special attachment for the same purpose. It is a useful tool for the wheelwright and for many kinds of rough work.

The Axe and Hatchet.—These tools (Fig. 24) are used for rough work only and often come in useful where a heavy hammer is required. Two of the commonest jobs for which the small axe or

Fig. 26.—Adze

hatchet is used are rough scribing and making wedges. Suppose, for example, that a board had to be fitted to a brick wall or a skirting board to an uneven floor, the board would be first scribed with the compasses (see Fig. 71, p. 42) and then chopped to the line with the axe or hatchet. The latter is the name given to a small axe.

In making wedges or plugs for insertion in wall joints, etc., for fixing purposes, the wedges are usually chopped to size with the axe. The wedge should be kept steady by pressing the knee against the hand holding the wedge (Fig. 25) Unless the wedge is held firmly and the axe used with care an accident may easily result.

The Adze.—This tool (Fig. 26) is used chiefly by wheelwrights and shipbuilders, but it is seldom used in ordinary woodworking. Just as the axe is used for vertical cutting, so the adze is employed for horizontal cutting and splitting.

Fig. 25.—Chopping Wedge (for Wall Plugs, etc.) with Axe. Note how the Wedge is Firmly Held by the Hand supported by Knee

Grinding and Sharpening Tools

To produce a cutting edge on all edge tools such as chisels, gouges, and planes, two processes are necessary: grinding on a grindstone and sharpening on an oilstone.

When tools are bought they are usually found to have been ground to the correct angle, but not to have been sharpened. So before using they have to be sharpened on an oilstone.

Chisels and plane irons are made up of two varieties of steel: a hard portion to form the actual cutting edge, and a soft portion to make the blade tougher, and thus prevent it from suddenly snapping. The built-up nature of the blade can easily be seen on examining a plane iron, the junction of the soft and hard steel being evident on examination (see page 67). The built-up blade, besides allowing of a keener cutting edge and providing strength, enables the blade to be ground more quickly.

The angle for grinding is about 15 degrees, as shown in Fig. 6, page 67,

Fig. 1.—Grinding Chisel: General Position (Water-can not shown)

whereas the sharpening angle is a little more than this, as shown.

Grinding.—This is done on a revolving grindstone, which may be worked by hand or power. Opinions vary as to whether the grindstone should be turned away from the operator or towards him; many workmen prefer the stone to revolve towards them, as it is the quicker method, but is the more dangerous one. The blade to be ground is simply pressed on the stone at the correct angle, and the revolving stone grinds the tool.

It is necessary to keep the stone wet, which is generally done by allowing water to drip on it from a can above. If the stone is not kept wet the blade gets hot and loses its hardness. A usual sign when the blade is getting too hot is that the edge turns a dark blue. Thus dry grinding is liable to "temper," that is, reduce the hardness of a tool.

Holding the tool in the hands whilst

grinding is usual (see Figs. 1 and 3), but it is tedious and requires much practice to produce a correctly ground bevel. The blade is therefore often levered against the stone as in Fig. 2, which shows a good method, one that is quick and safe to use if the stone is revolving upwards from where the chisel is placed; on the other hand, if the stone is revolving downwards there is a marked tendency for the blade to be dragged downwards and the fingers trapped; hundreds of accidents have occurred when using this method,

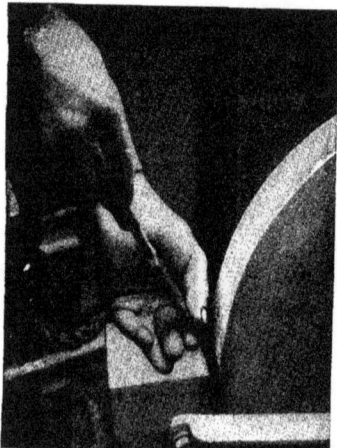

Fig. 2.—Grinding Chisel held Downwards, Grindstone Revolving Upwards

and it should be avoided as positively dangerous.

Various devices have been invented for holding the tool at the correct angle for grinding, but few of them have "caught on" for ordinary use.

Probably the best of them is shown in Fig. 4; a frame is pivoted to one side of the grindstone and the blade to be ground is fixed in this frame. More pressure can be used by this method, but the weight of the frame itself is sufficient to keep the blade in contact with the grindstone. A good finish is obtained by this device, and previous experience is not necessary.

The tool-grinding rest shown by Fig. 7 is a cheaper device, but not so good. Though a better and straighter angle could be obtained by the beginner with this rest than without it, its use will absorb both time and effort, as part of the pressure on the stone is taken by the rest itself.

In grinding chisels or gouges, care should be taken to use the edges as well as the centre of the stone, which otherwise is rendered unsuitable for grinding wide plane irons. But even though every care is taken, the grindstone will require "levelling" on the edge periodically. When it gets worn out of the circle, say ½ in., it should be trued up; this is best done when the stone is dry. The uneven wear may be due to soft places in the stone or to keeping part of the stone under water. The grindstone is levelled by pressing the end of a piece of hard iron or steel pipe, say a piece of old cycle tube, against the edge (Fig. 8); the tube is held firmly on a rest (not shown) and moved to-and-fro across the uneven edge of the revolving stone. Sometimes two old flat files or two short pieces of flat bar iron and a piece of stout hoop iron about 18 in. long are used; lay the hoop iron between the other pieces, allowing the end to project about ¼ in., and with this tool turn the stone away. Turn over the tool occasionally to keep a good cutting edge presented to the stone.

Grinding may be thoroughly well done on an artificial or manufactured wheel, say of emery or carborundum. Gouges (inside ground) cannot be conveniently ground on a grindstone, and they require one of the stones just mentioned, especially shaped for the purpose.

Oilstones.—There are many varieties of oilstones. The favourite brand is probably a "Washita" stone, obtainable in various degrees of hardness, "soft," "medium," or "fine." The last-named puts the finest edge on the tool, but it requires the most time to do so. The "soft" is the most rapid for sharpening, but wears quickly and does not give so keen an edge. Either a "medium" or a "soft" is the best for average work.

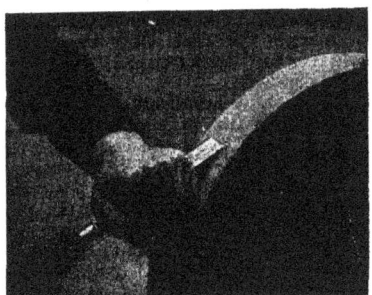

Fig. 3.—Grinding Chisel: The More Usual Position

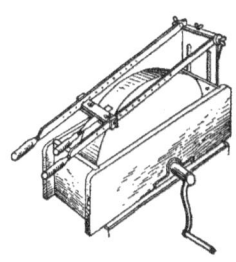

Fig. 4.—Adjustable Tool-grinding Appliance Fitted to Grindstone

Fig. 1 on page 73 illustrates the well-known treadle-driven grindstone. In many small shops this is being replaced by a geared high-speed grinder (see Fig. 5 herewith) employing a corundum grinding wheel used dry (power-driven corundum wheels are, of course, available). The hand-driven wheel requires the services of two persons—one to turn the handle and the other to hold the tool

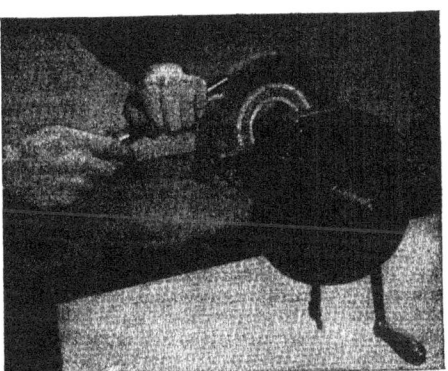

Fig. 5.—Using a Hand-driven Geared Corundum Grinding Wheel

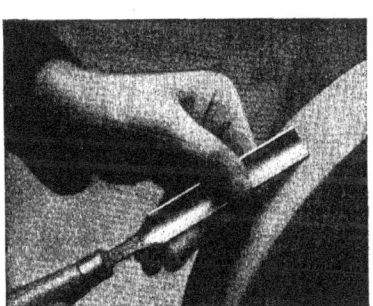

Fig. 6.—Grinding Gouge

Fig. 7.—Plane Iron in Tool-grinding Rest

There are many other good varieties of stones, some natural and some artificial compositions. Most of the natural stones are quarried and sawn. The Arkansas and Washita stone is found in Arkansas

Fig. 8.—Levelling Grindstone with End of Steel Tube. (The Tool Rest is not shown)

and is quarried in summer. It is sawn by plain bands of steel without teeth, the cutting element being a stream of sand and water that is poured over the stone as it is being sawn.

The Arkansas stone is similar to Washita, but more costly and finer in grain. It is largely used for sharpening surgical instruments. Charnley Forest and Turkey oilstones are suitable for woodworkers' tools, give a fine cutting edge, but are slow-cutting.

The India oilstone is an artificial stone manufactured in America. It is made in "fine" and "medium" grades, the latter being suitable for woodworking tools. "Combination" India oilstones are made of two parts, one face medium and the other face coarse grit. The coarse side can be used for very dull tools, and the edge finally rubbed up on the medium side.

Carborundum artificial stones can be had in various makes, sizes, and grades.

Water is used instead of oil for some stones, but most stones require oil; ordinary machine oil will do and is commonly used, but neatsfoot oil—an animal oil—is the best.

The oil keeps the pores of the stone from becoming clogged with the finely ground steel, lubricates the stone, and prevents the blade from becoming so hot as to "lose its temper," that is, lose its hardness.

A special oil-can is used to hold the oil. There are two varieties of "non-leak" cans that are in common use. Both of them have a pin in the nipple that stops up the passage when the can is not being used. In one can (Fig. 8A) the pin is pressed away from the outlet when pressing the can bottom with the thumb. In the other type the pin (projecting from the end of the nipple) is pressed on the oilstone to let the oil out of the can.

Oilstones may be bought separately or in ready-made boxes. A rough box may be easily made (it is usually "chopped out of the solid," see Fig. 9) and the stone fixed in by making it a tight fit or bedding it in white lead ; the latter is preferred as it prevents the stone being easily broken.

Two small nails are often knocked in the bottom of the box and left projecting about $\tfrac{1}{16}$ in., and filed to sharp points. The points stick in the bench top and prevent the oilstone sliding about whilst using.

After a stone has been in constant use for a few months it gets hollow in the centre and lumpy at the ends. In this state it is unsuitable for sharpening tools, particularly plane irons, and it therefore needs to be " rubbed down."

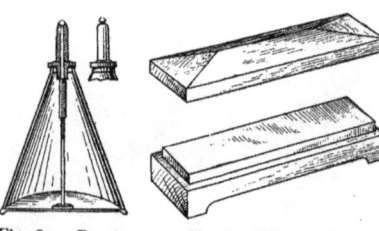

Fig. 8A.—Bench Oil-can

Fig. 9.—Oilstone Box Cut from the Solid

" Rubbing down " an oilstone is accomplished in two ways : on the grindstone, or on a flat stone. The grindstone is the quicker method, the oilstone simply

GRINDING AND SHARPENING TOOLS

being held against a side of the grindstone whilst the latter revolves. Rubbing the oilstone on a flat stone is a longer process on it, using water as a lubricant, and often a handful of sand to quicken the cutting. The sand being gritty and

Fig. 10.—Sharpening Plane Iron: Usual Method

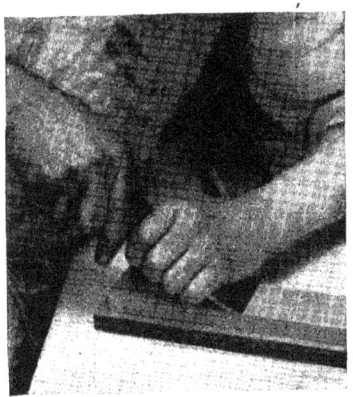

Fig. 11.—Holding Plane Iron to give more Pressure

Fig. 12.—Sharpening Chisel: Correct Angle

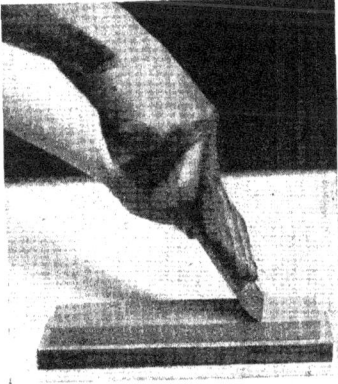

Fig. 13.—Sharpening Plane Iron: Angle too Steep

but gives a better result. The stone (as a door-step, preferably before fixing it in a building) should have a coarse grit. The oilstone is simply rubbed to-and-fro sprinkled on the stone enables the superfluous material on the oilstone to be rubbed away more quickly. Another method is to rub the stone on a sheet of glasspaper or emery cloth laid on a flat surface.

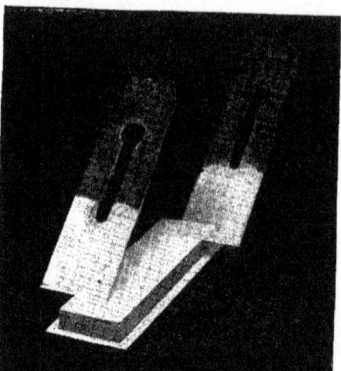

Fig. 14.—Showing the Sideways Movement as the Blade is Pushed Along

Sharpening or Setting Edge Tools.
—The sharpening of a plane iron is done

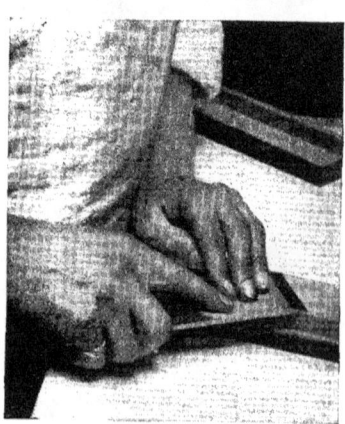

Fig. 15.—Taking Off the Burr

in the same way as sharpening a chisel; in fact, a plane may be simply described as a chisel fastened in a block of wood or iron. The adjusting of the plane iron

Fig. 16.—Testing the blade for Sharpness with the Thumb

in the stock of the plane will be dealt with in the chapter on planes.

First as to the correct way of holding the tool whilst sharpening. Fig. 10 shows the usual method of holding a plane iron. The right hand is chiefly used to push the blade forwards and backwards, and the left hand to press the edge on the stone

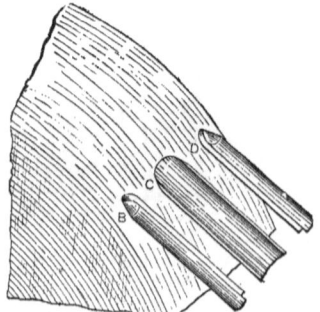

Fig. 16A.—Grinding a Gouge; B, C and D indicate Rotary Movement of Tool

but more pressure can be put on the blade by holding the left hand, as in Fig. 11.

GRINDING AND SHARPENING TOOLS

Care should be taken to hold the tool at the correct inclination. Fig. 12 shows a chisel being sharpened at the correct simply gliding backwards and forwards. Avoid any up and down movements; this is the chief fault of the beginner,

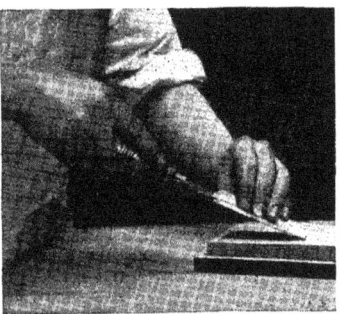

Fig. 17.—Sharpening Outside Ground Gouge

Fig. 18.—Sharpening Gouge: Another Method

angle, while Fig. 13 shows a plane iron held at too steep an angle. The best rule is to keep the angle of inclination as low as is consistent with easy sharpening. The lower the angle at which the tool is held the more metal has to be rubbed and is the chief defect to be guarded against.

The blade of a plane iron is not pushed straight up and down the stone, but somewhat across from corner to corner, as indicated in Fig. 14. This movement

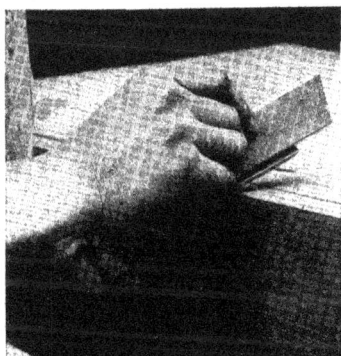

Fig. 19.—Removing Burr with Finger Slip

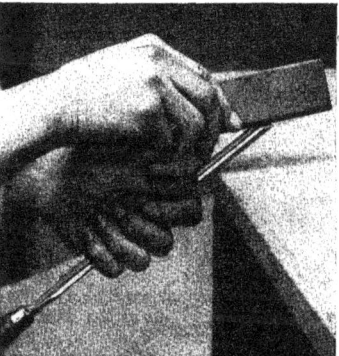

Fig. 20.—Sharpening Inside Ground Gouge with Finger Slip

away, but the finer and better the cutting edge.

The operator should endeavour to keep the right hand at a constant height, has been found to be the best for plane irons, as the edge is sharpened more evenly, but it is not so desirable for chisels, which may be moved practically parallel with the sides of the stone. In sharpening a chisel it should be rubbed on the stone

Fig. 21.—Sharpening Axe

towards the edges and not in the centre, or the stone will be worn hollow, and thus rendered unsuitable for the wide tools.

After about a minute's rubbing (for a plane iron, less time for a narrow chisel) the blade should be sharp. Sometimes a perfectly new chisel requires many minutes' work put into it. With sharpening, the edge will have burred over a little; the back of the iron is therefore laid quite flat on the face of the stone and rubbed gently backwards and forwards two or three times (see Fig. 15). The oil is wiped from the blade, which is then tested to see whether it is sharp enough. There are two methods of testing. Fig. 16 shows the edge being tested by drawing the thumb gently across the edge. This method puts slight cuts in the thumb and is really unnecessary, as the worker can see whether the edge is sharp or not simply by looking at it. A fine white line on the edge of the tool betrays that it is dull. If the edge cannot be seen, that is, if no white line can be seen, then the blade is sharp. The presence or not of the white line can be best observed by closely watching the edge as the iron blade is tilted backwards and forwards to catch the light. If the blade is found to be still dull it is rubbed again on the stone until judged to be sharp, and is then again tested.

Plane irons in constant use require sharpening about every twenty minutes, but the time they will keep reasonably sharp depends upon the kind of wood being planed and on whether it is quite clean. Dirty and gritty timber soon dulls a plane. Much depends on the quality of the steel blade.

Gouges are ground as illustrated in Fig. 6 (p. 75), and are rotated as in Fig. 16a.

"Outside ground" gouges are sharpened on an ordinary oilstone (see Fig. 17) by holding and pushing it like a chisel, but giving it a semi-rotary movement with the right hand to avoid getting any straight parts on the edge. Fig. 18 shows a different method, the gouge, in plan, being at right angles to the stone; a better edge can probably be obtained by this method but it is not as rapid as that shown in Fig. 17. The burr edge on the inside may then be removed by using a "finger slip" (see Fig. 19), which is a small oilstone with rounded edges (average size about 4 in. long, 2 in. wide, and tapering from $\frac{1}{2}$ in. to $\frac{1}{4}$ in. thick). But this removing of the burr edge is hardly necessary unless the job is a really high-class one.

Fig. 22.—Small Hand-driven Grindstone

"Inside ground" gouges cannot, of course, be sharpened on an ordinary oilstone, and the finger slip has to be used as in Fig. 20.

The axe and drawknife are usually

GRINDING AND SHARPENING TOOLS

sharpened by rubbing them with the oilstone; the axe is shown being sharpened in this manner in Fig. 21.

Grindstones : Selecting and Mounting.—Grindstones are mostly obtained from Yorkshire quarries, but may come from Derbyshire and Newcastle. The colour varies, but is usually a light grey or yellow.

A dark streak through the centre, or a dark patch on one side, indicates that the stone is much harder at those places than elsewhere; the consequence is, it will wear away faster at the softer parts and will therefore never be truly round for long together. It will wear lumpy, and at the dark places the tool that is being ground will glide over easily, and directly afterwards catch hold of the softer stone all at once, and "dig in."

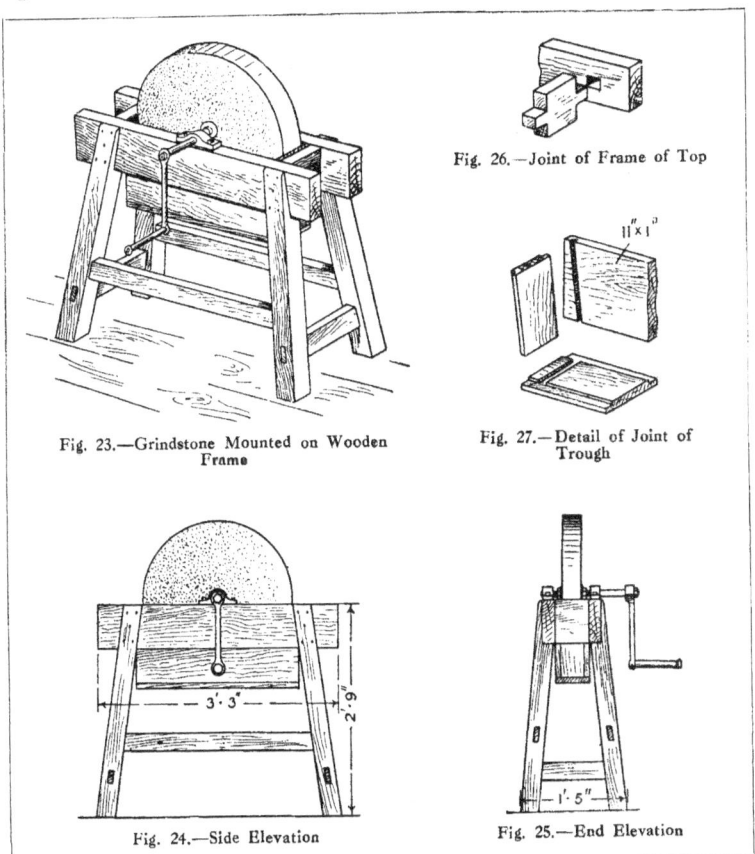

Fig. 23.—Grindstone Mounted on Wooden Frame

Fig. 24.—Side Elevation

Fig. 25.—End Elevation

Fig. 26.—Joint of Frame of Top

Fig. 27.—Detail of Joint of Trough

6—N.E.

A stone that shows flaws on the sides, as little smooth places running into it with fine cracks showing away from the ends, should be rejected, as such a stone will not stand frosty weather; a thick stone also is undesirable—one $2\frac{1}{2}$-in. or 3-in. wide on the face being ample for the average workshop, and one much smaller is suitable for occasional grinding—as it will tend to wear hollow and in that way always be a nuisance. A smooth stone with a bluish tint should be avoided, as such a one will work harder and smoother till it becomes like a glass bottle, and of no use at all for its proper work.

Test the stone with the thumb-nail, and if that should wear it down with a few rubs backwards and forwards and leave straight marks on the nail, this shows a good free-cutting stone.

A strong frame on which to mount it may be made of 3-in. by 3-in. stuff, with the legs well spread out and braced together about 6 in. from the ground. It is sometimes a great advantage to be able to step up with one foot when grinding a thick, heavy iron or axe.

A box to hold water to place under the stone should be provided. Some prefer a can fixed above to allow the water to drip on the stone, but this has the disadvantage of throwing the water on the ground and over the legs and boots of the grinder; others dislike the box below the stone, as the water always left in the box tends to soften that part of the stone which is immersed in it. This can be avoided by having the box loose and letting the two end pieces run up longer than the sides. Let these pieces be of the same width at the top as the rails in the ends of the frame, and with a pair of butt hinges hang one end to the frame.

Nail firmly to the other end of the box a leather strap, and punch half a dozen holes in it about 1 in. apart, the end with the holes projecting above the box, and screw a stout 2-in. screw centrally into the other end rail. By this means the box with the water can be used whilst grinding, and, when finished with, it can be dropped down a couple of holes so as to clear the stone. Thus all the advantages of a box, without its drawbacks, can be secured. It can also be easily dropped right down to the ground for cleaning out, or in the event of any small tool falling into the box, as sometimes happens.

A grindstone mounted on an ordinary wooden framework without the hinged trough device is shown by Figs. 23 to 27.

The various pieces should first be planed up true, and then set out for mortising, tenoning, and notching. The pieces from which the frame of the top is made are each 6 in. by $2\frac{1}{4}$ in., and are mortised and tenoned together as shown by Fig. 26, and are fixed with nails. The legs are of 3-in. by 3-in. stuff, and the lower parts are mortised to receive the tenons of the 3-in. by 2-in. rails. The upper ends of the legs are cut so as to fit against the side of the top frame, to which they are fixed with nails. The rails and legs are fixed together by wedging the tenons in the mortising, the joints being previously painted.

Fig. 27 shows the method of securing the ends, sides, and bottom of the trough. These are made from 1-in. stuff, and before nailing them together, all the parts in contact should be coated with white lead and red lead, in order to make the trough water-tight. The trough is fixed to the ends of the top framing with four stout brass screws. A hole in the bottom, fitted with a wooden plug, allows the water to run off when it is not wanted. The woodwork should receive two or three coats of good oil-colour.

A suitable spindle and handle, with bearings, can be purchased ready-made from most tool dealers.

MOUNTING A GRINDSTONE TO WORK BY TREADLE.

The accompanying illustrations show how a grindstone can be mounted on a trestle and worked by a treadle.

Figs. 28 and 29 show a grindstone mounted on a wooden frame, fitted with a trough, and the spindle cranked to receive the hooked end of a connecting rod; the other end of the rod is fastened through a hole in the foot lever. The

GRINDING AND SHARPENING TOOLS

length of the cranked part of the spindle should be about 5 in.; but the size and weight of the stone is the deciding factor.

A good method for setting the stone true is to make a square hole in the centre with corners having a large radius, as shown in

Fig. 28.—Treadle Grindstone, Side View

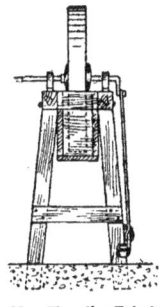

Fig. 29.—Treadle Grindstone, End View

Fig. 30.—Treadle Grindstone: Shape of Foot Lever

In Figs. 28 and 29 the crank is shown fastened to the spindle by means of a taper pin.

The shape of the foot lever is shown by Fig. 30, and other particulars can be obtained by reference to Figs. 28 and 29. Stiff bar iron or mild steel can be used, and a boss should be welded on the end

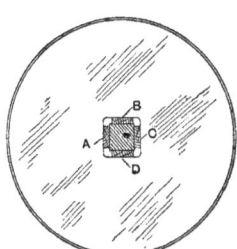

Fig. 31.—Method of Setting Stone True on Axle

that the pivot pin passes through. The looped end affords a grip for the foot, and if desired a series of chisel cuts can be made to prevent the boot slipping.

Fig. 31. The hole should be much larger than the square part of the spindle, to allow for the insertion of taper wooden wedges A, B, C, and D. The wedges can easily be adjusted if the stone does not run true.

A good form of spindle for a grindstone is shown by Fig. 32. The stone is mounted on the square portion A, and, after truing, secured by means of the flanges B and C. The faces of these should be hollowed out a little. If desired, two nuts can be used as shown, or one nut and a fixed collar. One advantage of having two nuts is

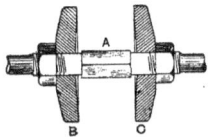

Fig. 32.—Detail of Spindle

that a thick stone can be easily placed central. Cast iron is a suitable material for the flanges or clamping plates, and mild steel for the spindle, etc.

The Plane

A PLANE in its simplest form consists of a blade fitted into a wooden or metal stock. The blade projects slightly below the bottom of the stock, and on being pushed over the surface of a piece of wood acts like a chisel and cuts into the wood, thus removing a shaving. Planes usually have a wedge or other device to hold the blade in position.

Though planes are not used as much as formerly, because of the introduction of machinery, particularly in modern well-equipped workshops, most woodworkers possess at least three planes: jack plane, trying plane, smoothing plane. These are known as the "bench planes," and are part of the necessary equipment of every woodworker.

The jack plane is used for rough work. If a piece of timber has to be planed the surface is first roughly "jacked" over, the trying plane is then used to make the surface straight and out of twist, and lastly the work is smoothed by the smoothing plane. In the case of a door or piece of framing, the jack and trying planes are used before the work is framed up and the "smoother" afterwards.

Jack Plane.—A jack plane (Fig. 1) is about 16 in. or 17 in. long, and the cutting iron is usually $2\frac{1}{8}$ in. or $2\frac{1}{4}$ in. wide. The stock and wedge are made of beech. The handle, which forms part of the body of the plane, is made from a separate piece of wood and glued in a slot formed in the top of the stock. Handles of planes are often broken—usually through knocking the plane accidentally off the bench on to the floor—in which case a new handle can be bought for a few pence, the old handle chiselled out of its slot, and the new one glued in.

Most planes are made of beech; in fact, all the wooden planes may be said to be of this timber; metal planes often have fittings and handles of rosewood or ebony. Beech is well adapted for planes; it is close grained, fairly hard, does not readily twist, and wears evenly.

On looking at the grain at the end of a plane the annual rings of the wood are easily seen. Crossing the annual rings, and nearly at right angles to them, are fine white lines called the medullary rays (*see* Fig. 2). If these white lines are at right angles to the sole, the plane will wear better and more evenly than if the lines were not upright. Of two planes that are about equal in other respects, choose the one with the more vertical medullary rays.

A plane should be "oiled" before using; this makes it heavier, lessens the friction, and thus makes the plane work easily. A reasonably heavy plane is better than a light one, as it works more solidly and does not require so much pressing down on to the work. If the plane, therefore, has not been oiled, or is too light, it should be soaked in raw linseed oil or other suitable oil until it is a suitable weight. This is usually done by suspending it in an oil tank. If this is inconvenient the cutter and wedge are

THE PLANE

taken out, the bottom of the mouth of the plane is stopped with putty, and the mouth filled with oil. After a few days the oil will have soaked into the plane; add more oil until sufficient has been absorbed. Planes are sometimes french-polished, but this is not necessary.

The plane iron, or cutter, is shown in Fig. 3, and, as described in the chapter on sharpening, is made of steel and iron, the steel being used to give a keen edge and the iron to give toughness to the blade and also enable it to be quickly sharpened.

Besides the cutter there is also a "back iron" (Fig. 4). This is screwed to the blade, the edge of the back iron being set back a little from the cutting edge of the blade. The back iron enables the plane to work better by increasing the stiffness of the blade and breaking the shavings as they are cut by the blade (*see* Fig. 5).

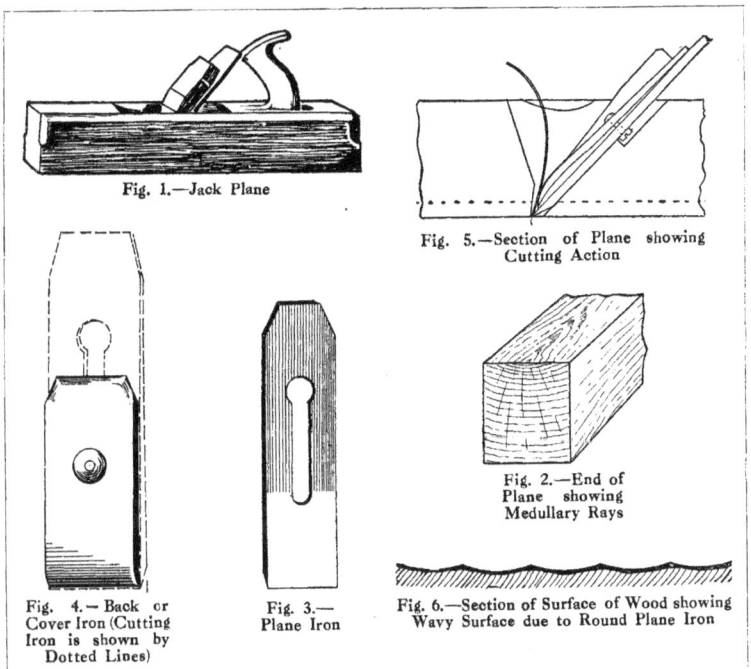

Fig. 1.—Jack Plane

Fig. 5.—Section of Plane showing Cutting Action

Fig. 2.—End of Plane showing Medullary Rays

Fig. 4.—Back or Cover Iron (Cutting Iron is shown by Dotted Lines)

Fig. 3.—Plane Iron

Fig. 6.—Section of Surface of Wood showing Wavy Surface due to Round Plane Iron

The amount that the back iron is set back from the cutting edge is important; for a jack plane it should be a bare $\frac{1}{8}$ in. The amount of "set back" is greatest for the jack plane; for the trying plane a slightly less amount is better, $\frac{1}{16}$ in. being usual, and for a smoothing plane a bare $\frac{1}{16}$ in. is used. The jack plane is for the roughest work, and therefore the set back is greatest for this plane; the smoothing plane being used for finishing off the work, and therefore for removing fine shavings, is set the finest.

The cutting iron of the jack plane should be ground slightly convex—about a bare ⅛ in. (see Fig. 7). This makes the plane work freely. Of course, this convexity of the plane iron causes the surface of the work to be wavy and uneven (see Fig. 6, which shows the unevenness exaggerated for clearness). This unevenness is afterwards removed by the trying plane and smoothing plane.

Fig. 7.—Edge of Jack Plane Iron

Fig. 8.—Edge of Trying Plane Iron

Fig. 9.—Edge of Smoothing Plane Iron

Fig. 8 shows the shape of the cutting iron for the trying plane, and Fig. 9 the shape of the smoothing plane iron. It

smoothing plane blade is straight, but with the corners taken off. These shapes

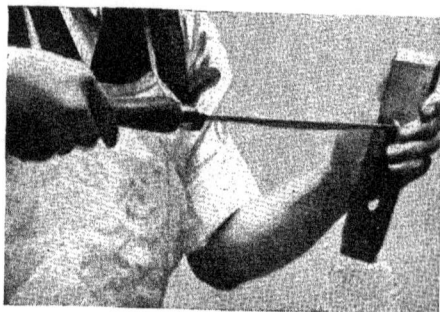

Fig. 12.—Unscrewing Plane Irons: Incorrect and Dangerous Method

of the trying plane and smoothing plane blades are not held to definitely, the smoothing plane often being of the shape shown for the trying plane. The main object is to remove the corners so that marks are not made on the surface of the wood whilst planing.

Taking Plane Apart.—When the jack plane requires sharpening it first has to be taken apart. The wedge and irons are loosened in two ways, as shown by Figs.

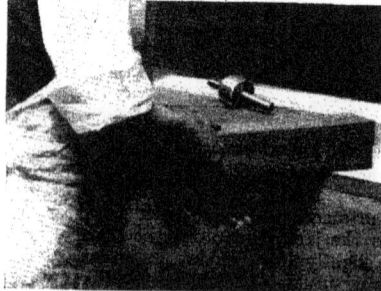

Fig. 10.—Loosening Plane Iron by Striking Plane on Bench

Fig. 11.—Loosening Plane Iron by Hitting End of Plane with Hammer

will be seen that the trying plane blade edge is the same shape as the jack plane, but with not as much curvature. The

10 and 11. The easiest method is shown at Fig. 10; take hold of the wedge and plane irons with one hand and the plane

THE PLANE

with the other, and hit the top of the front end smartly on the bench. This the other method, which consists of striking the front end of the plane sharply with the hammer. Whilst doing this the plane should be held with the thumb in the mouth on the irons and wedge, to prevent them dropping.

Now unscrew the back iron from the plane iron. This is usually accomplished by grasping the top end of the irons in the left hand and resting the cutting end on the bench (Fig. 13). Do not hold the irons in the left hand as shown in Fig. 12, as the screwdriver is liable to slip and

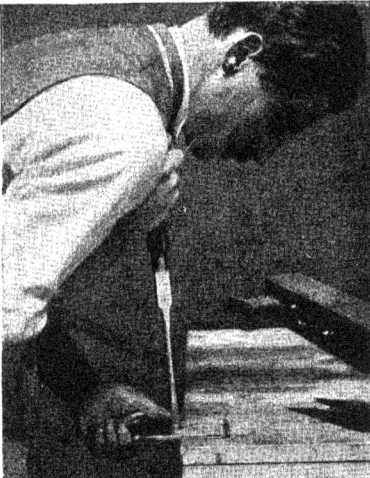

Fig. 13.—Unscrewing Plane Irons; Usual Method

Fig. 15.—Unscrewing Plane Irons by using Bench Hook

Fig. 14.—Unscrewing Plane Irons by using Plane Wedge

will loosen the wedge, and the wedge and irons are then withdrawn. Fig. 11 shows damage the hand. Sometimes the back iron screw is so tight that it cannot be loosened easily. In this case place the iron so that the back projection of the screw fits into the groove in the back of the wedge —the latter resting on the bench (see Fig. 14). By this method both hands can be used to the screwdriver if desired. A hole in the top of the bench or in the bench hook (see Fig. 15) will do instead of the wedge. An even better plan for very stiff irons is to screw them up in the vice; this will help to squeeze the irons together and loosen the screw; use the screwdriver with both hands.

When the blade is sharpened the irons with the left hand and the blade inserted (Fig. 18). The latter is pushed forward until the correct amount projects beyond the sole of the plane, as can be seen by

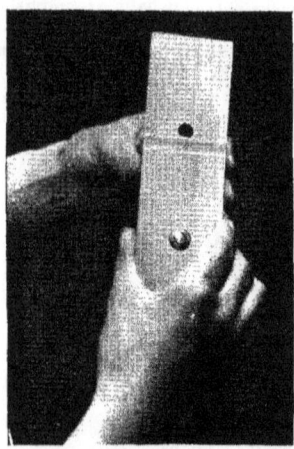

Fig. 16.—Putting Plane Irons in Position

Fig. 18.—Inserting Blade in Plane after Sharpening

Fig. 19.—Fastening Wedge in Plane

Fig. 17.—Plane Irons in Correct Position

are put together (*see* Figs. 16 and 17) by sliding the back iron up the plane and screwing together; the plane is then held sighting along the sole, as shown in Fig. 20. The wedge is now inserted with the right hand—the thumb of the left hand

THE PLANE

meantime keeping the blade in position—and then tightened with one or two taps from the hammer (Fig. 19). Whilst

Fig. 20.—Sighting Along Sole of Plane for Projection of Blade

tightening the wedge the iron may have slipped a little; sight down the sole of the plane; if the iron does not project enough give it a slight tap with the hammer; if it projects too much hit the top end of the plane gently (as when loosening the wedge). One or two adjustments like this may be necessary; finally, when the correct amount of iron projects beyond the sole, tap the wedge again with the hammer, and so make sure that the irons are securely held in the plane. Though at first one or two adjustments of the plane may be required as above, or the plane may have to be tried to see

if it takes off a correct thickness of shaving, an experienced workman can set the iron very quickly and correctly, often the first time and without trying it on the timber.

After years of wear and with repeatedly hitting with the hammer, the top end of the plane gets badly damaged. To prevent this a striking button, usually made of boxwood, may be fixed in the top end of the plane (see Fig. 21).

Adjusting a New Plane.—Planes, when first bought, or when using a new back iron or blade, and particularly when in the hands of an amateur or an apprentice, do not work easily. One of the chief faults is "choking up," that is, the shavings, instead of issuing freely from the mouth, stop up the mouth. The usual reason for this is that the back iron does not fit closely at the edge on to the plane iron, and, when planing, a shaving inserts itself in the small opening; an obstruction is thus formed and other shavings tend to stop in the mouth. The obvious cure is to file the back iron carefully until it fits the blade closely. The back iron should also be thin at the edge and smooth, so as to offer the least possible resistance to the shavings.

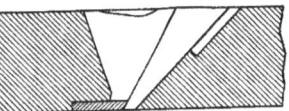

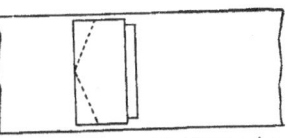

Fig. 22.—Re-mouthing Plane; An Alternative Mouthpiece is Shown Dotted

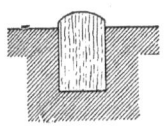

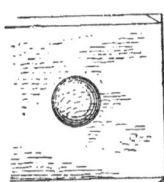

Fig. 21.—Striking Button in Plane

If the back iron is adjusted as described, the blade only allowed to project a little beyond the sole, and a smear of oil put on the sole of the plane—particularly if planing a highly resinous wood

Fig. 23.—Cutting Sole of Plane for Mouthpiece

like pitchpine—the plane will probably work all right.

"Clattering" is another defect, but it usually accompanies choking up, and if the latter is remedied the former defect is usually cured also. But sometimes "clattering" (anyone who has had a plane that "clatters" will know what this is—the plane, instead of removing shavings, clatters over the wood) is due to the blade not bedding down solidly on wood stock. If this is the case the wood should be carefully pared with a chisel until the blade beds properly.

There is often a temptation when a plane which has a narrow mouth chokes, as in a new plane, to chisel the mouth wider. This should be avoided.

Shooting and Re-mouthing a Plane. —After using for many months the sole of a plane wears uneven, and it then requires "shooting." This is done by taking a few fine shavings off the sole with the trying plane. Repeated shooting and wearing of the plane will cause the mouth of the plane to become wider, as illustrated in Fig. 5, which shows that the width of the mouth is greater along the dotted line. When this happens the plane requires re-mouthing, as shown in Fig. 22. Notice that the mouthpiece extends a little beyond the ends of the mouth. Boxwood is generally used for re-mouthing a plane. A plane does not work well when it has a wide mouth because the wood just in front of the cutting edge is not pressed upon by the sole of the plane. Figs. 23 and 24 show the sole of the plane being chiselled to receive a new mouthpiece. The method of using a jack plane will be dealt with in the next chapter.

Trying Plane.—This plane (Fig. 25) is very similar to the jack plane, the only differences being the shape of the handle —which is of the closed type—and the size. The trying plane is made long— average length about 22 in.—so that it will plane the wood straight. A short plane would sink into hollows, whereas a long plane cannot do so, but removes the lumpy parts and thus makes a level surface. The materials, methods of setting and taking apart, are the same as

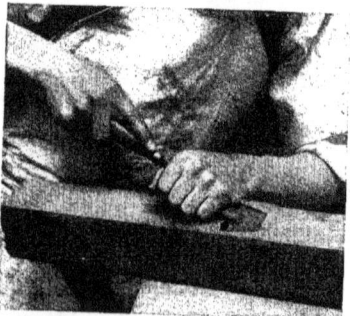

Fig. 24.—Chiselling Recess for Mouthpiece

for a jack plane, but the iron is wider— usually $2\frac{1}{2}$ in.—and the cap iron is set back only a $\frac{1}{16}$ in. from the cutting edge of the blade.

THE PLANE

A special type of trying plane is called a *jointer* or *panel* plane, the length being from 26 in. to 30 in. As the name implies, this plane is used for making joints—the are used. The smoothing plane is often used for convex curves if there is not much to do, but a hollow-soled compass plane is better. Concave work cannot

Fig. 25.—Trying Plane

Fig. 26.—Smoothing Plane

longer the plane, of course, the greater the tendency to plane the wood straight.

Smoothing Plane.—A smoothing plane (Fig. 26), as the name suggests, is for smoothing or finishing a surface. As the plane is not required to straighten the timber it is of a convenient size for holding and using. The usual size is about 8 in. long with 2¼ in. cutter.

The method of taking apart, re-assembling, and adjusting is the same as for the jack plane, except that owing to the shape of the smoothing plane the back end of the plane is hammered or knocked

be done with a smoothing plane, and therefore a compass plane is essential, though for small work a spokeshave (really a small compass plane) may be used.

Fig. 29 shows a wooden compass plane. Sometimes a stop for adjusting roughly to various curves is attached. In using this type of plane always keep the nose of the plane tightly against the work.

Adjustable compass (or circular) planes (Figs. 30 and 31) have an adjustable metal sole; these are preferable to the wooden type, as they can be more accur-

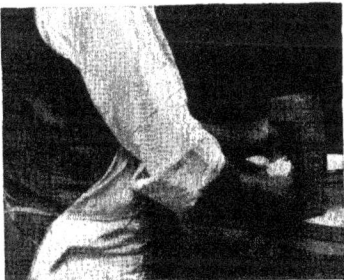

Fig. 27.—Loosening Plane Irons by Striking Back of Plane on Bench

Fig. 28.—Loosening Plane Irons by Hitting Back of Plane with Hammer

on the bench when loosening or setting (see Figs. 27 and 28).

COMPASS AND TOOTHING PLANES

When hollow or round surfaces have to be worked, planes with curved soles

ately adjusted to the curve either concave or convex. Fig. 31 shows a later and better variety than Fig. 30. The sole of the plane is adjusted to the correct curvature in each case by the screw at the top.

Toothing Planes.—In making a glued

joint between two surfaces, or in veneering, the surfaces are "toothed" with a toothing plane. The toothing simply roughens the surfaces, thus enabling the glue to adhere better. The plane in shape

Fig. 29.—Wooden Compass Plane or "Round Sole"

is similar to a small smoothing plane, the difference is in the blade, which is upright, has no cap iron, and is grooved at the back. Fig. 32 shows the blade, which has a series of **V**-shaped grooves at the back. When the blade is sharpened, like an ordinary plane blade, the edge will consist of a series of small teeth something like the edge of a saw. When the plane is used the teeth scratch the wood and give a better surface for holding the glue. The plane is used after the manner of an ordinary smoothing plane, but is pushed over the wood in all directions, with and across the grain.

REBATE AND BULL-NOSE PLANES

Rebate planes (see Fig. 33) are usually

Fig. 30.—Stanley Adjustable Compass Plane

called "rabbit" planes in the workshop, and are used for making rebates, or "rabbits." Where a circular saw is available the rebate is cut out by using the saw with the table raised, and the rebate is then cleaned up with the rebate plane.

Rebate planes are made in various

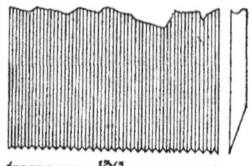

Fig. 32.—Blade of Toothing Plane

widths, ranging from $\frac{1}{4}$ in. to $1\frac{3}{4}$ in. A useful size is $1\frac{1}{4}$ in. The plane consists of three parts: body, blade, and wedge. There is no cap or back iron. The planes have either square or skew mouths. The latter type is the better—a skew mouth lets the shavings escape easily, thus preventing "choking," and a skew blade cuts better than a square one.

Rebate planes are not convenient tools for making rebates, but only for "cleaning up" rebates that have been cut by some other method. These methods will be described later, and include the circular saw, spindle, fillister, plough-cutting gauge.

Special rebate planes are used for some jobs. Suppose, for example, a "stopped" rebate had to be cut as in Fig. 33A. The best way to proceed would probably be to cut about 6 in. near the "stopped end" with the chisel and the rest with a

Fig. 31.—Victor Adjustable Compass Plane

plane. As, however, the rebate plane would not work close up to the stopped end, a special plane with its blade close

THE PLANE

to the nose is used. This plane (*see* Fig. 34) is called a *bull-nose* plane, and is made of metal. It is 3 in. to 4 in. in length, and is very useful. It should form part of every woodworker's kit.

The screw on the top of the plane enables it to be adjusted for any required depth of rebate. These planes are not much used, as a combination of the use of rebate plane and plough enables any

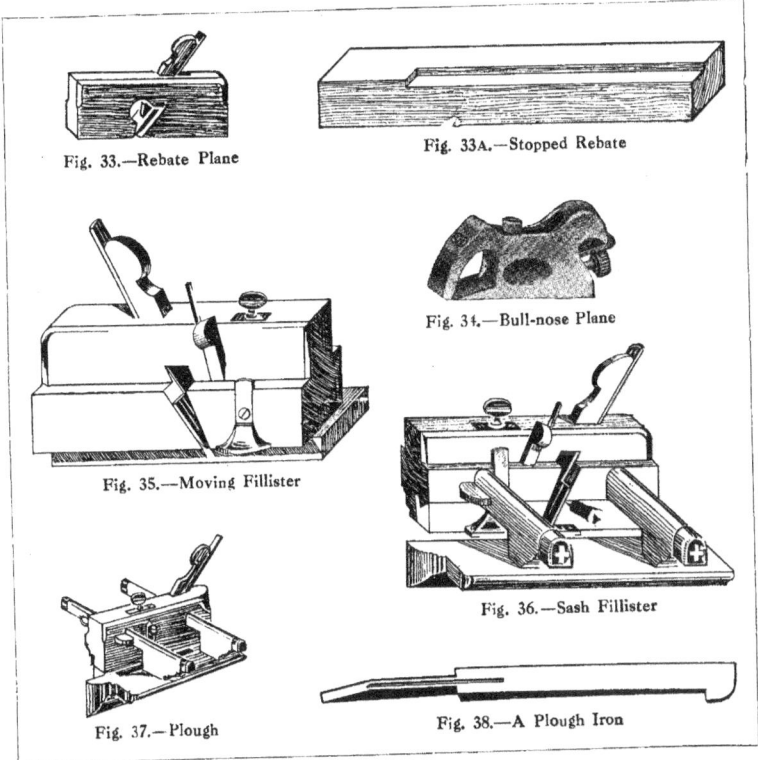

Fig. 33.—Rebate Plane

Fig. 33A.—Stopped Rebate

Fig. 34.—Bull-nose Plane

Fig. 35.—Moving Fillister

Fig. 36.—Sash Fillister

Fig. 37.—Plough

Fig. 38.—A Plough Iron

FILLISTERS AND PLOUGH

FILLISTERS are planes for making rebates. They consist essentially of a rebate plane with a movable fence, on the principle shown in Figs. 35 and 36. Two types are shown. The *Moving fillister* shown in Fig. 35 has a fence sliding on the sole of the plane, and the fence of the *Sash fillister* (Fig. 36) slides by means of stems through the body of the plane.

rebate to be cut, and a plough is necessary for making grooves.

THE PLOUGH (Fig. 37) is used for making all sizes of grooves and rebates. The blade, or " bit " is fastened into the body of the plane by a wedge; a side fence works on stems after the manner of the sash fillister, and a screw on the top of the plane determines the depth of the groove or rebate. A set of six or eight "bits" of various sizes is supplied with each plane (see Fig. 38). The method of using the plough is shown in Fig. 39. Take care to adjust the fence parallel to the "fin" of the plane.

JOINTING, MOULDING AND BEADING PLANES

Jointing or *matching* planes are made in pairs—one to cut the groove and the other the tongue (see Figs. 40 and 40A). A separate pair is required for each thickness of board. When making a tongued and grooved joint with match-

Fig. 39.—Using Plough

ing planes the joint should first be "made" (planed with the trying plane and adjusted to a fit), as the tonguing plane takes off an equal amount throughout the length of the board, and therefore if the pieces fit before being tongued and grooved they will fit afterwards.

Though moulding planes are not used in the workshop as much as formerly, a set of these planes is usually provided for "sticking" (moulding) short lengths, when it would not be worth while to "set up" a machine. The chief moulding planes are hollows and rounds, bead and ovolo planes.

A full set of hollows and rounds consist of 18 pairs, but about three "rounds" (see Fig. 42A) of various sizes are usually sufficient, except for very rare jobs. Hollows (Fig. 42) can be dispensed with if necessary, as the round portions of mouldings may be worked by the ordinary planes and then glass-papered to a finish.

Bead planes (Fig. 43) may be had in sizes to make beads from $\frac{1}{8}$ in. to 1 in. Planes for making small mouldings of

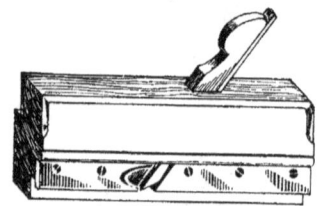

Fig. 40.—Grooving Plane

Fig. 41.—Blades for Matching Planes

Fig. 40A.—Tonguing Plane

standard patterns as Fig. 44 may be obtained, but these mouldings and others can be made without special planes, as will be described later.

METAL PLANES

Two or three metal planes have already been described, but there are numerous other types, chiefly of the Stanley make. An exceedingly useful metal plane is the block plane (Fig. 45). It is about the size of a small smoothing plane, and can be used with one hand (*see* Fig. 46); it is thus very convenient for planing

They are also more expensive and quite as liable to get out of order or get broken as, or even more than, wooden ones. The

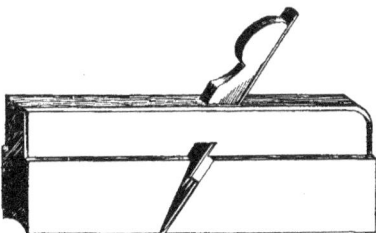

Fig. 42.—Hollow Plane

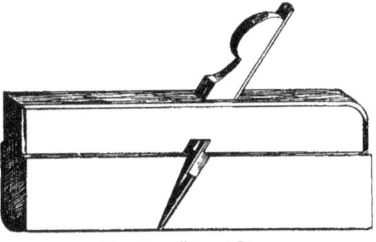

Fig. 42A.—Round Plane

mitres as well as useful for all kinds of small work. The width of the mouth can be adjusted by means of the screw at the front. The blade is secured in position by means of the cap, propelled backwards and forwards by the screw at the back, and adjusted sideways by the lever at the back. The blade of the block

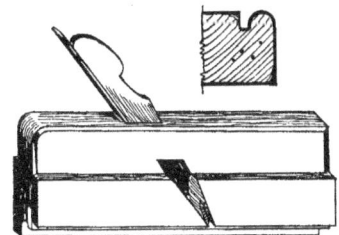

Fig. 43.—Bead Plane and the Beading Cut by it

plane is used with the bevel upwards, and the inclination of the blade is 20 deg. as against 45 deg. in ordinary planes.

Fig. 47 shows a block plane having the cutter at an even lower angle—12 deg. This angle enables the planes to be used with ease across the grain on hardwoods.

Large metal planes are not as largely used as was expected when they were introduced. The chief objection is that the metal " drags " on the wood, thus making the metal plane tiring to use.

average woodworker in this country nearly always has the three bench planes of wood, frequently an iron smoothing plane, usually a metal bull-nose and very often a block plane. Other metal planes are often met with, but though often very useful can hardly be said to belong to the average woodworker's equipment.

In order to avoid the excessive friction of the iron sole of metal planes, the sole is often corrugated as in Fig. 48. Another method of avoiding the " drag " of the metal is to have a plane with metal fittings and a wooden sole as in Fig. 49, which shows a Bailey jack plane and Fig. 50 a smoothing plane.

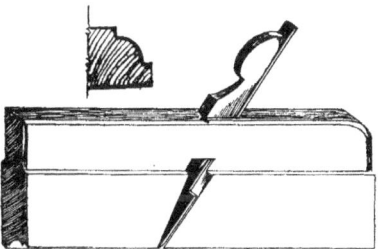

Fig. 44.—Ovolo Plane and Ovolo Moulding Cut by it

Fig. 51 shows a rebate plane with a square iron; the front part of the plane is movable and secured by the screw at the top. This plane is very suitable for shooting the shoulders of tenon joints, and is sometimes called a shoulder plane.

Fig. 52 is a small metal plane about

A Bailey adjustable jack plane is shown in Fig. 53. The illustrations give a plan and side elevation; a view of the seat for the blade, showing the screw for

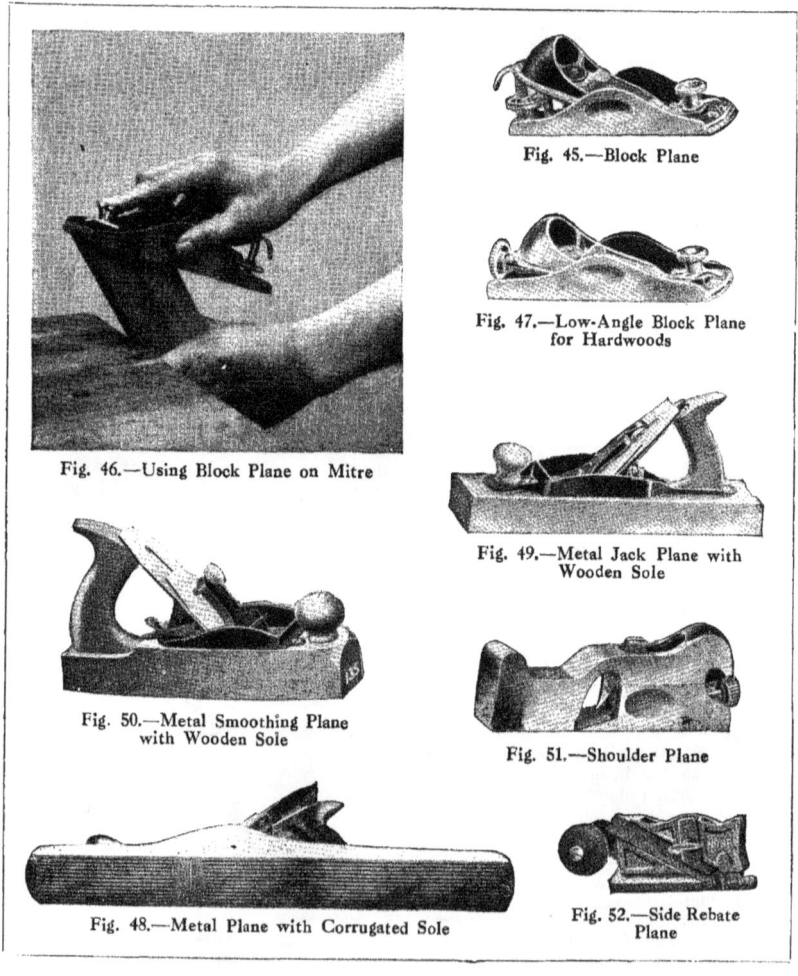

Fig. 45.—Block Plane

Fig. 47.—Low-Angle Block Plane for Hardwoods

Fig. 46.—Using Block Plane on Mitre

Fig. 49.—Metal Jack Plane with Wooden Sole

Fig. 50.—Metal Smoothing Plane with Wooden Sole

Fig. 51.—Shoulder Plane

Fig. 48.—Metal Plane with Corrugated Sole

Fig. 52.—Side Rebate Plane

4 in. long for planing the vertical sides of rebates; it has a reversible nosepiece, so that it will work closely up into corners when required.

propelling the blade and the lever for lateral adjustment; the cap; the plane irons; and the iron, cap, and seat together. The method of adjusting the

THE PLANE

Fig. 53.—Bailey Jack Plane, showing Parts Separated

Fig. 56.—Cabinet-maker's Block Plane

Fig. 57.—Handled Block Plane

Fig. 55.—Edge Plane

blade of metal plane is shown in Fig. 54.

Fig. 55 shows a cabinet-maker's edge plane; with the blade right at the end it can be worked close up into corners. A cabinet-maker's block plane with machined sides and suitable for fine work or with a shooting board is shown in Fig. 56.

Fig. 57 shows a block plane having a handle at the back so that the plane may be gripped and used comfortably.

Other special planes will be dealt with as they are required—notably the veneerer's and inlayer's toothing planes and router planes.

Fig. 54.—Adjusting Blade of Block Plane

SPOKESHAVES AND ROUTERS

A spokeshave may be described as a small double-handled plane for planing

The method of using the spokeshave is shown in Fig. 62. Always work "with the grain," as shown in Fig. 63, the arrows showing the directions in which the

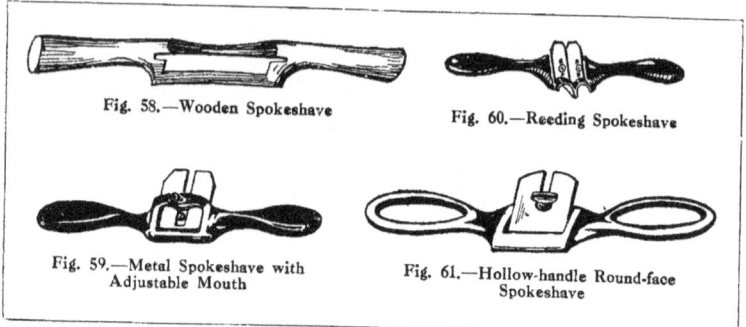

Fig. 58.—Wooden Spokeshave

Fig. 60.—Reeding Spokeshave

Fig. 59.—Metal Spokeshave with Adjustable Mouth

Fig. 61.—Hollow-handle Round-face Spokeshave

curves. It is made of either metal or wood, both types being largely used.

A wooden spokeshave is shown in Fig. 58. It consists of only two parts, the stock and the blade. The latter is sharpened with a finger-slip oilstone, as fully illustrated on another page, and is

Fig. 62.—Using Spokeshave

adjusted to take off the correct thickness of shaving by tapping the prongs, or the front, of the blade, with the hammer.

spokeshave should be pushed in order to avoid plucking up of the grain.

There are about four kinds of wooden spokeshaves: round faced for quick curves, flat faced for flat curves, brass-plated spokeshaves to prevent the mouth wearing, and spokeshaves with adjustable blades operated by thumb-screws.

Many varieties of metal spokeshaves may be obtained, with straight or raised handles, adjustable cutters, and types for quick curves (see Figs. 59 and 61).

A small spokeshave is usually better than a large one, as the small one will work both quick and large curves, whereas a large one is generally suitable only for big work.

A router is a tool after the manner of a spokeshave, but used for cutting trenches, reeds, and mouldings away from the edge of the timber or on curved work. Fig. 64 shows a router used for planing the bottom of trenches, say for shelving, stairs, etc. Special routers are mentioned on later pages.

Some routers have an adjustable fence so that grooves parallel to the edge of the timber can be cut.

Reeding and moulding tools are made in many varieties and consist usually of a two-handled body like a spokeshave,

THE PLANE

a sliding fence, and a number of adjustable blades for cutting various forms of mouldings, beads, and reeds. A reeding tool without a fence, but capable of taking for light routing out. A tool that is sometimes used for secret nailing is shown in Fig. 67. A ¼-in. chisel when attached to the body turns up a small shaving as

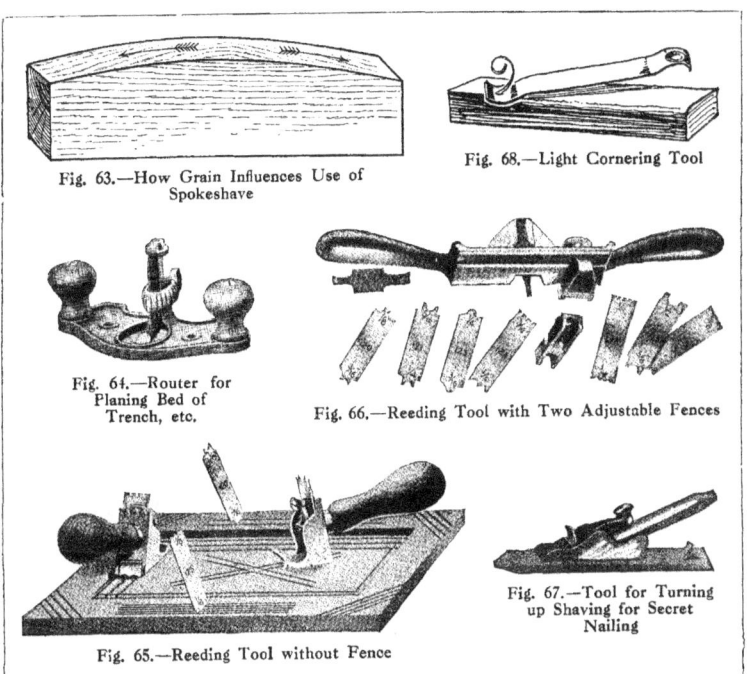

Fig. 63.—How Grain Influences Use of Spokeshave

Fig. 68.—Light Cornering Tool

Fig. 64.—Router for Planing Bed of Trench, etc.

Fig. 66.—Reeding Tool with Two Adjustable Fences

Fig. 67.—Tool for Turning up Shaving for Secret Nailing

Fig. 65.—Reeding Tool without Fence

various sizes of reeding tools, is shown in Fig. 65. A reeding spokeshave is shown by Fig. 60.

Fig. 66 shows a reeding tool with two adjustable fences—one for straight and one for curved work. It is also suitable shown on a later page; when the nail is driven the shaving is glued and pressed back into position.

Fig. 68 shows an American tool for easily removing a corner from a long strip.

Planing

THE object of planing is to make a piece of timber straight so that it does not twist, in order that it will fit into the required position, and also to make it smooth so that it may be painted, varnished, polished, etc.

rough," that is, make the surface fairly straight and smooth.

Figs. 1 and 2 show the method of using the jack plane. At the beginning of the stroke the left hand will have to press hard on the end of the plane, this pressure

Fig. 1.   Fig. 2.
Figs. 1 and 2.—Using Jack Plane, Beginning and End of Movement

Suppose a piece of timber, say about 3 ft. long, 4 in. wide, and 2 in. thick, is going to be used in the construction of a door or a piece of framing. Select the better side and place the timber on the bench and against the bench stop. First use the jack plane and take off " the

being released towards the end of the stroke. The right hand pushes the plane forward. If the plane takes off too much or too little—" too much iron " or " not enough iron "—the blade should be adjusted as described in the preceding chapter.

PLANING

A common fault in planing is taking too much off the end near the bench stop. To avoid this try to take less off this end and more at the beginning of the stroke. Generally, take as little off as possible; remember you can always plane a little more off, but you cannot put any on.

There is also a tendency to plane the surface round (convex in direction of length). With a piece of timber about 3 ft. long, it will be impossible to plane the surface hollow with a jack plane, except to a very slight extent depending on the projection of the blade. The best method of planing straight and avoiding planing round is to try to plane hollow. The surface can be tested for straightness with a straight-edge or by sighting as in Fig. 40 (p. 35). The piece of timber shown in that photograph is being sighted for straightness of edge. Shut one eye when sighting and simply "spy" along the edge of the wood; in this way the slightest irregularity can be detected. Sighting is a better and more usual method of testing than using a straightedge.

For straightness across the board the surface may be tested by holding the plane cornerwise as in Fig. 3; if the board is round or hollow light can be seen under the corner of the plane. A better method is to use the blade of the square as shown in Fig. 4.

Fig. 3.

Fig. 4.

Figs. 3 and 4.—Testing across a Planed Surface

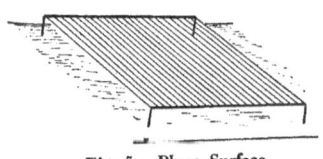

Fig. 5.—Plane Surface

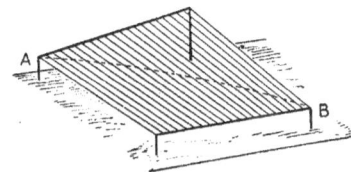

Fig. 6.—Twisted Surface

Twist.—Besides being straight the timber should be *out of twist*—that is, the surface should be a plane, or flat, surface. Beginners usually have some little difficulty in understanding what a plane surface (or a surface out of twist) really means. Suppose we have two rods perfectly level (as tested with a spirit level); see Fig. 5. Now suppose strings were connected, close together, from rod to rod: a plane surface would be thus formed. Consider now that only one of these rods was level and the other sloping and were connected by strings; we should thus get a twisted surface as in Fig. 6. Note that the strings and rods are *straight*—that is, all the edges of the surface are straight yet the surface itself is twisted.

A surface is tested for twisting by using a pair of winding strips as in Fig. 7. These strips may be about 18 in. long by 2 in. wide by ½ in. thick; the upper parts of the strips are usually bevelled to make the top edges thinner. If the surface

Fig. 7.—Using Winding Strips

twists, the winding strips will appear as in Fig. 9. It will be seen that the winding strips exaggerate the twist and thus make it easy to detect. The amount of twist may easily be estimated. Suppose that the right-hand end only of the back strip projects above the front one ½ in. (as in Fig. 9) and that the width of the wood is 4 in. and the length of the winding strips 16 in. The proportion of length of winding strips to width of surface is thus 4, and the amount of twist will therefore have been magnified four times; the amount of twist of the surface is therefore ⅛ in. Fig. 9 shows the surface with the amount of twist exaggerated for clearness.

To take the surface out of twist it will

Fig. 8.

Fig. 9.

Figs. 8 and 9.—Winding Strips on Plane and Twisted Surfaces respectively

PLANING

obviously be necessary to plane away the two thin wedge-shaped portions shown.

The workman does not calculate the amount of twist as given above, but guesses the amount to be planed off, then tests again, and so on until the surface is correct; but an understanding of the above theory will enable a more

twist though the edges are straight (*see* Fig. 6), but a twisted surface must be curved somewhere. For example, a line as A B (Fig. 8) passing on the surface from corner to corner will be convex. If a straightedge could be put in all directions on a surface so that it touched the surface at all points, then that surface would be

Fig. 10.—Observing whether a Small Surface is Twisted

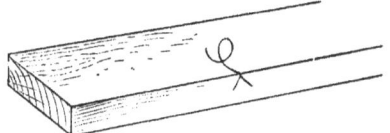

Fig. 11.—Face and Edge Marks

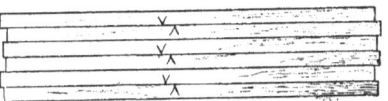

Fig. 12.—Edge Marks, showing how Pieces are arranged in Pairs when Setting Out

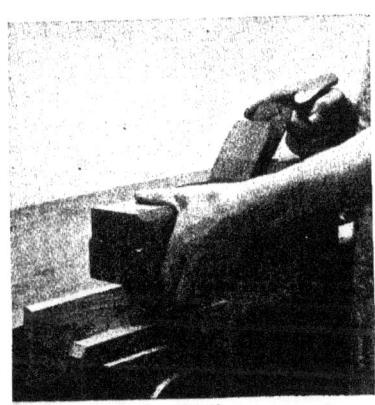

Fig. 13.   Fig. 14.
Figs. 13 and 14.—Edge Planing, with and without using Vice. Note Position of Fingers

accurate guess to be made. It is not often that an experienced man needs to use the winding strips more than twice on the same surface.

It has been shown that a surface may

out of twist. As, however, timber is usually very narrow in proportion to its length, any method of testing for twist with a straightedge is usually not reliable. (The surfaces of stonework are often taken out of twist with a straightedge alone, because stone surfaces are usually broader in proportion to length than timber surfaces.)

The jack and trying planes are often

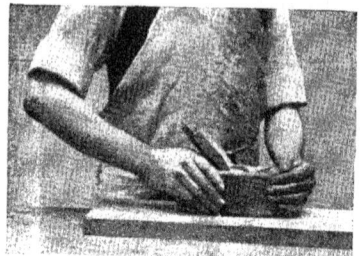

Fig. 15.—Using Smoothing Plane

used instead of winding strips; the planes are laid on their sides with the jack plane nearest the eye.

Another method of testing for twist, suitable for small stuff, is shown in Fig. 10. This method, which simply consists in holding the surface in a suitable position and looking at it, requires a little practice and care to use successfully.

After the "rough" has been taken off with the jack plane the trying plane is used for straightening and taking out of twist. When the latter has been accomplished the surface is "face marked" as shown in Figs. 11 and 12. The edge is now ready for planing.

Squaring the Edge.—Select the better edge, and place the timber, if it is thin, in the vice, or, if it is thick enough to stand up whilst planing, put it on the bench (see Figs. 13 and 14). Hold the plane as shown with the tips of the fingers of the left hand gliding along the side of the wood, so that the sole of the plane can be held steadily at right angles to the surface already planed. Test for straightness as in Fig. 40 (p. 35) and for squareness to the "face" by using a square. Hold the square and timber towards the light so that any light may be seen between the edge of the timber and the blade of the square. Either glide the square along the timber or test at intervals of about 6 in. If not square, plane the prominent parts; if correct, mark a "face edge mark" as in Fig. 12. This mark is usually a V pointing to the face side.

Planing to Correct Width and Thickness.—The third side, or rather the second edge, has now to be planed. Set the marking gauge to the required width of the piece of wood and gauge *on the face side, from the face edge.* Plane the third side (or second edge) to the gauge line; this will make the third side straight and the wood parallel. Test the edge with the square from the face side.

We now come to the last side or back. Set the gauge to the desired thickness and gauge both edges from the face side. Plane to the gauge lines. The timber is now said to be "trued up," that is, it is (1) straight, (2) out of twist, (3) square, and (4) the desired size.

In making any article, the pieces for the framework are first "trued up"; they are then "set out" for mortising, tenoning, moulding, etc., after which operations the framework is fastened together and finished off. This finishing varies with the class of work, rough work being simply planed; painted work being usually planed and glasspapered; and

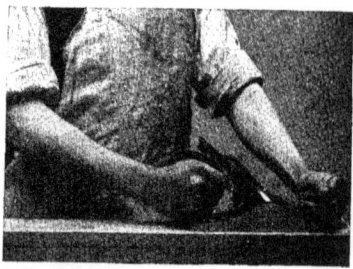

Fig. 16.—Using Metal Smoothing Plane

polished hardwood being planed, scraped, and glasspapered.

Thin stuff is not planed out of twist as it can be easily bent to the correct

PLANING

position; panels and similar stuff are simply planed smooth and to even thickness.

A surface is planed smooth by using the smoothing plane; the method of holding and using is shown in Fig. 15. In order to produce a smooth surface having no rough or "plucked up" grain, the two main points to be observed are to set the plane fine and to plane "with the grain." Remember that to set the plane "fine" the iron should project as little beyond the sole as is consistent with removing a suitable shaving, and

Fig. 17.—Section of Tree

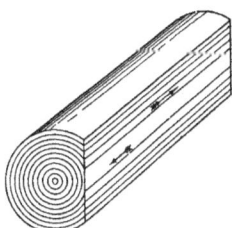

Fig. 19.—Obtaining Straight Grain

the set back of the cap iron should be as little as convenient. The blade should be kept sharp.

Fig. 16 shows a metal smoothing plane in use.

As the smoothness of the finished surface depends largely on planing with the grain, and as this is not understood thoroughly even by the majority of experienced workmen, the nature and cause of the grain of timber will now be explained.

Planing and the Grain of Timber.— On examining the section of a tree trunk as in Fig. 17 it is found to consist of annual rings. The tree is therefore made up, as it were, of a number of cylinders encasing each other. Of course, these cylinders are not straight or truly circular in section, but for the purposes of explanation let it be supposed that they are, as in Fig. 18. If a slice is cut off the trunk as Fig. 19, the grain of the surface will simply be a number of parallel straight lines. Now cut the trunk obliquely, and the section will be a number of ellipses, as in Fig. 20.

The surface in Fig. 19 may be planed in either direction, but the cut surface in Fig. 20 must be planed in the direction

Fig. 18.—Imaginary Tree

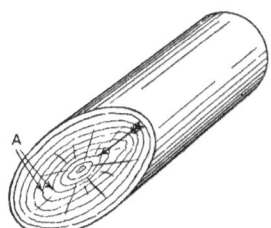

Fig. 20.—Tree Trunk Cut Obliquely

of the arrow or it will "pluck up"; planing in the direction of the arrow is called planing "with the grain," and planing in the reverse direction is "against the grain." If the surface is planed against the grain the blade of the plane tends to dig in the wood at the corners marked A, and a rough surface results.

Consider now an actual tree trunk: Fig. 21 shows the elevation of the trunk and Fig. 22 the plan of the end. Saw the trunk on the line A B. On taking away the portion cut off the view of the cut surface of the trunk will be as in Fig. 23. The direction in which the wood should be planed is shown by the arrows.

A rectangular piece of wood is shown in Fig. 24, the arrows showing the direction for correct planing. Note that if the surface were planed in the wrong edge to tell the correct direction for planing; this can be detected by looking at the grain on the surface and seeing how it rises to the surface.

The average woodworker spends a large proportion of his time in planing, and it is well worth while to understand the above theory of graining, as it will lead to better and quicker work But even the experienced craftsman is some-

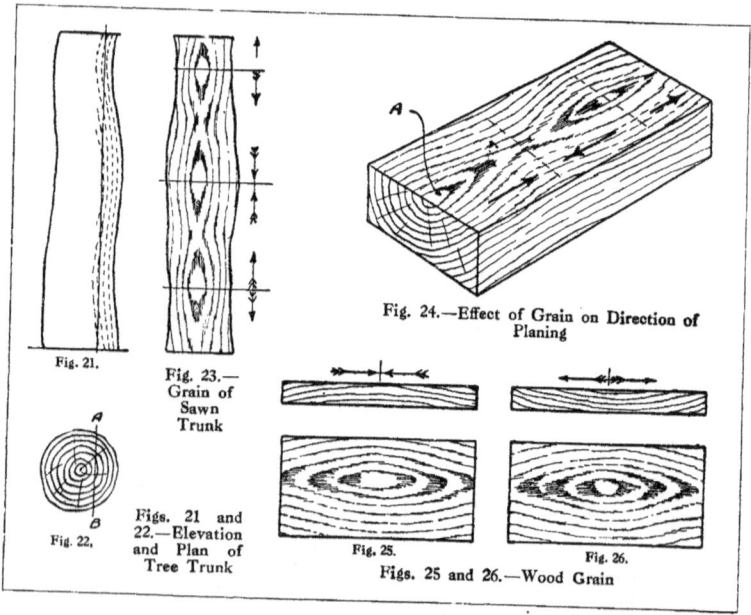

Fig. 21.
Fig. 23.—Grain of Sawn Trunk
Fig. 22.
Figs. 21 and 22.—Elevation and Plan of Tree Trunk
Fig. 24.—Effect of Grain on Direction of Planing
Fig. 25.
Fig. 26.
Figs. 25 and 26.—Wood Grain

direction there would be a tendency to pluck out the small piece A.

The directions for planing do not depend on the shape of the grain lines, but on how the grain rises to the surface of the wood; for example, in Figs. 25 and 26 the surfaces of the two boards are very much alike, but the grain on the edges show that the graining rises to the surface in a different manner. The arrows show the direction for planing. It is, however, not necessary to observe the times very hazy about grain; his usual method is to plane the timber regardless of grain, and then plane the plucked-up parts in the reverse direction, if necessary. This method may be excused for painted work; but for hardwood—say mahogany—if the grain is plucked up badly—and this is commonly done—much work with the plane and scraper is necessary before it is remedied. It is obviously a great advantage in planing curly-grained stuff to know, before the

PLANING

plane is put on the wood, which way the grain goes. The method of testing it in it to hold the strip is often used (see Fig. 31); the strip is thus kept in a

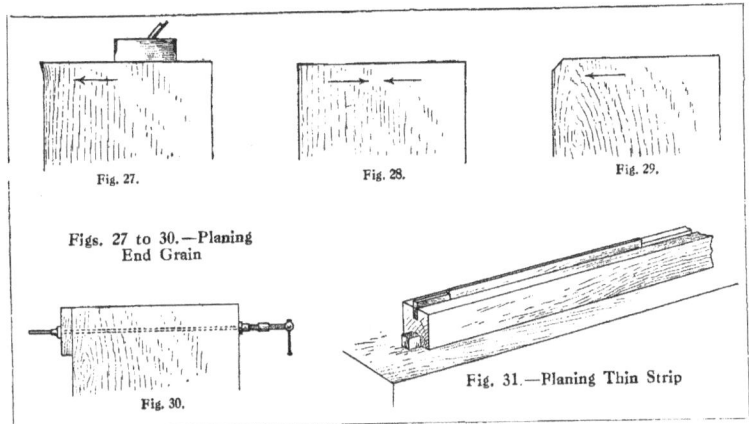

Figs. 27 to 30.—Planing End Grain

Fig. 31.—Planing Thin Strip

with the plane and the subsequent working up is wasteful of time, labour, and material.

Planing End Grain.—It might be said that there is one wrong method of planing end grain, and three correct ones, each of the latter being specially suitable under given circumstances.

If a piece of wood is planed on the end by pushing the plane along the *end* as if it were the *edge* of a board a small piece will probably be knocked off at the end, as shown in Fig. 27. The usual method is to plane from each end as in Fig. 28. Another way is to take a small corner off the far end with the chisel and then plane straight through as shown (see Fig. 29). The small bevel prevents any breaking. Of course, this method cannot be used where the end must be left perfectly square. Fig. 30 shows a further method, which consists in fastening (probably with a cramp) a bit of wood at the far end to prevent splitting and then planing straight through.

Planing Thin Strips and Panels.—When planing thin strips, particularly on the edge, a piece of timber with a groove

suitable position and can be planed with greater ease.

Fig. 32.—Testing Thickness of Panel with a "Mullet"

Panels are tested for thickness by means of a "mullet" or "mulleting piece" (see Fig. 32). This is a small piece of wood that is grooved at the same time as the framework, and therefore if the panels fit the mullet they will fit into their proper grooves.

In ordinary mechanical language, the "mullet" is a notch gauge.

In planing panels and suchlike stuff the object is to make them smooth and of even thickness so that they will fit neatly into their grooves. As the top of the bench is often rough and uneven, a "panel board" is sometimes used (see Fig. 33). This is merely a wide board about 4 ft. or so long, with a butting strip to act as a stop at one end. This strip is better than the bench stop when planing wide stuff.

In planing panels, and smoothing up generally, some workmen begin planing near the bench stop and work backwards; they argue that every time the plane is put down and a shaving begun a slight mark is made on the wood, and that in planing from the bench stop and working backwards these marks are avoided. This generally is not a matter of much consequence, but on the whole this method of beginning at the bench stop

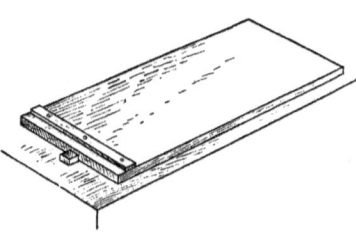

Fig. 33.—A Panel Board

end may be recommended, but for "smoothing" only.

The use of special planes will be dealt with later in connection with the processes for which they are required.

The Scraper

THE ordinary scraper (Fig. 1) consists simply of a piece of hard steel about 4 in. long and 3 in. wide and about $\frac{1}{16}$ in. thick. It may be purchased from the tool dealers or may be made from an old handsaw blade. Usually it is bought.

A scraper when properly sharpened does not merely "scrape" the surface of the timber, but planes it—something (but not exactly) after the manner of an ordinary plane. Fig. 2 shows the

and suchlike work when a proper scraper is not to hand.

Sharpening the Scraper.—As the scraper is not an amateur's tool and the sharpening demands considerable skill, this process will be described very fully. The object to be attained is to make the edge of the scraper straight, smooth, and square, and with just the long corners of the edges turned up slightly. By "corners," in this connection, is meant

Fig. 1.—Scraper

Fig. 2.—Action of Scraper

Fig. 3.—Action of Glass Scraper

edge of a scraper magnified, with the turned-up or "burred" cutting edges exaggerated. When using the scraper the turned-up sharp edge is pressed into the surface of the timber, and when the scraper is pushed along a thin shaving is removed.

A piece of glass is often used as a scraper. The edges of the glass are, of course, not turned up, but are extremely sharp and hard, and "bite" into the surface of the wood (*see* Fig. 3). Glass is not used as a regular scraper, but is very handy for finishing hammer shafts

not the two *ends*, but the two square arrises formed by the two faces of the steel meeting the square edge.

If the scraper is in very bad condition its edge must first be straightened and squared with a file (Fig. 4); a saw file is generally used, and is worked along the scraper so that the edge is kept straight. Care should be taken not to file the edge hollow, as it would not then cut in the middle; on the other hand, a slight convexity of edge does not much matter, and is, in fact, preferred by some woodworkers as it enables the scraper

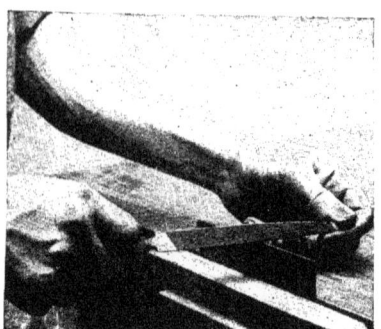

Fig. 4.—Filing Edge of Scraper Square

Fig. 7.—Removing Burr on Oilstone

to work easily in parts that are slightly hollow, and the outside corners do not then tend to "dig in."

The edge of the scraper is now rubbed on the oilstone as in Fig. 5; this tends to make the face of the stone hollow. Consequently the edge of the stone is often used as in Fig. 6. This latter method is recommended, as the edge of an old stone is usually straighter than the face. After about half a dozen rubs the scraper is next rubbed flat on the surface to remove any "burr" from the corners (see Fig. 7).

Now lay the scraper flat on the edge of the bench (as Fig. 8) and hold it firmly with the left hand. Take a piece of hard steel, such as a chisel or a gouge—a ⅜-in. or ½-in. gouge is very suitable—and, pressing the steel flat on the side of the scraper, rub it along the scraper about a dozen times. Turn the scraper over and repeat on the other side. A special scraper sharpener as Fig. 7A is sometimes used, but is hardly necessary.

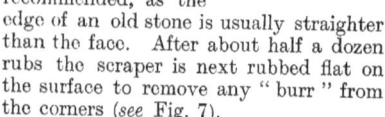

Fig. 7A.—Scraper Sharpener

Next hold the scraper upright on the bench as in Fig. 9; grasp it firmly and press it heavily on the bench; to avoid hurting the hand the top edge is often covered with the apron. Hold the sharpener tightly against the edge, at the bottom, with an angle of about 80 deg. between the sharpener and the scraper,

Fig. 5

Fig. 6

Figs. 5 and 6.—Rubbing Scraper on Oilstone

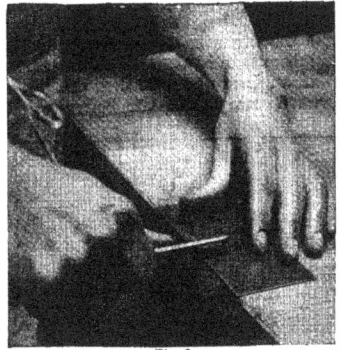
Fig. 8.

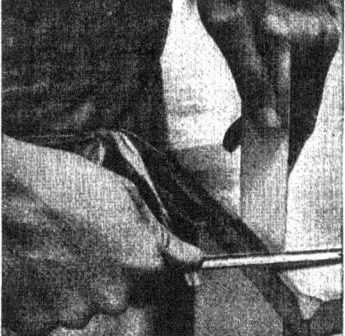
Fig. 9.

Fig. 8 (*above*).—Rubbing Side of Scraper with Tool

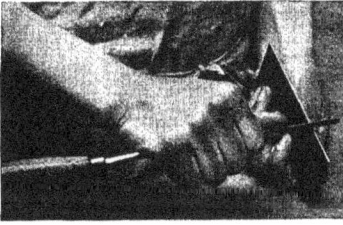

Fig. 9 (*above*).—Forming the Cutting Burr on the Scraper

Fig. 10.—Another Way of Holding Scraper when Forming the Burr

Fig. 11.

Fig. 12.

Figs. 11 and 12.—Two Methods of using Scraper

and bring the sharpener sharply upwards. Whilst doing this it is better to give a slight dragging action by pulling the hand away from the face of the scraper as the sharpener is pulled up-

Fig. 11. Grasp the scraper as shown, with the fingers round the front and the thumbs at the back. Incline the scraper at an angle of about 60 deg. and push it forward (away from the body), when a

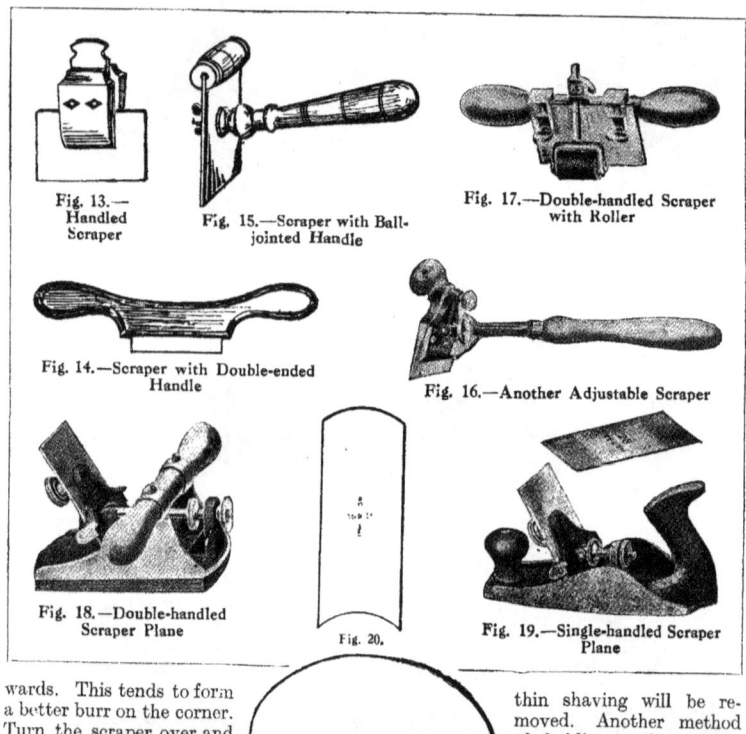

Fig. 13.—Handled Scraper

Fig. 15.—Scraper with Ball-jointed Handle

Fig. 17.—Double-handled Scraper with Roller

Fig. 14.—Scraper with Double-ended Handle

Fig. 16.—Another Adjustable Scraper

Fig. 18.—Double-handled Scraper Plane

Fig. 20.

Fig. 19.—Single-handled Scraper Plane

Fig. 21.

Figs. 20 and 21.—Scrapers for Mouldings.

wards. This tends to form a better burr on the corner. Turn the scraper over and repeat the process on the other corner. Fig. 10 shows another method of holding the scraper when burring the edge.

Usually, the two long edges are sharpened, thus providing four distinct cutting corners.

Using the Scraper.—Sharpening a scraper is a more difficult proceeding than using it; the latter is quite simple. The usual method of holding is shown in

thin shaving will be removed. Another method of holding and using is shown in Fig. 12.

Sometimes in scraping over a knot or other rough place it is an advantage to bend the scraper a little when using so that the edge will work into any slightly hollow part of the wood.

After using for a short time the scraper tends, through friction, to become hot and uncomfortable to hold. To overcome this discomfort the scraper is often

THE SCRAPER

fitted into a handle. Fig. 13 shows a handle fixed by means of a wedge at the top, and Fig. 14 shows a double-ended handle for grasping with both hands; the underside of the handle has a groove to receive the scraper.

Figs. 15 to 19 illustrate various Stanley scrapers and scraper planes. The handle in Fig. 15 is fitted with a ball joint so that it can be held at any angle to the blade; the top edge has a padding of wood, so that pressure can be applied downwards with the left hand without discomfort. Fig. 16 shows another form of adjustable scraper, and Fig. 17 illustrates a double-handled scraper with a roller at the back, which helps to relieve the strain on the wrists of the workman. A double-handled scraper plane is shown at Fig. 18, and a single-handed scraper plane at Fig. 19. Either of these adjustable tools can also be used as a toothing plane by inserting the blade shown above, Fig. 19.

For scraping mouldings a small curved scraper as in Fig. 20 or Fig. 21 is sometimes used, though mouldings are cleaned up chiefly by means of glasspaper, as will be described later.

It has been mentioned early in this chapter that scrapers may be made from old saw blades, but it should be noted that rusted and pitted steel is unsuitable, it being impossible to turn up a good cutting burr on metal spoilt by rust. The temper of a high-quality saw blade is just about right for the scraper since it allows of just—and only just—being filed, while at the same time it is sufficiently elastic to "give" very slightly in use. If the steel is hardened too much the result will be that, although it may be possible to turn up a burr, this will have no lasting qualities because of its brittleness, and resetting and resharpening will soon be necessary, while, of course, the quality of the work will also suffer. Many woodworkers have not seen a scraper correctly sharpened and used. It is very often used inefficiently even by craftsmen. Made of the right material, correctly sharpened and skilfully used, it becomes a true cutting tool capable of removing a long series of true shavings—not scrapings.

Timber: Its Growth and Properties

Introductory.—It is important for every craftsman to be acquainted with the natural characteristics of the raw material with which he works. It may, in fact, be doubted whether the highest craftsmanship can ever be attained without such knowledge. In so far as it is thorough, such practical knowledge will be scientific, although the craftsman may be but little acquainted with the technicalties or terminology of any science, and although he may only consider his material from a more restricted standpoint than the man of science may do.

As woods are never as homogeneous as metal may be, and vary in structure (and in the other characters dependent on it) not only according to the kind of species of tree from which they are derived, but also according to the situation in which, and the rate at which, it was grown, the age of the tree, and whether the wood be taken from the heart or from the exterior, from the butt end or from the top of the stem, it must always be more difficult to gain an accurate knowledge of this material than to measure the properties of a mass of iron, steel, brass or copper.

The worker in wood is not directly concerned with the botanical characters of trees, nor with the physiological uses of the wood to the living plant. He has, as a rule, neither flowers, leaves, nor bark to aid him in identifying the wood he is using; but deals only with "converted" material. So, too, the defects from which his material suffers, the insects that burrow into it, and the fungi which may bring about its decay, are not, for the most part, those that attack the living tree.

At the same time, the physical and mechanical characteristics of wood which determine its fitness for the various purposes of the craftsman are so dependent upon its mode of growth and its minute anatomical structure, that it is impossible to gauge those properties without reference to the natural history of the tree. It may be said in general terms that woods derive their utility from being soft enough to be cut, sawn or cleaved by ordinary hand tools, while stable or strong enough, and durable enough, to retain the form into which they are cut, under considerable strain, and for a long period without decay.

Sources of Wood.—The great class of flowering and fruit-bearing plants which includes grasses, lilies, orchids, screw-pines and palms, contains some plants with woody stems. Here, however, the bulk of the stem is soft, or, as in bamboos and other grasses, hollow; while the wood is in isolated strands crowded together towards the outside of the usually unbranched trunk. In the tropics palm-stems are often split for flooring or rough building, in spite of their splintery texture and very unequal wearing.

With this unimportant exception, woods are the produce either of the natural order *Coniferæ*, which includes pines, spruces firs, larches, cedars, junipers, yews, etc., or of the great class *Dicotyle-*

TIMBER: ITS GROWTH AND PROPERTIES

Fig. 1.—The Oak in Summer
Photo: G. Clarke Nuttall

dons. Though they agree, as we shall see, in the main principles of the growth of their stems, these two groups differ in several marked and generally recognized characters. The Coniferæ, or conifers, as they are styled in English, are so called because their seeds are not enclosed in a fruit, but are, as a rule, on the inner surfaces of a series of scales overlapping one another to form a cone. Fig. 6, on page 121, shows the cones of some of the best known conifer trees. Conifers have mostly very narrow, pointed, rigid leaves, and are, therefore, often styled "needle-leaved trees"; and, with the exception of the Yews, they have wood generally rich in resin. Fig. 5 shows the needle-shaped leaves of several conifer trees. Generally of rapid growth and of a structure which, compared to that of Dicotyledons, is simple, uniform, and of an even grain which renders it easy to work, their wood is commonly known as "soft" or "resinous." As a matter of fact, many Dicotyledons (or "broad-leafed" trees) grow as fast as conifers, and others, such as Willows, Poplars, and Horse-chestnut, have woods that are softer than some of the group technically known as "soft woods."

Broad-leafed trees are known as "hardwoods." They have their seeds enclosed in true fruits; their leaves are generally broad, with a network of branching veins; and their wood is of a more complex structure and, therefore, often more difficult to work than that of the conifers. Fig. 10 shows the leaves of a number of hardwood or broad-leafed trees.

Origin of Wood.—It may fairly be

Fig. 2.—The Oak in Winter
Photo: G. Clarke Nuttall

said that most of the properties for which we value wood are those which render it of use to the living tree. Its strength, combined with some elasticity and toughness, or power to resist various transverse strains, enables the living tree to support the weight of its own branches and foliage and to yield to the wind without snapping or being torn asunder. At the same time it is important to bear in mind, that in the living tree, wood is only formed gradually, and in its early stages of development performs functions other than these mechanical resistances to strain.

All the higher plants when young are alike built up of cells, minute sacs of cellulose, filled with protoplasm and combined into tisuses.

In the young stems and branches of trees the cells become elongated in the direction of growth, in a vertical direction, that is to say, in the stem, while still thin-walled and soft and retaining their protoplasmic contents. Those at or near the surface undergo a thickening of their walls with a substance that renders them highly elastic and impermeable, lose their protoplasm, and become cork. Those at the centre of the stem or branch merely lose their protoplasm, thus becoming physiologically dead, and are known as pith. This tissue may remain intact for some years, as in the Elder; it may become ruptured into a succession of transverse discs with intervening spaces, as in the shoots of the Walnut; it may dry up and be torn into longitudinal shreds, as in the withered winter stalks of Burdocks or Hemlock; or it may be recognizable in the centre of an old but sound stem, such as tnat of an Oak, 100 or 200 years old, as a line of loose dried powdery cells. It is then important, not merely as indicating that a plank is derived from the very centre of growth, but also that no decay has set in at that centre.

Between the young cork and the pith a ring of strands of cellular tissue undergo marked changes. The cells, or "elements" of which they are made up, are much elongated, so that they appear smaller than the other cells of the stem, when it is cut across, and have collectively a greyish effect amid the white tissue. In a cross-section of a stem—one, that is, cut horizontally or at right angles to the general direction of growth—these "bundles," as they are called, appear more or less wedge-shaped, with their broader ends towards the outside of the stem. The walls of some of the outermost and of the innermost elements in each bundle become thickened with ligno-cellulose, and they gradually lose their protoplasm. This change extends outwards and inwards to all the elements in the bundle except those forming a narrow line parallel with the circumference of the stem. This layer retains its protoplasm and persists throughout the life of the stem as a growing or "cambium" layer, its cells undergoing repeated tangential division — division, that is, parallel to the surface of the stem—and sometimes also transverse division.

The elements of the tissue between the bundles elongate radially, that is, from the pith outwards, and constitute what are known as the "medullary," or "pith," rays, familiar to the worker in ornamental woods as "mirrors," "silver-grain," or "figure." As the bundles do not develop in a perfectly straight course up the stem, this ray tissue is so divided up that it appears on the outer surface of the cylinder of wood when a tree is barked as a series of more or less elliptical patches with their longer axes vertical. It is when a stem is "quarter-sawn," that is, cut radially, that it is most conspicuous, appearing as a series of more or less interrupted lines or patches extending along the surface of the plank in the direction of the radius of the stem, as in what is termed "wainscot oak." These markings are also called the "silver grain."

In the second season's growth the active division of the cambium cells extends laterally in both directions across the pith-rays between the bundles. so that for the first time the central portion of the stem becomes thoroughly enveloped by a complete sheath of this soft protoplasmic tissue.

It is at this stage that we can first readily peel a twig, tearing as we do so through these cambium cells. The portion of the

TIMBER: ITS GROWTH AND PROPERTIES

stem from the cambium inwards to the pith is known collectively as the "wood." The outer surface of the wood of the peeled twig is sticky with the protoplasm of the torn cambium cells, and it is during the season of vigorous growth, "when the sap is up," that it is most easy to "bark" or "rind" logs.

Growth-rings.—During this second season of growth and each succeeding season, the cambium layer by the division of its cells adds new wood to the outside of the wood-cylinder, at the same time adding also to the pith-rays and, to a less amount, to the inner bark. It is to this method of growth by additions at the outside that the stems of conifers and broad-leafed trees owe the name "exogenous." In temperate latitudes, like our own, most broad-leaved trees shed their leaves in autumn; and, like the conifers, go through a period of rest, when, at the lower temperature, neither roots nor leaves take in much food; and the wood formed is thus distinctly divided up by pauses into annual rings.

In equatorial forests, where nearly all trees are evergreen and there is but little contrast of seasons, this division of each year's growth is less distinct, so that the term "growth-rings" is preferable for general application to "annual rings." These rings vary very much in width, even in different parts of the same tree; and they tell us so much about the nature and life-history of the tree that the first thing to do in examining a piece of wood, whether to identify the species to which it belongs or to study the history of its development, is to secure a cross-section showing them, cutting it smooth with a plane or a sharp knife. In young trees, grown in the open, and what the forester terms "thrifty," the growth-ring is widest near the butt, stump or base; but in older trees, especially when growing close together, it is narrowest at the base and at the apex, and widest towards the upper part of the tree. This is mainly dependent upon the area of the leaf-surfaces that contribute the food-supply by which the wood in any particular part of the stem is formed.

It must be remembered also that as the girth of the stem increases with age, the addition of a narrower ring of wood

Fig. 3.—The Pine

round the increased circumference may represent the formation of much more wood than a wider ring of less circumference.

In our ordinary forest trees, whether conifers or hard woods, rings half an inch wide seldom occur except near the centre, that is, representing the growth of the first few years, and in very thrifty specimens. The central twenty rings—that is, the growth of the first twenty years—in Pitch Pine may each be one-sixth to one-eighth of an inch wide; while the same number of rings at the outside of a large tree may only average a thirtieth of an inch each. These figures indicate, of course, an increase of diameter of the tree by a third, a quarter or a fifteenth of an inch in the year respectively. Twelve rings to the inch represents, in our latitudes, good thrifty growth; but slow-growing trees may not show half this; and stunted pines may have two hundred rings to the inch.

An exceptionally narrow ring in the series, or the defect known as "cup-shake," when the rings of two successive years do not cohere, may mark a season when the young leaves were stripped from the tree by caterpillars; whilst the sudden appearance of an increased width of ring often marks the admission of more light and air to the tree by the clearing away of some of its neighbours. The rings are seldom exactly circular, the centre of growth being, that is to say, excentric. This is especially the case with trees at the margin of a wood or where one side is in any way more exposed and thus forms less wood than the other. In the wood of horizontal branches more is formed on the lower side, under the influence of gravitation, so that the centre of growth, the pith, that is, is generally much nearer the upper surface of the branch and the rings are very elliptical.

Soft Wood.—So far a general description has been given of the stem of a tree, which is true alike of those of conifers and of those of broad-leaved trees. When, however, we come to look into the elements of which the wood is built up, we have to distinguish between the relatively simple wood of the former and the complex and varied woods of the latter.

The woods of the Coniferæ are mainly made up of elements known as tracheids, interrupted only by resin-ducts and by pith-rays so narrow as not to be recognizable by the naked eye. The tracheids are elongated, spindle-shaped, fibre-like elements, polygonal in transverse section and from a twentieth to a fifth of an inch in length, fifty to one hundred times their width. On their radial walls, that is on those parallel with a radius of the stem, and occasionally on other sides, they are marked by structures known as bordered pits, and they are themselves arranged in radial rows. Each of these rows is, in fact, the result of the repeated divisions of a single cambium cell. Their walls are thickened, the pits being merely spots at which no thickening of the original cell-wall has taken place. These pits allow of the more ready permeation of water from one element to another, the thickening being absent in the two contiguous elements on both sides of the cell-wall. A uniform absence of thickening at the same spot in successive thickening-layers forms a canal which, when seen in profile, will appear under the microscope as a more or less circular bright spot; but where each successive thickening-layer projects a little more over the unthickened spot a funnel-shaped canal is formed on each side of the wall, and the appearance in profile is of a bright spot surrounded by a less bright border. The first case is known as a simple pit, the second as a bordered one. The appearance of vertical rows of these double circles on the walls of the constituent tracheids enables us instantaneously to recognize a transparent sliver of wood when placed under a low power of the microscope—such, for instance, as a slice shaved from a lucifer match, in the direction of the grain—as being coniferous.

Early and Late Wood.—A cross-section of pine or spruce shows each growth-ring to consist of two parts, an inner, softer, light-coloured portion, and an outer, firmer, darker-coloured portion. The former is styled the spring, or preferably the early, wood; the latter, the summer, autumn, or late wood. The distinctness of colour of these two parts of the ring varies much in different species; and obviously, as the darker late wood is the stronger, the greater the proportion it bears to the whole, the heavier, harder, and stronger will be the wood.

This higher proportion of late wood occurs near the base of the tree, and after the first few years. In pitchpine for instance, it is stated to form often 45 per cent. of the wood at the butt and only 24 per cent. at the top, scarcely 10 per cent. in the earliest five rings, 40 to 50 per

TIMBER: ITS GROWTH AND PROPERTIES

cent. of the next one hundred rings, about 30 per cent. of the next fifty, and only 20 per cent. of the succeeding fifty rings.

When a pine log is sawn into planks, the sides of the middle plank may be taken as approximately radial sections, and on them the rings will appear as narrow parallel stripes alternately light and dark.

On the surfaces of other planks not passing through the centre—which are known as "bastard" planks—the rings appear as parallel but broader bands, with **V**-shaped lines towards the centre of each plank, while the bases of branches, or other projections, irregularities of growth, and the varying direction of the sawn surface with

Fig. 4.—The Douglas Fir   *Photo: H. Irving*

reference to the axis of growth, produce a charming variety of wavy and concentric bands of colouring. There is, for example, at Balmoral a room in which prayers are sometimes read which is panelled throughout with Scots Fir from the estate, which exhibits a wonderfully beautiful variety of figure.

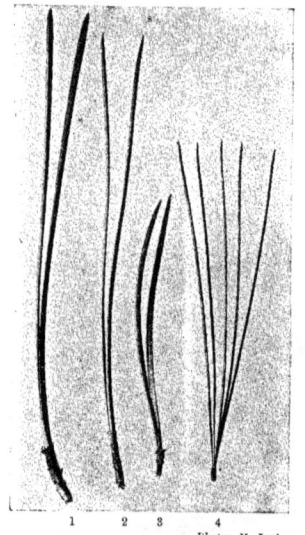

Fig. 5.—Needles of (1) Cluster, (2) Austrian, (3) Scots, and (4) Weymouth Pines

Heartwood and Sapwood. — The developmental history of the various elements of the wood is fundamentally the same. They are all formed from the cells of the cambium, they increase in size, their walls become more or less thickened ; but, as long as they retain protoplasmic contents, they behave as living cells. When they lose their protoplasm they cease to grow, though they may still act as conductive tissue, water and dissolved gases passing through them ; they still serve the important purpose of mechanical support ; nor is there any ordinary reason for their decay.

In the wood of Coniferæ, consisting as it does so largely of tracheids, it is these tracheids that convey water and air from the roots to the leaves, that store up starch in winter, and also support the weight of the tree. It is, however, only by the tracheids of the outer rings in a mature tree that all these functions are performed. This outer zone, generally from one to three inches across, and comprising some thirty to fifty annual rings, is known as the *sapwood*, or from its usually lighter colour, the *alburnum*, while the central mass is the *heartwood* or *duramen*. The deposition of tannin, gums, resins, etc., usually makes this heartwood darker in colour, especially in pines ; but in spruces and silver firs there is but little difference in appearance between the two portions.

The heartwood is so far physiologically dead that it only performs the mechanical function of contributing to the support of the weight of the tree. The thickness of sapwood varies not only in different species, but also in different individuals, in different parts of the same tree, or even in different parts of the same growth-rings. It is narrower near the base and towards the top of a tree than in the main part of the stem ; and it is wider in rapidly-growing trees, or in those grown in the open, as opposed to the crowded forest. In old trees the conversion of sapwood into heartwood proceeds more slowly. Thus, whilst in a pine a hundred years old only the outer thirty to sixty rings may be sapwood, in a tree of the same species 250 years old there may be seventy or eighty rings of sapwood.

Heartwood being heavier, and, on account of the smaller proportion of water that it contains, more durable, is generally the most valuable part of the tree, so that a high proportion of sapwood reduces the value of timber. Only for the manufacture of paper pulp is sapwood an advantage among coniferous woods. It is true, however, that sapwood can be more readily impregnated with chemical preservatives, and, when so impregnated, may equal

TIMBER: ITS GROWTH AND PROPERTIES

heartwood in durability and consequently in value.

Hard Woods.—It is the comparative simplicity of structure of coniferous woods, composed, as we have seen, almost entirely of tracheids in regular radial rows, which gives them a straight even grain, rendering them readily cleavable and easily worked with saw and plane ; while their resinous character renders them durable. Growing rapidly, on poor soil, and with a large proportion of straight timber, they are applicable to a great variety of uses, and both the demand and supply of this class of wood is enormous. Directly we begin to examine the woods of broad-leaved trees—those technically known as *hard woods*—we find that, though pith, cambium, growth-rings, sapwood and heart, early and late wood, and rays are all present as in coniferous wood, so that the general plan is equally exogenous, the wood itself is more complex, being made up of a greater variety of elements, and these elements not being, as a rule, in the regular rows presented by the tracheids of conifers.

Pith.—The outline of the pith when seen in a sound cross-section of a hard wood is often characteristic. It may be nearly circular, with an even margin, as in elm, or with a wavy outline, as in horse-chestnut, hawthorn or laburnum ; it may be oval, as in ash, maple, holly and plane ; triangular, as in alder, beech, and birch ; or five or six-sided, as in oak, poplar and willow.

Elements of the Wood.—It is, however, chiefly in the variety of the elements of which the wood is made up and in the varying proportions in which they are present that the hard woods differ from the soft woods. Instead of the functions of conducting water and affording mechanical strength being both performed by the same elements, as they are by the tracheids of the soft woods, these functions are separated in the hard woods. Vessels are always present to conduct liquid from roots to leaves, and mechanical strength is given mostly by wood-fibres. Some cellular tissue is generally also present, while tracheids may or may not occur.

Texture and Grain.—Two sets of characters of wood that are very often confused are texture and grain. Texture

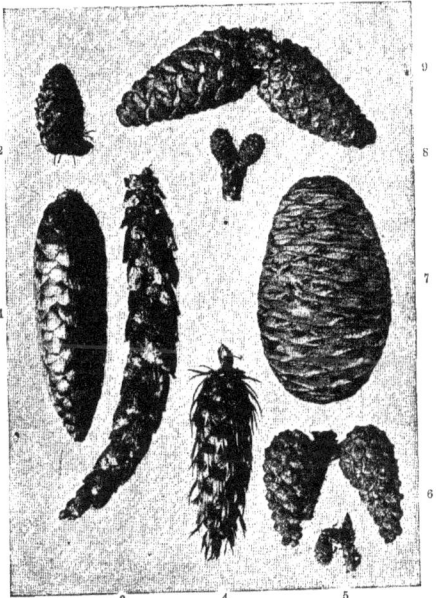

Fig. 6.—Cones of Conifers showing attitude in growth: 1, Spruce ; 2, Larch ; 3, Weymouth Pine ; 4, Douglas Fir ; 5 and 6, Scots Pine, first year and full grown ; 7, Cedar ; 8 and 9, Austrian Pine, first year and full grown

Photo: H. Irving

refers to the relative size of the elements of which the wood is made up ; grain to their direction and the width of the growth-rings. In texture wood may be either coarse, fine, even, or uneven. Coarse-textured wood has many of its elements large, as, for instance, the wood of Spanish Chestnut. Fine-textured wood has its elements mostly small, as in Willow or Poplar. Even-textured wood is that in which the elements are uniform in size, as in Box, Pencil Cedar, Horse-chestnut, etc.; uneven-textured, that in which they present marked contrasts in size, as when there is much difference between early and late wood, pitchpine and the ring-porous woods, oak, chestnut, elm, ash, etc., for example.

The various terms used by woodworkers in describing grain, such as coarse-grained, fine-grained, cross-grained, and spiral-grained, are not always employed in quite the same sense. *Fine-grained* should mean "with narrow growth-rings," that is slow-grown; and *coarse-grained*, with wide rings as the result of rapid growth; but in turnery and cabinetwork "fine-grained" is often applied to any wood susceptible of a high polish, that is practically to a hard or fine-textured wood; and "coarse-grained" conversely to wood that will not polish well, being soft, or of coarse texture. So, too, the term, *straight-grained* as applied to a tree or to unconverted timber should mean that the elements of the wood are parallel to the axis of growth; but when applied to a plank it means that its longer surfaces are parallel to the radius and the tangent of the stem, that is, that in cutting up the log the length of the plank has been kept parallel to the axis of growth. If this has not been done a "cross-grained" plank will have been cut from a straight-grained log.

As the strength of timber, especially in resisting a transverse or bending strain, diminishes in proportion as the plane of its elements deviates from parallelism with the longitudinal surface, this is most important in engineering or constructional work; and as, when split, wood cleaves in the direction of length of its elements, split wood is generally stronger—so far as such strains are concerned—than sawn stuff. Naturally cross-grained wood is produced when the elements are oblique and interlaced, not all lying in any one direction, so that, in working, the tool is sure to meet many of them at a wide angle with their longitudinal axis. This is notably the case with lignum-vitæ, which is employed accordingly for ships, pulleys, skittle-balls, mallets, etc. But whilst this cross-grained character need not interfere with the cleavability, or ease in splitting, of the wood, or diminish its strength when split, but may render it more tough, as the fibres will shrink in drying in the direction of their length, such wood will almost certainly twist or warp in seasoning. This is noticeably the case with the so-called "satin walnut," so that the cheap furniture made from it is unfit for employment in rooms in which fires are used, or other considerable changes of temperature are probable. Jarrah behaves in a similar manner when in thin planks.

It is not uncommon to find the elements arranged spirally round the axis of a tree, probably, in many cases at least, as the result of exposure to high winds.

Even-grain should apply to the regular circularity and uniform width of the growth-rings; but it has been described practically as one "that a sharp saw cuts directly through and leaves the surface compact and level"; while an "uneven" or "woolly" grain tears under the tool and leaves the surface rough with ragged ends of torn fibres. Perhaps the terms "smooth" and "rough" are preferable for these two conditions, "even" and "uneven" referring only to the regularity or irregularity of the growth-rings.

When the fibres undulate without crossing one another we get curly and wavy grain. When the folds or ridges are small and numerous we get the *curly* effect, frequent in maples; when the undulations are larger and less frequent we have the *wavy* structure. This is often found near the root or below the spring of large branches. The undulations of the elements are usually, but not always, in a plane tangential to the stem, so that the radial section is waved, but a tangential one smooth and exhibiting the ornamental grain. The exquisite grain of some sycamore and mahogany known as "fiddle-back" from its use in the case of the former, is of the nature of a wavy grain. Other variations of figure in mahogany are

TIMBER: ITS GROWTH AND PROPERTIES

known as "roe," "mottle," "cross-mottle," "dapple," "plum-pattern," and "curls." Two of the most beautiful pieces of wood known are a plank of Honduras mahogany, brought to England in 1816, now in Museum III at Kew, and one of satinwood from Ceylon, now at the Imperial Institute, London, to which the Grand Prix of the Paris Exhibition of 1900 was awarded.

The surface of the wood-cylinder, if the bark of a tree is removed, is seldom completely smooth, but is locally more or less pitted or channelled. These depressions on the surface can usually only be traced inwards through a very few annual rings. Such inequalities of growth in one year, that is to say, are generally made up in the next. In some woods, however, especially that of maples, these depressions are repeated year by year, although they are very slight in extent, generally less, in fact, than an $\frac{1}{8}$ in. in depth. In a tangential section they appear as rings or "eyes," in a cross-section as "pins." When numerous and small they produce the effect known as *bird's-eye* grain; and when wider, that known as *blister* or *landscape*. The latter name is appropriate, since the figure much resembles a contoured map.

Burrs.—On the stunted stems of shrubby plants, or the stumps of coppiced or pollard trees, or on the warty excrescences, known as *burrs*, produced on trees of various kinds by the attacks of mites or of fungi, numerous buds or rudimentary shoots appear, in no definite order. Each of these is a centre for the slow formation of growth-rings and the displacement of surrounding elements, so that—whether they grow out into the tangle of twigs known as a "witch's broom" or not—in the course of years a mass of wood several feet across may be formed, very dense, and with an irregular *gnarled* grain, somewhat resembling bird's-eye maple. Such burrs afford various very handsome kinds of veneer.

Knots.—A knot is the base of a branch, generally one the development of which has been arrested. Though a branch originates in a bud at the surface of the stem, it is not only added to year by year by newly formed wood so that it becomes a cone with its apex pointing towards the centre of the stem, but it also becomes embedded in the growth-rings of the stem

Spruce. Douglas Fir. Larch.
Scots Pine. Austrian Pine.
Photo: H. Irving
Fig. 7.—Shoots of Conifers

formed subsequently to its origin. The earlier the origin of the branch, the more deeply seated will be the knot.

The junction between the elements of the wood of the stem and those of the living branch differs on the lower and upper sides of the branch. Some elements from the stem bend outwards into the branch and are thus continuous with the elements of the branch; but the other elements of the stem bend round the base of the branch and continue beyond it, so that there is no such continuity of tissue between the upper side of the branch and the stem above as there is between its lower side and the stem below. When young trees are at all crowded together most of their earlier branches are killed, and the subsequently formed growth-rings of the stem do not then as a rule unite their growth with the base of the dead branch, but merely surround and embed it. If the dead branch is quite small it will form what is known as a *pin knot*, and may be closely *encased* by the newer wood and be covered over or *occluded* by its growth, while quite *sound*, so that no visible sign of its presence may remain on the outside of the stem or log. If, on the other hand, the branchlet decays, it may give rise to a rotting or *druxy knot*, which, though a source of extending damage to the wood, may be similarly concealed.

A less healthy surrounding growth often leaves larger knots *loose*, and sometimes they may have split radially or have begun to decay before they are occluded. If sound, a knot is usually harder than the surrounding wood; and in coniferous trees they generally become extremely resinous. The resin will often preserve them when the rest of the wood decays, so that they may be collected from a forest of dead trees as valuable fuel. The same resinous character will make them refuse to take paint or varnish. Small knots may impart an ornamental figure to wood. Burrs, in fact, consist largely of a crowded mass of such knots, presenting a series of small growth-rings, each with a central dark speck marking the pith.

As we have already seen, the outward and lateral bending of the elements below a large branch also produces handsome grain; but, in general, knots are defects, making the wood less easy to work or split and less able to withstand bending or pulling strains. For the structural reason just explained, it is found in splitting the wood of a stem that the knot splits with it if the split is started from below, but not if it be started from above.

Common defects found in converted timber will be dealt with in detail in a later chapter concerned with the conversion of tree trunks into commercial timber.

PROPERTIES OF WOODS

Though it is probably not altogether logical or scientific, it is convenient to group the characters of woods as structural, physical and mechanical.

Unquestionably the two most prominent characteristics that make up the appearance of wood are its grain and its colour. We propose, therefore, to begin the examination of the physical properties of woods by dealing with those properties that are most obvious to our unassisted senses, colour, lustre, odour, taste, resonance, and other forms of conductivity.

Colour.—When first formed, wood is nearly, if not entirely, colourless. The sapwood may become yellowish after a few years, but does not produce the varied tints of heartwoods. In not a few woods, such as silver firs, spruces, birches and horse-chestnut, there is little or no difference in colour between sapwood and heartwood; whilst in others there is a marked contrast. The deeper colour of the heartwood is due to the infiltration of resinous, gummy, tannin-like and other pigments into the walls and cavities of its elements; and, as these substances add to the durability of the wood, the depth of the colour is generally taken as a criterion of durability. There are many cases, however, where such infiltrating substances are not deeply coloured and where the heartwood may be durable without much deepening of colour.

Exposure to air and light darkens the colour of all wood, probably by the oxidation of the colouring-matters. This is strikingly seen in our common alder, the wood of which is white when growing, turns a deep pink on being felled, and finally becomes a light brown. Prolonged immersion in water produces various colour-changes in woods. They often turn grey, as in the spa wood or silverwood used for bric-à-brac. Yew, buried in peat, becomes a dark brown; whilst the tannin

TIMBER: ITS GROWTH AND PROPERTIES

Fig. 8.—The Ash in Summer
Photo: G. Clarke Nuttall

in oak combines with iron-salts in peat-water and dyes the wood jet black with a natural ink.

For some purposes wood is required to be free from colour. Perfectly white sycamore wood—known as Plane in the trade at Glasgow—is in demand for bread-platters, butter-moulds, and the rollers of mangles; and light-coloured woods are also preferred for spokes and tool-handles, under the mistaken generalisation that dark-coloured heartwoods, though heavy and hard, are brittle rather than tough.

Coloured woods, on the other hand, are specially valued for panelling, cabinet-making, furniture and inlaying —such as the black ebonies, rose-woods, mahoganies, walnuts, etc.

Scattered patches or streaks of discoloration, that is of colour unlike that of the rest of the wood, are usually symptomatic of disease. Dark stains may be partial decay, which may originate in the holes made by woodpeckers, followed by rain and fungoid growth. although it is doubtful whether such insect-eating birds would ever attack a previously sound tree. Such patches of discoloration are specially to be looked for at the butt ends of logs. If fungoid, these usually begin white, becoming later reddish-brown, or *foxy*.

The decay often begins at the pith, and may result in the destruction of all the heartwood, making the tree hollow, although the active growth of the cambium may continue. Decay may, however, originate in a broken branch, or some local injury from the outside, or by the accumulation of water and dead leaves. English oak, with such foxiness or incipient decay when first so affected, is in special demand as " Brown Oak " for ornamental use, in purposes in which the loss of strength is not of consequence.

Lustre or Gloss. — Wood being naturally translucent, its fibres, seen through its translucent surface, reflect a varying amount of light and so produce the lustre or gloss of the wood. A small degree of lustre is exhibited by most sound wood; but when wood is attacked by fungi it becomes

Photo: G. Clarke Nuttall
Fig. 9.—The Ash in Winter

more opaque and dull, or, as it is technically termed, "dead," instead of "live."

The natural lustres of sound woods differ much in degree, and true lustre must be distinguished from such merely superficial reflection of light as is obtained from any polished or varnished surface. Beech, plane, or American walnut, for instance, have so little natural lustre that they may be termed *dull*; spruce has a *pearly* lustre; lignum-vitæ, one that may be described as *greasy*; while the lustre that gives its name to the silver-grain of the "mirrors" of the pith-rays is very similar to that called "pearly" on the ordinary tangential section of spruce. Finally, the parallel and often curled fibres, visible through the light-coloured surface, give the beautifully *silky* effect that gives its name to satinwood.

Odour.—The production of an odour by wood implies the giving-off of some volatile substance. In many cases the smell is so slight or so evanescent as to escape notice; and it is generally more pronounced in moist green wood than in dry or seasoned material, and in heartwood rather than in sapwood. Prolonged exposure to air or submersion in water will usually deprive at least the exposed surface of the wood of its odour; but in other cases the scent will be again emitted for an almost indefinite time on the exposure of a fresh surface.

The turpentines of pines, larches, spruces and silver firs are volatile oils with resins dissolved in them, and their smell is known either as *resinous* or *turpentinous*. Cedar-wood oil, used for perfuming fine soaps, is obtained from the wood of the pencil cedar. Cedar is valued for cabinets, wardrobes, chests of drawers, etc., though the perfume soon leaves the exposed surface.

The cedar-wood of the English timber-trade is not coniferous; it is an ally of the mahogany, often known from its chief use as "cigar-box cedar." The wood is imported from Havana, Jamaica, and Honduras. It has a somewhat more peppery smell than that of pencil cedar.

Resonance.—It is mainly owing to its elasticity that wood can either receive from, or communicate to, the surrounding air the vibrations of which we are conscious as sound. The vibrations of the air, caused, for example, by the motion of the strings of a piano, can communicate themselves to a thin board, causing it to vibrate with the same intervals as the string and thus to transmit and reinforce the note. Any piece of wood struck by a hammer will give out a sound which will vary in pitch and in intensity according to the shape, size, kind, and condition of the wood. As musical sounds differ from mere noises essentially in being made up of regular periodic vibrations, it is obviously essential that the wood used in the construction of musical instruments should be, and should remain, as uniform in texture as possible.

Knots, resinous patches, sharply contrasted early and late wood in the growth-rings, as in our ring-porous hard woods, or alternating wide and narrow growth-rings, are, therefore, defects and would cause woods to be rejected for this purpose. That it may retain its form without twisting it is essential that the wood should be thoroughly seasoned; but the mistake has been made by some modern French makers of violins of using old and dry woods. Wood has its maximum elasticity, combined with stability, when just seasoned; and it was at this stage that the great Italian makers shaped their wood and protected it with their incomparable varnish. In order that each fibre of the wood may vibrate freely it is desirable that the wood should not be bent into shape or put in any condition of extreme or deforming strain. The belly of a violin is, therefore, cut from a thick piece of wood, and is not bent into shape.

Although any well-seasoned ornamental wood, such as rosewood, mahogany, walnut, or veneered material, may be used for the cases of pianofortes, it is most desirable that even in this part of the instrument there should be an absence of knots, contrasts of grain, joints, especially open ones, or other possible interferences with the regular transmission of the sound.

Conductivity.—The variation in the action of wood as a conductor of heat or electricity depends mainly upon the density and moisture of the wood, rather than upon any specific characters. Dry wood is a poor conductor either of heat or electricity. The wooden handles of metal tea-pots and of soldering-irons illustrate the former fact. As increased density increases the conductivity, the late wood is a better conductor than the early, and a section with the grain, affording continuous bands of late wood, will be a better conductor than one cut across the grain so that the bands of early and late wood alternate. It may, therefore, be worth while in the case of such handles as those just mentioned to see that the grain of the wood runs across the handle. Increase of moisture increases the conductivity both for heat and electricity. This is a matter of some practical importance. It has been found, for instance, that electric wires cased in wooden boxes may cease to be insulated if the boxes can become saturated. Such wood ought therefore to be filled with some preservative of a non-conducting character. Resins and oils being bad electrical conductors, porous and resinous woods are adapted for such purposes, which are being better met by other means.

especially with reference to the amount of water and air they contain but also with regard to their compactness, that is, the amount of woody or other solid matter in a given bulk. To speak more precisely, the weight of wood depends upon the

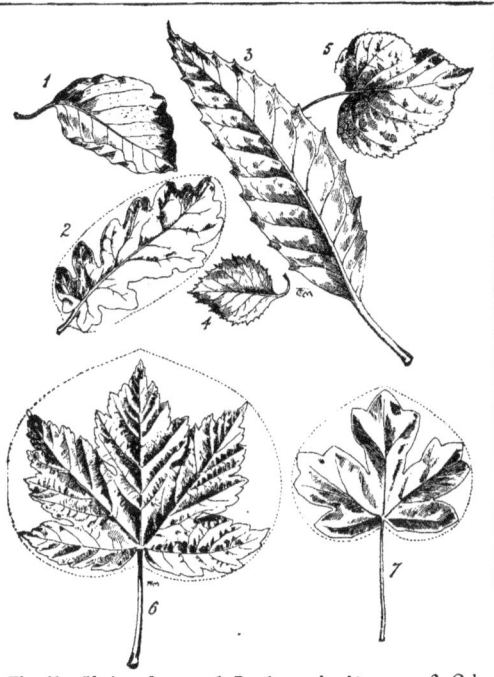

Fig. 10.—Various Leaves: 1, Beech—oval, edge wavy; 2, Oak—oblong, deeply wavy; 3, Sweet Chestnut—narrow, broadly sawed; 4, Birch—doubly sawed; 5, Lime—heart-shaped and oblique; 6, Sycamore—heart-shaped, five-lobed; 7, Maple—kidney-shaped, five-lobed.

WEIGHT, DENSITY AND SPECIFIC GRAVITY

Woods weighed in the mass vary immensely in their apparent weight, more closeness with which the wood-elements are crowded together, the density of the walls of the elements, and the nature of their contents. Most woods, with the exception of a few tropical species, float in water, and this is a matter of the greatest consequence with regard to the transport of newly felled trees from the forest to the port, and of much converted timber which is floated in rafts down the great waterways of the world. This floating is, however, due to the air imprisoned in the wood. A single wood-fibre dried and thrown into water will float, as will an empty bottle with a cork in it; but after a time it will become waterlogged and sink.

Undried sapwood will sink sooner than dried wood, because its elements are already more or less filled with water; and the more compact, slower-grown hard woods, especially those tropical species to which allusion has just been made—which have more crowded and thicker-walled element—will become waterlogged sooner than pinewood. The amount of water in woods varies not only in the species, but in the individual, in different parts of the same tree, and according to the extent to which it has been seasoned. No comparison of the weights of different woods can, therefore, be of any value unless this misleading factor, the moisture-content, has been as far as possible eliminated by kiln-drying. Many published weights of wood are rendered entirely valueless by the absence of any precise indication as to the amount of moisture present, such vague terms as "air-dried" being used, or even the distinction between sapwood and heartwood being ignored.

The substance of the wood, on the other hand, is, bulk for bulk, of very much the same weight in different trees, varying little below 1·5 or above 1·6 times the weight of water. A good-sized log of pinewood may float for months before the water will have filled most of the closed thick-walled elements of the heartwood; but a small fragment of wood cut across the grain, so that the elements are open to the access of water, will sink almost immediately. It is possible with such a fragment to determine the weight of the wood-substance with tolerable precision by immersing it in a series of liquids of varying specific gravity until we find one in which it neither sinks nor rises if immersed. To do this accurately, however, the wood should be boiled for some hours in calcium-nitrate or some zinc salt to replace all the water and air in its cavities. Another method has been adopted in which the wood is rasped to a fine powder, dried at boiling point, weighed and then put into a weighed bottle of water from which the air is exhausted and left for six days and then weighed.

If then we eliminate the moisture factor at least to a uniform degree by kiln-drying all samples, and take the actual density of the wood-substance to be the same in different woods, then differences in measured weight will depend mainly upon the amount of this wood-substance that may be packed into the unit of volume taken.

In practice the weight of wood is calculated from small sound specimens of heartwood (unless otherwise specified) ovendried at the boiling-point of water until their weight becomes constant. Various causes, however, such as rate of growth, may cause such wide variations that any single weight stated should be the average of many determinations; or if the extreme results are given they will commonly be found to be very far apart.

Density being thus the weight of a unit of volume, it is stated in grams per cubic centimetre, in kilograms per cubic metre or stère, or in pounds to the cubic foot. For commercial purposes the density of "air-dry" or "shipping-dry" wood is usually stated in pounds per thousand board-feet, a board-foot being one-twelfth of a cubic foot. If a wood weighs less than 24 lb. to the cubic foot it may be termed *very light*; if between 24 lb. and 30 lb., *light*; if between 30 lb. and 36 lb., *medium*; if between 36 lb. and 42 lb., *heavy*; if between 42 lb. and 48 lb., *very heavy*; and if above 48 lb. to the cubic foot, one of the *heaviest*.

We are inclined to think that the weight of a cubic foot, which is often represented as the value of W, is the most practically useful method of testing the density of woods; but it is very often given in the form of specific gravity. Specific gravity is the ratio of the weight of a substance to the weight of an equal volume of some substance taken as a standard. The standard we use for solids is distilled water

TIMBER: ITS GROWTH AND PROPERTIES

at the temperature at which it is at its maximum density, namely 4° centigrade (39 2° F.). At that temperature a cubic foot of water weighs 62·43 lb., so that if S.G. be used to symbolise specific gravity:

$$\frac{W}{62\cdot 43} = \text{S.G. or S.G.} \times 62\cdot 43 = W.$$

If we add to the scale of weights we have just given the corresponding specific gravities, and some examples, we get the following table:—

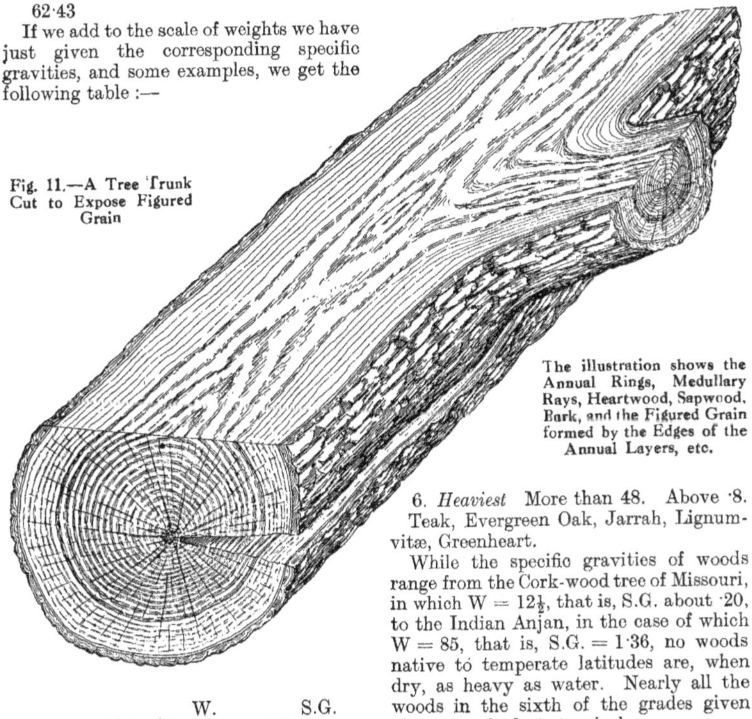

Fig. 11.—A Tree Trunk Cut to Expose Figured Grain

	W.	S.G.
1. *Very Light*	Not more than 24.	Not more than ·4.

Most Spruce, Willow, Poplar, Yellow Pine.

| 2. *Light* | 24 — 30 | ·4 — ·5 |

Linden, Chestnut, Canary Whitewood, Scots Fir, Pencil Cedar, Californian Redwood, Hemlock Spruce.

| 3. *Medium* | 30 — 36 | ·5 — ·6 |

Douglas Spruce, Sycamore. Satin Walnut.

| 4. *Heavy* | 36 — 42 | ·6 — ·7 |

Most Birch, Beech, Walnut, Elm and Ash.

| 5. *Very Heavy* | 42 — 48 | ·7 — ·8 |

Hornbeam, Hickory, Mahogany, Locust, White Oak, good Ash and Elm, Persimmon.

The illustration shows the Annual Rings, Medullary Rays, Heartwood, Sapwood, Bark, and the Figured Grain formed by the Edges of the Annual Layers, etc.

6. *Heaviest* More than 48. Above ·8. Teak, Evergreen Oak, Jarrah, Lignum-vitæ, Greenheart.

While the specific gravities of woods range from the Cork-wood tree of Missouri, in which $W = 12\frac{1}{2}$, that is, S.G. about ·20, to the Indian Anjan, in the case of which $W = 85$, that is, S.G. $= 1\cdot 36$, no woods native to temperate latitudes are, when dry, as heavy as water. Nearly all the woods in the sixth of the grades given above are, in fact, tropical.

Moisture-content.—We have already had occasion to refer to the constant presence of more or less water in wood as affecting its conductivity. It is still more important in its influence upon hardness, strength, and durability.

Water occurs in the sapwood of a living tree under three conditions. It forms more than 90 per cent. of the protoplasmic contents of the living cells; it saturates the walls of all the elements of the wood; and it occurs free wholly or partially filling the cavities of the cells, fibres, tracheids and vessels that have lost their protoplasmic contents. In heartwood it will only occur under the two last-mentioned conditions. In the freshly-felled wood of the tree which is known in the United States as white pine, in the Liverpool timber trade as yellow pine, and in our plantations as Weymouth pine, for example, water forms about half of the total weight of the wood; and it is estimated that of this amount less than 5 per cent. will be in the protoplasm of living tissue, 35 per cent. will be in the cell-walls, and 60 per cent., the free water or sap as it is commonly called, in the cavities of the elements that have lost their protoplasm. The amount will, however, vary greatly according to the species, the season of the year, and the part of the tree from which wood may be obtained.

While freshly-cut poplar has been stated to contain 44 to 52 per cent. of water, and oak, beech, elm and linden from 34 to 47 per cent., birch has been described with 30, ash and maple with 28 and 27 respectively, and hornbeam with only 18·6 per cent., though it may be doubted whether these figures have a general application. Water is probably at its maximum in the living tree when the roots are most active and the sap is rising. Thus, silver fir was found to contain 53 per cent. in January and 61 per cent. in April; Ash, 29 per cent. in January and 39 per cent. in April. As the proportion of water present diminishes gradually from the bark to the pith if there is no heartwood, or with a sudden reduction at the junction of heartwood with sapwood if heartwood is present, more water will be found, in proportion, in the younger shoots, twigs and branches than in the main stem, more in the upper part of the stem than in the lower, more in a young tree than in an old one.

The percentage of moisture present can be readily ascertained, but will appear at very different figures according to whether it is computed by comparison with the original or fresh weight of the wood or with reference to its weight when dried. A thin section of wood is sawn off, weighed carefully on a delicate balance, dried in an oven at the temperature of boiling water until its weight is found to be stationary, and re-weighed. The difference between the first or fresh weight and the final or dry weight is, of course, the amount of water given off. The percentage of moisture present with reference to the fresh weight will be

$$= \frac{\text{Fresh weight} - \text{dry weight}}{\text{Fresh weight}} \times 100.$$

Thus, if the dry weight is only half the fresh weight, 50 per cent. of that original weight was water. If, however, we refer the percentage of moisture to the dry weight, percentage of moisture

$$= \frac{\text{Fresh weight} - \text{dry weight}}{\text{Dry weight}}$$

$\times 100$, the moisture given off will be seen to be 100 per cent.

Winter-felled wood in Europe retains more than 40 per cent. of moisture until the end of the following summer, and even after being kept for several years in a dry place, as in what is known as "natural seasoning," from 15 to 20 per cent. may remain.

Except when there are extensive cracks or "shakes" in the wood, or when the wood is exceptionally sappy and the weather is warm, water does not escape from timber in a liquid form, but must be removed by evaporation. The rate at which this takes place under natural conditions depends upon the kind of wood, upon its structure, upon the size and shape of the piece, upon the area of the exposed surfaces, and whether they are radial, tangential or transverse, and upon the condition of the surrounding air as regards temperature, moisture, and movement.

Difference in the thickness of the walls of the elements is, for instance, apparently a reason why pine should dry faster than oak. Its greater relative surface causes an inch plank to dry more than four times as fast as one 4 in. thick, and more than twenty times as fast as wood 10 in. thick.

TIMBER: ITS GROWTH AND PROPERTIES 131

A cross-section may in an hour—from the open ends, that is, of the elements—give off four times as much water-vapour per square inch as a radial section will do. A high temperature will cause more rapid evaporation, even if the surrounding air is very moist.

Drying can take place to a considerable extent in hot steam and to some extent even in boiling water. Wind, however, by removing successive bodies of air laden with the moisture resulting from evaporation, will hasten the drying of timber.

If the air is artificially dried by the use of such chemicals as caustic lime, the wood, though parting with some moisture, will yet retain some ; and even if oven-dried at 120° F. will still lose more water at 200° F. It is impossible to remove all the water from the wood without destroying it ; so that, for practical purposes, wood is considered to be thoroughly dried when its weight remains unreduced at a sustained temperature of 212° F. (the boiling-point of water), although 2 or 3 per cent. of moisture will then remain in it.

The presence or absence of the free water in the cavities of the wood-elements does not apparently lessen or increase the strength of the wood, such effects being entirely due to the water with which the cell-walls may be saturated. The presence of this water renders these walls soft, pliable and weak ; its removal will increase the hardness, resilience, and strength of wood. Thus a small block of green spruce will, when dried, support a load four times as great as it would when wet. In large timbers, however, the resultant splitting or "checking," as it is termed, may entirely counterbalance any increase of strength due to drying. It is consequently unsafe, in calculating the strength of large timbers, to assume that they will be any stronger dried than when green. As examples of the gain in strength produced by drying, we may specially cite the soft-wood cross-arms for telegraph-poles, and the hard-wood spokes and handles in wheelwrights' and implement-makers' work.

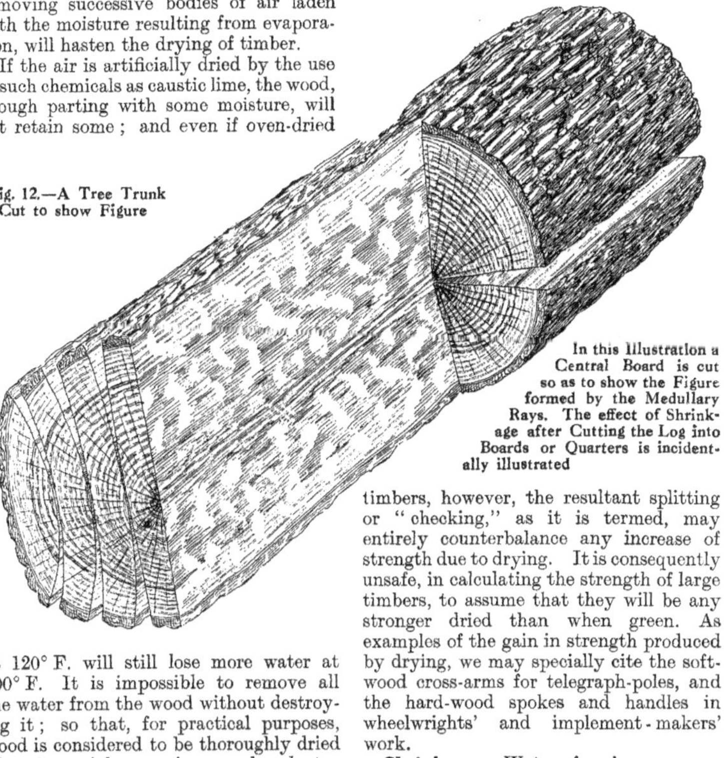

Shrinkage.—Water forming so considerable a proportion of the substance of living wood, it might be expected that a loss of water would bring about shrinkage. This is, however, not the result of the loss of the free water in the cavities of the

Fig. 12.—A Tree Trunk Cut to show Figure

In this illustration a Central Board is cut so as to show the Figure formed by the Medullary Rays. The effect of Shrinkage after Cutting the Log into Boards or Quarters is incidentally illustrated

wood-elements, but of that which saturates the cell-walls. The shrinkage mainly affects the width of the wood-elements, not their length ; but, as the elements of the pith-rays extend radially, in shrinking they contract in the directions of the height and width of the ray, thus producing some longitudinal shrinkage of the wood as a whole. In any case longitudinal shrinkage is small in its total amount, being greatest in woods with curly grain

Fig. 13.—Trunk and Bark of Oak
Photo: H. Irving

or broad rays, but not exceeding ·1 to ·3 per cent. of the total length.

Warping.—Even in the case of wood of uniform texture and straight grain, in which as a rule the distortion or *warping* due to unequal shrinkage will be reduced to a minimum, considerable shrinkage of this character may be produced by rapid unequal drying. Thus a plank of green wood exposed to the heat of the sun, or of a fire, will dry and shrink much more rapidly on the side exposed to the heat and curl up accordingly. Such warping, however, due as it is to a merely temporary inequality in the distribution of water in the plank, can generally be corrected by completing the drying process for the whole. On the other hand, warping due to such irregularities of structure as cross grain or spiral grain cannot as a rule be corrected. The so-called satin walnut or red gum jarrah, especially when in small pieces, and to some extent elm and beech, are liable, from the complex internal strains set up by their structure, to warp in various directions so that they become twisted.

We have already stated that shrinkage in length, that is with the grain, is far less than that which takes place radially. There is, however, another inequality in shrinkage of almost equal importance, that namely between the radial and the tangential direction. In the radial direction there is very slight shrinkage of the pith-rays, because that is their longitudinal extension ; but there is the lateral shrinkage of the tracheids or fibres of the wood itself. This latter, however, is made up of the shrinkage of longitudinal bands of late wood separated by bands of early wood that shrink less. On the other hand, in the tangential direction, that is, practically along the growth-rings, the greatly-shrinking late wood is continuous ; and consequently, as the late wood also represents as a rule the greater part of the wood-substance, the shrinkage in this direction is greater than that produced radially. The difference between radial and tangential shrinkage is generally in a ratio of about 2 to 3.

Splitting or Checking.—The more rapidly wood is dried, the greater is its tendency to split. When in the round, wood splits mostly in the direction of the pith-rays, that is, where the unequally-shrinking rays and wood are in contact. If a log is sawn in half longitudinally through its centre, the flat surface will, for the causes just explained, become convex. If a plank is cut from the middle of a log, that is, so as to include the centre growth-rings in its end section, when it is known as " box-hearted," both surfaces will be drawn into a convex curve and

TIMBER: ITS GROWTH AND PROPERTIES

some of the radial checks may open lengthways. If the half log just described be sawn into planks parallel to its flat surface, each of them will so shrink that the side nearer to the centre of growth will be convex, that nearer the outside, concave.

Cracks from the ends of converted timber may be prevented by stopping the drying at the ends with a coat of paint, by dipping the ends in melted paraffin, or gluing paper over them. Other substances, such as tar, linseed oil, or clay, are sometimes used for this sealing of the cut ends of the wood-elements, more especially in the case of valuable woods. Driving S-irons, or preferably thin steel clamps, into the ends of logs when the checks first appear is another method of preventing logs from splitting up. The most approved modern form of these irons is made by running a thin strap of iron with one tapered edge between cogs so as to crimp it into S-curves, which can then be cut to any desired length, the taper edge being readily driven into the wood.

Split wood is straighter in grain, and therefore more easily seasoned, without checking, than sawn timber. When it is to be sawn, timber will warp and check less if sawn as nearly as possible along the radii of the growth-rings, that is, "quartered," "rift-sawn," or "wainscot." On the Continent, it is usual in converting oak timber to take off two lateral "checks" from the log and a central plank with the usual "star-shake"—or radiating centre splits produced during growth—in it, these being considered as waste. The remainder is then sawn into planks parallel to the checks. The English method of quartering large logs is merely to saw the log longitudinally through the growth-centre in two directions at right angles to one another, the quarters being then sawn into planks parallel to either longitudinal section.

MECHANICAL PROPERTIES OF WOODS

The fitness of a wood for any particular purpose is never determined by one character alone, but invariably by its possession of two or more qualities together. Thus the spoke of a wheel must not only be "strong"—a somewhat vague quality—but must definitely be stiff to retain its shape under strain, hard, so that the tenons will not become loose in their mortices, and "tough" to resist shocks and twisting strains.

The mechanical properties of woods are, it has been well said, being continually put to the practical tests of everyday life. The stiffness, hardness and toughness of

Photo: H. Irving
Fig. 14.—Trunk and Bark of Scots Pine

every joist, rafter, window-sash, door-frame or flooring plank in our dwellings, of the chair we sit on, and of the boat or carriage in which we travel, are being tested by use as to the loads they can carry, or the other stresses they can withstand. So, too, every step we take in woodworking, from the splitting of firewood or of laths for thatching, or the "rending" of oak fencing, to the construction of the most delicate and elaborate piece of bric-à-brac, involves the practical, if unconscious, recognition of some of the mechanical properties of the woods we employ. At the same time mo t of these mechanical properties can be included under the general term "strength," and their detailed analysis and precise measurement chiefly concern the engineer and the builder of boats or of houses who deal with constructional timber, rather than the small woodworker.

Strength.—All measurements of the strength of timbers are determinations of their powers of resisting certain stresses, or forces tending to produce strains or changes of shape. There are, however, in these problems two complex sets of factors to be analysed, namely, the structure of the wood and the nature of the stress.

Stress, or distributed force, may be considered either extremely as the action of one body on another, or internally, according to the tendency of one part of the body acted upon to move with reference to another part. The intensity of stress is expressed in weights (pounds, tons), per unit of area (square inch).

Normal stresses which are considered as being exerted at right angles to an imaginary cross-section will be either *tensile*, or of the nature of a *pull*, or *compressive*, that is of the nature of a *push*. Such simple longitudinal stresses may be illustrated by a rod or rope stretched by force at each end, or by a block or short pillar compressed by opposite forces acting at its ends.

Strain is the change of shape produced by stress. In a simple longitudinal pull or tensile stress the deformation will consist of a lengthening in the direction of the pull, accompanied by compensating contraction in both directions at right angles to the pull. If the stress be compressive, the strain will similarly be a shortening in the direction of the push.

Any stress that tends to cause part of a piece of wood to slide upon an adjacent part will be a shearing stress or *shear*.

Transverse, Bending or Cross-breaking Strength.—The term "strength," when used without qualification, generally means the breaking weight under a bending test. The stress is in reality a complex one, involving compression on the upper or concave surface, tension on the lower or convex surface, and some longitudinal shear; but it is one which can be applied and measured with very simple machinery and with accurate results. Beams are subjected to transverse stress. The load that any beam will safely carry can be easily calculated, usually by means of a simple mathematical formula.

Flexibility.—It is a further instance of the complex structure of wood that we cannot simply define its property of flexibility. It is to some extent the negation of stiffness. Thus moisture softening wood renders it less stiff and more flexible, so that green woods are more flexible than dry. The interlacing of the elements in some woods, such as elm and ash, due to the independent elongation of each element, enables them to bend to a great extent without fracture, and thus, though stiff, they rank as flexible Hickory and ash are among the most flexible of woods, and, speaking generally, hard woods are more flexible than the stiffer conifers; but some of the characters of woods that are spoken of as flexible may, perhaps better be treated under the admittedly more complex character of toughness. As opposed to elasticity and to toughness, flexibility should mean merely the readiness with which wood can be bent (*pliability*) without rupture.

Toughness.—Though it is a term commonly used by woodworkers, toughness is not often defined, nor is it easy to define, being unquestionably used somewhat ambiguously. It is sometimes applied to a wood merely because it is difficult to split, which will often only mean that the fibres are interlocked, that is, that the wood is cross-grained. If a wood can be bent considerably in one direction without rupture, it ought, perhaps, only to be called flexible, but is often styled tough. Green willow shares such flexibility with ash, hickory and yew; but is not tough as they are.

Conversion, varieties, etc., of timber are dealt with in later chapters.

Glue and Gluing

To woodworkers in general a good understanding of glue and the best methods of using it is essential for the production of reliable work. Glue is made by boiling the skins, hoofs, and bones of animals and straining the product into coolers where it stiffens into a jelly. This is cut into thin sheets and dried on frames of wire netting. The marks of the netting can often be seen on the cakes of glue as bought.

The importance of gluing in woodworking, particularly furniture making, is underestimated. Good glued work with seasoned wood will last a hundred years or more, and a glued joint well made is as strong as the solid wood, to prove which statement it is only necessary to glue together two pieces of thin stuff (say $\frac{1}{2}$-in. boards), when it will usually be found that on trying to break the joint the boards will break elsewhere.

In many cases, however, the joints do not stand good, due to the wood being insufficiently seasoned, indifferent workmanship, careless gluing, or poor quality of glue. Either one or more of these causes are usually responsible for much rickety furniture, often when it has only been in use for a few years.

Varieties and Qualities of Glue.— Glue is manufactured in cakes of about 6 in. or 7 in. square, by $\frac{1}{4}$ in. thick, and sometimes oblong half that size. The varieties generally used are Scotch, English, and French; and although, as a rule, they are all good, the Scotch is acknowledged to be the best; that is, the strongest adhesive.

The cakes are often stamped with a name or brand by which they may be recognised as of reliable quality, and "Extra" means extra strength. It seems that the half cakes, unstamped, are not quite up to the standard, though they are often strongly adhesive and make an excellent glue. But it is only reasonable to expect that makers of a good glue will stamp their product.

In appearance glue should be of a clear amber colour when held up to the light; when cloudy it is usually inferior. In the cake form it is somewhat susceptible to changes of atmosphere. In a dry atmosphere it will be hard and brittle, and in dampness it will become pliable according to the degree of dampness. The least susceptible it is the better. A good cake of glue should never be extremely brittle; it should have some degree of toughness which can be tested by breaking it up. It has to be broken up in small pieces to "make off," which is done by wrapping in a piece of tough paper and smashing up with the hammer. This wrapping up is to prevent the pieces flying about as the glue is broken. The best glue is not so easily broken up small because of its toughness, even when it is quite dry. Glue that is very dark in colour or mouldy, or has an obnoxious odour should be avoided. The latter is glue gone bad, or the materials from which it was made had gone bad. It can be used very thin as size or for making size-colour (sc often required in furniture work) if not too bad; but sometimes the objectionable smell remains for a long time.

On the whole it is best to use glue sufficiently fresh for sizing even though

Fig. 1.—Section through Glue-pot

not up to the standard as regards adhesive properties. The standard quality will do for general woodwork and the extra strength when the occasion requires.

For some work the clearest possible glue should be obtained (the thin French glue, quite clear), notably in repairing veneered work in satinwood, bird's-eye maple, or other light woods; otherwise the joint is apt to show conspicuously.

Glue appears to be the same kind of substance now as that used on woodwork centuries old. It has served its purpose well, according to the skill of the workman in adapting it, and little thought seems to have been devoted to its improvement except in the last two or three years, during which "Croid" glue has become popular; this glue is not made of the traditional materials.

The ordinary glue has been taken for granted, and a considerable part of a woodworker's skill consists in his ability in using it. To do perfect work he must be able to judge its consistency, its temperature, etc., for each particular purpose. The atmosphere he is working in must be right, and he must know what to do should it be against him. For instance, in some pieces of woodwork many joints have to be managed at one gluing, and the worker cannot move too quickly to prevent the glue from chilling before all are safely cramped up. Although glue must be used amply, the least possible should be left between the united surfaces, because being susceptible to climatic influences, there should be nothing there to be affected, so long as the wood fibres are united. "Croid" is a liquid glue that "does not chill," being "used cold"; it thus gives much greater freedom in applying, and saves the trouble of heating the work, etc. Such a glue is extremely useful to have handy for emergencies, which are always happening; both for workshop and home use it can be handled with a much better chance of success by the average worker and the beginner. It saves heating up the glue-pot, or keeping it always ready on the stove. "Croid" glue is also claimed to "resist damp and heat," and to be the "strongest glue known." It has been used extensively in aircraft construction. "Croid" is used direct out of the tin, no glue-pot being used, which is very convenient.

However, the old glue-pot system has served well so long that it will not easily be superseded. The fact remains that at present there must be millions in use.

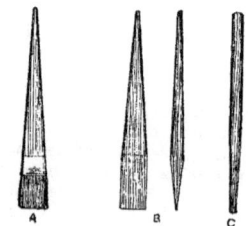

Figs. 2 and 3.—Glue Brushes and Sticks

It is a good plan to have a small-size glue-pot for general use, as it is handy for lifting about, is quickly heated up, and can be frequently changed; a large-size glue-pot is best for extensive work, veneering, etc.

In the cabinet-making factories the

GLUE AND GLUING

system is to keep a convenient number of glue-pots always ready on the stove, to be taken as needed; but for some classes of work, such as bamboo furniture making, the glue is so continually in use that each

Fig. 3A.—Glue Brush made by Hammering Piece of Cane

workman has a gas-ring and tube, with glue-pot, by his bench.

Heating the Glue.—The glue-pot (Fig. 1) is, as a rule, still the same simple appliance that has been used by generations of craftsmen. The receptacle for glue is suspended inside the outer vessel or water container (Fig. 1). Both inner and outer vessels are of cast iron, and will last for generations providing they are never burnt dry or get cracked. Indeed, it is surprising how many times they do burn dry without cracking. When that happens they should be allowed to cool gradually before putting water in.

There are two shapes as regards the glue-pan, the flat bottom and the cauldron, which has a round bottom and three stumps to stand on when lifted out of the water-container. It is frequently necessary to lift the glue out, and when put down anywhere the flat bottom makes a nasty wet mark; with the round bottom the wet dries off. This is an improvement in the hands of a careful workman, but the glue is more easily upset than in the flat-bottom pan.

A slight inconvenience occurs when the water boils over, making a splutter and a mess; but that is due to too much water or too much heat. When this happens the glue-pan is lifted up and a nail may be put under the flange rim to allow the steam to escape. In view of this some glue-pots are made having three small lugs under the flange which fit into corresponding recesses in the rim of the water vessel. When the glue-pan is turned with the lugs out of place the steam escapes and the water will not boil over.

There are special heaters for the glue-pots, consisting of an iron casing over the Bunsen gas-burner, for safety and to economise the heat. They are made to take a single glue-pot or double or treble.

Glue Sticks and Brushes.—For stirring the glue and applying it, glue-sticks are used, the most convenient shape being one made from a bit of $\frac{3}{8}$-in. wood dowel, thinned down to about $\frac{1}{4}$ in. at the wet end. This is used for gluing dowel-holes when jointing, and is always kept in the glue and used as a stirring stick. A flat stick is also useful, shaped similar to the blade of a putty-knife, for use in mortise holes and on tenons, etc. When the glue is "made off"—that is, in liquid—the glue brush is put in, being necessary for many purposes when the sticks are not suitable, such as applying glue quickly to "rubbed" joints, surface work, etc.

In many cabinet-making and furniture-repairing shops, a stick and brush are kept continually in the glue for applying

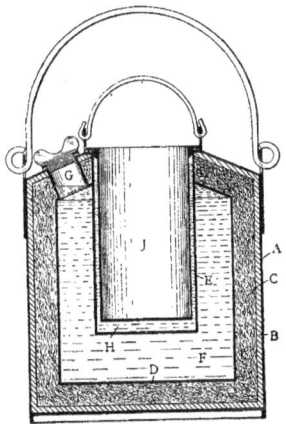

Fig. 4.—Three-vessel Glue-pot

it; these should be of a convenient shape and size. Figs. 2 and 3 show glue brush, etc.; A is a flat brush, 1 in. wide, which is very suitable. A handy shape for a glue-stick for gluing mortise holes, loose joints, etc.. is shown at B, whilst C shows a round stick, which is simply a piece of dowel made thinner at one end; it is useful for putting glue in dowel-holes, holes for spindles, etc.

Special glue brushes are obtainable from tool merchants. They are cheaper than paint brushes and, being iron bound, are more suitable. String-bound paste

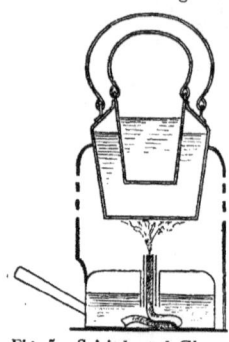

Fig. 5.—Spirit-heated Glue-pot

brushes are often used, but are apt to come undone. In any case, when the glue has set cold no attempt should be made to move the brush before thoroughly melting the glue into liquid again.

Glue brushes are sometimes made from a short piece of cane which is hammered out at one end, thus forming fibres or "bristles" (Fig. 3A).

Preparing Glue.—To prepare a pot of glue a cake must be broken up into small pieces, the smaller the better. The glue-pan should be about three-quarters filled with the glue, and water added to well cover, nearly filling the pan. The outer pot may be three parts filled with water, and with the glue-pan placed in it is boiled on the stove until the glue is dissolved. The more it is stirred the sooner it is ready; average time, within half an hour. The result should be a liquid resembling thin golden syrup. It can be thinned with water as required, and it is a common practice to use the hot water from the outer pot; but it should be clean. This water requires changing daily, otherwise it gets very rusty.

When the glue is boiled a white scum appears on the top. This is the impurity from the glue and should be removed with the glue stick.

A Patent Glue-pot.—Fig. 4 shows a patent glue-pot. It is not used for heating the glue, but for containing the glue after heating and keeping at as constant a temperature as possible; A represents the outside jacket; B is a layer of fabric keeping in position a layer of horsehair C. Between the inner and outer linings D and E is a space F to contain water. The inner glue-pot J fits so that a small annular space H is left for water; G is the filling nozzle.

A satisfactory makeshift glue-pot is provided by using a jam-jar or tin can in a saucepan of water.

Fig. 5 shows a spirit (methylated) heater for glue, and Fig. 6 a gas heater.

For preparing glue quickly, it can be obtained ready ground into powder form, 1 lb. to 1 pint of water for use as glue; 1 lb. to 1 gal. of water for use as size.

Another method is to have the cake glue always soaking in water to be partly ready for transferring to the glue-pots.

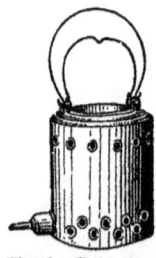

Fig. 6.—Gas-heated Glue-pot

Method of Gluing.—The quicker a joint can be properly glued and cramped up the better. The cramping tools should be set ready to hand, the glue quite hot and strong, but not stiff, inclining towards thinness than otherwise, and draughts of cold air avoided. The ends

GLUE AND GLUING

of the dowels may be slightly pointed and the holes slightly countersunk, the more quickly to go together, and if very tight-fitting, to avoid air compression it is advisable to take a shaving off the dowels, making a slight flat to allow the air to escape, unless the grooved dowels are used for the purpose. Inside the holes, the dowels, and meeting surfaces of the joint have to be glued, and should be made warm before applying glue of the right consistency for each particular purpose. Soft or open-grain woods absorb the glue more than those that are hard and close, so it can be used slightly stiffer. In making a rubbed joint of two boards edge to edge of very hard wood, the glue must be sufficiently thin and hot to scald the wood fibres up to unite together. Hardwood glue-blocks and braces do not hold so well unless they are toothed.

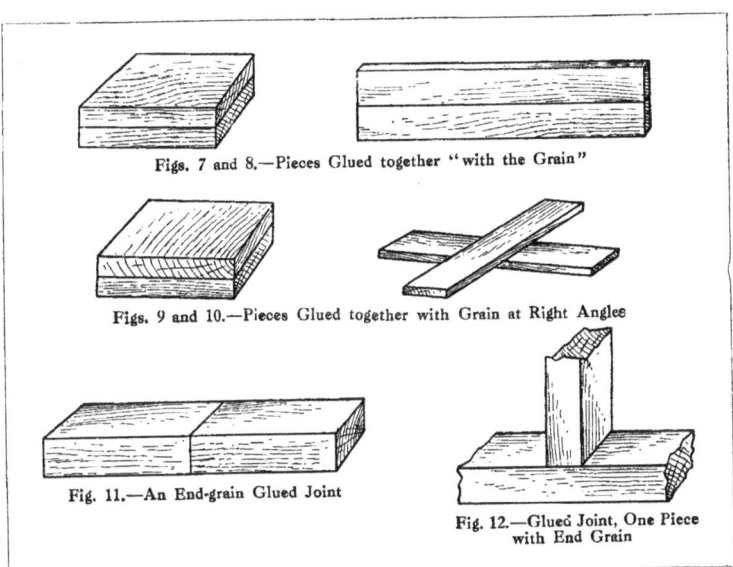

Figs. 7 and 8.—Pieces Glued together "with the Grain"

Figs. 9 and 10.—Pieces Glued together with Grain at Right Angles

Fig. 11.—An End-grain Glued Joint

Fig. 12.—Glued Joint, One Piece with End Grain

the glue amply and cramping up as close as possible. The fibres of the wood will be compressed into each other and united by the glue. The surplus squeezed out can be taken off and wiped clean with a rag wrung out of the hot water, though it is often left until set to be cut off with a sharp chisel. A glued joint should not be disturbed til' it is quite set.

In re-gluing a broken joint the old glue should be completely cleaned off.

Some judgment is necessary to have for veneered work it is worth the cost to have a good brush of a size that will spread the glue quickly and evenly over the surface without shedding a hair. The glue can be made thinner than required and strained through muslin, then boiled to the right consistency; but if the surface to be veneered is very absorbent, a sizing coat of the thin glue may be given.

Glued Joints.—Glue is a satisfactory means of union when pieces of wood have to be united with their grain as in Figs. 7

and 8, but not with it at right angles as in Figs. 9 and 10. It is not impossible to make a good glue joint with grain at right angles, but in ordinary work it is not done, the reason being that shrink-

Fig. 13.—Glued Dovetail Joint

age of either piece will break the joint. But apart from shrinkage, such a joint as in Fig. 10, depending on glue alone, could easily be pulled apart. On the other hand, joints as in Figs. 7 and 8 would, if properly made with good glue and kept dry, be as strong as a solid piece. End-grain joints, either when both pieces are end grain as in Fig. 11, or when one only is end grain as in Fig. 12, are never glued, except in a few instances where the glue can be regarded merely as an auxiliary not to be trusted. When glue is used on end grain the surface should be sized with a first coat of glue, which is allowed to soak in and dry before the final gluing is done, otherwise the glue is absorbed into the pores and fails to hold the joint.

Although pieces crossing as in Fig. 10 would never be glued, it is the common practice to glue such joints as Figs. 13 and 14, where the parts have their grain at right angles, but fit tightly in themselves, and can therefore be held together by glue securely enough for most purposes. Nevertheless, even in these cases, glue alone is not relied on if additional means can be employed without detriment to the appearance of the work. Glue is often used in addition to nails or screws, and in such cases clamping is unnecessary. Really good glue joints, however, are often spoilt if nails or screws are put in, because the perfect contact which has been made in squeezing out the glue is broken by driving nails or screws immediately after.

The method of exerting pressure to keep the parts tightly together while the glue is drying depends on the shape and size of the work. In some cases a convenient way is to put a weight on the top piece of wood; in others, clamps of some kind are better, and in others staples driven in, wedges arranged to act as clamps, or string bound round the parts may be suitable. Fig. 15 shows how a staple or dog is used. Its inner edges being tapered draw the parts together. It makes holes in the wood, which are objectionable sometimes, but frequently are not. A wooden handscrew is often used to hold the pieces together. It is adjusted with its jaws over the work, not quite parallel but wider apart at the extremity than at the back, and then tightening the back screw closes the points of the jaws by leverage. Metal clamps of various kinds and sizes are used also. When the surface of the work is large the clamps are often not put on it direct; but pieces of wood are interposed to equalise the pressure over a larger surface than the clamp jaws would cover.

A thin piece of wood wetted by glue on one face naturally warps; that is, the moisture makes it swell and become con-

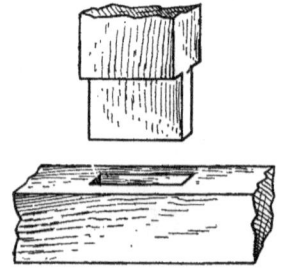

Fig. 14.—Mortise-and-tenon Joint, another Joint commonly Glued

vex on the wetted face and concave on the opposite one. If this is not prevented, the glue joint will open at the edges and remain so after the glue has set. If it is kept in close contact by pressure until

GLUE AND GLUING

the glue is dry enough to hold it, the joint will remain close. If it is not easy to apply the required pressure, the warping can sometimes be counteracted by wetting the outer face with water. If only a small thin piece has to be glued on, it is sometimes best to use a thicker piece than is wanted, and reduce it after the glue is dry. This is always advisable when the glued-on piece has to be pared or planed down thin at any of the edges, for a thin edge easily curls up when wetted on one side. Thick pieces of wood are not affected in this way. Fine wire nails driven part way in diagonally at intervals, to be subsequently pulled out, are sometimes used for keeping edges close while glue is drying.

Waterproof and Other Special Glues.—Besides the glues already mentioned, there are many varieties used for special purposes. Fish glue is obtainable in tubes and bottles, and is useful for small jobs. Seccotine is a strong, handy glue, and can be recommended for small work.

A good liquid glue can be made by breaking glue and soaking the pieces in acetic acid. Slightly heat the glue and add more acid until the required consistency is obtained.

Marine glue is useful for cementing different kinds of materials as leather, iron, glass, wood, etc. It is best bought ready made; it contains about 1 part of rubber and 20 of shellac, incorporated through the medium of 12 parts of coal-

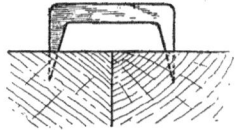

Fig. 15.—Use of Dog to hold Glued Work together

tar naphtha and evaporated to dryness. In using it should be warmed and applied sparingly.

Waterproof glue may be prepared by heating glue in the ordinary way and adding 1 part of bichromate of potash for every 2 parts of cake glue used; the glue thus prepared must be kept in the dark (say in a stone jar with a close-fitting lid) until required, because it becomes insoluble on exposure to light.

Procedure in making glued butt joints —work requiring some amount of craftsmanship for its successful accomplishment—is described in a later chapter.

Nailing, Screwing, and Bolting

THE parts of woodwork should, as far as possible, hold one another together. This is one of the chief secrets of the durability of old woodwork. The joints were fashioned so that they were interlocking, or so that they were held together by wooden pins. This method of making joints is expensive, and to-day nails, screws, bolts, glue and paint are used for fastening the parts of woodwork together. The suitability of each kind of fastening depends on the particular work.

Glue is used chiefly for internal work and furniture. Joinery, such as inside doors, cupboards, stairs, etc., are fastened together with glue and wedges. Windows and outside doors, which are subjected to damp, have the joints painted and wedged; the joints are also sometimes " pinned " with small pegs passing through the tenons.

Nails, generally speaking, are only used in inferior work or constructional carpentry. If used in good work the nails are kept out of sight.

Screws have a greater holding power than nails. They are therefore used where greater strength is desired, or where it may be required to pull the work to pieces at some future time. The chief method of fixing hinges and other ironwork is by means of screws. Bolts may be considered to be a special form of screw used where great security is desired. It is useful to remember that screws and bolts should be turned as the hands of a clock to tighten them up; the reverse to loosen.

Varieties of Nails.—There are many varieties of nails, as shown in Figs. 1 to 12. Probably the best nail for all-round purposes is the oval wire nail (Fig. 1). Because of being oval (really elliptical) in section it does not split the wood easily, and as its head is small it only leaves a small hole.

The oval nail does not hold as well as the round nail (Fig. 2), the head of the latter assisting to hold the wood as well as the friction on the shank. The head of the round nail is serrated or roughened to prevent the hammer slipping off the head when nailing. Oval nails may be obtained in the following sizes: $\frac{1}{2}$ in., $\frac{3}{4}$ in., 1 in., $1\frac{1}{4}$ in., $1\frac{1}{2}$ in., 2 in., $2\frac{1}{2}$ in., 3 in., 4 in., 5 in., and 6 in.

The shanks of both round and oval wire nails are roughened near the head so that they will hold better in the timber. Round nails are generally used for rough work. Wire nails, as the name implies, are cut from wire.

Floor brads, or cut nails (Fig. 5) are mostly used for nailing floor boards. The nails are made by simply punching them from a sheet of thin metal.

The wrought nail (Fig. 4) is very similar to the cut nail, but the shank tapers in both thickness and width, and the head is hammered to shape in manufacture. This nail is now little used.

The wire nails are of a bright colour, and the wrought or cut nails are dull.

The panel pin (Fig. 10) is a very handy type of nail, being really a very thin round wire nail with a small head. It

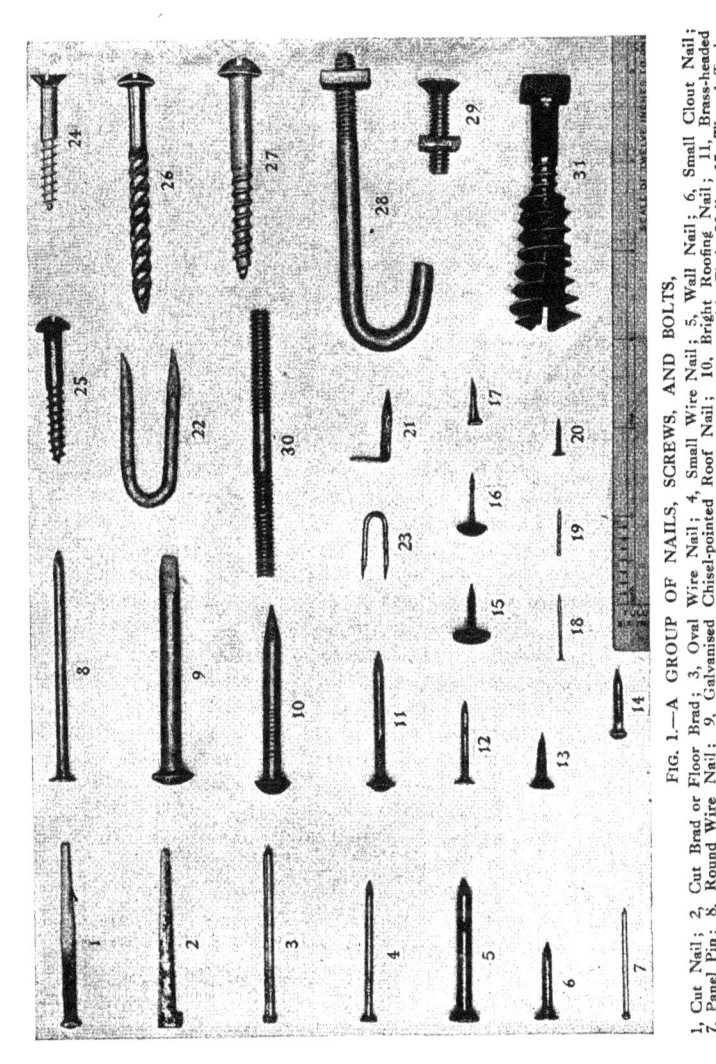

FIG. 1.—A GROUP OF NAILS, SCREWS, AND BOLTS.

1, Cut Nail; 2, Cut Brad or Floor Brad; 3, Oval Wire Nail; 4, Small Wire Nail; 5, Wall Nail; 6, Small Clout Nail; 7, Panel Pin; 8, Round Wire Nail; 9, Galvanised Chisel-pointed Roof Nail; 10, Bright Roofing Nail; 11, Brass-headed Nail; 12, Lath Nail; 13, Small Stout Tack; 14, Screw Nail; 15, Drugget Pin; 16, Chair Nail; 17, Tinned Tack; 18, "Cigar-box" Pin; 19, Small Pin; 20, Wire Gimp Pin; 21, Tenter Hook; 22, Fencing Staple; 23, Small Wire Staple; 24, Countersunk-head Wood Screw; 25, Round-head Wood Screw; 26, Bright Driving Screw-nail; 27, Galvanised Roofing Screw; 28, Galvanised Hook Bolt and Nut; 29, Small Bolt and Nut; 30, Double-ended Fixing Screw; 31, Expanding Wall-plug

is very useful for nailing beadings and other small work.

Needle points (Fig. 12) are simply needles

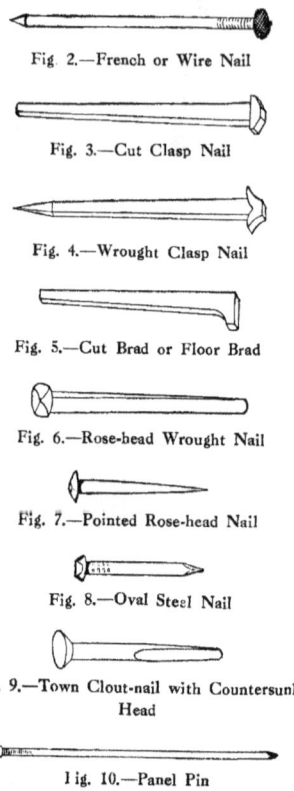

Fig. 2.—French or Wire Nail

Fig. 3.—Cut Clasp Nail

Fig. 4.—Wrought Clasp Nail

Fig. 5.—Cut Brad or Floor Brad

Fig. 6.—Rose-head Wrought Nail

Fig. 7.—Pointed Rose-head Nail

Fig. 8.—Oval Steel Nail

Fig. 9.—Town Clout-nail with Countersunk Head

Fig. 10.—Panel Pin

Fig. 11.—Veneer Pin

Fig. 12.—Needle Point

without the eye part. They are used for "nailing" very fine work. When a needle point has been driven as far as required into the wood a slight tap at the side breaks it off flush with the surface of the wood, and the needle point is practically invisible.

Clout nails are small round nails with large flat heads. This shape makes them very suitable for nailing roofing felt and similar materials.

Holding Power of Nails.—When a nail is driven into a piece of wood (Fig. 13) some of the fibres of the wood are broken and bent downwards, the ends of the fibres pressing against the sides of the nails; other fibres are pressed apart, and in the effort to maintain their normal course bind on the nail. These two forces hold the nail in the wood and prevent it being easily withdrawn. A nail does not hold as firmly when in the end grain of the wood.

If two pieces of timber are nailed together as in Fig. 14, the top piece is held to the nail by the friction on the sides of the nail plus the holding power of the head; the nail is only held in the lower piece by the friction on the sides. Nails should be used so that the holding power in each of the pieces of wood joined is about the same. The holding power of a nail is equal to the grip of the weakest side, just as the strength of a chain is the strength of the weakest link.

It follows that if a piece of wood $\frac{1}{2}$ in. thick has to be nailed to a thick piece of wood, then the length of the nail in the thick piece should be more than $\frac{1}{2}$ in. to make up for the holding power of the nail head on the other piece. If the nail is an oval wire nail having a small head, a suitable nail would be $1\frac{1}{4}$ in. long, but if the nail were of round wire with a large head, a $1\frac{1}{8}$-in. nail would be better. If the joint were as Fig. 15 with the nail going into the end grain, a suitable length for an oval nail would be $1\frac{1}{2}$ in., and for a round nail either $1\frac{1}{2}$ in. or 2 in.

If two pieces of equal thickness (as Fig. 16) have to be nailed together, it is obvious that, if nails that are just equal to the two thicknesses are used, the nails would pull out of the back piece fairly easily. Rather longer nails are

NAILING, SCREWING, AND BOLTING

therefore sometimes used and "clinched"—that is, bent over—on the back side. Clinching may be done by bending the nails down with the hammer after they have been driven, or by nailing the pieces together on an iron plate. The latter, where it can conveniently be adopted, gives a quicker and better job, and avoids splitting on the back side.

(pine, spruce, red deal, etc.) can be nailed without fear of splitting, but even with these woods if the nails are near the end of the piece (say in making a box) it is sometimes advisable to "bore for the nails" with a bradawl.

Hard wood can seldom be nailed without boring. It is better to bore in case of uncertainty, but the hole should be less

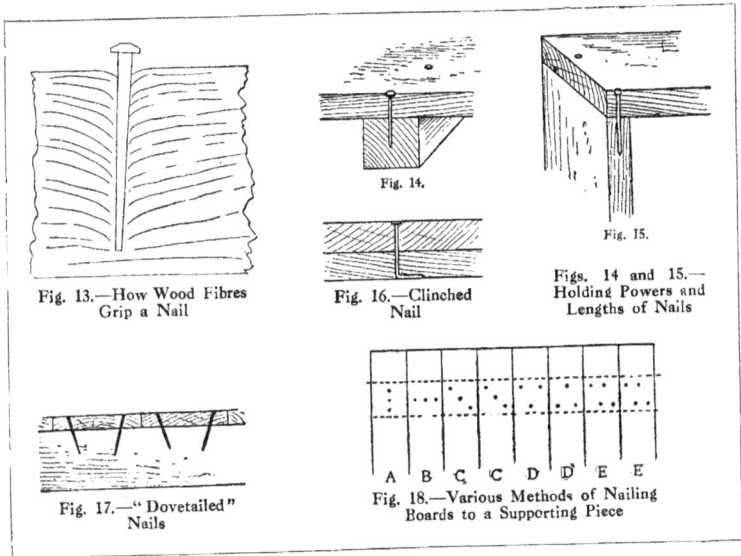

Fig. 13.—How Wood Fibres Grip a Nail

Fig. 14.

Fig. 15.

Figs. 14 and 15.—Holding Powers and Lengths of Nails

Fig. 16.—Clinched Nail

Fig. 17.—"Dovetailed" Nails

Fig. 18.—Various Methods of Nailing Boards to a Supporting Piece

Another method of making the nails hold better is to drive them on the slant as in Fig. 17. This is sometimes called "dovetailed nailing," and it is clear from the illustration that boards nailed in position in this manner cannot be as easily pulled apart as when the nails are driven parallel.

Preventing Splitting.—The chief difficulty that a beginner experiences in nailing is splitting the wood and thus spoiling the job. The trained craftsman knows from experience when the timber is likely to split.

Generally speaking, most soft woods

than the shank of the nail so as not to lessen appreciably its holding power. The thinner the nail and of course the less likelihood there is of splitting the wood.

In nailing boards or battens it is better to zig-zag the nails to avoid splitting and to give greater holding power. Fig. 18 shows various methods of nailing boards to a supporting piece; A is incorrect, as the nails would tend to split the board, and would not hold the boards to the bearer at the edges; B shows a rather better method, but this would tend to split the bearer; C and D show correct methods; E shows an excellent method, using four nails to a board.

Nailing.—The actual operation of nail-

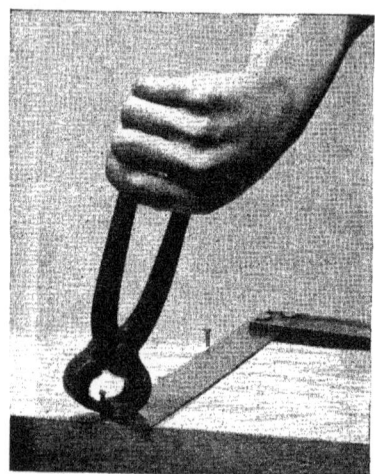

Fig. 19.—Using Blade of Square to obviate marking work when using Pincers

ing is very simple, and expertness depends upon practice. One or two hints may, however, be useful. A common fault of the beginner is that he holds the hammer too stiffly and too near the head. Grip the hammer as near the end of the shaft as convenient and let it fall freely, hitting the object with a sharp rap. The amateur usually seems to retard the fall of the hammer just as it is hitting the nail, etc.

When driving nails there should be something substantial beneath or behind the work to receive the impact of the blows and prevent vibration. Thus, in a case where a nail has to be driven horizontally, with nothing for the work to bear against, it is a great advantage to hold a block of metal or another hammer against the opposite side. It is not the pressure which this exerts, but its resistance. Without it, and with the work only steadied by the left hand, the nail would require at least twice as many blows, and even then the parts might not be held so tightly together, besides which the vibration at each blow might have injurious effects elsewhere. Nailing on the bench should be done over one of the bench legs. Nailing on the ground should be done on solid ground rather than on a boarded floor.

Hammer Marks after nailing are the chief sign of the amateur. The hammer-head is ground slightly round, and if it only lightly hits the wood surface no mark is made. Care should be taken in driving nails, as hammer marks are difficult to remove. If the "dent" is wetted and left overnight it will have risen somewhat by the morning, and may be glasspapered level.

There is a good method of nailing mouldings, etc., to avoid hammer marks, by using the blade of a square under the nail and gliding the hammer on the blade of the square.

A common cause of hammer marks is

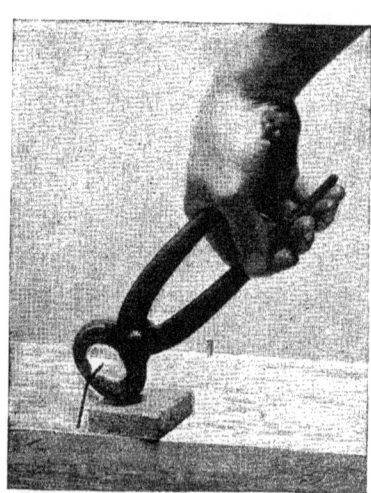

Fig. 20.—Using Scrap of Wood as a Prizing Piece

that the "face" of the hammer becomes greasy and thus readily slips off the nail and hits the wood. In this case the hammer should be cleaned by simply rubbing on the floor.

NAILING, SCREWING, AND BOLTING 147

Withdrawing Nails.—A nail has often to be withdrawn from timber, owing to the nail going crookedly into the wood,

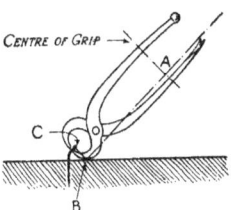

Fig. 21.—The Pincers as a Lever

or to bending due to the nail "catching" a knot or the wood being too hard. As soon as it is found that the nail is not "going" straight enough it should be pulled out, as the further it is driven in the more difficult it is to get out.

There are three tools used for withdrawing nails : the claw of a claw-hammer, a nail puller, or the pincers.

A pair of pincers is really a double lever. Firstly, by gripping the pincers tightly in the hands a good grip of the nail is obtained. If the nail has a large head this part of the operation is easy, but if the nail has no head it is difficult to keep a firm grip on the nail.

Secondly, keeping a firm grip on the pincers they are levered over with the

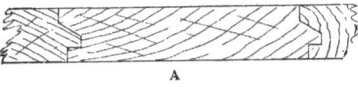

Fig. 22.—Round Nail-set or Nail-punch

Fig. 23.

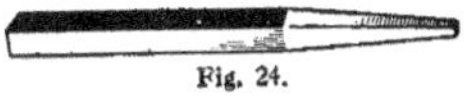

Fig. 24.

Figs. 23 and 24.—Square Nail-sets

jaw of the pincers pivoting on the surface of the wood. This operation is shown in the diagram (Fig. 21). The power of a pair of pincers depends on the proportion of length A B to the length B C. In the diagram A B is 6 in. and B C is 1 in. ; the power or mechanical advantage of the pincers is, therefore, 6 —that is, for every 1 lb. pressure put on the pincers there is a pull upwards on the nail of 6 lb. If, with the pincers of the proportions shown, it requires 50 lb. pressure to pull the nail out, then the nail has a holding power of 300 lb.

In pulling out a nail there is a danger of marking the wood with the pincers levering on the surface. This does not matter in rough work, but in good work it should be avoided by placing the blade of a try-square between the pincers and the wood surface as in Fig. 19. A bit

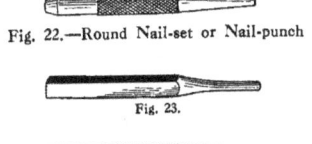

Fig. 25.—Secret Nailing applied to Floorboards

of wood is sometimes used instead of the blade of the try-square—also to give better purchase (*see* Fig. 20).

Punching.—In good work, nails are usually "punched" about ⅛ in. below the surface of the wood. In painted work the nail holes are then filled with putty, and "stoppings" of various kinds, as will be described later, are used in varnished and polished work.

Three varieties of nail punches are shown in Figs. 22 to 24. The punches vary a little in shape, some being square and others round. A convenient shape of punch end is made by filing small flat surfaces on a round punch ; this shape is useful, because it is very similar to the hole made by an oval nail.

Usually the punch has a flat end, but many are now made with a cup-shaped end so that the punch will not easily slip off the nail. It is usual for a woodworker to have two (sometimes three) sizes of punches to suit various sizes of nails.

Secret Nailing.—In good-class work it is desirable not to have the heads of the nails in the face of the work even if filled in with a good stopping. Moulding hould be nailed as much out of sight as possible. Floor boards are often secret-nailed through the tongue. Another method of secret nailing is to lift up a small splinter or shaving of wood with a narrow chisel, drive the nail, and then glue and press the shaving back into position. A special tool for lifting a shaving for this method of nailing is shown in Fig. 67 (page 99). Tongue-and-groove boarding is sometimes secret-nailed, a special form of this joint being shown at A and B (Fig. 25).

to hold a red-lead or other packing so as to make a watertight joint at the screwhole. Iron screws can be had blued, japanned, tinned, galvanised, and brassed or coppered finish; and screws made of brass or copper may be oxidised to match different colour bronzes, or nickelled, or silvered.

For use in hard wood, or in any situation where they may have to be withdrawn from time to time, countersunk screws are often provided with a cup or socket (Fig. 28A), which fits accurately under the head. This socket is ribbed on the outside that it may not turn in the wood; its office is to enable the screw to be extracted without trouble and without marking the wood surface.

The thickness of screws is measured by a gauge on which (unlike the wire gauge)

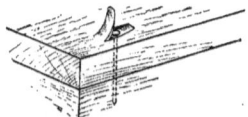

Fig. 26.—Secret Nailing

SCREWS AND SCREWING

Types and Sizes. — Wood screws are made of iron, brass, copper, and gun-metal, and are supplied with different shaped heads. The countersunk (Fig. 27) is the sort most often seen, and is used where a flush surface is required. The round head (Fig. 27A) is mainly used where the material is too thin to allow countersinking, but it is also employed for the sake of appearance, and the raised head (Fig. 27B) is a modified combination of both the former sorts. Other forms of head are made, such as cheese and ball shapes, but they are seldom required by woodworkers. In Figs. 27 to 27c, A denotes number and size, and B length.

A gutter or spout screw, shown in section in Fig. 28, is used for fixing ogee spouting to a facia board; it will be seen that there is an annular groove underneath the head; this is intended

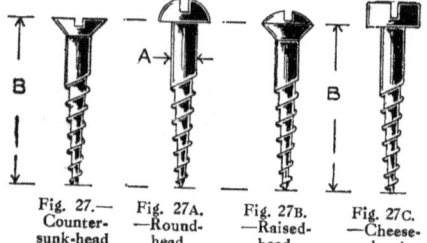

Fig. 27.—Counter-sunk-head Screw

Fig. 27A.—Round-head Screw

Fig. 27B.—Raised-head Screw

Fig. 27C.—Cheese-head Screw

the higher the number the larger is the diameter of the screw (see table in first column of page 15).

Japanned round-head screws are largely used for thumb latches, barrel bolts and rim locks; the most useful sizes are ¾ in. by 8, 9; 1 in. by 9, 10; 1¼ in. by 10; 1¾ in. by 11; and 2 in. by 12.

A useful range of sizes of brass screws with countersunk heads would be ½ in. by 4; ⅝ in. by 5, 6; ¾ in. by 6, 7, 8; 1 in. by 7, 8, 9; 1¼ in. by 8, 9, 10; 1½ in. by 10, 11; 2 in. by 11, 12.

Handrail screws (Fig. 29) are made with parallel and with swelled centres; they are used for jointing up sections of wood handrail. They have a square nut at one end and a round nut at the other, the

NAILING, SCREWING, AND BOLTING

latter nicked around its periphery so that it may be tightened up when in position by a small chisel ; the object of the swelled centre is to fill the hole in the wood rail tightly, and so prevent

Fig. 28.—Gutter or Spout Screw

Fig. 28A.—Screwhead Cup or Socket

any slackness at the junction. Dowel screws (Fig. 30) are, as the name implies, used for dowelling up two pieces of wood ; they are used amongst other purposes for fixing ornamental ends on curtain poles.

Corrugated fasteners (Fig. 31) are pieces of steel having a chisel edge on one side and are corrugated in section ; the corrugations are not parallel, but inclined towards each other at the top so that when they are driven across the joint between two pieces of wood they have a tendency to bring the two edges closer together.

Screws made by different British firms are sufficiently alike in gauge for the accompanying table—which has been calculated from data supplied by the leading makers—to be relied on :—

Number or size of screw	1	2	3	4	5
Diam. of shank in parts of an in.	.066	.080	.094	.108	.122
6	7	8	9	10	11	12	13
.136	.150	.164	.178	.192	.206	.220	.234
14	15	16	17	18	19	20	21
.248	.262	.276	.290	.304	.318	.332	.346
22	23	24	25	26	27	28	29
.360	.374	.388	.402	.416	.430	.444	.458
30	31	32
.472	.486	.500

The range from one size to the next is .014 in., and in the absence of a table the following easily-remembered formula will enable the diameter of any desired size to be ascertained : Diameter = (.014 × No.) + .052 in. For example, (.014 × 16) + .052 = .224 + .052 = .276 in. = diameter of No. 16 screw, and (.014 × 32) + .052 = .448 + .052 = .5-in. diameter of No. 32.

The diameter of the head is twice that of the neck or shank.

Numerous lengths are obtainable in each size from ¼ in. upwards in the smaller sizes up to 9 in. in No. 32. Larger sizes can be obtained to order, but are not stocked or gauged.

The length of a wood screw is the distance from the point to the portion normally flush with the surface of the material into which it is driven. Dowel screws are measured from point to point.

Boring for Screws.—Screws are used in cases where work may have to be taken

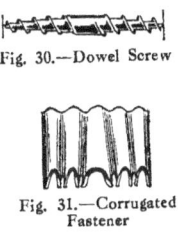

Fig. 30.—Dowel Screw

Fig. 31.—Corrugated Fastener

Fig. 29.—Handrail Screw

apart again and where a very secure hold is necessary accompanied also with the means of gradual tightening. In some cases the avoidance of the shock of nailing is an advantage. In the attachment of metal to wood, nails are usually quite unsuitable, as the tightness of their hold cannot be adjusted or relied on.

Holes are almost invariably bored for screws. This is because it is undesirable to have the smooth parallel part of the screw a very tight fit in the wood, as it may prevent the joint from closing perfectly. Fig. 32 shows two pieces of wood screwed together, the screw shank fitting loosely into the top piece. A hole for a screw is bored completely venient, but is much slower and rather more liable to split the wood. The holes are bored completely through the first piece of wood before it is adjusted on the

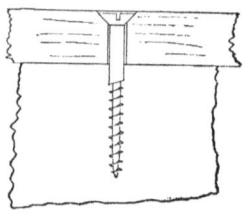

Fig. 32.—Diagram Showing Cramping Action of Screw Properly Inserted

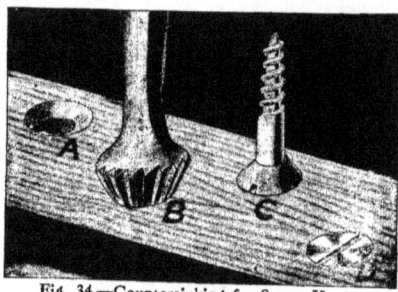

Fig. 34.—Countersinking for Screw Heads

through the first piece of wood, and may or may not be continued into the second piece, depending on the size of the screw. The screw thread cuts its own way, and the hole it enters must be smaller in diameter, and may be shorter than the distance to which the screw will penetrate. The hole must be bored relatively larger in hard wood than in soft. Fig. 33 shows at A a screw inserted in the ordinary way, and at B a deeply countersunk screw, C and D show respectively the way the holes are bored for these, though in the first instance screws are often put in without making the shallow countersink shown at C, the screw simply being tightened until it has forced its way flush.

A shell bit (illustrated later), fixed in a brace, is generally used for boring screw holes. Sometimes a gimlet is more con-

second, and any projecting splinters or burr on the joint surface are removed with a chisel before the joint is closed. Then the smaller holes in the second piece are made with a bradawl or gimlet or bit passing through the upper and larger holes. If the wood is soft and the screws small, no holes are bored in the second, but the screws are started and steadied by a tap with a hammer, and are run in with a screwdriver or screwdriver-bit in a brace, the latter being preferable when a large number of screws are being inserted. The small handdrill on a later page is very convenient for boring screw holes. Screws are sometimes greased before insertion to prevent rusting and to make them turn easier.

Countersinking.—The reason for countersinking is generally to get the heads well below the surface; but if a hole is

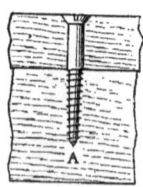 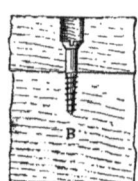 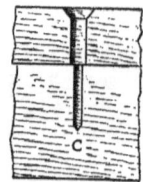 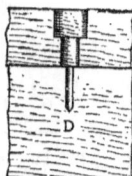

Fig. 33.—Boring for Various Screws

NAILING, SCREWING, AND BOLTING

not countersunk, the screw head in forcing its way level will twist and break the fibres of the wood more or less around the head, and, except in rough work, the appearance of this is objectionable.

Countersinking is done with the brace and bit as shown by Fig. 35, or with a gouge or chisel, as in Figs. 36 and 37. The countersinking is effected by beginning with the chisel at one side of the hole and twisting it so that it scoops out the countersink. The bit-and-brace method is neater and quicker. Fig. 34 inserted in a screw hole. The plug is driven in as far as possible and then cleaned off level with the surface.

In screwing parts together a side pull as well as a direct squeezing together of

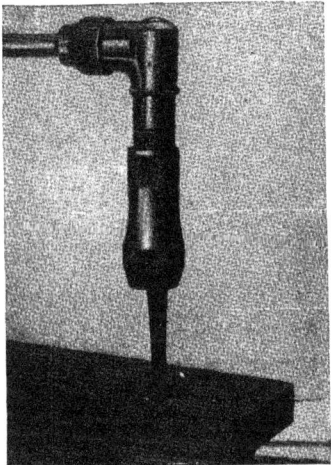

Fig. 35.—Countersinking with Brace and Bit

A shows a hole countersunk with a brace bit; B shows the bit; C shows the screw, and D shows the screw in position. A deep countersink as at B and D (Fig. 33) is made with a centre-bit before the hole for the body of the screw is bored. The reason for a deep countersink may be to avoid using extremely long screws, but frequently it is to allow the holes to be plugged with wood after the screws are in, the grain of the plugs usually running the same way as that of the plugged surface. Fig. 38 shows a wood plug being

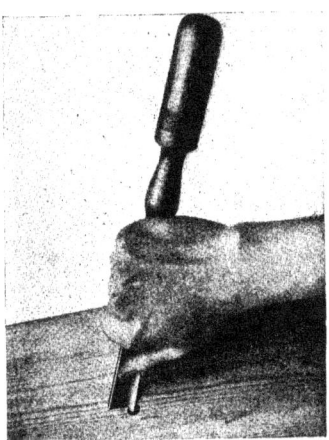

Fig. 36.

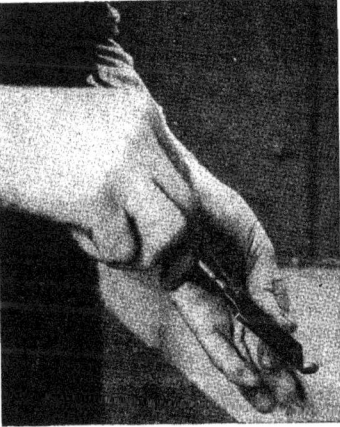

Fig. 37.

Figs. 36 and 37.—Countersinking with Gouge and Chisel respectively

the joint can be exercised when desirable. This is done by boring the small hole in the second or under piece of wood out of centre in relation to the upper hole, as in Fig. 39. The screw then tends to

Fig. 38.—Wood Plug for Screw Hole

pull the holes concentric, and strains the parts in the direction desired. The reason for doing this is to pull a shoulder, as in Fig. 39, into the closest possible contact. With the holes concentric it might be slack or slightly open.

Spacing of Screws.—The positions and distances apart of screws require some judgment to decide. The rule, both with screws and nails, is that they should be much farther apart when arranged in a line with the grain than in a line across the grain, as illustrated at E (Fig. 40). This is because a row of screws very close together in the line of the grain might split the work, and because the wood being so much weaker across the grain than lengthwise needs to be attached at a greater number of points.

Points of attachment are more neces-

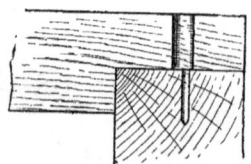

Fig. 39.—Method of Pulling Shoulder into Close Contact by Eccentric Boring

sary near edges than in the middle parts of large areas. F, G, H, and J (Fig. 40) show various arrangements of screw holes in strips or battens which have to be screwed to a surface. F is so narrow that the holes must be central. G has the holes arranged diagonally, the idea being that when screwed to a surface with the grain at right angles the screws would be about equally spaced across the grain in the latter surface, and so would hold it better, and no two screws would come in line in that grain. This has the disadvantage of an irregular appearance in the narrow piece, and also that two of its corners are not held uniformly with the other two ; but sometimes the screws at the corners are made uniform, and the diagonal arrangement limited to the

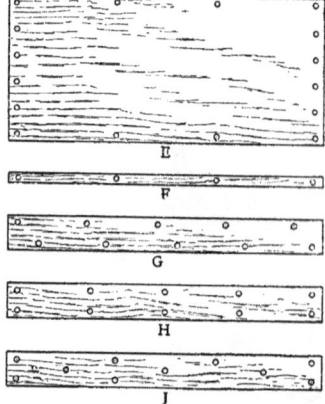

Fig. 40.—Screwing on Strips, Battens, etc.

intermediate ones, this also having an unsymmetrical appearance.

In a moderately wide strip the arrangement at H would generally be preferred, and in a still wider strip the arrangement at J is a good one. Fig. 41 shows arrangements of screws in members crossing each other. These would be equally applicable for nails, bolts, and screws. Where a single point of union is sufficient it would be central as at A. The next stage is to use two at opposite corners as at B. After this, four as at C or five as at D would follow, depending on the size of the work and the strength required. In the arrangement at E one member is

NAILING, SCREWING, AND BOLTING

wider than the other, and the points of attachment are modified to suit. At F the members are not at right angles, and therefore with two points of union the parts together securely, as to prevent side movement while the screws are being inserted. Slight adjustments can, if necessary, be made with a hammer before all

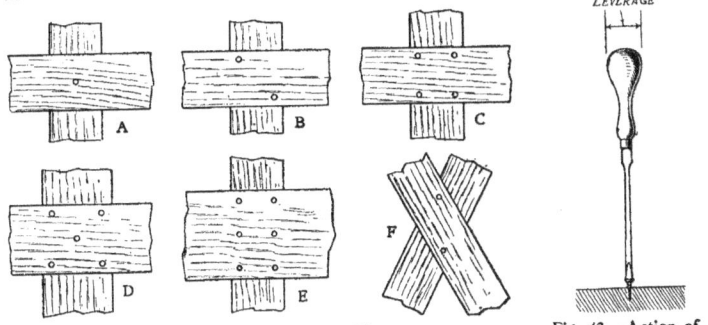

Fig. 41.—Screwing on Cross Pieces

Fig. 42.—Action of Screwdriver

screws would be inserted at the corners farthest apart.

When a number of screw holes have to be bored their positions are usually marked with pencil first as some guide to symmetrical spacing. Occasionally the distances apart are equalised by measurement, but generally the workman trusts to his eye. Sometimes screws have to be inserted behind or beneath, while the pieces in front are held or temporarily secured in place by other means. These other means may be clamps or fine nails or bradawls, the two latter being put in diagonally at the edges of the piece, and pulled out after it has been screwed. They are used not so much to hold the

the screws are in and before the final tightening of any of them.

The Action of a Screwdriver.—A screwdriver may be described as a lever for turning screws. When the thread of the screw has got a hold in the fibres of the timber the turning of the screw causes it to worm its way into the wood, this action being largely helped by the gimlet point of the screw.

Fig. 42 shows a screwdriver; the theoretical power of the lever action will be proportional to the breadth of the handle—the broader the handle, the more powerful the screwdriver. In practice, however, the difficult part of screwing is not turning the screwdriver, but

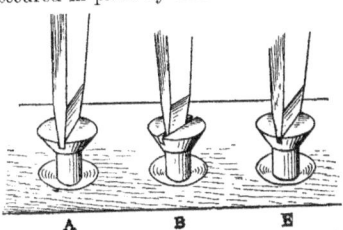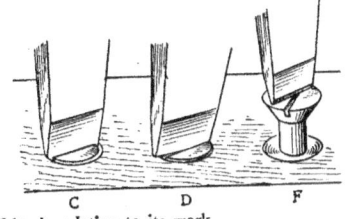

Fig. 43.—Width of Screwdriver Edge in relation to its work

THE PRACTICAL WOODWORKER

holding the end of the screwdriver in the slot of the screw. When a screw has been driven the slot should be as perfect as before use. A badly damaged slot in a

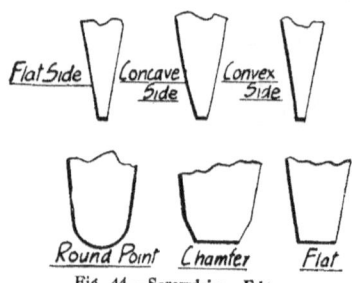

Fig. 44.—Screwdriver Edges

screw is the " hall-mark " of the amateur. Too great stress cannot be laid on this point. Once let the screwdriver slip off the head and the screw is more difficult to drive and more difficult to pull out, besides being evidence of inexpert workmanship.

To prevent the screwdriver slipping off the head of the screw it is necessary to hold the screwdriver tightly against the screw, paying more attention to this point than to turning the screwdriver. The edge of the screwdriver should fit the screw, as at A (Fig. 43). The edge should not be too narrow (as B) or too wide (as C). In the latter case the edges of the screwdriver tear up the edges of the timber unless the screwdriver is canted as D. The edge should not be filed as E, or it will be liable to jump out of the slot as in F.

In order to obtain as much leverage as possible with the screwdriver, there must be, as already explained, as much contact as possible within the slot in the screw head. It is thought that very few workers grind their screwdrivers correctly. The correctly-ground screwdriver has flat sides and a flat point, as shown in Fig. 44. The others shown are incorrect. More often than not it is the fault of the screwdriver that a screw cannot be extracted. When the point of a screwdriver is round or chamfered, or if the sides are convex or concave, the torsion or twist of the hand merely tends to lift the end from the slot.

Fig. 44A shows how to hold the screwdriver on the emery-wheel or grindstone.

Generally speaking, a long screwdriver is better than a short one. The reason for this is somewhat obscure, as, theoretically, the nearer the pressure is to the screw, the easier should the screw revolve. It is contended, however, that it is impossible to hold a screwdriver perfectly upright, and the slightest inclination is bound to have a lever effect on the screw. Hence it is quite clear that the longer the lever is, the easier will the screw move.

Types of Screwdrivers.—The ordinary types of screwdriver is shown in Fig. 45. Some screwdrivers have round spindles with the end only ground flat; there are various shapes of handles.

The chief difficulty about using a screwdriver (with one hand) is to keep a pressure maintained on the screw and yet to glide the hand round the handle to turn it round. This difficulty is obviated in the case of the ratchet screwdriver (Fig. 46), a light grip on the handle being maintained and the handle turned backwards and forwards, the ratchet letting

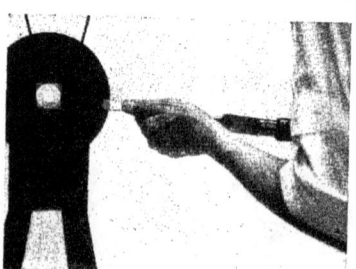

Fig. 44A.—Grinding a Screwdriver

the handle slip round on the backward turns.

The spiral screwdriver is shown in Fig. 47. Pressure on the top causes the spindle and screw to revolve. To drive screws by this method it is only necessary to press the screwdriver on the screw.

NAILING, SCREWING, AND BOLTING

This is obviously a quick and easy method and very useful where a lot of small screws have to be driven. It is not very suitable for a large screw, as the point tends to fly out of the slot of the screw.

The brace and screwdriver bit is a quick method, and is particularly suitable when large screws are being used. With this method a great leverage can be easily exerted and the difficulty is to keep the bit in the screw slot. Where possible,

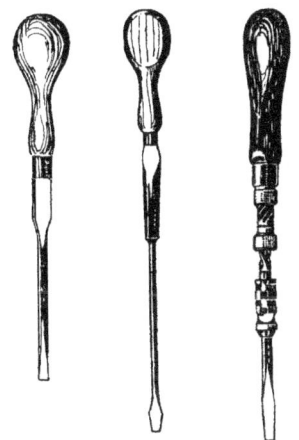

Fig. 45.—Two Screwdrivers   Fig. 47.—Spiral or Automatic Screwdriver

Fig. 46.—Ratchet Screwdriver

put the weight of the body on the brace. It will be found better to use the ratchet (on the brace) and only sweep the brace handle backwards and forwards through a quarter of a turn. If the brace is used horizontally, press the handle up and down through a quarter turn. More power can be exerted on the screw in this manner.

A woodworker usually possesses two or three screwdrivers of various sizes to suit different sizes of screws.

Withdrawing Screws.—A screw is usually more difficult to withdraw than to drive owing to the wood fibres having "set" round it, or the screw having rusted, or to the screw slot being filled with paint, varnish, etc. The usual way of "starting" a difficult screw is to place the screwdriver in position and then rap it smartly with the hammer. This will loosen the rust on the fibres and drive the screwdriver well into the screw slot. Try to avoid the screwdriver slipping, because once it slips out of the slot it will slip out easier the next time.

If the above method fails put a few drops of paraffin on the screw, which will tend to loosen the rust. A redhot poker pressed against the head of the screw will often cause the wood fibres to shrink a little and loosen the screw.

Fig. 48.—Coach Screw

Screws are often damaged whilst being inserted, a frequent happening being that one side of the screw head comes off. The screw should at once be turned back either with the screwdriver or pincers. If a screw happens to break off close to the surface of the wood so that the pincers cannot get a grip, it might be necessary to punch the screw right into the wood with a nail punch and then "peg" the hole up. The damaged screw could perhaps be removed by boring round it with a shell bit, the bit being a little larger than the shank of the screw.

Coach Screws.—A coach screw (Fig. 48) is like an ordinary screw but with a square head that can be turned with a wrench. They are generally of a larger size than ordinary screws, and are mostly used for rough or temporary work.

BOLTS AND BOLTING

Bolts are made with various shapes of heads and nuts, the commonest type having a cup head (round or snap head) and a square nut, as in Fig. 49 Other types are shown in Fig. 50 to Fig. 56. The cheese-head has little projection and does not interfere with other parts of the work. The countersunk head is used vent it from " eating " into the wood. A washer under the head is also sometimes used, but this is not essential. Holes for bolts up to ⅜ in. diameter may be bored

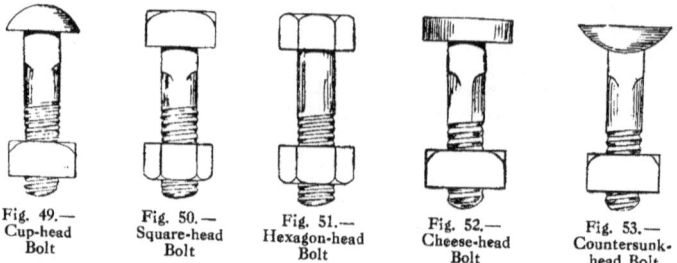

Fig. 49.—Cup-head Bolt
Fig. 50.—Square-head Bolt
Fig. 51.—Hexagon-head Bolt
Fig. 52.—Cheese-head Bolt
Fig. 53.—Countersunk-head Bolt

where the bolt head has to finish flush with the surface.

Bolts are made in many lengths and thicknesses, ranging from 1 in. to 12 in. long. Bolts for woodwork are usually made with a square shank just under the head; this prevents the bolt turning when the nut is being tightened up.

Holes for bolts should be bored so that

with a shell bit; over that diameter it is better to use a twist bit.

It will be noticed that the nut has its edges slightly rounded on one side. Where the nuts are not seen it is better to use the rounded edges near the work as this gives an easier turning movement. Where the nuts are seen the rounded corners may be placed outermost to give

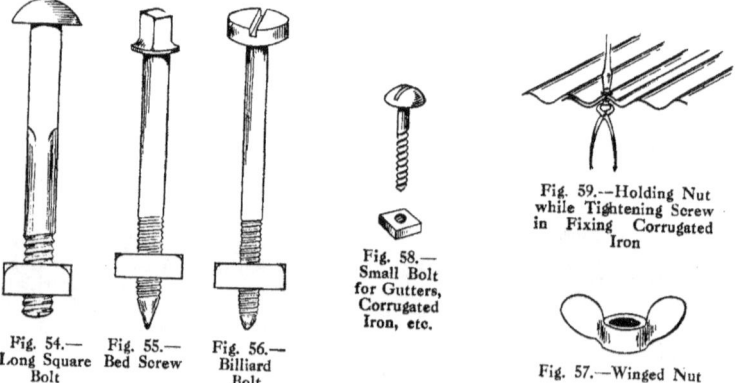

Fig. 54.—Long Square Bolt
Fig. 55.—Bed Screw
Fig. 56.—Billiard Bolt
Fig. 58.—Small Bolt for Gutters, Corrugated Iron, etc.
Fig. 59.—Holding Nut while Tightening Screw in Fixing Corrugated Iron
Fig. 57.—Winged Nut

the bolt will go in easily; the gripping power of a bolt is obtained by the pull between the head and the nut. Washers are generally used under the nut to prevent a better appearance, and to be more convenient for passing traffic, etc.

Office desks, etc., that have to be constructed in such a manner that they may

NAILING, SCREWING, AND BOLTING

be taken apart for removal, are sometimes fixed together by bed-screws (Fig. 55) or billiard bolts (Fig. 56). The heads are sunk in the woodwork, and are usually covered by turned wood bosses fitting tightly into the circular hole which accommodates the head of the bolt. The former are screwed up by an old-fashioned bed-key, the latter by a strong turnscrew. The winged nut (Fig. 57) is used in connection with ordinary bolts for more temporary work, which has to be constantly taken to pieces and re-erected, such as market stalls, adjustable fittings, and furniture of various kinds; they are easily tightened or released by the fingers without the help of tools.

Bolts and nuts are measured in the hardware trade as from under head to point, but if it is remembered that the thickness of the nut equals the diameter of the bolt it is easy to conform to the manufacturer's system of measurement; thus a bolt required to pass through 9 in. of material, if desired to be of $\frac{1}{2}$ in. diameter, must be $9\frac{1}{2}$ in. long, if of 1 in. diameter must be 10 in. long, although, of course, when bolts are particularly ordered 9 in. *between head and nut*, the correct size would be supplied, but the order would need to be exactly worded.

Small bolts, as in Fig. 58, are used for fastening gutters, corrugated iron, etc., and Fig. 59 shows how the nut is held while the screw is driven tight.

Chamfering, Bevelling and Rounding

A CHAMFER means the removal or breaking of an angle, as in Fig. 1, by planing a narrow flat at, say, an angle of 45 deg. with the main surfaces. It is done to improve the appearance of the work, or occasionally to diminish risk of damage to sharp corners of wood. A chamfer is the simplest and quickest way of doing this. In rough work neither exact angle nor width of chamfer is taken account of, the workman judging by his eye alone.

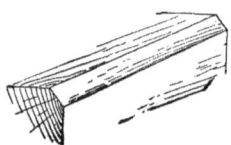

Fig. 1.—Chamfer

The work is done with a jack or smoothing or small iron plane, or with a chamfer plane.

A chamfer may run entirely round an outer edge, as in Fig. 2, but it is more frequently used on the inner edges of panelled framework, as in Fig. 3, and in the latter case the chamfers are almost invariably stopped, as shown, a short distance before they reach the corners.

The four common forms of "stop" are shown at A, B, C and D in Fig. 4, A being a curve dying into the straight, and B a flat angular stop. The stop at C is a variation of B, a small face being left at right angles to the chamfer; D is an ornamental stop consisting of a small semi-circular projection left on the chamfer adjoining, or a little distance away

Fig. 2.—Chamfered Surface

from, the stop. A chisel is used to produce the stops, and is used flat on the surface, as in Fig. 5, for the flat stop, and the reverse way, as in Fig. 6, for the curved stop. A special template, somewhat similar to a mitre template, is sometimes used for cutting stops.

Chamfer planes (a metal chamfer plane is shown in Fig. 7) are useful when a great deal of chamfering is being continu-

Fig. 3.—Chamfered Framing

ally done, but for occasional work they can very well be dispensed with. Their principle is that of a sole, Fig. 7A, which

CHAMFERING, BEVELLING AND ROUNDING

fits over the right angle of the work to be chamfered, and a cutter adjustable for depth, so fixing the width and angle of the chamfer automatically. Adjustments for different widths of chamfer are made either by raising or lowering the cutter or by moving the sides of the plane in relation to each other, according to the type of plane. Some are made in spokeshave form. These can be used for curved chamfers.

Another advantage possessed by chamfer planes is that they will cut right up to the end of a stop chamfer. An ordinary plane with a front extending some distance beyond its cutter could not do this, but could either only be used on non-stopped chamfers, like those in Figs. 1 and 2, or would only work as far as the cutter would go towards the stop, the rest being finished with a chisel or spokeshave or a bullnose plane. The latter is shown in use on a chamfer in Fig. 8.

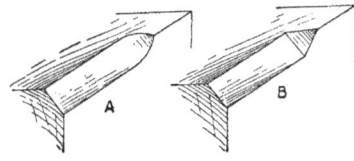

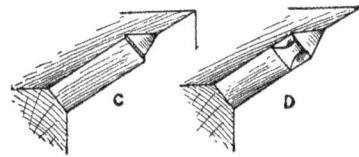

Fig. 4.—Various Forms of Stops for Chamfers

Fig. 7.—Chamfer Plane

It is an open-sided metal plane from about 3½ in. to 7½ in. long, with a cutter about 1¼ in. wide. It is, of course, used for much other work besides planing chamfers. Its front extends only ¼ in. or ⅜ in. beyond the cutting edge, and this enables it to plane within that distance of a stop or shoulder on the work in front of the plane. Another type of plane, useful for stop-chamfering because it can be worked right up to the stop, is shown in Fig. 55, page 97.

When a chamfer plane is not used and a reasonable degree of accuracy is desired it is necessary to mark lines to plane to. In other circumstances a gauge would be the proper tool to mark them with, but lines cut into the surface at each edge of the chamfer could not be properly removed and would show more or less after the work was finished. Therefore pencil lines are preferred, which even if

Fig. 5.—Cutting Flat Stop

Fig. 7A.—End View of Chamfer Plane

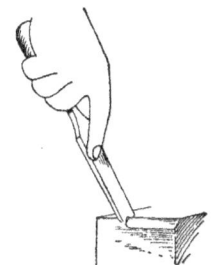

Fig. 6.—Cutting Curved Stop

not planed out can be obliterated in glasspapering.

If the chamfer is at the angle of 45 deg. these lines would be at an equal distance

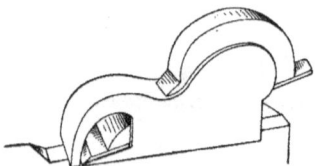

Fig. 8.—Using Bullnose Plane

from the edge of the wood, the distance depending on the width of chamfer desired. If not at 45 deg. one would be at a greater distance than the other. A pencil line may be gauged by notching a piece of wood to the required distance and drawing it along the work with a pencil held against it, as in Fig. 9 ; or the pencil can be held and drawn along with only the finger to keep it at uniform distance (Fig. 10). Lines could, of course, be measured and ruled if preferred.

As chamfers in ordinary work seldom

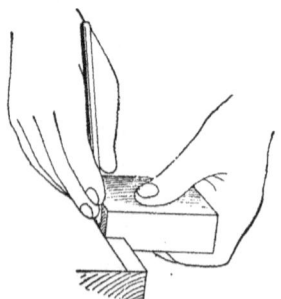

Fig. 9.—Drawing Lines for Chamfering, using Chamfering Gauge

exceed ½ in. in width a drawknife is not often employed, but the first rough cut is made with a chisel when a plane is considered too slow. More or less chisel work is always necessary in finishing the ends of stop chamfers. On end grain most, or even all, the material may be removed with a chisel, as in Fig. 11, though in most cases a plane would be used for finishing. The majority of chamfers run with the grain, the chief exceptions being the ends of a block of wood, as in Fig. 2.

Instead of a plain flat angle, chamfers are sometimes made more ornamental by beading or moulding them, as in Fig. 12. This has to be done with special planes or attachments to chamfer planes.

Occasionally curved work, either concave or convex, is chamfered, and then, of course, the chamfers follow the curve.

Fig. 10.—Drawing Lines for Chamfering, using Finger as a Guide

A flat plane cannot be used in such cases, but a spokeshave is the usual tool to employ, as in Fig. 13. It must be used in a direction which will not tear up the grain.

Bevelling.—Bevelling means the planing or chiselling of surfaces which are not at right angles with each other. A chamfer, of course, is an instance, but it is not called a bevel, because it is merely an ornamental detail. A bevelled surface is usually of equal importance with other main surfaces of the work and is not adopted for ornament. It may be necessary in forming a joint, or the shape of

CHAMFERING, BEVELLING AND ROUNDING

the work may require it. It may be at the angle of 45 deg., which is sometimes distinguished by being called a mitre full size in front view and end view on a sheet of paper or a board, and the bevel can be set to the angles thus obtained and

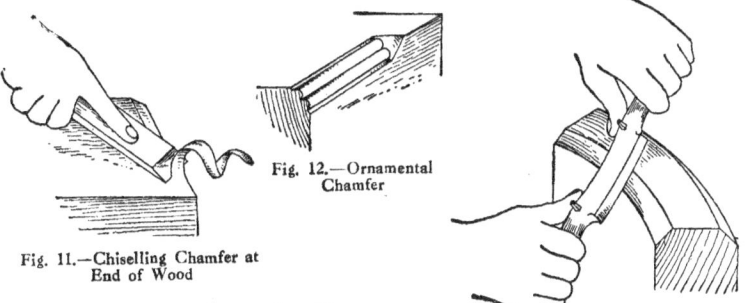

Fig. 12.—Ornamental Chamfer

Fig. 11.—Chiselling Chamfer at End of Wood

or it may be at any other angle. Lines may be marked for working to, or an instrument called a bevel is set to the required angle and used for testing as the work proceeds. Fig. 14 shows such a test being made on an edge which is bevelled in relation to the faces of the work. It is generally easier and more accurate to use a bevel in such a case than to mark lines for planing to. Fig. 15 is an instance where the lines would be marked on the work even if a bevel was used for testing the angles afterwards. It represents octagonal blocks marked out ready for cutting. The bevel is used both for marking lines with and for testing.

Fig. 16 shows a more complex system of bevels; in fact, the right angles which are the general rule in woodwork are entirely absent. The angles in this case cannot be obtained from a protractor, as they are in most work. Generally in ordinary work a certain angle, perhaps 45 deg., is wanted and the bevel can be set to it on a protractor or on a set square of that angle, or it can be easily obtained by direct marking out. In a case like Fig. 16 the angles themselves are usually not specified, but only the dimensions of the article are known. The splayed tray or box must be a certain size at the top and a certain size at the bottom and a certain depth. This must be marked out

Fig. 13.—Using Spokeshave to Curved Chamfer

used in preparing the pieces of wood, measurement and bevel tests being equally important in the process. (The bevels to which the joints have to be sawn cannot be obtained directly from the front or end views, but must be obtained geometrically, as will be described later.)

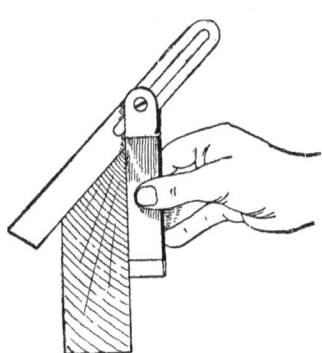

Fig. 14.—Testing Edge with Bevel

Mitreing, or fitting parts at the angle of 45 deg., occurs so frequently that there are a number of tools and appliances specially designed for that angle, as will be explained in a later chapter.

Rounding.—Angles may be rounded instead of chamfered. Rounding also

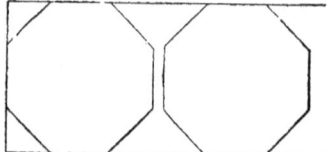

Fig. 15.—Marking Octagonal Blocks

includes larger curvatures and may be done for other reasons than improved appearance. Rounding is usually done with flat cutters, such as ordinary planes, chisels or spokeshaves. There is a class of planes made for the purpose, usually kept in pairs and termed "hollows" and "rounds" (*see* Fig. 42, page 95). With them, rounding is done with a concave cutter and sole of a certain radius. It can be used also on quicker radii than its own but not on flatter curves, just as a gouge or round soled plane is useful on any curve of larger radii than its own.

An ordinary flat plane can be used on any convex curve which is straight in the direction of planing. If the latter direction is curved a spokeshave is used. Rounded surfaces, unless they are turned in a lathe, require more glasspapering than flat ones, because the cutting tools used, are usually flat instead of fitting the curve, and the latter becomes really a

Fig. 16.—Splayed Box

series of narrow flats, the ridges of which must be removed by glasspapering.

There is some variety in the forms of

rounded angles. A corner with square edges may be cut to a radius, as in Fig. 16A. An end may have one of its angles rounded,

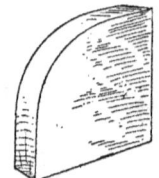

Fig. 16A.—Rounded Edge

as in Fig. 17, leaving the others square, or the rounding may be continued as in Figs. 18 and 19. An edge may be semi-circular, as at A, Fig. 20, or have small radii at the edges with flat between, as at B. Pieces of this cross-section may be curved lengthwise in addition to the transverse curve. The corner of a table, for instance, may be a quarter circle in plan and a semicircle the other way, and the quarter circle may be of any radius within reason, from a corner which might almost be glasspapered or rasped off, to a considerable sweep which would necessitate the use of a saw.

Except for very small radii dividers or compasses are used to strike the curves for the cutting tools to work to. Where this cannot be done, or sometimes in addition to this, a template is made for testing the accuracy of the radius as the work proceeds. The template is either a quarter circle or half circle, as in Fig. 21, and may be of thin wood or card.

Fig. 17.—Rounded Corner

A rounding along the edge of a piece of wood with the grain is easily planed. If of large radius it may first be roughed

CHAMFERING, BEVELLING AND ROUNDING

with a drawknife or chisel, or even with a hatchet. When the curve is large and end grain is involved, as in Fig. 16A, a saw is used in the first place. A keyhole removed with a spokeshave followed by glasspaper on a flat rubber, or glasspaper only may be used. Both spokeshave and glasspaper should be worked only in the

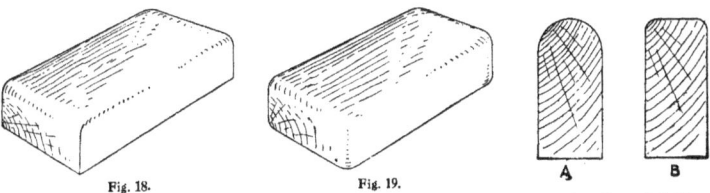

Figs. 18 and 19.—Rounded Corners   Fig. 20.—Rounded Edges

saw or bow saw may be run round the curve just clear of the line, but more frequently a single straight cut is made, as indicated in Fig. 22, with a tenon saw. If the radius is very large other cuts may be made after, as dotted in Fig. 22. This is quicker than cutting it all with a chisel.

A curve which includes end grain is direction in which the grain cannot be torn up. Concave rubbers are seldom used in glasspapering rounded surfaces, but when surfaces are concave a round rubber is generally essential. The important thing in rounding is to produce a neat and uniform curve with no trace of tool marks. A curve which does not die properly into a straight looks bad but is often seen, not only in the work of amateurs but of those professional carpenters and joiners who are accustomed chiefly to a rough class of work.

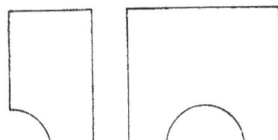

Fig. 21.—Templates

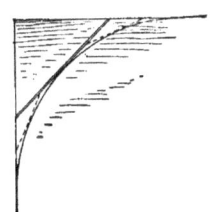

Fig. 22.—Cutting Large Rounded Corner

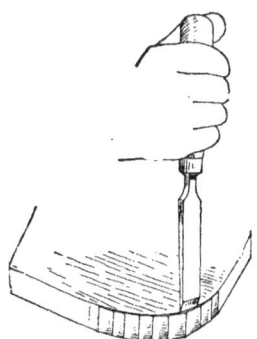

Fig. 23.—Chiselling Corner

chiselled in the position shown in Fig. 23; this leaves a number of more or less perceptible flats (Fig. 23). These may be Occasionally a comparatively large outside radius is wanted where there is only a limited thickness of material, and this may necessitate some building up. Thus a corner may be treated, as in Fig. 24, when the interior is concealed. If an inner as well as an outer curve is required the method in Fig. 25 may be adopted, or for a still larger curve it may take the form shown in Fig. 26. Where this is unsuitable a segmental corner piece may be inserted, as in Fig. 27.

Rounding Poles and Rollers.— Lengths of wood circular in section may

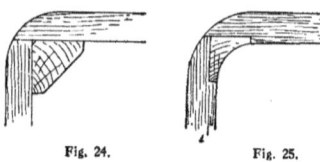

Fig. 24.   Fig. 25.

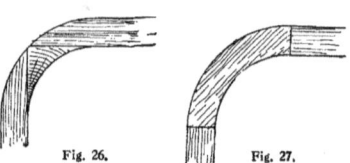

Fig. 26.   Fig. 27.

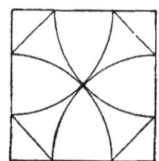

Fig. 28.—Setting Out Octagon

be turned on the lathe or may be worked by hand by using the plane. If made by hand the square piece is first planed octagonal in section. The octagon is usually marked on each end of the timber,

Figs. 24 to 27.—Methods of Forming Corners

and an easy method of constructing the octagon is shown in Fig. 28. First draw the diagonals of the square, and then with compass point on a corner of the section and radius equal to half the diagonal, describe an arch. Repeat for the other four corners. Join the points thus obtained.

When the timber has been planed octagonal the corners of the octagon are then planed off, giving a sixteen-sided figure in section. The wood will then be approximately circular and can be finished with glasspaper. If the pole or roller is a large one perhaps a little more planing would be necessary, or a "hollow" plane could be used with advantage before glasspapering.

Rebating

THE terms "rabbet" and "rabbit" mean the same thing as rebate and are often used. But rebate is probably the original and more correct word. The cutting of rebates is often necessary in woodwork, generally in the formation of joints. It means the cutting of a step or shoulder along the edge of a piece, as in Fig. 1, in most cases transversely to the grain. Usually the end of another piece fits into this at right angles, as in Fig. 2. The advantage of the rebate in such a case is that the outer surfaces of

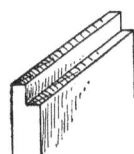

Fig. 1.—Rebate

the parts remain flush, when if simply depending on nails or screws and a plain butt joint they might easily be forced more or less out of position by a blow or severe pressure.

Generally the lines of a rebate are marked before commencing to cut. The wood has usually been planed to the required thickness, width and length, so that the lines can be gauged. Sometimes the rebated end is not finished to length but is left roughly sawn so that the end grain can be trimmed flush after the parts are together. In such a case the distance in of the rebate from the end cannot be marked with a gauge, but lines must be

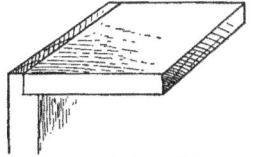

Fig. 2.—Rebated Joint

squared across. When the lines are marked a cut is made with a tenon saw slightly outside of the line, as in Fig. 3, and nearly or quite to the depth of the rebate. This makes it easy to rough-away most of the wood with a chisel and finish with a rebate plane. That

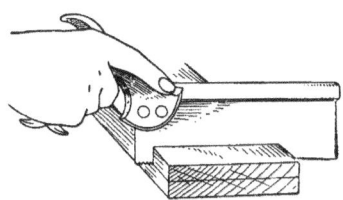

Fig. 3.—Cutting Rebate

is the way of working when no special planes are available, and it is a quite satisfactory method to adopt for just occasional rebating.

A chisel may be used in the vertical position (Fig. 4) or horizontally (Fig. 5). The first is generally more convenient on narrow pieces and the second on wide ones. As a precaution against chiselling

used carefully. Special planes, such as the fillister, trenching or grooving plane, router, and plough, can be set to cut to a required depth and will go no deeper, so that lines are unnecessary. More will

Fig. 5.—Paring Rebate Horizontally

be said about the use of these planes a little further on; some of them have already been referred to.

A rebate plane is used as in Fig. 7. As it is an open-sided plane it cuts close to the shoulder of the rebate. It usually has a skew mouth, that is, the cutter moves forward in a diagonal position instead of at right angles with the sides of the plane body as in most other planes. This enables it to make a cleaner cut across grain and reduces risk of splitting away the farther edge of the work. The usual width of the rebate plane is 1¼ in., but narrower ones are made for planing grooves of less width. Strictly speaking, a rebate has a shoulder at one side only

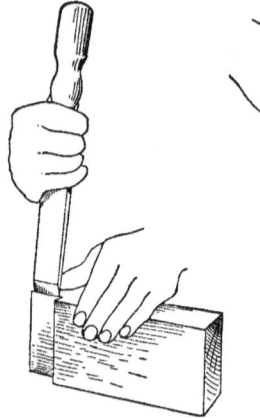

Fig. 4.—Chiselling Rebate Vertically

or planing below the gauge line it is usual to cut down exactly to it, as in Fig. 6, before the intermediate surface is levelled. Chisel and plane can then be used to reduce to the level required without continual examination to see when the line is reached, for it is easy to see when the bevelled portion at each edge has been removed, and the chief thing to be careful about is to get a

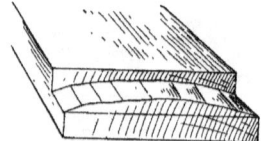

Fig. 6.—Ensuring Correct Depth of Rebate

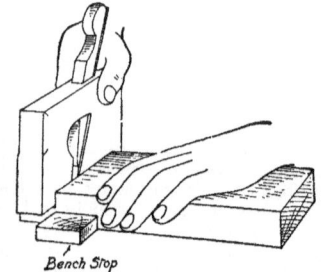

Fig. 7.—Using Rebate Plane

straight surface from one to the other. With a plane this is done almost automatically; but a chisel, of course, may go too deep in the intermediate part if not

and is open at the other, as in all the examples shown. When it does not occur at the end or edge of a piece but at an intermediate place, necessitating a

REBATING

shoulder at each side, it becomes a groove or trench, but a rebate plane can be used for planing it. Rebates and grooves, however, are not always planed. In many cases they can be cut entirely with a chisel. If they are short it may be quicker

Fig. 8.—Cleaning Inner Angle of Rebate with Chisel

to finish with a chisel than to change from chisel to plane, for a skilled worker can cut as straight with a chisel as with a plane on a short distance. In either case it is advisable to test for straightness with the edge of a try square blade or with the side of the chisel itself.

A chisel is often used for cutting the shoulder of a rebate, or the sides of a groove, exactly to the scribed or gauged line, as a sawcut to the line is rather too rough and inaccurate for some work. Therefore $\frac{1}{16}$ in. or so is left for chiselling and the chisel is used in the vertical position already illustrated. It is set exactly on the line and forced down to the depth of the rebate in a series of cuts, with a slight diagonal or side movement of the chisel simultaneously with the downward movement. In a rebate (though not in a groove) a rebate plane could be used on the end grain, but as a rule a chisel is preferable. End grain is not easy to plane, and the risk of splitting at the far edge is consider-

able. The shoulder of end grain cannot be chiselled till after the main body of material is cleared out of the rebate. A chisel is necessary also for cutting well down into the angle of the rebate in finishing the latter, for the saw is often stopped slightly short of the full depth, or if it is not the plane cannot always clear shavings completely out of the angle unless the fibres of end grain are severed by drawing the edge of the chisel along. Fig. 8 shows the inner angle of a long rebate being "cleaned," the chisel being drawn first along one side of the rebate and then along the other side.

On very wide pieces a chisel lying on its face, as in Fig. 5, may not be long enough to reach across, perhaps not even half way if worked from opposite sides. In such cases, of course, a plane is essential, and some of the roughing must be done with the chisel face upwards in a tilted position.

When a rebate runs parallel with the grain a sawcut need not be made. Most of the material can be roughed out with a chisel, and a rebate plane can be used

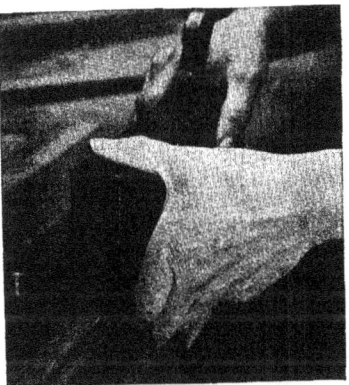

Fig. 9.—Using Temporary Guide whilst Making Rebate

in the ordinary position on the horizontal face and lying on its side to plane the other face. Or a strip of wood can be nailed temporarily or clamped to the line as a guide for the side of the plane to work against (*see* Fig. 9).

Rebate planes are not restricted to the wooden pattern shown in Fig. 7. There is some variety in the shapes and sizes of metal ones. The ordinary bullnose and the badger plane (a large rebate plane open at one side only; *see* Fig. 10) can be used on rebates of greater width than the rebate plane. So also can the jack and other ordinary planes if the surface next to the shoulder of the rebate has first been finished with a plane that cuts right up to it. But rebates are usually limited to about the width of a rebate plane. If much wider they would probably not be called rebates, but would be for the purpose of making halved or

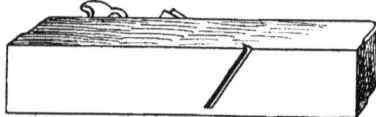

Fig. 10.—Sole of Badger Plane

half-lap joints, while if wide and not constituting joints it would in many cases be better to build them up by putting a piece or pieces on rather than to cut away solid wood.

Use of Fillister Plane.—A plane specially designed for cutting rebates is the fillister (Figs. 35 and 36, page 93); it differs from the rebate plane in having a side fence, and in its more elaborate forms it is adjustable for depth of cut and has a slitting cutter in advance of the main cutter, so that even across grain it can be used without making a sawcut or marking lines for planing to. But it is used mainly for cutting rebates with the grain, which are often required in joinery, in window sashes, for instance, and in other framework.

There are three types of fillister—the sash fillister (Fig. 36, page 93) which looks very much like a plough, and is designed for planing a rebate on the opposite side of the wood to that which the fence slides against. There is the moving fillister (Fig. 35, page 93), intended for planing rebates on the same side as the fence; and there is the standing fillister, which is not adjustable.

A rebate with the grain may be started by ploughing a groove with a plough at the distance and to the depth required

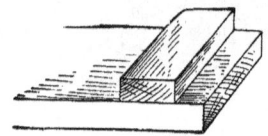

Fig. 11.—Built-up Rebate

and clearing the remainder of the rebate with any planes that are available. If necessary two or more grooves may be ploughed side by side. There are a few other planes intended primarily for cutting grooves, but these are suitable also for finishing rebates. But, as already mentioned, all special planes for work of this character can be dispensed with by a beginner or by anyone who does such work only occasionally. Their value also has been reduced by the fact that where such work is turned out in quantity it is not done by hand but by machine. A great deal of rebating and grooving can be done with a circular saw which is provided with a rising and falling table. It is set so that the top of the saw stands up to the correct distance for

Fig. 12.—Built-up Rebates

cutting to the depth required, and a fence on the table acts as a guide in pushing the wood over the saw.

Built-up Rebates.—A rebate may be built up instead of cut in the solid. Examples are shown in Figs. 11 and 12, the attached pieces being nailed or screwed on. The method in Fig. 11 is common in

REBATING

some rather rough classes of work, and where it can be adopted it often economises both material and time. The method in Fig. 12 is an alternative to cutting a rebate all round a piece of wood. The smaller piece is planed to width and length and nailed on the other. A rebate at the ends, or at the sides only, could be formed similarly, but as a rule it is better to cut it in the solid. The rebate in a door frame, into which the door fits, is often built up. The lid of a box or chest often fits a rebate which is built up, as shown in Fig. 13.

Fig. 14 is an instance of a rebated joint where the parts are not at right angles. The bead shown is not an essential feature of it, but beads are often used in such

Fig. 13.—Section of Box showing Built-up Rebates

places to avoid the unsightly appearance of a joint in a plain surface. The wood may shrink and the joint open slightly, but the beads make this almost unnoticeable. Instead of a bead the edges of the joint are sometimes chamfered. This type of rebate usually runs with the grain.

Occasionally a shallow rebate may be cut round the edges of a large piece to avoid planing down the entire surface to a thickness required. A rebate may or may not be wanted, but a certain uniform thickness at the edges is important and the piece of wood available may be considerably thicker and perhaps not uniform in thickness. Or it may be warped and a lot of planing would be necessary to make it true on both faces. Some work can be avoided by planing one face true, gauging from this, and going round the edges of the other face with a rebate plane. In large boxed-up foundry patterns this is common.

The inner edges of panelled frames are sometimes rebated instead of grooved. Glass in a wood frame nearly always fits in a rebate. The advantage is that it

Fig. 14.—Rebated Joint

can be inserted after the frame is together and can be replaced if broken. But in a rebate the inserted panel or glass requires something to keep it from falling out. This may take the form of a nailed-in moulding or bead, as dotted in Fig. 15.

Rebates are not invariably straight but may have to follow a curve. The equivalent of a rebate often occurs in turned work and is easily cut, but it is comparatively rare in bench work and is more troublesome, because it must generally be cut rather tediously with gouge and chisel, assisted perhaps with tools of the router class, which are made in considerable variety of form. There is one kind (Fig. 66, page 99), made in spokeshave form, with an adjustable fence to keep the cutter at a fixed distance from the edge of the work. It can be used for curved rebates or grooves. Another is the side router. Routers are used chiefly for finishing work already roughed with a chisel. Compass rebate planes, which have curved soles and sides, are also used.

Stopped Rebates.—Instances sometimes occur when a rebate must have a stopped end instead of running the full

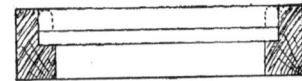

Fig. 15.—Rebated and Beaded Frame

length of the edge it is cut in. Fig. 16 is an example in cabinet work where the appearance of a rebate at the front edge is considered objectionable, and therefore it is stopped and the corner of the fitted-in piece notched to suit, so that, viewed from the front only, the method of jointing is concealed. Occasionally there are other reasons for stopping a rebate, and sometimes the stop may be formed by building-up methods. In rebated frames, for instance, as in Fig. 15, the rebate must stop at the inner corners. This does not necessarily mean that it cannot be planed through in preparing the pieces. On the two pieces that fit between the rebates would go full length. On the other also it might be stopped, or it might be planed through and made good afterwards. If the corners were mitred it would go through on all four pieces alike. When the corners are tenoned or halved methods of forming the rebate may vary. A safe method for a beginner is to put the frame together and mark and cut the rebate afterwards, mainly with a chisel, but using suitable planes as far as possible; the same method of cutting would be adopted for the stopped rebate in Fig. 16. In the case of a rebated frame the neatest way is to plane all pieces through and modify the joint so that the rebate is stopped, as in Fig. 17.

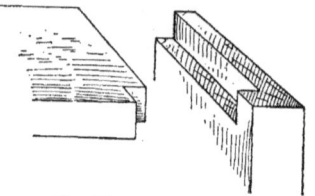

Fig. 16.—Stopped Rebate

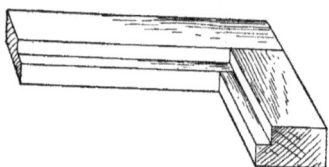

Fig. 17.—Method of Jointing Rebated Frame

Grooving, Ploughing and Tongueing

A GROOVE may be wide and shallow, as in Fig. 1, or narrow and deep, as in Fig. 2. The first is used in framing and boxing up and fitting the ends of shelves into

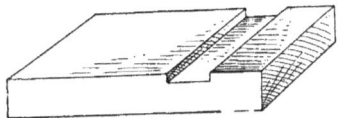

Fig. 1.—Trench or Groove

uprights, and similar work where pieces alike in thickness or nearly so are united at right angles, as in Fig. 3. The second is used mainly in the edges of boards to receive thin tongues or strips of wood,

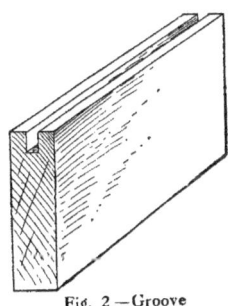

Fig. 2 —Groove

projecting and fitting a similar groove in the next board, as in Fig. 4. Both types of groove are very commonly employed in woodwork. The difference in their proportions makes it necessary to adopt different methods in cutting them. The first can be treated in a number of different ways. Without special tools it can be cut in the way described for rebates. It is first marked out by squaring lines across with penknife or scriber to indicate the width of groove, and its depth is marked with a gauge. Two cuts are then made with a tenon saw, allowing a little for chiselling exactly

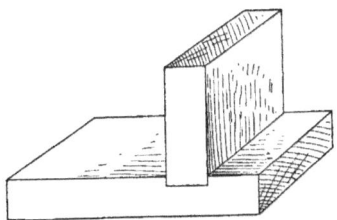

Fig. 3.—Grooved (or Housed) Joint

to the lines, and the wood between the sawcuts is cleared out with a chisel and finished with a rebate plane. In wood about an inch thick grooves of this kind seldom exceed $\frac{1}{4}$ in. in depth. In thinner wood they would often be less, for deep grooves weaken the piece in which they are cut.

The trenching or grooving plane (Fig. 4A) is designed specially for grooves of this class. Like the fillister for rebates, it is adjustable for depth and has a slitting cutter for the side of the groove. It is a narrow plane, ranging from ¼ in. to ⅜ in. wide, but, of course, can be used in wider grooves. The side rebate is another plane used for planing the edges of grooves in widening them. There is also a great variety of other planes of the rebate and shoulder and router class which can be used in most grooves of moderate size. The sash fillister can be used also in a groove which its fence allows it to reach to, and the same is true of the plough when a groove runs with the grain.

plough has the advantage of adjustability and it possesses a set of cutters of different widths. It can be set to cut to a certain depth, and has an adjustable fence at one side which acts as a gauge in keeping the cutter at a fixed distance from the edge of the wood, so that when the plough is set for the work it will cut the groove without any necessity for marking out or measuring. It will not cut across grain, like the fillister and trenching planes, though it is occasionally used on end grain, but practically all its work is in cutting narrow grooves with the grain.

Fig. 4A.—Trenching Plane

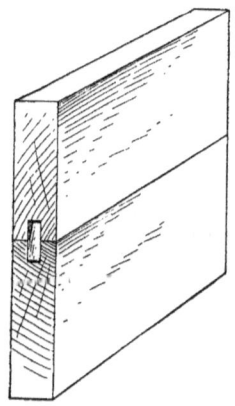

Fig. 4.—Grooved and Tongued Joint

The Plough.— In hand work the plough is the only suitable plane for making grooves for tongues, as shown in Figs. 2 and 4. An exception to this, however, is the matching planes (Figs. 40 and 41, page 94). These are made in pairs, for this work only, and are not adjustable like the plough. One forms a groove of definite size in the edge of a board and the other forms a tongue to fit it on the edge of another board. The tongue then is not a separate strip like the example in Fig. 4. But very little of this kind of ploughing and tongueing is done by hand now, and matching planes are seldom used. A

Sometimes it is convenient to use it in commencing wide grooves and rebates. Fig. 39, page 94, shows a plough in use. When used on considerable lengths of wood it is best to work it in a series of comparatively short strokes, just as with the ordinary surface planes. But ploughing is commenced at the front end of the wood and gradually worked backwards.

Grooves for the reception of tongues are required on so large a scale that most of this work is done by machinery. Boards for partitions, large panels, floor boards, and boarding for covering large surfaces, could not be grooved and tongued economically by hand, and so the latter is restricted to small amounts in details of joinery and other work, where it is seldom a case of fitting a number of boards edge to edge but of making grooves in pieces which are not of the proportions available in prepared boards.

The plough illustrated in Fig. 37, page 93, is only one of a number of types. But in all alike there is a set of interchangeable cutters, ranging from about ⅛ in. to 1¾ in. in stages of 1/16 in. There is a vertical metal plate running the length of the plane, less in thickness than the narrowest cutter. The lower edge of this plate is the sole of the plane and bears on the bottom of the ploughed groove,

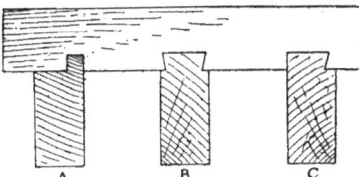

Fig. 5.—Three Types of Grooved Joint

enabling the thickness of shaving to be adjusted suitably. The fence determines the distance of the cutter, and of the groove it cuts from the side of the wood. The fence may have either screw or wedge adjustment, the type shown in Fig. 37, page 93, being adjusted by means of wedges. To set the plane the wedges are loosened, the plane set, and the wedges tightened by tapping them with the hammer. The depth of the groove is determined by a vertically sliding stop at the side of the metal plate. This is raised and lowered by turning the thumb-screw seen on the top of the plane. When the stop bears on the upper surface of the work the plough ceases to cut the groove any deeper.

Returning to grooves of the class shown in Figs. 1 and 3, which usually run across grain, there are some variations in the form they may take. Fig. 5 shows three ways in which such a groove may be modified, each having some advantage of its own. The width of the groove shown at A represents only about one-third the thickness of the piece fitted into it. This is done sometimes in corner or edge joints as an alternative to a rebate; or it may be employed when the fitted-in piece comes so near an edge that a full width groove would leave very short and consequently weak grain beyond. Another, and sometimes the chief advantage, is that the piece fitted in is secure from lateral displacement by having a shoulder to bear against on each side instead of only on one side as in an ordinary rebate. The plough is suitable for cutting such a groove when it runs with the grain. If across grain a plough could not be used because it would tear up the surface too badly. The groove could be sawn and chiselled and finished with other planes, or a special plane called a dado groove could be used, or a narrow trenching plane.

The grooves at B and C in Fig. 5 are dovetailed, so that the inserted piece cannot pull directly out, but must be slid in or out in the longitudinal direction of the groove. There may be a double-sided dovetail, as at B, or a single-sided one, as at C. These are rather troublesome to cut, and are only adopted in high-class work when the additional security they afford is very desirable. The groove would first be cut in the ordinary way to the width of its narrowest part and then undercut with a chisel to the extent of the vee. The parts fitting into them are treated similarly, the dovetail being usually cut with a chisel. Grooves of this kind can be built up by nailing on strips that have had their edges bevelled, or the grooves may be machine-cut.

Figs. 6 and 7 show methods of jointing boards edge to edge when it is considered desirable to have more than the ordinary

Fig. 6.—Rebated and Tongued Joint

Fig. 7.—Double-tongued Joint

provision against an open crack right through the joint, which might occur if the tongue in an ordinary tongued joint became split. In Fig. 6 the joints in the opposite faces of the boards are not opposite each other. In making this joint by hand one edge of each board has a tongue and the other a corresponding groove. The tongue is formed by cutting two rebates which are dissimilar in distance in from the edge. On the other edge the groove may be ploughed either before or after the single rebate has been cut. Fig. 7 has its outer joints opposite each other but has a tongue and groove side by side on each edge of the board. In this case two rebates and a groove are cut in each edge. As a rule, of course, the edges would be machine-cut, a revolving cutter of the correct profile being employed and a large number of boards done.

Besides the various grooving planes already mentioned there are combination and universal planes. These are provided with a large number of cutters and adjustments which adapt them for a great many different operations, They are entirely of metal, and necessarily rather complicated and expensive compared with the single purpose planes. Some are limited to various grooving operations,

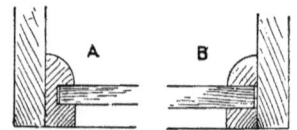

Fig. 8.—Two Methods of Securing Drawer Bottom

such as ploughing, rebating, slitting, matching, with perhaps beading. Others include different kinds of simple moulding, and chamfering. As many as 50 or 60 different cutters may be supplied with a plane of this class, the large number, of course, being accounted for, not being of different shapes, but because the commonly used shapes are in sets of different widths or curves. The best plane of this type is the Stanley Universal plane which will be described later in a special chapter.

Grooves, like rebates, are sometimes built up instead of cut out. Fig. 8 shows two examples where a drawer bottom fits in a groove which is not cut in the sides of the drawer itself but in attached pieces. At A a separate strip is grooved and attached to the side of the drawer. At B two strips are used and the groove is not ploughed at all, but is formed by

the space between them. These methods are generally adopted for strength when the sides of the drawer are too thin to be ploughed deeply enough, or when the drawer has to contain heavy articles.

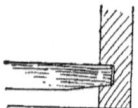

Fig. 9.—Usual Method of Fixing Drawer Bottom

The ordinary method, with no building up, is shown in Fig. 9. Fig. 10 shows a method of fitting panels into frames when a flush surface is required on one side, and a groove central with the thickness of the panel would come too close to the edge of the frame. The edge of the panel is rebated so that the projecting tongue and the ploughed groove it fits into are as far as possible from the edge of the frame.

Varieties and Uses of Tongues.— A tongue is a strip of wood for fitting into a ploughed groove. In cross section it is generally about $\tfrac{3}{8}$ in. by $\tfrac{1}{4}$ in. It is usually long enough to go in as a single piece the full length of the joint, but there is no objection, as a rule, to making up the length by inserting two or more shorter strips end to end. As a separate tongue must go halfway into each of the pieces

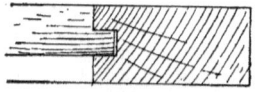

Fig. 10.—Flush Panel

it unites its width must be nearly double the depth of the ploughed groove in the edge of each piece; it should not be quite double or there might be some risk of its preventing a close joint between the pieces. When it is formed solid on the edge of one piece and fits into a groove in the other it should still not quite reach to the bottom of the groove. This is indicated in preceding illustrations

GROOVING, PLOUGHING AND TONGUEING

where tongues fitting in grooves are shown.

A tongue is not used because it is of any value in holding parts together. Its purpose is partly to keep the outer surfaces flush by preventing side movement in relation to each other, and partly to avoid an open crack right through the joint if the latter is not quite close. Wood is liable to shrink or to swell as it loses or acquires moisture, and therefore absolutely tight joints are not always possible or desirable. A tongue in the joint allows shrinkage, but it is a barrier to a direct passage through.

In work where grooving and tongueing is done on a large scale tongues are sawn to size on a circular saw. Width and thickness must be exact, but length is anything that happens to be convenient. If sawn by hand some amount of planing is necessary afterwards to get the thickness exact and uniform, but the edges can generally be left as sawn. Usually the thickness of the board they are cut from would represent the width of the tongues, and this would be quite near enough without gauging and planing to width. Exceptions might occur in very fine and exact work or when the tongues are wider than they are wanted. In thickness a tongue should be a reasonably close fit in its groove but not so tight as to require driving in.

The grain of a tongue usually runs lengthwise, but exceptions to this are sometimes made. It may run either crosswise or diagonally, in which case, of course, the loose tongue is very weak transversely and can easily be snapped off anywhere. But when inserted this weakness does not matter; in fact, unless the joint is very short the tongue has to be inserted in short lengths, because long ones across grain are unobtainable. The advantage of having the grain across instead of lengthwise is that it cannot split down the middle as a tongue with longitudinal grain might. Tongues with cross grain may be cut from a board the same thickness as the tongue, or a thicker board may be used and the strips sawn down into two or more afterwards.

The advantage of diagonal grain is that longer strips can be cut diagonally than at right angles across a board, and there is also slightly less risk of breakage, because there is a greater length of grain to split when it is diagonal than when it is direct across the strip.

The tongued joint may be glued or may be simply put together without glue, the latter being commonest. A joint is glued when a single piece would be preferred if it could be obtained wide enough. The reason for gluing is to make a practically solid piece. But the risk of shrinkage makes it impossible to glue

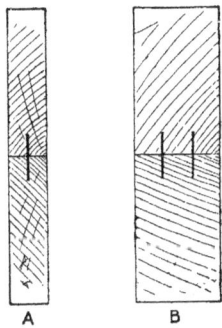

Fig. 11.—Metal Tongues

up very great widths and at the same time prevent them from warping and splitting. Therefore a number of narrow pieces, each free to shrink independently of the others, is the best way in many cases, and the joints are not glued.

When glue is used in edge joints there is no great advantage in using a tongue as well, and in the majority of such cases it is omitted. To make a good glue joint it is necessary to have the wood surfaces in tight contact everywhere with only a thin film of glue between. This is done by pressing and sliding the parts over each other to squeeze all superfluous glue out, and then usually by clamping until the glue is dry. When a tongue has to be inserted one of the grooved pieces is held in the vice, as in making an ordinary edge glue joint, and the tongue is glued in and secured with a few nails to keep it from moving endwise while the other piece is being adjusted on it. Plenty of glue is applied to the edges of both pieces, and they are fitted together and the upper one slid a few inches each way with as much downward pressure as possible and finally adjusted with its ends flush with the ends of the lower piece. Then clamps are applied to keep the joint squeezed together and it is laid aside for a few hours to dry.

Metal tongues are sometimes used instead of wood. They do not require a ploughed groove, but can be inserted in a sawcut, which is usually made with a circular saw. They are not only strong themselves, but the narrow groove they require diminishes risk of breaking the ledges of wood on each side of the groove. A central tongue may be used, as at A in Fig. 11, or if the joint is wide two tongues may be inserted, as at B. In very wide joints two wooden tongues are sometimes used similarly.

Shooting and Mitre Cutting

Shooting Square Work.—When it is required to joint-up thin boards to form panels, etc., this may be done by overhand planing, or shooting as it is sometimes termed. Each board is fixed in turn in the vice and the edges planed straight and square as shown in Fig. 1 (*see* also Figs. 13 and 14, p. 103). When one piece is placed on the other the surfaces forming the joint should touch each other the whole length, and the broad surfaces should be in one plane, so that when a straightedge is applied it will touch both of them, as illustrated by Fig. 2.

Construction of Shooting Boards.—The method described above is difficult and requires a deal of skill, and is not convenient where much jointing and thin-edge planing is required; therefore the shooting is generally done with the help of a shooting board, which in size may vary according to the purposes for which it is required. A useful size is made by having a 9-in. or 11-in. by ⅞-in. board for

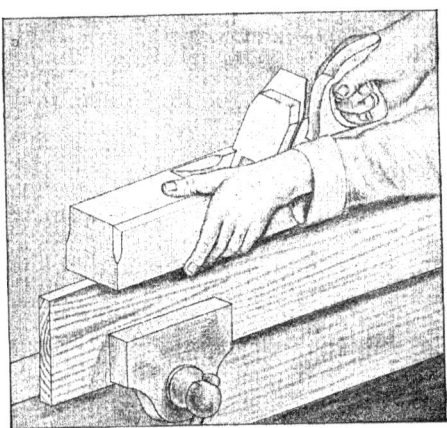

Fig. 1.—Overhand Planing or Shooting

Fig. 2.—Testing Jointed Boards with Straightedge

the base. A piece 5 in. to 7 in. wide and ¾ in. thick is fixed on the top of this. The length may be from 2 ft. 6 in. to 4 ft. A stop made of hardwood is housed into the top board, as shown in Fig. 3. Shooting boards are liable to warp, as shown exaggerated at Figs. 4 and 5, which causes the plane to shoot the edges of the work out of square; this can be obviated by screwing ledges to the underside are tried together their face sides are not in one plane, as shown in Fig. 9; whereas, if the face of one piece is placed downwards on the shooting board and the other piece upwards, they come together, as shown in Fig. 10.

Shooting Edges at an Angle.—When it is required to plane edges at an angle other than a right angle, if the material is ¾ in. or more in thickness the

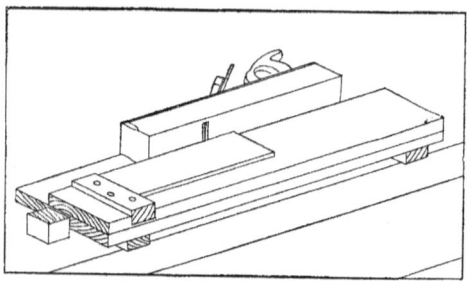

Fig. 3.—Using Shooting Board

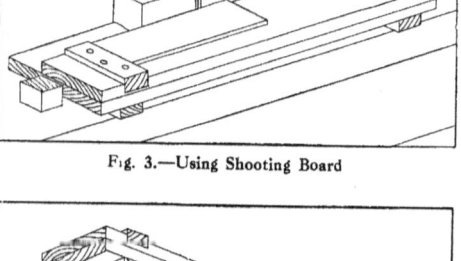

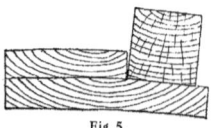

Figs. 4 and 5.—Faulty Construction of Shooting Boards

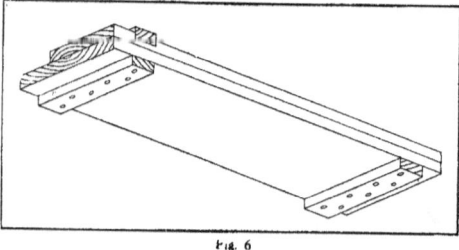

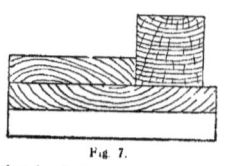

Figs. 6 and 7.—Shooting Board prevented from Warping by Ledges

(hardwood being the best for the purpose) and so keeping the board true, as shown at Figs. 6 and 7.

Using the Shooting Board.—It sometimes happens that the edges of the work are not shot quite square owing to the shooting board wearing or warping or to the face of the plane not being at right angles to the side that is on the rebate of the shooting board (Fig. 8). Then if the face side of each piece is placed on the shooting board and planed, when they work is frequently done by overhand planing. A bevel is then set to the required angle and applied to the ends of the stuff, as shown at Fig. 11, and marked. The work is then planed to the lines and also to fit the bevel (Fig. 12) which is frequently applied during the process of planing.

Shooting Block.—For thinner material a shooting block is more convenient. Where there are only one or two pieces to be done, just one or two blocks of

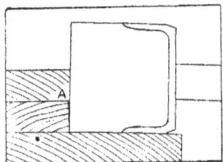

Fig. 8.—Shooting Out of Square

Fig. 13.—Built-up Shooting Block for Bevelling Edges and Ends of Work

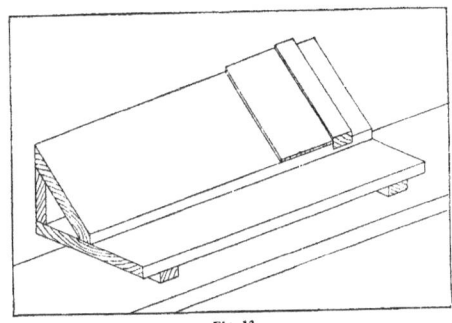

Fig. 13.

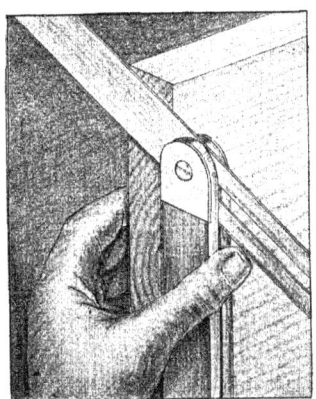

Fig. 11.—Applying Bevel to End of Board for Marking

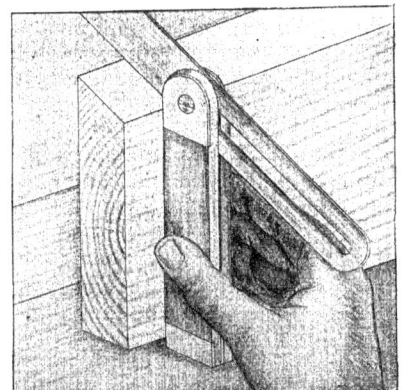

Fig. 12.—Testing Planed Edge with Bevel

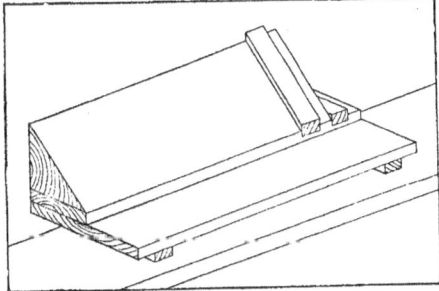

Fig. 14.—Movable Block Dowelled to Ordinary Shooting Board

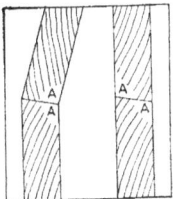

Fig. 9. Fig. 10.

Fig. 9. Placing Boards Together so that Adjacent Angles are Equal

Fig. 10.—Placing Boards Together so that Opposite Angles are Equal

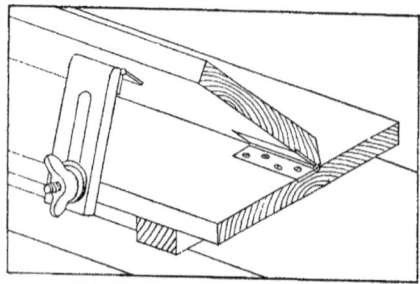

Fig. 16.—Adjustable Shooting Block

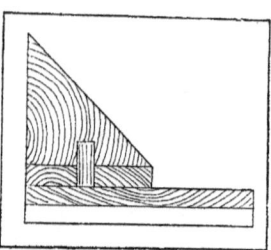

Fig. 15.—Section through Movable Block showing Dowel

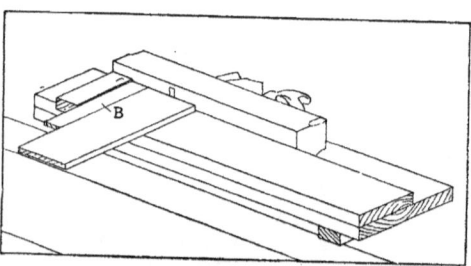

Fig. 17.—Shooting End grain

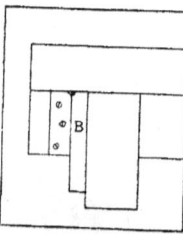

Fig. 18.—Using Piece to Prevent Breaking of Corner

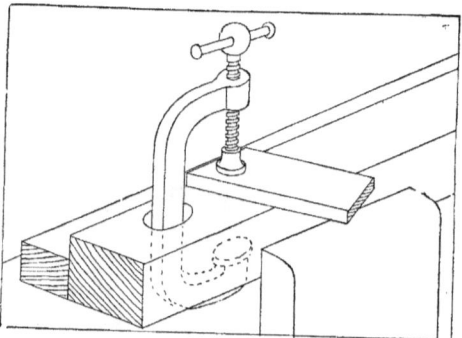

Fig. 20.—Shooting Block with Adjustable Stop

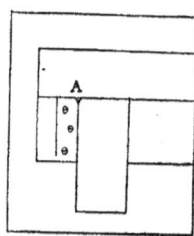

Fig. 19.—Faulty Method, Corner Broken

SHOOTING AND MITRE CUTTING

wood cut to the particular angle and temporarily screwed to the shooting stop becomes worn and does not properly support the corner of the work, and

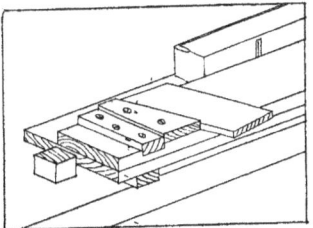

Fig. 20A.—Shooting Ends at an Angle

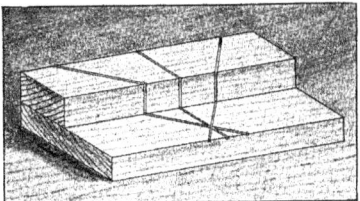

Fig. 21.—Ordinary Mitre Block

block will probably be found sufficient. But when there are a number of pieces to be done accurately, then it will generally pay to have a more or less permanent block. Fig. 13 shows a block built up. Figs. 14 and 15 illustrate a solid triangular piece trued up to the desired angle; by means of three or four dowels it can be made readily to fit on or be taken off an ordinary shooting board. Fig. 16 shows one end of a very useful and simple form of adjustable shooting block which can be set to any angle within its limits.

the fibres forming it become broken, as at A, Fig. 19, by the plane-iron edge.

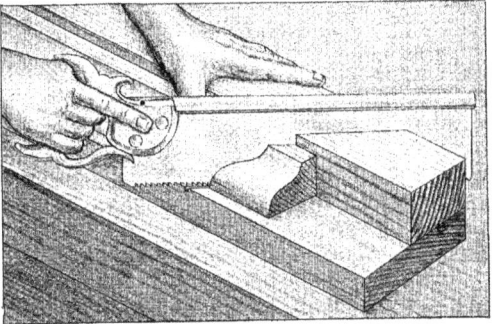

Fig. 22.—Cutting Mitre

Shooting End Grain.—Fig. 17 shows

Therefore it is a good plan to have an

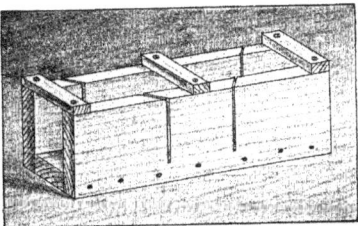

Fig. 23.—Ordinary Mitre Box

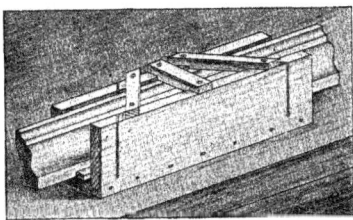

Fig. 24.—Moulding in Position in Box

the operation of shooting end grain square to an edge. After a time the end of the

intervening piece, as shown at B, Figs. 17 and 18, then the end of the work and

THE PRACTICAL WOODWORKER

this piece are shot together, which prevents the corner of the work being damaged. This matter has already been alluded to in the chapter on general planing.

Shooting Ends at an Angle.—When it is required to shoot ends at an angle a wedge-shaped piece can be cut to the proper form and fastened to the ordinary shooting board, as shown at Fig. 20A.

A very convenient kind of shooting block with adjustable stop is represented by Fig. 20. The block is bored and pared so as to receive a strong form of G-cramp, which will hold the stop firmly

Fig. 26.—Mitre Trimming Machine

Fig. 25.—Adjustable Guides to Box

at any desired angle, and which can be quickly altered as found necessary.

CUTTING MITRES

Mitre Cut or Mitre Block.—In Fig. 21 is shown the ordinary mitre cut made of two pieces of wood; these are fastened together by a little glue and also are nailed from the underside of the base. This is a very useful form of mitre cut for general purposes, particularly for small mouldings, and the work and block can be held together by the left hand, as shown in Fig. 22.

Mitre Box.—The ordinary mitre box is shown in Fig. 23. This is used for deeper and larger mouldings than can be cut by the mitre block. Fig. 24 shows a cornice moulding in position. This kind of mitre box can be used for different sizes of mouldings by inserting a fillet of the proper width, as shown.

Fig. 25 illustrates a mitre box with metal guides, which are screwed upon the edges as illustrated; they can be adjusted to suit any thickness of saw; as they greatly reduce the wear of the cuts in the box, truer mitres can be cut for a much longer period. The metal guides can also be obtained for cutting square ends, and may be

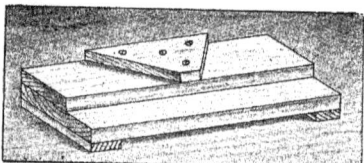

Fig. 27.—Ordinary Mitre Shoot with Solid Fence

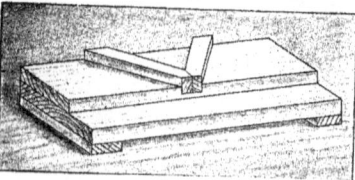

Fig. 23.—Mitre Block with Two Stops

SHOOTING AND MITRE CUTTING

used at the end of the box as shown or in pairs at the top of the cuts.

Metal Mitre Cut.—There is a number of excellent, and, of course, expensive, mitreing machines on the market, but probably one of the handiest is illustrated by Fig. 26. It will cut mouldings of a good size and mitres at any angle within the compass of the machine. It cuts mitres true and smooth, obviating any necessity of shooting. A much later chapter will deal in detail with the use of this and similar simple machinery.

Fig. 30.—Improvised Shooting Block

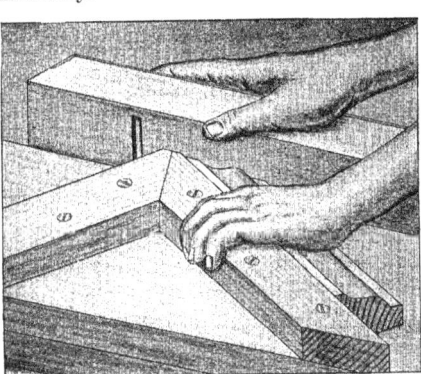

Fig. 29.—Shooting Mitre

SHOOTING MITRES

Mitre Shoots.—The two common kinds of mitre shoots are shown in Figs. 27 and 28. The base is shown battened, or ledged, underneath so as to prevent warping, which would cause untrue mitres. The handiest kind is that shown by Figs. 28 and 29, because the work and the mitre stop can be grasped firmly together, as shown at Fig. 29.

Shooting Blocks.—A very useful improvised block is shown at Fig. 30. A piece of wood is screwed to the top of the bench and its surfaces well planed so that it is quite square with the side of the bench; then a fillet is screwed to the side of the bench almost touching the screw and at the mitre angle with the piece s. The upper end A may be thicknessed out as shown. Then by holding the plane on the skew so that the iron cuts the mitre whilst the other part of the sole of the plane is kept firmly on the piece s, as will be seen, the bench vice can be brought into use to hold the moulding firmly.

Fig. 31.—Good Form of Mitre Shooting Block

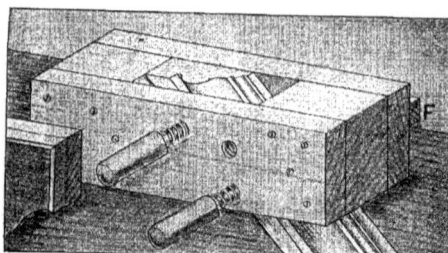

Fig. 32.—Another Kind of Mitre Shooting Block

Fig. 31 illustrates a most useful kind of shooting block which will hold mouldings of different sizes. If desired, this kind can be bought ready-made with either a wooden or steel hand-screw.

The shooting block shown by Fig. 32 has its advantages, being simple to make and also suitable for being held firmly in the bench vice. To prevent slipping, a fillet F can be fixed at the back of the block so as to rest on the top of the bench as shown.

Of course, in using this kind of block great care must be taken to have the plane irons set very fine and to hold and use the plane so that the mitre of the moulding is cut by the iron and not the surface of the block.

During recent years many accurate mitreing appliances constructed of steel have been introduced. For example, Fig. 33 shows an appliance especially made for use with a steel plane, and it will be noted that the angle of mitre is adjustable. Still other appliances will be mentioned in

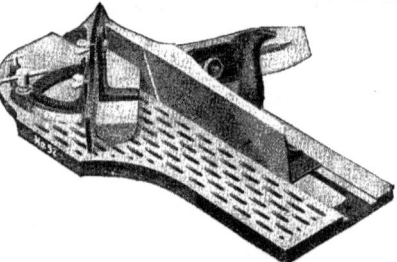

Fig. 33.—Metal Shooting "Board"

connection with special applications of mitreing discussed in later chapters.

Timber: Conversion and Seasoning

Introductory.—A tree should be felled in its prime. If it is prematurely cut down the larger quantity of sap-wood causes too much wastage, and if it is allowed to grow too old it is inferior in toughness and strength. The oak tree is mature for felling between eighty and a hundred years' growth; ash, elm, and larch between sixty and a hundred years; the poplar between forty and fifty years. Spruce and pine trees are felled between seventy and a hundred years of age.

As the sap is drawn up the tree for nourishment during the spring and descends in the autumn the tree is at its driest period during the winter, which is the time, in temperate climates, chosen for felling trees. There is, however, always a large amount of sap remaining in the tree, which is of such a quantity that its weight is half as much as the timber itself; that is, when dry timber loses about one-third of its weight. This condition for practical purposes is not generally attained, and is only approached and approximated for the best cabinetwork and joinery.

SEASONING TIMBER

When drying or seasoning timber shrinkage takes place circumferentially, the shrinkage in diameter being comparatively small. The annual rings shorten, and if the timber is left whole in the log too long many vee-shaped shakes will appear and spoil the timber. To prevent this happening, the log is sawn into planks to the desired thickness and stacked for drying, and the timber then seasoned either by natural or artificial methods.

Natural Seasoning.—Though the use of drying kilns is increasing the bulk of our wood is still seasoned in the open air. If kept in the air long enough, the moisture content of the wood finally comes into equilibrium with that of the surrounding atmosphere, and the wood is said to be air-dried. The rate of drying varies, of course, with the time of year, species of wood, size and form of piece, and method of piling. Certain of these factors may be controlled or utilised in a way to hasten the drying process and lessen the likelihood of defects appearing.

Sawn timber generally is dried by being piled in stacks with air space between the boards. In forming the stacks the boards usually are laid flat, with strips called "stickers" (or "skids") between courses or layers. A space also is left between each board in a layer and the adjacent board to provide for circulation of air throughout the stack. Flat or horizontal piling may be of two kinds: (a) With the ends of the boards toward the alley—endwise piling, and (b) with the sides toward the alley—sidewise piling. Figs. 1 and 2 illustrate the two methods. The stacks are arranged to slope from front to rear, and to lean forward so that water dripping from the top falls to the ground without trickling down over the courses below. With either method of piling the stacks should be so located in the yard that the prevailing winds blow through them rather than against the ends.

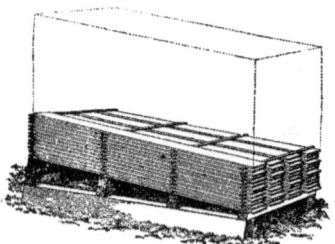

Fig. 1.—Endwise Piling of Timber

Most timber manufacturers and dealers use the endwise method of piling. A number, however, have adopted the sidewise method, which has certain advantages in the matter of air circulation. In endwise piling the stickers obstruct the passage of air from back to front of a course, while in sidewise piling the passages from front to rear are clear. Water which forces its way into the pile is more efficiently drained in sidewise piling, and the likelihood of sticker rot and discoloration due to the accumulation of moisture, dust, and dirt against the stickers is lessened.

The bottom boards in a stack rest on skids, which in turn rest on foundations, preferably of stone, cement, or metal. Pieces containing rot should never be used for foundation timbers or skids, or allowed to remain in the pile. The vicinity of the pile should be kept clear of weeds.

The use of cement and metal foundations is especially feasible in retail timber yards and in those maintained by wood-using factories. In retail yards, where economy in space often is the essential thing, the piles are high and a particular space usually is allotted to each class or species of timber. In factory yards timber often is held for a number of years before being used. In such cases the frequent renewal of wooden foundations under timber piles entails considerable expenditure of time and money, to say nothing of the danger of infecting the wood by bringing it in contact with partly rotted foundation timbers. For these reasons foundations of a more permanent character are constantly growing in favour in retail and factory yards.

Kiln-drying.—Timber is kiln-dried when there is need for seasoning it quickly, or when the manufacturer does not wish to carry large stocks in his yard. A kiln is used also to further dry partially air-seasoned or even fully air-seasoned material, for special uses.

The main problem in kiln-drying is to prevent the moisture from evaporating from the surface of the pieces faster than it is brought to the surface from the interior. When this happens the surface becomes considerably drier than the interior and begins to shrink. If the difference in moisture content is sufficient the surface portion opens up in checks.

The evaporation from the surface of wood in a kiln can be controlled to a large degree by regulating the humidity, temperature, and amount of air passing over the wood; and a correctly designed kiln, especially one for drying the more difficult woods, should be constructed and equipped in a way to ensure this regulation.

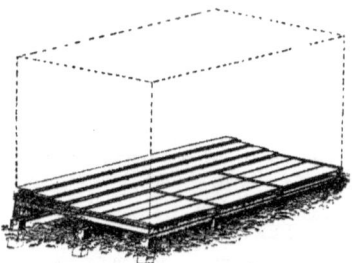

Fig. 2.—Lengthwise Piling of Timber

A dry kiln may consist simply of a box in which timber can be heated, or of a good-sized building or group of buildings (battery) containing steam pipes, condensers, sprays, and various air passages

TIMBER: CONVERSION AND SEASONING

capable of adjustment to regulate the amount of ventilation.

Kilns for drying timber may be divided into two classes: (a) compartment kilns (Fig. 3) and (b) progressive kilns (Fig. 3A). In compartment kilns the conditions are changed during the drying process, and all timber in the kiln is dried at one time. The conditions at any time during drying are uniform throughout the whole kiln. In a progressive kiln conditions at one end differ from those at the other, and the timber is dried progressively by being passed through the kiln. Compartment kilns are used when it is desired to dry timber of various sizes and species, while progressive kilns are used where uniform stock is handled.

Seasoning Timber Strips.—An apparatus for seasoning small strips is shown in Figs. 4 to 7. The smaller the cross-section of the strips to be seasoned, the less time is required to complete the process. Possibly if the strips are very small, say 1¼ in. by 1¼ in. or 1 in. by 1 in., a day in such an apparatus as that illustrated herewith would render them fit for all ordinary purposes.

A rectangular structure, the walls of which could be made of coke breeze concrete, is lined inside with sheet asbestos or coated with fireclay. The concrete walls are reinforced with light wrought-iron bars to increase the strength and rigidity of the structure. The dotted shading in Figs. 4, 5, and 6 represents the walls of the structure. The two central vertical walls are so arranged as to leave a space (c, Fig. 4) between them, and a horizontal wall shuts off the lower portion c of this space from the top portion.

At the back end of the structure a boiler B (Figs. 5 and 6) is fixed at a slightly lower level by making a pit. This boiler could be obtained from any of the makers of horticultural heating apparatus. Flow and return pipes are connected with this boiler, as shown in Fig. 5. The air in the chamber c is thus brought to a very high temperature. The heated air from c is allowed to pass alternately into each of the two drying chambers E (Figs. 5 and 6) by means of slides s, operated from handles H at the front of the structure. Thus, when the timber is stacked in one of the drying chambers E ready for seasoning, the slide s (Fig. 6) is withdrawn, as shown, and the hot air allowed to pass from the chamber c through the opening o into one of the drying chambers E. Meanwhile, the other slide s_1 is closed as shown, and so shuts off the hot air from the drying chamber from which the dry timber is to be removed. The moist air from the drying chambers E and E passes through an aperture F into a hollow chamber D at the rear end of the structure, into which the fumes from the boiler F

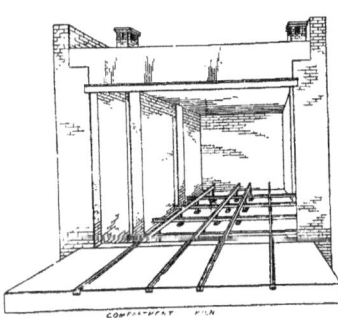

Fig. 3.—A Compartment Kiln for Timber Drying

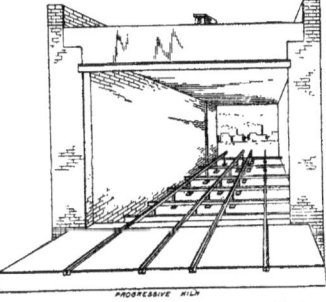

Fig. 3A.—Progressive Kiln for Timber Drying

are also carried. This ensures a good draught up the flue J.

Fig. 4, which is partly a vertical section and partly an elevation, represents the front end of the apparatus. The doors shutting off the drying chambers are arranged in such a way as to keep the hot air from escaping. The doors may be made to lift up to open, as shown; or they may be hinged in the same way as an ordinary oven door. If made to work vertically, some method of counterweights must be arranged to take off the weight of the door in lifting.

In order to avoid the necessity of stacking the timber each time in and around the drying chambers, trolleys are provided. These are constructed with flanged wheels and run on rails. The sides of the trolleys should not be solid, but should be of iron, bolted together in such a way as to leave ample space for the hot air to circulate around the timber. Near each end of the trolley are fixed U-shaped iron uprights, as shown in Fig. 7.

After having placed the bottom layer of strips horizontally on the bed of the trolley a bearer is dropped down at

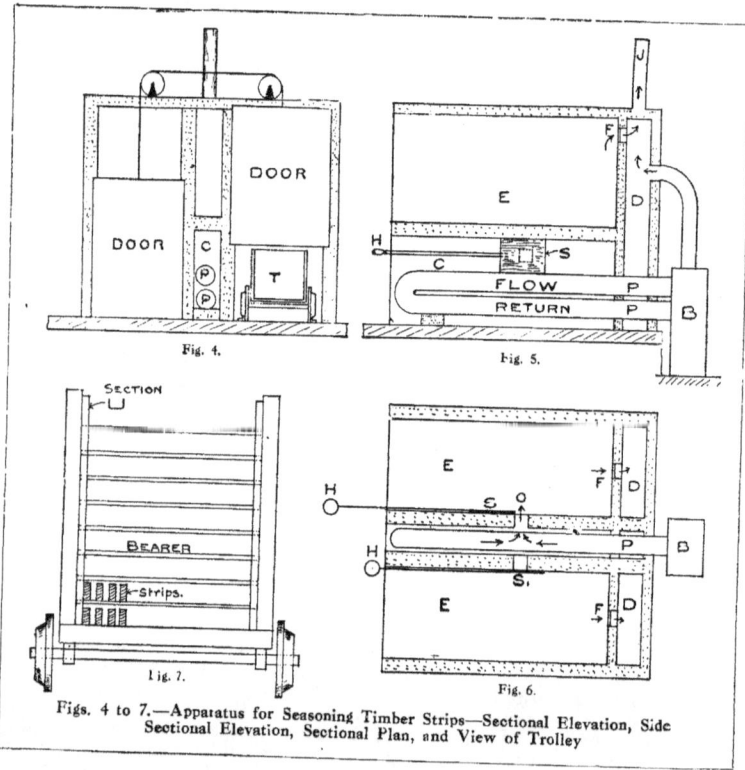

Figs. 4 to 7.—Apparatus for Seasoning Timber Strips—Sectional Elevation, Side Sectional Elevation, Sectional Plan, and View of Trolley

TIMBER: CONVERSION AND SEASONING

each end between the two U-shaped uprights until it rests upon the first layer of strips. The next layer of strips is

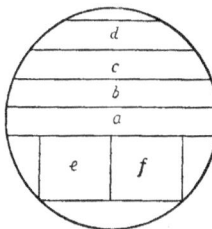

Fig. 8.—Log Cut into Planks and Beams

then laid transversely on these bearers and another pair of bearers dropped into position, and so on until the trolley is loaded. While this trolley is being loaded up in this way the other loaded trolley is within the closed drying chamber into which the hot air from c has been admitted through o (Fig. 6), by withdrawing the slide s. A considerable amount of time is saved in this way, and the operator is kept busy for the greater part of the time.

If an anthracite stove, such as the "Esse," is used it would only require attention once a day, and would feed

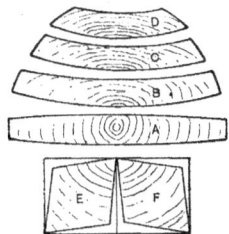

Fig. 9.—Effect of Shrinkage on Sawn-up Log

itself automatically, keeping the heat at a steady height continuously day and night. Thus a trolley loaded up during the day could be run into the chamber at night and safely left until early morning,

when it could be withdrawn and another —loaded by someone working a night shift—could then be run into the other chamber.

By making the structure sufficiently long from the front to the boiler end it could be made to accommodate two trolleys in each of the drying chambers, or four altogether. The number of strips handled would thus be increased greatly without any undue amount of extra labour or of initial expenditure.

Fig. 10.—Beams Cut Square with Tree

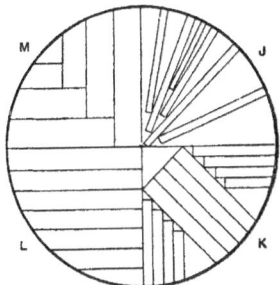

Fig. 11.—Converting Oak Log to "Silvergrain" Panelling, Quarter-stuff, etc.

CONVERSION

Conversion of timber is the operation of sawing the log into planks, deals, battens, etc., and this is generally done before seasoning. The subsequent shrinkage is noticeable in the portions when cut as illustrated. Take, for instance, a log cut into planks and beams shown in Fig. 8. The middle piece a, when dry, will remain practically the same width and of the same thickness in the middle. The thickness of the edges will diminish a trifle as shown exaggerated in A (Fig. 9). The piece b will take the shape of B. Owing to the shortening of the rings, this piece will shrink in its width more on the upper surface than the surface next to the heart of the tree, giving the plank a curved shape as shown. This also will be a trifle thinner at the edges than in the middle; *c* and *d*, following the same action, are shown; the shrinkage in width is more marked, but they keep more parallel in

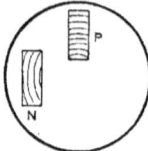

Fig. 12.—Getting Beam or Joist from Log

thickness. The tendency to distort with rectangular-shaped pieces is shown in E and F; if the rectilinear shape is to be preserved they must be cut square with the tree, as in G and H (Fig. 10).

If boards are required that will not shrink in width, nor warp untrue, they must be cut, as shown in Fig. 11 at J. This method is also pursued in cutting oak panelling to obtain the full figured silver grain. It is an expensive method of converting timber, because it entails more waste, but most of the vee pieces can be utilised for feather-edged tiling laths and for oak fencing, etc. A more economical method to approximate the above

where strength is a more important matter than shrinkage, it has been proved the best to cut tangentially to the annual rings as at N in Fig. 12; this is stronger than when cut as at P.

Deals are cut from the Scandinavian fir trees according to the size of the log, as shown in Figs. 13 and 14. A method of cutting pitch pine and other timbers, for panelling, tangentially to the rings is seen in Fig. 15. The log, instead of being cut into halves or quarters, is first cut to a square balk, which is then gradually reduced as the boards are sawn off. The deciding factors as to the method of cutting up the log are its size, the amount of sap-wood to cut off, and the presence of any particular defects of knots, shakes, or decay.

MARKET SIZES OF TIMBER

The terms given to the various size timbers in market forms are as follow: A balk varies from 12 in. by 12 in. to 18 in. by 18 in.; whole timbers from 9 in. by 9 in. to 15 in. by 15 in; half timbers from 9 in. by 4½ in. to 18 in. by 9 in.; scantling from 6 in. by 4 in. to 12 in. by 12 in.; quartering from 2 in. by 2 in. to 6 in. by 6 in.; planks from 11 in. to 18 in. wide and from 3 in. to 6 in. thick; deals from 9 in. wide and from 2 in. to 4½ in. thick; battens from 4½ in.

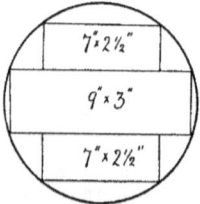

Fig. 13.—Converting Fir Log to "Deals"

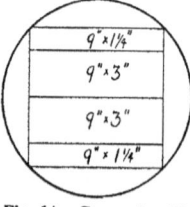

Fig. 14.—Converting Fir Log to "Deals"

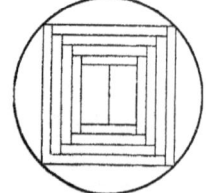

Fig. 15.—Converting Pitch-pine Log to Panelling

advantages is shown at K. For ordinary boarding, sometimes known as "quarter-stuff," it is cut as at L; M is the best method of cutting "thick stuff." When cutting the log for beams or joists, or

to 7 in. wide and from ¾ in. to 3 in. thick; strips and laths from 4 in. to 4½ in. wide and from ½ in. to 1½ in. thick.

Pine and spruce timbers are sold by standard hundred, by the load, and by the

TIMBER: CONVERSION AND SEASONING

square of 100 ft. super. The Petersburg standard is 120 pieces of 6 ft. by 11 in. by 3 in.; the Christiania standard is 120 pieces of 11 ft. by 9 in. by 1¼ in.; and the London standard is 120 pieces of 12 ft. by 9 in. by 3 in. Calculating the volume of timber in the Petersburg standard, which is the one in general use, gives 165 cub. ft., so that the 120 pieces are equal to a balk 12 in. by 12 in., 165 ft. long. When buying timbers of other sizes this method of calculating is convenient. Supposing scantlings were brought, 9 in. by 4 in., it will be seen that this section of 36 sq. in. is one-fourth the area of the section of the balk, 12 in. by 12 in.; therefore, to make the standard the length would be four times as long as 165, which is 660 ft. A load is 50 cub. ft., so that $3\frac{3}{10}$ loads make a Petersburg standard.

Boarding is generally reckoned by the standard of 100 ft. super., so that the length of boarding required to make 100 sq. ft. varies inversely as its width, that is, the narrower the boarding the greater the length will be to give the standard area. This area is equal to 100 ft. of boarding 1 ft. wide, or if it were 6 in. wide these will be 200 ft. in length. Boarding, however, is generally sold in widths of 7 in., 9 in., and 11 in., which must be brought to the fraction of a foot so as to divide into the area of 100 sq. ft. For instance, 7 in. = $\frac{7}{12}$ ft., 9 in. = $\frac{9}{12}$ ft., 11 in. = $\frac{11}{12}$ ft. 100 ÷ $\frac{7}{12}$ = 100 × $\frac{12}{7}$ = 171¾ ft., the length of boarding required 7 in. wide.

When buying timbers by any other standard of measurement the cubical contents or volume can be obtained from the measurement given.

"Mixed timber" implies defective deals from the first quality mixed with seconds.

Fir timber, sometimes imported as "hand masts," is the longest, soundest, and straightest trees when topped and barked, circumference from 24 in. to 72 in. "Spars and poles" have a circumference less than 24 in. at the base. "Inch masts" are those having a circumference of more than 72 in., and are generally dressed to an octagonal form. "Ends" are less than 8 ft. long. Scaffold and ladder poles are from young trees of larch and spruce, and average 33 ft. long. Rickers are about 22 ft. long and under 2½ in. in diameter at the top end.

Calculating Contents of Timber Logs.—When measuring log timber, either round or square in section, it is quite customary to multiply the length of the log by the square of a quarter of the girth

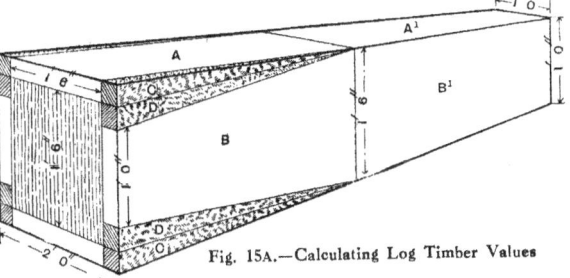

Fig. 15A.—Calculating Log Timber Values

—the girth being taken at the middle of the log.

For example, suppose a log measures 20 ft. long and is 8 ft. in circumference at the centre of its length; then, a quarter of 8 ft. equals 2 ft., and 2 ft. multiplied by itself (or squared) equals 4 ft., and this multiplied by the length of the log gives the cubical contents as 80 ft.

This method of measuring — shortly expressed by the formula $L \times \left(\frac{girth}{4}\right)^2$ — while being quite proper for some forms of timber, is by no means accurate when applied to all forms; it, however, has the great advantage of being simple to work and easy to understand. Even in those cases where this rule does **not** properly apply, the approximate result that it gives is often of greater value to the timber merchant than would be a solution arrived at by calculating the areas of circles, or by reducing logs from pyramidical to imaginary rectangular forms.

With circular tree-trunks that do not taper, the actual contents may be found by employing the formula $L \times \dfrac{girth^2}{4\ \pi}$; but calculations involving the use of π are troublesome, to say the least, and, should the log taper considerably, the difficulty of determining the actual contents by this method becomes greater still. Moreover, the actual contents of round timber, whether parallel or tapering, is always a fictitious quantity in the eyes of a timber buyer.

Considerable waste must occur during conversion, and the question really is, not how much stuff does the log contain, but how much of it is realisable. Thus, for example, a round log 20 in. in diameter equals 314 sq. in. in sectional area ; but, converted into a square log, the sectional area will equal only 201 sq. in., which more nearly represents to the buyer the timber value of the log. This loss in conversion, amounting to at least one-third of the original bulk of the log, happens only when the squaring is done by axe.

If the logs are sawn square, the slab pieces are then of some value, and the actual loss will not be more than about one-fifth of the original bulk. Now the quarter-girth method of measurement (on preceding page) places the contents of a round log without taper about one-fifth lower than they really are ; compared with accurate measurement in the above instance the result is as 1·00 is to 1·24 . . ., and gives very approximately the merchantable contents of the log. Not only is this method the safest to follow in connection with the measurement of round timber, but, as the form of any timber to which it may be applied more nearly approaches parallelism and squareness, so the results become more and more accurate, until, with perfectly square and parallel timber, the quarter-girth method gives a perfectly accurate result.

Applied to square tapering logs, the quarter-girth method, though not quite accurate, is still approximately correct and fair in its results. Taper in a log invariably means loss to the buyer ; more taper means more loss. As if to compensate for this drawback, the quarter-girth method of measurement gives a contents result that is proportionately lower and lower as the taper in a log increases. So that here again, while the actual contents may, of course, be readily determined by considering the log as the frustum of a pyramid, the answer so afforded is often not so desirable nor so useful to the purchaser as one that more nearly represents the converted working possibilities of the log.

The diagram (Fig. 15A, p. 191) is intended to show the amount of material that is neglected or given to the buyer when such a piece is measured by taking the quarter-girth at the centre as a basis. The log represented is supposed to taper uniformly from 2 ft. at the large end to 1 ft. at the small end. At the middle of its length the quarter-girth measures 1 ft. 6 in., but, strictly speaking, there is more than sufficient wood at the large end to compensate for deficiencies at the other.

The wedge-shaped pieces A and B (Fig. 15A), when folded back into the positions A[1] and B[1], would exactly bring the log up to a 1-ft. 6-in. side from end to end. It will be seen, therefore, that an amount of material represented by the shaded portions C and D is left unaccounted for when measuring by quarter-girth ; but, as before stated, except in rare circumstances, this extra material would be no real gain to the buyer.

DISEASES AND DEFECTS OF TIMBER

Decay of timber usually commences with the decomposition of the sap-wood ; this takes place in either *wet rot* or *dry rot*. Wet rot reduces the timber to a snuff-coloured powder. It may occur in the growing tree or when the timber has been placed in positions where it has become saturated with rain. Wet rot is caused most frequently by a fungus which

TIMBER: CONVERSION AND SEASONING

germinates in moist ground around the roots of a tree. This eats into the tree, feeding first on the new tissue of wood, then on the sap in the cells of the rings and medullary rays until the whole is reduced to a soft spongy mass. The rot grows until finally the tree falls because of its undermined foundation. Timber that has been partially destroyed by wet rot can be distinguished by red spots; if the decay is advanced, by dull yellow soft patches with clear white spots having a small black speck in the centre of each.

Dry rot is caused by the growth of fungi, which commences to grow on timber under favourable conditions, germinating and eating into the timber and destroying its constituents. Timbers of buildings are attacked in this way when enclosed without sufficient ventilation, and in a warm, humid atmosphere, especially if any green

Fig. 16.—Cup Shake in Log

sap-wood is left on the timber. When no visible sign of dry rot exists it may be detected by boring into the timber and inspecting the dust. Sometimes dry rot appears only in the form of reddish spots, which upon being scratched show that the fibres beneath have been reduced to powder.

To preserve timber from decay, there are several elaborate but effective methods of impregnating the pores of the wood with chemicals that resist these fungi, exclude moisture, and are proof against the attack of insects; but for general purposes, if the timber is well seasoned and well ventilated, any decay will be prevented. If the timber is exposed to the weather it should be protected by painting; tarring or charring the surface if buried in the ground. Posts should be placed in the ground in an inverted position to which

they grew, so as to oppose the rising of moisture into the cells of the wood.

Dry rot is the worst and most common disease of timber. It very often attacks ground floors, built-in cupboards and other

Fig. 16A.—Cup Shake in Balk

work which is insufficiently ventilated. The remedy is to cut away the diseased parts and replace with well-seasoned timber free from sap-wood and preferably treated with creosote oil. Ventilation should be supplied so that a current of fresh air has access to all sides of the timber.

Good wood should look bright and have a fresh smell. It should be cut from the heart of a sound tree, uniform in substance, straight in fibre, free from large or dead knots. The surface should not be woolly or clog the saw; it should also have a silky lustre when planed.

Sound timber should be sonorous when struck; a dull, heavy sound denotes decay within. The wood should not be water-logged, softened, or discoloured by being floated. Good timber should be free from the following defects:

Cup shakes (Fig. 16), which occur between the annual rings in the spring

Fig. 17.—Heart Shake in Balk Fig. 18.—Star Shake in Balk

wood, due to the inner portion of the tree shrinking from the outer portion. This often occurs in the resinous pine and fir trees, but they are generally very small and not a serious defect. *Heart shakes* (Fig. 17) are splits through the heart of the tree. They are often very small, but sometimes extend right across the tree. They are common with most timbers, but they can be prevented if timber is not allowed to lie too long in the log. *Star shakes* (Fig. 18) are splits radially from the centre of the tree, which sometimes increase in width to the outside. If the log is allowed to get into this state the timber is useless for planks, scantlings, etc.

Upsets (Fig. 19) are caused by the growing tree receiving a blow (say another tree falling against it). *Twisted fibres*, as in Fig. 20, are caused by the wind twisting the tree. Timber with twisted fibres is unfit for good work, as after it has been sawn to shape it has a tendency to

Fig. 19.—Upset

Fig. 20.—Twisted Fibres

twist back again. *Waney edges* are due to the round surface of the trunk being left on the edges of the cut plank, as in Fig. 21. *Foxiness* is a reddish or brownish tint showing that the timber is beginning to decay. *Doatiness* is a speckled stain found chiefly in beech and is a sign of decay. It is caused by unseasoned timber

and by exposure for a long period to a stagnant atmosphere.

The rain may have penetrated a hole or hollow in the bark where a branch has been cut off, or some other cause which has started decay in parts. Even when the general defects are not visible, the

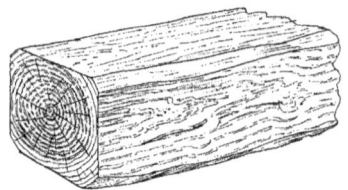

Fig. 21.—Waney Edges

experienced eye can detect the inferiority of the timber by the looseness of fibres, especially on the end grain, which can be verified by testing its lightness in weight.

The following lists comprise the broadleaf woods, which are mostly hard woods, and the conifers approximating the needle-shape leaves, which are generally soft woods :—

BROAD-LEAF WOODS.

Oak	⎫ Medullary	Teak.
Beech	⎬ rays clearly	Satin Walnut.
Sycamore	⎭ visible.	Poplar.
Ash.		Bass.
Elm.		Birch.
Mahogany.		Greenheart.
Black walnut.		

CONIFERS.

White fir or spruce.	Pitch pine.
Red or yellow fir.	Cedar.
American yellow pine.	Larch.

Rasps, Files and Glasspaper

Cutting Action of a File and Rasp.—The action of a rasp or file in removing material is purely one of abrasion. It is argued that strictly speaking its cutting action is that of incision, but if this is so the well-known abrasive action of a grindstone should be included under this head. Rasping and filing is the operation of cutting by the friction between a hard medium with multiple cutting edges and inch so that each tooth has less work to do and hence removes less material.

Fig. 1 shows the teeth formation of both a rasp and file drawn to exaggerated proportions, from which it will be readily manifest how and why a rasp gives a rough and a file a smoother finish. The semi-circular leading face of the rasp tooth gives a greater frictional cohesion between rasp and wood, which explains

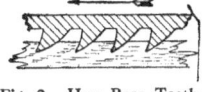

Fig. 2.—How Rasp Teeth Cut

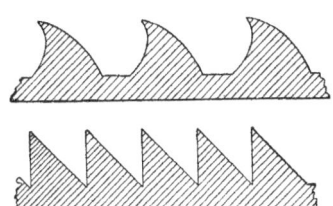

Fig. 1.—Teeth of Rasp and File Respectively

Fig. 3.—How File Teeth Cut

the softer material it is desired to reduce. A rasp is used to remove the greater amount of the irregularities on a surface (its particular sphere of utility will be propounded later), whilst a file is used after the rasping operation for smoothing down the grain and roughness raised by the coarser action of the rasp. In order, therefore, that this result may be effected, a variation in the number as well as the formation of the teeth of a file as compared with a rasp is given to it, the file having a greater number of teeth to the

the resultant coarse yet rapid finish. Fig. 2 shows the rasp, as pressure is applied, taking hold of the material, and Fig. 3 a file under similar conditions. Whereas the cutting or leading face of each rasp tooth offers great resistance to motion by reason of its formation, a file more nearly approaches chisel action, which is responsible for its softer cut.

It must, of course, be understood that a wood file or rasp will not cut metal, as its degree of hardness is much lower than a metal-cutting file.

THE PRACTICAL WOODWORKER

The Manufacture of Files and Rasps.—Files are both hand and machine cut, the hand cut being more expensive but of longer life than the machine cut. As has been previously explained, the formation of the teeth is decided by the purpose for which the file is intended, but in all cases the process of manufacture is the same. Bars of steel, rolled to sizes most appropriate for the size of file being made, are cut into file blanks. "Tanging" is the next operation, consisting of cutting the pointed end on which the handle is driven, and which is effected, as is the following operation of truing by a steam hammer.

The blanks are next annealed in a furnace made for that purpose, remaining therein for about three hours at a temperature of 760° Fahrenheit. The blank is then sufficiently soft to be cut. The brightening or burnishing operation follows, and is effected by either a sandblast, grinder, or (in the case of awkward patterns) by filing. In all files having a flat face the latter has to be machine ground, when the file is ready for cutting.

The file-cutter delivers his blows (made with a 6-lb. hammer) upon a chisel ground to give the desired form to the file teeth (the blank being strapped to a block), at the rate of from 120 to 150 blows per minute; even so, no inaccuracy can be detected either in the depth or angularity of the cut. Sometimes the backs of the teeth are sand-blasted to improve the cutting qualities. The hardening is an interesting process; the file is first dipped into a brewery by-product known as "grounds," which prevents the teeth from oxidising or burning off. After heating it is plunged into a brine bath, which removes any scale formation. After scouring to clean it, the tang is tempered by dipping in a bath of molten lead.

Forms of Rasps and Files and Special Uses.—Rasps as used by the woodworker are usually of the half-round variety with one flat face (Fig. 4), whilst cabinet-makers use a somewhat finer variety, as in Fig. 5. They usually range

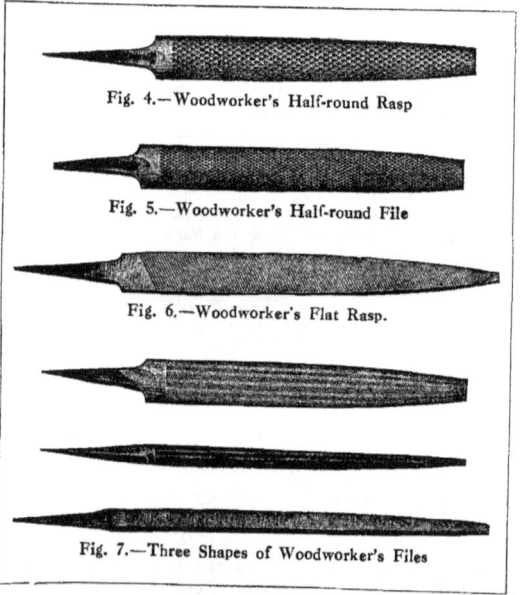

Fig. 4.—Woodworker's Half-round Rasp

Fig. 5.—Woodworker's Half-round File

Fig. 6.—Woodworker's Flat Rasp.

Fig. 7.—Three Shapes of Woodworker's Files

from 6 in. to 14 in. in length, and, as previously stated, are used to remove the greater amount of unevenness—the file afterwards being used to smooth the surface down; but rasps as a general rule are seldom resorted to where a chisel, spokeshave or plane can be used. In fact, rasps are only used to give evenness to curved surfaces and others that are inaccessible to the regular truing tools, as

RASPS, FILES AND GLASSPAPER

it is thereby possible to reduce the "high places" to a common level and also to operate more locally than with a spokeshave, etc. This is especially true when spokeshaving end-grain, where a cutting tool tends to cut in a series of jumps. Rasps may be purchased flat on both sides (Fig. 6), but their utility is not so general as the half-round variety.

Of the files used in woodworking the selection shown in Fig. 7 can be taken as representative; they are square, flat, half-round and round. The difference in the cut of the teeth will be noticed, files being what is known as "cross cut," that is to say, a series of intersecting cuts are made across the file; this eliminates

Fig. 8.—Adjustable Handle for Files and Rasps

Fig. 9.—Riffler

the tendency of single-cut files to follow the path of least resistance, viz. the direction of the cut, the cutting thrust thus being balanced. The round file is chiefly used for cleaning out holes of circular or curved form which are too small to admit a cutting tool, and similarly the square file is brought into use when a small slot or opening has to be cleaned out. Where delicate overlay or fretted work has to be finished a file is invariably used, irrespective of the size of the opening, since the lighter pressure required for filing renders the work less liable to fracture across slender connecting pieces. When end-grain cannot be satisfactorily smoothed by plane or chisel, filing is often resorted to to give a finished appearance; but generally speaking a filed surface lacks the smoothness of a planed one.

In carved or sunk work the riffler file is brought into use (see Fig. 9); this has its ends upturned to enable the pressure from the hand to be applied from a higher plane than that on which it is desired to operate. One end is rasp cut and the other file cut. Experience decides exactly where a file may be used—to use one where a cutting tool may be used is regarded with disfavour in the woodworking trades.

In the making of cutters for moulding planes and machines, the filing flush of nail heads, the removal of burrs, etc., which are jobs frequently falling to the lot of the woodworker, metalworker's files must of necessity be used. It is wise to select those which will cover the greatest range of work, as the infrequency with which they are used does not warrant the carrying of a full range. The "three-square" file for saw sharpening, and which has been referred to in an earlier chapter, should, of course, form part of those chosen. Plane irons, chisels, etc., are seldom made of solid steel, but have a thin steel face forming the cutting edge autogenously welded to a softer body. It saves considerable time when the chisel or plane iron requires grinding to "relieve" the softer portion with a file, leaving only the hardened cutting edge to be ground and the filed portion to be just levelled by the grindstone. An adjustable file handle (Fig. 8) which will take a variety of tangs is a useful acquisition.

Glasspaper, Sandpaper, Agate Paper, etc.—Glasspaper, sandpaper, etc., are further abrasive agents used in connection with the finishing of woodwork, but to a greater and more general extent than rasps and files. Glasspaper consists of particles of crushed glass secured to the paper by an adhesive. The crushed glass is passed through a series of screens or sieves, the various sizes of the particles thus being classified and used to form the various grades of paper. The powdered glass is shaken over the paper (which has previously been covered with glue) by means of a sieve, any superfluous powder being afterwards shaken off. Sandpaper and emery cloth are manufactured in a similar manner, differing only in the fact that sand or emery is used in place of glass powder. Different makers adopt different methods of classifying glasspaper, but the most general scheme (from fine upwards) is 0, 1, 1½, F2, M2, S2, 2½, 3, the letters F, M, and S standing for fine, medium, and coarse in that particular grade. A fine grade, known as "flour" (owing to its fine cutting grains), is used when a fine surface is required. Glasspaper (erroneously termed "sandpaper" by many) is by far most generally used, sandpaper being almost unobtainable; glasspaper has the better cutting qualities of the two, which probably accounts for this. The M2 and 1½ sizes are commonly used, roughing down with the coarser and finishing with the finer size.

The main use of glasspaper is to prepare a smooth surface to receive the finishing agent, which will be either polish, paint or varnish. Unless the surface were so prepared tool marks made by the plane, hammer, etc., would show through and mar the finished appearance. After the first coat of paint or varnish is applied (if this form of finish has been chosen), glasspaper is again used to remove finally the grain raised by the brush and the swelling of the grain. As each succeeding coat of paint is applied the grade of glasspaper used should be proportionately finer, until by the time the last coat is applied the surface has become so smooth that no further abrasions is necessary. While glasspaper will effectually obliterate tool marks, it should not be used to remove a great amount of material—its function is merely to remove that small portion which the ordinary cutting tool is not sufficiently sensitive to remove.

Using Glasspaper.—In order to obtain the greatest possible service from glass-

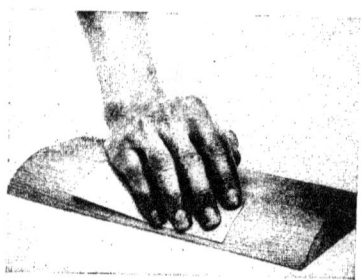

Fig. 11.—Glasspapering Convex Surface

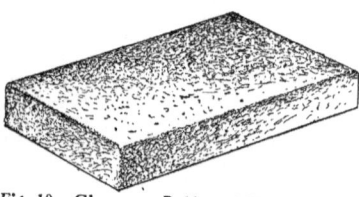

Fig. 10.—Glasspaper Rubber of Wood or Cork

paper it should almost always be wrapped round a wooden block. This prevents the paper "cockling" and so cracking off the cutting particles. Moreover, the pressure from the hand is more evenly distributed and covers a wider area than when used without a block, with consequent less exertion to surface the wood.

The simplest rubber is the ordinary rectangular block (Fig. 10) of either wood or cork, round which the paper is wrapped; its usual size is in the neighbourhood of

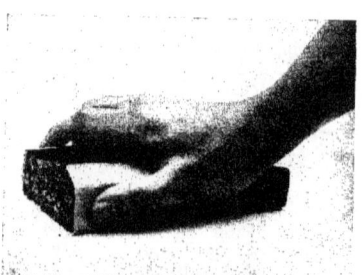

Fig. 12.—Glasspaper Rubber in Use

5 in. by 3 in. and 1 in. to 1½ in. thick. Sometimes a wooden block with a linoleum pad (Fig. 13) glued on the bottom is used. It is used in line with the grain

of the wood except in certain circumstances when it may be used across grain; in the latter case the marks of the glasspaper are much more noticeable. Patternmakers frequently surface their woodwork by rubbing first across grain, and finally with the grain. For work that is to be painted the wood may be papered at an angle of 45° across grain. The sharp edge on a piece of woodwork should be preserved and not rounded by the glasspaper.

Sometimes when mouldings have to be glasspapered a rubber of wedge formation (Fig. 14) is used to work into the inner angles, while curved moulding surfaces should have a rubber made to the proper contour. For an elaborate moulding a number of rubbers to fit the various "members" may be used. Convex edges (Fig. 11) may be glasspapered without a rubber by using the hand as shown.

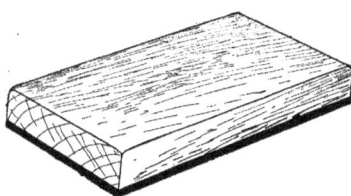

Fig. 13.—Glasspaper Rubber Soled with Linoleum

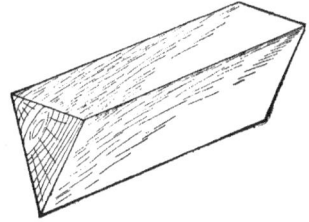

Fig. 14.—Wedge-shaped Glasspaper Rubber

There are many mechanical devices for glasspapering, such as revolving endless belts with glasspapered surface, glasspapering machines (consisting of a revolving wooden disc covered with glasspaper), and also glasspapering devices that may be used in the lathe; these will be dealt with in a later chapter.

Making Mouldings

It is often necessary to work mouldings by hand to match others already in use, or to avoid stock patterns; and as such should be worked very exact to design, they must be done systematically, or the result is a failure, and it must be admitted that the result in the majority of cases is nothing else.

In the first place, the wood from which the moulding is to be worked must be planed up properly. That is, it must be faced up truly, squared, and gauged to width and thickness just as carefully as though it was to be used for high-class joinery. On each end of the wood a true dotted line; but a better way is to plough a series of grooves, as in Fig. 2, taking them quite down to the marks, so that they will form guides as to the depth of the various hollows, etc. The next proceeding should be to take off the surplus wood in the form of chamfers, bringing it to the section shown in Fig. 3, after which a very little work with hollows and rounds will bring it to the section required, and it will be the same throughout—a very important point and one not often attained.

The accompanying photographs (Figs. 7 to 9) show these several stages in the

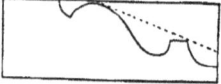

Fig. 1.—Section of Moulding to be Worked

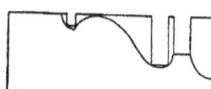

Fig. 2.—First Stage of Working

Fig. 3.—Second Stage of Working

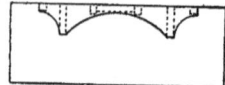

Fig. 4.

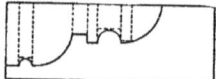

Fig. 5.

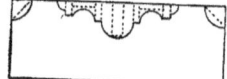

Fig. 6.

Figs. 4 to 6.—Sections of Other Mouldings; Dotted Lines indicate How the Mouldings are Worked

section of the required moulding must be marked, as shown in Fig. 1. After this is done, the usual procedure is to chamfer off the waste wood, as shown by working of an actual piece of moulding made to the section for the purpose of this article, the time taken being half an hour.

MAKING MOULDINGS

To ensure success, each operation should be taken down to the mark at once; the temptation to leave a little piece on for finishing must be resisted, as it only means extra work and less satisfaction in the end.

Figs. 4, 5, and 6 show three other sections of moulding, the dotted lines showing where the necessary grooves have to be made to ensure successful work.

Curved mouldings can be worked by hand as easily as the straight; but as planes cannot be used for these, a somewhat different procedure is necessary and this is where a scratch-tool is sometimes used.

The working of curved mouldings differs from the straight ones here described, in that it is impossible to use the plough

Fig. 7.—First Stage of Moulding

and rebate plane to remove the surplus wood, and it is here that the scratch-tool is found useful. The better way in making a curved moulding of any description, whether curved on plan or in elevation, or both, is to work on the woodcarving principle, that is, correctly to mark out the shape and pattern of the moulding and to cut down to the lines direct, and to clear away the surplus wood with sharp chisels and gouges. By working on this principle the wood is cut cleanly, and all that has to be done to get a smooth finish afterwards is to paper off the tool marks, which, if the tools are sharp and in capable hands, will be easily accomplished.

Fig. 10 shows a short piece of wood curved on plan, with the section of the required moulding marked on the end.

Three parallel lines are also shown on the flat surface to serve as guides in what may be called outlining the moulding.

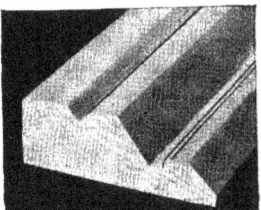

Fig. 8.—Second Stage of Moulding

Two of these lines are guides in forming the quirk of the moulding, while the other, in conjunction with one on the curved edge, forms the guide in cutting out the square portion shown white.

Fig. 11 shows the roughing out as done, the double chamfer being cut down exactly to the mark, forming a parallel vee of equal depth throughout, and the rectangular portion cut away so as to leave a level surface for the flat member of the moulding as shown. In Fig. 12 the corner of the before-mentioned square is bevelled off down to the shape line, and the double chamfer altered into a hollow at one side and a round at the other, the two meeting in a sharp quirk at the bottom.

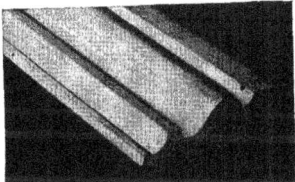

Fig. 9.—Finished Moulding

The extreme corner of the flat is also chamfered off down to the lines as a preliminary operation to forming the hollow at the thin edge of the moulding.

The hollow portion of the ogee has now to be formed with the gouge, also the hollow at the edge of the moulding, and the

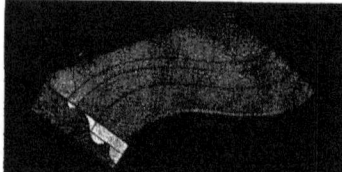

Fig. 10.—Wood for Curved Moulding, Shaped and Gauged

sharp corners on the round part of the ogee removed with a sharp chisel, when the moulding will have the appearance of Fig. 13. The finishing is done with glasspaper of not too coarse a grade, using shaped blocks, and taking particular care not to rub off the sharp corners. Providing that the shaping has been done carefully, and sharp tools used, very little papering is needed; and if care has been taken to cut to the marks and not beyond them, also to keep to the correct depths, the moulding will be found to be very even in section throughout.

Should there be small sunk members in the moulding to be worked, they should be cut down as evenly as possible, shaping the sides to the correct outline, and then to get the depth right with a level surface on the sunk portion, an improvised router

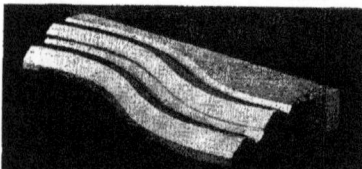

Fig. 12.—Corners Chamfered Off and Hollows Roughly Cut Out

may be formed by passing a small chisel of the required width through a piece of wood, allowing it to project to the required depth, so as to scrape the sunk part level and smooth at the same time. If the chisel is sharp and care is taken in using it, the part will be left as smooth as though it is planed.

At all times the material for mouldings which have to be worked by hand, especially curved ones, must be of good quality, perfectly dry and seasoned, free from sapwood, knots or shakes. If these points are looked after, careful work will do the rest.

On no account should the work be left a little away from the mark at first to allow for finishing. This means failure or a great deal more work to make a good job. Each successive operation must go down to the mark at once, and then the

Fig. 11.—Wood Roughed Out and Small Flat Member Formed

finished article will be of correct section, and if it has to intersect with other mouldings will require no cleaning off at the joint. If this latter is needed to any great extent, good work is impossible.

The Stanley "Universal" plane is very useful for making moulding by hand. This plane is fully dealt with in the next chapter, while machines for moulding will find a place in a much later section.

Developing Shape of a Moulding Iron.— Let the shaded part of Fig. 14 represent the moulding to be worked. It will be obvious that a plane cutter made exactly as a counter-part of the moulding outline would not cut a correct replica of it, because the inclination or pitch angle of the iron would cause it to lose

MAKING MOULDINGS

its dimensions, and the depth of the moulding would be shallower and the curve also flatter than the given section.

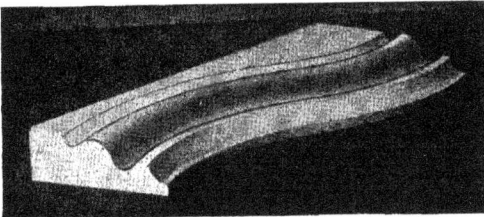

Fig. 13.—All Hollows Formed and Mouldings Shaped Generally, Ready for Finishing

A simple experiment to substantiate this can be made. Drill a 1-in. hole in a piece of wood, and cut a 1-in. round rod to slide freely in it. Now cut the end of the rod obliquely on one end to an angle of 45° to the rod axis. The shape of this oblique end, it will be seen, is elliptical, yet every point on its circumference will touch the inside of the hole into which the rod fits. If the oblique end of the rod is imagined to be a flat plane-iron shaped similar to the oblique end (elliptical, it will be readily seen that in order to shape a circular groove with an inclined iron, the latter must be proportionately *longer* in form length.

To develop the form of the cutter, first draw the moulding section to full scale, and erect a line vertically X Y, just touching the extreme edge of the moulding. At right angles to this draw the line A B, intersecting X Y at O. From this latter point draw in the pitch of the moulding iron (this must be measured with a bevel protractor from the iron-seating in the mouth of the plane).

Now, from a convenient number of points along the curve of the moulding erect vertical lines, which are continued down until they cut the moulding-iron pitch line. With O as centre project these points with the compasses until they cut the line A B, and from the intersecting points on A B erect vertical lines.

Next transfer the points on the contour of the moulding obtained by the erection of the vertical lines cutting the pitch line, and the intersection of these with the vertical lines erected from O B gives the corresponding points of the iron. A curve drawn passing through these points gives the required shape.

It will be clearly noticed that the iron is the complementary or opposite curve of the moulding; it is obvious that the hollows in the moulding must be cut by a "round" in the iron. It should further be seen to that ordinates are erected from depth points, as L and M, for reasons previously stated.

In ordinary circumstances the pitch angle is about 45°, but for hard wood it is

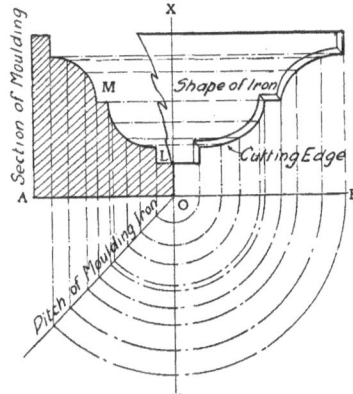

Fig. 14.—Obtaining Shape of Plane-Iron to Make a Given Moulding

recommended to be flatter or less than this, the angle decreasing as the wood increases in hardness.

The Stanley "Fifty-Five" Plane

THE Stanley "55" Plane (Fig. 1) sometimes called the Stanley Universal Plane, is a combined plough, matching, rebating, slitting, and moulding plane. Fifty-two cutters are supplied with the plane, and a further forty-one cutters may be obtained from stock. The plane is mostly made of nickel-plated metal except the handle and fences, which are of rosewood.

Parts of the Plane.—A view of the plane is shown in Fig. 1A, the important parts being designated by letters.

The Main Stock carries the cutter, cutter adjustment and cutter bolt, slitting tool, depth gauge and handle, and provides a bearing for one side of the cutter. The Sliding Section has an adjustable steel runner and gives a bearing for the other side of the cutter. It slides on the arms secured in the main stock. The adjustable runner can be raised or lowered so that cutters can be used having one side higher or lower than the side in the main stock. To form an additional bearing the Auxiliary Centre Bottom is used in connection with irregular shaped cutters, and also as a depth gauge for the matching cutters. It can be adjusted for width or depth, and when required should be attached to the sliding section.

The **Fences** can be used on either side of the plane and the rosewood faces tilted to any desirable angle up to 45

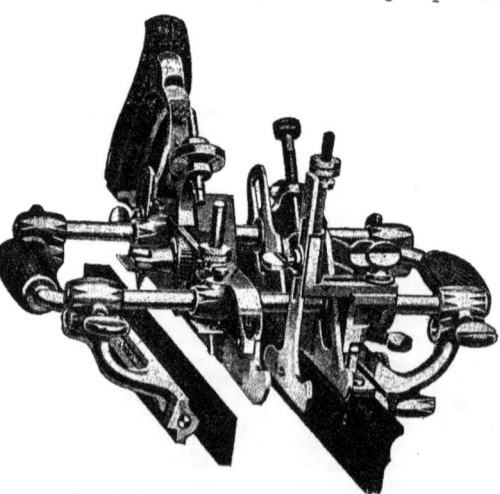

Fig. 1.—The Stanley "55" Universal Plane

degrees. The fence to the right may be regulated by the screw for extra fine adjustment. The other fence is machined on the outside, so that when reversed it gives an extended reach for centre beading

THE STANLEY "FIFTY-FIVE" PLANE

wide boards. **Arms** are used to carry the fences and sliding section at the position desired. Two sets of arms (one 8½ and one 4½ inches long) are provided with each plane.

A **Cam Rest** can be fastened on either the front or back arm between the sliding section and the right-hand fence, and acts as a rest when the fences are wide apart as in centre beading. When the auxiliary centre bottom is in use, the cam rest provides additional support when required and should be placed on the rear arm.

The Fences.—The fences are of metal with adjustable rosewood faces attached to form the bearing surfaces, and are used to guide the plane along the work. The plane should stand at an exact right angle to the edge of the work as in Fig. 2. To ensure this the rosewood faces must be adjusted to come parallel with the *side* of the cutter.

If the plane is tipped as shown in Fig. 3 the groove will work away from the fence as it goes deeper, and owing to the wood acting as a wedge between the cutter and the fence, the plane will bind. If tipped as shown in Fig. 4 the groove will work towards the fence as it goes deeper, thus forcing the fence away from the wood. The grooves made are indicated by the dotted lines in the two figures, and show that good work is impossible under these conditions.

The rosewood faces are attached to the metal fences by means of two machine screws, consequently any slight variation from a right angle can be readily overcome by simply loosening these screws and changing the angle of the faces—taking care to see that the screws are tightened when the faces are properly adjusted. Special forms can be attached to the rosewood faces if desired.

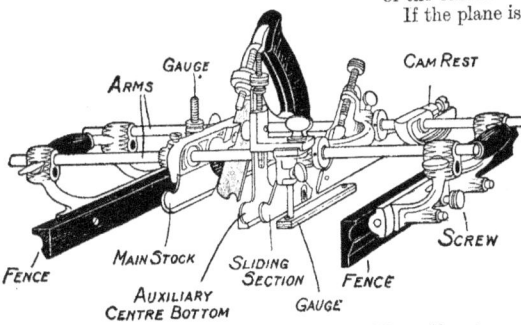

Fig. 1A.—Stanley "55" Plane with Chief Parts Named

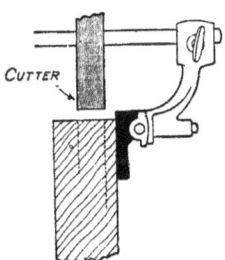

Fig. 2.—Plane Correctly Held at Right Angles to Work

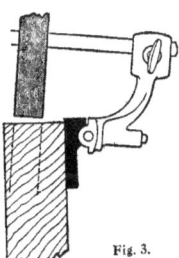

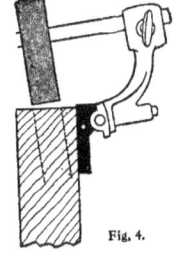

Figs. 3 and 4.—How Incorrect Holding (Tipping) of the Plane Causes Grooves to be on the Slant

The fences are provided with upper and lower arm-holes. The upper holes allow the fences to slide under the cutter to regulate the width of cut required—as in rebating. The lower holes can be used where the work is such as to require a narrow fence.

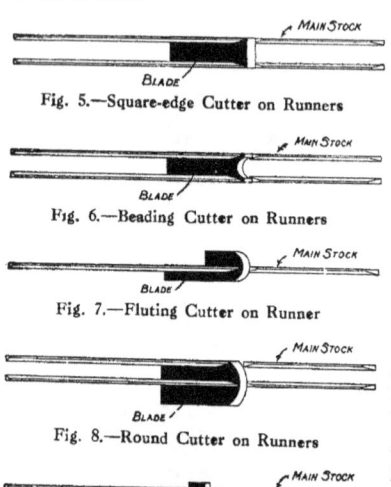

Fig. 5.—Square-edge Cutter on Runners

Fig. 6.—Beading Cutter on Runners

Fig. 7.—Fluting Cutter on Runner

Fig. 8.—Round Cutter on Runners

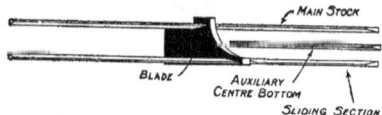

Fig. 9.—Ogee Cutter on Runners

It is advisable to use both fences where possible, as by so doing the plane may be kept true to the work with slight effort. Where only one fence is in use, care should be taken to see that it is kept close up to the edge of the stuff being worked.

The Runners.—These are thin plates of steel attached to the main stock and the sliding section, and are used to form the bearings for the cutter. For the purpose of illustrating their proper position when in use, bottom views of these runners set to use cutters of various forms are shown.

When a square edge cutter or beading cutter (Figs. 5 and 6) is used, the main stock and sliding section runners are both required. With the fluting cutter (Fig. 7) the main stock runner only is needed, the cutter being recessed on one side so that the runner will come to its highest point. In using a round cutter (Fig. 8) both main stock and sliding section runners are required, the sliding section being set to the centre of the cutter and its adjustable runner set to govern the thickness of shaving to be removed. The auxiliary centre bottom is not required for the cutters shown in Figs. 5 to 8.

With an "Ogee," or any cutter that has an irregular cutting edge, with one side extending below the other (Fig. 9), the auxiliary centre bottom should be used to form an additional support. This auxiliary centre bottom can be readily adjusted sidewise by means of the angle iron to which it is attached, and for depth by the adjusting nut on its stem. Where the bearing surface for the auxiliary centre bottom is ¼ in. or more in width an additional support called a sole plate is furnished, to be attached to the bottom of same.

Cutters and Depth Gauges.—Near the upper end of each cutter a slot or hole is made to engage with a pin located near the end of the adjusting screw on the main stock.

The proper way to set the cutter is as follows: First—Loosen the cutter clamp (Fig. 10) and place cutter in position with slot on pin. Adjust by means of

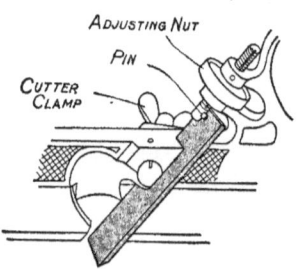

Fig. 10.—Setting a Cutter

adjusting nut, and tighten cutter clamp, then bring up the sliding section and secure it as required.

Care should be used in adjusting the sliding section where the cutter is to be

THE STANLEY "FIFTY-FIVE" PLANE

used its full width, to see that the side of the cutter extends beyond the runner only enough to give clearance (Fig. 11).

Fig. 11.—Setting Cutter to give Clearance

Fig. 12.—Cutter Set to give Excessive Clearance

The channel in which the cutter rests in the main stock regulates this on the right-hand side.

If too much clearance is given (Fig. 12) through allowing the sides of the cutter to project too far beyond the sliding section runner the cutter will scrape the sides of the groove, making a rough uneven cut, as well as causing the plane to

shown in Fig. 14, setting gauge F on main stock first and then gauge J on sliding section. Gauge F should always be clamped with the slotted screw to lock it securely in position.

How to Hold the Plane.—One of the most important points to be observed for the successful working of the plane is the way in which it is held, and the following explanation will enable the user to understand the best way in which this may be done.

As the plane is held in both hands (Fig. 15), the tendency with the beginner is to push as much with the left hand as with the right, the result being that the plane will be drawn over to the left away from the stock, making good work impossible.

The plane should be pushed forward with the right hand only, the left hand being used to keep it steady and hold the fence up to the work. The palm of the left hand should rest on the fence handle, the thumb passing over and resting on the front arm—the fingers being against

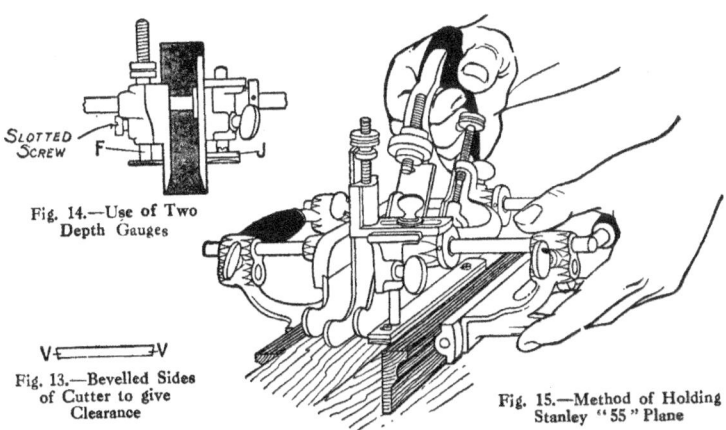

Fig. 14.—Use of Two Depth Gauges

Fig. 13.—Bevelled Sides of Cutter to give Clearance

Fig. 15.—Method of Holding Stanley "55" Plane

work hard. The sides V (Fig. 13) of the cutter are given only a slight bevel, which is for clearance only and not for cutting.

As a rule it is best whenever possible to make use of both depth gauges as

the lower part of the fence. The natural tendency of the hand when holding the plane in this way is to guide it correctly.

The directions already given in regard to setting the different parts and the various adjustments of the plane will apply for all kinds of work that it may be used for.

Rebating.—For this work insert a cutter of greater width than width of

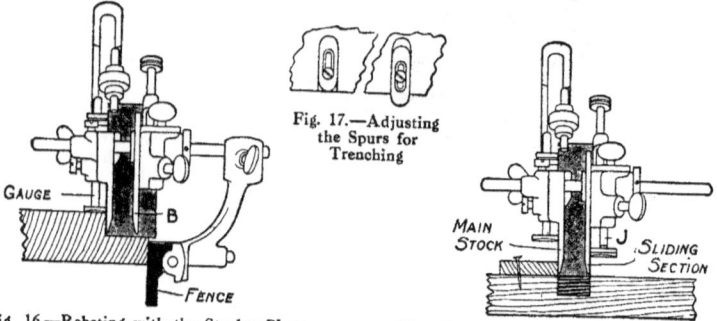

Fig. 17.—Adjusting the Spurs for Trenching

Fig. 16.—Rebating with the Stanley Plane

Fig. 18.—Trenching with the Stanley Plane

rebate wanted and move sliding section B to about ¼ in. inside the outer edge of rebate as an extra support. This will bring the sliding section inside the edge of the cutter.

Now attach the fence, putting same on the arms through the upper holes so that it will slide under the cutter the required distance to give the width of rebate wanted (Fig. 16). The depth gauge regulates the depth of the rebate.

Trenching.—As the plane has to work across the grain in trenching, "spurs" are necessary in front of the sides of the cutter to score the wood and thus prevent the tearing of the stock. These spurs are set in the sides of the main stock and sliding section.

Loosen the screws, securing the spurs so that they will drop into position (Fig. 17) with cutting edges extended beyond the runners fully the thickness of shaving to be removed, and tighten screws. Insert a plough cutter of the same width as width of trench wanted, and move sliding section up to cutter until spur is in line with its outer side. When so located there will be no danger of the cutter tearing the side of the groove.

Insert depth gauge J in sliding section,

as shown in Fig. 18, and set it to regulate the depth of trench.

Nail a strip of wood on the board in which the trench it to be cut to guide the plane. The fences of the plane are not used, and should be removed unless the trench can be worked from the edge of the board.

Ploughing.—When used as a plough, set the sliding section runner as described on page 206. The width of grooves are in no way confined to the width of the cutters supplied, as it is possible to make a groove

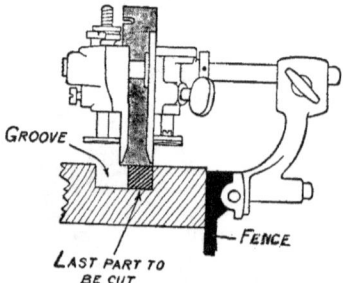

Fig. 19.—Ploughing with the Stanley Plane

of any width by working it twice or more, one cut running into the other. In making these extra wide grooves it is necessary that the fence should first be set to work to the side of the groove which

THE STANLEY "FIFTY-FIVE" PLANE

is farthest from the edge of the wood against which this fence is to bear (Fig. 19). If this is not done there will be difficulty in keeping the fence up to the

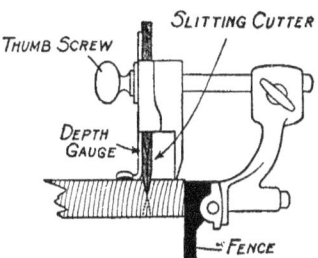

Fig. 20.—Slitting with the Stanley Plane

wood when running the second part of the groove.

It is also best to use a cutter of comparatively narrow width when making extra wide grooves, instead of a cutter nearest to the width of the finished groove, as in making the last cut the cutter has a tendency to "run off" where there is only a narrow strip left to be taken from

Slitting.—(See Fig. 20.) For cutting strips from thin boards a cutter is provided which will perform the work more rapidly than if a saw were used. The slitting cutter is inserted in a slot on the right side of the main stock just forward of the handle. The depth gauge is placed over the blade and both cutter and gauge fastened by the thumb-screw. The fence gauges the distance of the cut from the edge of the board.

Thicker boards can be cut by first running the cutter partly through on one side, reversing the timber, and completing the cut on the other side.

Matching.—To make a tongue on boards of any thickness from $\frac{3}{4}$ in. to $1\frac{1}{4}$ in., a tonguing tool or cutter is provided.

This cutter is recessed on one side so that if used on either a thin or thick board the runners may still be kept on the wood when regulating position of tongue (Fig. 21).

The auxiliary centre bottom C is used as a depth gauge to regulate the height of tongue. The position of the tongue is regulated by the fence.

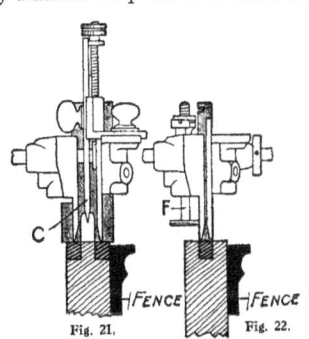

Figs. 21 and 22.—Matching (Tonguing-and-grooving) with the Stanley Plane

the side of the groove. The two depth gauges should be used in work of this kind, or the bottom of the groove may finish unevenly unless more than ordinary care be taken.

14—N.E.

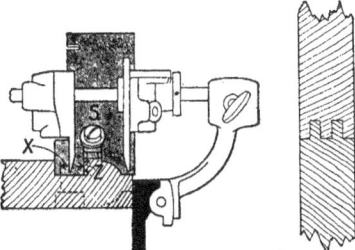

Fig. 24.—Sash-moulding with the Stanley Plane

Fig. 23.—Section of Double-tongued Joint

To make the groove use the $\frac{1}{4}$ in. plough cutter. The fence regulates the distance of groove from face of board and gauge F the depth (Fig. 22).

If double-tongued joints are wanted, as in Fig. 23, they may easily be worked by using plough cutters to make both members.

Sash Moulding.—For this work a cutter of a design known as "Ovolo" is provided which carries its own depth gauge s, secured in the required position by means of a set screw on the gauge (Fig. 24).

The moulding can be worked on a strip of wood of the necessary width and thickness by cutting one side first, then reversing the strip and repeating the operation on the other side. When worked in this way the depth x of the rebate of the moulding is regulated by the fence and the width z by the gauge s on the cutter. The other portions of the moulding are fixed by the shape of the cutter.

A more satisfactory way, especially for ease in holding the timber, is to work the moulding on the two sides of a board of suitable thickness. The depth x will here be obtained by cutting off with a slitting cutter or saw.

Beading.—Fig. 25 is an illustration of the plane with a beading cutter inserted, and the fence properly set for the working of an ordinary bead.

To cut a bead on the edge of a board, bring up the sliding section so that the bevel of the runner will allow the cutter to take off a shaving of the same thickness as that on the side in main stock (Fig. 26). This bevel will allow only the thinnest shaving possible to be taken off by the part of the cutter forming the quirk.

The fence must be set so that it comes exactly to the inner point of the cutter, as shown in Fig. 25. This will bring the outside face of the bead to the edge of the board. Set the depth gauge on the main stock so as to allow the bead to be worked down to the proper depth below the surface of the wood.

It is always advisable when working beads and similar mouldings to finish them well below the surface of the wood, so that any subsequent cleaning off the surface will not change their form (Fig. 27).

The bead should appear in section as

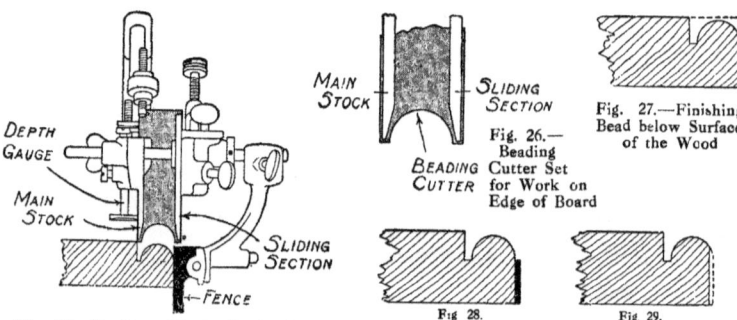

Fig. 25.—Beading with the Stanley Plane

Fig. 26.—Beading Cutter Set for Work on Edge of Board

Fig. 27.—Finishing Bead below Surface of the Wood

Figs. 28 and 29.—Badly-formed Beads

Fig. 27, the round gradually merging into the straight without a break.

The first attempt may result in a bead, as shown in Fig. 28, necessitating the planing off of the edge (see dark line) to form a perfect bead; or worse still, as in Fig. 29, which cannot be made into a properly shaped bead. The fault in the first instance is caused through the fence not being brought up to the point of the cutter; in the second instance through its being set inside the point of the cutter.

Fig. 30 shows the section of a centre bead. It can be worked at any required distance up to eight inches from the edge of the board by using the longer set of arms regularly furnished with the plane and reversing the fence. Extra long arms can be furnished on special order which will permit of a bead being

THE STANLEY "FIFTY-FIVE" PLANE

worked at even a greater distance than eight inches from the edge of the board.

When making a bead near the edge of a board the cam rest is not necessary, but when beads are made at any distance from the edge it will be found convenient and of great assistance, as it will tend to prevent the fence from sagging. It should be placed on the front arm.

Fig. 31 is a section of *reeds* worked in the same way as the bead in Fig. 30 by using the reeding cutters for small sizes, and by working a series of centre beads for larger sizes. When working centre beads, the bead which will be farthest from the edge against which the fence bears should be worked first. If this is not done there will be difficulty in working the succeeding beads so that they will properly connect with those first made.

Fig. 32 shows a section of the "Torus" bead. This is easily worked by first forming the centre bead at the required distance from the edge of the board, and working the square or quirk with one of the narrow plough cutters. This cutter should always be the full width of the square, so that no further work is needed to level it down. A section of the plane as set to work the square is shown in Fig. 33.

The working of a return bead (Fig. 34) of a good shape is often a puzzle with the ordinary wooden bead planes. With the "55" the bead is first made on the edge of the board (Fig. 35) so that a small quirk is left on the face side, as shown in Fig. 35A. The bead is then finished by setting the plane with the depth gauge so adjusted as to exactly take off this superfluous quirk on the face side and no more (Fig. 36). This will come easily, as the first part of the bead is worked true from the face side, and the depth gauge will regulate the other part from the same surface.

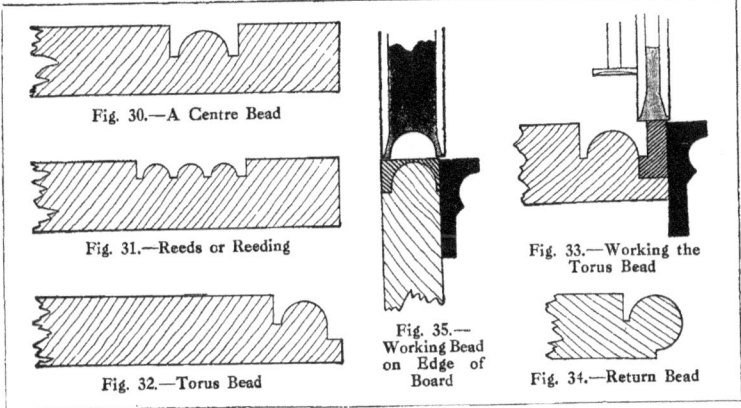

Fig. 30.—A Centre Bead

Fig. 31.—Reeds or Reeding

Fig. 32.—Torus Bead

Fig. 33.—Working the Torus Bead

Fig. 35.—Working Bead on Edge of Board

Fig. 34.—Return Bead

Figs. 37 and 38 show sections of small mouldings which can be worked on the edges of boards of suitable thickness and then cut off to the thickness required, as shown by dotted lines. Fig. 39 shows how to make round rods of any size by working a bead from both sides of a board. If the board is of the right thickness and the depth gauge set correctly, the rods come off so as to require very little finishing.

In beading matched boards (Fig. 40) the ordinary fence cannot be used as the tongue is not always of the same width. Instead use the gauge, placing same in the socket on the front of the sliding section. The adjustable bottom on this gauge can be moved under the sliding section runner, thus bringing the bead to the edge of the board if no quirk is desired. In either case it gauges on the edge of the work, above the tongue.

Chamfers.—For working a right-angle chamfer (Fig. 41) both fences are used, the wood faces being set at right angles to each other, or forty-five degrees with the cutting edge of the cutter.

and give the advantage of the fine adjustment on the fence used as a gauge. Fig. 41 shows plane assembled this way.

The width of the cutter should be a little more than the width of the chamfer. Bring the auxiliary centre bottom near the centre of the cutter and set the sliding section so as to form a bearing for the

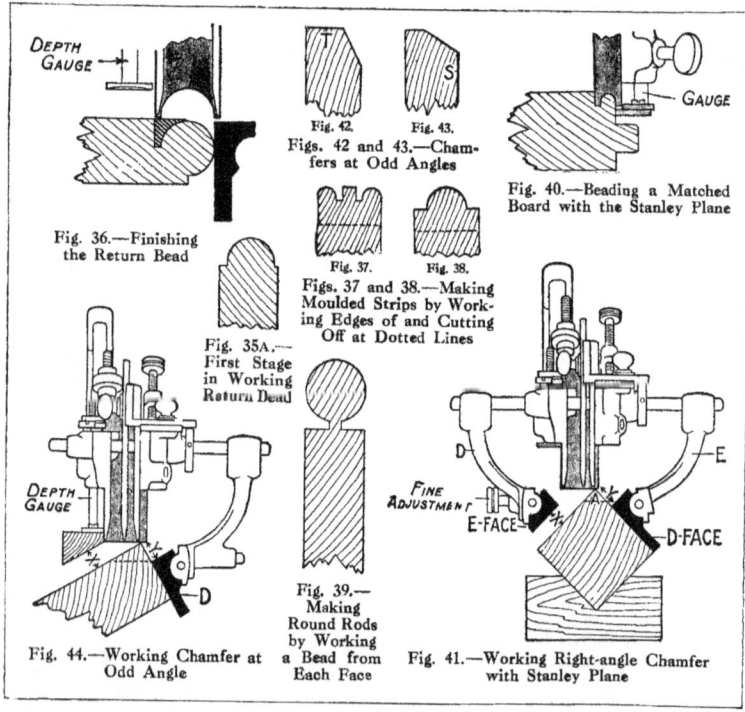

Fig. 36.—Finishing the Return Bead

Figs. 42 and 43.—Chamfers at Odd Angles

Fig. 40.—Beading a Matched Board with the Stanley Plane

Figs. 37 and 38.—Making Moulded Strips by Working Edges of and Cutting Off at Dotted Lines

Fig. 35A.—First Stage in Working Return Bead

Fig. 39.—Making Round Rods by Working a Bead from Each Face

Fig. 44.—Working Chamfer at Odd Angle

Fig. 41.—Working Right-angle Chamfer with Stanley Plane

first cut, locating it just inside the corner of the wood A. For width of chamfer set the fence so that the distance (x) from the fence to the work will be the same as the distance (y) from the corner of the work to the finished chamfer.

Where a number of right-angle chamfers of the same size are to be made it will be of advantage to change the rosewood faces on the fences, and to change the fences, putting D on the right-hand side of the plane and E on the left. This will bring the wide face on the bearing side

For making a chamfer at an odd angle the fences are used as regularly assembled (Fig. 1A, page 205). Set the rosewood face

THE STANLEY "FIFTY-FIVE" PLANE

on fence D to the angle required for the bevel of the chamfer (Fig. 44). Work from the edge T of boards for chamfer as in Fig. 42, and from the side (S) for chamfer as in Fig. 43. While fence E can be used to gauge the width of chamfer, better results will be obtained by using the depth gauge, attaching a wood face of proper shape to the bottom of same, as shown in Fig. 44.

Moulded Chamfers.—Arrange the plane as shown in Fig. 45, the two fences forming the bottom support and being in contact with the work at all times.

The patterns of mouldings shown in Figs. 46 to 49 can be easily worked in this way by inserting suitable cutters, all being done at one working, except Fig. 49, which is done in two.

For stop chamfering (Fig. 50), nail stops on work against which the runners will strike, thus governing the point where chamfer is to begin and end. The plane should be set and worked as for moulded chamfers (Fig. 45), using a straight cutter a little wider than the width of chamfer desired.

In working chamfers, either plain or

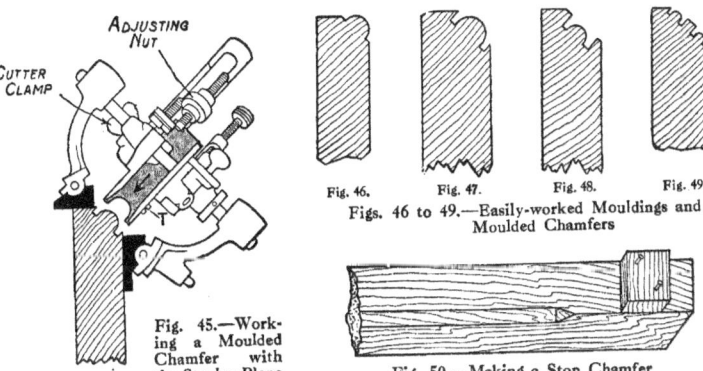

Fig. 46. Fig. 47. Fig. 48. Fig. 49.
Figs. 46 to 49.—Easily-worked Mouldings and Moulded Chamfers

Fig. 45.—Working a Moulded Chamfer with the Stanley Plane

Fig. 50.—Making a Stop Chamfer

Slightly lossen the cutter clamp and draw back the cutter before starting the work.

It is necessary as the work progresses to feed down the cutter, as the moulding is made on the face of the chamfer. This can be done by slightly turning the adjusting nut between each shaving. If the fence were used as a gauge the cutter would move parallel with the face of the stock and the form of the moulding be entirely lost.

It is also necessary to give the cutter an extra support on the sliding section to prevent it working to one side. This is done by putting screw T in the sliding section runner, bringing the head close up to the cutter. This screw will be found in the main stock below the back handle.

moulded, it is best to support the wood in notched blocks whenever possible (Fig. 41). This permits of the plane being held in a horizontal position.

Hollows and Rounds.—In working *convex* mouldings or rounds the main stock and sliding section runners should be at the extreme points of the cutter (Fig. 51), when they will gauge correctly the thickness of the shaving to be taken off. In working *concave* mouldings or hollows, set the adjustable runner on the sliding section to form a bearing for the cutter at its lowest point, as in Fig. 52.

Thumb mouldings can be worked with the hollow and round cutters when curves having a rather large radius are desired. Mouldings having curves of smaller radius can be worked to better advantage with the fluting and beading cutters. First, cut the hollow on the face of the board (Fig. 53); second, form the round on the edge of the board (Fig. 54). The auxiliary

Fig. 51.   Fig. 52.
Figs. 51 and 52.—Setting Cutter for Convex and Concave Mouldings respectively

Fig. 54.—Second Stage in Working Thumb Moulding

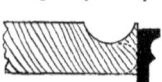 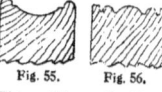

Fig. 53.—First Stage in Working Thumb Moulding

Figs. 55 and 56.—Mouldings Worked with Hollows, Rounds and Beading Cutters

centre bottom should be used in finishing the round or bead.

The two mouldings shown in Figs. 55 and 56 are worked with the hollow and round cutters and beading cutters. In working mouldings such as Fig. 57, the depth gauges and fence can be readily set so as to bring the concave and convex parts of the moulding together, and the correct section accurately obtained.

The mouldings shown in Figs. 58 and 59 are worked from both edges of the board, being careful to work the member farthest from the edge first. In Fig. 60 the face of the moulding must first be worked to the required curve, but not to a fine finish, and then the rounds worked, as in Figs. 58 and 59, changing the wood face on the fence to the proper angle. Fig. 61 can be worked by using one of the fluting cutters; and Fig. 62 is simply a repetition of Fig. 60 in reverse order, worked in the same way.

Mouldings.—In working all mouldings it is of the utmost importance that the fence be kept firmly to the wood, but particularly so in working quarter hollows (Fig. 63), owing to the tendency of the cutter to force the fence away from the wood, due to the fact that the runners come partly on the curve of the moulding. In mouldings of these forms the auxiliary centre bottom can be used to advantage as an additional support, especially on large mouldings.

With reasonable care, and setting the cutter so that it only takes off a thin shaving, one will find little if any difficulty in forming perfect mouldings. By setting the fence so as to leave a narrow strip of wood between the fence and the cutter, as shown in diagram of Roman ogee (Fig. 64), the plane will be much more easily held up to the work. Having completed the moulding, the extra material can be removed with an ordinary plane.

Reverse ogees (Fig. 65) and quarter rounds (Fig. 66) having squares or quirks

Fig. 57.—Moulding Requiring Careful Setting of Gauges and Fence

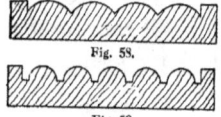

Fig. 58.

Fig. 59.

Figs. 58 and 59.—Mouldings Worked from both Edges of Board

Fig. 60.—Mouldings on Board of Concave Section

Fig. 61.—Moulding Worked with Fluting Cutters

Fig. 62.—Moulding on Board of Convex Section

to deal with can be readily worked without leaving any extra material, as shown in Fig. 64.

In working the quarter hollow with bead (Fig. 67) and the Grecian ogee

THE STANLEY "FIFTY-FIVE" PLANE

(Fig. 68), the sliding section should be brought to the inside of the bead; the bead serving to hold the fence up to the work.

It is possible to make quarter hollow (Fig. 69), but first the part shown by dotted lines must be rebated out and the fence set at exactly the right position to bring the cutter to the angle.

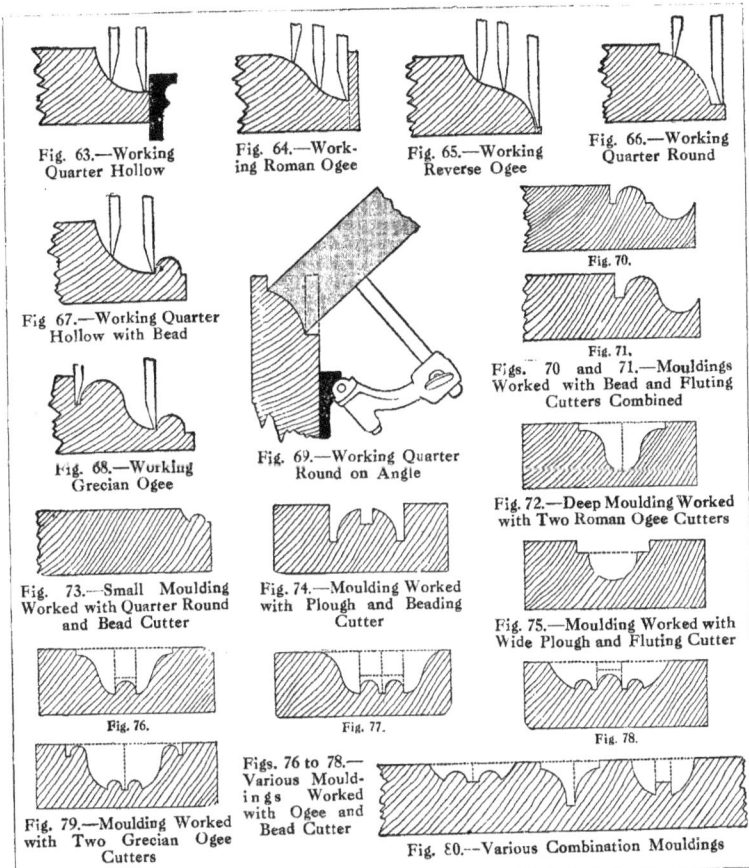

Fig. 63.—Working Quarter Hollow

Fig. 64.—Working Roman Ogee

Fig. 65.—Working Reverse Ogee

Fig. 66.—Working Quarter Round

Fig. 67.—Working Quarter Hollow with Bead

Fig. 68.—Working Grecian Ogee

Fig. 69.—Working Quarter Round on Angle

Fig. 70.

Fig. 71.

Figs. 70 and 71.—Mouldings Worked with Bead and Fluting Cutters Combined

Fig. 72.—Deep Moulding Worked with Two Roman Ogee Cutters

Fig. 73.—Small Moulding Worked with Quarter Round and Bead Cutter

Fig. 74.—Moulding Worked with Plough and Beading Cutter

Fig. 75.—Moulding Worked with Wide Plough and Fluting Cutter

Fig. 76.

Fig. 77.

Fig. 78.

Fig. 79.—Moulding Worked with Two Grecian Ogee Cutters

Figs. 76 to 78.—Various Mouldings Worked with Ogee and Bead Cutter

Fig. 80.—Various Combination Mouldings

and quarter round mouldings of practically any shape and size and to any angle by using a hollow or round cutter of suitable size and curve and setting the rosewood face of the fence to the angle desired

While the working of mouldings, requiring two or more operations to complete, is easy, care must be used in setting the fence and depth gauges in order that the different members will properly work

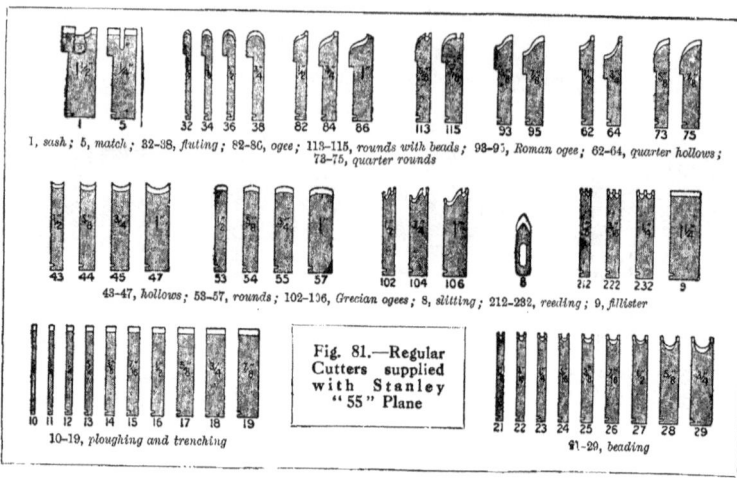

Fig. 81.—Regular Cutters supplied with Stanley "55" Plane

into each other. If this is not done their symmetrical appearance will be lost.

In Figs. 70 and 71 are shown the sections of two slightly different mouldings, both of which are formed by the use of a bead and fluting cutter in combination. The only difference in the two mouldings is that in Fig. 70 the fence is set so that the beading cutter will leave a small square or quirk between the members, and in Fig. 71 the fence is set so the two members will join without a quirk, thus forming a continuous curve.

Fig. 72 shows a deep moulding of rather unusual section, made by using one of the Roman ogees from one edge of the wood, then reversing the wood and using the same cutter from the opposite edge, being careful to set the fence so that the two grooves exactly meet at the bottom, thus forming one moulding.

The small moulding (Fig. 73) is suitable

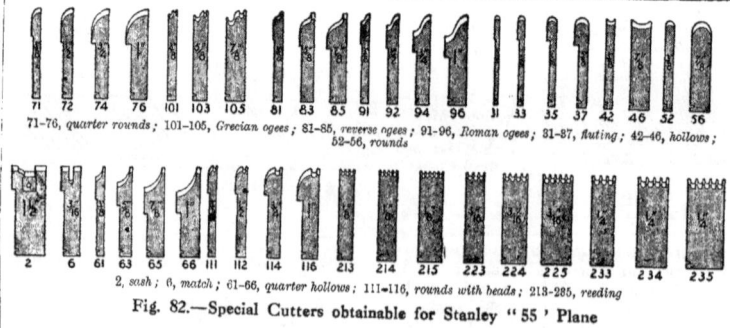

Fig. 82.—Special Cutters obtainable for Stanley "55" Plane

THE STANLEY "FIFTY-FIVE" PLANE

for edges of doors and panelling in various kinds of cabinet work. It is made with one of the quarter rounds with bead, the depth gauge being used to prevent the cutter from working down to its full extent.

Fig. 74 is worked with a plough and a beading cutter. The groove should be made first, finishing with the bead. This ensures sharp corners at each side of the groove. Fig. 75 is worked with a wide plough cutter and a fluting cutter. The fluting cutter should be used to make the hollow groove first, in order that the

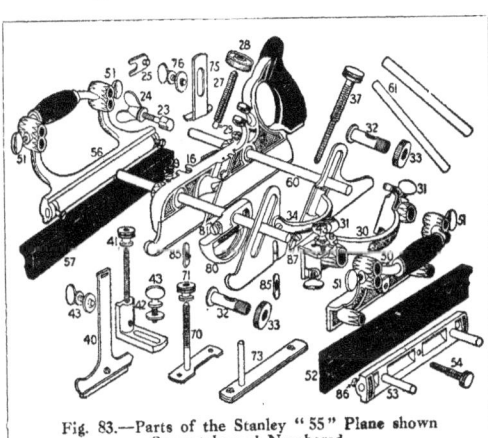

Fig. 83.—Parts of the Stanley "55" Plane shown Separately and Numbered

edges of the groove will be sharp on the finished moulding.

Fig. 76 shows a moulding similar to Fig. 72, but instead of the ogees coming together, they are divided by a bead. To make this, the ogees are worked from opposite sides, keeping them far enough apart to leave the width of the bead intact; then reduce the extra wood remaining to the required depth with a plough cutter, and form the bead in the usual way. Fig. 77 is worked the same as Fig. 76, using the quarter round with bead, but not working it to its full depth. Fig. 78 is worked the same as Fig. 76, first using the ogee from opposite sides, but far enough apart to leave room for the two beads which are to be made with a regular beading cutter. Fig. 79 is made with a Grecian ogee from both edges of the work, the cutter being worked to its full depth.

Fig. 80 shows three more sections of mouldings; the first from the left being made with the quarter round with bead but not carrying the cutter down to its full depth. The middle one is formed by using the quarter hollow cutter in the same way. The one to the right by the quarter round, the fence being set so that a small upstanding square is left at the bottom. If the square is first made to the proper height with a plough cutter, thus removing some of the waste stock, the working of the quarter rounds will be materially aided.

The depth gauges form important factors in the proper working of these mouldings, as it is very evident that if these are not set exactly right the cutter will damage the first member worked. Both gauges should be used.

The examples shown are merely to give an idea of the way combination mouldings are formed, and to give the workman suggestions that will enable him to form practically any shape of moulding desired.

Fig. 81 shows the regular cutters supplied with the plane. The numbers underneath the cutters should be given when ordering cutters for this plane from the makers.

Fig. 82 shows special cutters that may be ordered by specifying the numbers. Cutters of practically any form can be used in the plane, which the operator can make from blanks or order from sketch.

All the parts of the plane are shown separated in Fig. 83. In ordering repair parts the number of the part should be given.

Halved, Lapped, Notched and Housed Joints

UNLESS woodwork joints are neatly and well made, the best after-finish cannot conceal a clumsy effect, nor can proper strength and durability be expected. The careless worker often relies on tightening with the cramp, or on slight alterations when fitting, but by far the most satisfactory and least time-wasting way is to follow sound and craftsmanlike principles from the start.

trated instructions will be given for constructing all the ordinary kinds of joints employed by skilled artisans, besides numerous others of an unusual and unique type.

Halved Joints.—Figs 1 to 17 show simple examples, in wood of rectangular section, of joints commonly met with in carpentry and cabinet work. They are very easy to make, and, in some cases

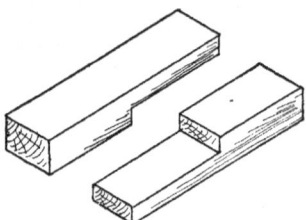

Fig. 1.—Straight Half-lap Joint

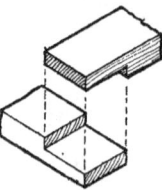

Fig. 2.—Angle Half-lap Joint

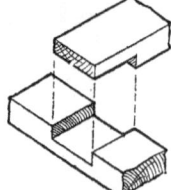

Fig. 3.—Tee Half-lap Joint

The number of different joints employed in woodworking is surprisingly large. Joiners, carpenters, cabinet-makers, wheelwrights and many other trades each have their own favourite methods, and, oddly enough, often have distinctive ways of making what is really the same joint. Even national variations are met in the work and tools of one country as compared with another.

It is here proposed to deal with many descriptions of jointing in such detail as to be practically helpful. Fully illus-

are quite as suitable as more difficult joints. The straight half-lap joint (Fig. 1) can be used for lengthening posts or rails in hut-building, etc., also for forming wall plates, joists and rafters for roofs, floors, and temporary structures. It is readily set out. A marking gauge, marking knife (or pencil) and square are employed in setting out the pieces. As the name of the joint indicates, the depth of each piece cut away is half the thickness of the wood, and in cutting down with the tenon saw care should be taken to

HALVED, LAPPED, NOTCHED AND HOUSED JOINTS

keep inside the line; the four cuts are made with a tenon saw. The terms "halved" and "lap" are often used interchangeably; but, as a matter of fact, while a halved joint is always a lapped one, a lap joint is not invariably with a flush face. A familiar instance is the Oxford frame, and the centre of a barrow-wheel may also be cited. In making Tee and cross half-joints, the parts should be gauged to a width, so that they may be set out with the cer-

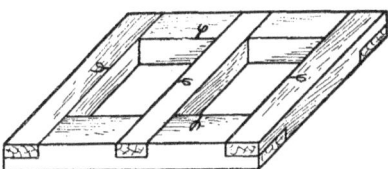

Fig. 4.—Lapped Frame with Tee-stretcher

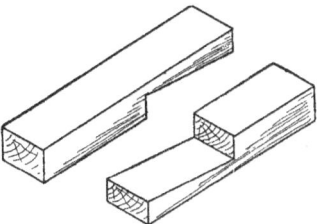

Fig. 6.—Straight Bevelled Half-lap Joint

halved. Fig. 2 shows the angle half-lap joint, suitable for corners or angles in framework, and in framed grounds for the fixing of joinery.

Tee and Cross Half-lap Joints.—The Tee half-lap (Fig. 3) is useful where a rail meets a post, or post meets sill, in the framework of huts. Fig. 4 shows a square frame halved at the angles, and with a Tee stretcher fitted at the middle. The sinking for the Tee joint is marked out for the width and gauged for depth; then, after making the usual saw-cuts, the waste is removed with a paring chisel,

tainty of fitting truly. When marking for the width of sinking, care must be taken that the saw kerfs are not too far apart. It is better to have the slot too narrow rather than too wide, and fit the joint afterwards by planing the opposite piece or paring the joint. But this precaution should not be depended upon to give good work. It is only suggested that it is better to have the joint a little tight rather than a little

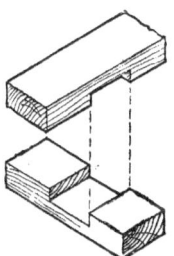

Fig. 5.—Cross Half-lap Joint

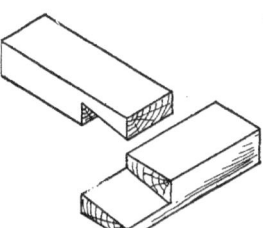

Fig. 7.—Angle Bevelled Half-lap Joint

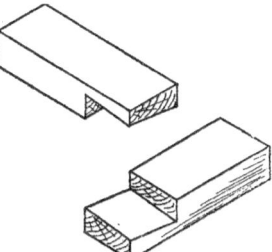

Fig. 8.—Double Bevelled Angle Half-lap

used either horizontally or vertically, as proves most convenient.

The cross half-lap (Fig. 5) is obviously a double Tee, and is very handy where pieces are required to cross each other

slack. The former can be remedied, but the latter cannot. The aim should be to saw the joint right first time, and so that the pieces can be fitted together "hand-tight."

Bevelled Half-lap Joints. — Examples of this useful joint are shown by Figs. 6, 7, and 8. It is occasionally employed for heavy framing work, wall plates, sills and binders, to withstand a pulling stress, also in good half-timbering for the exterior of Elizabethan-style houses. The marking down and across is similar to the simpler form of lap, but a tapered piece of wood is used as a template for the depth, instead of the gauge, though the latter is sometimes used as well, to give the right starting point for the taper.

Dovetail and Diagonal Half-lap Joints.—The dovetail half-lap may be regarded as a Tee half-lap modified to resist a lateral pull (see Figs. 9 and 10). It is extensively used in cabinet work. The pin part should be made first, commencing as for an ordinary lap joint, then sawing the shoulders to the necessary angle and carefully finishing with the chisel. The pin half is next held over the piece for the socket, the sinking accurately marked, as in Fig. 11, squared down, sawn sparely so as to fit the pin tightly (see Fig. 12), and the waste chiselled out. Fig. 13 illustrates a similar joint designed to resist an upward pull. An adaptation of dovetail and half-lap joints will be seen in Fig. 14, which

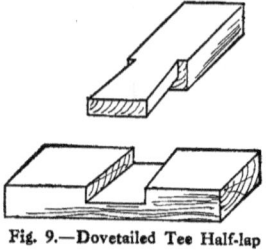

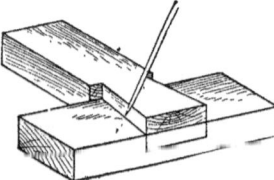

Fig. 9.—Dovetailed Tee Half-lap

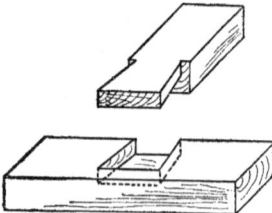

Fig. 10.—Stopped Dovetailed Half-lap

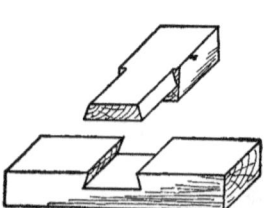

Fig. 11.—Marking Sinking from Pin

Fig. 12.—Sawing Dovetail Socket; note Saw-kerfs in Waste Wood

Fig. 13.—Dovetail Half-lap for Upward Pull

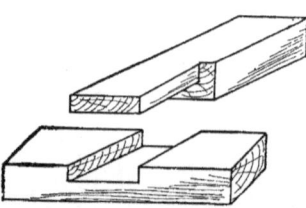

Fig. 14.—Dovetailed Acute-Angle Half-lap

HALVED, LAPPED, NOTCHED AND HOUSED JOINTS

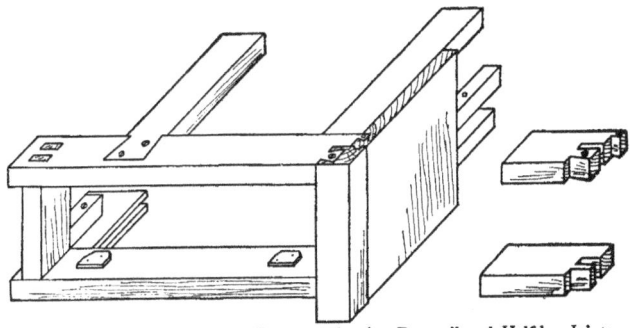

Fig. 15.—Portion of Chest of Drawers, showing Dovetail and Half-lap Joints

shows the same kind of joint as in Fig. 10, but not having the two pieces at a right angle; this is known as diagonal halving. Fig. 17 is a cross diagonal joint.

The corners of the frame illustrated in Fig. 18 are secured by bevelled half-lapping, while in the centre are two diagonal crosspieces or braces. To set out the latter, the sliding bevel is used to take the exact angle, which is then transferred to the first portion of the cross. The second piece is then laid on the first and marked in. The marked piece is now gauged for depth and cut; the other being next laid in position in the halving and marked to fit in the usual way. To insert the completed cross into the frame, one is laid on the other and the positions marked for all the cuts, the depths on both frame and cross-ends being then gauged.

In Fig. 16 we show the application of the ordinary form of the ship-lap joint (there is a more complicated form of this joint which will be described later); this is only suitable for use between two absolutely fixed posts or something similar,

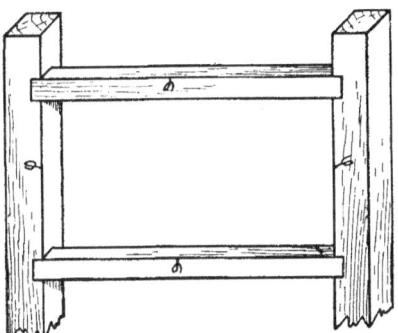

Fig. 16.—Posts and Rails with Ship-lapped Joints

but in such positions it is a handy way of fixing rails or uprights. The reason why it is necessary that the timbers between which this joint is used must be rigidly fixed is, the joint being made on the slope and fixed with nails, these latter have the tendency to force the posts or other timbers apart, thus destroy-

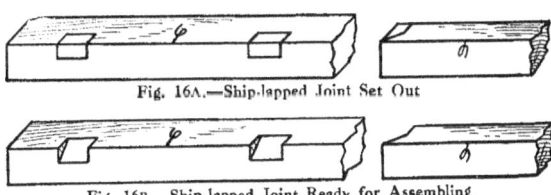

Fig. 16A.—Ship-lapped Joint Set Out

Fig. 16B.—Ship-lapped Joint Ready for Assembling

ing the stiffness and also opening the back part which should fit close up to them.

The ship-lap joint consists of a bevel lip fitting into a sloping recess, and the setting out is as shown in Fig. 16A, while the two parts after cutting are shown in Fig. 16B. This is really a carpenter's joint, and is rarely applicable to any other branch of woodworking, though exceptions occasionally crop up. This joint

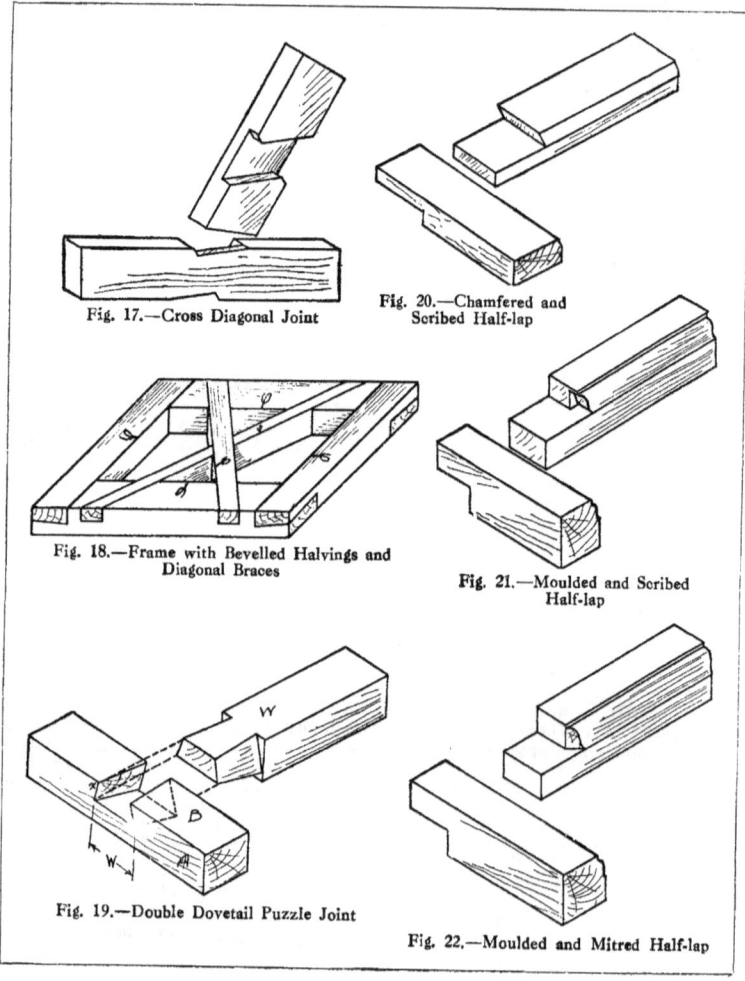

Fig. 17.—Cross Diagonal Joint

Fig. 18.—Frame with Bevelled Halvings and Diagonal Braces

Fig. 19.—Double Dovetail Puzzle Joint

Fig. 20.—Chamfered and Scribed Half-lap

Fig. 21.—Moulded and Scribed Half-lap

Fig. 22.—Moulded and Mitred Half-lap

HALVED, LAPPED, NOTCHED AND HOUSED JOINTS

is also largely localised, being very common in the south of England, but rarely seen in the Midlands and the North.

A puzzle joint, dovetailed both ways,

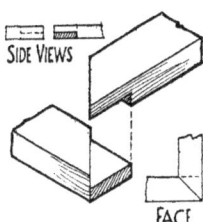

Fig. 23.—Plain Mitred Half-lap

is shown by Fig. 19. It is of the same kind as seen in Fig. 14, with the difference that the two pieces have to be separated by a slanting, downward pull; this causes the apparent dovetail on the face B. The joint is made by first gauging the edge A half-way down; on this line the width w is set out, and the dovetail is marked on faces A and B. The bevel

manner and the other piece next marked, keeping the lines full for fitting. It is as well if the joint is fitted tight. Sur-

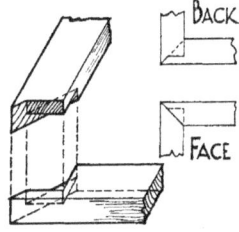

Fig. 24.—Stopped and Mitred Half-lap

prisingly many people are deceived by this joint.

Moulded and Chamfered Half-lap.—Figs. 20, 21, and 22 show moulded and chamfered pieces with half-lap joints,

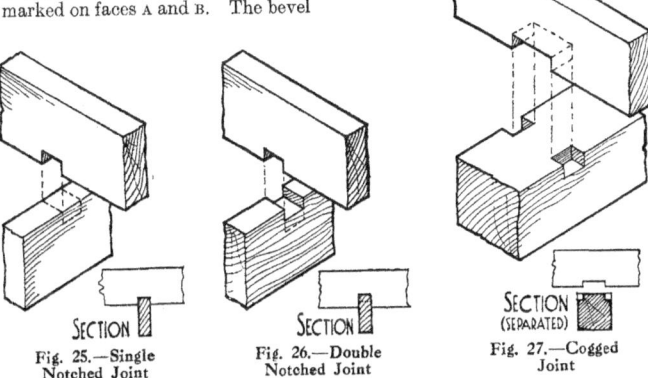

Fig. 25.—Single Notched Joint

Fig. 26.—Double Notched Joint

Fig. 27.—Cogged Joint

x is then transferred to the opposite edge, w is squared over to the same edge, and the work is gauged down at the point where the bevel and square lines intersect. Cutting out is done by sawing down and chiselling out the waste in the ordinary

Figs. 20 and 21 being scribed and Fig. 22 mitred. The scribing and mitreing referred to will be discussed later when dealing with mortise and tenon joints. Figs. 23 and 24 are examples of mitred half-lap joints, that seen in Fig. 24 being stopped

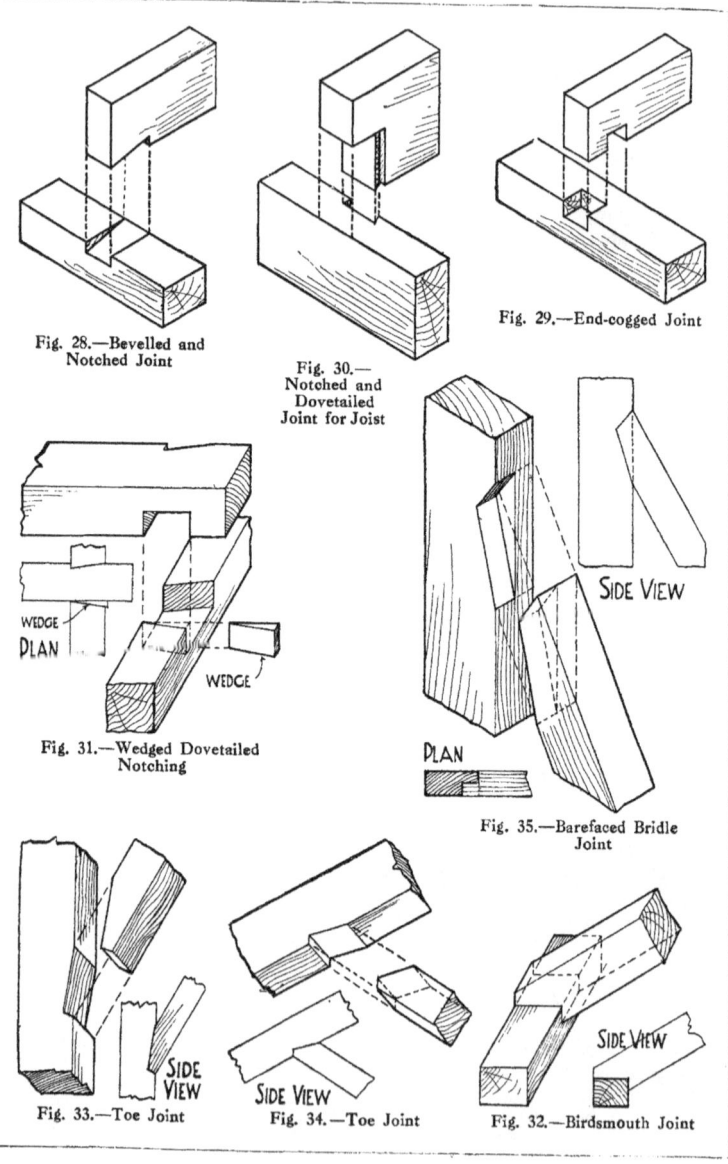

HALVED, LAPPED, NOTCHED AND HOUSED JOINTS

to prevent the end grain of the wood showing, as would be required for picture frames.

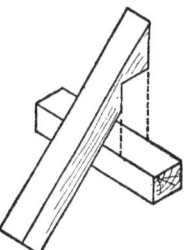

Fig. 36.—Falling Birdsmouth Joint

Fastening Halved or Lap Joints.—For securing all manner of halved or lap joints glue, nails, screws, or a combination of such can be employed. Much, of course, depends on the particular purpose, the nature of the strain to be met, and whether or not appearance has to be studied.

Notched Joints.—Numerous varieties of these are illustrated by Figs. 25 to 39. Though sometimes met with in ordinary woodworking, their chief use is in con-

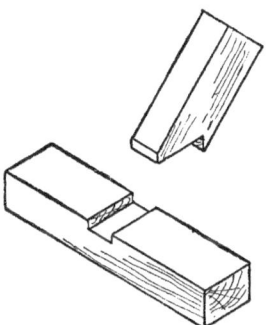

Fig. 37.—Sunk Birdsmouth Joint

structive carpentry, such as the framework of wooden buildings, cycle sheds, photographic and cinema studios etc.,

also in the making of rough benches and brackets. Figs. 25, 26, and 27 are examples of single and double notching, employed for fitting joists into floor

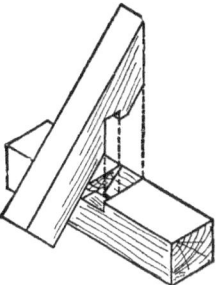

Fig. 38.—Notched Birdsmouth Joint

binders. The depth having been marked with a gauge or template, and the width from the work itself, the rest is merely a matter of sawing and chiselling. Fig. 27 is also known as a cogged joint, and is used with extra heavy beams. Figs. 28 and 29 are end-notched joints, employed at the ends of joists, or when a cross rail is notched on to a wall plate or head piece in framed or stone buildings.

Fig. 30 shows the end of a roof joist or purlin notched into a beam or rafter in such a way as to withstand a tensile

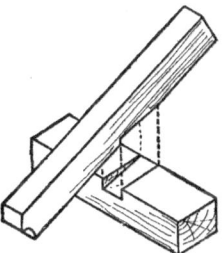

Fig. 39.—Bevelled and Notched Joint

pull. This is a good manner of binding a building. Fig. 31 illustrates another method of jointing to resist a pull by driving a wedge into the joint. This may be considered as a cross half-lap, modified into a locking and wedged dovetail.

Figs. 32 to 39 show more kinds of notching, which can be used, graded from the simple to the rather complex,

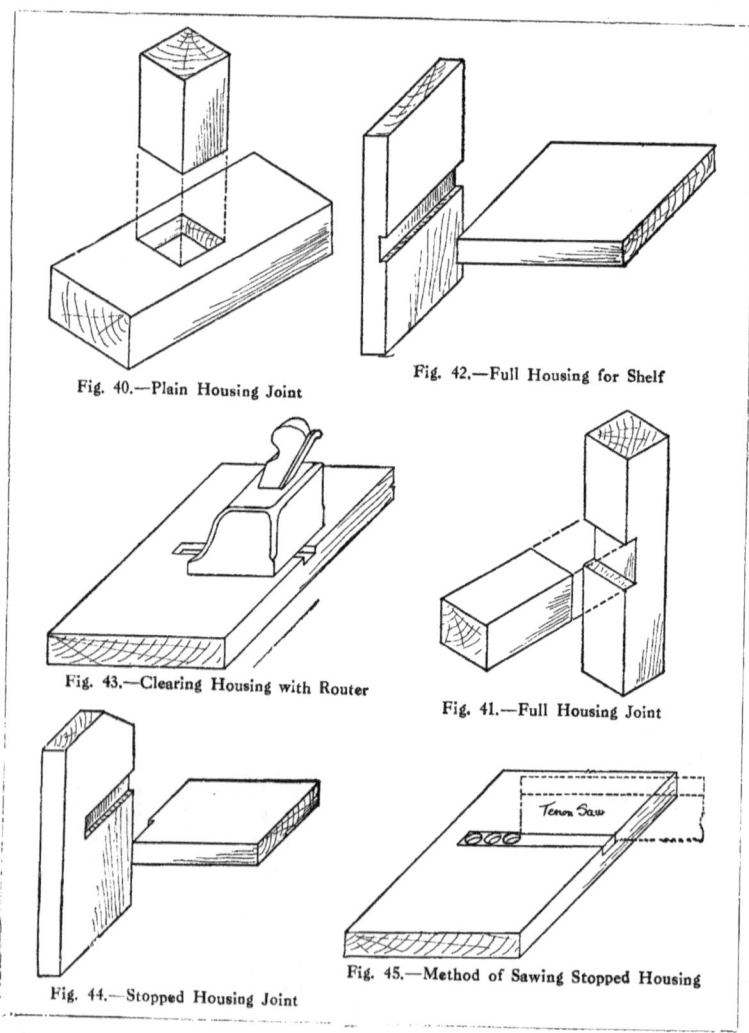

Fig. 40.—Plain Housing Joint

Fig. 42.—Full Housing for Shelf

Fig. 43.—Clearing Housing with Router

Fig. 41.—Full Housing Joint

Fig. 44.—Stopped Housing Joint

Fig. 45.—Method of Sawing Stopped Housing

HALVED, LAPPED, NOTCHED AND HOUSED JOINTS

to suit the greater or lesser importance of the work in hand. It is thought that the drawings are sufficiently explicit to render explanation needless, inasmuch as the joints are all derived from one or other of those already described. Some of them, it will be seen, may if desired be formed with the saw alone, but generally the chisel also is needed. The main thing necessary is to make sure of careful angling and accurate fitting.

Housed Joints.—Housing may be defined as sinking the end of one piece into a notch or groove cut in another for its reception. It is chiefly used for the ends of shelves, and for posts, rails, etc. Figs. 40 to 42, 44, and 46 to 52 illustrate different housing joints. Fig. 40 shows a post housed into a sill; though this

depth, the lines are sawn down, with the saw kerfs inside the waste wood, to the gauge marks. The core or waste is next taken out nearly to the depth with a narrow chisel, and the trench is often finished with a router, or "old woman's

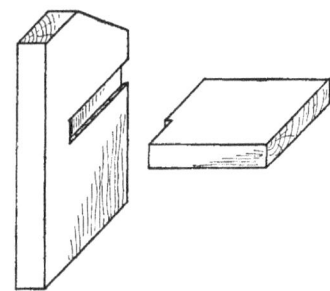

Fig. 47.—Dovetailed and Stopped Housing

tooth," to a flat bottom as shown by Fig. 43. The chisel in the router is adjustable to any desired depth. By the foregoing method the sinking is left visible on the front edge of the upright; it looks decidedly better if this is avoided

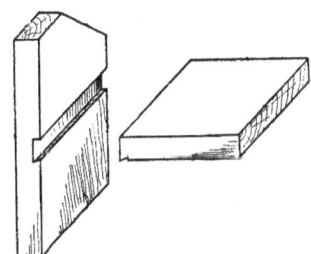

Fig. 46.—Dovetailed Housing Joint

ought only to be done when the top also is fixed, otherwise the depth is insufficient for rigidity. The recess may be set out from the bottom of the post itself, and is then chiselled away like a mortise, keeping well inside the marked lines to ensure a tight fit.

Fig. 41 is typical of the rail and post joint, as in the case of a door post and head for a hut framework or partition. It is fastened by nailing from the back.

Figs. 42, 44, and 46 to 48 show five methods of housing shelves into the upright ends of a bookcase or cabinet. In setting out, the parallel lines for the sinking should always be marked exactly to the thickness of the shelf. Then, for the plain housing (Fig. 42) having gauged to the

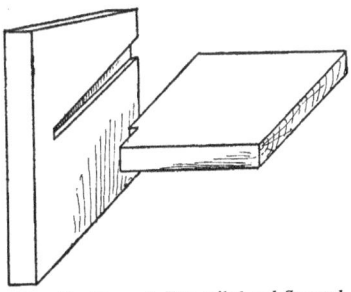

Fig. 48.—Tapered, Dovetailed and Stopped Joint

by "stopping," as seen in Fig. 44. The latter may be done by gauging the width of the stopped end, and using the saw slantwise on the marked parallel lines till the cut reaches the stop and is the right depth at the other end; the sinking is then finished with a chisel. Another way is to get a start for the tenon saw by boring three or four holes with a centre bit to the width and depth of the groove, these holes being afterwards cut out square with the mallet and chisel. The saw can now be inserted and the groove finished off with the router (*see* Fig. 45).

A stronger joint, to resist an endways pull, is obtained by dovetailing or bevelling one edge of the housing, as seen in Figs. 46 and 47, the first being plain and the second stopped. The best method, however, as used for good furniture, is a stopped, dovetailed and tapered joint (*see* Fig. 48). When well fitted, glued, and driven in from the back this makes a perfect joint, both as regards strength and appearance. This joint requires no nailing.

A type of tenoned and housed joint used between a newel post and hand-rail is illustrated by Fig. 49. In a thick newel post, shrinkage is almost certain to occur, which causes the joint at the shoulder to open. This defect is prevented by housing the whole of the hand-rail into the post to a depth of about ⅜ in., which permits the post to shrink or expand at will. To do this a mortise and tenon is first made. The tenon is inserted and the rail marked round with a marking awl, the housing for the rail being finally cut with mallet, chisel and scribing gouge.

The housed joint between the pulley

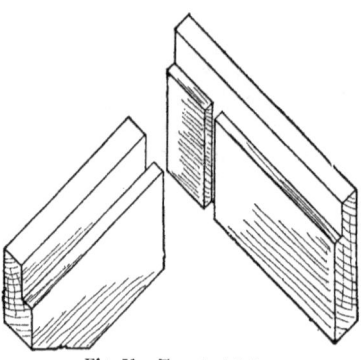

Fig. 51.—Trenched Joint

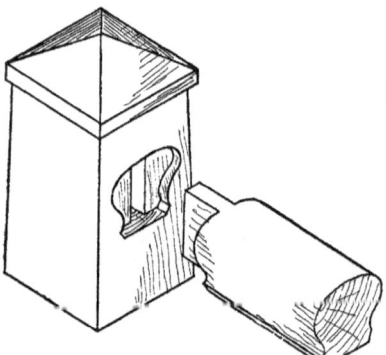

Fig. 49.—Housed and Tenoned Joint

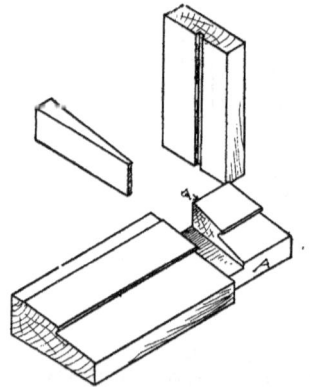

Fig. 50.—Wedged Housing Joint

stile and bevelled sill of a double-hung sliding-sash window frame is shown by Fig. 50. The housing is tapered, and is cut wider than the thickness of the stile, in order to allow the insertion of a wedge behind the latter, as indicated. The trenching is often set out, squared over, and cut before rebating and bevelling the sill, so that the try-square and gauge

HALVED, LAPPED, NOTCHED AND HOUSED JOINTS

may be used. The pieces notched at the sides marked A are cut out for the reception of the outside and inside linings, is nailed from the upper side of the head.

Fig. 52 illustrates the housed trenching

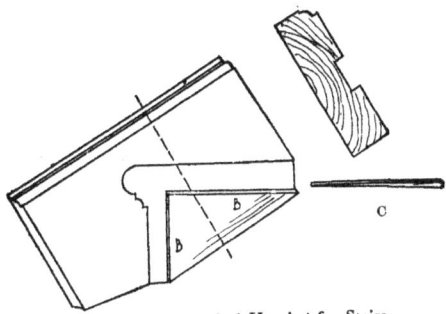

Fig. 52.—Trenched Housing for Stairs

which form the box for the sash-weights to slide up and down in.

Fig. 51 shows the joint between the head and side of an ordinary inside door casing to be fixed in a brick or stone opening. This joint is fitted tightly and of a stair string to receive the step ends. It will be noticed that the sides marked B are out of parallel in order to admit a glued wedge C besides the step end, to ensure a good fit on the top side of the tread and a rigid fixing.

Edge and Angle Joints

Glue Joints.—What are known as glue joints are those which depend chiefly, or, at any rate, to a large extent, on gluing for their adhesion and strength, though not necessarily to the exclusion of other factors. These comprise butt, slotted screw, tongued and grooved, feathered, and keyed joints. They are mostly used to join up boards to a greater

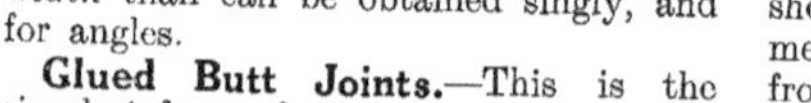

Fig. 1.—Butt Joint Correctly Made

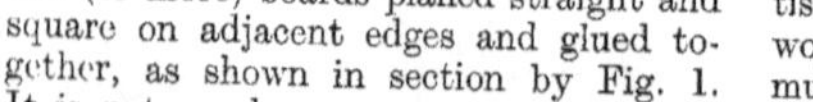

Fig. 2.—Butt Joint Badly Made

width than can be obtained singly, and for angles.

Glued Butt Joints.—This is the simplest form of glue joint, consisting of two (or more) boards planed straight and square on adjacent edges and glued together, as shown in section by Fig. 1. It is not nearly so easy as it looks. In making such a joint, especially when a fairly long one, the patience and skill of the novice, and sometimes of the professional, are taxed to the utmost, and it often happens that when the two boards fit closely together they are not straight on the face, appearing instead as in Fig. 2. The remedy, of course, is further careful planing.

Should the wood be over ¾ in. thick, the joints are best made with the boards fixed in the bench vice, the trying plane being held with the fingers of the left hand under the plane face, and the finger tips running along the face of the board so as to act as guides and keep the plane iron in the middle, either for the whole length of the board or for a portion only, as may be needed, and for good jointing aim should always be made for the final shaving to be the full length of the board. The feet should be placed to facilitate walking in the direction of the length.

The trying plane used for jointing should be in good condition. The cutting iron should be as thin as possible and only very slightly round on the edge, while the back iron should be set down to within the merest trifle of the cutting edge of the front iron. The shavings taken off will then be no thicker than the thinnest tissue paper. Rough, " near enough " work will not answer; indeed, the joints must fit exactly together, and this is achieved when no light can be seen through the joint. This is most important.

For thinner boards and very short joints there is no better way than the " underhand " method of using the plane. This necessitates the employment of a shooting board (see Fig. 3 and also the chapter on mitreing), a handy appliance which should be found in every workroom. The main portion A may be 9 in.

wide by 1 in. thick; it must be straight and out of twist. The part B on which the plane works should project about 3 in., and is screwed to the under side

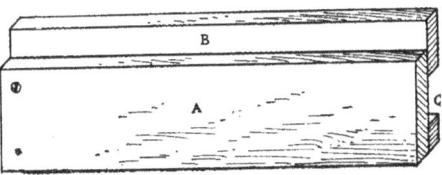

Fig. 3.—Shooting Board

of A. The strip C, of the same thickness as B, is merely to make the board level. Fig. 4 is a sectional view, with the plane and work in position.

One of the pieces to be jointed should be laid on the shooting board face upwards, while its fellow must be "shot" face downwards, to counteract the state of things indicated in Fig. 2, which might be caused by the curvature of the plane making the edges slightly out of square.

The edges of the boards should be tested with the try-square, and by holding the two surfaces in contact between the worker and the light. The parallelism of the boards when together should also be verified by laying a straightedge across.

The glue employed for the joints must be of the best quality and comparatively freshly made. It should be used as hot as possible.

A great many people undoubtedly make it too thick, under the impression that it will be stronger, whereas the exact reverse is the case. The glue should run off the brush like thin paint.

Undoubtedly the best way to put glue joints together is by "rubbing"; that is to say, the two edges are glued liberally, and then the two boards are rubbed to and fro in contact, as shown in Fig. 5, so as to rub as much of the surplus glue out of the joint as possible, and incidentally to rub it well into the pores of the wood. For joints of any length assistance is required, otherwise it is difficult to keep the boards flush at the sides and ends. As the to and fro movement becomes stiffer, proving that the glue is beginning to set, the boards are brought finally into correct adjustment, and should

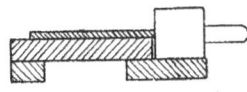

Fig. 4.—Section of Shooting Board in Use

then be no more interfered with till set hard.

When more than two boards are to be joined at one time (as in Fig. 1), the upper joint should be made first; then, while these two boards are held vertically, the under edge can be glued, as well as the upper edge of the next board, and the two already joined rubbed down on the single one. If the contrary order is adopted, the first joint is sure to be broken. It is, however, better to let one joint set before making another. A glued joint is sufficiently set for careful handling in two hours, and is practically at maximum strength in two days.

The correct numbering of the joints as

Fig. 5.—Rubbing a Glue Joint

they are fitted up is very important, so as to ensure that the tested surfaces are those that will be glued. The system shown in Fig. 6 cannot fail to give satisfaction. It consists of straight marks and crosses made over each joint, so that each adjacent half is alike, but reversed. All numbering is best done before the jointing, and invariably on the best side of the wood.

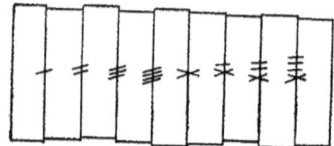

Fig. 6.—Correct Way of Numbering Joints

Steel dogs (Fig. 7) are very useful to strengthen the joints when set, especially in compound work. They cannot be depended on to pull the joints together, but are of much help towards holding them after rubbing so that they may be more freely handled. Fig. 8 shows the dog in use.

After making the joints the boards should be stood aside very carefully, so that the air can circulate freely between them. Fig. 9 illustrates a series of six joined boards, set away to dry with strips between. These strips must be parallel and should bed evenly on each board. They may be employed singly for short joints, but for anything over 3 ft. long it is best to have two strips between each board.

Slotted Screw Joint.—This is a butt joint having hidden screws driven into keyhole slots (see Fig. 10). It is used principally by cabinet-makers. The

Fig. 7.—Steel Dog

Fig. 8.—Method of Using Dog

screws are inserted at intervals along the edge of one of the boards to be jointed, leaving the heads projecting about ⅜ in. Holes are bored in the edge of the other board so that the screw heads will fit into them, and slots are made leading from the holes, as shown, of the right size to take the shank of the screws. On placing the two boards together with the screw heads in the holes, and then forcing the top board to the right, the head of each screw will, as it were, dovetail itself into the wood and hold the joint together. When driving in the screws they must be made to lean slightly so that they will draw the joint together rather than apart; thus the left-hand screw in the illustration is wrongly inserted, the other being correct. It is also usual before finally gluing the joint, and after it has been tried up, to give the screws half a turn, thus ensuring a close joint.

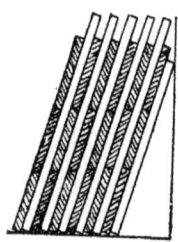

Fig. 9.—Stacking Boards after Gluing

Rebated Joint.—In this joint (Fig. 11) an open groove is cut at each edge to be joined, usually with a rebate plane. The edges require to be as carefully trued up as for the ordinary butt joint, and are glued in much the same way.

Tongued or Feathered Joints.— Either tongued or matched joints are now generally insisted on in preference to the glued butt. The first is illustrated in section by Fig. 12. A groove of equal width and depth has to be cut in both pieces with a "plough." This is a plane having a narrow iron, an adjustable fence to keep the groove at the right distance from the edge of the work, and usually also a device for regulating the depth.

To use the plough the fence is set by means of the two wedges to bring the iron in the middle of the wood (unless otherwise desired), while the gauge for the depth is adjusted by means of the

EDGE AND ANGLE JOINTS

thumbscrew at top. The board is then fixed in the bench vice, and, holding the plough as shown in earlier pages, working is started to and fro on a portion at the

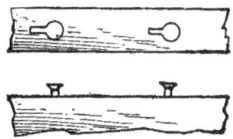

Fig. 10.—Details of Slotted Screw Joint

far end till almost deep enough. Next, stepping backwards, another short section is done, and so on, till the near end is reached. Lastly, one or two pushes are given along the entire length. Unless the grooves are made true, the effect of the finished joint will be as indicated exaggeratedly by Fig. 13, and the tongue will be of more trouble than use.

The tongues, or feathers, are thin planed-up wooden-strips, usually cut parallel with the grain, though some prefer them cut across. Opinion is divided as to which is best. If good three-ply wood is available it makes excellent tongues, combining the advantages of both the parallel and cross varieties, but to prevent the grain stripping the outside ply should be parallel with the wood to be glued up.

For a perfect joint it is requisite that the tongue should fit just closely in the

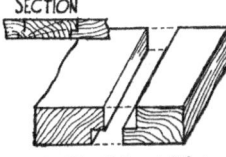

Fig. 11.—Rebated Joint

grooves without being tight, and be slightly less in width than the combined depth of the two grooves, so as not to bind when the joint is glued up. Such

a joint is shown sectionally by Fig. 14, and it will generally prove more difficult to divide than the surrounding wood. To make tongued joints easy to rub when gluing, the tongues should be planed slightly uneven in thickness, so that one edge fits tightly while the other will be loose enough to allow the board to be rubbed to and fro. The tight edge is obviously inserted first.

To glue the tongue, lay it on the joint and rapidly cover one side with glue, then turn it over and do the other side, after which it should be tapped into its

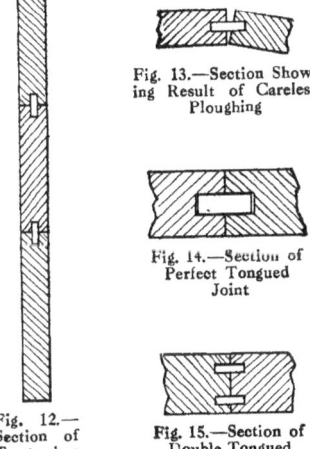

Fig. 12.—Section of Tongued or Feathered Joint

Fig. 13.—Section Showing Result of Careless Ploughing

Fig. 14.—Section of Perfect Tongued Joint

Fig. 15.—Section of Double Tongued Joint

groove. Then the two edges of the board are glued with the projecting tongue and the joint rubbed quickly.

In very thick material it may be advisable to use double tongues, as shown sectionally in Fig. 15, which is preferable to using a single thick one. In that case, the two grooves should be ploughed from the same side of the wood, otherwise they will probably fail to coincide, and crippled tongues would result.

Rebated and Filleted Joint.—This may be regarded as an open-grooved

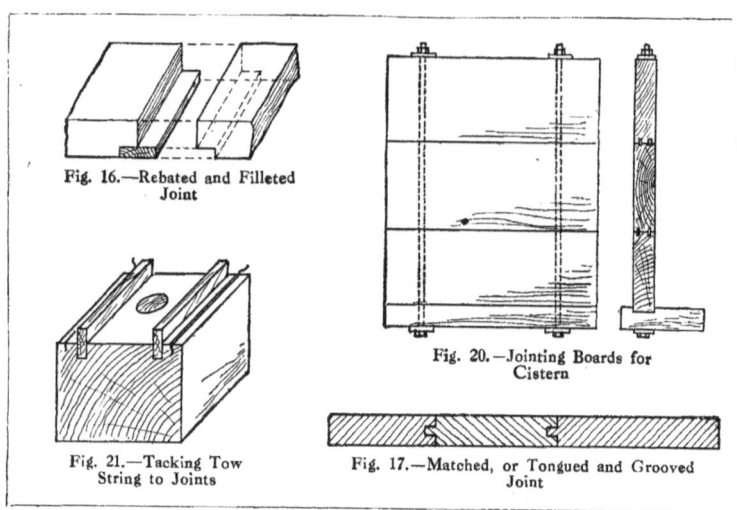

Fig. 16.—Rebated and Filleted Joint

Fig. 20.—Jointing Boards for Cistern

Fig. 21.—Tacking Tow String to Joints

Fig. 17.—Matched, or Tongued and Grooved Joint

tongued joint. It is suitable for work of which only one side shows, and which is not subjected to a bending strain. It is illustrated by Fig. 16.

Matched Joints.—This type of joint (Fig. 17) is also known as grooved and tongued; but, while the groove on one board is cut with a plough as before, the tongue is formed on the other board itself by means of a tonguing plane, which cuts a rebate on each edge, leaving a projecting piece between. The two are usually sold together as "matching planes" (see Figs. 18 and 19). The

Fig. 18. Fig. 19.

Figs. 18 and 19.—Using Matching Planes

EDGE AND ANGLE JOINTS

boards should be accurately shot and fitted before the matching is done, when, if the planes are in good condition, the joint will fit as well as it previously did.

Watertight Joints for Cistern.—Figs. 20, 21, and 22 show a method employed for constructing wooden cisterns, suitable for the water storage of a country house. The thickness of material may be from 1½ in. to 4 in., according to the size of the tank. Red deal, elm, oak, and pitch pine are suitable woods to use for this kind of work. The planking should all be brought to the same thickness, the groove being ploughed from both faces with the same setting. This can only be done when the timbers have been machined to thickness.

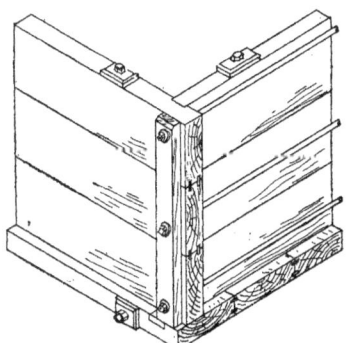

Fig. 22.—Bolting End of Cistern

Having made and fitted the joints, two lengths of tow string are tacked to them, as shown by Fig. 21, the whole being given two coats of priming paint before putting together.

In boring the holes for the long bolts it is better to bore from each edge to ensure true alignment. The end of the tank is put together in a similar way, being then fitted between and housed into the sides and bottom to an equal depth. Two or three lengths of tow should also be nailed on to the bottom of the grooves.

The end is kept in position by long bolts passing through the sides, and through stout pieces planted at the ends of the latter, as in Fig. 22, in order to

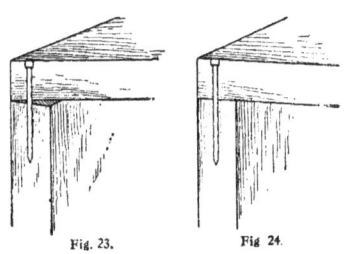

Fig. 23. Fig. 24.

distribute the pressure and keep the sides straight.

Angle Joints.—When nailing together end and side pieces, as for the angles of a box, care should be taken to select nails of the right length. For nailing into the end grain, the length should equal from 2½ to 3 times the thickness of the first piece of wood. The distance apart should be at least equal to the thickness of nail, and it is better to slope the nails slightly towards each other; this is known as "lock nailing." Figs. 23 to 26 show the result of badly fitting nailed butt joints.

In cutting the ends of boards care

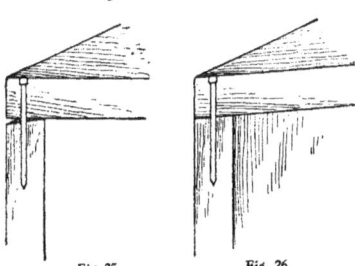

Fig. 25. Fig. 26.
Figs. 23 to 26.—Examples of Badly Fitting Nailed Joints

should be taken that the tenon saw is kept at a right angle to the stuff. It is much better to shoot the ends on the shooting board, ascertaining at the same

236   THE PRACTICAL WOODWORKER

time that opposite sides are of equal length, to ensure a true rectangle in the finished box.

When using this joint in furniture making it is better to nail and glue it; also, if the job permits, fixing glued

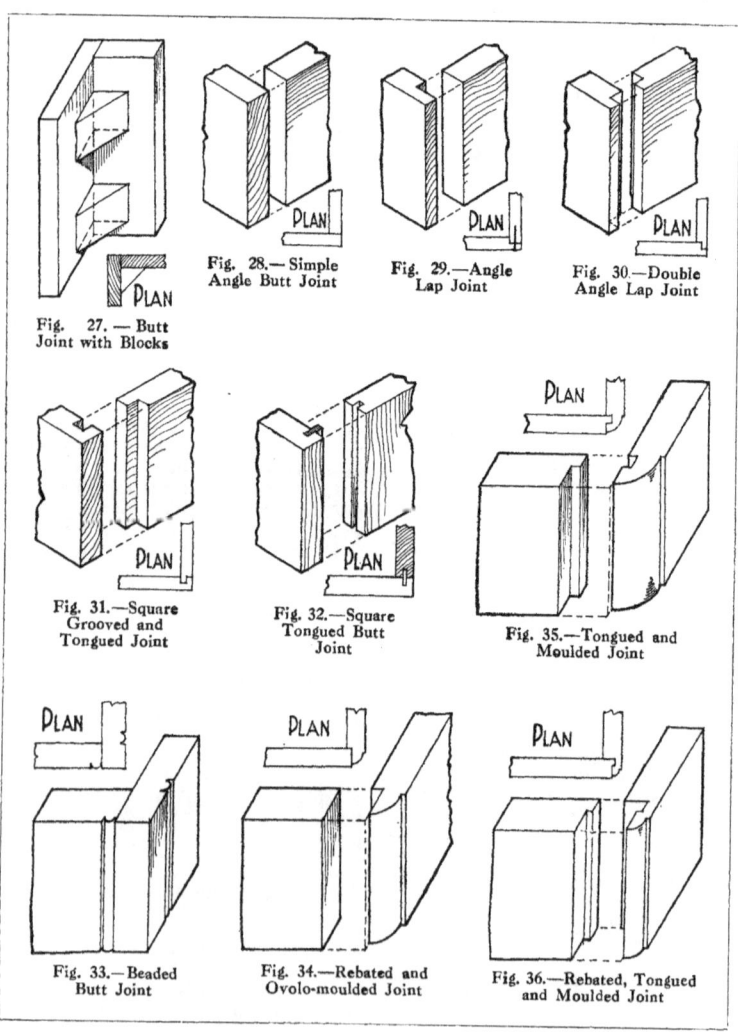

Fig. 27.—Butt Joint with Blocks
Fig. 28.—Simple Angle Butt Joint
Fig. 29.—Angle Lap Joint
Fig. 30.—Double Angle Lap Joint
Fig. 31.—Square Grooved and Tongued Joint
Fig. 32.—Square Tongued Butt Joint
Fig. 35.—Tongued and Moulded Joint
Fig. 33.—Beaded Butt Joint
Fig. 34.—Rebated and Ovolo-moulded Joint
Fig. 36.—Rebated, Tongued and Moulded Joint

EDGE AND ANGLE JOINTS

blocks into the internal angles, as in Fig. 27. Fig. 28 shows a simple angle butt joint ready for nailing or screwing. Fig. 29 illustrates the use of a rebate in one piece to receive the end of the other; this gives more surface for gluing and resists an inward pressure better, also it especially if a very thin hardwood cross tongue is employed.

Ornamental Angle Joints.—Sometimes, as for furniture, both butted and tongued joints are finished with a bead or moulding. Figs. 33 to 36 are typical examples. These joints are otherwise

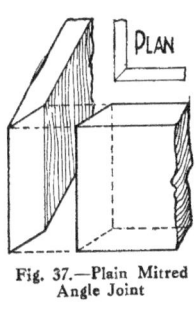

Fig. 37.—Plain Mitred Angle Joint

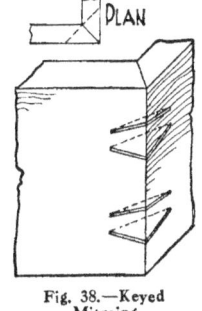

Fig. 38.—Keyed Mitreing

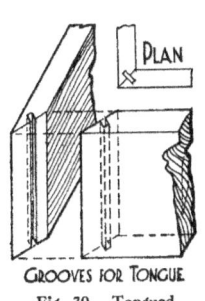

Fig. 39.—Tongued Mitreing

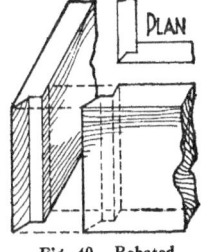

Fig. 40.—Rebated Mitreing

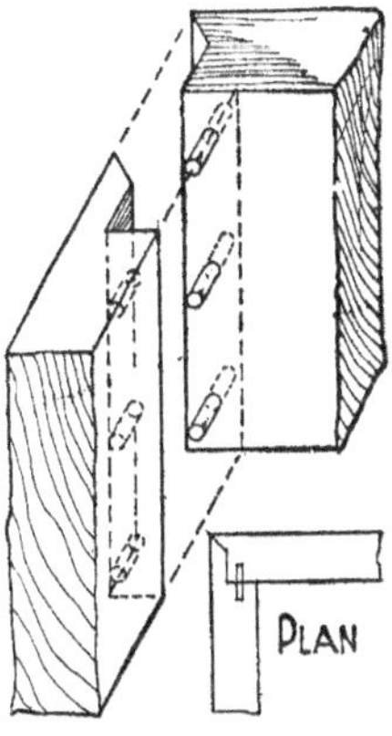

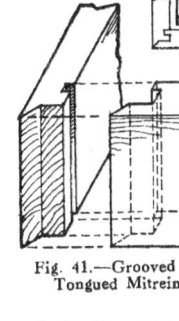

Fig. 41.—Grooved and Tongued Mitreing

Fig. 42.—Rebated and Dowelled Mitre Joint

may be nailed in two directions if desired. A slight variation of the previous example, but a little stronger, is shown by Fig. 30.

The grooved and tongued angle joint seen in Fig. 31 is a very good form, but there is a danger of the short end-grain lap breaking off. It is, however, strong and serviceable when used as a side angle joint and glued. Fig. 32 illustrates an excellent joint, made in the same way as already described.

Mitred Angle Joints. —Figs. 37 to 39, and 40 to 42, show six methods of joining the ends of boards to form mitred angles. The plain mitreing (Fig. 37) and the keyed mitreing (Fig. 38) are used for skirting or plinth boards. Where extra strength is required with no details of the jointing showing, as in a plinth base for heavy furniture, such as a wardrobe on which the carcase stands, the joints illustrated by Fig. 39 and Figs. 40 to 42 are employed. The appearance of the tongued mitre joint (Fig. 39) when finished is shown by Fig. 43. Fig. 44 indicates how the pieces are put together in the bench vice when grooving with the plough in order to have a face at 90° for the fence. By gluing triangular pieces to the face of each board a good seating may be provided so as to cramp up the joint effectively, as seen in Fig. 45. The rebated and dowelled joint shown in Fig. 42 is specially adapted for thick work, and gives particularly strong results. These joints can also be used for friezes, fascias, etc., on furniture and joinery fixings.

Obtuse Angle Joints.—Figs. 46 and 47 show two ways of dealing with a joint at an obtuse angle for either side or end grain. The rebating, grooving and moulding are discussed elsewhere, and need not here be explained. Fig. 48 illustrates a composite grooved and tongued angle joint, planed to a curve, as might be useful for skirting, a bottom stair, or a plinth to furniture.

It must be borne in mind that the strength and rigidity of all this kind of jointing depends wholly upon a good tight fit and the best quality glue, properly applied.

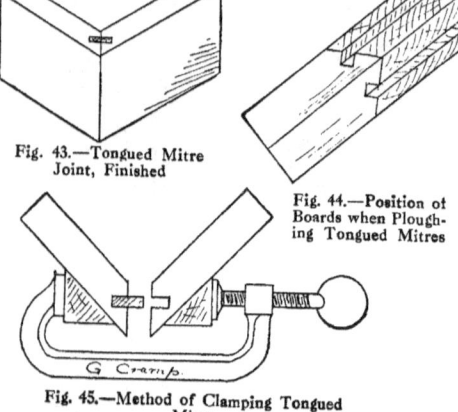

Fig. 43.—Tongued Mitre Joint, Finished

Fig. 44.—Position of Boards when Ploughing Tongued Mitres

Fig. 45.—Method of Clamping Tongued Mitre

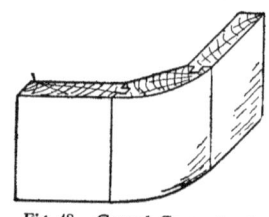

Fig. 48.—Curved Grooved and Tongued Joint

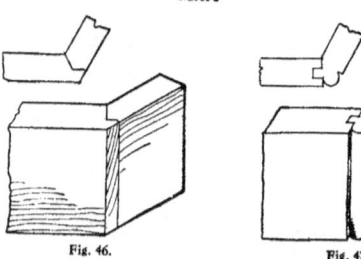

Fig. 46.   Fig. 47.

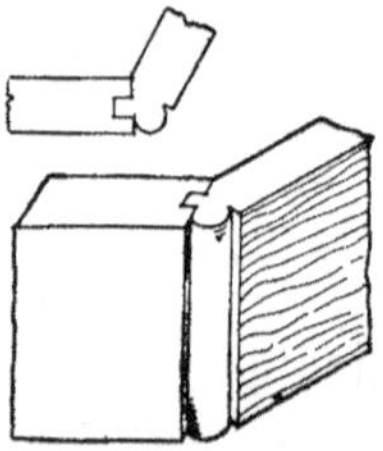

Figs. 46 and 47.—Obtuse Angle Joints: Rebated and Tongued

Dowelled Joints

Uses of Dowelled Joints.—In a dowelled joint, holes are bored in line at a right angle with the two surfaces to be connected, and into these are inserted glued wooden pins. When properly done, the result is very strong and rigid, besides being quickly executed and effecting a saving of material; but if carelessly carried out it readily comes apart. In some cases dowels are used for parts intended to be removable, as in cornice

Fig. 1.—Wheelwright's Dowel

Fig. 2.—Ordinary Dowel

fitments, piano fronts, and extra leaves for dining tables. Another typical use of this joint is by the wheelwright, who inserts dowels into the ends of the curved wooden sections, or felloes, where they meet; not to hold the felloes to the wheel, but simply to keep them flush at the joints. The felloes are really held on the wheels by wedges inserted in the tenons formed on the ends of the spokes, and also by the iron tyres. The kind of dowel used for wheels is nearly spindle-shaped, as shown in Fig. 1. When, however, the dowels are required to hold the parts together entirely, by the aid of glue alone, they must be cylindrical, as in Fig. 2.

Making Dowels.—These should be of sound, well-seasoned, straight-grained material, preferably hardwood, and usually beech. A convenient method is to saw blocks two or three times the required length, and to split them into roughly rectangular sticks. The latter are then planed, first to a square section, next hexagonal, and finally circular. A handy

Fig 3.—Dowel Box

device to hold the sticks while planing is illustrated by Fig. 3. The dowels are then cut to length, and the square ends trimmed as seen in Fig. 2, to facilitate driving in. This is best done with a dowel-pointer used in the brace, but a knife or chisel can be employed. Some workers flatten one side of the dowels, or cut a narrow **V**-groove along them, to allow the escape of air and surplus glue, but others consider this unnecessary, and do not recommend it.

The dowels can be gauged to size and shaped up by passing them through a round hole in a piece of wrought-iron plate, letting the hole remain as left by the drill. Fig. 4 shows such a dowel plate, mounted on a 1-in. thick hardwood block with various sizes of holes. The wooden base serves to keep the dowel vertical as it is driven through the iron plate. Dowels can also be turned in the lathe, or they may be purchased. They should not be too smooth; a slight roughness improves the strength of the joint.

Marking Boards for Dowelling.—For dowelling the edges of two boards together, first see that the surfaces meet truly, as if for an ordinary glued butt; then fix them back to back in the bench vice. Mark the centre of each board lengthways with the gauge, from opposite sides, and measure off the positions for

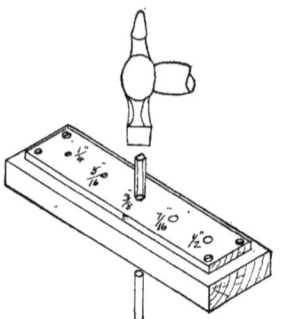

Fig. 4.—Dowel Plate, showing Method of Use

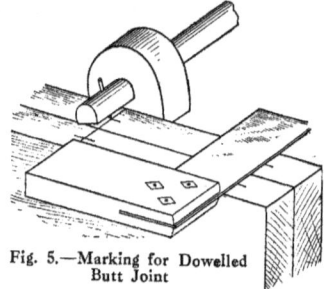

Fig. 5.—Marking for Dowelled Butt Joint

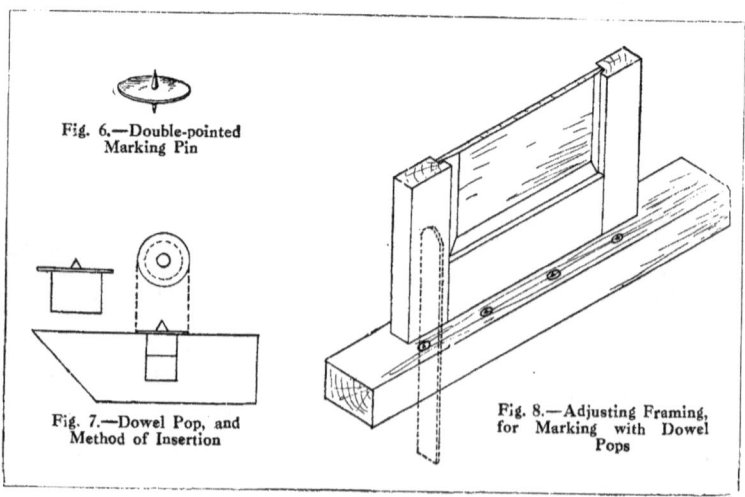

Fig. 6.—Double-pointed Marking Pin

Fig. 7.—Dowel Pop, and Method of Insertion

Fig. 8.—Adjusting Framing, for Marking with Dowel Pops

DOWELLED JOINTS

the dowels, from an inch or two to a foot distant, according to the work. Square these marks across the edges, and where the squared lines cut the gauged lines will be the points for boring. This method is illustrated by Fig. 5.

It is not always practicable to mark the two edges together, as, for instance, when a piece of woodwork is already partly made up. In such a case, some workmen use a kind of double drawing-pin (Fig. 6), having a point each side. One point is driven into the fixed portion where the dowel is to come, and the other piece to be joined is laid over the projecting point and tapped gently down. This obviously gives two marks exactly in line.

Dowel Pops.—Another good plan for marking the centres when boring dowel holes, used in Yorkshire, is to employ "dowel pops" (Fig. 7), of various sizes, usually cast in brass. Suppose it is the base of a wardrobe that requires dowelling. The holes are bored at suitable places in the base, away from shakes or knots, and the dowel pops are inserted, resting on their thin flanges. Next the framing is placed in position, resting on the projecting points of the pops, as shown in Fig. 8, measuring the equality of each side space and testing for flushness with a straightedge. A sharp tap is lastly given with a mallet on the top of the framing, when the points of the pops make impressions at the bottom of the latter, showing clearly where to bore for the dowels.

Marking Dowels for Panelled Work.—One method often adopted when making a length of panelling, such as is illustrated by Fig. 9, is to set out as for mortise and tenon joints (that is, by marking the width of one piece on the edge of the other), and then to measure and make fresh marks inside these at the proper distances for the dowels, squaring them across. A gauge mark is also made along the length of the wood to give the distance from the edge. The points where the inner lines cross the central line will then be the places to insert the point of the

Fig. 9.—Length of Panelling to be Dowelled

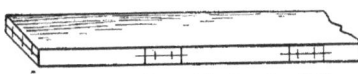

Fig. 11.—Old Way of Setting Out Rail

Fig. 10.—Old Way of Setting Out Muntin for Dowelling

boring bit. This way involves a great deal of needless setting out, as will be recognised from Figs. 10 and 11, which show one of the muntins, or upright divisions between the panels, and a portion of the top rail set out in this manner. There is, too, some opportunity for error or mistake.

A much better plan is to set out the timber as shown by Figs. 12 and 13, the first being the rails and the second the stiles and muntins. The marks indicated are all that are necessary, with the exception that the lines on the muntins (the middle pieces in Fig. 13) must be squared over as a guide to cutting off, while those on the middle rail will need squaring over on to the other edge of the wood. The muntins might, of course, be in two pieces, to obviate the waste of the two or three inches at the middle rail, as well as for convenience in converting. The setting out of the actual holes is done by means of a dowelling template.

made as illustrated in Figs. 14 and 15, the stock being of hardwood and the tongue of brass. The full length may be about 3 in., and the other parts in proportion. The tongue may be about $\frac{1}{8}$ in. thick, and the series of small holes

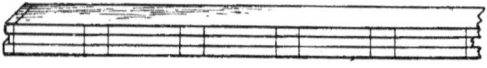

Fig. 12.—Better Method of Setting Out Rails

Fig. 13.—Better Method of Setting Out Stiles and Muntins

shown should be drilled truly, for on this will depend, in a great measure, the accuracy of the work set out with the tool. The tongue is screwed in the stock as shown in the section (Fig. 15), and both parts of the latter must be in the same plane, so that the tool can be used from either side, as occasion requires. In drilling the holes in the tongue it is also necessary to get them an equal distance from either end, and equally spaced, for the same reason.

The method of using the template is explained by Fig. 16. The tongue is placed level with one of the squared-over marks and the stock against the face side, when the dowel hole can be marked through a hole in the plate with a fine bradawl. The correct hole to use, in the present instance is that indicated by a cross at the left of the illustration. To finish the marking, slide the template to the right, as shown by the dotted lines, and mark through the corresponding hole at the other end. This is the manner of setting out for the muntins : that for the top or bottom rails is done as shown at the right, the two crossed holes being marked with the template in one position.

When setting out on, or for, wider rails, the template can be moved along, using the holes already marked as a guide, until the whole ground is covered ; thus Fig. 17 shows a wide rail set out for six dowels, while Fig. 18 shows the end of a thicker rail, in the setting out of which two rows of holes in the template are used, alternately near the face and the back. This will be found much preferable to using stouter dowels.

When making panelling with dowelled joints, do not forget the grooves in which the panels will fit. The dowels should be kept well clear of these, as shown by the dotted lines in Fig. 19. It will, of course, be understood that the dowel holes must be bored before the grooves are made, otherwise there would be great difficulty in getting them correct.

Dowelling Chairs, Tables, etc.—For dowelling the legs of tables or chairs or the rails of a cabinet framing into the stiles, a template may be made from a piece of thin zinc, the exact size of the end to be joined. Three small holes are pierced in this, and it is then laid in position on the leg or stile and the holes

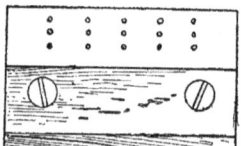

Fig. 14.—Plan of Metal Dowelling Template

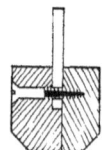

Fig. 15.—Section of Metal Dowelling Template

Fig. 16.—Method of Using Template for Setting Out

pricked through, as shown by Fig. 20. The other side of the template is used for marking the end of the rail. The holes

DOWELLED JOINTS

should be irregularly spaced, certainly not all in line.

Dowelling Doors.—To mark the centres for dowels in light doors, such

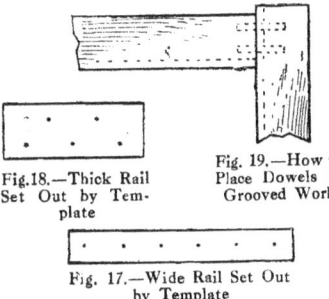

Fig.18.—Thick Rail Set Out by Template

Fig. 19.—How to Place Dowels in Grooved Work

Fig. 17.—Wide Rail Set Out by Template

dowel holes should fit those in the template as nearly as possible, without being actually tight.

Dowelling Felloes on Wheels.—

Fig. 21.—Wooden Dowelling Template for Doors

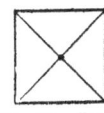 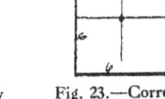

Fig. 22.—Faulty Method of Marking Felloes for Dowels

Fig. 23.—Correct Method of Marking Felloes

as those of sideboards, cupboards in wash-stands, chiffoniers, etc., the wooden template illustrated by Fig. 21 will be found useful. It should be of hardwood and equal in length to the width of the door rail, the projecting part being as wide as the thickness of the rails and stiles. The holes should be the same distance from each end. In use, it simply needs to be held on the ends of the rails, which it fits, while marking the holes with the bradawl, being then transferred

Fig. 22 shows the method often adopted to obtain the boring mark for dowels in wheel felloes, which may sometimes be useful for other circular work. With this it is necessary, however, for all the felloes to be true to size, a comparatively rare state of things. Therefore, a better way of getting the correct spot is that indicated in Fig. 23, where the face side

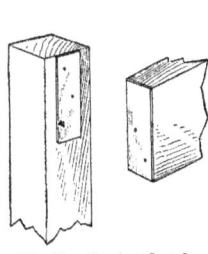

Fig. 20.—Setting Out for Dowels in Table or Chair

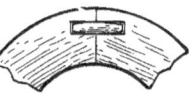

Fig. 25.—Felloes Correctly Dowelled

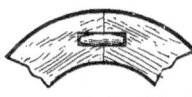

Fig. 24.—Felloes Joined, with Dowel Too Low

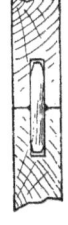

Fig. 26.—Section of Perfectly Dowelled Joint

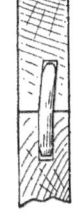

Fig. 27.—Joint with Bent Dowel, through Faulty Boring

to the side edges of the stiles, to mark the corresponding holes near the top and bottom.

The bradawl employed for marking

and the inside of the felloe are gauged from, the crossing of the lines being the right spot for boring. The holes should be bored at a right angle to the end of the felloe. It will be noticed that the mark is higher up in Fig. 23 than in Fig. 22. The former is correct, for if the

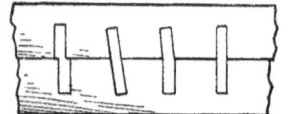

Fig. 28.—Diagram showing Various Faults in Dowels

Fig. 29.—Plan showing Holes Before and After Opening

dowel is too low down there is a risk of splitting off the lower corner of the felloe, where the grain is cut across. Figs. 24 and 25 will make this clear.

Boring Holes for Dowels. —The bit for boring dowel holes should be in good working order, a short-length twist bit being best. The right size for most work is $\frac{5}{16}$ in., though the $\frac{1}{4}$-in. or $\frac{3}{8}$-in. size may occasionally be found convenient. The bit must be kept truly vertical to the surface, or the joint will be unsatisfactory. Till expertness is gained, a try-square applied to the drill will be of assistance as a test. Fig. 26 is a section of a perfectly dowelled joint, where the two holes are bored to exactly the right depth and parallel with the sides of the wood, so that the dowel exerts its full holding power without being crippled in any way. Fig. 27, on the other hand, shows the effect of one of the holes being bored slightly out of parallel; in such a case the joint has to be forced together and held until the glue has set. Even then the dowel is crippled and its holding power much diminished.

Besides being parallel with the sides of the wood, it is equally important that the holes should be truly at a right angle to the joint the other way. Fig. 28 shows a series of four holes bored for dowels, that on the extreme right being as it should be. The second is bored correctly in the lower part but badly in the upper; therefore the dowel will be more or less crippled in putting the joint together. In the third, the dowel will be quite straight when in place, but it will have to be bent to get it to enter,

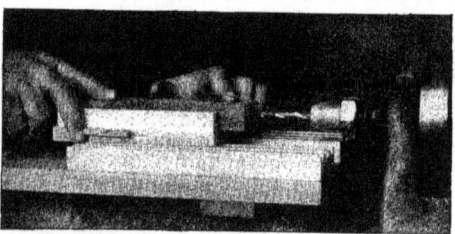

Fig. 31.—Method of Using Boring Fitment

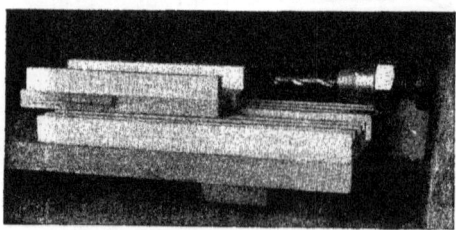

Fig. 30.—Fitment for Boring Dowel Holes in Lathe

and will probably be injured in doing so; the fault here is that both holes are bored badly, though in such a way that one compensates the other. This kind of compensation is very undesirable, but sometimes cannot be avoided. In the last case, the extreme left, the holes partly miss each other, either through faulty setting out or extremely careless boring. When this occurs, the holes should be plugged up and re-bored, for if left as it is the dowel will prove worse than useless.

DOWELLED JOINTS

The holes must be bored to a correct depth, a little over half the length of the dowel, to allow for glue and any trifling roughness at the bottom. Thus, with dowels $2\frac{1}{4}$ in. long, the holes should be $1\frac{1}{4}$ in. deep. With a good twist bit this may be gauged by counting the turns given, after testing the depth of the first hole. Another way is to place a wooden stop over the bit, or to use a metal bit gauge (*see* Chapter on Boring), to check it at the right distance down. A cylindrical piece of hardwood may be used, bored along the middle and furnished with a set screw to tighten it. It is as well to open or countersink the tops of the holes very slightly, as indicated by the second hole in Fig. 29, and seen sectionally in Fig. 26, this helps considerably in putting together and forms a sinking for surplus glue. The opening can be done with a snail or rose bit used in a brace.

Boring Dowel Holes in the Lathe.—If a lathe is available it forms an ideal appliance for making dowelled joints, obviating a great deal of the setting out, dispensing with a template, and, what is perhaps the best recommendation of all, boring the holes absolutely straight and true. The necessary fitment can readily be constructed to fit any lathe, and may be adapted to any thickness or width of material. The only parts which cannot very well be manipulated in the lathe are extra long pieces, owing to the room required; but in such cases the two methods are easily worked together, the long portions being bored in the ordinary way, as already described, and the shorter ones for the same job being drilled in the lathe.

The complete fitment is illustrated in Fig. 30, and the method of using it in Fig. 31; while Figs. 32 to 34 explain how it is made. Fig. 32 is a plan, and Fig. 33 a section, of the fitment in position on the lathe ready for work, the lettering being similar in each. The lathe bed is shown at A, while B is a clamp for bolting the fitment in place (two are required, one near the front and the other near the back). At C are cross-pieces, and to these the actual bed of the fitment, D, is screwed from underneath. On the top of the bed and level with the sides are fixed the two pieces E, provided with longitudinal and parallel grooves. In these grooved pieces slides the adjustable holder shown in Fig. 34. This latter consists of the two side pieces F, on the bottom of which are formed projections that will just fit into the grooves in E, these projections being nearer to one side than the other, as indicated. On the top of the pieces F are screwed strips G, level with the outside edges. To keep the two side portions of the holder in position, and yet allow them to be divided easily and quickly, so that they will fit into any of the

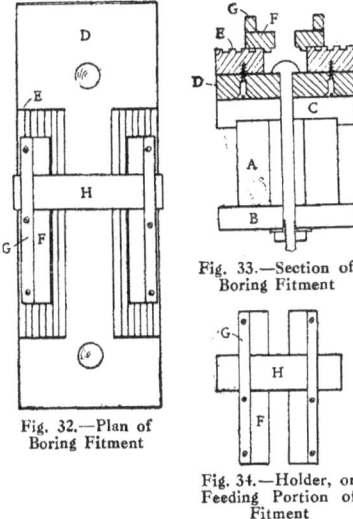

Fig. 33.—Section of Boring Fitment

Fig. 32.—Plan of Boring Fitment

Fig. 34.—Holder, or Feeding Portion of Fitment

grooves in E, a cross-bar H is sunk into the pieces F, so that it is level with their upper surfaces and passes under the strips G, thus retaining them rigid and parallel, and at the same time permitting a lateral adjustment.

The fitment must be so fixed on the lathe that the centres are midway between the pieces F when the latter are in any pair of grooves. In the section (Fig. 33) the guides are completely inside, that is as close together as possible; while in the plan (Fig. 32) they are in the middle groove.

The wood to be bored lies in the rebates formed by the pieces F and G, therefore the whole fitment must be built up according to the lathe, so as to bring the surface of F about ⅜ in. below the actual lathe centre, when it will be right for working on any thickness of material from ¾ in. to 1¼ in.

To use the fitment the sliding piece should be placed in suitable grooves to bring the holes the correct distance from the edges, and then fed up to the drill, as in Fig. 31, working from each of the pieces G, and, if more than two holes are wanted, resetting after the first boring. The face side of the material must be downwards during the boring operations, and a guide mark should be made to act as a depth gauge. For boring rails or other horizontal parts, another sliding holder, similar to Fig. 34, is required, in which, however, the pieces G are shortened at the front, so that the wood to be bored can rest directly across F. The rails must be set out on the side opposite where the holes are to be. The marks are then placed to the inside of the shortened pieces G, and the fitment used as before.

The best tool for boring in the lathe is an ordinary twist drill. This will be found to act very quickly and easily; the sizes also will fit the stock dowels better than is the case with twist bits. The drill, of course, needs to be fixed in a chuck.

Gluing Dowels.—The parts being bored and ready to put together, the dowels cut off and trimmed, and the glue at hand (which should be slightly thinner than usual), the holes in one piece are

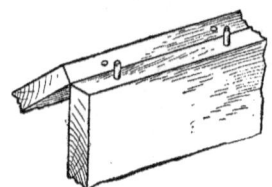

Fig. 35.—Parts of Dowel Joint in Position for Gluing

glued inside, using a round stick instead of a brush. The dowels are also touched with glue at one end, and then driven gently home into the glued holes. The other part is now held against the first, as shown in Fig. 35, the two edges and the projecting halves of the dowels being rapidly brushed with glue, allowing a little to run into the holes. Lastly, the pieces are fitted promptly together with pressure, and cramped up tightly till set.

Some workers prefer "cold" or liquid glue for dowelling, since it does not set so quickly, but more time must elapse before the joints can be depended on to bear usage.

Mortise and Tenon Joints

The Mortise and Tenon Joint.—This joint, in one or other of its numerous forms, is the most important and probably the most used of all where strength and rigidity are required. It is of great value to carpenters, joiners, cabinet-makers, cart and coach builders, wheelwrights, shipwrights and aircraft workers. An advantage of this kind of joint is that it seldom needs reinforcing by metal fastenings.

The making of simple mortise and tenon joints in material of rectangular section will first be dealt with; then a number of examples will be given showing their application in different kinds of work, with hints for setting out and making.

Closed Mortise and Tenon.—One of the most common forms of this joint is the ordinary closed tenon, so called because the tenon is surrounded by wood on all four sides. Fig. 1 shows the setting out of the mortise, Fig. 2 the setting out of the tenon, Fig. 3 the mortise made, Fig. 4 the tenon cut, and Fig. 5 a section of the complete joint secured by a pin, though the latter is often omitted.

Using Mortise Gauge.—Save in exceptional cases, it is usual for the tenon to be one-third the thickness of the material, or thereabouts. While it is certainly possible to do the setting out merely by measurement, it saves much time and trouble to employ a mortise gauge (Fig. 6), for marking the two

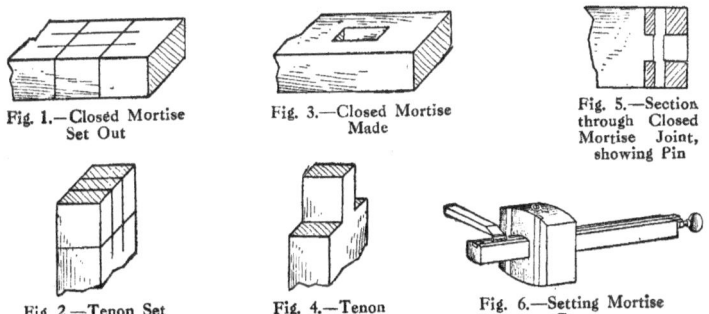

Fig. 1.—Closed Mortise Set Out

Fig. 3.—Closed Mortise Made

Fig. 5.—Section through Closed Mortise Joint, showing Pin

Fig. 2.—Tenon Set Out

Fig. 4.—Tenon Cut

Fig. 6.—Setting Mortise Gauge

parallel lines on opposite faces of each piece, and on the end of the tenon portion. Except for large mortises, the width consists of single cuts with the chisel, hence the gauge requires setting to the

Fig. 7.—Beginning with Chisel on Bored Mortise

width of the latter by turning a nut at the end of the gauge stem, which regulates the distance between the two marking pins. The arrangement for setting the pins, however, varies in different patterns of gauges. The sliding stock is then moved till its face is the correct distance from the inner pin, and the screw tightened up. The lines indicating the length of the mortise and tenon respectively are measured and squared over on all four faces.

An ordinary marking gauge may, with a little care, be used to set out mortises and tenons by marking single lines from opposite sides, if the exact position for these is first measured centrally and the gauge set accordingly. This, however, presupposes that the wood is of uniform thickness and with truly parallel sides. It is better if only a marking gauge is available to set the gauge twice and work from one side only.

Cutting the Mortise.—The easiest way of making a mortise is to bore out part of the waste before using the chisel. A small piece of work may be held in the bench vice, while longer or very heavy pieces are best laid on two trestles. The back side should always be done first, and both sides should be bored from if the mortise goes right through the wood. It will be noticed in Fig. 7 that a third hole is bored. This is advisable in a longer mortise; in fact. as much of the wood as possible should be bored away, thus reducing the chisel work.

One often sees the method of mortising shown in Fig. 8 recommended, a small wedge-shaped piece being taken out in the middle and continued each way until the ends of the mortise are reached, when these are cut down square. This method is not a good one, as the chisel has to be reversed between each stroke, and it is impossible to remove so much of the waste wood as is desirable.

A better way is to commence nearly close up to the end of the mortise nearest the worker, cutting perpendicularly and as far in as the chisel will enter without using undue force. Then move the chisel back without reversing, and make another cut, removing the loose wood at the same time. Bring the chisel back to its first position, making another perpendicular cut, then take in a further piece towards the other end, and so on, till the whole length of the mortise has been done. The successive strokes are indicated in Fig. 9, and shown in plan by Fig. 10. By this

Fig. 8.—Incorrect Method of Chiselling

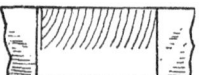

Fig. 9.—Correct Method of Chiselling

Fig. 10.—Plan of Correct Chiselling

method practically the whole of the wood is removed as it is cut away, while the work is done very quickly and cleanly.

Faults in Making Mortises.—Fig. 11 represents in section lengthways a series of mortises, of which N is the only perfect one. Here the ends are straight through from top to bottom—a result, unfortunately, but seldom found, even in

MORTISE AND TENON JOINTS

the best work. At O is seen the most usual product, in which the ends of the mortise are both cut under, as a rule purposely on the principle that the tenon will fit at each side and nothing else matters. That is true to a certain extent; but if the undercutting is overdone there is a risk of driving out the wood at the back when fitting together.

The faults shown at P and R are caused by carelessness or want of judgment, and the remedy is fairly obvious. The section shown in S is sometimes made intentionally, and is called a wheelwright's mortise. The idea is that the tenon being forced into the mortise causes the wood, as it were, to clinch itself, and needs no further fixing; but the notion is rather far-fetched, and such a joint cannot be very secure.

There is more excuse for making mortises of a bad shape at the ends than at the sides, but the latter also is by no means uncommon. In Fig. 12 are illustrated a series of finished mortises, of which T alone is satisfactory. The effect of U is that the holding pin cannot be so strong, owing to the tenon and the sides of the mortise not being in close contact; but in V the case is different, there being grave danger of splitting the work when putting the joint together. The slovenly cutting seen at W has very little influence on the completed joint; nevertheless, it should be avoided. In X the faults are glaringly apparent, and the wood will almost certainly split. The last two mortises are tapered, being wider at the top than at the bottom. In one case the right-hand side of the mortise has been made sloping and in the other both sides are inaccurately cut.

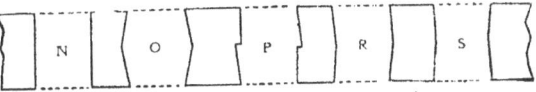

Fig. 11.—Faults in Mortising (Endways)

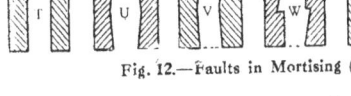

Fig. 12.—Faults in Mortising (Sideways)

Fig. 13.—Starting Tenon

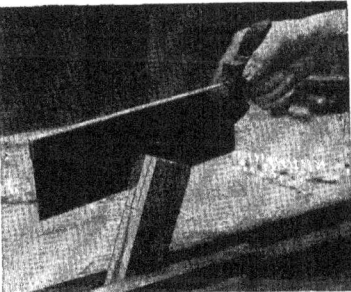

Fig. 14.—Making Tenon—after Reversing Wood

The last-mentioned batch of faults will only occur in the larger mortises. The narrow ones, being cut to the width of the chisel, must come out the full width, but it is just possible to make the mistakes shown at V and W.

Sawing the Tenon.—Figs. 13 and 14 illustrate the commencement of sawing a tenon. The first shows the slight cut across the corner at the face side ing at the face side is to have the finishing cut there also. In the case of very long tenons the wood may have to be reversed four times instead of two,

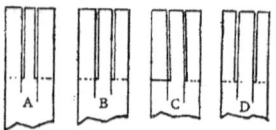

Fig. 15.—Various Faults in Sawing Tenons

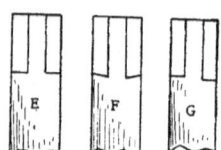

Fig. 16.—Various Faults in Cutting Tenon Shoulders

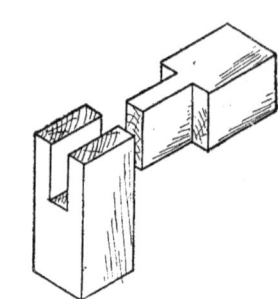

Fig. 19.—Finished Slot Mortise Joint, ready for Fixing

or edge, and the second indicates the position of the saw leading from this cut to the opposite side, after the timber has been reversed. This latter cut should gradually be run down on the side

but it is better if the cuts begin and finish on the face side.

In making a shoulder cut the saw at first is held with its point down, the hand being then gradually lowered until the saw is horizontal, and the cutting proceeded with until it meets the tenon

Fig. 17.—Slot Mortise Set Out

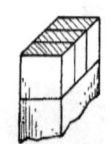

Fig. 18.—Setting Out Tenon for Slot Mortise

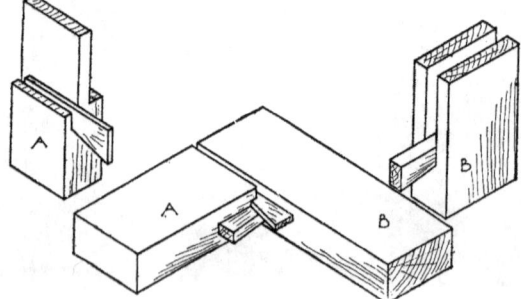

Fig. 20.—Adjustable Slot Mortise and Tenon Joint

of the tenon nearest the operator, when the timber may be again reversed and the cut continued to the shoulder lines; or the cut may be finished at the second operation. The object of start-

cut, when the "cheek" will drop off. Unless it is a "barefaced" tenon, the other side is then done in the same way.

Faults in Sawing Tenons.—It is usually impressed on beginners that they

MORTISE AND TENON JOINTS

must learn to cut to the lines, and, of course, the advice is good; but it is quite possible to obey it literally and yet be far from correct, especially when sawing

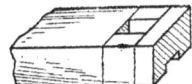

Fig. 21.—Closed Haunched Mortise

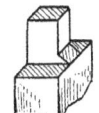

Fig. 23.—Tenon with Secret Haunching

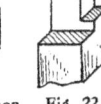

Fig. 22.—Haunched Tenon

tenons. In Fig. 15 are shown a series of tenons sawn in, but with the shoulders uncut; and of these only one is right, though all are sawn to the lines. Thus A is cut on the inside of the lines, which will make the tenon too thin; B is inside one line and outside the other, while C commences in the same way and crosses the lines. The correct method is seen at D, where the cuts are made on the outside of each line, leaving the tenon the full thickness to fit properly in the mortise.

Fig. 16 illustrates the right and the wrong way of cutting shoulders for tenons. Thus, E is correct; each shoulder is sawn in exactly to the mark, and will as the term is; in consequence they will fit on the outside only, and if any considerable amount of cleaning off is required the result will be an open shoulder. At G the cutting is worse still, one shoulder being sawn on the one side of the mark and the other on just the opposite, the effect being that only one shoulder will fit.

Slot Mortise and Tenon.—In this joint, also known as the "open" type, the mortise is merely a slot cut in the end of a piece of timber, so that the tenon can be driven in from the side. Fig. 17 shows the setting out of such a mortise, and Fig. 18 the setting out of the tenon, while Fig. 19 illustrates the finished joint ready for fixing together. It is often used in making door frames.

Adjustable Slot Mortise and Tenon.—Fig. 20 illustrates the familiar device employed to stretch the canvas for oil paintings. The shoulder is grooved out against the face of tenon with a ½-in. chisel and sloped to fit a ½-in. wedge, as shown at A on the left; while the slot mortise is made with a sloping end to receive a wedge full width, as at B on the right. The canvas is then tacked on to the frame and the wedges driven up till the required tension is obtained.

Haunched Mortise and Tenon.— In cases where the end of the mortised piece has to be cut off level with the tenoned piece, and a slot mortise is not suitable, the joint is "haunched," that is, the mortise is made shorter than the

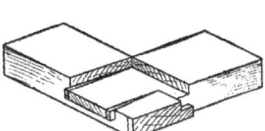

Fig. 24.—Cut-away View of Wedged Haunched Tenon

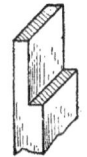

Fig. 25.—Barefaced Tenon Cut

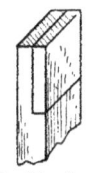

Fig. 26.—Setting Out Barefaced Tenon

Fig. 27.—Section of Barefaced Mortise and Tenon Joint

fit on the inside as well as on the outside. The shoulders at F are started at the lines but the cutting is continued "under," actual width of the tenon, as in Fig. 21, while the tenon itself is cut away, as in Fig. 22. The tenon is first sawn the full width, as for the ordinary type, then the haunch is marked off and the small block of waste sawn away. The recess in the mortise to receive the haunch is sawn to the lines with the end of the tenon saw and finished with the chisel. Another form, known as secret haunching, is shown by Fig. 23 ; in this the haunch does not show on the end. Haunched joints are often secured by wedges at each side of the tenon, for which purpose the ends of the mortise are made a little

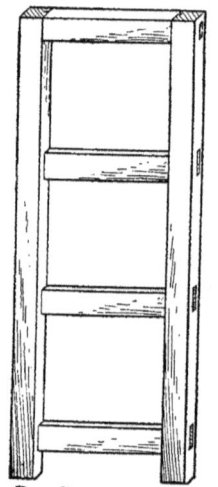

Fig. 28.—Door Frame, with Ordinary and Barefaced Tenons

wider and slanting outwards, as seen in the cut-away view (Fig. 24).

Barefaced Tenons.— A barefaced tenon has only one shoulder, the other side being flush with the face, as indicated by Fig. 25. Fig. 26 shows how the tenon is set out, the setting out for the mortise being readily understood from the section of the complete joint (Fig. 27). The barefaced tenon is used when one side of a rail has to be flush with the stile or post, while the other side is set back ; as, for instance, when it is desired to fix matchboarding across the lower rails of a frame, such as is shown in Fig. 28. In that case the lower rails have barefaced tenons, while the top rail is the same thickness as the stiles, and has ordinary tenons. The barefaced joint is also useful when a stouter tenon is desirable than the thickness of the material would otherwise allow, as in the rails connecting table tops.

Stub or Joggle Tenon.—When a tenon does not pass right through the material it is known as a stub or joggle tenon. These are only employed to keep the tenoned piece laterally in position, and are seldom required. Fig. 29 is typical of such.

Oblique Mortises and Tenons.— These are more difficult and require careful setting out. Fig. 30 illustrates a rectangular frame in which two oblique braces are inserted. Fig. 31 shows the method of setting out the rails (note that the face marks are both on the inside) ; while Fig. 32 shows the top rail tenoned and haunched. The bottom rail (Fig. 33) does not require haunching. The stiles should be set out as a pair in the same way as the rails ; one is shown in Fig. 34 with the mortises set out, including that for the brace, while Fig. 35 shows the cut mortises. In actual practice, however, only the mortises for the rails would at first be set out and made. The frame would then be knocked together, so that the braces can be laid on i in the position they will eventually occupy, when the mortises can readily be marked on the stiles and rails, as well as the shoulder lines on the braces, after which it is only necessary to square the various lines across to get the complete setting out.

Fig. 36 shows one brace after the various marks have been squared over and connected, and also gauged for cutting the tenons ; while Fig. 37 shows the same brace after the tenons are cut. Before inserting the braces it is necessary to cut the tenons at the longest point to a right angle with the shoulders, and also to cut them parallel with the latter, thus bringing them to the shape seen in Fig. 38. The reason for cutting the oblique tenons

MORTISE AND TENON JOINTS

as described is to give them a much firmer abutment, and also to simplify making the mortises, as will be understood by reference to Fig. 39, where the method temporarily to the face of the work, so that the bit may be held vertically and enter at a right angle. This is illustrated by Fig. 40, where A is the stile to be

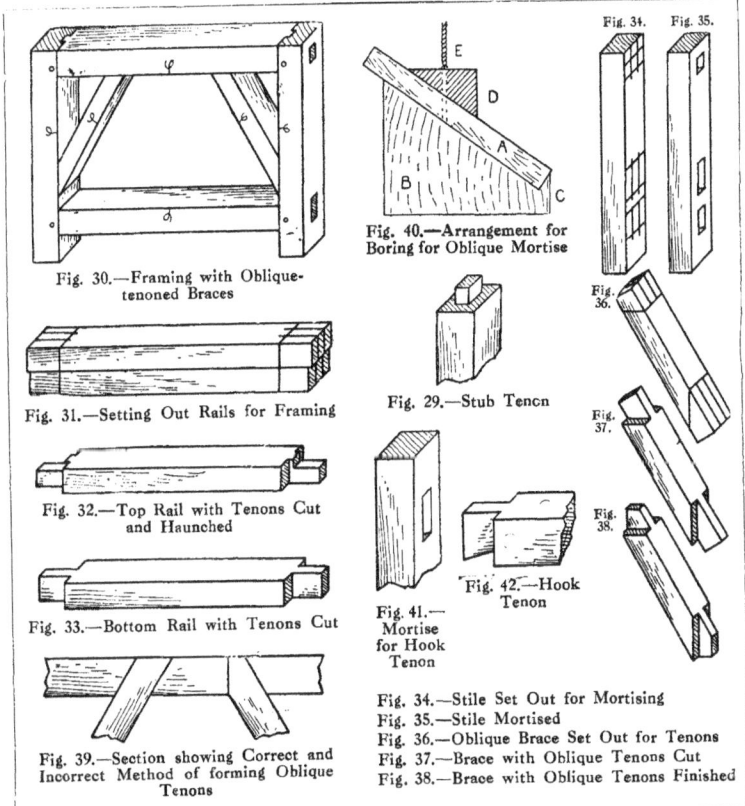

Fig. 30.—Framing with Oblique-tenoned Braces

Fig. 31.—Setting Out Rails for Framing

Fig. 32.—Top Rail with Tenons Cut and Haunched

Fig. 33.—Bottom Rail with Tenons Cut

Fig. 39.—Section showing Correct and Incorrect Method of forming Oblique Tenons

Fig. 40.—Arrangement for Boring for Oblique Mortise

Fig. 29.—Stub Tenon

Fig. 42.—Hook Tenon

Fig. 41.—Mortise for Hook Tenon

Fig. 34.—Stile Set Out for Mortising
Fig. 35.—Stile Mortised
Fig. 36.—Oblique Brace Set Out for Tenons
Fig. 37.—Brace with Oblique Tenons Cut
Fig. 38.—Brace with Oblique Tenons Finished

recommended is seen on the right, and the direct way on the left, both being in section.

In making oblique mortises it is a good plan to support the piece at a suitable angle in a box or cradle, or on an inclined plane, fixing a wedge-shaped block mortised, B an inclined plane having a stop C, D a block secured to the stile, and E the bit. Or, in some cases, the stile and block might be clamped in the bench vice at the required angle, placing a piece of waste at the back of the hole to prevent splintering.

Hook Tenon.—Figs. 41 and 42 show respectively the mortise and tenon forming a hook or dovetail joint. The mortise is made on the bevel at one end, or rather side, the tenon being cut to fit. Since the mortise obviously has to be the full width of the tenon, a space is left into which a pair of folding wedges can be inserted which hold the joint very firmly together, while, at the same time, it may easily be unshipped if desired.

It is often made long enough to project on the other side, and a hole is cut to receive a tapered key or peg.

Tusk tenons are also employed in general carpentry, especially in collapsible bookcases, garden frames, etc., in which case the tenon is often made thicker, and the hole for the peg or wedges cut through the face side of the wood, instead of through what may be called the flat or top of the tenon.

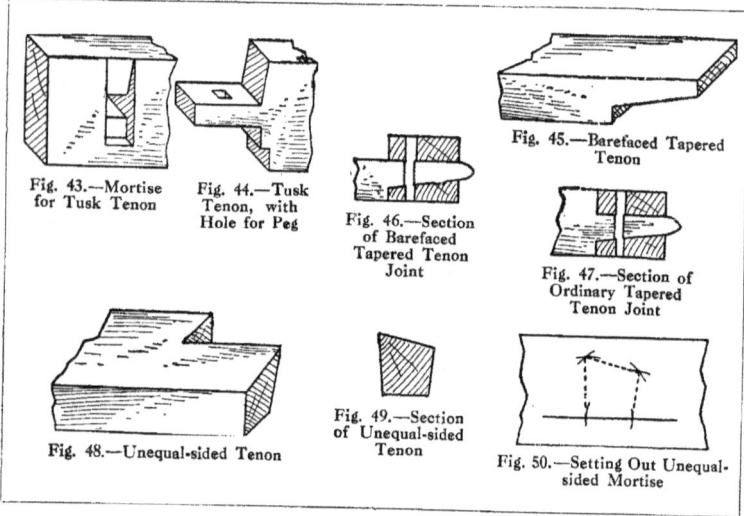

Fig. 43.—Mortise for Tusk Tenon
Fig. 44.—Tusk Tenon, with Hole for Peg
Fig. 45.—Barefaced Tapered Tenon
Fig. 46.—Section of Barefaced Tapered Tenon Joint
Fig. 47.—Section of Ordinary Tapered Tenon Joint
Fig. 48.—Unequal-sided Tenon
Fig. 49.—Section of Unequal-sided Tenon
Fig. 50.—Setting Out Unequal-sided Mortise

Tusk Tenon.—Fig. 43 shows the mortise made ready to receive a "tusk" tenon, while Fig. 44 shows the tenon ready for insertion. This kind of joint is used in building construction for the framing of floor joists. It will be noticed that though the mortise is so small as to weaken the joist very little, yet the tenon takes a very strong bearing owing to the recess made below the mortise and the sloping cut above it. As a rule the setting out of this joint is done by placing the tenon in the middle as regards the depth of the joists and allowing it to be one-seventh of the depth only in thickness.

Tapered Tenons.—Some workers have a particular fancy for the tapered tenon; but while there are undoubtedly a few points in its favour for special purposes, it is not advised for frequent use. Great care must be taken in setting out to get the tenons accurate, for if too tight they will act as wedges and split the wood, while if too slack they depend entirely on the pin for security. In Fig. 45 is shown a barefaced tapered tenon, such as would be used for framing up the bottom of a wheelbarrow or farm cart, while Fig. 46 is a section of the joint finished. A similar tapered joint, but

MORTISE AND TENON JOINTS

with the ordinary double shoulders, is shown by Fig. 47. In all cases the upper side should be parallel with the face of the wood.

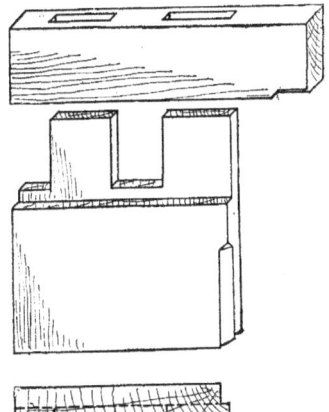

Fig. 51.—Double Tenon Joint for Bottom Rail of Door (shown on its side)

Unequal-sided Tenons.—An unequal-sided barefaced tenon is shown by Fig. 48, and in section by Fig. 49. The mortise is set out as illustrated by Fig. 50, in which the straight line represents the face. On this is marked off the width of the tenon in the proper position, then, with a sharp pair of compasses, the width of the tenon is taken from back to front at each side and transferred to the wood, using the points already marked to work from, and striking arcs as shown. Next, the diagonals of the tenon are taken each way and transferred to the wood as before, lastly connecting the points where the arcs cut each other, as indicated by the dotted lines. A mortise made to these marks will be found to fit the tenon exactly.

Double Tenons. In the case of wide timbers, such as the middle and bottom rails of panel doors, it is not desirable to run the tenons the whole width, which would not make either a strong or satisfactory job on account of the excessive shrinkage which would take place, leaving the tenons slack. Furthermore, the stile is weakened by having such a wide mortise. To overcome these disadvantages double tenons are used. Fig. 51 shows the double-tenoned joint between the stile and bottom rail of a 2-in. house door. Fig. 52 shows the setting out for the tenons, and also for the muntin mortise in the middle. It is a good rule to limit the width of the tenon to six times its thickness. The haunch at the bottom edge is to allow of enough end grain wood being left in the stile to wedge against. The small tongue forming the lower haunch, and the one between the tenons, are to keep the rail from warping, and also prevent light coming through the door should the joint open a little. It is a merit of double tenons that four wedges may be used, instead of only two.

Fig. 52.—Setting Out Double Tenons

Fig. 53.—Double Tenon for Middle Rail (on Left)

Fig. 54.—Compound Double Tenon for Mortise Lock

The middle rail of a door should be haunched in the centre alone, as seen on the left in Fig. 53; the two haunches required for the lower rail being shown on the right for comparison. The dotted lines indicate where the grooves for the panels will come, and, in actual practice, rails only of doors to be fitted with mortise locks. When it is known which way the doors will hang, these tenons would be made on the lock side alone;

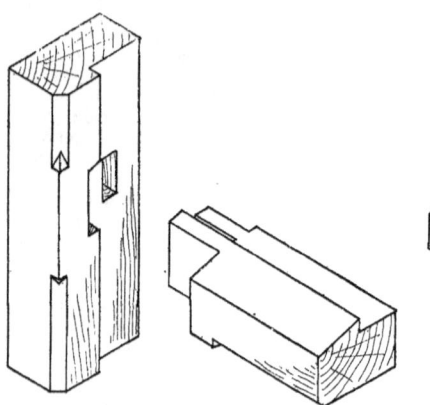

Fig. 55.—Double-tenoned Joint for Transom Rail

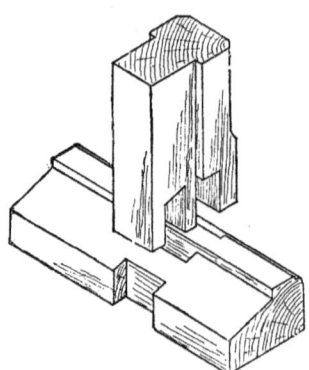

Fig. 57.—Tenoned and Bridled Joint

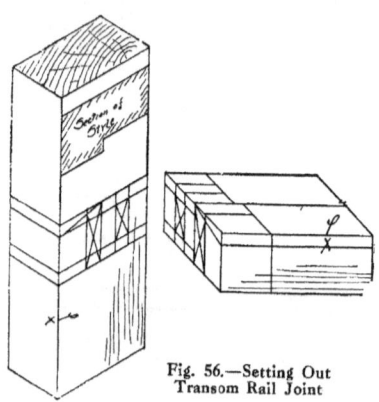

Fig. 56.—Setting Out Transom Rail Joint

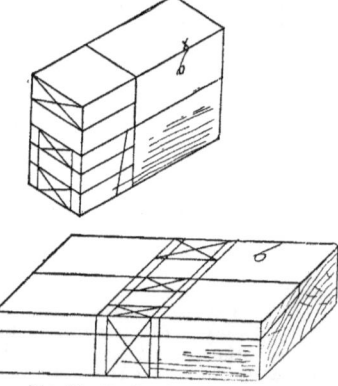

Fig. 58.—Setting Out Tenoned and Bridled Joint

these should be made before the shoulders are cut.

Fig. 54 illustrates another form of double tenon, set out on the right and made on the left, as used in the middle but in the absence of definite information it is best to prepare both sides, as shown. It is also advisable to cut the mortise for the lock in the rail itself before putting the door together.

MORTISE AND TENON JOINTS

Fig. 55 shows the joint between transom rail and stile of an outside cottage door frame, rebated, weathered and chamfered, where, on account of the great thickness, a different kind of double tenon is called for. It will be noted that the tenons are not the same length, and that the near one is bevelled on its top edge to correspond with the weathered slope of the transom rail. When setting out for rebated and grooved framing, it is well to let the tenons coincide with the grooves and with the edge of the rebate. In this case the near tenon finishes level with the rebate. Fig. 56 illustrates how to set out shoulder and gauge lines in the square stuff, for all tenons and mortises should be cut before rebating, chamfering or moulding is begun.

A somewhat related type of joint, though not a double tenon, is seen in Fig. 57. This shows a post tenoned and bridled into the sill, as in the case of a French window. When finished, the shoulder lines are, of course, vertical. Fig. 58 indicates how this joint is set out on the square. Wedges can be inserted from the bottom side of the sill into the middle tenon, and it is advisable that an oak pin should be driven through the whole joint from front to back. Previous to wedging up, the joint should be well coated with thick paint.

Locking Tenons.—Fig. 59 shows the method of tenoning when the rails are continued through a post in such a manner that the latter is continued in one piece from top to bottom. An example of this kind can be seen in the doorpost and transom rail of a vestibule, and

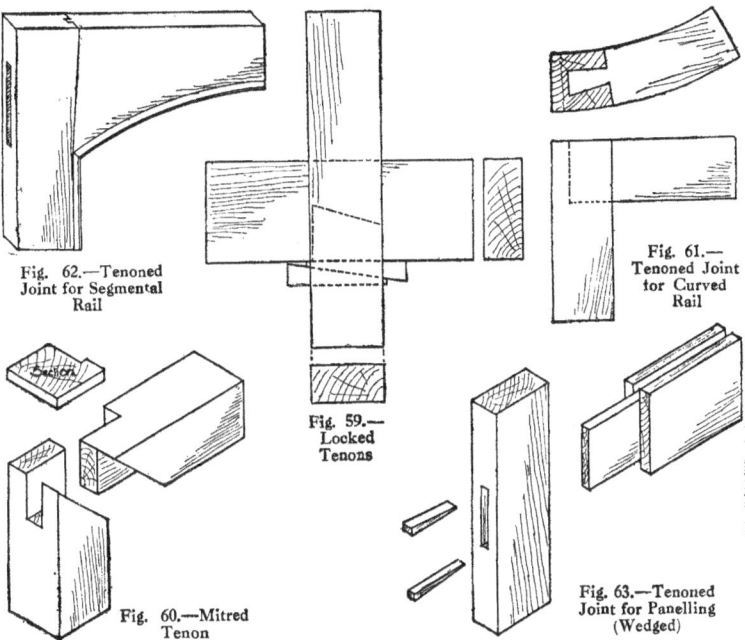

Fig. 62.—Tenoned Joint for Segmental Rail

Fig. 61.—Tenoned Joint for Curved Rail

Fig. 59.—Locked Tenons

Fig. 60.—Mitred Tenon

Fig. 63.—Tenoned Joint for Panelling (Wedged)

sometimes in a large casement window. The tenons are made first in the usual way, being then cut and bevelled to fit each other, as indicated by the dotted lines, thus forming a locked joint. The mortise is cut wider than the rail, in order to let the bevelled tenons pass each other into position, and the extra space is filled up with a pair of folding wedges glued before insertion.

Mitred Tenon.—A mitred tenon may sometimes be needed in picture and other frames. A typical instance is shown by Fig. 60, the section displaying the rebate for the glass and picture.

Tenons for Curved Work.—Fig. 61 illustrates the joint for a door or window rail, curved in plan with the stile. The dovetail tenon is first cut on the curved rail, being then rested on the end of the stile, flush to the face, and marked round with an awl. The stile can now be gauged and the mortise slotted with tenon saw and chisel.

Fig. 62 shows how the segmental top rail of a glazed panel door is jointed to the stile. The bevelled shoulder will be noted from the full width of the stile at the top to the depth of the quirk in the moulding, which has been struck on the solid material. The shoulder lines should be marked on the square stuff, and the tenon cut before the curved cut is made and rebated to receive the glass. It will be seen that the tenon is haunched.

Tenons for Grooved, Beaded, or Moulded Work.—Fig. 63 shows the joint between rail and stile in ordinary

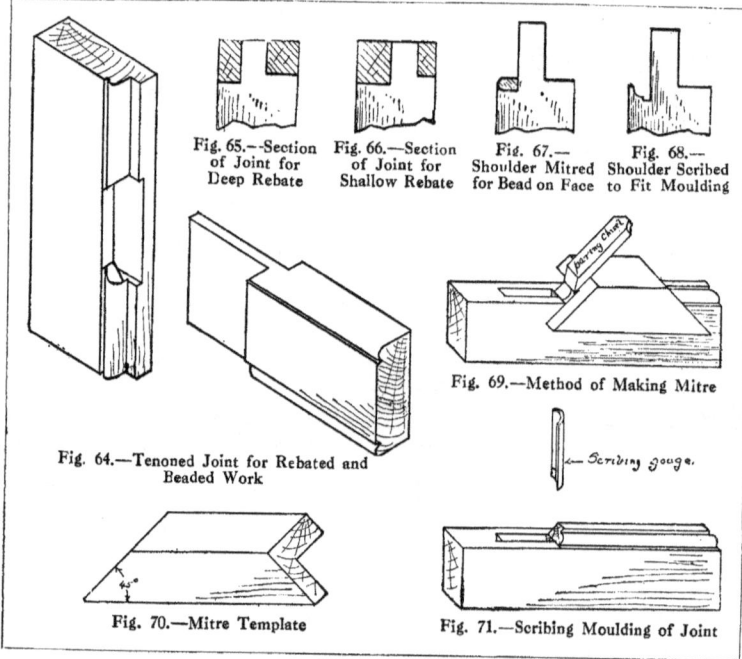

Fig. 65.—Section of Joint for Deep Rebate
Fig. 66.—Section of Joint for Shallow Rebate
Fig. 67.—Shoulder Mitred for Bead on Face
Fig. 68.—Shoulder Scribed to Fit Moulding
Fig. 64.—Tenoned Joint for Rebated and Beaded Work
Fig. 69.—Method of Making Mitre
Fig. 70.—Mitre Template
Fig. 71.—Scribing Moulding of Joint

MORTISE AND TENON JOINTS

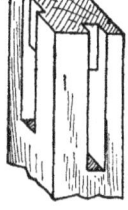

Fig. 72.—Mortises for Table-leg Joint

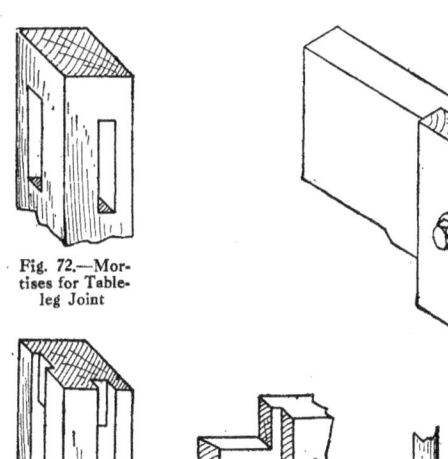

Fig. 77.—Bolted Table-leg Joint

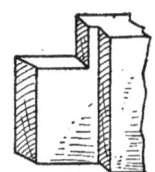

Fig. 73.—Haunched Mortises in Table Leg

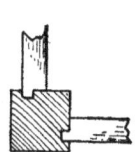

Fig. 74.—Rail with Haunched and Mitred Tenon

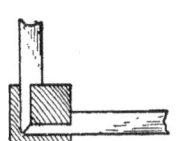

Fig. 75.—Top View of Table-leg Joint

Fig. 76.—Section of Table-leg Joint

panelled framing, as in a door or dado frame. It will be noted that the tenon is narrower by the depth of both the top and bottom grooves in the rail made to receive the panels.

Fig. 64 shows the middle rail tenoned into the rebated and once-beaded stile of a cupboard frame. This kind of joint requires tenon shoulders of unequal length. The following general principles will make the procedure to be followed in such cases clear. Thus, when there is only a rebate to be considered the shoulders are cut to fit into the rebate, and the tenon so cut as to bring one side level with the latter. Fig. 65, for instance, illustrates the joint in section for a deep rebate, and Fig. 66 that for a shallower one. When there is a moulding on the side opposite the rebate, both shoulders have to be longer, so that one fits to the rebate while the other is mitred or scribed to fit

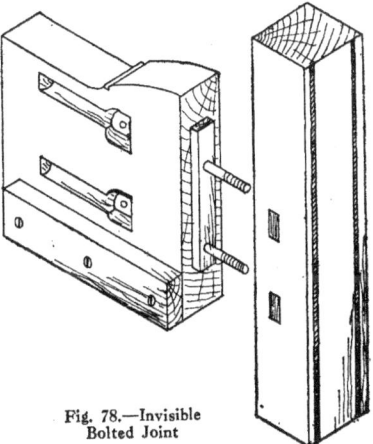

Fig. 78.—Invisible Bolted Joint

the moulding. Fig. 67 shows a shoulder mitred to fit a corresponding bead on the mortised head, and Fig. 68 shows the scribed joint to fit to a moulded head. Returning to the joint illustrated in Fig. 64, the method of mitreing is in- in two directions at right angles is shown by Fig. 72. Barefaced tenons are used, and the mortises continued till they meet. Fig. 73 shows the leg with the haunchings cut, while Fig. 74 illustrates one of the rails tenoned and haunched,

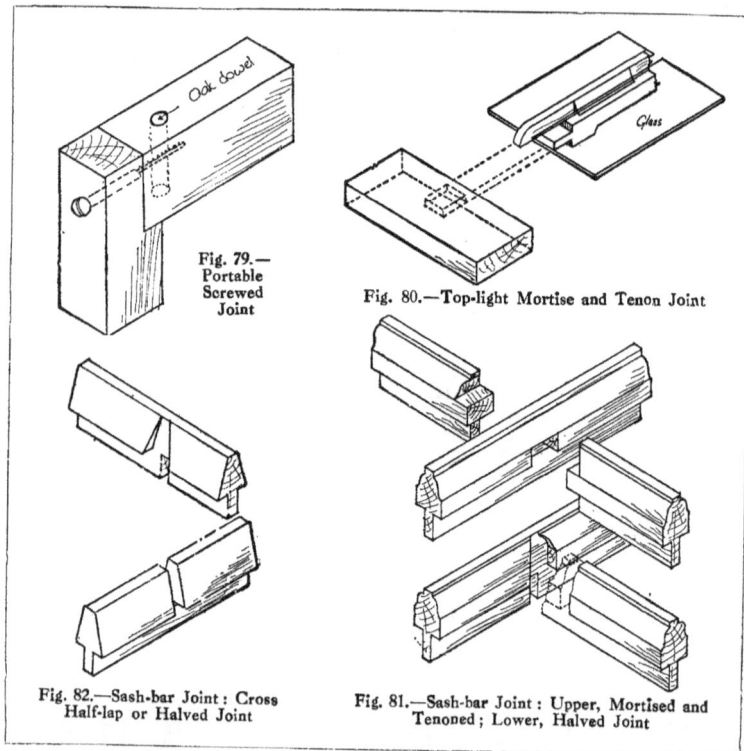

Fig. 79.—Portable Screwed Joint

Fig. 80.—Top-light Mortise and Tenon Joint

Fig. 82.—Sash-bar Joint: Cross Half-lap or Halved Joint

Fig. 81.—Sash-bar Joint: Upper, Mortised and Tenoned; Lower, Halved Joint

dicated by Fig. 69. This is done with a paring chisel, guided by a template (Fig. 70) cut to an angle of 45°. The method of using this mitre template is shown in Fig. 47, page 36. Fig. 71 shows the scribed portion being shaped with a scribing gouge.

Table-leg Joints.—A table leg or corner post mortised to take side rails the end being mitred to get the advantage of as much length as possible. Fig. 75 is a top view of the finished joint, and Fig. 76 a section showing the mitred ends of the tenons, which should be kept just short enough not to touch each other.

Bolted Table-leg Joints.—Fig. 77 shows a bolted barefaced tenon joint,

MORTISE AND TENON JOINTS

suitable to connect the rails and leg of a strong table or work-bench. This method is often employed in portable buildings to allow of the structure being taken down and stored away in pieces. The wooden framework of machinery is also mostly put together in this fashion, and many examples may be met with when visiting a flour-mill or an up-to-date dairy. The hole for the bolt is made after the tenoned rail is inserted into the mortise, and the nut is then sunk into the back of the rail. Great care should be exercised in fixing the nut true and firm, so that it will not shift when the bolt is withdrawn.

Another type of joint, with bolts arranged not to show from the outside, is illustrated by Fig. 78. The bolts have cylindrical heads with holes drilled through. This enables a nail punch to be inserted and the bolt screwed into the nut, which is sunk into the post and plugged up with the same kind of wood, selected to follow the graining. This joint is often met with in wooden bedsteads. The tenon is only needed to take the dead weight off the bolts, the latter themselves sufficing to hold the joint tight.

Portable Screwed Joint.—Fig. 79 shows a portable joint, just notched or stub-tenoned together, and held in position with a long round-headed screw. A hardwood dowel is glued and driven through the rail to receive the thread of the screw, which acts like the nut on a bolt. This joint is suitable for light framework, such as a meat-safe or dog kennel.

Sash-bar Tenon Joints.—Sash-bars require special treatment. Fig. 80 illustrates the joint between a rebated and chamfered sash-bar and the bottom rail of a skylight. It will be seen that the portion above the glass is continued over the bottom rail.

When making a long skylight, such as the glass covers for garden frames, it is better to let the tenon go right through the top and bottom rails and to wedge them up in the ordinary way, long tenon and short tenon alternately.

Figs. 81 and 82 give two methods of jointing moulded and rusticated sash-bars. The first is mortised and tenoned together, and is mostly used with thick bars, which are here shown scribed. The second is really a variation of the half-lap joint, with moulded and sloping sides cut to fit.

Fox-wedged Mortise and Tenon Joints.—In certain work it is not expedient for the tenons to go through the wood for wedging, and equally impossible to use pins. In such cases, carpenters and joiners generally adopt the method

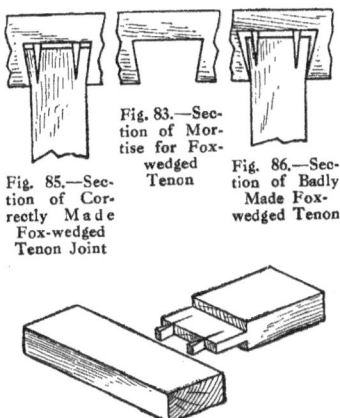

Fig. 85.—Section of Correctly Made Fox-wedged Tenon Joint

Fig. 83.—Section of Mortise for Fox-wedged Tenon

Fig. 86.—Section of Badly Made Fox-wedged Tenon

Fig. 84.—Fox-wedged Tenon Ready For Driving In

known as "fox" or secret wedging. This consists of making the mortise wider on the inside than the outside, by the thickness of the two wedges, as shown sectionally in Fig. 83. The rectangular tenon is made a little shorter than the depth of the mortise and saw kerfs are cut in the end; then the parts are glued, the wedges inserted, as in Fig. 84, and on knocking the tenon in the wedges are forced home by coming against the inside of the mortise. In consequence, the tenon is expanded into what is practically a dovetail, as illustrated by Fig. 85.

Fox-wedged joints are more or less successful according to whether the wedges and the sloping sides of the mortise are correctly made, and it often turns out that they are not. One common cause of failure is shown sectionally by Fig. 86, where the wedges are not large spandril frame under the stairs in a hall. If the tenons had to be cut out of the solid rail parallel to the bottom, the mortise holes would be so acute as to be almost useless; they would also be extremely difficult to cut. This is overcome by inserting two loose tenons, as in-

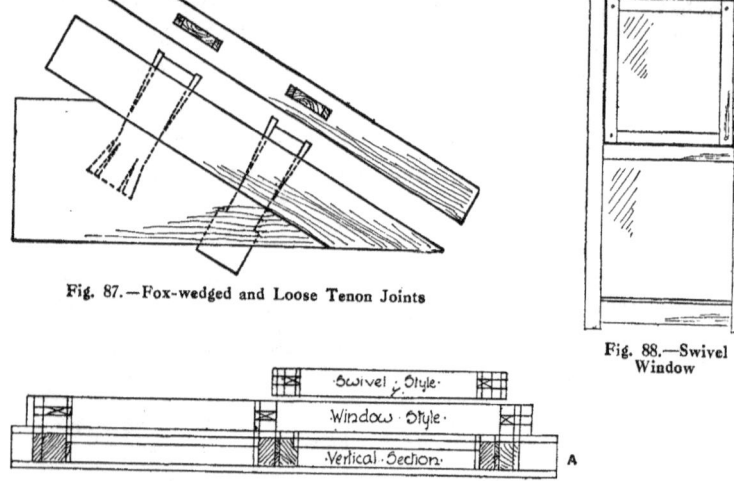

Fig. 87.—Fox-wedged and Loose Tenon Joints

Fig. 88.—Swivel Window

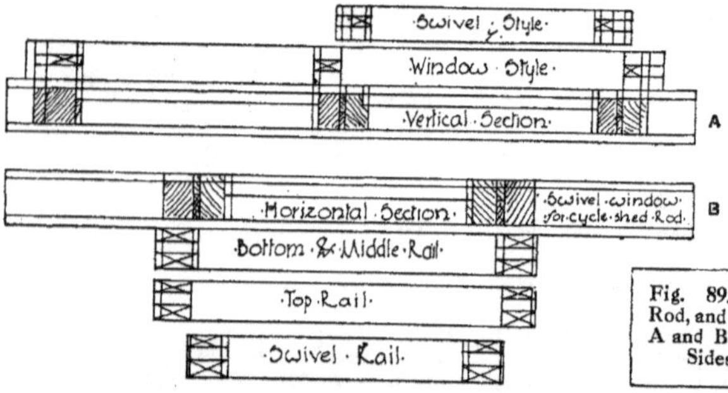

Fig. 89.—Setting-out Rod, and Method of Use; A and B show the Two Sides of the Rod

enough to expand the tenon to the full extent of the mortise, with resulting looseness. When, on the other hand, the wedges are too thick, there is risk of breaking off the sides of the tenon, or even of splitting the rail.

Fig. 87 shows a good way of joining the sloping piece and bottom rail of a triangular panelled frame, such as the dicated, one being fox-wedged while the other is shouldered and slipped in from the bottom. The whole can then be glued and cramped up, which gives a very strong joint.

Use of the Setting-out Rod. — For repetition work a setting-out rod saves much time. As an example, Fig. 88 is the elevation of a small swivel

MORTISE AND TENON JOINTS

window for a cycle shed in 1½-in. thick material. All stuff should first be planed straight, true and square, and to the right width and thickness. The setting-

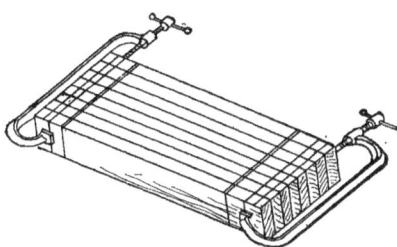

Fig. 90.—Cramping Work while Setting Out

out rod is next prepared in 2 in. by ⅛ in. wood, planed up smooth and with straight, parallel edges. Fig. 89 shows both sides of the rod when set out, allowing for the rebating and jointing The same illustration also indicates how to apply the rod to the squared pieces, transferring the shoulder lines from rod to stuff. The gauge lines and bevelling are also shown. Setting-out work will be dealt with in the chapter on drawing, and in numerous examples later.

The pieces should first be mortised and tenoned ; secondly rebated and the bottom rail weathered ; thirdly fitted together joint by joint and finally glued, wedged up, and cleaned off with the smoothing plane.

ensures accuracy, and makes all identical parts, such as stiles, rails, muntins, etc , equal in length.

Wedging Mortise and Tenon Joints.—All kinds of tenons used in joiners' work are best secured with glue and wedges, unless they are of sufficient thickness to make a pin more suitable. As a rule, joints where glue is employed should be wedged, while others should be pinned. There are exceptions, but they are few, and rarely found in practical work.

In Fig. 91 are given sectional examples of how and how not to cut out the "wedging" for a mortise and tenon joint. Thus at H a double tenon is inserted in mortises where the wedging is cut out very abruptly. so that the wedges have not a fair opportunity. At I is seen the opposite extreme, a parallel wedging, which is very unlikely to make a strong joint. The correct wedging is shown at J ; it reaches nearly through the wood with an easy taper, hence correctly-made wedges will fit throughout the whole length.

At L, in Fig. 92, is illustrated a properly-cut wedge. Too often they are made as at M, or at even a greater angle, which will not be satisfactory in use.

Pinning Mortise and Tenon Joints.—For ordinary pinning, the joint is well cramped up while boring the hole through the tenon and the two cheeks of the

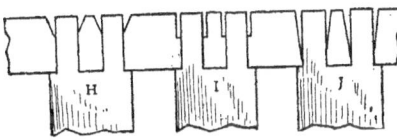

Fig. 91.—Section through Tenons and Mortises; Correct and Incorrect "Wedgings" to Mortises

Fig. 92.—Right and Wrong Forms of Wedges

It is more convenient, when a number of similar, or nearly similar, pieces have to be dealt with, to clamp them at the ends, as seen in Fig. 90, while the setting-out markings are squared across. This

mortise, for doing which a brace and bit is used. A slightly-tapering wooden pin, a shade larger than the hole, is then driven tightly in and cut off flush. This does not make so strong a joint as "draw-boring," to be next described.

Draw-boring.—The best method of pinning is first to bore the hole through the mortise only. The joint is then put together and the position of the hole marked on the tenon by inserting the point of the bit. Next, the pieces are taken apart, and a mark is made on the tenon a trifle nearer the shoulder, as at B in Fig. 93, where A is the one originally made. The tenon is now supported on a piece of waste, the bit inserted at B and a hole bored. On again putting the joint together the holes a e obviously out of line, as seen in Fig. 94. A tapered steel pin, specially supplied for the purpose, is driven through, as in Fig. 95, which naturally has the effect of forcing the holes into line and thereby tightening up the joint. The steel pin is lastly removed and a wooden one substituted.

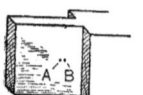

Fig. 93.—Diagram showing Where to Draw-bore the Tenon

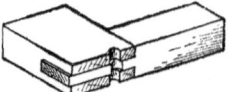

Fig. 94.—Draw-bore Holes Out of Line

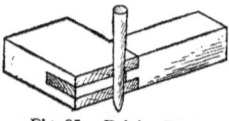

Fig. 95.—Driving Draw-bore Pin through Joint

In the case of a slot mortise shown on an earlier page (see Fig. 19), the hole in the tenon should not only be closer to the shoulder, as before described, but should, in addition, be a little farther away from the inner edge, so as to force the tenon up to the end of the mortise. This is usually a trap for the inexperienced.

The displacement of the central hole in draw-boring must be only of the slightest, or there is a risk of splitting the pin, or possibly of breaking the tenon. A few trials will soon show how much to allow.

Scarfing and Other Joints

Scarfing Joints.—Scarfing joints are used to connect timbers in length, and might better be termed splicing joints. They are numerous, varying from the simple to the elaborate, according to the part they have to play. Thus, for a wall plate, a common halving joint is all that is needed; while in heavy constructional carpentry, as for lengthening posts, beams, struts, tie-pieces, etc., something much more substantial and secure is essential.

The joint should always be selected

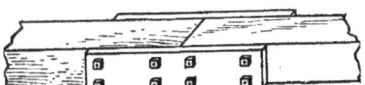

Fig. 1.—Butt Joint with Fish-plates

to suit the particular work in hand. Thus, in the case of a tie beam there is a pulling or tensile strain; a girder is subject to a bending strain; a column to compression, while any of the foregoing might also have to resist a shearing strain, or sliding pressure.

Fig. 1 illustrates a very simple form of scarfed joint, in which the two pieces are merely butted together and held in position by a couple of fish-plates bolted on the sides. It is satisfactory for work not subject to vibration, and supported entirely by a wall or by columns at short intervals. If movement is likely, the bolts will wear the wood and the joint will fail. Since stout plates and bolts are imperative, it is only suitable for heavy work. When plates projecting outside are inadmissible, the joint may

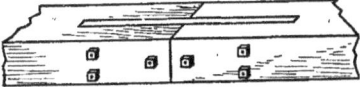

Fig. 2.—Butt Joint with Central Fish-plate

be made as in Fig. 2, a slot being cut in the middle at each end and a single plate inserted. This takes longer, and is not so strong.

Splayed Scarf Joint.—Fig. 3 shows a splayed scarf joint, or plain splice. It is easy to make, but is only used in light work, as, for instance, the joint between the ash bend and straight in the leading edge of an aeroplane, for splicing broken cart shafts, broken oars, etc. In dry work the pieces are secured by screws and glue; while, where wetting is likely,

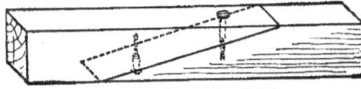

Fig. 3.—Splayed Scarf Joint

bolts, iron plates and screws are necessary. The splice should be at least 9 in. long, or, better still, 1 ft. If the pieces are equal in size the setting out may be done by measuring off the required distance, squaring over, and connecting the lines diagonally; otherwise one piece should be cut first and the other marked

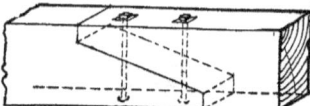

Fig. 4.—Splayed Scarf with Shoulders

by it, laying them out in a straight line while doing so.

Splayed Scarf with Shoulders.—Fig 4 shows a splayed scarf joint with shoulders and bolt fastenings. This is suitable for heavy work and will resist a lengthways push better than the simple splayed joint.

Birdsmouth Splay Joint.—Fig. 5 illustrates the birdsmouth splay joint,

Fig. 5.—Birdsmouth Splay Joint

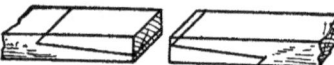

Fig. 6.—Setting Out Birdsmouth Splay Joint

Fig. 7.—Finished Parts of Birdsmouth Splay Joint

which to some extent resists a bending stress. Fig. 6 shows the setting out, and Fig. 7 the two parts ready for putting together. If several of these joints are required it is worth while making a template, especially with timber of unequal size.

An elaboration of the preceding is the splayed scarf with folding wedges and inclined shoulders (Fig. 8). The hardwood wedges pull the pieces together tight, helping to take any tensional stress

that may be put on, and thus relieving the bolts. It is used in bridge building, shoring, strutting, etc. Fig. 9 shows the employment of the same joint in an

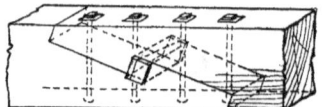

Fig. 8.—Splayed Scarf with Folding Wedges

aeroplane, for the main plane spar, which is too long to be in one piece. It is cut, fitted in close contact, glued, wedged and dowelled, as shown, forming a very strong joint indeed. This and all other aeroplane joints are wrapped round with glued tape, for extra strength.

Slot Mortise and Tenon Scarf.—This joint (Fig. 10) is one of the strongest and most useful in carpentry, and is suitable for splicing very large timbers. Although easy to make, it is important that the parts should fit correctly without being tight, otherwise there is a difficulty in putting together. Fig. 11 shows how to set out the joint. The width is divided into four parts, and a series of equal lengths are measured off, usually six inches each. In Fig. 11 only three of these are shown to save space, but in Fig. 10 four have been used, two in the middle and one at each end, the joint being thus 2 ft. long. Obviously it could be made longer by having five divisions, three being in the centre, as shown by Fig. 12. The best way of putting together is to drop one piece into position while the other is

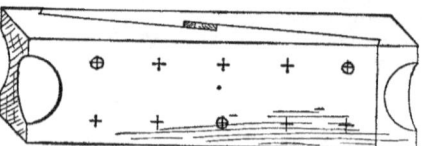

Fig. 9.—Splayed Scarf Joint for Aeroplane Work

lying in place. Fig. 13 shows the two parts ready for doing so. Pins and draw-boring are mostly used for fixing, though bolts are sometimes employed.

When boring the pin-holes, prior to marking, two should be bored through the slot mortises in each piece. This type of joint may be further strengthened, if desired, by making certain members pointed, as indicated by the dotted lines.

Tabled Joint.—Fig. 14 shows a tabled joint, practically a hook halving. It is easy to make, and is useful where longitudinal lapping 1 ft. at each side of the joint and having four bolts run through. The fishplates should be the same width as the beam, so that the bolts may be placed zigzag, while the thickness of the plates should be about one-quarter the depth of the beam. Like the preceding joint, certain parts may be pointed if preferred, as shown dotted in Fig. 15.

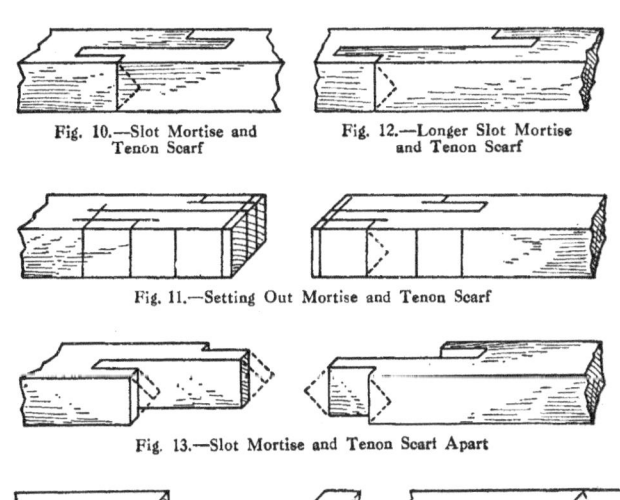

Fig. 10.—Slot Mortise and Tenon Scarf

Fig. 12.—Longer Slot Mortise and Tenon Scarf

Fig. 11.—Setting Out Mortise and Tenon Scarf

Fig. 13.—Slot Mortise and Tenon Scarf Apart

Fig. 14.—Tabled Joint

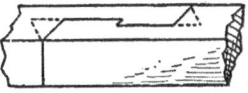

Fig. 15.—Finished Tabled Joint, showing Pointing

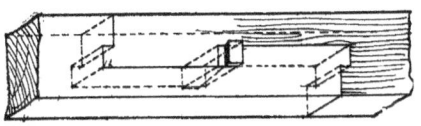

Fig. 16.—Tabled Joint with Folding Wedges

An elaboration of the tabled joint, with folding wedges, used in heavy engineering work, is shown by Fig. 16. Another one, very similar, but having a vertical check to prevent side motion, is illustrated by Fig. 17. When well made this is very effective and needs no other fastening than the folding wedges, but if constructed in a slovenly manner it cannot be recommended. Fig. 18 shows the pieces apart. The seating for the wedges should be so cut as to allow a

tudinal stresses (tension and compression) are encountered, but not so good for a lateral bending strain. It is greatly improved by the addition of wooden fish-plates at the top and bottom, over-

slight amount of draught, so that the parts will be forced together when the wedges are driven in.

Double-splayed Scarf Joint.—A double-splayed scarf joint with shoulders at top and bottom is illustrated by Fig. 19. It should only be used when there is substantial support immediately underneath, and should be fixed by bolts and straps, as seen sectionally in Fig. 20.

posts, each piece has what are actually two stopped rebates cut in it, as shown by Fig. 22, one quarter of the area of each section being cut away at alternate corners.

Hammer-headed Key Joint.—This strong and useful joint, illustrated by Fig. 23, consists of a slot so cut in the two pieces as to accommodate a hammer-headed key, sufficient space being left for the insertion of four folding wedges, which pull the joint up tight. In making it great care should be exercised. The key should first be made, in hard wood of a non-splitting nature, and the recess marked direct from the key, making allowance for wedges and fitting. When placing the wedges, note that they are in contact from top to bottom of the hole

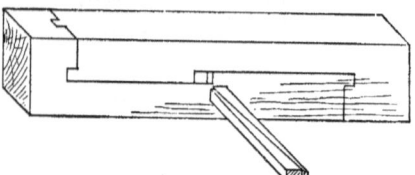

Fig. 17.—Joggle Halving Joint

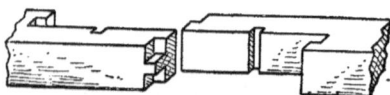

Fig. 18.—Parts Cut for Joggle Halving

Fig. 19.—Double-splayed Scarf Joint

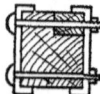

Fig. 20.—Section of Bolts and Straps for Double-splayed Joint

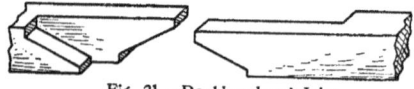

Fig. 21.—Double-splayed Joint Apart

If bolts are employed without straps, and there is the least movement, the wood will gradually wear away and the joint loosen. The two pieces, ready for fixing, are shown by Fig. 21. To set out, divide the length into five parts, taking two parts for each splay and leaving one in the middle for the square. The total length may vary from eighteen to thirty inches.

MISCELLANEOUS JOINTS

Double-halved Longitudinal Joint.—In this, which is very suitable for heavy

on their sloping sides, otherwise they will tend to tilt the joint out of truth.

Fig. 24 shows the application of a hammer-headed key joint to a circular-headed frame.

A simpler joint for connecting two light curved pieces end to end, when no great strain is expected, is by means of a double dovetail key (see Fig. 25).

Screwed Joints for Curved Work.—When part of the woodwork is hidden behind brick or stone on one side, and has plaster or wood linings on the other, an easy way for joining curved pieces is by a screwed-on overlapping piece, as

SCARFING AND OTHER JOINTS

shown by Fig. 26. This method is very extensively used in the building trade.

The joint where the straight side of a window or other frame meets the curved head may be treated as in Fig. 27. Here glue is employed as well as screws.

Handrail Bolts and Dowels.—A very strong type of joint, used in handrailing, heavy curtain poles, wooden curb fenders, etc., is shown by Fig. 28. The bolt holds the pieces close, while the dowels prevent rotation. The nuts are

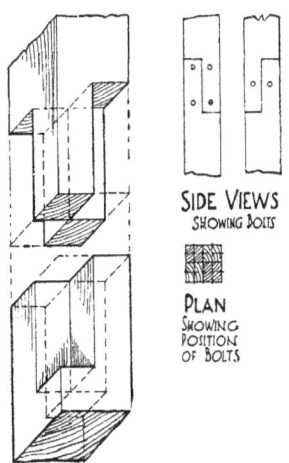

Fig. 22.—Double-halved Longitudinal Joint

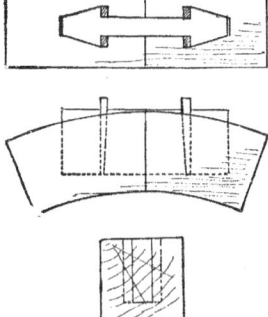

Fig. 24.—Hammer-headed Joint on Curved Frame

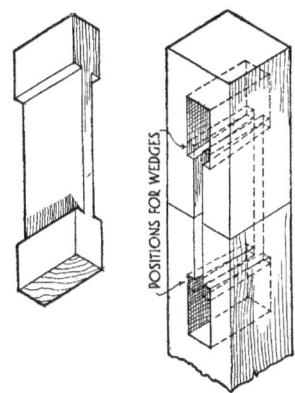

Fig. 23.—Hammer-headed Key Joint

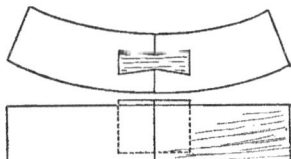

Fig. 25.—Curved Joint with Double Dovetail Key

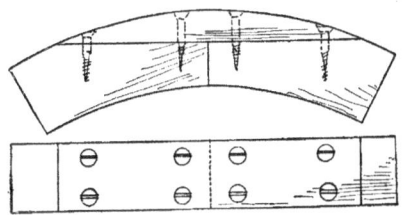

Fig. 26.—Lapped and Screwed Joint in Curved Frame

circular, with grooves cut round the edges, to facilitate tightening with hammer and punch.

Screw Dowel for Walking-stick.—of the screw shank, and continued forward with a smaller bit so as to allow the thread to catch. The holes must be big enough or the stick will split; but, on

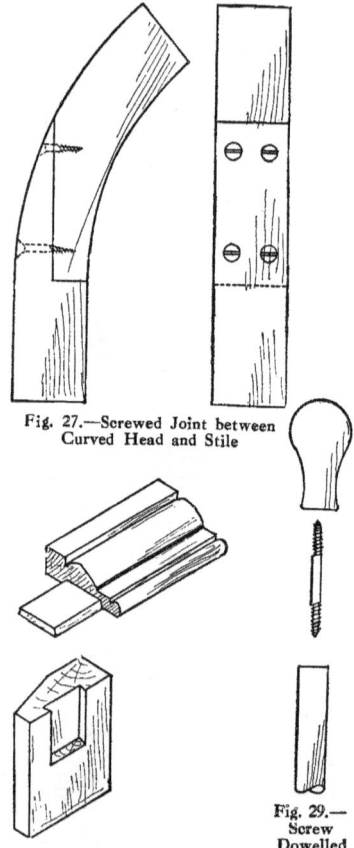

Fig. 27.—Screwed Joint between Curved Head and Stile

Fig. 29.—Screw Dowelled Joint

Fig. 30.—Architrave Joint

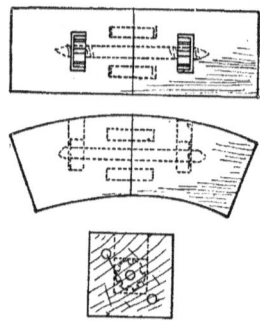

Fig. 28.—Curved Head Jointed with Handrail Bolts and Dowels

the other hand, if made too large, the pieces will soon come apart, as most people have had melancholy experience. The joint is fixed by glue.

Architrave Joint.—Fig. 30 shows a good way of jointing the bottom end of an architrave with the plinth block

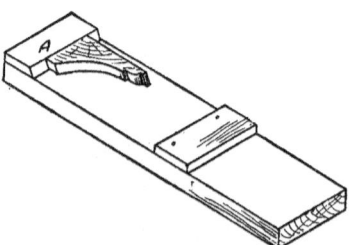

Fig. 31.—Planing Board for Short Breaks in Mouldings

of a door or window. It is held in position by glue and screws.

Short Breaks in Moulding.—Fig. 31 illustrates the planing board used for

The usual method of attaching the handles to umbrellas and walking-sticks is indicated by Fig. 29. A hole is bored in each piece the width and half the depth

SCARFING AND OTHER JOINTS

making short breaks in mouldings, as when continuing a cornice round a pilaster. A small piece of moulding, or several such, has to be cut, which is too short to be held in the vice or on an ordinary shooting board. In such cases it can be planed by placing on the special board against the bevelled stop A, as shown, nailed. The same principle can be adapted for cornices, picture and dado rails, etc.; it is also often employed in cabinet-making, where rounded corners are required instead of the sharp arris of the mitre.

Simple Scarfing Joints.—In making furniture and fittings boards are some-

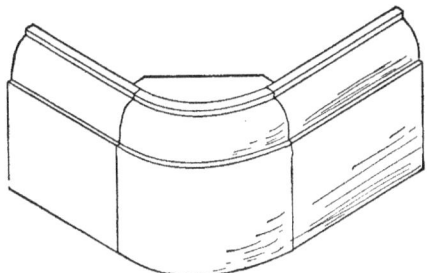

Fig. 32.—Joint for Curved Skirting

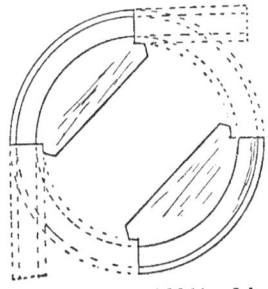

Fig. 33.—Method of Making Joint for Curved Skirting

and nailing it down, punching the nails in a little.

Joint for Curved Skirting, etc.—An excellent and very substantial method of jointing skirting or other mouldings round circular corners is shown by Fig. 32. A block of wood is turned in the lathe to the same profile as the moulding, and is then cut as indicated in Fig. 33, rebating it at each side to receive the straight pieces. In fixing, the back part of the corner block is sunk into the brickwork, plugged and

times required to be lengthened where, from the fact that the work is otherwise supported, simpler methods than those previously dealt with will very well suffice. In mantel-boards and small shelves, for instance, two or three dowels will answer quite satisfactorily; in table-tops mere gluing and cramping will do; while in further cases, rebates, grooves and tongues, half-lapping, or adaptations of some of the other joints already described may be used.

Mitre Joints

The ordinary "mitre" is a joint at 45°, as, for example, the corner of a picture frame, the pieces of wood being at right angles. If the pieces to be jointed together do not meet at right angles then the mitres will not be at 45° but at some other angle.

The cutting and shooting of mitres was dealt with in a previous chapter, and

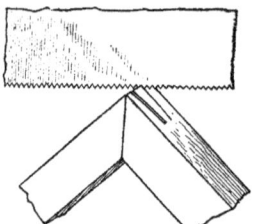

Fig. 1.—Making Saw Kerfs for Keys

mitreing and framing pictures will be treated later. In this section only the chief forms of mitred joints will be described.

Keyed Mitred Joints.—In joinery and cabinet-making the simple glued mitre would not be strong enough, but has to be strengthened, most commonly by inserting keys or tongues. To make a keyed joint, the two parts are fixed together accurately in the vice, and saw kerfs are cut across at the corners, as shown by Fig. 1. It is better not to make the kerfs parallel, but slightly converging, so as to form a kind of dovetail. Having then glued and cramped the joint, pieces of hardwood veneer are glued and driven in the kerfs, any projecting portions being trimmed flush when set. Another way is to leave the keying till after the joint has been glued up. The grain of the veneer should be at a right angle to the joint.

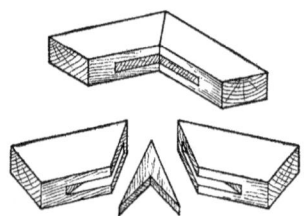

Fig. 2.—Thick Inside Key for Mitre Joint

If the keys are not to show they may be placed inside the corners. The two pieces to be joined are fixed back to back in the vice and marked carefully for the kerfs from each of the faces. A single key of a pointed or arrow-head shape is best.

Thicker and more substantial keys can be used to fit mortises cut at the mitres, an inside example being shown by Fig. 2. The length of the mortise is measured on the end and edge in both pieces, and squared across. The width of the mor-

MITRE JOINTS

tise is then marked with a mortise gauge. Kerfs are now made along the gauged lines and the waste chiselled out. The keys are planed to the right thickness and cut to the arrow-head shape to fit, being then glued, inserted, and the joint cramped till set.

False Tenons for Mitred Joints.—Another type of key used in mitre joints is known as a false tenon (see Fig. 3). The one illustrated is square and shows outside, but other shapes may be employed. The method of making this joint is practically the same as that in the preceding paragraph, save that

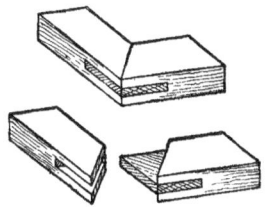

Fig. 3.—Mitre with False Tenon Joint

the saw kerfs for the mortise finish on a line at a right angle with the sides.

Screwed Mitre Joint. — A stout screw may be used to strengthen a mitre joint, a hole being bored just deep enough to countersink the head completely, and stopped up to match the wood after the screw is driven in.

Other Mitre Joints. — Variations of other joints are frequently used for mitred corners. Thus lapped, tenoned, rebated, or grooved and tongued mitres are often met with. These, however, have already been discussed elsewhere. The dovetail-keyed mitre joint (Fig. 4) is more difficult to pull apart than the ordinary types. Dovetail-tenoned mitres, which are still stronger, will be considered when dealing with dovetail joints.

There only remains the case of mitres

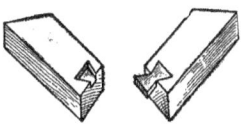

Fig. 4.—Dovetail-keyed Mitre Joint

at other angles than 45°. Fig. 5 shows a six-sided or hexagonal frame with mitred joints. To do work of this kind accurately it is best to prepare a mitre box or block having saw kerfs at the required angle. The sum of the angles in a regular polygon is equal to twice as many right angles, less four, as the polygon has sides. Hence, the sum of the angles in a hexagon = $(90° \times 12) - (90° \times 4) = 1080 - 360 = 720°$. Therefore one of the angles $= 720 \div 6 = 120°$, and the joint is, of course, half the angle, $= 60°$. A shooting board having a triangular block to suit the work is also necessary. The angle of the block facing the shoot should be equal to two right

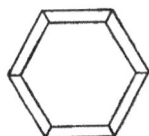

Fig. 5.—Hexagonal Mitred Frame

angles, less twice the angle of the joint. In the present instance this would be $180 - 120 = 60°$. Therefore an equilateral triangle could be used, whose angles are each 60°.

Plain Dovetail Joints

Different Kinds of Dovetail Joints. —The term dovetail joint is almost self-explanatory. It is really a tenon or "pin" of inverted wedge shape, fitting into a similar mortise or socket, and being, therefore, locked in all directions save one. It is important in joinery and cabinet-making, but seldom used in carpentry. Single dovetails, such as the dovetail half-lap, dovetailed housing, notching, etc., have already been dealt with. There now only remain to consider the various descriptions of multiple dovetail joints, as mostly seen on drawers and boxes.

Generally speaking, the first method is best, since it displays less end grain on the part most seen (the front), and is therefore neater.

Much of the strength of the dovetails depends on the size and angle of the pins. It is a mistake to think these gain by being large and clumsy. They should be as light as possible, and spaced pretty

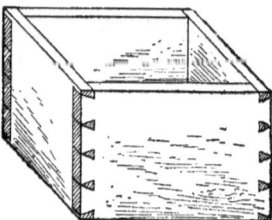

Fig. 1.—Correctly Dovetailed Box

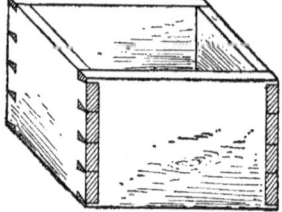

Fig. 2.—Box Incorrectly Dovetailed

Ordinary or Box Dovetail. — Two ways of arranging this are shown by Figs. 1 and 2. In the first, the pins are cut on the end or side pieces, the mortises or sockets being made in the front and back. In the second, the contrary is the case; the pins are on the front and back, while the mortises are in the ends.

closely together. Some fancy that an obtuse angle is an advantage. It certainly may have greater holding power, but since the grain of the wood is cut more across in making the pins, there is grave danger of these splitting out when the joint is put together. Thus, the setting shown in Fig. 3 is preferable to that in Fig. 4, both for the reasons given and as regards appearance. A very coarse dovetail, only suitable for carpentry, is shown set out in Fig. 5.

Provided all is done carefully and in due sequence, the box dovetail is quite

PLAIN DOVETAIL JOINTS

easy to make. There is an unsettled controversy whether the pins should be made first, or the sockets. The second

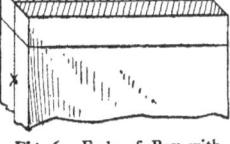

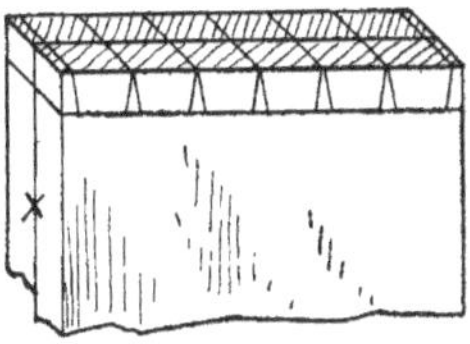

Fig. 3.—Dovetails Correctly Set Out on Front and Back of Box

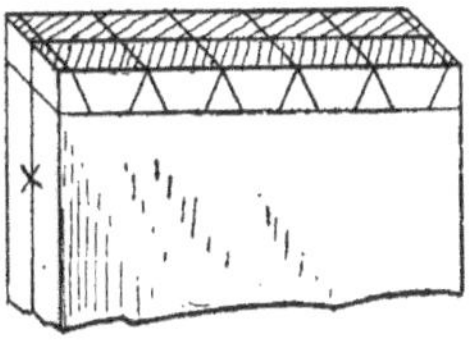

Fig. 4.—Dovetails Faultily Set Out

Fig. 6.—Ends of Box with Scribed Shoulder Line

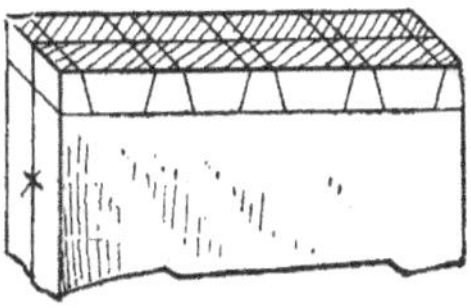

Fig. 5.—Carpenter's Coarse Dovetails, Set Out

way is the quicker, and will therefore be dealt with before the other.

"Sockets First" Method of Dovetailing.—The pieces having been planed, smoothed, and the ends shot true, the back and front are put face to face, in the same position they will occupy when finished, and are fixed together with slight brads, keeping the face edges flush. A line is then scribed all round at a distance from the end equal to the

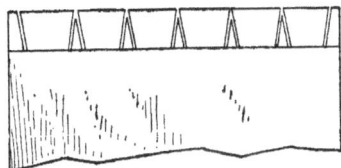

Fig. 7.—Dovetail Sockets Sawn in on Front and Back Piece

thickness of one piece, as shown in Fig. 6. At the two ends of the line mark off half the width of a mortise or socket, then divide the intervening space into as many equal parts, plus one, as there are to be whole sockets. Thus, for five whole sockets there should be six equal divisions. From each dividing line mark off on both sides half the width of a socket and with a bevel set to the correct angle, say 10°, set out the inclined lines, as in Fig. 3. Square the lines across ends (Fig. 19), and, if considered necessary, mark bevels on the other side. Now, with a tenon or dovetail saw, according to the fineness of the work, make kerfs by the side of the lines in the waste, as shown by Fig. 7. In this illustration each pair of saw kerfs meet at the top, but it is sometimes preferred to have the top of the socket a little wider, in which case the cuts would be slightly separated. Having set out and cut the saw kerfs at both ends of the boards, the two are taken apart,

Fig. 8.—Method of Marking Pins on Box Ends

ready to use for marking the pins on the end pieces.

The speediest way of doing this is that illustrated by Fig. 8. One of the end pieces to be marked is fixed upright in the bench vice with the outer side towards the worker. The front or the back piece is now laid on this at a right angle,

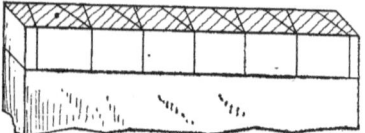

Fig. 9.—Pins Marked and Squared Down

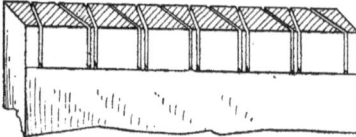

Fig. 10.—Pins Sawn In

inside downwards, with the edges quite level, and the pins can then be marked on the end grain with the point of the saw by inserting the blade in the groove, as

Fig. 11.—Removing Waste from Socket with Bow Saw

shown. Before removing, both pieces should be crossed or numbered for identification when putting together.

The pins are now squared down from the marked lines on the ends to the shoulder lines, as in Fig. 9, and saw kerfs are made to the latter, taking care, in this case, to go a trifle outside the marks in the waste, say about $\frac{1}{32}$ in., to ensure a good fit, and keeping the cuts parallel with the squared down lines. Allow a little less for the two half dovetails, since if these are tight there is a risk of splitting at the ends. Having reached this stage, the pins will appear as in Fig. 10.

The waste in the sockets may then be removed with a small bevel-edge chisel, or, if they are large, the bow saw may first be employed to cut out as much as possible, as shown by Fig. 11, finishing

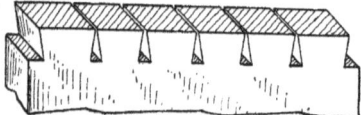

Fig. 12.—Sockets or Mortises Completed

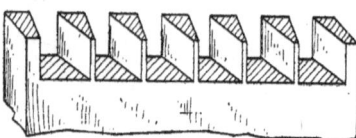

Fig. 13.—Pins Completed

up with the chisel. The half sockets at the ends are, of course, removed with the tenon saw. The sockets when completed should present the appearance seen in Fig. 12. The pins are next finished by cutting out the waste, in a practically similar way, when they will look as shown by Fig. 13. If all has been properly done, the joint should be an exact fit, and only need gluing.

To put together, take one of the ends and glue the pins well and promptly. Stand it on end on the bench and place the front or back piece on it, according to the identification marks previously made, then gently tap it with a hammer until the pins have entered. Next, glue the pins on the other end and engage them in the same way. The two joints now require to be driven home quickly.

PLAIN DOVETAIL JOINTS

using a heavy hammer and a fairly stout piece of wood as a buffer, as shown by Fig. 14. The wood block should be placed directly over the dovetails until the pins are level, or come through, and then, if necessary, set just inside them.

The first two joints having been driven home, the whole is turned over and the remaining piece is put on in the same way. In cases where the bottom of the box or drawer fits grooves made all round in the sides, it is obviously inserted before fixing the last piece.

"Pins First" Method of Dovetailing. — While an expert worker will find the "sockets first" system most expeditious, it is perhaps not the best for the beginner, who will usually meet with less difficulty and fewer mishaps by adopting the "pins first" method, at any rate until some dexterity has been gained.

Here the boards or pieces to be joined are planed up and shot true at the ends, as before, and are gauged with a shoulder line all round at a distance equal to the thickness of the material. Next, on the shoulder line and at the outer side of the wood measure off at each end half the thickness of the thinnest side of the pin. With the compasses or dividers divide the intervening space between these marks into as many parts, plus one, as there are to be whole pins (see Fig. 15), and on each side of these divisions mark off half the thickness of the pin, as shown.

Any slight inaccuracy at this stage will affect the appearance but not the fit of the dovetails.

Next, square down from these marks, as illustrated by Fig. 16, and, with the bevel set to the required angle, say 10°, mark for the ends of the pins, as indicated in Fig. 17; to do which it is best

Fig. 14.—Putting Dovetail Joint Together

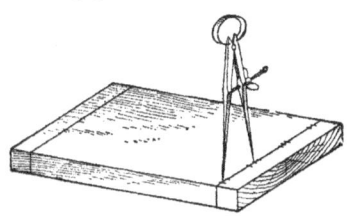

Fig. 15.—Spacing Pins with Dividers

Fig. 16.—Squaring Down the Pins

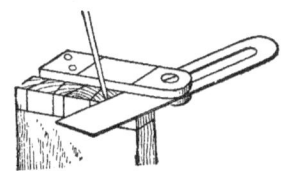

Fig. 17.—Marking Ends of Pins with Bevel

to fix the work in the bench vice. It is preferable also to square down the lines on the other side of the face.

Then, with the tenon or dovetail saw, make kerfs on the ends outside the lines in the waste, down to the shoulder marks, as seen in Fig. 18; then, with a sharp point, such as that of an awl or of a marking knife, the shape of the pins is marked on the other piece. The ends are next squared across (as in Fig. 19, but singly), and the dovetails are repeated

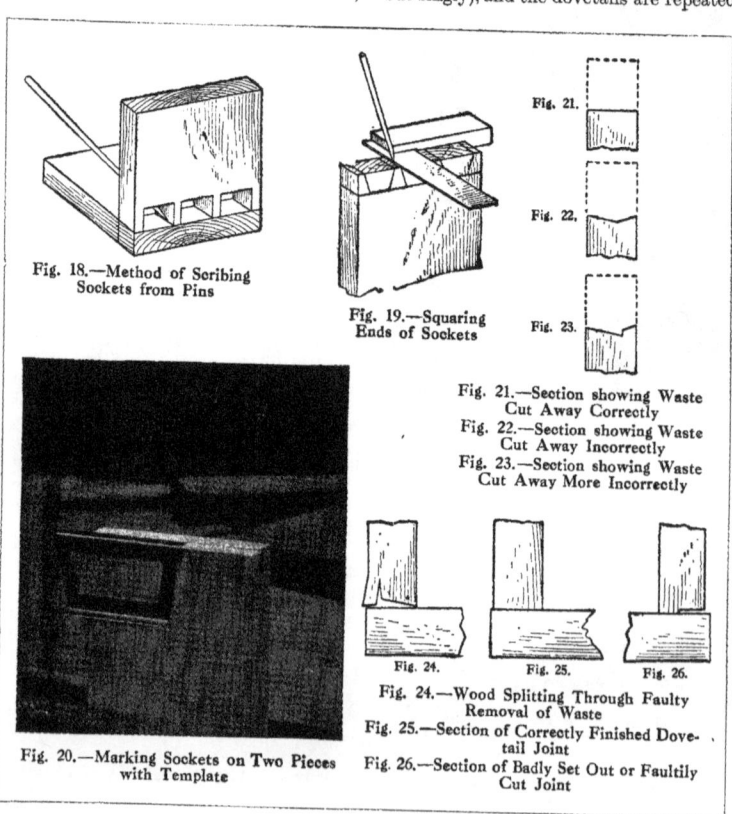

Fig. 18.—Method of Scribing Sockets from Pins

Fig. 19.—Squaring Ends of Sockets

Fig. 21.—Section showing Waste Cut Away Correctly
Fig. 22.—Section showing Waste Cut Away Incorrectly
Fig. 23.—Section showing Waste Cut Away More Incorrectly

Fig. 20.—Marking Sockets on Two Pieces with Template

Fig. 24.—Wood Splitting Through Faulty Removal of Waste
Fig. 25.—Section of Correctly Finished Dovetail Joint
Fig. 26.—Section of Badly Set Out or Faultily Cut Joint

and remove the waste with the chisel, aided, if required, by the bow saw, as before described.

From the finished pins the sockets may now be marked out. The piece for the sockets is laid flat on the bench, and that having the pins is rested vertically on it, on the other side, though this is sometimes omitted. The sockets are lastly cut in a similar way to the pins.

Dovetail Templates. — Instead of using the bevel it is a convenience to have a template of wood or metal, set to the angle desired by the worker, which

PLAIN DOVETAIL JOINTS

should not be less than 10° or more than 15°. Fig. 20 illustrates a metal template, by which the sockets may be marked with accuracy. By putting the dovetailed portion of the template uppermost, it can obviously be employed to mark the pins also, one piece at a time.

Faults in Cutting Dovetails.—In removing the waste between the pins the finishing cuts should be taken on the outside. It will be found at first that there is a tendency to break the wood up instead of cutting it cleanly. To guard against this the chisel must be very thin and sharp, especially with soft wood. The cut should be straight through from side to side, as seen in section in Fig. 21, though it is, of course, performed half from one side and half from the other. Too often the section turns out to be as in Fig. 22, and the joint will tend to open when cleaning off; or, worse still, the section may be as in Fig. 23, when a portion of the wood will be driven out on putting the work together, as shown in Fig. 24. When the setting out and cutting are correct, the finished section will be as in Fig. 25; but if the setting out is careless, or the cutting is carried in beyond the mark, the result will be as shown by Fig. 26.

reducing the risk of splitting when putting together. The projecting ends are levelled when cleaning off.

Applications of Simple Dovetailing.— Fig. 28 illustrates a dovetailed tenon joint, such as might be used for a window or similar frame. It hardly

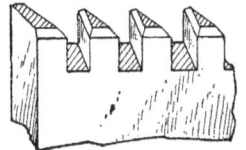

Fig. 27.—Extra Long and Pointed Pins

calls for any explanation. It is the joint commonly used between the meeting rails and stiles of vertically sliding sashes.

Fig. 29 shows the employment of dovetails in carcase work for furniture, when the top board is full width, including the legs. This type of joint is only used when the carcase end is a single board, and not a panelled frame.

Box Pin or Lock Joint.—This joint, sometimes wrongly classed as a dovetail, is extensively used for small boxes, often

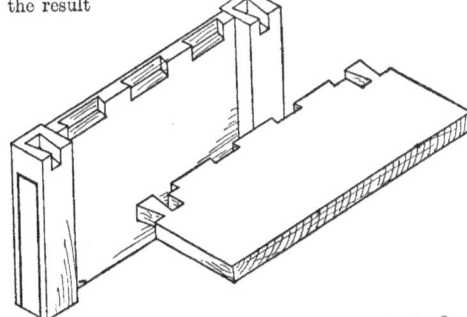

Fig. 28.— Dovetailed Tenon Joint   Fig. 29.—Dovetailed Carcase of Small Stand

Pointed Pins.—Some workers prefer to set out the pins a little longer than required, on the ground that this permits the ends to be pointed, as shown by Fig. 27, and makes fitting easier, besides

cut in numbers by machinery. As will be seen by reference to Fig. 30, it consists of a series of alternate notches and square-sided pins on each piece, interlocking and all of the same width. It is a good rule to make the pins as wide as they are thick, though with thin material this is

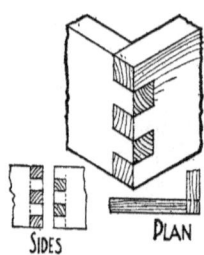

Fig. 30.—Box Pin Joint

not always adhered to. To set out, adjust the cutting gauge to the thickness of the stuff, and scribe a shoulder line all round at the ends of each piece. The dividers are now also set to the thickness, and a number of equal divisions stepped off on the shoulder line of one piece, these marks being squared up to the end. The two pieces are then clamped together in the bench vice, and the division lines squared over the ends of each, and down to the other shoulder line. Before removing, pencilled marks should be made to indicate the notches or parts to be cut out, seeing that the notches on one piece are opposite the pins on the other. The pieces are then taken from the vice and sawn in close to the lines, the waste in the notches being lastly cut out with the chisel and mallet, and finely pared to finish. When doing a number of such joints, a metal template will save much time in setting out.

Lap and Secret Dovetail Joints

Lap Dovetail Joint.—This is chiefly used by cabinet makers for drawers, being seldom required in joinery or carpentry. Unlike the box dovetail, the end grain only shows on the sides, and is not visible at all on the front, as illustrated in Fig. 1.

When this joint is to be employed it is usual to have the front of the drawer thicker than the sides, and to make the length and width of the pins equal to the thickness of the sides. Therefore, to set out, the marking gauge is adjusted to the thickness of the sides, and a shoulder line A (Fig. 2) is scribed all round at the end of the front. A line B is also scribed along the edge, placing the gauge stop against what is to be the inside of the front. At the same time, a shoulder line may as well be marked all round at the front end of the sides. As will be gathered from Fig. 1, the pins are made on the front and the sockets in the sides.

To set out the pins, mark off half the thickness of the pin from each end of the shoulder line A (Fig. 2) on the front, and with the dividers carefully divide the intervening space into as many parts, plus one, as there are to be whole pins. At each side of these divisions mark off half the thickness of the pin. Then square down the latter marks to the end, as shown by Fig. 3. With either the bevel or a template the dovetails are now marked on

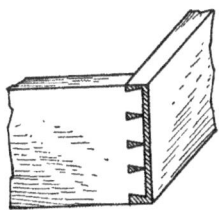

Fig. 1.—Lap or Drawer Dovetail Joint

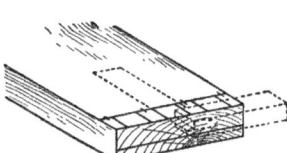

Fig. 3.—Squaring Down the Pins

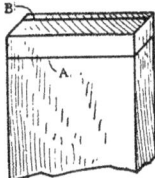

Fig. 2.—Scribing Shoulder and Edge Lines on Front

the edge, as shown in Fig. 4. Expert workmen usually dispense with the marking.

Next with the dovetail saw held on the slant, kerfs are made slightly outside the lines previously marked, as far as both the gauge lines, the remaining waste being then removed with the chisel. The finished pins should appear as indicated in Fig. 5. It is important to keep the cuts vertical, and not to let them slope outwards as seen in Fig. 6. If that is allowed the joint will fit badly, and there

281

may be a tendency for the half-pins to split at the ends.

The sockets in the sides of the drawers are marked from the front, placing the end grain of the front towards the end of the side, in the correct position for going together when finished, as shown by Fig. 7.

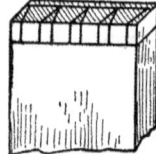

Fig. 4.—Pins Completely Set Out

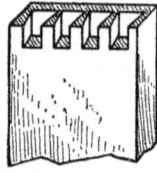

Fig. 5.—Finished Pins for Lap Dovetail

An alternative method is to complete the sockets first in the side pieces, and from them to mark the pins on the front (see Fig. 8). Note that, in this case, the front should be fixed upright in the vice, and the side supported over it at a right angle, its end level with the gauge line on the top edge. The piece is then removed, the marks squared down on the face, and the pins cut as before described.

Double Lap Secret Dovetail Joint. —In the single lap dovetail, just dealt with, the sockets are like those of the ordinary box dovetail, only the pin portion displaying any difference, in the lap that prevents a front view of the dovetails.

The double lap dovetail, however, as its name implies, has a lap on each piece; or, more correctly, a lap on one and a stopped end on the other, so that the dovetails are altogether hidden, the external appearance being as shown in Fig. 9. It is, therefore, a form of secret dovetail. The front and sides may conveniently be of equal thickness. Sometimes the pins are made on the front piece, and sometimes on the sides. Logically, it is best to place them on the front of a drawer, from which the greatest pull comes when opening, since the dovetails then help to resist this.

To set out the pins on the front, adjust the marking gauge to the thickness of the stuff and scribe a shoulder line on the inside at the ends, and over at the top and bottom edges, as shown by Fig. 10. Next, adjust the gauge to about one-third the thickness, and scribe a second line parallel with the others, marking it also on the end edge. The pins are then set out with the dividers on the shoulder line, in the manner already described, squared up to the edge, and the dovetails marked on the end with a bevel or template as far as the outer line. With secret dovetails the pins and sockets may be equal in size, or nearly so. The pins can now be sawn in on the slant with the dovetail saw, taking care the cuts are kept vertical,

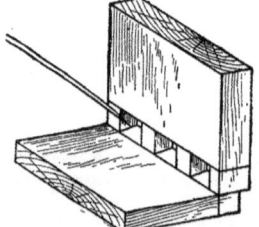

Fig. 7.—Marking Sockets from Pins

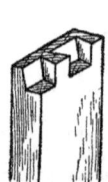

Fig. 6.—Sloping Spaces Between Pins

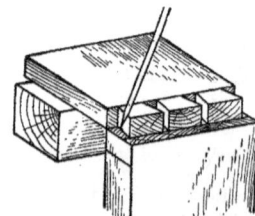

Fig. 8.—Marking Pins from Sockets

and the waste removed with the chisel, appearing at this stage as in Fig. 11. Cuts are now made with the tenon saw down both the outer lines on the end and edge (see the dotted line in Fig. 11)

LAP AND SECRET DOVETAIL JOINTS

until they meet, leaving a lap, as seen in Fig. 12. Some workers prefer to saw away the rebate first before setting out and cutting the pins.

Fig. 9.—External Appearance of Double Lap Secret Dovetail

Fig. 10.—Setting Out Drawer Front for Double Lap Dovetail

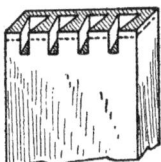

Fig. 11.—Pins Cut for Double Lap Dovetail

To set out the sockets on the sides, adjust the gauge (in this case) to two-thirds the thickness, and mark a shoulder line at the end and on the side edges. Also, placing the gauge stop against what will be the inside of the piece, mark a line on the end edge. The sockets may now be scribed from the pins, as shown in Fig. 13, by placing the side piece level on the bench and standing the front piece vertically upon it, with the rebate close against the edge. The marked lines are next squared over, up to the gauge line on the edge, when the waste may be removed with saw and chisel. The finished sockets should appear as in Fig. 14. When put together, the corner

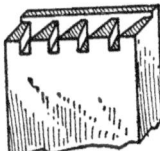

Fig. 12.—Pins Cut and Rebate Formed

Fig. 14.—Finished Sockets for Double Lap Dovetail Joints

of the double lap dovetail joint is often rounded for better effect.

Secret Mitred Dovetail Joint. — It may reasonably be objected to the double lap dovetail that it looks ex-ternally too much like a mere lapped angle joint. On this account it is not much used, since there is but little more trouble in making the mitred dovetail joint, now to be described. As will be seen from Fig. 15, the outside appearance of this is much more satisfactory than either of the two preceding joints.

Both the front and side pieces are set out at first as for the double lap dovetail (see Fig. 10). The pins may then be set out and cut, as in Fig. 11, and the rebate formed, as in Fig. 12. Next the rebates are cut out on the side pieces, leaving these for the present square.

The two parts are then placed one on

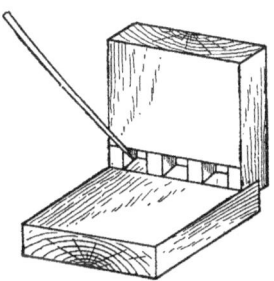

Fig. 13.—Marking Sockets from Pins for Double Lap Dovetail

the other, as shown by Fig. 16, when the sockets can be marked from the pins, as illustrated in Fig. 17. The difference of treatment now commences. First the two projecting laps should be trimmed to an angle of 45°, either by cutting with a chisel or preferably by using a rebate plane. In the former case, the best way is to cut a mitred edge on a piece of board at the correct angle, and to clamp this shortened pins cannot have so strong a hold; while, since the mitre only shows at the top, there is nothing whatever gained by carrying it all along, save that the joint is somewhat easier to make.

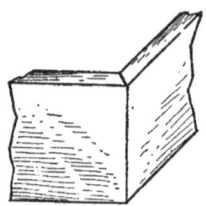

Fig. 15.—External Appearance of Secret Mitred Dovetail Joint

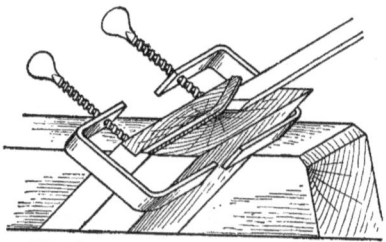

Fig. 18.—Paring Mitre on Lap with Chisel

to the work, as shown by Fig. 18, to act as a guide for the paring chisel. The alternative method of using the rebate plane is illustrated by Fig. 19. The pins and mitred rebate will now appear as in Fig. 20. Next, the half pin at the top end is mitred down, in continuation of the mitre on the lap; there is no need to mitre the bottom half pin unless desired. Figs. 21 and 22 show two secret mitred dovetail joints finished.

Mitred-Through Secret Dovetail Joint.—There is another form of mitred dovetail joint, beloved by the theorist rather than the practical man, in which the ends are mitred throughout. Fig. 23 shows how the pins appear when this is done, while Fig. 24 shows the corresponding sockets. It is self-evident that the

Setting out is commenced in the same way as for the other form of mitred dovetail (see Fig. 10). Then the two rebates are made, the pins set out on the front, and the rebate mitred. In cutting the pins the saw cuts are taken at an angle of 45°, and the waste is chiselled out at

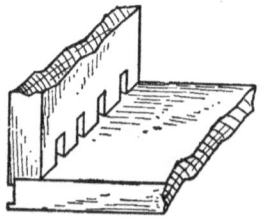

Fig. 16.—Placing Front on Side to Mark in Sockets

Fig. 17.—Marking Sockets from Pins.
(Note in this method the End Mitres are sawn before the Sockets are Marked)

the same angle, to give the result shown in Fig. 23. The sockets are now marked from the pins, cut out, and the whole end planed to a mitre at 45°, as in Fig. 24.

LAP AND SECRET DOVETAIL JOINTS

Oblique Dovetail Joints. — Sometimes it is required to use dovetail joints on a rectangular frame having inclined sides. In such a case it is necessary to set out the whole in plan and elevation, Shoulder lines are now set out parallel to the inclined ends, and the dovetails for the pins are spaced and set out on the end edge of one piece, noting that the centre lines of the pins should be parallel

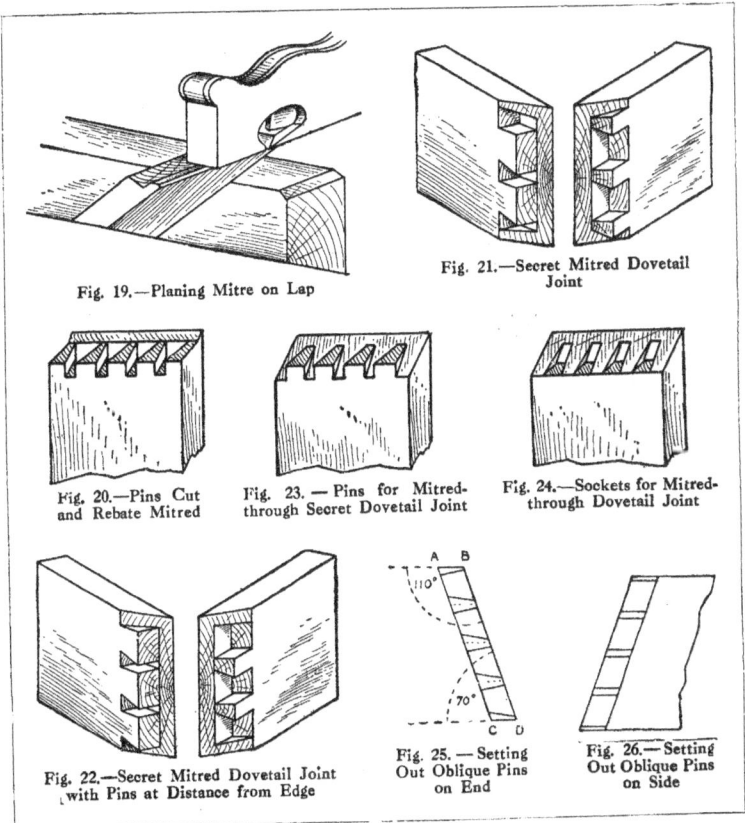

Fig. 19.—Planing Mitre on Lap

Fig. 21.—Secret Mitred Dovetail Joint

Fig. 20.—Pins Cut and Rebate Mitred

Fig. 23. — Pins for Mitred-through Secret Dovetail Joint

Fig. 24.—Sockets for Mitred-through Dovetail Joint

Fig. 22.—Secret Mitred Dovetail Joint with Pins at Distance from Edge

Fig. 25. — Setting Out Oblique Pins on End

Fig. 26.— Setting Out Oblique Pins on Side

to find the requisite angles for the ends of the four pieces, and for the bevels at top and bottom. The pieces are then cut and planed to these angles and carefully tested to make sure that they go correctly together.

with the bevels at both the top and the bottom.

The pins are then carried down to the shoulder by lines also parallel with the top and bottom, and may be cut out, being next used to mark the sockets.

Suppose, for instance, the frame or box is to have four sides, all inclined at 70° to the base. Then, Fig. 25 shows the end of one of the sloping sides. A B and

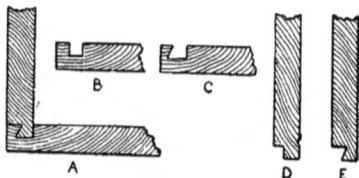

Fig. 27.—How Dovetail Grooves and Tongues are Cut

C D being the bevelled edges at top and bottom.

It will now be obvious that the angle of the bottom bevel is equal to the inclination of the side (70°); while the top bevel is equal to 180° minus the angle at the base, or, in this case, 180 − 70 = 110°.

Fig. 25 indicates the pins set out on the end, the dotted centres of the pins

sides of which have half-dovetail tongues all along their lower edges, and fit into half-dovetail grooves at the bottom, as shown in section at A (Fig. 27). The sides themselves are similarly dovetail-tongued and grooved at the corners. This is practically the same joint as the dovetail housing used for shelves. On a small scale, it may be executed by first making square grooves in the bottom, as at B, and then undercutting one side of the groove with a chisel, as at C. The tongues would be cut first as rebates, as at D, and next chiselled in at one side to fit the grooves, as at E.

The proper way, however, of making the grooves is to do the tongues with a special rebate plane having the iron and bottom set to the correct angle, and furnished with a side stop; while the grooves are cut by tilting the board and doing the dovetail side with a plough plane, having the iron sharpened to the required angle.

The board is then levelled and the square side of the groove done with another iron.

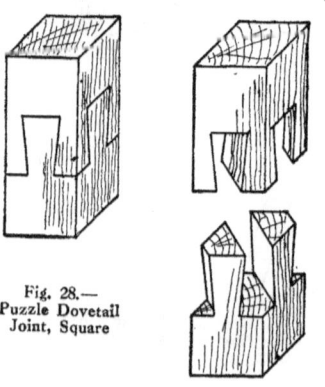

Fig. 28.— Puzzle Dovetail Joint, Square

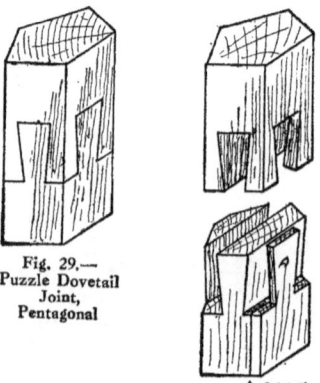

Fig. 29.— Puzzle Dovetail Joint, Pentagonal

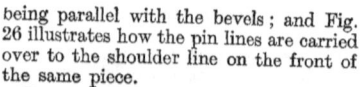

being parallel with the bevels; and Fig. 26 illustrates how the pin lines are carried over to the shoulder line on the front of the same piece.

Dovetail Grooves and Tongues.— One now and then comes across boxes the

Puzzle Dovetail Joints. — Fig. 28 illustrates a puzzle joint in dovetailing two pieces end to end. It is best made in different coloured woods. The pins and slots are marked on the sides of the square, as shown, and cut out sloping with due

LAP AND SECRET DOVETAIL JOINTS

allowance for fitting. The joint is then glued up and cleaned off.

Fig. 29 shows a more difficult puzzle joint, and the way to make it is not so obvious as in the previous case. The section is a pentagon, and one is naturally perplexed as to where the other end of the odd pin can be. To construct this joint, two pairs of adjacent sides are marked with pins and slots, and cut out.

The side marked A is a false dovetail, being cut out as shown, and split with a broad chisel along the line indicated. The joint is then fitted without piece A and glued up. Piece A is now glued, inserted, and cramped up close in the split join till the glue sets. The joint is lastly cleaned up with a smooth plane and polished.

This puzzle joint looks well if made in sycamore and black walnut, the latter being the one to split. A piece of straight-grained wood must be chosen.

Ledges and Clamps

Ledges.—Whereas cramps are merely used to tighten up joints while the glue is setting, and are then removed, there is a somewhat analogous method employed for the permanent security of boards jointed together, and known as ledging. It is familiar in common doors composed of grooved and tongued boards, in which case the ledges are merely nailed or screwed across, as shown in Fig. 1. A better form, used for drawing-boards, makes allowance for shrinkage. The middle of the ledge is fixedly screwed, but countersunk slots are cut for the side screws, as illustrated in Fig. 2. Then, if the joints should open, the outer screws can be loosened, the board cramped up, and the screws again tightened. Dovetailed and other forms of ledges are also employed for different purposes.

Buttoned Ledges.—These afford a convenient means of adjustment to coun-

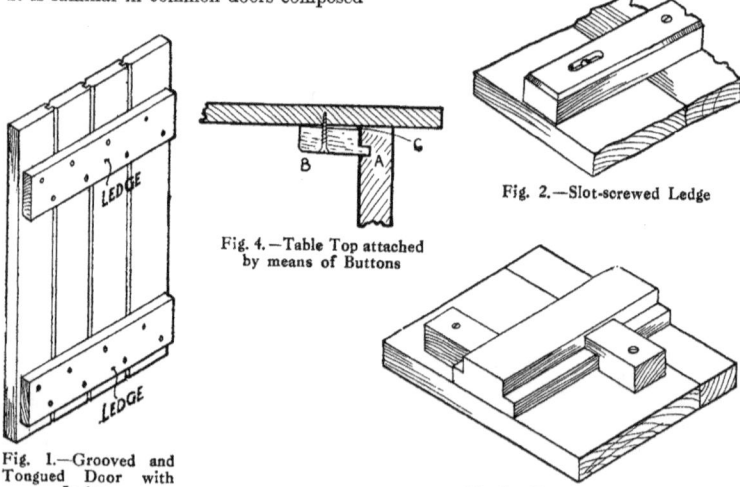

Fig. 1.—Grooved and Tongued Door with Ledges

Fig. 2.—Slot-screwed Ledge

Fig. 4.—Table Top attached by means of Buttons

Fig. 3.—Buttoned Ledge

LEDGES AND CLAMPS

teract warping due to shrinkage. Thus, in Fig. 3, the ledge has rebates, over which fit the projecting ends of screwed-on wooden buttons. By tightening one of these or loosening another, as may seem expedient, the work may be rendered flat.

thus ensure a close joint between top and rail. This will be understood from the slight space left at c, purposely a little exaggerated.

Clamped Ends.—These must not be confused with the cramping previously referred to. A clamp is an end piece

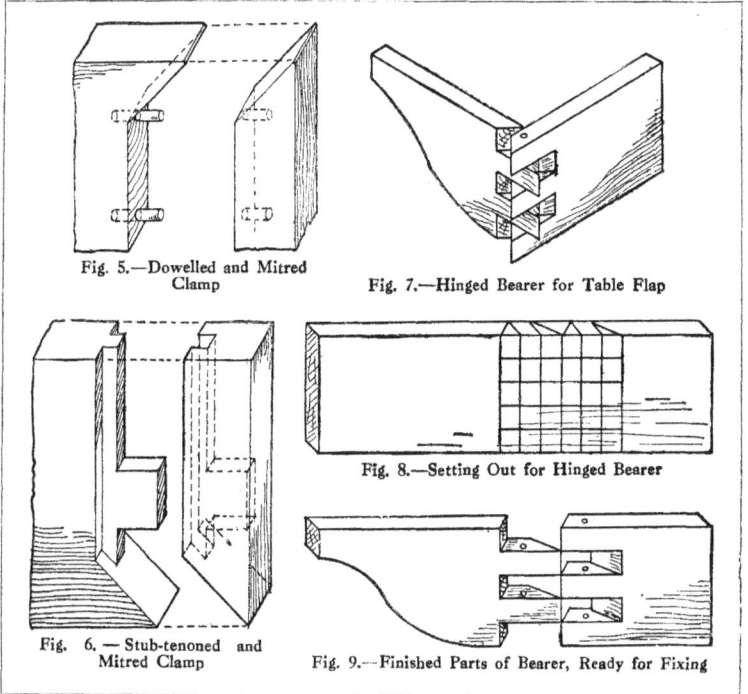

Fig. 5.—Dowelled and Mitred Clamp

Fig. 7.—Hinged Bearer for Table Flap

Fig. 8.—Setting Out for Hinged Bearer

Fig. 6.—Stub-tenoned and Mitred Clamp

Fig. 9.—Finished Parts of Bearer, Ready for Fixing

An application of the buttoned ledge provides a good way for attaching a table top to the rails. Grooves are cut in the latter, as seen at A in Fig. 4, into which fit the projecting ends of the buttons, one of these being shown at B. The shoulder of the button should be narrower than the distance of the groove from the upper edge of the rail, in order to give a tension to the screw and table top, and having the grain lengthways, and is used to prevent warping or twisting, besides giving a neater appearance. The ends of drawing-boards, blackboards, etc., will occur to mind as typical examples. The most usual form is probably the tongued and grooved; but rebates, dowelling, and haunched tenons are also employed; all these joints are usually glued and none of them should present any difficulty to those who have followed the instructions already given under these heads.

For the backing of cupboards and wardrobes a tongued and grooved joint is used without gluing, the outer boards being secured to the framing instead. This allows for shrinkage or expansion due to dryness or dampness.

Mitred Clamping.—To avoid the end grain showing at the corners in cabinet work, mitred clamping is sometimes adopted, which may either be dowelled, as in Fig. 5, or stub-tenoned, as in Fig. 6. The first hardly requires explanation. For the second, the clamp is grooved with the plough and mitred at each end. The haunched tenons and mitres are then set out on the other portion of the work, on which the clamps are to fit, and the waste removed with tenon saw and chisel. The rebate plane may be partly used for the haunching, if long. The clamp is now laid over the tenons and marked for cutting the mortises.

Hinged Bearer for Table Flap.—In concluding this survey of woodwork joints it may be of interest to describe the manner of making the hinged bearer for a table flap, illustrated by Fig. 7. In one sense this is not properly a joint, yet in another it may certainly be considered so. Fig. 8 shows how it is set out, and Fig. 9 how it is cut. Having bored the holes in line in each piece, an iron rod is lastly inserted to form the hinge-pin. Take care to saw just inside the waste to ensure a good fit.

Boring Tools and Their Uses

THE BRADAWL

THE chief boring tools are the bradawl, the gimlet, and the brace and bit. For small holes, say up to about $\frac{1}{8}$ in. or $\frac{1}{16}$ in., the bradawl (or sprigbit) is generally used, particularly if the holes are only a few in number. When nailing softwoods, say with nails up to about 2 in. to $2\frac{1}{2}$ in. in length, and if there is a danger of splitting owing to the nails being near the edge, the nails are "given a start" by boring part-way with the bradawl. Screw holes in softwoods are bored in the same way. Holes for nails or screws, in hardwoods are bored with the bradawl only if they are very small, the brace and bit being generally used for larger ones.

The common type of bradawl is shown in Fig. 1. It consists of three parts: the handle (preferably ash, but often beech), the ferrule of brass, and the blade

Fig. 1.—Ordinary Bradawl

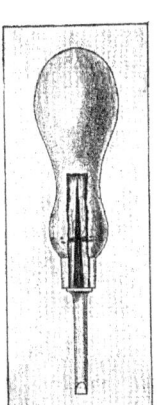

Fig. 2.—Section of Bradawl having Pin through Tang

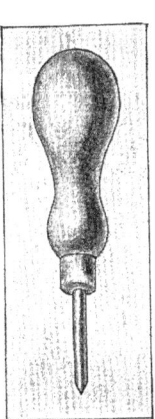

Fig. 3.—Bradawl Secured by Ferrule

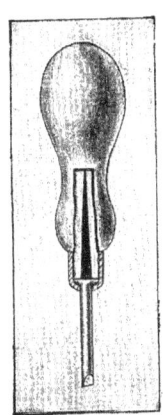

Fig. 4.—Section of Bradawl Secured by Ferrule

(or prong or bit). The blade has a tang which fits into the handle. Between tang and blade is a shoulder which prevents the blade being driven into the handle. Fig. 2 shows a section of a

Fig. 5.—Bradawl and Tool-pad with Wing-nut Adjustment

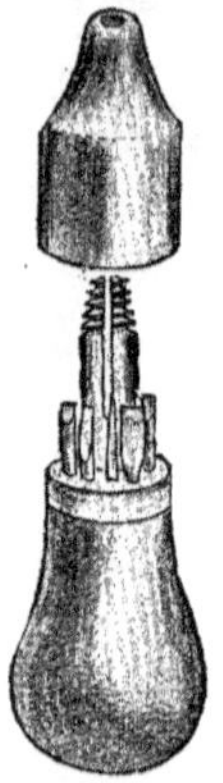

Fig. 6.—Bradawl and Tool-pad

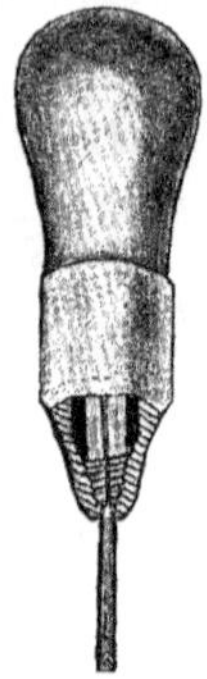

Fig. 7.—Section of Bradawl, showing how the Jaws Grip the Blade

bradawl having a pin passing through the handle and tang and thus preventing the blade from being easily withdrawn from the handle, this being a decided advantage.

Fig. 3 shows an even more securely fixed blade than the type shown in Fig. 2. After the tang is driven into the handle the cup-shaped ferrule is driven on the handle and holds against the shoulder of the blade (see Fig. 4). The tang is then fastened with one or two pins.

There is a number of types of bradawls with detachable blades, as shown in Figs. 5, 6 and 7. Sometimes these elaborate bradawls are known as "tool-pads." The "bits" (or tools) often comprise a small screwdriver, gimlets, reamer, etc.

In the type shown in Fig. 5 the "bits" are kept in the hollow handle, which is usually made of boxwood and has a screw top. The various bits are quickly fixed in the jaw or chuck by means of

the wing screw. Care should be taken not to hit the handle of this tool-pad with the hammer, as being hollow it is easily split.

Fig. 6 shows another variety of bradawl and tool-pad. The shanks of the tools fit into the jaws, the top of which is screwed and tapered. On screwing the cap into position the jaws are forced together and grip the shank of the bit, as indicated in Fig. 7.

Using the Bradawl.—Before using, the bradawl should be sharpened. This is usually done by filing the end bevelled from both sides, the bevels being about $\frac{1}{4}$ in. long. The end, of course, is an *edge*, like a chisel, not a point. A *pointed* bradawl is a mere pricker; it cannot bore. A saw file is generally used for sharpening, though the bradawl could be ground on a grindstone or flagstone if desired. A

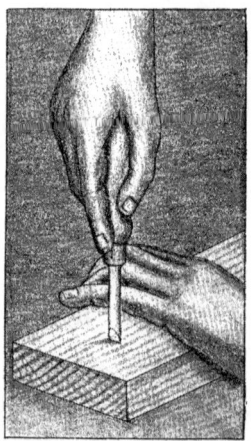

Fig. 8.—Correct Method of Using Bradawl

keener edge may be given by a few rubs on an oilstone, but this is usually not considered worth the trouble.

The cutting edge of the bradawl should be held across the grain (Fig. 8) and pressed into the timber. Whilst pressing on the bradawl it should be slightly

BORING TOOLS AND THEIR USES

rotated to and fro with an arc-like movement; it should not be turned completely round as in the case of a gimlet. Very often it is driven into the wood with the hammer, as in Fig. 9. This method undoubtedly requires less effort on the part of the workman, but there is a being held by the left hand and the handle of the bradawl grasped with the right hand, which exerts a lifting action and at the same time a slight arc-like motion.

If the bradawl is driven into a piece of timber with its edge in the direction of the grain it acts as a wedge and the

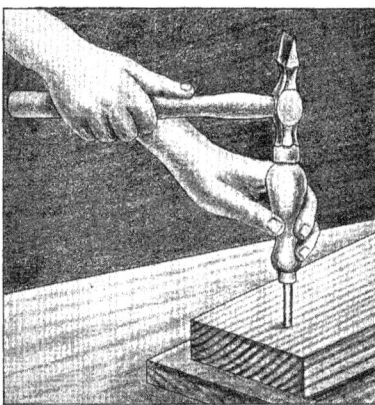

Fig. 9.—Driving Bradawl with Hammer

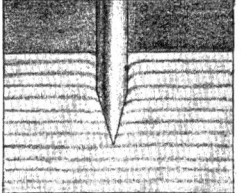

Fig. 12.—Boring Action of Bradawl

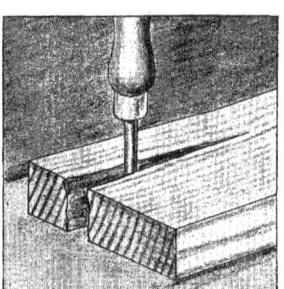

Fig. 11.—Timber Split with Bradawl owing to Incorrect Usage

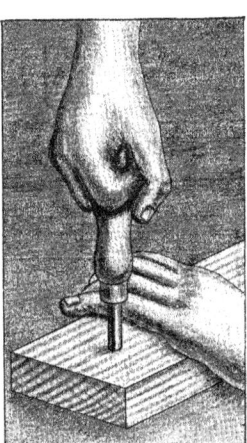

Fig. 10.—Withdrawing Bradawl

likelihood of the handle of the bradawl being split, and there is also difficulty in withdrawing the tool.

The usual method of withdrawing the bradawl is shown in Fig. 10, the timber wood is likely to split, as in Fig. 11. If the edge of the blade is held across the grain there is no wedge action tending to split the wood and the edge also cuts the fibres, thus making a cleaner and larger hole than when the edge of the blade is parallel with the grain. Besides this cutting action there is also a crushing action, the fibres being compressed and bent downwards, as indicated in Fig. 12.

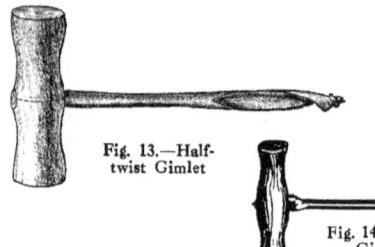

Fig. 13.—Half-twist Gimlet

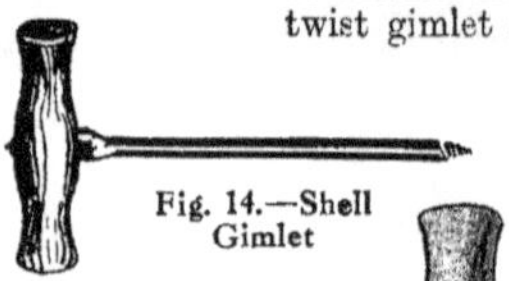

Fig. 14.—Shell Gimlet

GIMLETS

A gimlet is a self-contained boring tool (like a bradawl), but having a twisted or threaded point that forces its way into the wood. In boring a hole with a bradawl continuous pressure has to be applied, but in the case of a gimlet, after it has once been started, the worm end "eats" its way into the timber. The handle is therefore shaped so that a fair amount of turning effort can be applied.

The steel portion of the gimlet is made in various shapes. Fig. 13 shows a common form known as a half-twist gimlet. A shell gimlet is shown at Fig. 14, the bit being a straight shank, half circular in section, with a twist at the end. Fig. 15 shows an auger bit, and Figs. 16, 17 and 18 further illustrate an ordinary form of twist gimlet in course of use.

Using the Gimlet.— To bore a hole with a gimlet it has to be turned con-

Fig. 15.—Auger Gimlet

stantly in one direction (like the hands of a clock). Fig. 16 shows the usual way of holding when starting to bore. The gimlet is at first rotated and pressed down at the same time. When the point and the cutter have entered the wood, and provided the wood is not too hard or

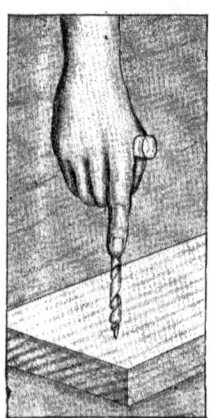

Fig. 16.—Starting Gimlet

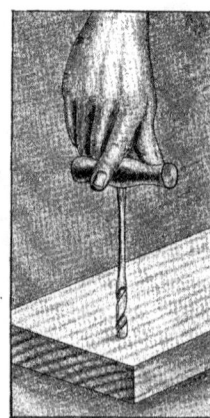

Fig. 17.—Boring with Gimlet

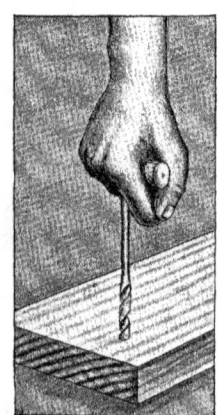

Fig. 18.—Withdrawing Gimlet

BORING TOOLS AND THEIR USES

the gimlet dull, the gimlet can be turned more quickly by the thumb and finger, as indicated in Fig. 17.

worker possesses a brace and bits or a handdrill and two or three bradawls, gimlets are hardly necessary, and, in fact,

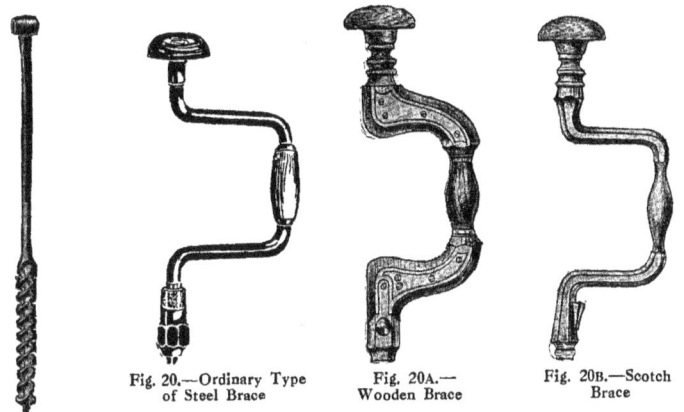

Fig. 19.—Auger, Gedge's Pattern

Fig. 20.—Ordinary Type of Steel Brace

Fig. 20A.— Wooden Brace

Fig. 20B.—Scotch Brace

The gimlet is withdrawn by grasping the handle (Fig. 18) and using a combined lifting and rotating action; this will bring out the core and leave a cleaner hole. The process just described often has to be repeated several times when boring hardwood or thick softwood.

Care should be exercised in the use of all gimlets when boring near the end of the wood, as they exercise a splitting action. This is especially the case when they become worn and blunt and thus do not cut properly; extra effort is then exerted which brings into play the wedge-like form of their ends, which tends to force the fibres apart instead of cutting them, thus splitting the timber.

Gimlets do not appear to be as much used nowadays as formerly. If a wood-

inadvisable. The chief advantages of the gimlet are its small size and small price.

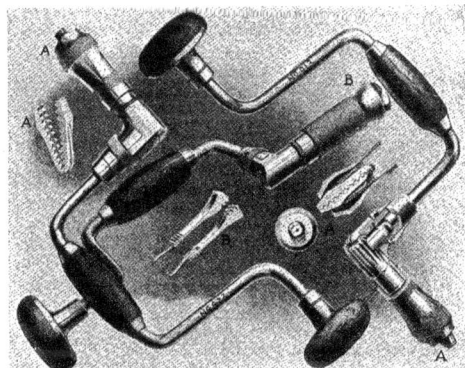

Fig. 21.—Examples of Ratchet Braces and Fittings

An *auger* (Fig. 19) might be described as a large gimlet used for boring large and long holes in carpentry, etc. The handle may either fit through a hole in the auger shank or the latter may be shaped like a brace bit and fit into a special adjustable handle.

Fig. 22.—Further Examples of Ratchet Braces and Fittings

BRACE AND BITS

A brace is a tool for holding and rotating bits for boring holes and other purposes. The common simple type is shown in Fig. 20. It consists of three parts: the jaws (or chuck), the head, and the crank. Formerly the bit was fastened in the jaws by means of a thumbscrew, as in the old-fashioned wooden brace in Fig. 20A, or by a spring catch as in Fig. 20B, but the usual type of jaws on modern braces is as shown in the illustration. The bit is inserted between the jaws, which grip the bit between them when the jaw cap is screwed down on to the jaws. This latter operation is accomplished not by turning the jaw cap, but by holding it still with the left hand and turning the crank of the brace with the right hand.

Very often the jaws are serrated, as shown in Figs. 21 and 22, in which case they are known as "crocodile jaws," to get a better grip on the bits.

The power of the brace depends on the "sweep" of the crank—the bigger the sweep the more powerful being the brace. The sweep is the diameter of the circle that the crank describes. A 10-in. sweep is a usual size, though 8 in. is fairly common. Other sizes of braces may be also obtained. Though more turning power can be exerted when the crank is large, it is found in practice that a 10-in. sweep gives enough power for all ordinary purposes. The handle of the crank and the head are usually made of rosewood. In good makes the head runs on ball-bearings.

Many braces, in fact, probably the majority in use by professional workmen, are now fitted with a ratchet. Stanley ratchet braces are shown in Figs. 21 and 22; the letters in the illustrations show to which braces the various fittings belong, parts A belonging to brace A, etc. The ratchet is simply a catch or

Fig. 23.—Boring Hole with Ratchet Brace in Floor near Wall

device which, at will, enables the crank to be rotated without rotating the jaws and bit. This adds greatly to the utility

BORING TOOLS AND THEIR USES

of the tool. Fig. 23 shows a hole being bored in the floor near a wall with a ratchet brace and a twist bit. A hole could not be easily bored in this position with an ordinary brace, as the crank of forming part of the tool, the bit can be turned at a higher speed than with a brace, and, further the turning of the handle of the drill does not have a strong tendency to pull the drill and bit out

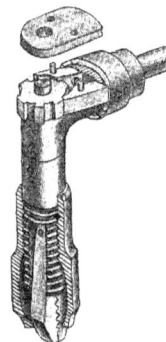

Fig. 23A.—Sectional View showing Ratchet and Jaws

Fig. 23C.
Figs. 23B and 23C.—Angular Bit Stock and How to Use It

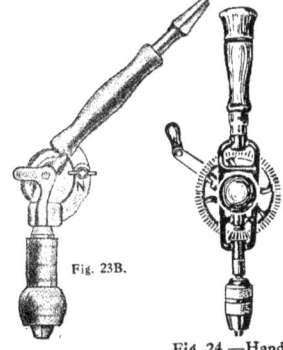

Fig. 24.—Hand Drill

the brace could not be turned continuously. With the ratchet brace, the ratchet may be so adjusted that on turning the crank clockwise the bit is turned. When the crank has thus been turned as far as possible, that is, until it comes in contact with the wall, it may be turned backwards, during which latter turn the bit remains stationary. The crank is again turned clockwise and turns the bit, and so on until the hole is bored. The ratchet may also be adjusted so that the ratchet misses on a clockwise turn and grips on the anti-clockwise turn. Fig. 23A gives a pictorial view showing how the ratchet works; the crocodile jaws are also clearly shown in the illustration.

Figs. 23B and 23C show an angular bit stock; it is an alternative to the ratchet brace in awkward positions; N (Fig. 23B) is the clamp.

HAND DRILL

This tool (Fig. 24) is better for many purposes than the brace, and deserves to be better known. Owing to the gearing of its correct direction. These are two decided advantages. The tool is recommended to both amateurs and skilled craftsmen.

BRACE BITS

There are many varieties of bits, different patterns having been found necessary for boring holes under differing conditions, such as size of hole and kind

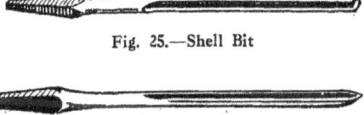

Fig. 25.—Shell Bit

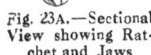

Fig. 26.—Spoon Bit

of timber. Other bits are necessary for drilling and enlarging holes in metal fittings for woodwork and for other purposes.

Shell Bit.—This bit (Fig. 25) is the simplest and mostly used type of bit.

It is employed only to bore small holes (up to about ⅜ in. diameter) generally for screws and nails. It is sharpened by

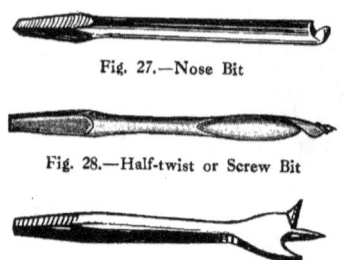

Fig. 27.—Nose Bit

Fig. 28.—Half-twist or Screw Bit

Fig. 29.—Centre Bit

filing the end. This bit has less tendency than any other type of bit, when boring a hole through a piece of wood, to splinter the back side, but even with this it is better to safeguard against splintering by holding a scrap of timber to the other side of the wood. This warning applies particularly to such jobs as boring the holes for a keyhole.

The shell bit has to be forced into the wood by continual pressure. If the hole is deep or in hardwood it is customary, after boring a little distance, to withdraw the bit whilst still turning in the same

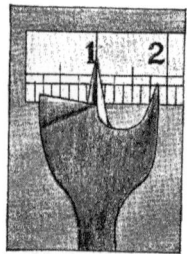

Fig. 30.—Obtaining Size of Centre Bit

direction, so that some of the "core" is withdrawn. If it is attempted to bore a deep hole without withdrawing some of the core at intervals the bit will get very hot and the brace difficult to turn, there being also a possibility of boring an unsatisfactory hole.

Spoon Bit.—Fig. 26 shows this bit to be similar to the shell bit except that the cutting end is spoon-shaped. It is a little quicker in action than the ordinary

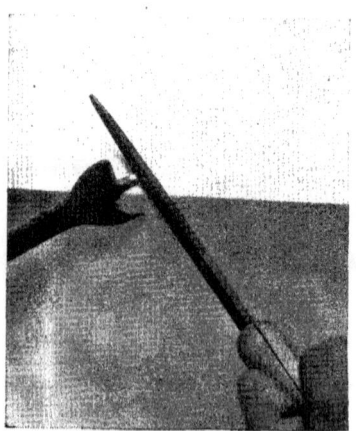

Fig. 31.—Sharpening Point of Centre Bit

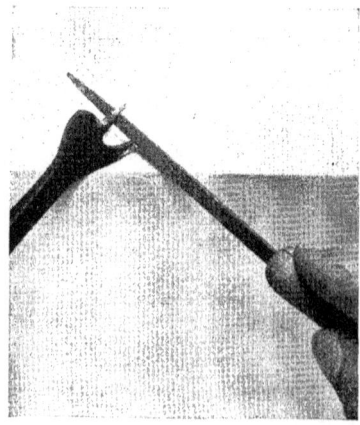

Fig. 32.—Sharpening Nicker of Centre Bit

BORING TOOLS AND THEIR USES

shell bit, but the end is soon damaged by "running against" a nail.

Nose Bit.—This is another variety of shell bit (*see* Fig. 27) possessing the same merits and demerits. Both spoon and nose bits are useful for boring with the grain, and the shape of the end enables the core of the hole to be easily withdrawn.

Half-twist Bit.—This bit (Fig. 28) is often known as a "screw bit" because it is used in "boring for screws," for which it is particularly suited. It is self-propelling, and is therefore not fatiguing to use. As the bit starts at a point and gradually thickens in the shank it exerts

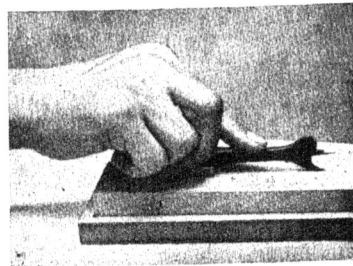

Fig. 33.—Removing Burr on Nicker of Centre Bit

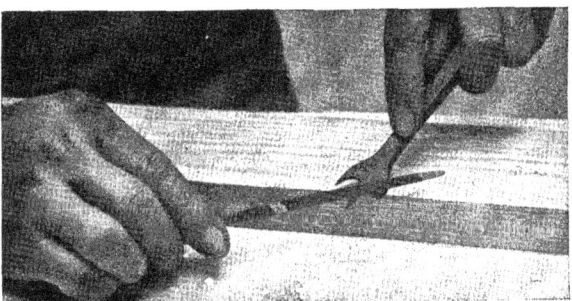

Fig. 35.—Filing Cutter of Centre Bit

a wedge-like action when boring, and care is therefore necessary to avoid splitting the wood.

Centre Bit.—This bit is of a distinct type from the preceding bits, its action in cutting a hole being quite different. A centre bit (Fig. 29) consists of three parts : the centre pin, which forms an axis or guide when cutting the hole ; the outside point or "nicker," which marks the rim of the hole and cuts the wood fibres ; the cutter or scoop, which removes the wood after the manner of a revolving chisel. The "size" of a centre bit is twice the distance from the centre pin to the nicker. For example, in Fig. 30 the distance from the centre of the bit to the nicker is $\frac{7}{8}$ in. and therefore the size of the bit is $1\frac{3}{4}$ in. The distance from the centre pin to the outside of the cutter should be *slightly less* than $\frac{7}{8}$ in. so that the side of the cutter will not rub or scar the side of the hole, thus giving a clean cut. The size of a centre bit should therefore be determined, as in Fig. 30, or a trial hole bored and measured.

As there are

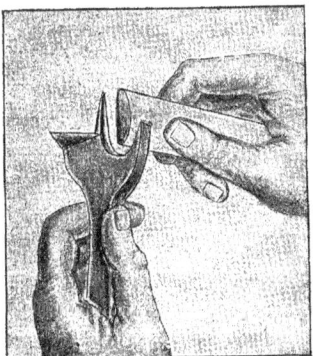

Fig. 34.—Using Finger Slip to Sharpen Centre Bit

three parts to a centre bit there must be three operations in sharpening. First the point should be sharpened by filing, as in Fig. 31, if necessary. Fig. 32 shows how the nicker is filed—on the *inside*, not on the outside. If the latter were filed the size as well as the cutting properties of the bit would be spoiled. The nicker should also be sloping on the edge so as to cut easily. Sometimes the " burr " on the outside is carefully removed on the oilstone, as in Fig. 33, or the nicker finished with a " finger slip," as in Fig. 34, but these last two operations are hardly necessary except in very high-

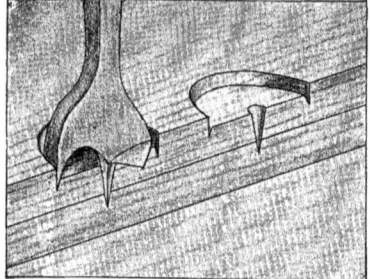

Fig. 36.—Boring with Centre Bit: First Operation, shown partly in section

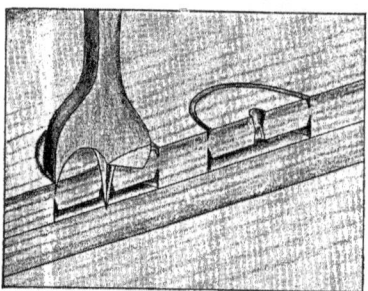

Fig. 37.—Boring with Centre Bit: Second Operation, shown partly in section

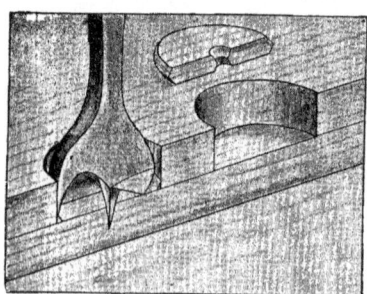

Fig. 38.—Boring with Centre Bit: Third Operation, shown partly in section

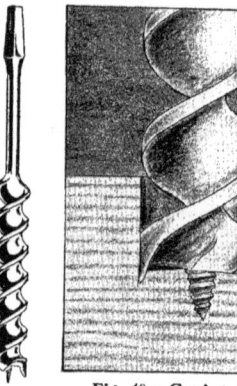

Fig. 39.—Twist Bit: Jennings' Pattern

Fig. 40.—Cutting Action of Twist Bit

class work. Lastly, the cutter is filed, as in Fig. 35. The filing must be done on the top side of the cutter, otherwise the bit will not " bite " into the wood when in use.

A hole may be bored with a centre bit right through a piece of wood without splitting if a piece of wood is held against the wood where the bit comes through, as recommended when boring with the shell. It is usual, however, to bore from both sides of the wood. Figs. 36, 37 and 38 show a slight variation of the usual method of boring from both sides. Preferably the work is placed on or against a piece of waste wood, though this could be dispensed with. The hole is bored

BORING TOOLS AND THEIR USES

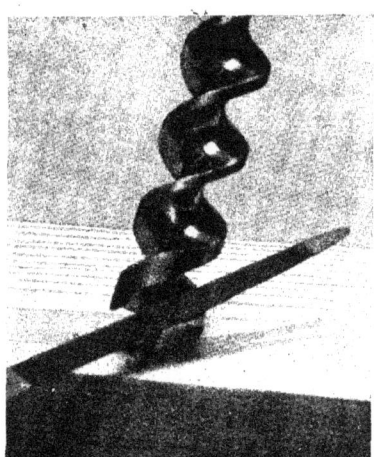

Fig. 41.—Filing Cutter of Twist Bit

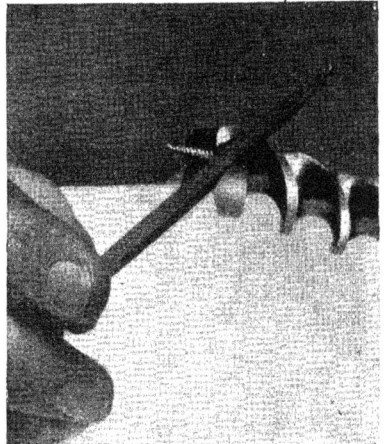

Fig. 42.—Filing Nicker of Twist Bit

until the centre point projects a little through the back of the wood, as shown in Fig. 36. The work is then bored from the other side a little so that the nicker makes a circular cut, as indicated in Fig. 37. The work is turned back to its first position and the boring continued, when a circular piece should come out as shown. If the bit is sharp and held at right angles to the face of the work the hole will be true and smooth.

The ordinary type of centre bits have to be forced into the wood by constant pressure, but a special type with a screw centre point may be obtained. This is occasionally used for large holes, and as the screw end tends to pull the bit into the wood the work is made easier.

Twist Bits.—These bits have both a twisted point and a twisted shank. When the bit " gets a start " it forces its way into the wood. No pressure is usually required on the head of the brace and it is only necessary to turn the crank. The worm point " eats its way " into the wood, this action being assisted by the spiral shank. The cutters at the end of the bit cut the wood after the manner of a centre bit—though this action varies a little with the type of twist bit used. Compare, for example, a Jennings' twist bit and a Gedge's twist bit. Twist bits are self-clearing, as the cuttings ascend the spiral shaft to the top of the hole.

In the Jennings' twist bit (Fig. 39) the end works on the principle of the centre bit, but has two nickers and two cutters— and, of course, a screw centre point. Fig. 40 is a sectional view of a piece of wood partly bored, showing the front edge of one cutter and the edges of the nickers. This twist bit is sharpened with a file

Fig. 43.—Twist Bit : Gedge's Pattern

Fig. 44.—Twist Drill Bit

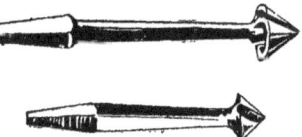

Fig. 45.—Wood Countersinks

after the manner of a centre bit; see Fig. 41, which illustrates how a cutter is sharpened, and Fig. 42, which shows a nicker being filed.

There are other twist bits of slightly varying design, but they usually belong to either of the two preceding classes. A dowel bit is a short twist bit. Fig. 44

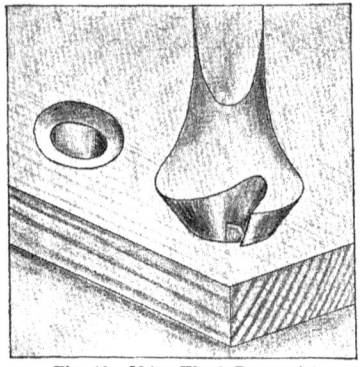

Fig. 46.—Using Wood Countersink

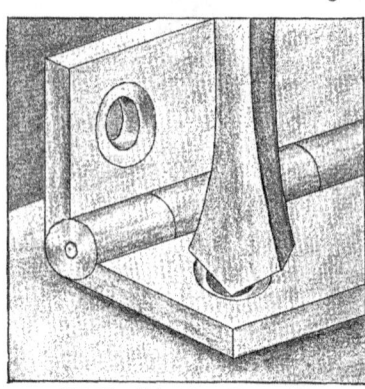

Fig. 50.—Using Iron Countersink

Fig. 47.—Countersink for Brass

Fig. 49.—Iron Countersink

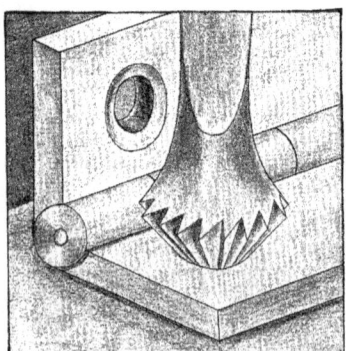

Fig. 48.—Using Countersink on Brass Hinge

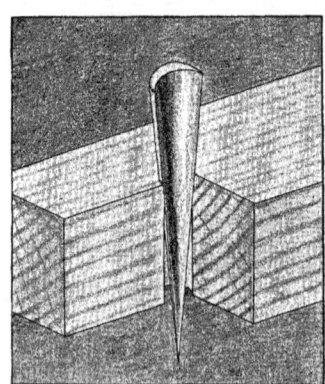

Fig. 51.—Using Wood Reamer

Gedge's bit (Fig. 43) is a twist bit very similar to the preceding but with a different shape of cutter end, which is formed by two curved wings. It is sharpened with a small round (rat-tail) file.

shows a twist drill bit that is very useful for boring hardwood in any direction of the grain without much fear of splitting.

Countersinks.—These bits are of various types, and are used for counter-

BORING TOOLS AND THEIR USES

sinking screw holes in wood or metal. Fig. 45 shows two types of countersinks for *wood*. The ordinary type is shown in use in Fig. 46. It will be seen that the bit has one cutter only. This bit should be sharpened with a rat-tail file. Fig. 47 represents a countersink for brass; it is shown in use on a brass hinge in Fig. 48, from which illustration it will

Reamers.—These are used for enlarging holes already made. There are three chief types. Fig. 52 shows a reamer for wood, which is after the manner of a tapering shell bit and should be sharp on the edges. Fig. 51 shows the wood reamer in use.

A metal reamer (Fig. 53) is like a long pyramid in shape and has four cutting

Fig. 52.—Wood Reamer

Fig. 55.—Screwdriver Bit

Fig. 53.—Iron Reamer

Fig. 56.—Forked Turn-screw Bit

Fig. 54.—Using Iron Reamer

Fig. 57.— Expansion Bit (Clarke's Patent)

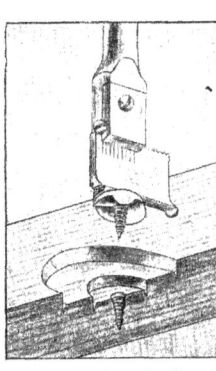

Fig. 58.—Boring with Steer's Screw Adjustment Expansion Bit. The Wood is shown in Section.

Fig. 59.— Forstner Bit

be seen that the bit has a number of cutters; these should be sharpened, when required, with a small saw file. Very often this bit is used for countersinking timber, particularly hardwood, as it usually leaves a cleaner hole than the wood countersink.

A countersink for iron is shown in Fig. 49, and in use, countersinking the holes in an iron hinge, in Fig. 50. It is sharpened with a file or on the grindstone.

corners. In Fig. 54 the end of the reamer is shown enlarging a screw hole in a metal hinge. This reamer though supposed to be specially for iron is also suitable for brass, etc.

A special reamer for brass, semi-circular in section and tapering in length like the two former types, is sometimes used. It is, however, not necessary, and the iron reamer will do the work equally well.

Screwdriver Bit.—This bit is shown in Fig. 55 and is very useful for driving screws, particularly if the screws are numerous or large in size. The chief difficulty when using the brace and screwdriver bit is not to turn the brace or screw but to keep the bit in the nick of

Expansion Bits.—The ordinary type of expansion bit (Clarke's patent) is shown in Fig. 57. The principle is quite simple: an adjustable wing cutter slides in a groove; the projection of this cutter gives the radius of the hole, the cutter being fixed in any desired position by means of

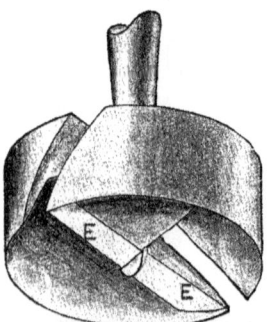

Fig. 60.—Steer's Expansion Bit, showing Parts Separated

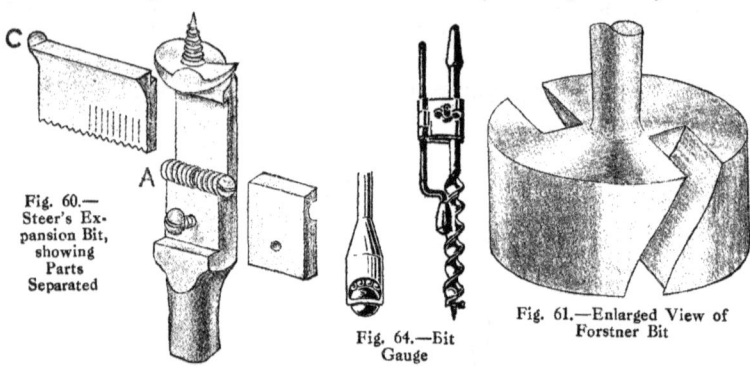

Fig. 64.—Bit Gauge

Fig. 61.—Enlarged View of Forstner Bit

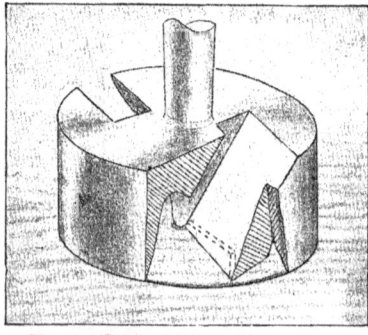

Fig. 62.—Forstner Bit, showing Cutting Edges

Fig. 63.—Sectional View of Forstner Bit, showing Cutting Action

the screw. It is better when dealing with tight screws to use the ratchet and turn the crank backwards and forwards through a small arc.

A forked screwdriver bit is shown at Fig. 56, and is used for tightening saw screws and other screws of the same kind, as already shown in the chapter on saws and sawing.

a screw. One expansion bit will cut holes within certain limits only, two useful sizes being a small one cutting holes between $\frac{1}{2}$ in. and $1\frac{1}{2}$ in. and a larger one boring from $\frac{7}{8}$ in. to 3 in.

In the screw-adjusting expansion bits (see Figs. 58 and 60), turning the side screw A with a screwdriver modifies the distance of the circular cutter c.

BORING TOOLS AND THEIR USES

Forstner Bit.—This bit (Fig. 59), unlike other bits, is guided not by its centre but by its circular rim. It will bore any arc of a circle, and will bore in any direction regardless of grain or knots and leave a smooth surface. It is particularly useful for recessed work.

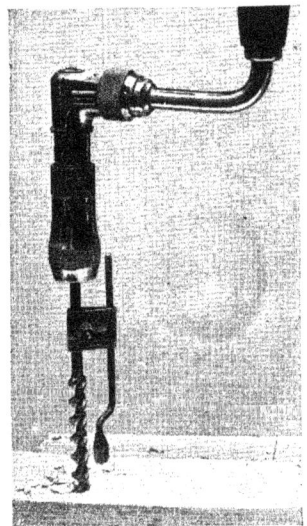

Fig. 65.—Using Bit Gauge

Fig. 66.—Dowel Sharpener

Fig. 67.—Extension Bit

A small three-cornered, or flat, file is used for sharpening it. Figs. 61 to 63 illustrate clearly the action of the bit; E indicates the two cutting edges.

Bit Gauges.—When boring holes, say for dowels, they have to be of a certain depth. The correct depth can be obtained in various ways. If there are not many holes the two following methods may be used : (1) count the number of turns of the brace to bore the first hole

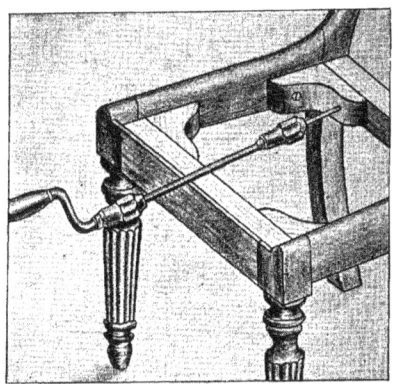

Fig. 68.—Using Extension Bit

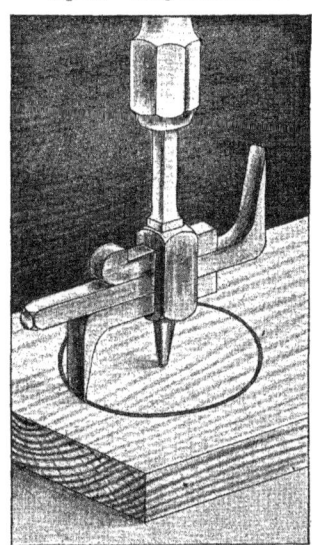

Fig. 69.—Disc Cutter in Use

of correct depth and give the other holes a similar number of turns ; (2) mark the bit with chalk, a pencil or a file.

Fig. 64 shows a gauge (and enlarged

detail) for attaching to the side of a bit, and Fig. 65 shows the gauge in use. Bit gauges for countersinking are also used, so that the countersinking will accurately receive the head of the screw.

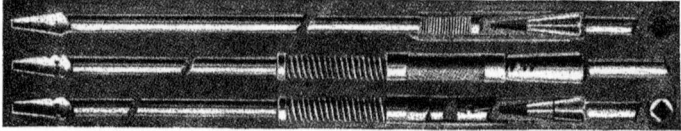

Fig. 70.—Extension Bits

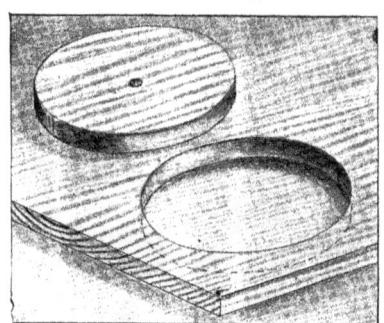

Fig. 71.—Circular Disc Cut Out

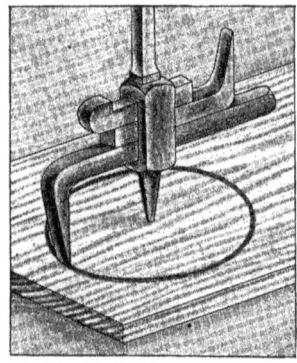

Fig. 72.—Cutting Circular Recess or Disc with Disc Cutter

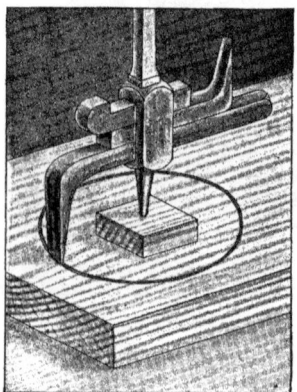

Fig. 73.—Method to Avoid Making Hole in Centre of Recess

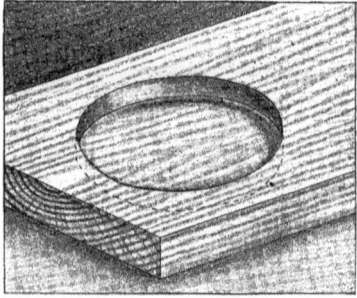

Fig. 74.—Circular Recess as Cut with Disc Cutter

BORING TOOLS AND THEIR USES

Other Bits and Devices.—A bit for pointing the ends of dowels is shown in Fig. 66.

Figs. 67 and 70 show various patterns of extension bit holders. These will extend the brace bit, enabling it to be

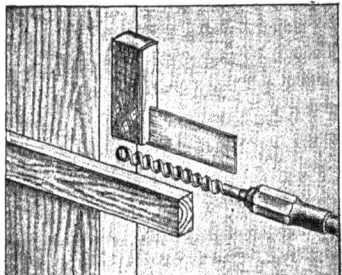

Fig. 75.—Boring at Right Angles to Edge

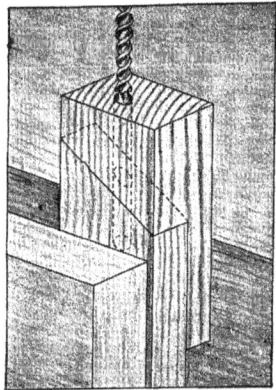

Fig. 76.—Boring Mitre

used for boring through walls, floors, etc., where the ordinary bit will not reach. Fig. 68 gives an example of their use.

A disc cutter bit is often found useful for cutting small wheels and discs. It consists of a centre point and a sliding nicker which can be adjusted according to the size of disc required. Fig. 69 shows the cutter being used to cut a hole (or alternatively, a disc) from a thin board. Fig. 71 shows the finish of the operation. The disc cutter is also useful for cutting circular recesses that are too large for a centre bit. The circular side is first cut, as in Fig. 72, by chiselling. If it is desired to avoid a mark in the centre a piece of waste wood should be used, as in Fig. 73. The finished recess is shown at Fig. 74.

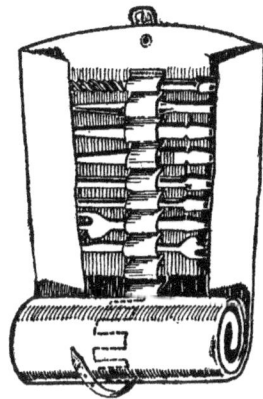

Fig. 77.—Case for Holding Bits

Boring at Right Angles to an Edge.—When boring for mortise locks and similar purposes care has to be exercised so that the bit goes in the right direction. This is best tested by a straightedge, as shown at Fig. 75. The bit must also fit the blade of a try-square as shown.

Boring at an Angle to a Mitre.—To bore accurately a hole at a mitre is somewhat difficult; but it can easily be done by a guide piece, as shown at Fig. 76.

A case or roll for holding bits is shown in Fig. 77. Some woodworkers prefer a case with longer pockets so that the bits cannot come in contact with, and damage, each other.

A Few Elementary Examples

COMBINED BOOK TROUGH AND STOOL

THIS chapter gives designs and descriptions of a few useful articles for the home. Though the articles are not elaborate the parts will have to be made carefully and accurately to ensure neat work.

The first example is a book trough as in Fig. 1. It will require one piece called A 1 ft. 7 in. by 9¼ in. and ⅞ in. thick, two pieces B 12½ in. by 7¼ in. and ⅞ in. thick, one piece C 1 ft. 4 in. by 3⅜ in. and ⅝ in. thick, and one piece as last but 7¼ in. wide.

The first piece specified above forms the top shelf, and should be finished 1 ft. 6½ in. by 9 in. by ¾ in. It will need two chases or housings ¼ in. deep cut into it exactly as shaded and figured in Fig. 4, and should also be chamfered all round on the underside as shown in section by Fig. 6, where a very small chamfer is shown at D, this giving a more durable edge than if this were simply a thin fillet.

For the uprights the two pieces B will be required. Each should be finished 12¼ in. by 7 in. by ¾ in., and worked as in Fig. 3. This shows them cut square at E, housed ⅜ in. deep (Fig. 5) for the two sloping shelves at F, and pierced with a trefoil at G. The trefoil can be cut mainly with a brace and bit, and consists of a 1¼-in. sided equilateral triangle having a 1-in diameter circle struck from each of its points (see Fig. 7).

The sloping shelves forming the trough are at right angles to one another, and can be prepared from the two pieces C, the whole work being accurately and tightly fitted, glued up, and screwed or nailed.

A USEFUL SCULLERY FITMENT

The scullery fitment shown by Fig. 8 is easily constructed. The top projecting

Fig. 1.—Book Trough and Stool

rail acts as a rack for saucepan lids, the lower shelf as a draining rack for light articles, and a shelf for the accommodation of brushes, etc.

The materials required are 6 ft. of matchboarding and 4 ft. of 2-in by 1-in. planed deal. Wood 4½ in. wide and ½ in. thick can be used in place of the match-

A FEW ELEMENTARY EXAMPLES

boarding if desired. In fact, by altering the design to suit, any odd pieces of timber could be utilised.

Take the piece of deal in hand first, and from it cut two pieces 1 ft. 6 in. long. These form the sides. Cut the matchboarding into 2-ft. lengths, and saw one of the pieces down the centre. These two strips form the top and bottom rails, which must be half-dovetailed into the sides. Fig. 9 shows the position of the dovetails, half of the front rail and shelf being cut away for that purpose. This completes the frame. Take the piece of deal left over from the sides, cut two pieces 4 in. long from it, and shape as at A (Fig. 10). The recess in the top (which provides for the reception of the projecting rail) is 1½ in. by ½ in. These pieces are fastened to the frame, 3 in. from the top, with screws inserted from the back. Cut a rail 1½ in. wide from one of the two remaining pieces of matchboarding, and nail or screw across the frame in the recesses. Cut two pieces from the other portion of matchboarding 5½ in. long and 2½ in. wide, and let these into the sides 1¼ in. from the bottom, and slope slightly upwards about 1 in. in 6 in. To these supports three 1½ in. rails, which can be cut from the remaining piece of matchboarding, should be nailed across, as shown in Figs. 9 and 10. The beaded edge of the matchboarding can be left on, and used with effect, as shown at B (Figs. 9 and 10).

It is recommended that the rack be left plain, though it could be varnished if thought at all desirable.

BOOT AND SHOE RACK

A rack for boots, shoes, and slippers, which would be useful in almost any house is shown by Figs. 11 to 14. It can be

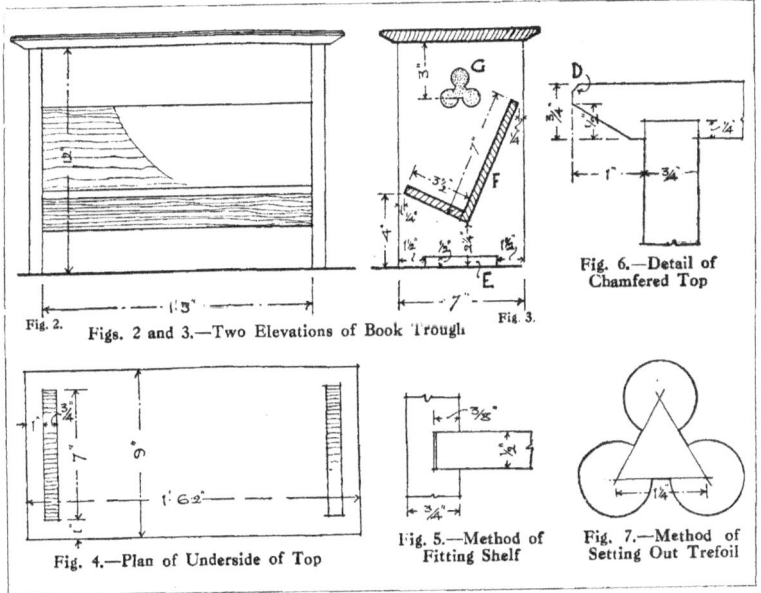

Figs. 2 and 3.—Two Elevations of Book Trough

Fig. 6.—Detail of Chamfered Top

Fig. 4.—Plan of Underside of Top

Fig. 5.—Method of Fitting Shelf

Fig. 7.—Method of Setting Out Trefoil

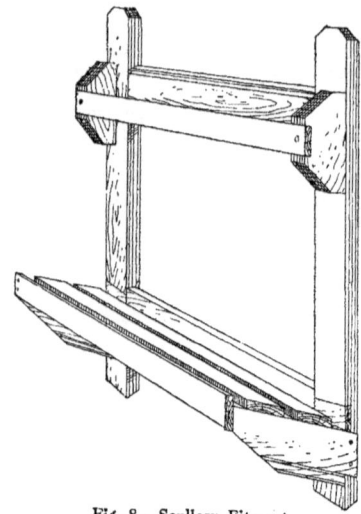

Fig. 8.—Scullery Fitment

First prepare the rails. Plane them square, and take off the sharp corners to form a slight chamfer. Shoulder and tenon each end ready for the ends, which can then be prepared with the mortises, and cut out the bottoms, as shown in Figs. 12 and 13. Space them out as shown, the two top rails for children's boots and slippers being closer together than the others. When the mortises are cut, gently drive on the ends and wedge the rail tenons. Across the back screw three braces A (Figs. 11 and 13), round off the back edges, as at B in Fig. 14, and then screw on the top from the underside, the ends being gouged for the screws.

At the front, immediately below the top, place a rod of wood or $\tfrac{3}{16}$-in. diameter iron suspended by brass hooks, as at C in Fig. 13, on which to fix a curtain to cover the whole.

The thicknessing fillet along the top can next be fixed, and the rack is then ready for painting, or staining and var-

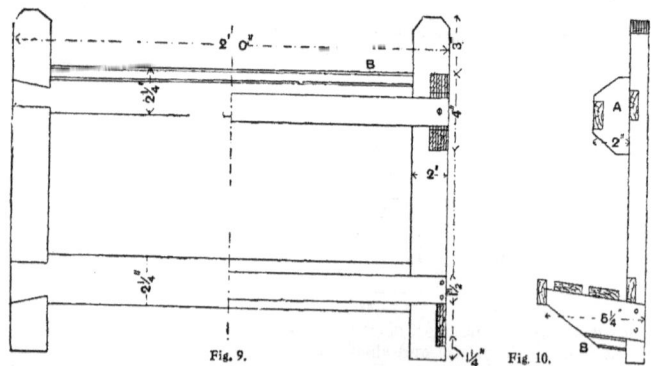

Figs. 9 and 10.—Front and End Elevations of Scullery Fitment

made of $\tfrac{3}{4}$-in. yellow pine or sound red deal, and requires two ends, 2 ft. 9 in. by 11 in. by $\tfrac{3}{4}$ in.; one top, 4 ft. by 12 in. by $\tfrac{3}{4}$ in.; three braces, 3 ft. 6 in. by 3 in. by $\tfrac{1}{2}$ in.; six rails for shelves, 3 ft. 7 in. by 2 in. by 1 in.; and one thicknessing fillet to be mitred round the lower edge of the top, 6 ft. by $1\tfrac{1}{4}$ in. by $\tfrac{7}{8}$ in.

nishing. Rails are preferable to solid shelves, as they admit of a free current of air to dry the soles of the boots.

PHOTOGRAPH STAND

The miniature easel, or stand for photographs (Fig. 15) has quite an attractive

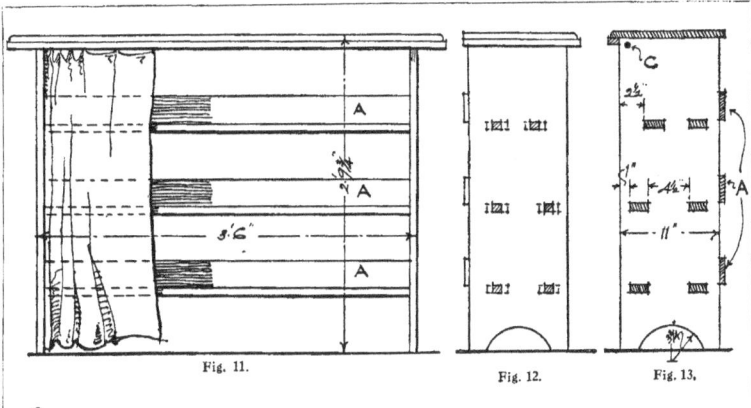

Fig. 11.

Fig. 12.

Fig. 13.

Figs. 11 to 13.—Front and End Elevations and Vertical Section of Boot and Shoe Rack

Fig. 14.—Plan of Boot and Shoe Rack (Top Removed)

Fig. 15.—Photograph Easel-stand

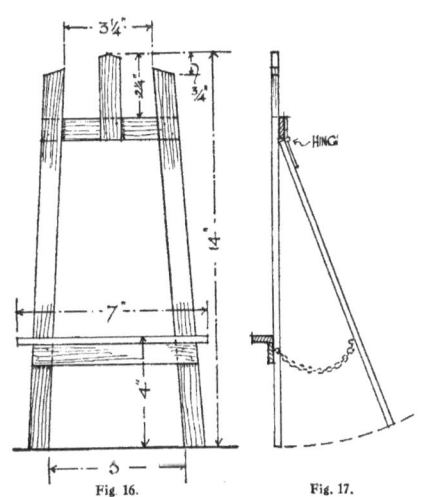

Fig. 16.

Fig. 17.

Figs. 16 and 17.—Front and Side Elevations of Photograph Easel-stand

appearance, and can be used in widely different sizes. It presents an opportunity for utilising odd pieces and scraps for which it might otherwise be difficult to find a use, and the sizes given in Figs. 16 and 17 require about 5-ft. run of stripwood of about, say, ¾ in. or ⅝ in. by ₁₆/₃ in. or other convenient dimensions.

folded in half and the pieces interweaved so that the one half of a folded piece of paper is between the folds of the next higher piece, and the other half between the folds of the next lower piece. Fig. 19 shows several pieces as they lie in the box. It will be seen that there is a slot in the bottom of the box, running across

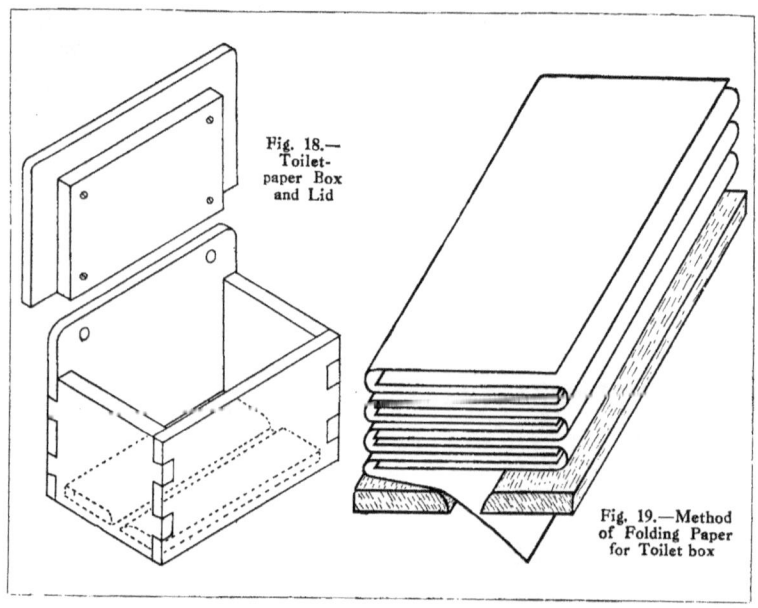

Fig. 18.—Toilet-paper Box and Lid

Fig. 19.—Method of Folding Paper for Toilet box

Fine wire brads filed off smooth will give suitable fixing; or round-headed brass screws might be employed. The support should be hinged rather than rigid, and the extent of its opening limited by a small length of chain or ribbon at the bottom.

A BOX FOR TOILET-PAPER

A box in which home-cut toilet-paper may be kept tidily and conveniently is shown by Fig. 18. A pile of paper having been cut to size, each piece is

the centre lengthwise. A portion of the bottom piece of paper is passed through this slot and hangs down underneath the box. When this piece is pulled out it brings with it a portion of the next piece, ready to be pulled out in its turn, and so on until the contents of the box is exhausted.

Suitable outside dimensions of the box are as follows: Sides, 4 in. high by 4½ in. long; front, 4 in. high by 7 in. long; back, 5½ in. high by 7 in. long. The thickness of the sides may be ½ in.; the front and back ⅜ in. The bottom is ⅜ in. thick

A FEW ELEMENTARY EXAMPLES

and is in two pieces, separated in the centre lengthwise by about ½ in. to form the slot. The pieces may be simply screwed together, or jointed and glued as shown. The lid consists of two pieces of wood, screwed together, the underpiece fitting down into the box, and the top piece projecting over the sides and front of the box about ⅛ in. The underpiece may be ½ in. thick, the top piece ⅜ in. In the top portion of the back two holes are bored, as shown, for hanging the box on nails or hooks driven into the wall. When finished the box may be stained and varnished.

A box of the size described will take paper 5¾ in. by 7 in. When cutting the paper, time will be saved by arranging a pile of paper, marking out the size on the top piece, and cutting through the lot with a sharp knife, using a straight-edge as a guide.

MINCING OR CHOPPING BOX-BLOCK

A box-block, as illustrated by Fig. 20, on which meat, vegetables, etc., can be minced with an upright chopper, can be made with a piece of ash 1 ft. 1½ in. by 9⅞ in. by 2 in. (marked A in Figs. 22 and 23), two ends of deal 11 in. by 6 in. by ½ in. (B in Figs. 21, 22, 23), one side of deal 1 ft. 3 in. by 6 in. by ½ in. (C, Fig. 23), and one side of birch 1 ft. 2 in. by 4 in. by ⅜ in. (D, Figs. 20 and 23).

Plane the block to thickness, and square the sides and ends. The fence above the block, 1 ft. 1¼ in. long by 9¾ in. wide, inside measurement, should first be "cogged" together, as at E in Fig. 3. Then separate the three pieces and rebate them to a depth of ⅛ in., so as to fit over the block. This forms a close joint, and prevents the minced stuff working down between the block and the fence. The two end pieces are grooved for a loose side of ⅜-in. birch (D); this lifts out to enable the minced contents to be readily removed from the block. Pierced holes to facilitate lifting are required in the ends as shown.

The inside of the box-block should be glasspapered clean, and the outside sized and varnished, when it will be ready for use.

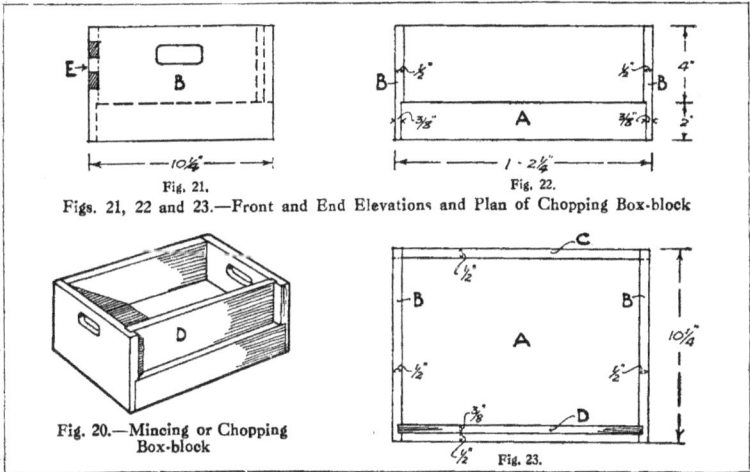

Figs. 21, 22 and 23.—Front and End Elevations and Plan of Chopping Box-block

Fig. 20.—Mincing or Chopping Box-block

LETTER BOX

The letter box, suitable for fitting to a front street door, shown by Fig. 24, is fairly simple to make, and its usefulness will be quite apparent. The box is made entirely of wood; hard or softwood may be used, but hardwood will, of course, be preferable. A slot through which the letters may pass into the box is cut in the door rail; the slot is 7 in. long by 1¾ in. wide. A small door having a glass panel is fitted at the bottom of the box, by means of which the letters are removed from the box. In making the box, wood ½ in. thick should be used. The sides are cut so that when finished they are to the dimensions given in Fig. 25. The top and bottom are 8½ in. long and should be wide enough to overhang the sides ¼ in. at the front. The top and bottom are dovetail-grooved to the ends of the sides. Joints as shown by Fig. 26 are used, and the width over the sides is 8 in. The back of the box is in two portions, as shown in Fig. 25, and it is rebated into the back edge of the sides, as shown by Fig. 27. The front of the box is grooved into the sides, joints as shown by Fig. 28 being used. The front of the box finishes 5 in. up from the bottom to allow for the door. These portions of the box should be cleaned up, and finally fixed together with glue and nails. In fixing together, first fix the front into the sides, then the top and bottom, and finally the back.

The door of the box is framed together, as shown by Fig. 29. The framework is 1 in. wide by ½ in. thick, and is put together with mortise-and-tenon joints as shown. The framework is beaded and rebated, and the glass is held in position in the rebate with small fillet pieces, as shown in Fig. 29. The door is hung with a pair of small butt hinges, and should be fitted with a small mortise lock and key. Small fillet pieces are fitted to the interior of the box to act as stops for the door, as shown in Fig. 25. Two small metal plates are fixed to the top and bottom of the box, as shown in Figs. 24 and 25, and the box is fixed to the door with screws, which pass through these plates.

The interior of the box should remain in the natural state of the wood; but the exterior should be polished or painted. The letter-box plate and flap may be of copper, about 20 B.W.G. being a suitable thickness. The plate is cut to the dimensions given in Fig. 30, and is shaped as shown by Figs. 30 and 31. A small bead is worked round the edges, and four screw holes are provided in the plate. The opening in the plate for the flap is 6 in. long by 1½ in. wide, and the flap should be slightly larger than the opening in the plate. The plate and flap are hinged together, as shown in Figs. 30 and 32. The hinge pin is ⅛ in. in diameter, and the edges of both the plate and flap are curled round a piece of wire of this dimension. The wire is then withdrawn, and the hinge is jointed up in the usual manner by cutting out the portions which are not required, as shown in Fig. 32. The letters should then be worked on the flap, this, of course, being done on a pitch block. The hinge pin is then fitted, and finally the plate and flap are cleaned up and lacquered. The plate is fixed to the door with four round-head screws.

MAKING IRONING BOARDS

Skirt boards are made of various sizes, but a most suitable one is 5 ft. long by 1 ft. 5 in. wide at one end and 9 in. at the other.

In making a board of this kind, an important defect to guard against is the tendency which the board has to warp and cast after being used for some time. Fig. 33 shows the side of a board with cross ends which have cross-tongued joints, and also a dovetail key to prevent warping or casting.

This is an advantage, as the board is kept level and fair. Fig. 34 is a plan. The board should be covered with a piece of white felt or flannel, which can be fixed by tacking the edges, as shown in Fig. 35. These boards, like ironing tables, are covered with blankets and sheets.

Polishing boards are made in the same way as skirt boards, and are of uniform

A FEW ELEMENTARY EXAMPLES

size and width. A suitable size is 1 ft. 6 in. long and 1 ft. wide. These boards are best made of hardwood, on account of the extra pressure given when the polishing iron is used. When the board is only used for this work there is no need to cover it. Fig. 36 shows a polishing board with cross ends made of birch.

The joints are formed with cross-tongues, as in the skirt board.

Boards are made for the double purpose of ironing and polishing. In this case the covered side is used for the first-mentioned work, and the back of the board is taken for the polishing.

A sleeve board is a tapered board about

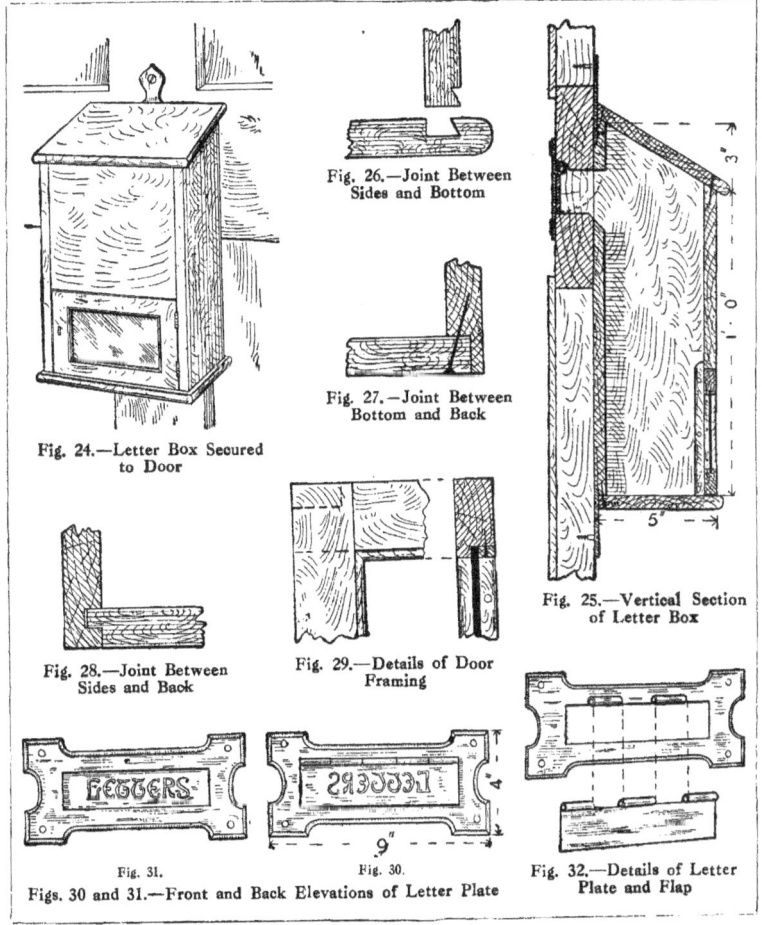

Fig. 24.—Letter Box Secured to Door

Fig. 25.—Vertical Section of Letter Box

Fig. 26.—Joint Between Sides and Bottom

Fig. 27.—Joint Between Bottom and Back

Fig. 28.—Joint Between Sides and Back

Fig. 29.—Details of Door Framing

Fig. 32.—Details of Letter Plate and Flap

Fig. 31. Fig. 30.
Figs. 30 and 31.—Front and Back Elevations of Letter Plate

1 ft. 6 in. long and 4 in. to 5 in. wide at one end, decreasing to about 2 in. towards the other end. The tapered board can either be fitted to an upright stand or on a bracketed stand, as shown in Figs. 37 and 33. The top of the board 6 in., shaped as in Fig. 38, the bracket 9 in. by 6 in., the ironing board 1 ft. 9 in. by 6 in., and the two vertical straps 7¼ in. by 2 in. by ⅝ in. In jointing together the various parts, the vertical straps should be dovetailed to the back end of the sole

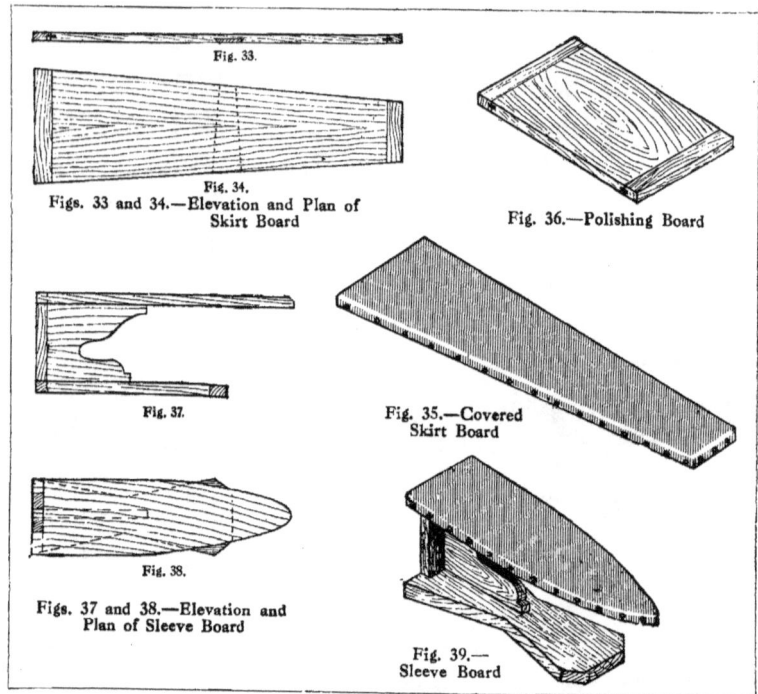

Figs. 33 and 34.—Elevation and Plan of Skirt Board

Fig. 36.—Polishing Board

Fig. 37.

Fig. 35.—Covered Skirt Board

Fig. 38.

Figs. 37 and 38.—Elevation and Plan of Sleeve Board

Fig. 39.—Sleeve Board

should be covered to provide a soft surface for ironing. It is used, as its name indicates, for the ironing of sleeves of various sizes and shapes, especially for the fuller parts that cannot be made to lie flat on the table. The usefulness of the sleeve board depends on the make; one with a strong bracketed stand of the size given is very useful.

In making a sleeve board, as in Fig. 39 yellow pine should be used. Five pieces are required, the sole piece 1 ft. 4 in. by piece and the ironing board, with a sufficient space apart to allow the bracket to pass in between them. The ironing board and sole piece should then be well screwed to the edges of the bracket. The top of this board should also be covered with white felt or flannel.

A NEWSPAPER RACK

The handy newspaper rack shown complete by Fig. 40 will look well if made of

A FEW ELEMENTARY EXAMPLES

oak, American walnut, or satin walnut. Fig. 41 shows the joint of the uprights into the horizontal bearers, and Fig. 42 the hidden housing for receiving the slats to form the floor.

The three frames of bars and slats A, B and C should be made separately, according to the finished measurements given. The top and bottom bars and the two uprights should be joined together with mortise-and-tenon joints, and the slats (five in number, $\frac{1}{2}$ in. by $\frac{1}{4}$ in.) should be let in the top and bottom rails for $\frac{1}{4}$ in.

Fig. 42 shows how the stopped housing joint L is made for the four slats, 6 in. by $\frac{1}{2}$ in. by $\frac{1}{4}$ in., forming the floor. These bearers should be secured by means of small screws run into the bottom rail. The whole should be polished, and a handle (see Fig. 40) attached to the central division.

HINGED TABLE-FLAP

A side-table hinged to fold flat against a wall when not required is often very

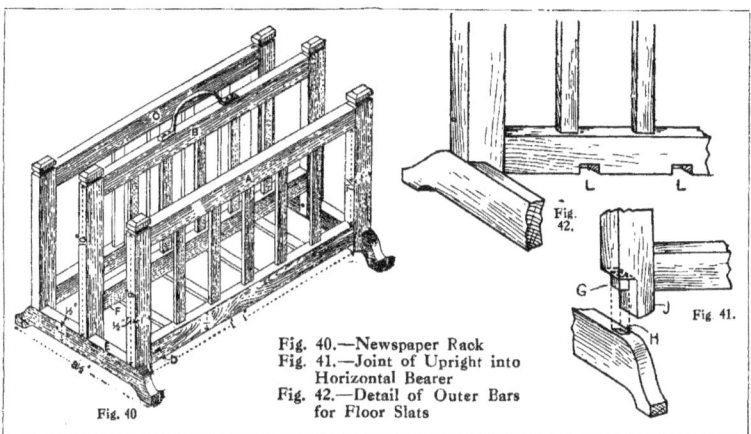

Fig. 40.—Newspaper Rack
Fig. 41.—Joint of Upright into Horizontal Bearer
Fig. 42.—Detail of Outer Bars for Floor Slats

The central division is 1 in. higher than the two outside frames, as it gives the rack a better appearance. The lower bar should be so arranged that the lower edge D should be $\frac{1}{4}$ in. lower than the upper edge of the bearers E, so as to allow for the slats which will form the bottom coming on a level with the edge E. The lower bar F of the central division should be 1 in. higher than the two outer frames, so as to clear the floor slats.

Fig 41 shows how to make a strong and neat joint to support the uprights. A pin G, cut as shown, is let into a mortise H, while a support J comes inside the horizontal bearers, and is fastened to the same with a screw as shown at K.

useful in kitchens and elsewhere, and can be made very efficiently by following the instructions here given.

The first consideration—and a very important one—is the fixing of the brackets to the wall surface. If this happens to be boarded the matter is simplified ; but in most cases when plastered brickwork occurs, holes must be made and very tightly filled with small wooden plugs, to which the work can be nailed or screwed. In the event of the wall proving to have lath and plaster or wooden uprights (or "studding"), the latter must be located by sounding and a few trials with a small bradawl, and the work spaced out in such a way that it can be fixed to them.

To work in strict accordance with the illustrations, fix to the wall in the desired position three lengths of 2½-in. by 1-in. deal, as at C and D in Fig. 50, the first two being 1 ft. 6¾ in. long and 2 ft. 4½ in. apart. For a first-class job they can be halved to the horizontal piece D and chamfered on the exposed edges, although these points are not essential. Next very securely screw on a ledge, as at E in Figs.

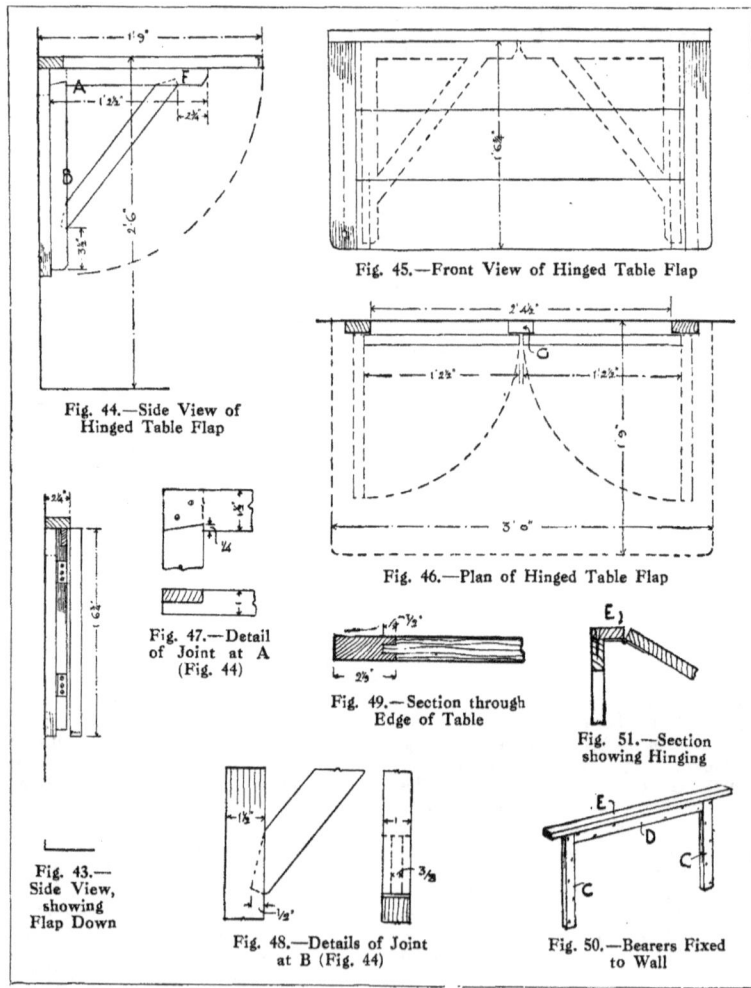

Fig. 44.—Side View of Hinged Table Flap

Fig. 45.—Front View of Hinged Table Flap

Fig. 46.—Plan of Hinged Table Flap

Fig. 47.—Detail of Joint at A (Fig. 44)

Fig. 43.—Side View, showing Flap Down

Fig. 48.—Details of Joint at B (Fig. 44)

Fig. 49.—Section through Edge of Table

Fig. 50.—Bearers Fixed to Wall

Fig. 51.—Section showing Hinging

A FEW ELEMENTARY EXAMPLES

50 and 51, $2\frac{1}{4}$ in. by 1 in. and 3 ft. long. This is also shown in Figs. 43 and 44, the latter giving a comprehensive view of one of the two "gallows-brackets" required. These are built up of about $1\frac{1}{2}$-in. by 1-in. stuff, dovetail-halved at A, and angle-tenoned at B and F in accordance with Figs. 47 and 48. When ready they should be hinged to the uprights in Fig. 50 in the manner shown by Figs. 45 and 46, the former showing how they just clear one another when folded back, and the latter a small stop on the wall at G to avoid any forcing of their hinges. They should just work easily under the small top ledge.

Dealing next with the table-top itself, this measures 3 ft. by 1 ft. $6\frac{3}{4}$ in. by 1 in. and has its two outer corners rounded. It is intended to be composed of three widths, cross-tongued together and "clamped" at the ends with pieces $2\frac{1}{2}$ in. wide, as in Fig. 49. Observe that when in use the join between the boarding and the clamp comes centrally over the bracket. If it did not receive this support it would be as well to continue the tongue (seen in Fig. 49) right through the clamp in two places, as tenons about 3 in. wide. Alternatively, for an inferior job, the flap could be composed of boarding on "ledges" across each end, these being only 2 in. wide in order to clear the brackets, unless the flap is increased a little in length to suit them. In each case the flap should be hinged from the underside, as explained by Fig. 51, and if of the clamped variety should have two small stops, against which the brackets would strike when opened to the full right angles. Some workers may find it more convenient to hinge the flap and ledge together before the latter is screwed finally in position; but it may be found necessary to take a little out of the tops of the brackets in order to clear the hinges.

The following is a list of the material required: Bearers, $2\frac{1}{2}$ in. by 1 in. 5-ft. 6-in run (6 ft. if halved at angles); brackets, $1\frac{1}{2}$ in. by 1 in., 8-ft. 6-in. run; ledge, $2\frac{1}{4}$ in. by 1 in., 3-ft. 3-in. run, flap, $6\frac{1}{2}$ in. by 1 in., 8-ft. 3-in. run; $2\frac{1}{2}$ in. by 1 in., 3-ft. 3-in. run; 1-in. oak cross-tongue, 5-ft. 6-in. run.

Box and Packing Case Construction

THE standard deals from which the spruce boards of which packing cases are made run 7 in., 9 in., and 11 in. in width by $2\frac{1}{2}$ in. and 3 in. in thickness. A 3-in. deal sawn into three planks by two saw-cuts makes 1-in. material. A one-cut $2\frac{1}{2}$-in. deal makes $1\frac{1}{4}$-in. material, while $\frac{3}{4}$-in. material is made by three cuts in a 3-in. deal. Thus the nominal thickness is always scant by about half the thickness of the saw, a 1-in. board being actually about $\frac{7}{8}$ in.

The case-maker is bound to charge for timber consumed, and if this cuts to waste the customer pays. It is therefore best that the latter receives the advantage of the extra inch or two removed. It usually makes for better packing or the inclusion of more goods without extra charge. The lengths of deals vary considerably; but if any quantity of cases are required of similar dimensions, it is often possible to arrange with the case-maker as to economical length. The price received for firewood in the shape of short ends does not compensate for their unnecessary manufacture.

Taking the usual widths, 7 in., 9 in., and 11 in., and remembering that width and depth of the case is alone considered for the moment. By assembly of boards in three widths without cutting the following dimensions are possible: 7 in., 9 in., 11 in., 14 in., 16 in., 18 in., 20 in., 21 in., 23 in., 27 in., 28 in., 29 in., 30 in., 32 in., 33 in., 34 in., 36 in., 38 in., 40 in., 42 in., 35 in., 37 in., 39 in., 41 in., 43 in., 39 in., 45 in., 47 in., 51 in., and 55 in. It will be seen that there is less exact choice in the smaller dimensions than in the larger. Anyone interested can follow out the permutations and combinations open to the integers 7, 9, 11 throughout the entire series possible to cases. Twelve feet and 14 ft. are usual lengths, and aliquot or fractional division of the normal lengths is desirable. If, for instance, the length of the case is 5 ft., it is obvious that 12-ft. boards are not an economy. Short ends 2 ft. or under are of little, if any, use except as firewood.

It must be remembered that planking width for the top and bottom measures are external. Internal depth and plank width are equal, and the length of ends is the internal size of the case. The total length of the case is, of course, external measurement, and the ends themselves are invariably thicker than the rest of the planking. When permitting the normal widths these facts must be borne in mind. Also that battens add to superficial measurement.

By rational consideration of the limitations set by his material to the case-maker, in very few instances is it necessary to cause serious wastage, for which it must be remembered the customer has to pay. If some attention be given to the subject it will frequently be found that an extra couple of inches may be added to accommodate standard planks at no extra cost. Such addition is not detrimental to packing—on the contrary, it is advantageous; it allows the use of more woodwool or other packing material, or the enclosure of extra goods.

Take an instance of fifty cases each 7 ft. 6 in. long, which have to be made up from 12-ft. boards. It is obvious that to utilise the cut portions the case-maker has to wait for a 4-ft. 6-in. order. If he utilises them for a 3-ft. 9-in. order there is a wastage (less firewood value) of 25 super ft. His customers unquestionably have to pay for this if he remains solvent.

The matter receives more attention when quantities of the same size case are dealt with, since by adjustment of dimensions the cost can be materially reduced. At all events, it pays to consult the case-maker before fixing the dimensions, if a large sum be involved. The basis on which cases are charged is that of superficial area. This differs considerably from the cube feet contained. The following figure show this clearly:

Dimensions of case in feet (Internal).	Cube feet contained (Internal).	Total superficial feet neglecting board thickness and battens.
4 × 4 × 4	64	96
3 × 3 × 7	63	102
2 × 2 × 16	64	136
4 × 2 × 8	64	112
1½ × 6 × 7	63	123
1 × 10 × 6	64	128
3 × 4 × 5½	66	111

If charges for similar thickness of approximate date be considered on this basis, the puzzle as to their fairness or otherwise becomes clearer. If added to this the matter of standard planking relative to dimensions is considered, the facts may be startling. The case-maker is blamed in too many instances where blame is not due. He must perforce charge up the timber used, whether this is in the finished cases or wasted as firewood. It is, of course, totally impossible to avoid some wastage; but more might

be done to conserve timber resources by a realisation of the facts, and the foregoing may serve a national no less than a utilitarian end. The nearer to cube dimensions the cheaper the case, and in most instances where two of the dimensions are similar and no undue disproportion exists, the case will be found little more expensive than the cube.

A cube case is extremely awkward to handle, and for this reason alone should not be employed. It is evident by calculation that little is sacrificed by making the length exceed the width and depth. Provided that the length does not exceed the sum of width and depth, its relative cost is not increased unduly. It is worth pointing out that for large cases where strength is also a prime consideration, the over-sea transit case may be tongued with hoop iron. This course sacrifices less of the inherent strength of the boards, and adds very greatly to its ability to resist damage.

ROUGH BOXES

An ordinary box is generally regarded as the simplest article that a woodworker can have to construct, yet there are a good many wrong ways, as well as a right way, of doing it. If illustrations of how not to do it were given here they would be more numerous than those showing how to do it.

The arrangement of the parts in Fig. 1 shows the correct and professional way of making a small rough box. The ends are about twice as thick as the other parts, and fit between the sides. The sides and ends are first nailed together, and then the bottom is nailed on. The top corresponds with the bottom in being the full outside length and width of the box. Lines of nails running across the grain, as at the ends, are closely spaced, running with the grain, as in nailing along the sides of top and bottom the nails are much farther apart. If the box measures the same in each direction, the ends are shorter than the sides only by the amount required for lap at the joints, that is, the combined thickness of the two side pieces. If the box is longer one way than the other, the length of the ends corresponds with the shorter inside measurement, and the length of the sides with the longer plus the thickness of the ends. In depth the sides and ends are alike, and represent the inside depth of the box.

Ends are made thicker because it gives greater rigidity and greater thickness for receiving the nails. In the sides, top and bottom, increased thickness has not such an advantage as in the ends. The effect would be the same if the sides were made thick and the ends thin, and the ends overlapped the sides; but this would be less economical of material, because the ends are shorter than the sides and consume

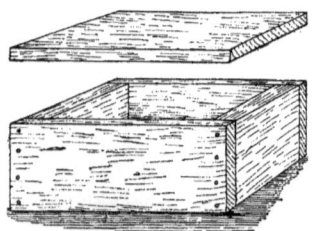

Fig. 1.—Method of Putting a Box Together

less thick material. Exceptions occur when ends and sides are alike in thickness, and in a more highly finished class of work than that dealt with here it is the rule to make them alike. The reason for spacing nails closely across the grain, and at long distance with the grain, is that in the first case the wood may split or warp, and requires to be secured at close intervals. It has very little strength in this direction. But along the grain, nails needlessly close add nothing to the strength of the box, and may, by their excessive number in one line of fibres, split the piece into which they are driven.

Fig. 2 shows methods of jointing box corners alternative to nailing; A is a dovetailed corner and B a lock corner. There are many other ways of jointing, but none that is used much in box construction. The dovetailed joint is not often used for rough boxes. The lock corner is used a great deal for small boxes. In factories dovetails and lock corners are cut by machines. The lock corner is never made by hand; dovetails occasion-

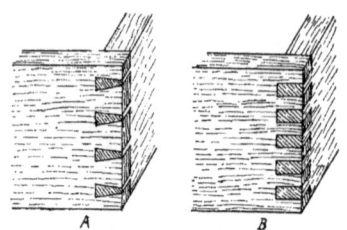

Fig. 2.—Dovetail and Lock Corner Joints

ally are. Both of these joints are glued, and not nailed. Bottoms and covers have to be nailed on even when the corners are locked or dovetailed.

Only small boxes can be made of single widths of wood. Large cases always have to be built up of a number of pieces edge to edge, to make the widths required. This is because there is a limit to the width of wood obtainable; but a box is just as strong, and there is no objection at all to building up in this way in rough

Fig. 3.—Ordinary Type of Packing Case

boxes. In highly finished work it involves the extra trouble of gluing the pieces edge to edge; but otherwise they are simply placed together, often with slightly open joints. It is essential to have the lengths right, end-grain joints in boxes, and in most other work, being out of the question. Bottoms and covers are usually wider than the sides and ends, and therefore, as boxes go up in size, the necessity for building up in widths occurs first in the bottom and

BOX AND PACKING CASE CONSTRUCTION

covers. This is because a shallow-box is usually more convenient than a deep one of equal capacity. It is an advantage to have the sides and ends in single pieces, because it simplifies the work of nailing them together; but a bottom or cover can be nailed on almost as quickly and

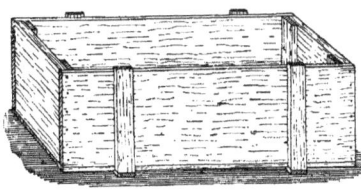

Fig. 4.—Packing Case with Cleats on all Parts

easily if it consists of half a dozen pieces as it can when in a single piece.

When above moderate dimensions in boxes, it becomes necessary to use cleats or battens crosswise on the grain, both to strengthen the box and to facilitate building it up. The need for these arises as soon as the sides and ends exceed a width easily obtained in single pieces, say more than about 12 in.; but even single pieces above this width need stiffening with cleats, and cleats serve a further purpose of thickening up the ends or sides

Fig. 5.—Packing Case with Corner Cleats

at the corners, so giving a larger joint surface and permitting the use of thinner wood. The thick ends shown in Fig. 1, therefore, become unnecessary when cleats are used, as in Fig. 3. The latter shows a first stage where cleats are used on the ends only. This type of box probably occurs more frequently than any other.

Its ends can be built up of two or more widths, which are held together by nailing on the cleats. There is no difficulty then in nailing the sides to these, also in more than one width, but without any need for cleats. The bottom and cover also can be nailed on without cleats, and in as many separate pieces as happens to be convenient.

Fig. 4 shows how a much larger class of box or case is made. Here the areas are so great that cleats are used on all parts. A rather remarkable point to be noticed here is that it is the great length and not the widths that makes cleats necessary on the sides and bottom and top; for no matter how wide these latter happened to be, they would, if not very long, be amply secured by the nailing at the ends. But when the length is considerable they are not capable of withstanding a severe blow in the middle part without springing or perhaps even breaking, either of which might damage the contents of the case. An alternative would be to use much thicker wood; but the increase would have to be so great that it is far better to use thin wood and put cleats across to stiffen it. The number of cleats used depends on the size of the case. Cleats may be outside or inside. Very large cases always have outside cleats. In Fig. 4 the ends are shown cleated on the inside, which is a variation from the method in Fig. 3. Both are equally good; but in some instances inside cleats might interfere with the packing of goods in the box.

The arrangement shown in Fig. 5 is occasionally seen, but is much less common than that in Fig. 3. It is best suited for comparatively deep and narrow boxes, as the grain of the ends then runs the longest way of the pieces, which is advisable in all woodwork. The cleats would generally overlap at the ends as shown.

CRATES

Crates have alternate bars and spaces, but are otherwise constructed in the same way as large boxes. First the article to be crated is measured, and the position of the ends of the crate in relation to it decided, the ends being usually the parts of smallest area. A pair of these is made by cutting a number of bars to the length required, and laying them side by side with spaces between, and nailing other bars or cleats on at right angles to hold them together. The construction of the crate then proceeds in the same way as with a closed box, except that bars are nailed on instead of continuous wood for sides, top, and bottom. More bars or cleats at right angles may be put on these. When the area is large, they are often put on diagonally to keep the crate from being knocked out of square.

In all cases, the nails which hold cleats are longer than the double thickness of wood, so that their points can come through and be clinched. Nails in other parts, going into an unlimited depth of wood, should be in length about three to four times the thickness of the wood through which they are driven.

In nailing a box together, its squareness is determined when the bottom is being put on. Previous to this the sides and ends are in a rickety condition, and may be forced very much out of square in relation to each other. As soon as the bottom is on, the box is rigid, but is not necessarily square unless precautions are taken to see that it is so at an early stage in the nailing on of the bottom. If the bottom is in a single piece and is sawn square, all that need be done is to see that it is nailed on correctly; but if it is in a number of separate widths, the box should be tested before the nailing of the first piece is completed. Testing is done with a square or by measuring diagonally across corners. If the latter shows alike in opposite directions, the box is square. If slightly out, it must be forced right before any more nails are put in.

PACKING CASES

A large packing case as used by large business houses for packing and sending hardware goods abroad should be made in the following manner. It will be supposed that the dimensions of the sample case are to be 4 ft. long, 2 ft. 3 in. wide,

and 1 ft. 6 in. deep. It must be remembered that the case will have to be $\frac{1}{8}$ in. smaller in each dimension. The reason for this is that "hold space," which is charged by the cube foot, shall not be exceeded, as the excess charge on a number of cases would be a heavy item.

The case should be made of rough 1-in. boards 8 in. and 9 in. wide, and fastened with $2\frac{1}{2}$ in. wire nails. Begin with the bottom ledges, of which in this case there are three. Fig. 6 shows them spaced. These are of 8-in. board cut off $\frac{1}{4}$ in. shorter than the actual width of the case; that is, $\frac{1}{8}$ in. off each side, so as not to project beyond the sides of the case. These boards will thus be 2 ft. $2\frac{3}{4}$ in. long. Next cut off two pieces of 8-in. stuff and one piece of 9-in. board 3 ft. $9\frac{3}{4}$ in. long

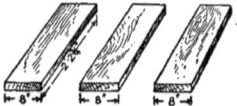

Fig. 6.—Bottom Ledges for Packing Case

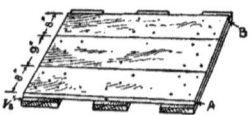

Fig. 7.—Packing Case Bottom

to make the bottom boards. By cutting these boards 3 ft. $9\frac{3}{4}$ in. long this allows 2 in. for the two 1-in. end pieces. Place these pieces side by side on the ledges, as in Fig. 7, with the 9-in. board in the centre as shown. They should be nice and square, with the ledges projecting each side $\frac{7}{8}$ in., and the nail right through both the bottom boards and ledges and into the floor. This will keep all firm while building up the case. Now measure across the bottom (from A to B, Fig. 7) to get the length of the first two boards for the ends. These are of 8-in. stuff. Stand these upright at the ends of the bottom boards, with their edges on the floor, and nail right through into the side of the end

BOX AND PACKING CASE CONSTRUCTION

ledges, with two nails opposite the end of each board, and one nail into the end of each bottom board as well. Having fixed the first two end boards as shown in Fig. 8, get out the first two side pieces. Take a stick and measure from A to B for these, and be sure and lay the stick on the ledges where the side is to go, not 8-in. pieces to finish the sides. Nail and clinch as before. Having finished building the case, lever it up from the floor with a piece of board. Turn the case upside down and clinch all the nails in the bottom. Also put a couple of nails through the ends of each ledge into the sides, and the case is ready for being

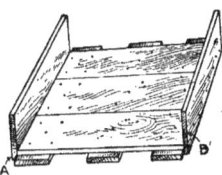

Fig. 8.—Packing Case with Ends Partly Fitted

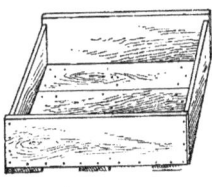

Fig. 9.—Packing Case with Ends and Sides Partly Fitted

Fig. 10.—Packing Case with Corner Cleats Fitted

higher up the end pieces already fixed, as these might be standing either in or out a little, and so prevent the true measurement being taken. Fig. 9 shows the first two side pieces nailed in position, and also how the side boards stand about 1 in. higher than the ends, thus breaking the joints. Next get four inside corner cleats, as shown in Fig. 10. These are 1 in. by 4½ in. and 1 ft. 6 in. long, less the thickness of the lid, the bottom boards, and the ledges underneath the bottom boards, and ⅜ in., to allow for the 3 in. of stuff, as before explained. Therefore, these cleats will be 1 ft. 2⅝ in. long. Having cut these to length, place them in the four corners, as shown in Fig. 10, and nail edgewise, first through the ends, then through the sides, and clinch inside.

Then continue the building of the case to the top of the cleats, putting a piece of 9-in. above the 8-in. piece at the ends, and packed. Then the lid is made and nailed on (Fig. 11). As a rule, the lid requires no ledges. A 1-in. board is simply nailed across the case lengthwise, and cut off at the end of the case. If extra

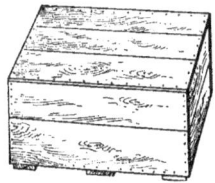

Fig. 11.—Packing Case with Lid

strength of lid is required, a piece of 4½-in. stuff is let into the sides across the top of the case, so that it is flush with the top before the lid goes on. The lid is then nailed on as before described.

Drawing and Other Boards

A GOOD drawing-board should be light, perfectly square, true on its surface, free from knots and shakes and from any tendency to warp. Fig. 1 shows a back view of an engineer's drawing-board. It has a $\frac{3}{4}$-in. pine top of standard size, with two $3\frac{1}{2}$-in. by $\frac{5}{8}$-in. oak ledges screwed at the back to prevent warping. The screws are fitted into slotted metal plates, upon which they slide freely and so prevent the board splitting during shrinkage. As a further prevention against any tendency to "cast," the underside of the board is furnished with a series of shallow grooves from 2 in. to 3 in. apart and one-third of the thickness of the board deep. These grooves, by destroying the continuity of the fibres of the wood, materially reduce

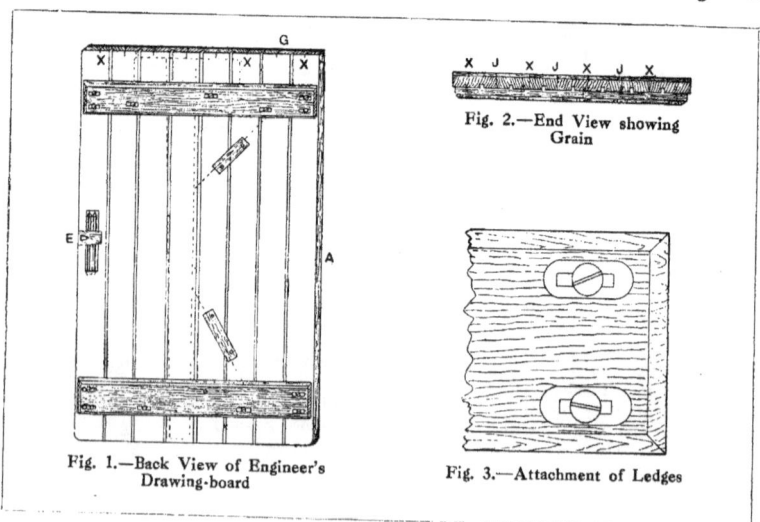

Fig. 1.—Back View of Engineer's Drawing-board

Fig. 2.—End View showing Grain

Fig. 3.—Attachment of Ledges

the pull of the top on the ledges, and enable the latter to be made thinner than would otherwise be possible; consequently, the board is lighter. The grooves may be of any width, from a saw kerf to $\frac{3}{8}$ in., but must not be made at a joint.

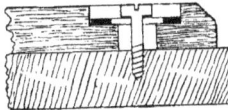

Fig. 4.—Section of Ledge

The left-hand, or the working hand of the board, is slipped or inlaid with a piece of ebony to prevent the **T**-square wearing the edge hollow. This slip, in machine-made boards, is usually grooved in at about $\frac{1}{4}$ in. below the upper surface of the top; this, however, is not its best

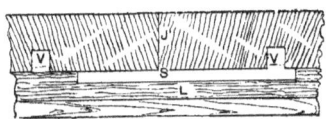

Fig. 5.—Part Cross-section of Drawing-board

position, and it should be placed, as shown in Fig. 6, flush with the surface, the ebony slip G being glued and fixed with wood sprigs in a small rebate.

The grain of the slip must run lengthwise across the board to furnish a smooth surface for the square to work against,

Fig. 6.—Section of Drawing-board at Slipped End

and it is obvious that, as this piece cannot shrink endwise, the board would split during shrinking unless some means were provided to give the necessary play. This is done by running several tenon saw kerfs down the end of the board just through the slip, as shown at x (Fig. 1). the spaces between the cut ends affording sufficient room for subsequent contraction.

The joints in the top should not be ploughed and tongued, and need not be dowelled if the board is glued up in pieces not more than 5 in. or 6 in. wide. Particular attention must be paid to the position of the annular rings. To enable a board to maintain a true surface the rings must run, as shown in Figs. 2 and 5, at right angles, or nearly so, with the surface; if a piece of stuff is used with the rings running parallel with the surface the board cannot keep flat.

Machine-made boards are usually planed dead-true on the surface; some draughtsmen, however, prefer to have one slightly convex in both directions, as this allows

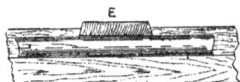

Fig. 7.—Section of Pencil Well

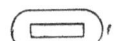

Fig. 8.—Metal Slot-plate

the paper to bed much better and the **T**-square to travel easier. The convexity must only be slight, say a bare $\frac{1}{8}$ in. for an imperial or larger board, and $\frac{1}{16}$ in. for smaller sizes; the method of producing it will be explained later.

Two little accessories introduced in the board shown by Fig. 1 will be found useful to technical students who have to carry their own boards to drawing classes. The first is a provision for carrying the **T**- and set-squares at the back of the board; the positions are indicated by dotted lines. The blade of the **T**-square passes through slots in the ledges, as seen at s (Fig. 5), shallow recesses being made in the interior of the ledges to receive the bases of the set-squares, and two thin rebated fillets to receive their hypotenuse edges. The set-squares are placed in position first, and are then secured by the **T**-square, which should fit accurately into the slots. At E (Fig. 1) a receptacle for pencils is shown. This is a well cut as long as a pencil, ⅞ in. wide and ⅜ in. deep (see Fig. 7), one end being undercut to receive the pencil ends, whilst at the middle there is a small slide having dovetailed edges and a thumb notch at the outer end.

Fig. 9.—Section Through Simple Drawing-board.

In making such a board, the first thing to be decided on is the size, which should be 1 in. wider and longer than the standard size of drawing paper. The sizes of paper most frequently used are half-imperial, 15 in. by 11 in.; royal, 24 in. by 19 in.; imperial, 30 in. by 22 in.; and double elephant, 40 in. by 27 in. Of these, perhaps imperial is the most useful, and the board should therefore be 31 in. long, 23 in. wide, and a full ¾ in. thick. The wood used should be American yellow pine, thoroughly seasoned, dry, and free from knots, shakes and sapwood. Assuming the boards to be 11 in. wide, three pieces 2 ft. long will be required; these should be ripped down the middle and jointed with the outside edges together, and mixed—that is, no piece must be glued to the piece from which it was ripped. After shooting, plough the grooves V (Fig. 5) ¼ in. deep down the centre of each piece on the worse side; then glue up, using two cleats. When dry, plane the back true, gauge to the thickness, and face up the front.

If a convex surface is required, take some thin stuff and prepare a hollow straightedge having the required sweep, which may be obtained by a compass plane, or even by a trying plane with the iron set coarse. Work the face of the board down lengthwise to fit the template. The cross convexity is obtained by preparing the ledges by the same template, and drawing the board round with the screws.

The next thing to be done is to square the board off to size; the edge marked A (Fig. 1) is shot straight, and the opposite edge is gauged parallel and shot. The end G is squared from the edge A. If a square of sufficient length is not at hand, a line may be drawn at right angles as follows : Mark its beginning and measure 12 in. from it on the edge A; take a straightedge and set off 9 in. on its edge, put the straightedge on the board with one end to the beginning of the line, and place it in such a position that the 9-in. mark is exactly 15 in. from the 12-in. mark, measured diagonally; it will then be square with the edge. The other end can be squared in a similar manner.

Prepare an ebony slip, 2 ft. long and ¼ in. square, and sink a rebate a shaving less across the end to receive it. The slip is glued in, the best way to hold it up whilst drying being to fix a piece of stuff on the bench to rest the end of the board against, and to screw another fillet 1 in. clear of, and at a slight angle to, the other end, so that a long wedge may be driven between the fillet and the slip, tightening the latter up throughout its length. After the glue is dry and the superfluous wood cleaned off, put half a dozen cleft ebony sprigs through the face, making the holes with a fine bradawl ; also make a saw kerf between each groove, as shown in Fig. 1.

The ledges, which should be of mild, straight-grained American oak or Honduras mahogany, straight or convex on the face, as desired, should be gauged 3½ in. wide by ⅜ in. thick, and cut them off ½ in. short of the width of the board. Work a ¼ in. chamfer all round, as shown in Fig. 3, and bore the screw holes a trifle wider than the screws, and ½ in. long. The centre screw in each ledge is not slotted. The slot-plates are formed of brass or zinc (see Fig. 8), 1¼ in. by ½ in. by 1/16 in. The screws have squared heads, No. 5 in size. The plates should be sunk into the edges to such a depth that the heads of the screws are flush (see Fig. 4).

The board may then be glasspapered in the direction of the grain and given a coat of hot size on both sides, the ends being given two coats to prevent damp entering the pores. In Figs. 1. 2. and 5

J indicates the joints in the boards, X the saw kerfs, E the dovetailed slider, S the slot in the ledges, L the ledge, and V the grooves for preventing casting.

grooved fillets into corresponding grooves and tongues formed in the ends of the board. The grooves in the board should be exactly central, and should be slightly

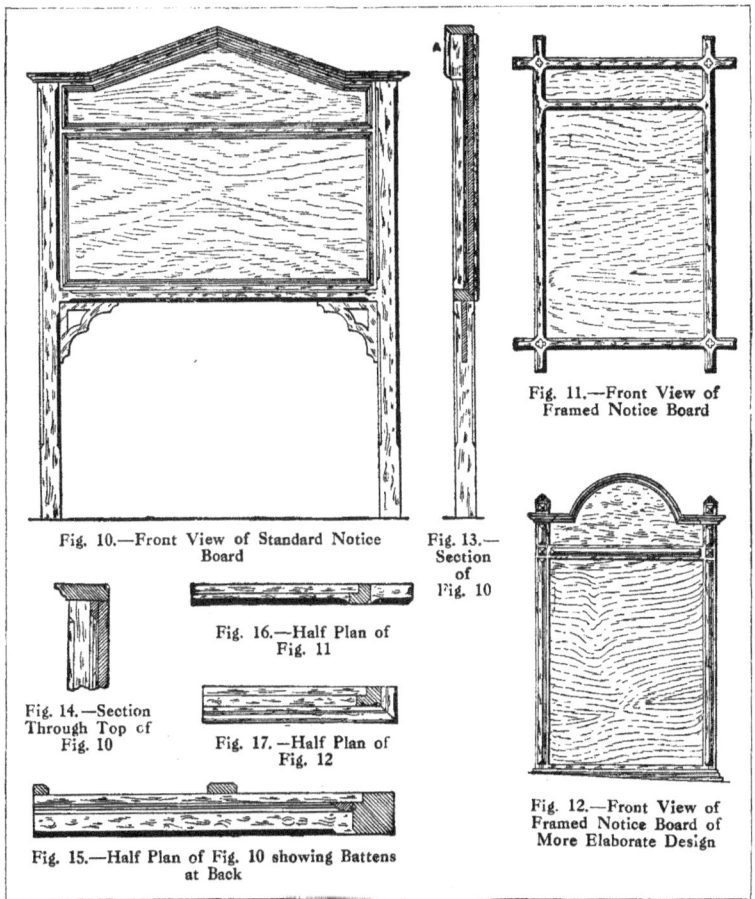

Fig. 10.—Front View of Standard Notice Board

Fig. 11.—Front View of Framed Notice Board

Fig. 12.—Front View of Framed Notice Board of More Elaborate Design

Fig. 13.—Section of Fig. 10

Fig. 14.—Section Through Top of Fig. 10

Fig. 15.—Half Plan of Fig. 10 showing Battens at Back

Fig. 16.—Half Plan of Fig. 11

Fig. 17.—Half Plan of Fig. 12

Another method of constructing a drawing-board at much less expense, although equally good, is shown by Fig. 9. It consists in fitting two shaped hardwood

more than one-third of the board's thickness. The tongue and groove in the fillet should fit accurately, and be reversible so that each surface of the board may be used. The width of the fillet will depend on the size of the board. Oak, beech, or Spanish mahogany are the most suitable woods for the purpose, and the fillets should be fitted rather tightly at first to allow for shrinkage. A little French chalk rubbed in the grooves will facilitate the removal when altering the positions of the fillets.

NOTICE BOARDS

The notice board shown by Figs. 10, 11 and 12 are suitable for public or other buildings. The board shown at Fig. 10 is mounted on standards, and those shown at Figs. 11 and 12 are suitable for attaching to the wall.

The standards for Fig. 10 are 4 in. square in section, sunk into the ground a distance of 3 ft. 6 in., and extend 7 ft. above the ground line. The cross rail is 4 in. by 2 in. in section, tenoned into the standards 3 ft. 6 in. up from the ground line ; the width over the standards is 6 ft. The bracket pieces are 1 in. thick by 1 ft. long each way, tenoned into the standards and cross rails. The edges of the standards and cross rail are stop-chamfered, as shown at Fig. 10.

The panelling is 1 in. thick, and should be of well-seasoned, straight-grained stuff free from knots and shakes ; it is rebated into the standards and cross rail, and fixed with screws. The rise of the board in the centre, at the top, is 9 in. The joints of the panelling are grooved and tongued, and strengthened with three battens, 3 in. by 1 in., fixed to the back with screws. The top is 5½ in. wide by 1¼ in. thick, jointed round and fixed to the top of the panel and standards, the front edge being moulded as shown. A moulding 2 in. wide by ¾ in. thick is mitred round the edges and across the panel at the top, dividing it into two portions. The top portion is intended for the name of the building or institution, and the bottom for the usual notices. Fig. 13 is a vertical section of the board, Fig. 14 an enlarged detail of the top at A, and Fig. 15 is an enlarged half plan.

The board (Fig. 11) is of very simple construction, and consists of a frame half-lapped together with a panel rebated and fixed to the back. The stiles are 2 in. squares in section, and the outside dimensions over the stiles when framed together are 4 ft. 8 in. high by 3 ft. wide. A frieze rail 2 in. deep by 1 in. thick is lapped 6 in. down from the top rail and fixed with screws. The front edges of the stiles are chamfered as shown, and the back edges are rebated 1 in. square for the reception of the panel, as shown at Fig. 16. The panelling is 1 in. thick, fixed to the frame with screws.

Fig. 12 shows a more elaborate board suitable for fixing to the wall. The outside dimensions are height 5 ft. and width 3 ft. The side stiles are 2½ in. wide by 2 in. thick, bottom rail 3 in. deep by 2 in. thick, and top rail 2½ in. deep by 1 in. thick. The frame is mortised and tenoned together, the height over the rails being 3 ft. 9 in. The faces of the top and side pieces are cut to represent raised panels, and the bottom rail and stiles are rebated 1 in. square to receive the panelling, which is fixed with screws. A moulding 1½ in. deep is mitred round the top, and a moulding 2 in. deep is mitred round the bottom. A half plan of this board is shown in Fig. 17.

ROLL OF HONOUR

This Roll of Honour, a photograph of which is shown in Fig. 18, is suitable for a church, club, or office, and is intended to be reproduced in oak with an oiled and wax-polished finish. The work is not too difficult for any craftsman to undertake, and if carried out to the dimensions shown, it will be large enough to contain up to forty names ; but the size could be varied to meet individual requirements. It is very important that the wood should be quite dry, and carefully selected.

The back is framed and panelled. The stiles A (Fig. 20) are 3 ft. 8½ in. long by 2⅛ in. wide by 1⅛ in. thick ; top rail B 2 ft. 5 in. long by 6 in. deep by 1⅛ in. thick, shaped as shown in Fig. 21, and bottom rail C 2 ft. 5 in. long by 5 in. deep by 1⅛ in. thick, shaped as shown in Fig. 22. The

DRAWING AND OTHER BOARDS

framework is mortised and tenoned together, as shown in Fig. 20, the tenons on the top and bottom rails being haunched in ¼ in. from the inner edges to allow for the grooves which are cut to receive the panel. The grooves are ⅜ in. wide by ¼ in. deep. The stiles are made up to the wide (Fig. 19), and of the section shown in Fig. 23. The frets G are 2 ft. long by 2¼ in. wide at the bottom shaped out to ½ in. wide by ¾ in. thick, and are grooved into the outer edges of the framework (see Fig. 23). In cutting the frets, ¼ in. extra in width must be allowed to form

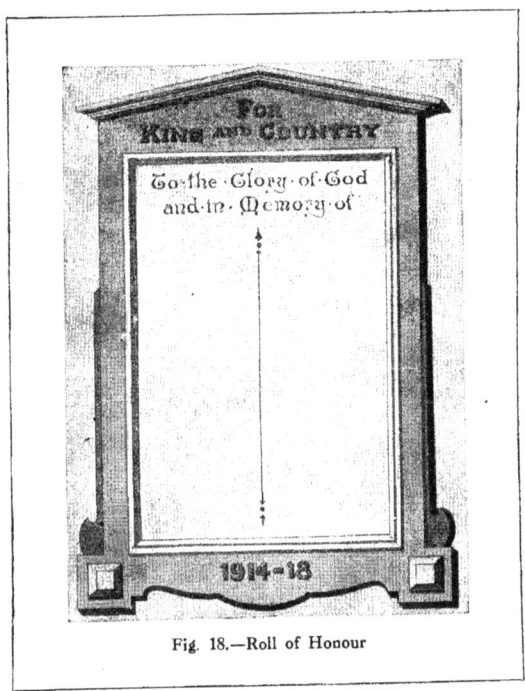

Fig. 18.—Roll of Honour

required width at the bottom with pieces D, which are glued in position. The panel E is ⅜ in. thick, grooved into the edges of the framework, as shown in Fig. 23. If it should be necessary to use two pieces to make up the width required, it will be best to use pieces of equal width so that the joint will be exactly in the middle. The joint should be tongued (see Fig. 23).

The moulding F, which is mitred around the inner edges of the framework, is 1 in. the tongues which fit into the grooves. The top moulding is made up with capping pieces H, 2⅜ in. wide by ½ in. thick, underneath which are mouldings J, 1 in. square, and of the section shown in Fig. 24. Raised and chamfered blocks K (Fig. 19) are fixed at the lower corners of the framework to form a finish, the blocks being ½ in. thick, and of the shape and section shown in Fig. 25.

The inscription on the top rail and the

dates on the bottom rail are intended to be cut in wood letters about ¼ in. thick. The size for the letters and figures may be gathered from Figs. 21 and 22, and the cutting should be done with a fret-saw. Some care should be exercised in marking out and cutting the letters and figures. They are glued in position, and may either be left plain or gilded. The wording on the panel, together with the list of names,

Dealing with the preparation of these laths it is done very easily and simply by a rebate plane, or it could be done with a saw, chisel, and mallet. The detail of the sinking of rebate is shown in Fig. 27, ¼ in. deep and ¼ in. wide being sufficient. These rebates on the outside pieces should be stopped at the top to ¾ in. of the length of the lath at each end. This will be obvious on reference to Fig. 26. All

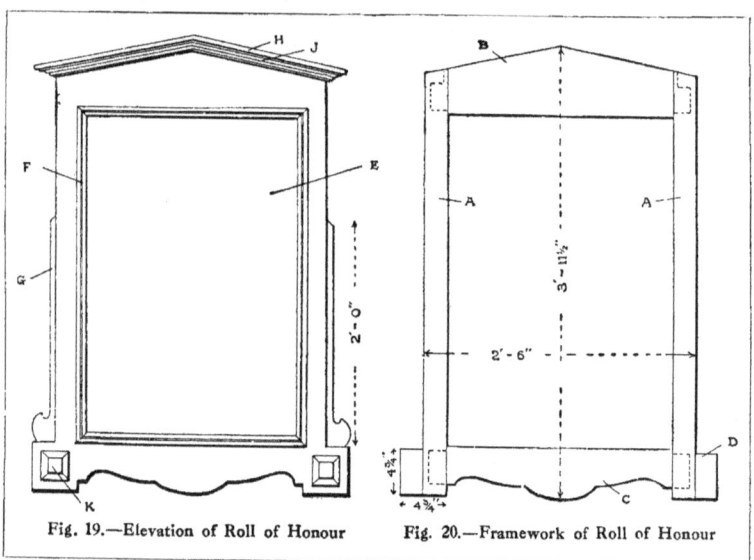

Fig. 19.—Elevation of Roll of Honour   Fig. 20.—Framework of Roll of Honour

should be in gold letters, a suitable style of lettering being shown in Fig. 21.

EMERGENCY POSTER BOARDS

The following are ideas for the construction of emergency notice boards.

Fig. 26 shows a board fitted with double rebated or grooved laths dividing it into sections, and surrounded on the outside edges with a similar piece of wood, but prepared with a single rebate on the inside edges. For an average board about 14 ft. of 1-in. by ½-in. wood lath is required.

could be finally nailed on with the exception of one of the outside ones, which should be screwed on after the movable slips are in position.

It is now seen that a frame is prepared to receive these latter, composed of cuttings of linoleum obtained at very small cost. Preferably it should be brown, grey, or any of the darker shades, of course without pattern on its surface, and being divided into sections; almost the smallest odd piece left over after covering a floor will be sufficient, whereas if covered in one difficulty might be experienced in getting a piece large enough. The suggestion of its being mounted by nailing on three-ply wood or "Venesta" secured from discarded tea boxes, applies more to the very thin qualities of linoleum, although possibly it would be a wise course in any case to stiffen the linoleum in this manner.

diagram, namely, to keep the lettering straight. Of course, a damp cloth will easily remove the chalk when alteration or adaptation is required.

Dealing with alternative schemes, a complete set of four alphabets on small sections could be prepared the height of

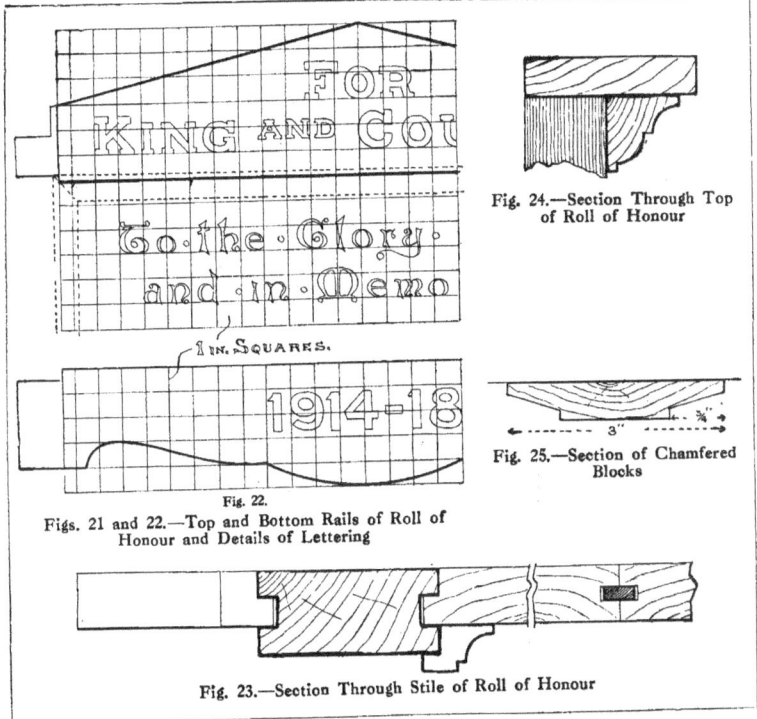

Fig. 24.—Section Through Top of Roll of Honour

Figs. 21 and 22.—Top and Bottom Rails of Roll of Honour and Details of Lettering

Fig. 25.—Section of Chamfered Blocks

Fig. 23.—Section Through Stile of Roll of Honour

When the board is complete the woodwork should be given two coats of paint to preserve it from weather.

In Fig. 26 the top section is suggested for chalking the name of a publication, while the remaining three sections may be used for the contents of the same. There is a further advantage of the sections as shown by the word "Victory" on the grooved laths apart and slipped in, in order to form any words desired. Half spaces should be provided each side of the letters. One does not suggest laboured lettering or anything of that sort, but just presentable wording. In this case the outside lath shown screwed on in Fig. 26 should be hinged with a small lock or catch to the intermediate laths, so as to

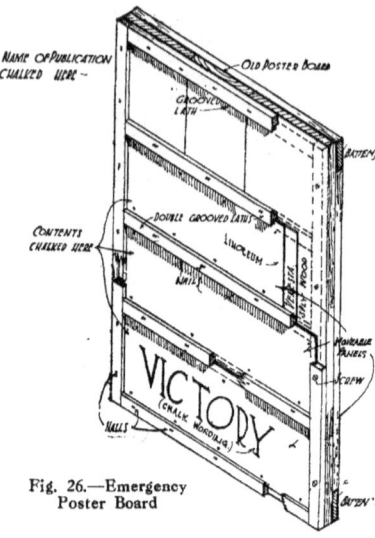

Fig. 26.—Emergency Poster Board

prevent unauthorised persons removing the letters.

Another method of displaying news is with a blackboard and chalk. A good preparation for making a durable and suitable surface is ivory or drop black, gold-size, with a little emery powder to roughen and so take the chalk. To make a sound job, a clamped board with shot edges should be made, and painted both sides with the above preparation. The next example shows a typical black board.

MAKING AND PAINTING A BLACKBOARD

To make the clamped blackboard shown by Figs. 28 and 29, best pine, free from knots and with a close grain, should be used. Material about 1 in. thick should be obtained, and this will be finished to about ⅞ in. The board should be formed by jointing up two, three, or more 11-in. boards, depending, of course, on the particular size required. The best results are obtained if the joints are ploughed and a cross-tongue is inserted, all the joints being glued, of course. When the glue becomes hard, prepare the clamps. These are usually about 3 in. wide. The mortises in the clamps should be made and the inner edges ploughed to receive the haunching (see Fig. 30), after which the tenons and haunchings at each end of the board should be set out and made. Next glue the mortises and tenons, and fix the clamps by wedging the mortises and tenons together, after which each surface should be planed off true and smooth.

In painting a blackboard it should be remembered that all gloss should be absent, as unless the lighting of the room is very favourable a board having a glossy surface is sure to cause annoyance and trouble. A glossy board reflects the light, and, in consequence of this, it

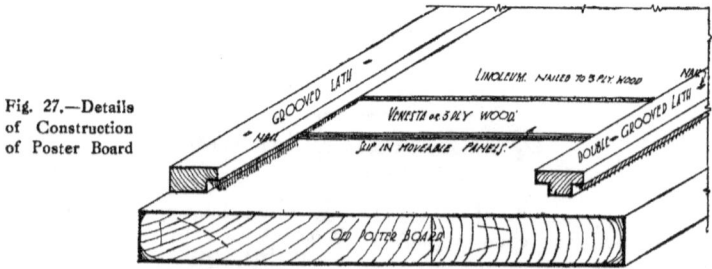

Fig. 27.—Details of Construction of Poster Board

will be found that from some part of the room, at any rate, chalk marks on the board cannot be seen clearly. The following recipes and instructions are given as the result of much experimenting. The

DRAWING AND OTHER BOARDS

compositions here given are all applied over two, or preferably three, good coats of colour made with white-lead, boiled oil, black pigment, and turpentine. Glass-paper each coat, which should be quite dry before the next is applied.

turpentine and 1 part of japan gold-size, and dilute with turpentine.

(3) Give two coats of black mixed with boiled oil; smooth, when dry, with flour emery-paper, then coat with black mixed merely with turpentine.

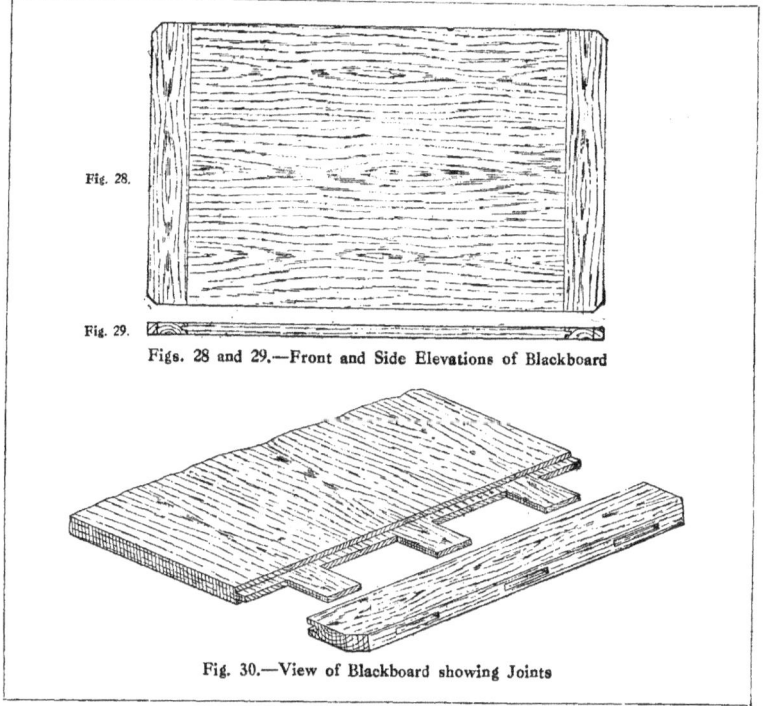

Fig. 28.

Fig. 29.

Figs. 28 and 29.—Front and Side Elevations of Blackboard

Fig. 30.—View of Blackboard showing Joints

(1) Give a coat of flat drop black and japan gold-size containing ½ lb. of flour emery to 1 pt. of black pigment. When dry, coat again; but add a part of turpentine to 3 parts of gold-size used in the former coat.

(2) Coat thinly but evenly with common black and driers and 2 parts of linseed oil to 1 part of turpentine. When dry, spread quickly a mixture of 3 parts (by measure) of best ivory black ground in

(4) Give two coats of paint containing an excess of driers. Glasspaper the board after the first coat.

(5) Give two coats of varnish colour, containing just enough varnish to produce an "egg-shell" gloss. When thoroughly hard, rub down with felt and pumice powder, and leave for a few hours before using.

(6) The board should be well sized, and then coated twice with oily, dark lead colour or common black paint. Before

twenty-four hours have elapsed, apply a mixture of ivory drop black ground in turpentine, japan gold-size, or copal varnish, and enough turpentine to give a thin watery consistency. This should produce a flat and lustreless black surface.

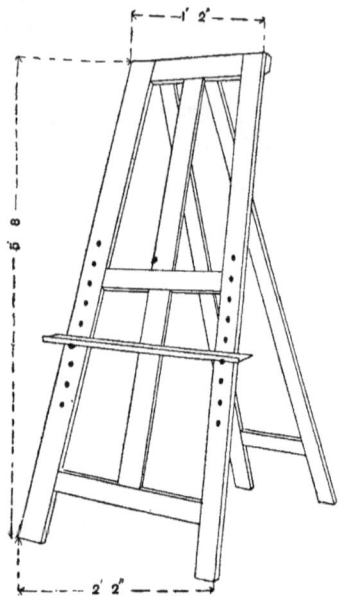

Fig. 31.—Sketch of Easel

AN EASEL

The easel shown in Figs. 31 and 32 is suitable for studio or schoolroom. It is simple but rigid in construction. The wood may be spruce, yellow pine, or pitchpine, and should be about 2½ in. by 1 in. in section. All the framework is mortised and screwed together. When

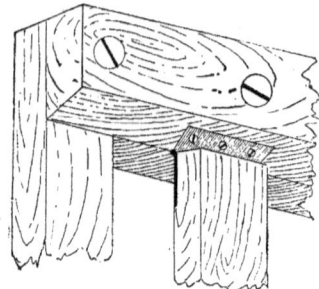

Fig. 32.—Detail of Hinged Leg

making the front part the rails are driven on to the centre stiles (muntins) and the outside stiles then cramped into position.

The detail shown in Fig. 32 gives the method of hinging the double leg. A cross piece is screwed to the top of the easel to receive the hinges. This cross piece is bevelled on the lower edge, the amount of bevel determining the limit of the spread of the legs, which should not exceed about 2 ft. from the front legs. The hinges are preferably screwed on the face of the legs as shown, but if screwed on the *ends* of the legs the screws should be not less than 2 in. long; even then, they may not hold very well, but this will depend largely on the quality of the timber.

Holes are bored in the front of the easel to hold pegs which support the board. A ledge is shown in the general view (Fig. 31), and this is useful for holding such things as chalk, instruments, painting materials, etc.

Plain Tables

EASILY-MADE KITCHEN TABLE

THE strong and serviceable kitchen table shown by Fig. 1 is of easy construction, and one that can be put together in a few hours.

The method of jointing is entirely different from the usual variety, rendering given for the parts are for a table with a top of the dimensions mentioned: they can, of course, be adjusted according to requirements. Fig. 2 shows how the sides of the table are halved together for fitting into the legs, the joint being shown complete in Fig. 3.

Fig. 1.—Kitchen Table with Drawer

the making extremely simple, even to a beginner, the sides being merely halved together and slotted into the legs. Being simple to prepare, a greater degree of accuracy can be secured by a beginner, and consequently stronger joints obtained when glued up than by an ill-fitting mortise-and-tenon. The measurements

Begin by cutting the sides, the shape and measurements for which are given in Fig. 4. These are prepared from boards 6 in. by ¾ in. Set the shapes out very carefully, for the success of the table will depend very largely on their fitting well. The simplest way, after truing up the planks, will be to set out a rectangle

Fig. 2.—Joint of Leg of Kitchen Table

measuring 3½ in. by 3 in. at the bottom lower corner of each piece and saw it out, afterwards setting out and cutting away the slots for halving the pieces together, these being cut in the lower edge of the long sides and the top of the short ones. After cutting the joints the sides may be fitted together, as shown in Fig. 2, the next item being to cut the slots in the top of the legs.

Prepare four pieces of 2½-in. quartering 2 ft. 4½ in. long, two lines being scored on each face in the centre at a distance of ¾ in. apart. This is done most accurately and simply with a marking gauge. Set the stock of the gauge ⅞ in. from the spur, and then proceed to score the lines in the manner shown in Fig. 5, the stock of the gauge resting against the edge of the wood whilst the tool is worked away from the operator, just enough pressure being applied to cause the spur to enter the wood. The lines are carried across the end in the manner indicated in the illustration, and then a line is carried at right angles right round the wood 3 in. from the top (see Fig. 6). Saw down to this line, when the waste can be easily chiselled out, the result appearing as in Fig. 2. See that the bottom of the cut-out part is rasped quite flat.

Before gluing up the joints the legs can be planed to a taper if desired, and the hole cut for the drawer in one side. In the table shown by Fig. 1 this is made in one of the long sides, and measures 2 ft. 2 in. long by 2¼ in. wide. To cut out, set out the shape and drill a 1-in. hole with brace and bit at each corner, and then saw out with a pad-saw, afterwards rasping quite square and true. The framework can now be glued up with hot glue and the work allowed to dry. Fig. 7 shows the work at this stage, with the addition of the drawer supports, which are next applied. Screw a strip c to project ½ in. above the bottom of the opening for the sides of the drawer to rest on, and then cut slots in this to take the drawer supports, the other ends of which rest on slotted brackets screwed to the opposite side of the table.

Fig. 8 shows a drawer of simple construction. The front is of ¾-in. stuff, the sides and back of ⅜ in. Rebates are sawn in the front to receive the sides, which measure ½ in. less in depth. Along the lower edge of the sides nail narrow strips to which the bottom of the drawer can be nailed. The strips need only be of very thin material, the back being cut to rest on it. Complete with a pair of handles. Should a drawer with an extended front, such as shown, be employed, the drawer bearers indicated in Fig. 7 will need to be fixed in a position for the sides to rest on, and narrow strips nailed along the outer edges to serve as guides. Fig. 9

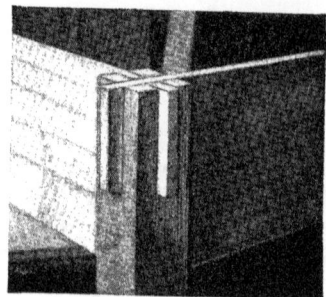

Fig. 3.—Leg of Kitchen Table Fitted

PLAIN TABLES

gives an underside view, showing the manner of framing together the top of the table, which could conveniently consist of ¾-in. matchboarding edged round with 2-in. by ¾-in. strip, with a piece of similar strip across the middle. In fitting the table-top a piece will be required to be taken out of the top of each projection of the sides (see A, Fig. 7), also slots ¾ in. by 2 in., shown by B, from the centre of the long rails, to enable the top to rest flat.

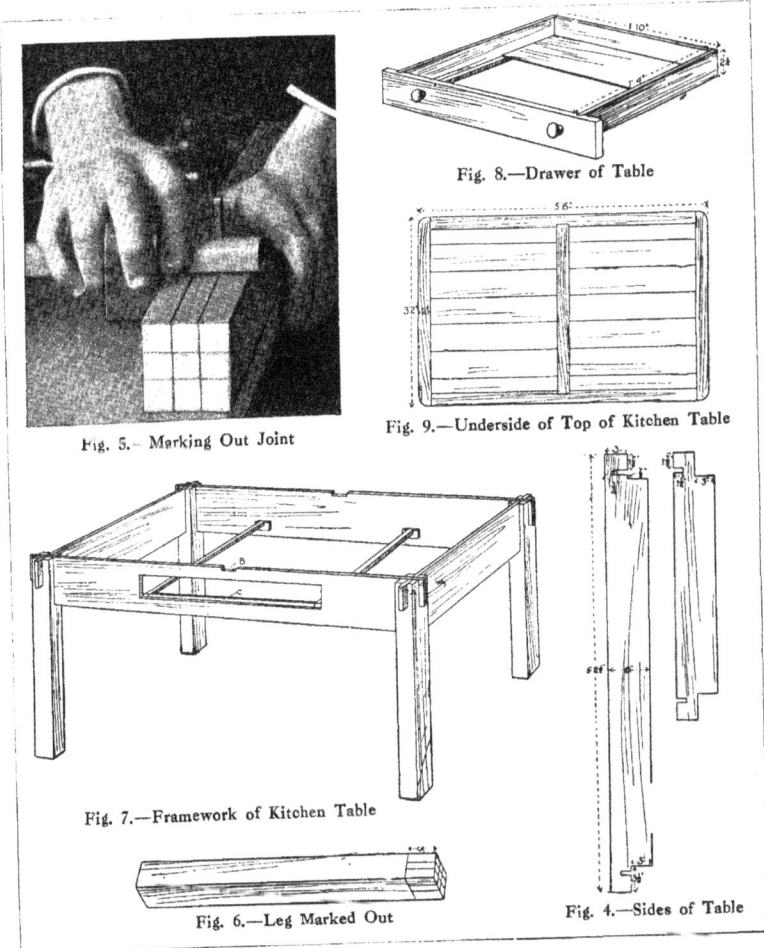

Fig. 5.—Marking Out Joint

Fig. 8.—Drawer of Table

Fig. 9.—Underside of Top of Kitchen Table

Fig. 7.—Framework of Kitchen Table

Fig. 6.—Leg Marked Out

Fig. 4.—Sides of Table

TABLE WITH DETACHABLE LEGS

The table illustrated (Fig. 10) will be found very convenient for packing away when not required; and though easily taken apart and re-fitted, is quite strong and firm. Fig. 10 is an elevation and Fig. 11 a plan of a table 3 ft. 2 in. long by 1 ft. 8 in. wide by 2 ft. 6 in. high. Should a wider table be required, a leaf may be fitted on one or each side; the addition of two 9-in. leaves would make it square.

The table is made of oak throughout, and the following is the material required: For the top, four pieces 3 ft. 2 in. long, 5 in. wide, and ¾ in. thick; for the rails, two pieces 2 ft. 7⅞ in. long, and two pieces 1 ft. 1¾ in. long, all 5 in. wide and ⅞ in. thick; for the corner pieces, four pieces 4½ in. long, 5 in. wide, and ⅞ in. thick; for the legs, four pieces 3 ft. 5 in. long,

2½ in. wide, and 2¼ in. thick. There will also be required four ⅜-in. iron bolts, nuts, and washers, and two and a half dozen 1-in. iron screws.

The top is ¾ in. thick, and is joined together in widths (see Fig. 11) to make up 1 ft. 8 in.; the narrower the boards are the better; but that, of course, means more work. The boards are either tongued and grooved (end-grain tongues), or dowelled, and well glued and cramped. When properly set and dry, the top is squared up to length and breadth. If leaves are to be fitted, the corners should be left square; if not, they should be rounded. The lines for the positions of the 5-in. by ⅞-in. rails A (see Figs. 10 and 12) are then marked on the underside, 1¼ in. and 2 in. from the edges, the ends of the rails being 3½ in. from the edges. The four rails are worked to the width, and the edges carefully squared. The

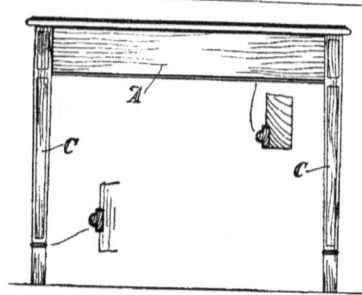

Fig. 10.—Elevation of Table with Detachable Legs

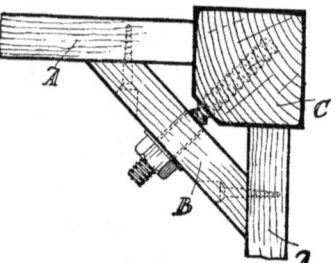

Fig. 12.—Enlarged Detail of Corner

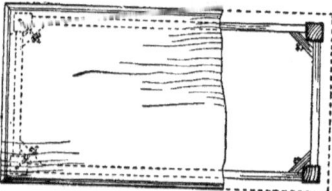

Fig. 11.—Plan of Table showing Part of Top Removed

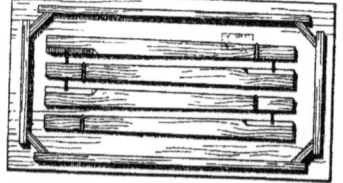

Fig. 13.—Underneath Plan of Table when Packed

PLAIN TABLES

two side rails are cut 2 ft. 4¼ in. long, and the two end rails 1 ft. 1¾ in.; care should be taken that the ends are perfectly square from both the top and the sides. The rails are glued to the top, and further secured with stout 2-in. iron screws. The screw-heads are let down ⅛ in., and a clean hole the size of the head is bored with a centre-bit to enable a dowel to be glued over the head.

Fig. 12 is an enlarged section of one of the corners. The angle pieces B are 4½ in. 3½ in. long, with a wood-cut screw at one end 2 in. long and an iron-cut thread, 1 in. long, with a nut at the other. The bolts are worked into the legs with the aid of the nut, which acts as a temporary head, after which the nut is taken off. Holes are bored in the angle pieces large enough to let the bolts pass through easily, their centres being 2½ in. from the edges.

The legs having been placed in position, the bolts are passed through the angle

Fig. 14.—General View of Side-table

long by 5 in. wide by ⅞ in. thick, with the ends cut to a true mitre, and are glued and screwed to the top and to the side-rails. The legs C (see also Fig. 10) are 2 ft. 5¼ in. long. The upper part for 9 in. is planed up 2¼ in. square, the lower part being tapered to 1¾ in. at the bottom. The middle part of the legs may be left square with a small chamfer taken off each corner, or turned, reeded, or fluted. On the upper inside corner, for a depth of 6 in., a chamfer is taken off, ⅞ in. from each edge, which gives a face ⅞ in. wide (see Fig. 12); while 2½ in. from the top of the leg a hole is bored square from this face to take a ⅜-in. wood-cut screw. The bolts used are ⅜ in. in diameter by pieces. A washer is then placed over the bolts, and the nuts put on and worked up steadily, so that they bear an equal strain. This makes a very rigid frame. Should there be signs of racking at any time, this may be remedied by tightening the nuts. If there is any difficulty in obtaining the bolts, ⅜-in. coach screws, or handrail screws, may be used instead. When disconnecting the parts, the nuts are removed, and the legs taken off and stowed under the top of the table, as shown in Fig. 13, which is an underneath plan of the table packed ready for removal. By this method of construction the cutting of mortises and tenons is avoided, and much time saved.

SCULLERY SIDE-TABLE

The kitchen or scullery side-table illustrated in Fig. 14 is shown and described precisely as actually made; but would naturally be modified in detail in order to suit particular cases. Fig. 15 is a front view.

To construct the table, first frame up the two ends, each of which comprises two 2-in. square legs connected by two 2-in. by 1-in. rails, as at A and B in Fig. 18. The latter portions could be a little thicker if desired, and are intended to have tenons ½ in. thick, mortised into the legs in such a way that the rails will be ¼ in. thick back from their outer faces. The tenons are best if mitred ready for the longer rails, as shown on plan in Fig. 19, the joints being further explained by the isometric views in Fig. 20, where it will be observed that the upper tenon has to be "haunched," that is, reduced to one half the height of the rail, in order to leave a secure margin of wood above the mortise at the extreme top of the leg.

The next step should be to prepare four long rails as at C and D in Fig. 15, similar in size to the previous ones and tenoned into the legs in precisely the same way, the mitred ends meeting those of the shorter rails as shown in Fig. 19. Before the long top rails are fixed, the shelf (Figs. 15, 16 and 17) should be prepared from ¾-in. stuff. It is 11 in. by 3 ft. 8 in., notched to fit against each leg as at E in Fig. 20, and can probably be obtained in one width. The tenons of the rails can be pegged, screwed, or wedged, and the shelf fixed from below by means of screws put obliquely through the top inner edges of the rails.

For the table-top two widths dowelled or cross-tongued together will be requisite. It should be out of 1-in. stuff, with its front corners cut to quadrants of about 2-in. radius, and arranged in most cases to overhang 1 in. along the back edge. It can be fixed as before described, or by means of "buttons" fitting in grooves in the rails, allowing for a little expansion or contraction, and it will be advisable to slightly round off all exposed angles.

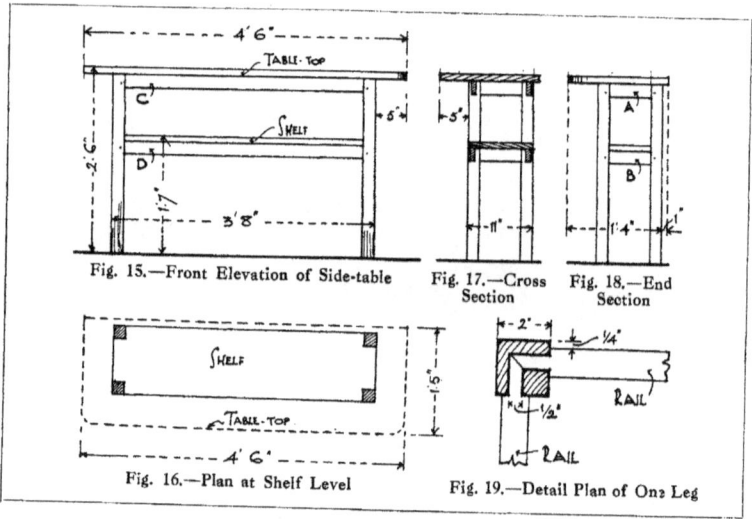

Fig. 15.—Front Elevation of Side-table   Fig. 17.—Cross Section   Fig. 18.—End Section

Fig. 16.—Plan at Shelf Level   Fig. 19.—Detail Plan of One Leg

PLAIN TABLES

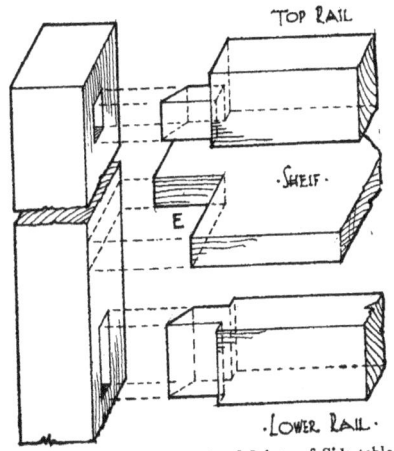

Fig. 20.—Isometric Sketch of Joints of Side-table

Either a clean natural surface, a sized finish, or an application of varnish would be suitable for the type of work; but this matter may be left to individual taste.

DETACHABLE TABLE

The kitchen table shown in Fig. 21 can be taken apart in several sections. The dimensions given are suitable for an ordinary cottage kitchen; but the same construction and dimensions of the several parts are applicable to tables up to 9 ft. by 5 ft. top surface, with the one exception of the legs, which should be increased in size sectionally when the length of the table exceeds 5 ft. Figs. 22, 23 and 24 show side and end elevations and plan respectively.

The top can be made from sycamore, good white deal, or fir, which can be got in 11-in. widths, and should be free from knots, sap, and shakes. White deal or fir is preferable to yellow deal or pine, as it always scrubs clean and white, and does not become discoloured. The wood should be 1 in. thick. A fillet 2 in. by 1 in. is mitred at the angles, and screwed on the underside of the top all round the edges, the joint being broken by a bead worked on the fillet if desired. This not only serves to protect the edges of the top, but gives it a substantial appearance.

The legs may be constructed of white or yellow deal 3 in. square, and they can be turned, or square and tapered as shown. Fig. 28 shows the mortise and dovetail notch to receive the rails. There are four bolts (one in each leg), which should be about 8 in. long and $\frac{3}{8}$ in. to $\frac{1}{4}$ in. in diameter; they should have snap-heads, having a slot cut across them with a file, for the purpose of inserting the blade of a screwdriver when turning them either in or out. The long-side rails are also of deal $6\frac{1}{2}$ in. wide and 1 in. thick, grooved on the inside for the buttons for attachment to the top (see Fig. 25); a hardwood cleat (as at A in Figs. 26, 27 and 28) is fitted into a notch, and well

Fig. 21.—Detachable Kitchen Table

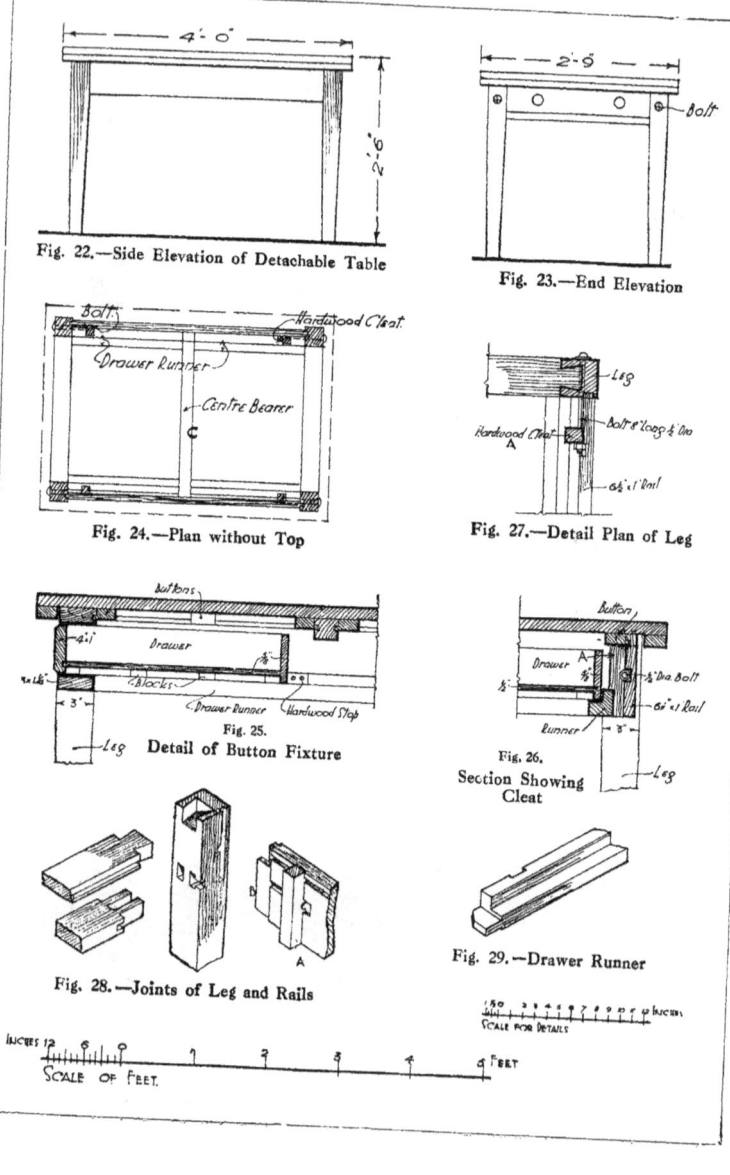

Fig. 22.—Side Elevation of Detachable Table
Fig. 23.—End Elevation
Fig. 24.—Plan without Top
Fig. 27.—Detail Plan of Leg
Fig. 25.—Detail of Button Fixture
Fig. 26.—Section Showing Cleat
Fig. 28.—Joints of Leg and Rails
Fig. 29.—Drawer Runner

PLAIN TABLES

glued and fixed with screws, a hole being bored through it to accommodate the belt. The tenon at the end B (Fig. 28), which is about 1¼ in. long by ⅝ in., should fit easily into the leg. The upper cross-rail is ploughed on the inside for buttons, and is dovetailed to drive into the top of the legs; the lower rail has two tenons about 2½ in. long by ⅜ in., which should be secured permanently to the legs by well gluing; they are made of deal 3 in. wide by 1¼ in. thick (see Fig. 28).

The centre bearer C (Fig. 24) is about 1 in., with lips to fit into grooves in rails; they should be secured to the top with stout brass screws to prevent rusting in, which would occur if iron were used. The side rails should be fitted into their respective legs, and marked by cutting with a chisel Roman numbers on the inside to correspond, and the holes for the bolts should now be bored.

All that is necessary in taking the table apart is to slack the screws with a screw-driver, and, turning the buttons round, disengage them from the rails, lift off the

Fig. 30.—Perspective View of Simple Table

2 in. by 1¾ in. in section, and has a lip tenon to fit into a mortise in the long rails at the middle of their lengths, and should be grooved for buttons. The drawer-runners are 2 in. by 2 in. in section, and are rebated to form a guide for the drawers (Fig. 26); they are notched to fit over the cleat for the bolt (see Fig. 29). A hardwood drawer stop, about ¾ in. by 1 in., is screwed into the rebate, as shown in Fig. 25. The front of the drawer measures 4 in. by 1 in., each side 4 in. by ⅝ in., and the back 3 in. by ⅝ in.; they are dovetailed together. The bottom is ½ in. thick, and fitted into grooves in the front and sides, and nailed on to the back. The sides and front should be secured to the bottom by glued blocks underneath, as shown in Figs. 25 and 26, and the buttons should be of hardwood, 4 in. long by 1½ in. by

top, take out the bolts, and draw off the united pairs of legs at the ends, leaving the long rails, centre bearer, and runners in separate pieces. The reverse method is adopted in re-erecting the table.

SIMPLE TABLE

This table (Figs. 30 to 33), while unusual in construction, combines the advantages of strength, lightness, and economy of material with that of being easily separated into several portions convenient for storage or transit. It is perfectly suited for kitchen and other purposes.

The dimensions given in the following list are approximately those of parts worked ready for fitting together. The top measures 6 ft. by 3 ft. 3 in. and 1 in. thick, composed of any convenient number (probably four) of widths; these should

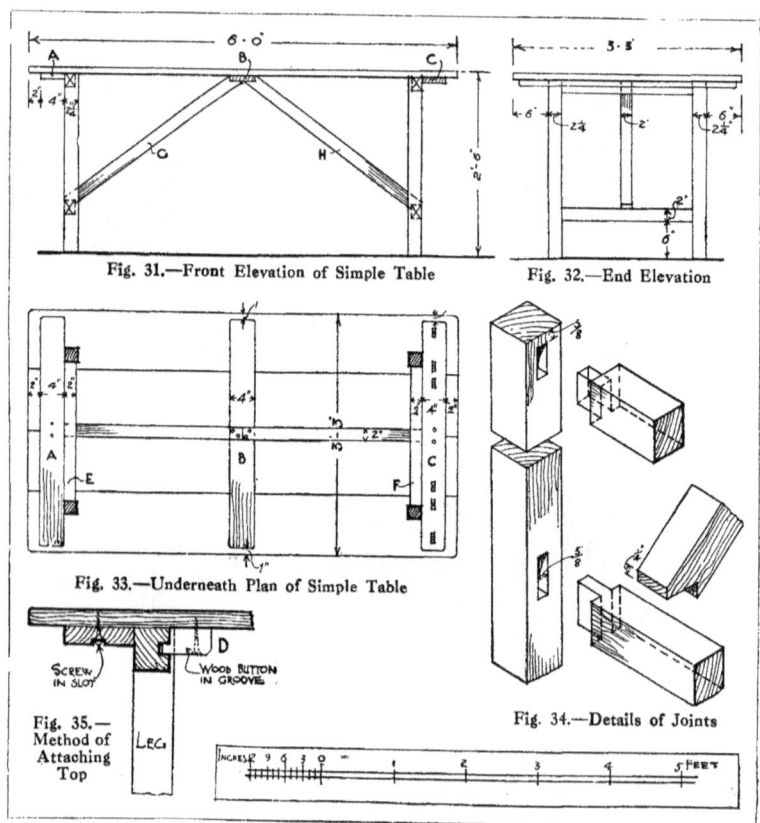

Fig. 31.—Front Elevation of Simple Table
Fig. 32.—End Elevation
Fig. 33.—Underneath Plan of Simple Table
Fig. 34.—Details of Joints
Fig. 35.—Method of Attaching Top

be joined up with oak cross-tongueing, and have three 4-in. by 1-in. ledges, as A, B and C in Figs. 31 and 33. These ledges should be slot screwed except in the centre of their lengths, in order to allow a slight movement without splitting. For the under-framing, four legs 2¼ in. square and 2 ft. 5 in. long; four rails about 2¼ in. by 2 in. and 2 ft. 1½ in. long; two struts about 2 in. by 2 in. and 3 ft. long; six or eight "buttons," as D (Fig. 35), about 3 in. by 1½ in. by 2 in.

The top has already been sufficiently described so that the next part to require mention will be one of the two end framings. It is set out and dimensioned in Figs. 31 to 33, and the two rails should be fixed flush with the outer faces of the legs. They are fixed by means of tenons ⅜ in. thick and mortised about 1½ in. into the legs, the upper joint being "shouldered" or kept down about ⅝ in. from the actual top surface of the leg as shown (Fig. 34), while the tenon of the lower one is of the same depth as the rail. When ready, the

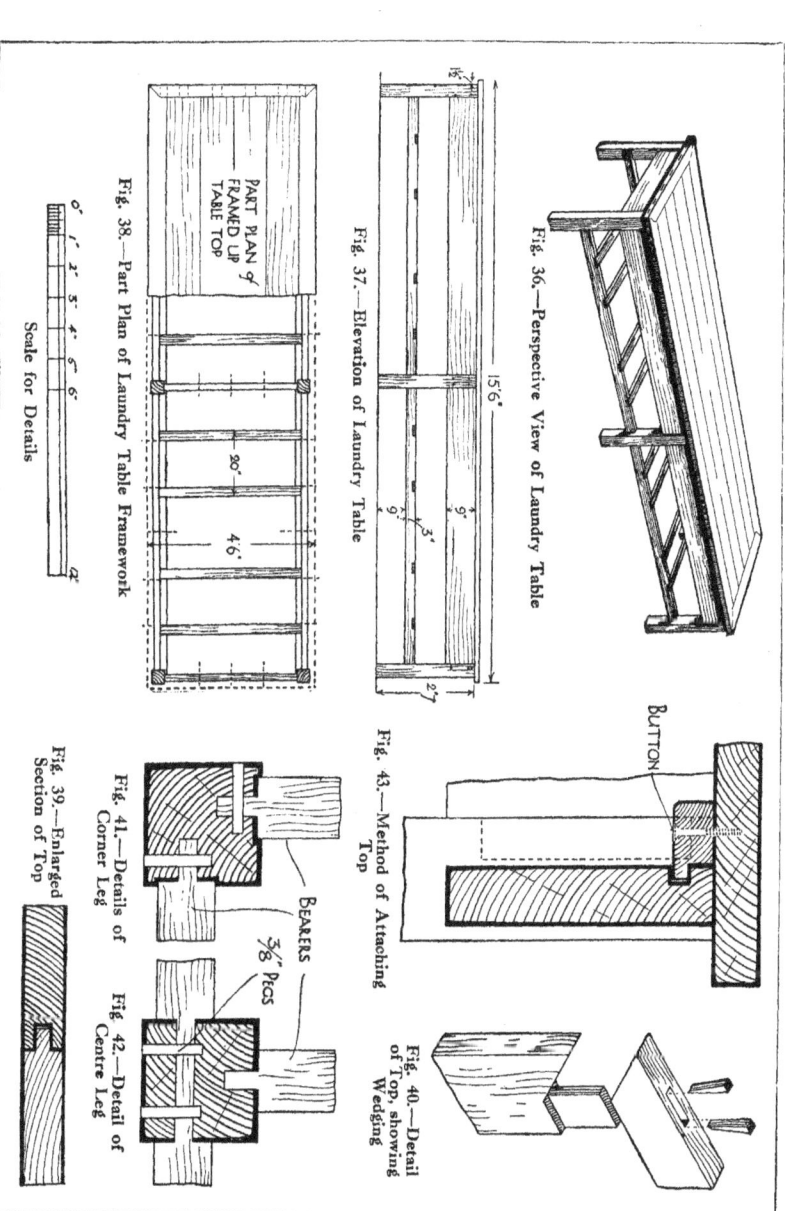

Fig. 36.—Perspective View of Laundry Table
Fig. 37.—Elevation of Laundry Table
Fig. 38.—Part Plan of Laundry Table Framework
Scale for Details
Fig. 39.—Enlarged Section of Top
Fig. 41.—Details of Corner Leg
Fig. 42.—Detail of Centre Leg
Fig. 43.—Method of Attaching Top
Fig. 40.—Detail of Top, showing Wedging

top should be reversed and laid flat, the end framings placed in position as at E and F in Fig. 33, tight up against the end ledges of the top, held there with one good screw near the centre of each top rail, and then secured with "buttons," as at D in Fig. 35, fitting a groove in the side of the top rail and screwed through to the boarding.

This done, the table will be comparatively strong but lacking rigidity, which is imparted to it by the addition of struts, as at G and H in Fig. 31. Each of these should be of full length, birds-mouthed to fit the lower rail and the central ledge, and secured to each with two 2½-in. screws, thus producing a perfectly firm table.

IRONING TABLE FOR LAUNDRY

The illustration (Fig. 36) shows a good ironing table suitable for a laundry. An elevation is shown in Fig. 37 and a plan of the framework with the top removed is given in Fig. 38.

The timber generally, except the table-top, should be of the best yellow deal free from large knots or defects, and thoroughly seasoned. All joints should be well made and put together, where possible, with oak pins, thus avoiding the use of nails. The top is of 1½-in. white deal tongued-and-grooved battens (see Fig. 39) framed together as shown in Figs. 36 and 40, the end tenons being wedged up tightly. The legs are 4 in. by 4 in., grooved for the rails, as shown in Fig. 41, while the rails are 9 in. by 2 in. The side rails are in one length, and checked out to fit the top of the centre leg and pinned (see Fig. 42). The cross-rail in the centre of the table is of 9-in. by 2-in. stuff, with a tenon formed on each end for two-thirds of its depth, to fit the top of the centre leg, as shown in Fig. 43. Plough-goove the rails all round for twenty-nine hardwood buttons, placed as indicated by broken lines in Fig. 38. These buttons are fixed with brass screws, as shown in Fig. 43.

The racks underneath for linen baskets are formed of 3-in. by 2-in. rails halved on to legs, and 3-in. by 1-in. bearers fixed 1 ft. 2 in. apart. All the edges should be arrised.

Domestic Woodware

BATH SEAT

To make a bath seat as shown in Fig. 1 procure a piece of teak $1\frac{7}{16}$ in. thick, from which the following sizes can be cut: Two pieces $8\frac{1}{4}$ in. by $8\frac{1}{4}$ in.; seven pieces $15\frac{1}{2}$ in. by $1\frac{3}{8}$ in.; and four pieces 5 in. by $1\frac{1}{4}$ in. Two pieces of brass are also required, each 7 in. long, $\frac{3}{8}$ in. wide, and $\frac{3}{16}$ in. thick.

Proceed now with the planing of each piece to the finished size shown in Figs. 2 and 4, being careful to have all the edges squared to ensure accurate work when setting out the mortise-and-tenon joints. The length of the spars for the seat should now be set out, and the position of the tenons marked off. The same operations should be carried out with the four hangers, and then it is possible for the cutting of all tenon joints to be done at the one time. Next proceed with the cutting of the shoulders and the ripping of the tenons. Then the position of the mortises can be marked off on the side pieces. This part should be most carefully done, as the proper working of the seat depends entirely on each spar being its exact distance apart.

The mortises should now be cut out, after which the side pieces should be cut to the tapered outline given in Fig. 4, the corners rounded, and the face arris chamfered as in Fig. 5, where the parts are shown ready for fixing together. Then plane the hanger to a round section. This is best done by taking the corner off first to form an octagon, and then by easy stages converting the polygonal figure into a complete circle. The position of the long $\frac{3}{16}$-in. slot in each of the spars (see Figs. 2 and 4) should now be set out, care being taken that all the gauging is done

Fig. 1.—View of Bath Seat

from the one side. To cut out the slots, the simplest plan is to bore a number of holes at the one end, sufficient to allow a port saw to pass through. Then a sawcut can be made for the remainder of the work, and the slot pared out from both sides to the gauge marks with a chisel.

The spars are now ready for rounding so as to form a comfortable seat, and can be bored for fixing to brass bearing plates. All the pieces should now be carefully planed with the smoothing plane, and the surfaces finished with glasspaper. To put the seat together, glue and wedge the tenon joints together, putting four spars into the one side piece and three into the other. The ends of tenons should now be pared off, and the surfaces finished.

Next set out the holes on the brass plates (Fig. 6), and if there is any difficulty in the boring, this could be done by a local smith. The seat is now ready to be fixed together, and to do so put the spars in position, as shown in Fig. 3, and pass the respective brass plates through the slots

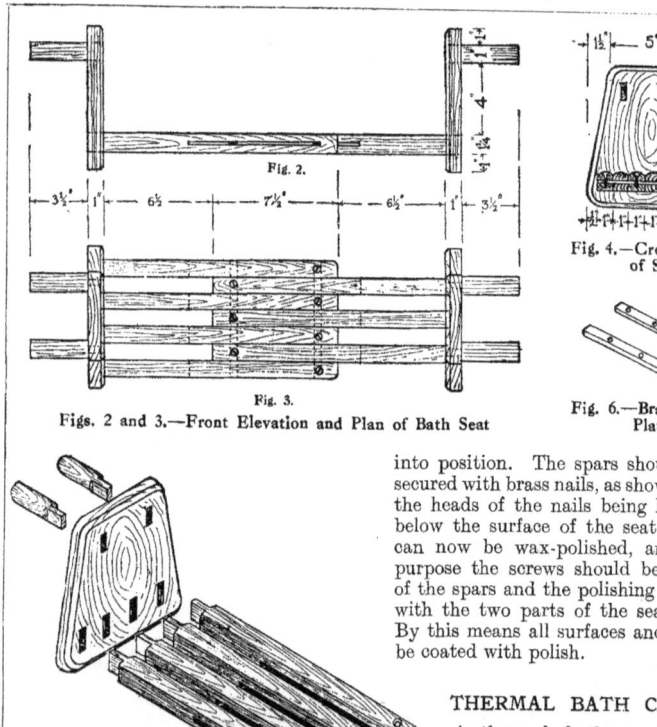

Figs. 2 and 3.—Front Elevation and Plan of Bath Seat

Fig. 4.—Cross Section of Seat

Fig. 6.—Brass Bearing Plates

Fig. 5.—Hangers, Side Piece and Spars of Seat

into position. The spars should then be secured with brass nails, as shown in Fig. 3, the heads of the nails being left slightly below the surface of the seat. The seat can now be wax-polished, and for this purpose the screws should be taken out of the spars and the polishing carried out with the two parts of the seat separate. By this means all surfaces and edges will be coated with polish.

THERMAL BATH CABINET

A thermal bath, sometimes recommended for the cure or alleviation of specific complaints, consists of an enclosure inside which the patient can stand or sit and be surrounded by steam, chemical vapours, or hot dry air, or be exposed to the action of radiant heat in a dry atmosphere. The portable cabinet shown by Fig. 7 consists of a bottom or floor, four sides, and a cover for the top and sloping parts. Such cabinets can be made of sheet metal

DOMESTIC WOODWARE

or wood; the latter is usually preferred, as it does not conduct heat so readily as metals, which are, however, better for a high temperature, but buckle and twist very much when heated, and this prevents the joints fitting properly unless strengthened with iron plates. The wood should be light and thoroughly seasoned. All woods swell on being wetted, and shrink on drying; but American whitewood or red pine, or any wood which contains very little resin and is free from knots, can be used. The bottom, or floor, may be 3 ft. by 2 ft. 9 in.

The edge of the back may be fixed to the bottom with dowels, as shown in Fig. 8, the upright edges of the back being rebated for fitting to the side pieces, as in Fig. 9.

At the top of the back a piece of $\frac{3}{4}$ in. stuff (Fig. 10) should be hung on brass butts with gunmetal pins, so as to fold inwards when the cabinet is taken to pieces (see Fig. 11). The ends of the folding top piece should have caps (see Fig. 12) to lap over the sides and help to keep them in their positions. The half-circle (see Fig. 10) should be to a radius of $2\frac{1}{2}$ in. to

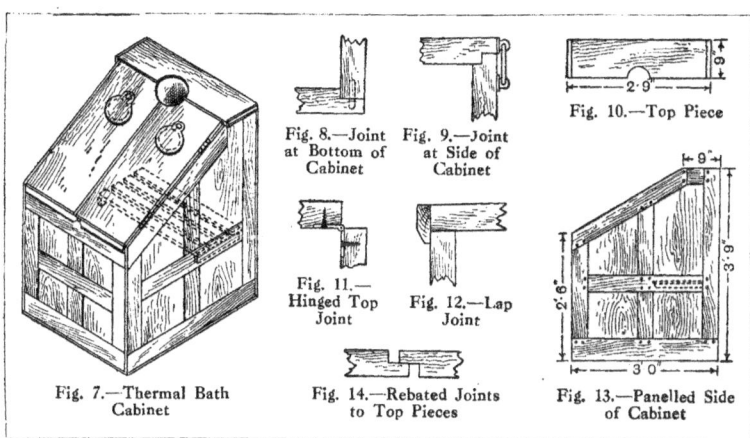

Fig. 8.—Joint at Bottom of Cabinet
Fig. 9.—Joint at Side of Cabinet
Fig. 10.—Top Piece
Fig. 11.—Hinged Top Joint
Fig. 12.—Lap Joint
Fig. 7.—Thermal Bath Cabinet
Fig. 14.—Rebated Joints to Top Pieces
Fig. 13.—Panelled Side of Cabinet

by $1\frac{1}{4}$ in. thick, and battened to keep it from warping and twisting. The edges should be rebated all round to receive the bottom edges of the four sides, as shown in Fig. 8; the dotted lines represent oak dowels. The back may be framed and panelled, the stiles and rails being of 1 in. stuff, and the panels $\frac{3}{8}$ in. or $\frac{1}{2}$ in. thick. The frames and panels are best flush inside. Any mouldings on the outsides of the panels should be worked out of the solid stiles; but if they are planted on they should be nailed to the stiles and rails, so as to allow freedom for the panels to expand and shrink. The framing should be pinned together, no parts being glued.

3 in., the edges being carefully rounded to avoid chafing the user's neck.

The sides may be panelled, as shown in Fig. 13, the upright edges being rebated to the back, and secured by a brass staple and hook on brass plates fixed a few inches below the top of the cabinet. The dotted lines in Fig. 7 show the lattice work seat, which should rest on fillets. The seat can be omitted, and a chair used instead; but the seat, if used, should not be painted or varnished. The two halves of the sloping top are to be hung to the sides by brass butts, and have easy fitting rebated joints (see Fig. 14) at the top and centre. If these joints are fitted too tight they will probably lock when the three flap pieces are all opened together by the bather rising to get out of the bath. Cappings (as in Fig. 12) may be fixed on the bottom ends of the sloping flaps to lap over the front piece and hold it in position. Corners cut out of the sloping flaps complete the hole for the user's neck and elled similar to the back and sides, and fitted in the same way, except that it should not be fixed or held together with bits or fastenings of any kind, as it is important that the bather should be able to leave the cabinet very quickly if necessary. In the hinged top a special opening may be made for a thermometer to indicate

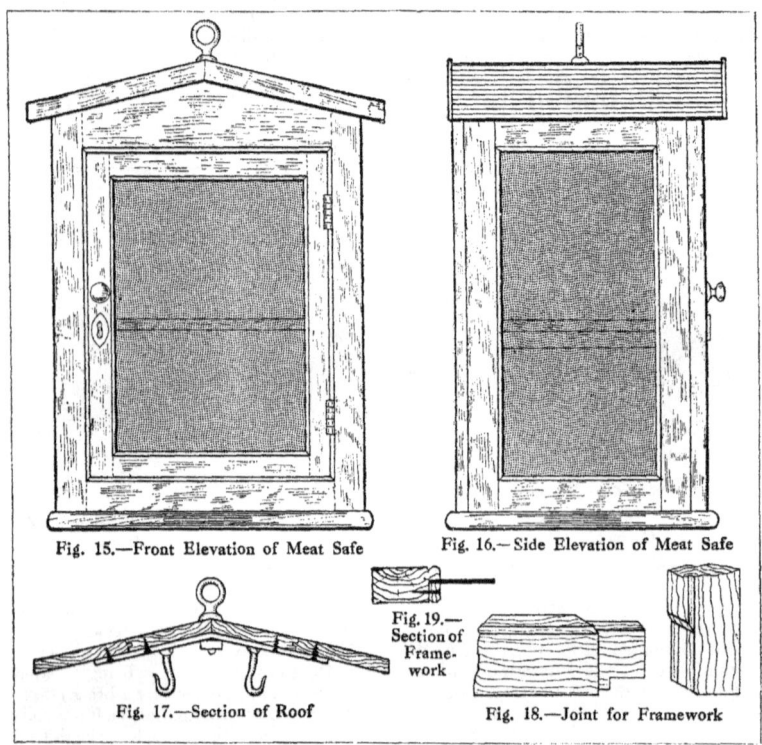

Fig. 15.—Front Elevation of Meat Safe

Fig. 16.—Side Elevation of Meat Safe

Fig. 17.—Section of Roof

Fig. 19.—Section of Framework

Fig. 18.—Joint for Framework

5 in. holes for the hands must be made in each a few inches lower down. Covers for the hand-holes are made out of ½ in. or ⅜ in. stuff and turn on hardwood pins with heads. The covers can be fixed inside, and be under the control of the bather.

The front of the cabinet should be panelled the inside temperature. Wood thermal cabinets should not be painted, but for a finish they can be stained and varnished.

MEAT SAFE

The meat safe shown at Figs. 15 and 16 can be made of deal. It is fitted with

DOMESTIC WOODWARE

a shelf which divides it into two compartments, the upper one being fitted with hooks at the top, as shown in Fig. 17. The sides and front are covered with perforated zinc, which allows of a free passage of air.

The general dimensions are : width, 1 ft. 6 in.; depth, back to front, 1 ft. 3 in.; height to underneath side of the roof, 2 ft.; rise of roof in the middle, 2 in. The framework of the front and side frames is 2 in. by ⅞ in., mortised and tenoned together as at Fig. 18. The back

eye bolt, which has a ⅜-in. spill through the roof fixed with a nut underneath.

PROVISION SAFE

The safe illustrated by Figs. 20 to 22 can be built up of stuff 2 in. or 1½ in. square to the sizes shown, the joints being simple tenons of the usual character.

It will be noted that the ends have a middle horizontal rail A (Fig. 21) not present on the back. This serves to sup-

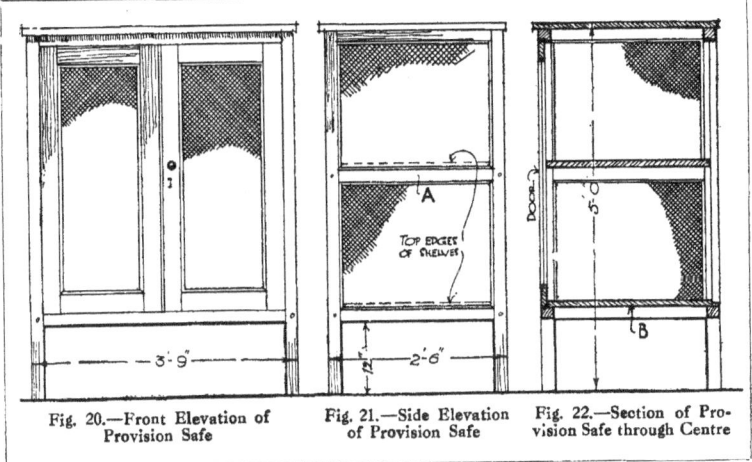

Fig. 20.—Front Elevation of Provision Safe   Fig. 21.—Side Elevation of Provision Safe   Fig. 22.—Section of Provision Safe through Centre

is ⅝ in. thick, and the bottom ⅞ in. thick. The framework of the door, 1½ in. by ⅞ in., mortised and tenoned together, is hung with two 2-in. butt hinges and is fitted with a lock and key. The framework of the front door and side frames is boxed out on its inside edge ⅜ in. by ½ in. to receive the perforated zinc, which is fixed in position by fillet pieces, as shown at Fig. 19. The roof is ⅝ in. thick, and should be covered with zinc to prevent water penetrating into the inside of the safe. The hooks in the top are of ⅜-in. round iron riveted into a 1-in. by ¼-in. iron plate. The safe is hung by means of an

port the shelf. For the top, ¾-in. tongued boarding projecting ½ in. all round will suit, while the 1-in. bottom is supported by the four bottom rails, as at B in Fig. 22. The doors are formed of 3-in. by 1-in. stuff halved at the angles, rebated, and beaded down the meeting stiles, and without rebates on the inner edges, the wire panels to these and also to the sides and back being secured by means of a double bead all round. Only a single bead on the outside will be required at the sides against the edges at the bottom and middle shelf. A single bead also at the head, together with the edge of the bottom shelf, will serve as stops for the doors, as in Fig. 22.

Fig. 23.—Fitment for Cutlery Drawer

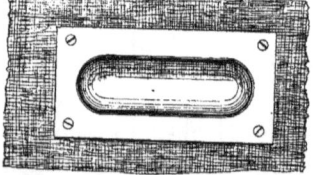

Fig. 25.—Flush Handle

TARNISH-PROOF FITMENT FOR CUTLERY DRAWER

The fitment and drawer are shown by the photographic reproductions (Figs. 23 and 24).

The drawer in this case is about 18 in. square by 6 in. deep, and the fitment is intended to serve the purpose of a knife-box, to be lifted out with the contents as required. Because of this, two finger-place handles, the same as used for sliding doors (see Fig. 25), are let flush into the outer sides of the two partitions of the fitment. Also, to allow for the drawer to be pulled out to the full extent and no farther, a stop is put at the upper edge of the drawer back to come against the inside edge of the front bearer rail of the drawer place. This latter is about 2 in. wide, and it happens

that there is a space of about 2½ in. between the back of the recess and the drawer when closed. Thus it allows for the stop to be made of a piece the length of the drawer back by 2 in. wide by ⅞ in. thick, with a strip of beading 1¼ in. by ⅜ in. screwed on one edge. This stop is fixed with three screws through the drawer back (see Fig. 26); but these screws must be slacked to allow the stop to drop a little to put the drawer in place and then tighten up.

The fitment is made 4 in. deep, the space between the bottom and the drawer bottom being used as a press for the table linen, which is another convenience. It consists

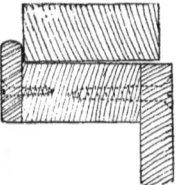

Fig. 26.—Drawer Stop

of a box made in common deal ½ in. thick, with two partitions, and a bottom of three-ply or other thin board. It should fit easily, but neatly, into the drawer, allowing for the felt with which the wood is to be covered. The box is first

Fig. 24.—View showing Fitment Open

made and put together with screws—1¼ in. No. 4 for the sides and ⅝ in. No. 4 for the bottom. The handles may be fitted into the partitions. It is then taken apart for covering with green felt. The bottom is to be covered on the inside only, fixed with glue applied to the board just sufficient to fix the felt, taking care to have it the right consistency so as not to work through.

The two partitions are covered on both sides over the top edge, the felt edges meeting under the lower edge of the wood. The felt for the four box-sides should be cut to cover both sides and edges, allowing fully ½ in. over at the ends of the two longer pieces, also about ½ in. to lap under the bottom. It must be fixed first on the inner sides and lower edges only; then the parts must be screwed together and the felt glued over the outer sides. There are three lids of three-ply wood, each covered all over with the felt, having flat handles of the same material fixed with nickel-headed stud nails. Before putting into use, the fitment should be allowed several days in dry air to make sure that all moisture has evaporated.

EASILY-MADE SMOKER'S CABINET

This small hanging cabinet can be of ½-in. stuff throughout, oak or mahogany for preference. Its upright portions comprise two sides of the dimensions given, shaped top and bottom to some such contours as those in the illustrations, and a couple of uprights as at A in Figs. 28 and 29, these latter serving to tie the sides and shelves together. The top and bottom shelves are of the same width as the sides, into which they should be stop-housed, and they should be notched out at their back corners to fit the uprights A, which are also shaped top and bottom. For

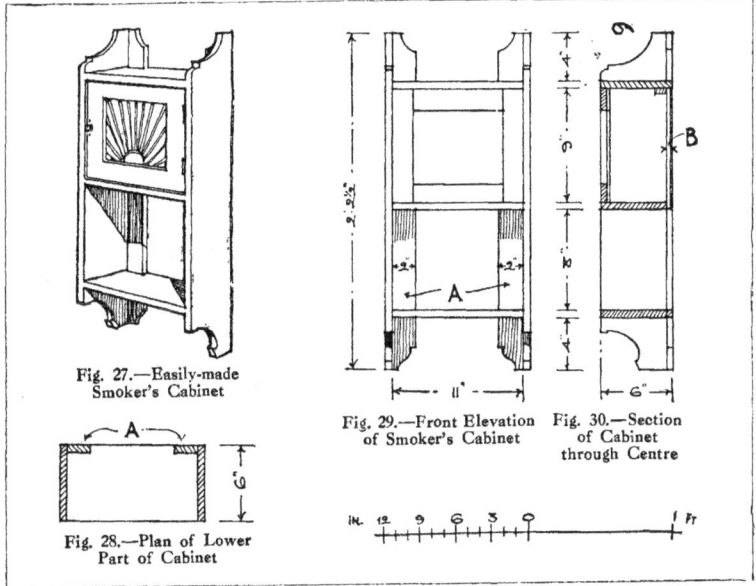

Fig. 27.—Easily-made Smoker's Cabinet

Fig. 28.—Plan of Lower Part of Cabinet

Fig. 29.—Front Elevation of Smoker's Cabinet

Fig. 30.—Section of Cabinet through Centre

the central shelf a piece 5⅛ in. wide should be used, so that in this case the notching just mentioned will not be required. The uprights A are nailed or screwed to both sides and shelves, and for a good job it would be desirable slightly to rebate the sides to take them neatly, instead of having simply a butt joint, although this is not essential.

The back of the cupboard can be filled in with three-ply or other thin form of panels, and should be fixed to the back of the middle shelf and to a fillet along the underside of the top shelf, as shown at B in Fig. 30. The fillet might with advantage be continued down the inner sides of the cupboard, which can be fitted up with a shelf, pipe-racks, or compartments as desired. The door can be panelled, or built up with good three-ply having sham framing applied on its face. To add a touch of interest the panel may well be decorated in some way best suited to the craftsman. A simple conventional device, such as the rising sun shown in Fig. 27, can very easily be carried out in gesso, repoussé, leaded glazing, or painted ornament; or a framed and glazed picture might be incorporated.

HANGING CLOTHES AIRER

Three views of the clothes airer are given in the illustrations, Fig. 31 being a side elevation, Fig. 32 a plan, and Fig. 33 an end elevation.

The two 10-ft. runners A are each made up of three pieces, two 3 ft. 4½ in. by 2½ in. by ¾ in., and one 3 ft. 3 in. by 2¼ in. by ¾ in.; these are joined together with strong brass bagatelle-table or desk hinges, as shown at B, care being taken that the hinges are fixed on opposite edges of the runner so that one end folds over the top and the other underneath. An enlarged detail of the hinged joint is shown at Fig. 34. Opposite one hinge on each runner must be screwed a brass plate 5 in. by ¾ in. by ⅛ in., as shown at C, to keep the whole in perfect alignment. These plates must be removed when the airer is to be folded. The brass plates will not be required if the method of jointing shown at Fig. 35 is adopted. A cheaper and easier method of making the joints of the runners is shown at Fig. 35. The pieces are halved together, and fixed with six brass countersunk head whitworth screws and nuts. This makes a good strong job; but the dimensions given above will have to be slightly modified.

The over-all length of the hanging rods is 2 ft. 5½ in., four of them being ⅞ in. in diameter, and the remaining fifteen ⅝ in. in diameter. The large ones are shouldered down to ⅜ in. in diameter, which is the size all the holes should be drilled, by $\tfrac{1}{16}$ in. deep, and the small ones tapered for 1 in. down to ⅜ in. in diameter at the end; and if made of softwood, will be found to be a good driving fit in the ⅜-in. hole. The rods are afterwards fixed with 1½-in. brass nails. Four strong screw eyes will be required and two single and one double screw pulleys, 1½ in. in diameter, with 12 yards of thick blind cord. The airer folds up to 3 ft. 4½ in. by 2 ft. 6 in. by 7½ in., and weighs only about 9 lb. A coat of size and clear spirit varnish will improve its appearance.

BABY'S PLAY-PEN

The pen shown in the photographs, Figs. 36 and 37, is 2 ft. 6 in. high, which is higher than usually made, and the gate is quite an unusual feature, to save having to stride over it in the event of a child having to be reached quickly. Another point is the wide rail or plinth which comes down to the floor and so prevents toys from getting pushed underneath; this is further improved by fixing rubber draught-proofing on the lower edge. It folds up, as shown by Fig. 38, in a different way from other kinds. The size is 4 ft. 6 in. square.

The wood used is whitewood, except the top rails and the gate fastening piece, which is of birch. The lower rails are 5 in. wide, and the top rails 2 in. by ⅞ in., the rounded bars being ⅝ in. in diameter. These latter can sometimes be bought in hardwood, ready made, in lengths of about 3 ft. Each frame may be made the same, with eleven bars, equally dividing

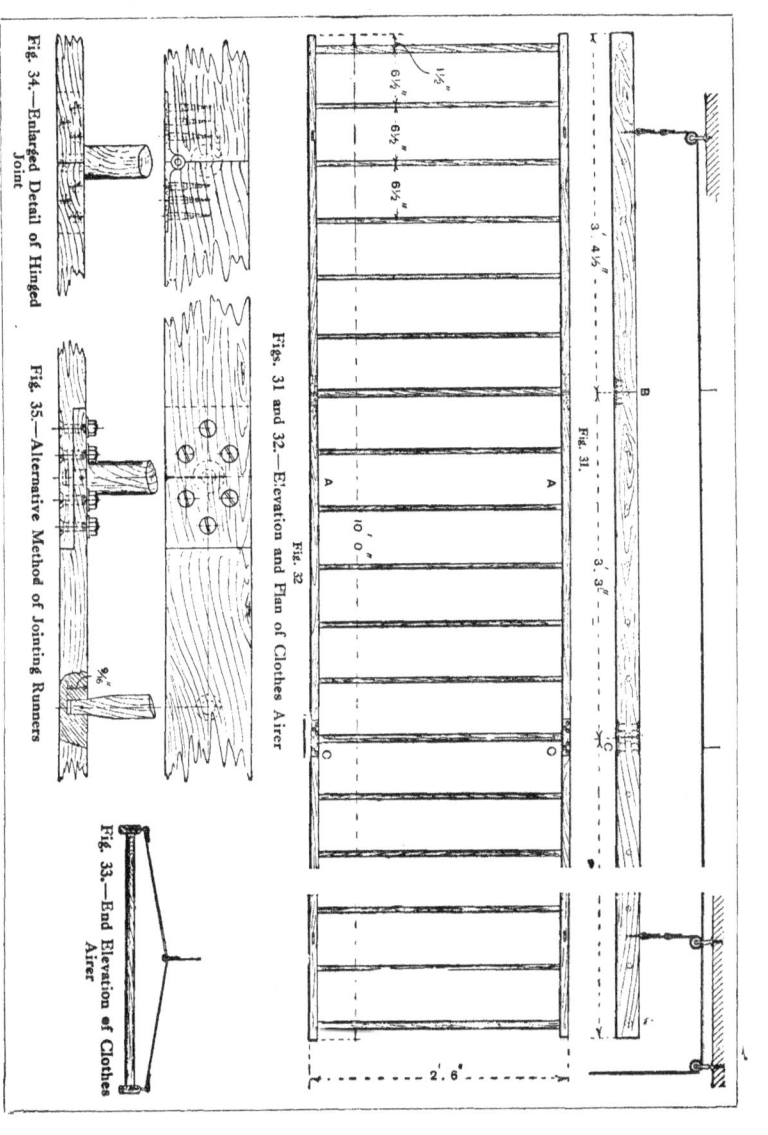

Figs. 31 and 32.—Elevation and Plan of Clothes Airer

Fig. 33.—End Elevation of Clothes Airer

Fig. 34.—Enlarged Detail of Hinged Joint

Fig. 35.—Alternative Method of Jointing Runners

the space with a pair of compasses to decide the points on the rails where the bars must be let in direct about 1 in. deep. This is shown in Figs. 39 and 40, in which will be seen the shape of the top rails, the upper edge being made round, and the lower corners also rounded off. All square corners should be rounded off. In boring the holes for the bars, a clean-cutting twist- or centre-bit should be used, and it is

Fig. 36.—Baby's Play-pen

Fig. 37.—Play-pen with Gate Open

essential to keep square with the rail. When all are ready they may be quickly glued up, making certain that they are quite straight and square before being left to set.

The metal fittings required are: three pairs of common iron hinges (Fig. 41), one pair (Fig. 42), two thumbscrew fasteners (Fig. 43), two screw-eyes (Fig. 44), a snap-latch (Fig. 44), and a plate catch for same (Fig. 45). It is sometimes not so easy to get these things exactly as required ready made, so one had to adapt the nearest obtainable. There should be no trouble about the hinges (Fig. 41), but with Fig. 42 something slightly different might have to be used, or a pair could be altered or made at a small extra cost. Figs. 43 and 44 are stock articles, also Fig. 45, in different shapes and sizes. The plate catch (Fig. 46) is made from a piece of sheet brass sufficiently pliable to work, but hard enough to keep rigid. Fig. 45 shows the inner side of the latch, the outside being shown in Fig. 47.

In Fig. 48 is shown the method of hinging the frames together and fixing with the thumbscrew fasteners. The four hinges (Fig. 41) are screwed on the inner sides of the rails as at A (Fig. 48), but they may be let in level if desired. The two hinges (Fig. 42) are put on the outer sides of the rails, and should be let in, as shown at B. Also, they have to be reversed, the inner side out; therefore it is necessary to countersink the screw holes at the other side. The fasteners must have the screw plate let into the ends of the two rails, the plain plate being let into the outer side of the other rails for the thumbscrew heads to tighten up against.

The place for the gate may then be marked for cutting out. This is on the same frame as the thumbscrews. The top rail has to be cut through just a little inside the fourth bar from each end and the lower rail the same, but only half-way through the width. Before cutting the rails, the hinges may be put on the inner side of the rails, let in level, and screwed. They have to be taken off, of course, to cut the rails; but on being replaced the gate will fit true without any further fitting (see Fig. 49). The closing ends should be cut on the slant, as shown in Fig. 50, which also shows the method of hinging the clamp (to carry the snap-latch) with the screw-eyes and screws. Fig. 51 shows how the snap-latch and catch are fitted.

To close up the play-pen, the thumbscrews must be taken out, and these two frames closed inwards; then the two pairs of frames thus formed can be closed outwards, that is, to bring the two outer sides together. The top rails should

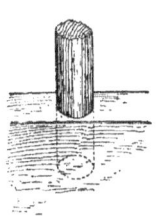
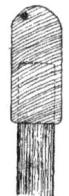

Fig. 38.—Play-pen Folded Up

Fig. 39.—Method of Fitting Bars into Rails

Fig. 40.—Section through Upper Rail

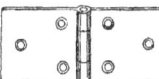

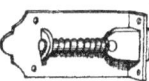

Fig. 41.   Fig. 43.   Fig. 44.   Fig. 45.   Fig. 46.

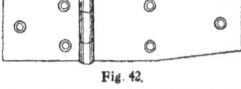
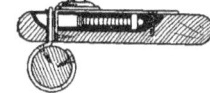

Fig. 42.

Figs. 41 to 46.—Metal Fittings

Fig. 51.—Section through Clamp and Bar at Latch

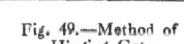

Fig. 52.—Plan of Pen Folded Up

Fig. 49.—Method of Hinging Gate

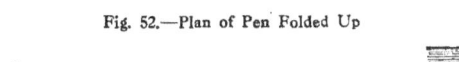

Fig. 50.—Plan of Portion of Upper Rail and Hinged Clamp at Closing of Gate

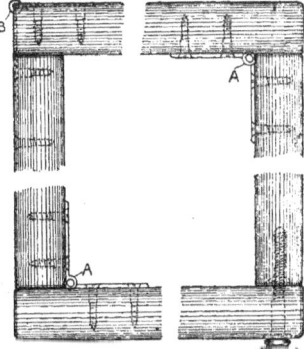

Fig. 48.—Showing Method of Hinging and Fixing Frames Together

Fig. 47.—Photograph of Snap-latch and Catch Fixed in Position

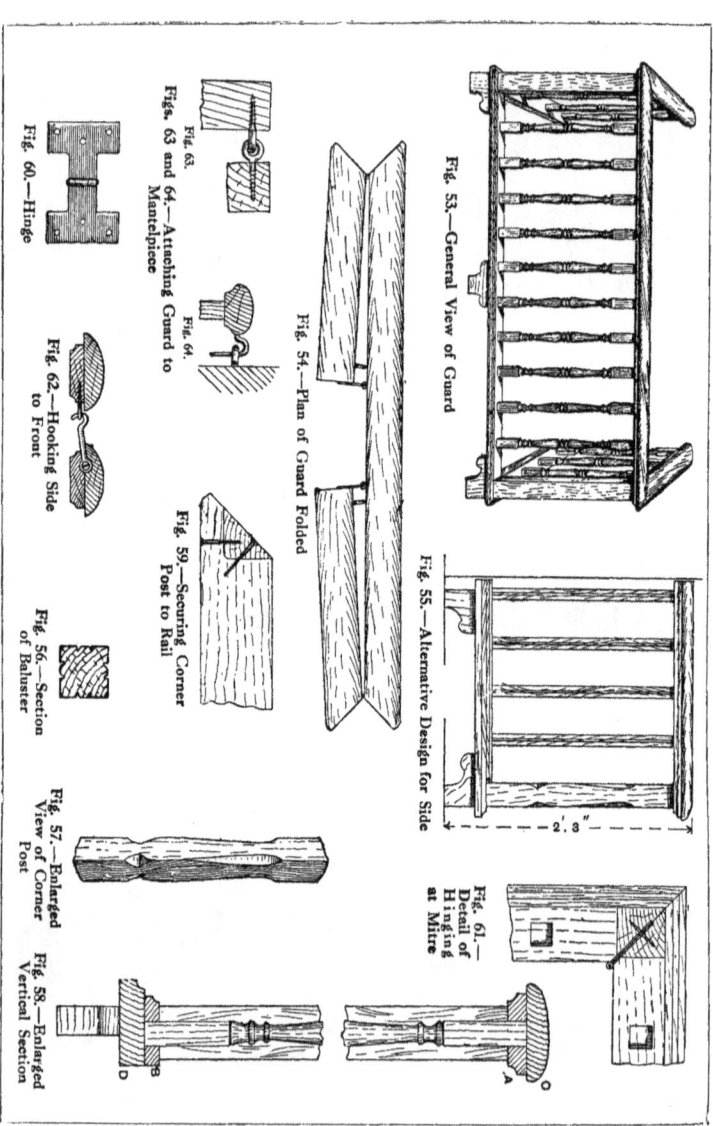

DOMESTIC WOODWARE

present the appearance shown by Fig. 52. The woodwork can be finished with french polish and spirit varnish.

FOLDING FIRE-GUARD IN WOOD

Although wood does not seem an ideal material for a fire-guard, yet by keeping to the dimensions given in the accompanying illustrations, the fire-guard will be a sufficient distance from the fire to avoid any danger from overheating. Fig. 53 is a general view of the guard, while Fig. 54 is a plan showing the side fences folded and hooked to the front rail of the fence. In Fig. 55 is given an elevation of the end fences, showing an alternative design. In Fig. 53 ordinary turned stair balusters are shown in conjunction with plain corner posts of stuff 2 in. square, while in Fig. 55 straight balusters 1 in. square in section and centre reeded, as shown in Fig. 56, are used; the corner posts are chamfered as indicated in Fig. 57, giving them a unique appearance.

Begin with the corner posts, cutting them 1 ft. 10 in. long from stuff to finish 2 in. square; next saw them through the diagonal longitudinally. Also prepare two lengths 4 ft. 6 in. long by $2\frac{3}{4}$ in. wide and $\frac{7}{8}$ in. thick, and four pieces of similar stuff 2 ft. 3 in. long for the sides. These lengths can be cramped together in pairs, marked off, bored, and the holes squared out to receive the balusters, which should fit them fairly tight. These battens are shown at A and B (Fig. 58). When the balusters are in position a capping C and a plinth D are attached to hide the flush ends of the balusters, and also to improve the finish. The half post is housed to the plinth batten D and B, and secured to D with screws, as shown in Fig. 59. The half post is also slightly reduced on its two right-angle faces at the top end, and is then housed to the batten A, while the cap piece C is carried over the top end and mitred, as shown in Fig. 54. The battens have a small cavetto mould worked on their edges; but, in the absence of a suitable moulding plane, an ordinary chamfer would do as well.

The two side fences are next treated in a similar way. The mitres should be adjusted to make the side fences lie at right angles with the front. Two pairs of special hinges (see Fig. 60) will be required. They are recessed to and screwed to the halves of the posts. The rivet of the hinge should stand out just clear of the inner angle of the top capping; the lower hinge should also be fixed in the same vertical plane with the top hinge, the method of fixing being clearly shown in Fig. 61. The side fences are retained in their folded position by an ordinary brass hook and eye (see Fig. 62). At the corner and centre of the plinth are fixed small shaped brackets or feet, 3 in. high by 6 in. long and 1 in. thick. The corner brackets are mitred at their angles of meeting, but are independent of each other in closing.

If the mantelpiece is constructed of wood, the method of attachment by hook and eye, as shown in Figs. 63 and 64, will be effectual. If the mantel is of stone, slate, or cast-iron, then the hook could be attached to the lower rail, and the eye screwed to the skirting boards; or the wall could be plugged to receive the eye, the hook being fixed to the top rail. The guard should be stained, and, when dry, rubbed with linseed oil.

WOODEN CURB FOR A FIREPLACE

The curb shown by Figs. 65 and 66 entails in its construction a certain amount of skill, but not so much that would make it too difficult for anyone who has a fair knowledge of woodwork. Alternate designs are shown in the sections (Figs. 67 and 68), and if desired the bevelled portion of the curb could be ornamented with carving.

The top, front, and bevelled portion are of hardwood $\frac{1}{4}$ in. thick, placed on the body of the curb to give it its design, thus rendering it easier to make than would be the case if it had to be worked out of the solid. The curb being made this way can be of yellow pine or red deal for the body. The latter is made as follows:— Take two pieces of wood, rough sizes, 3 ft. $8\frac{1}{2}$ in. by $4\frac{1}{2}$ in. by $2\frac{1}{8}$ in. respectively, the first for the front pieces, and the second for the two end pieces; plane and finish to 4¼ in. by 2 in. Before proceeding to bevel the pieces it is advisable to make the half-lap joints at the ends of each piece of wood (see Fig. 69). The size of the curb is given in Fig. 66; of course, the sizes may be adapted for any fireplace.

Now bevel each piece to the required angle as shown. This can be done best by drawing out full size the section as shown in Fig. 67, taking the measurements from the inside on the top to where the bevel begins on the front edge. Gauge a line along the top and front, join these on the end of each piece of wood, and this will show the amount of waste that is required to be planed off. When this is done, cut the two end pieces from the short piece, and make them the required length. Screw them together temporarily, and when they are true with each other, glue and screw together and work off the end pieces to the bevel of the front piece. The ¼-in. pieces of hardwood, oak, walnut, or mahogany, or any other wood to match the furniture of the room, may now be fixed. Put the bevel pieces on the end first, and finish these to the front bevel. Next the front piece, and plane the waste wood off flush to the top and front. Fix on the top pieces, mitre them at the corner, and then add the front and side pieces. In addition to gluing on the ¼-in. pieces, it is advisable to fix them with fine sprigs or needle points to make them secure.

To give a nice finish, as well as to protect the wood from the fire, it is necessary to line the inside of the curb with sheet brass or copper, which may be finished in antique repoussé style.

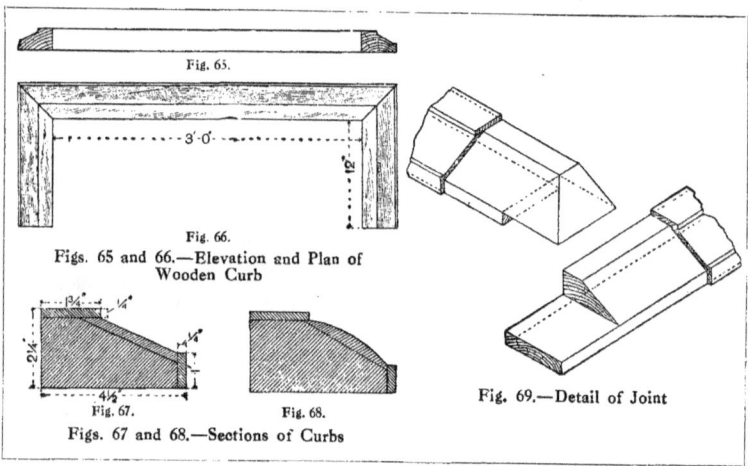

Fig. 65.

Fig. 66.

Figs. 65 and 66.—Elevation and Plan of Wooden Curb

Fig. 67.   Fig. 68.

Figs. 67 and 68.—Sections of Curbs

Fig. 69.—Detail of Joint

BOX PEDESTAL FOR BOOT CLEANING

An article which serves as a receptacle for brushes, etc., and at the same time to rest the foot upon when cleaning a boot is shown by Figs. 70 and 71. It can be made by anyone who is handy with tools, and will be appreciated by members of the household.

The size may be as required; but the one shown is 1 ft. 3 in. high by 1 ft. 2 in. square. A suitable wood is common whitewood of ⅞-in. thickness, although "spruce shelving" or any other deal boards would do. The whitewood has

DOMESTIC WOODWARE

Fig. 70.—Box Pedestal for Boot Cleaning

the advantage of being obtainable in wide boards, which saves jointing, besides being more solid than deal and nearly as cheap, and makes a better article. A board 9 ft. long by 1 ft. wide is more than enough, and will allow for working out some of the knots that might be in the board. Two of the sides must be cut 1 ft. 1 in. long, and two $11\frac{1}{4}$ in. long, all 1 ft. wide. When smoothed and squared up they may be nailed together with $2\frac{1}{2}$-in. oval wire nails. It is best to drive one or two nails first straight, to fix them exact, then "skew" the other nails, as in Fig. 72, for which the wood should be pierced with a suitable bradawl. Whilst being nailed, it should be observed that the box is keeping square, and then the nails may be punched a little below the surface.

The bottom will require a 1 in. wide strip nailed on to make it 1 ft. 1 in. square, and it may be secured with 2-in. wire nails, which need not be "skewed" as they do not go into the end-grain wood. The lid is the same as the bottom, but slightly larger, to overhang about $\frac{1}{8}$ in. all round when it is fixed with 2-in. butt hinges. On the edges of the lid a half-round nosing of $1\frac{1}{4}$-in. by $\frac{1}{2}$-in. section, is fixed with nails ($1\frac{1}{2}$-in. ovals); but at the hinged edge it must be no wider than the thickness of the top, as shown at A in Fig. 73, where also is shown the bottom edged with the half-round slips, and the top covered with thick linoleum; but this is not put on until the painting is done. The slips are mitred at the corners and rounded, as in Fig. 74.

In Fig. 73 is also seen drawer knobs put on as feet; also the handles made from pieces of wood 7 in. by $1\frac{1}{2}$ in. by 1 in. They are simply bevelled off at the ends and top edge, and cut out on the innerside corner as a slot for the fingers (*see* Figs. 75 and 76), and are fixed with a screw and two sprigs at each end. About 4 in. from the top is a loose shelf B (Fig. 73), with a hole in the centre for lifting it out. It rests on triangular blocks fixed at each corner with a screw, as at C. *See also* Fig. 77, which also shows the outer corner well rounded off. The box may be painted green outside and white inside, all the nail holes being filled with putty after the first coat is dry. A piece of plain green thick linoleum is fixed

Fig. 71.—Pedestal Open

on after the second coat, with fine wire nails round the edges to fix it down close. Two more coats may be given, going over the linoleum as well, especially round the edges. Plenty of time should be allowed for the paint to get dry and hard.

DUSTLESS CINDER-SIFTER

Fig. 78 shows a dustless sifter which can be easily made and operated, and by the use of which a considerable saving will be effected.

The sifter has an outer box, into which the sifter proper fits and works on two runners screwed to the sides. A cover having overhanging edges fits over the box and the sifter is worked by a handle projecting through the box. The ashes are placed in the sifter, the cover is closed, and a few backward and forward movements of the handle complete the sifting operation. The cover should not be removed for a few seconds to allow the dust to settle. The sifter shown is of handy dimensions, but a larger or smaller size can easily be made from the instructions. The selection of wood is of no account, as almost any kind ¾ in. thick will be suitable; even the wood from an old packing box could be used.

The outer box is nailed together to the dimensions given in Figs. 79 and 80, the ends fitting within the sides, and the bottom fitting over the sides and ends. The runners (see Figs. 79 and 80) on which the sifter works are 1 in. deep by ¼ in. thick, screwed to the sides of the box in the position shown in Fig. 81. The cover (Fig. 82) is cut slightly larger than the box, say a full ⅛ in. in both length and breadth, while the overhanging edges are 2½ in. deep by ½ in. thick, mitred at the corners and nailed in position.

The sifter is made to the dimensions given in Fig. 83. The ends fit within the sides, and the sides and ends are nailed together. For the bottom of the sifter a piece of meshed wire having about ½-in. meshes will be required. It should be ¾ in. larger all round than the opening in the sifter. The edges are turned over, and the wire is fixed to the sifter with wood fillets nailed in position, as shown in Fig. 84. The sifter should work freely in the box, and it is moved by an iron handle

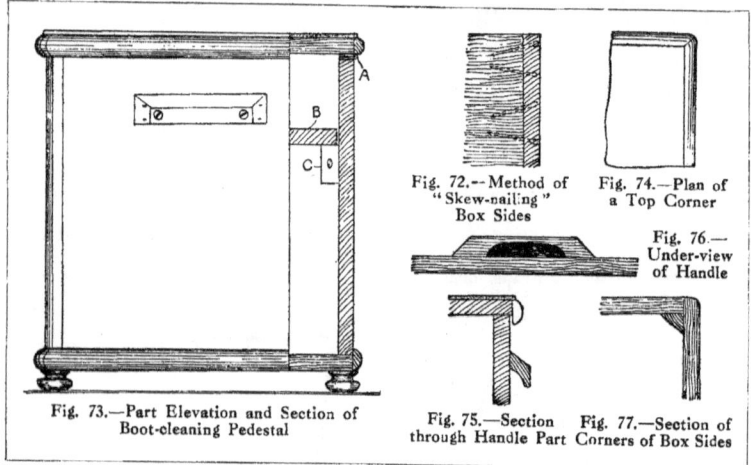

Fig. 73.—Part Elevation and Section of Boot-cleaning Pedestal

Fig. 72.—Method of "Skew-nailing" Box Sides

Fig. 74.—Plan of a Top Corner

Fig. 75.—Section through Handle Part

Fig. 76.—Under-view of Handle

Fig. 77.—Section of Corners of Box Sides

DOMESTIC WOODWARE

similar to that shown by Fig. 85. This handle should be of ⅜-in. round iron, having a foot at one end provided with two screw holes for fixing to the sifter, and a bow at the other end. A notch must be cut in one end of the box to allow the handle to work, and also in the cover.

An iron handle could be fitted to the cover, as shown in Fig. 82, and two handles (Fig. 86) could be fitted to the sides of the box to enable it to be moved more easily.

Fig. 78.—Dustless Cinder-sifter

A couple of coats of paint will make the sifter more durable.

FIRELESS COOKER

A fireless cooker or hay-box is shown complete by Fig. 87. It consists of a wood box which is built up with four sides and a bottom, while a cover is hinged to the top edge of one side. The cooker must be fitted with a suitable metal stew-pan, and this is packed in hay, as shown in Fig. 88, while a hay-stuffed cushion is made to fit above the stew-pan.

The cooker as shown in the illustrations is made up with a front and back A and B, which are framed up as shown in Fig. 90. The framework in each case consists of four rails which are 1 ft. long by 2 in. wide by ¾ in. thick, and are framed together with half-lapped joints similar to that shown by Fig. 91. The half-lapped joints will not be very difficult to cut. They should be marked off with a square and marking gauge, and cut with a tenon saw ; while fixing them together they should be secured with glue and a couple of nails or screws. The front and back frames are lined on the inside with ¼-in. boards, which are nailed to the framework. For this purpose there is nothing better than ply-wood.

The front and back must now be connected with two sides C (Fig. 89), each 1 ft. 2 in. long by 1 ft. deep by ½ in. thick of ply-wood, and they are nailed or screwed to the side rails of the front and back framework. The bottom D may also be of ply-wood, and it is 1 ft. 2 in. long by 1 ft. 1 in. wide by ½ in. thick, nailed or screwed to the bottom edges of the front, back, and sides. Two handles E are arranged at the front and back as shown in the illustrations. These handles should be 1 ft. 1 in. long by 1 in. deep by ½ in. thick, and they are simply nailed or screwed in position. The cover F is framed together, as shown in Fig. 92, and is covered on the inside with a ¼-in. panel in a similar manner to the front and back. The side rails of the framework are 1 ft. 2 in. long by 2 in. wide by ¾ in. thick, and the top and bottom rails are 1 ft. 1 in. long by 2 in. wide by ¾ in. thick. The rails are half-lapped and screwed or nailed together, as shown by Fig. 91, while the panel is simply nailed or screwed to the framework. The cover is hinged to the back B with a pair of 2-in. butt hinges, and a catch similar to that shown by Fig. 94 is arranged at the front to secure the cover.

The hay-stuffed cushion which is fitted to the upper portion of the interior of the cooker should be about 4 in. deep, and may be made up as shown by Fig. 93. For the top of the cushion cut a piece of wood 1 ft. square by ½ in. thick, so that it will fit between the sides of the cooker. The hay stuffing is held in place with a linen

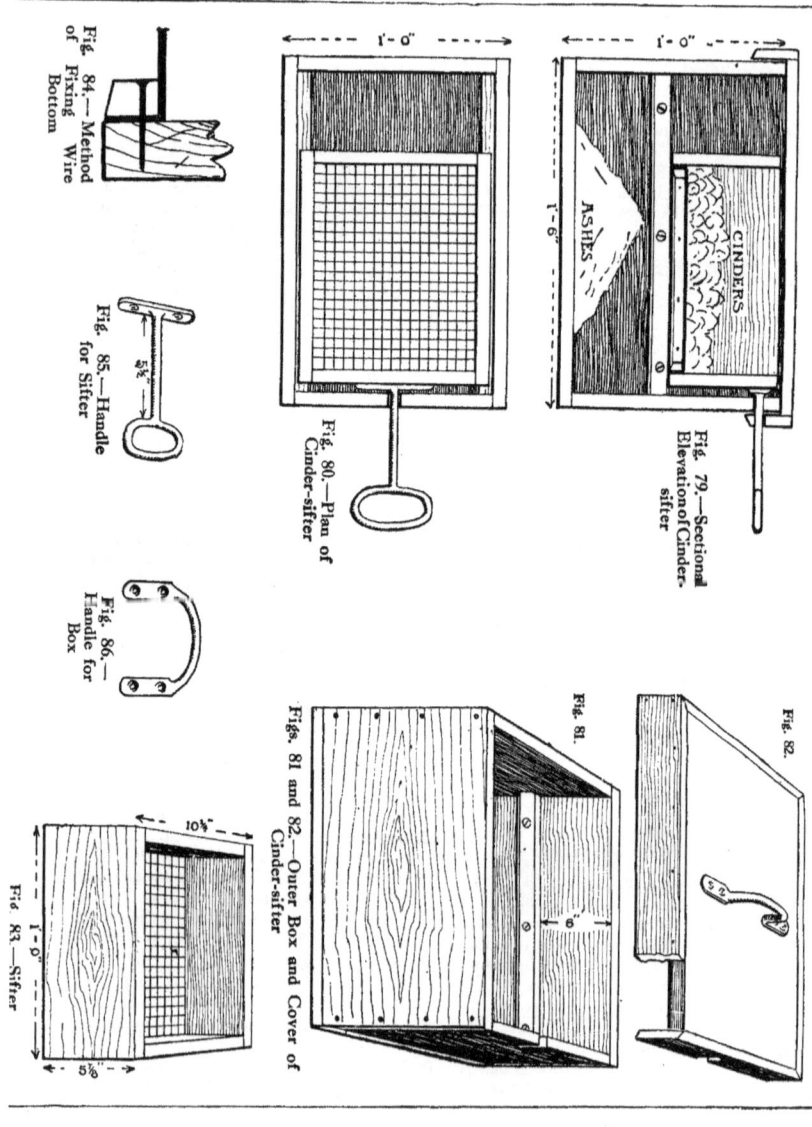

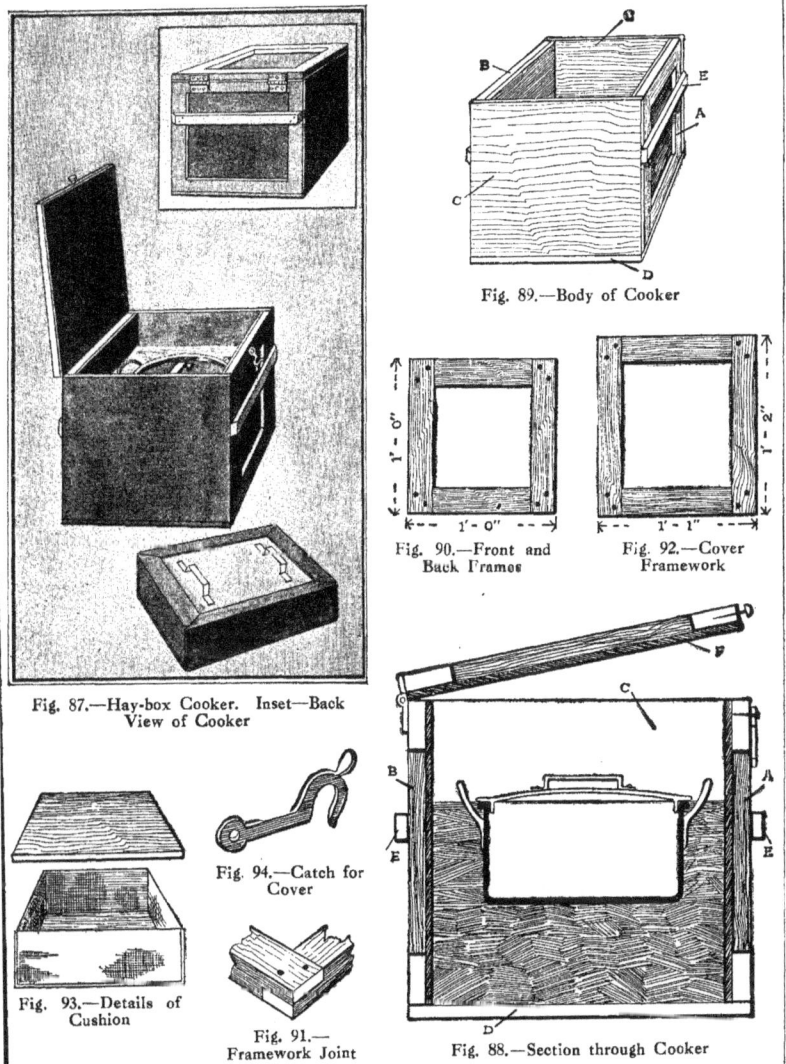

Fig. 89.—Body of Cooker

Fig. 90.—Front and Back Frames

Fig. 92.—Cover Framework

Fig. 87.—Hay-box Cooker. Inset—Back View of Cooker

Fig. 94.—Catch for Cover

Fig. 93.—Details of Cushion

Fig. 91.—Framework Joint

Fig. 88.—Section through Cooker

covering, which is made up in the form shown in Fig. 93, and is nailed to the upper face of the board which forms the top of the cushion. Two tape handles could be arranged on this board, as shown in Fig. 87. The stew-pan which should be used in the

Fig. 95.—Stew-pan for Cooker

cooker should be similar to that shown by Fig. 95. It should be of enamel-ware or, better still, aluminium, and should be 2-qt. size. The stew-pan is arranged in the cooker, as shown in Fig. 88, and is packed in hay, which should be stuffed fairly tight round the pan. The pan is placed so that when the cushion is fitted over the pan, and the cover is closed, the cushion will fit tightly on the pan.

The method of using the cooker is no doubt well known. The stew-pan containing the food to be cooked is simply brought to the boil on the gas or fire, and is then placed in the hay-box cooker. The time required to cook in this way will, of course, vary with the nature of the food being treated ; but the great saving in fuel will be very evident to everyone. The cooker, when complete, could be stained and varnished.

WOODEN BATH

At first sight, the advantage of using wood as a material for a bath may appear somewhat doubtful ; but in some cases there certainly are advantages, though there is no economy as regards first cost. Wood is lighter as regards weight than iron, and a bath of wood can be removed or even stood on end out of the way when not in use. It is stronger and more durable than zinc, and has the same advantage over this as over iron, while with both zinc and iron there is the question of paint or enamel ; but with the wood neither need be used.

The length and width here given will be found sufficient for all purposes; but these dimensions may be reduced to a certain extent to suit. The depth may be anything from 12 in. to 15 in., the latter being preferable, as with this depth the water is not so liable to splash over.

Timber of the best must be used ; no knots or shakes must be allowed, and the sides, ends and bottom must each consist of one piece only.

The construction is simple, but good work must be put in or the joints will not be water-tight. The sides of the bath project 1 in. beyond the ends, and are trenched to take the latter, the trenches being made the full width to take the ends. The latter should each be marked into its place and numbered, thus ensuring a perfect fit, which cannot be certain if done in any other way. The subject of determining and setting out bevels is adequately treated in a later chapter.

The trenches need not be more than a ¼ in. deep; but they must be equal throughout, and in cutting them the marks must be left on the wood, so that the ends will drive in tightly. When the trenches are finished, the four parts can be fitted together, and the whole planed off level at what will be the bottom of the bath, after which the grooves can be made for the tongues which fit into the bath bottom (Fig. 101) and the sides (and ends).

As may be seen in the sections (Figs. 97 and 99), the grooves must not be made parallel with the sides of the boards, but at right angles to the edges after these have been planed off as previously instructed, otherwise the tongues could not fit in tightly. Fig. 98 shows how the tongues should fit when the bath is together, and Fig. 100 shows one of the sides with the trenches made and the grooves in the edge ready to receive the tongue.

All the grooves made, the sides and ends may be put together permanently, fixing them with brass screws inserted not more than 3 in. between.

When fitting the tongues into the groove fit these in the sides first, then trench the side tongues, as in Fig. 98, so that the

DOMESTIC WOODWARE

end tongues will fit into them tightly as shown.

The trenches in the bottom should be set out by measurement, and must be made as true as possible, so that the bottom will fit on the tongues without any need for easement, but just friction tight. The bottom will be fixed on with brass screws in the same way as the sides were fixed to the ends, and if the trenching has been done truly, the joints should

Nothing has been said as regards putting anything in the joints to make them watertight, the whole of the joints being simply wood to wood, and depending on the close fitting for their water-tight qualities. The writer considers that this is all that is required, and has no hesitation in stating that if done properly the bath will come up to expectations. At the same time, if any readers feel that they would prefer to use some safeguard in the joints, the

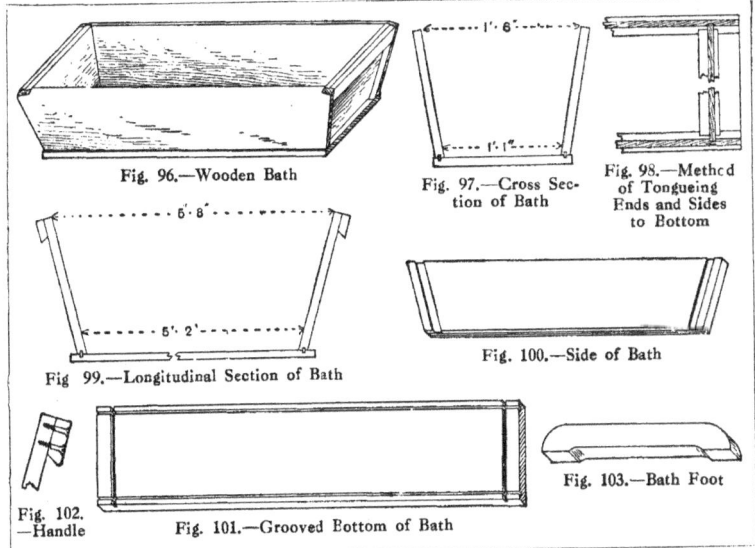

Fig. 96.—Wooden Bath
Fig. 97.—Cross Section of Bath
Fig. 98.—Method of Tongueing Ends and Sides to Bottom
Fig. 99.—Longitudinal Section of Bath
Fig. 100.—Side of Bath
Fig. 102.—Handle
Fig. 101.—Grooved Bottom of Bath
Fig. 103.—Bath Foot

come up closely without any trouble, and without need for any undue force.

Supplementary pieces to form handles should be screwed to the ends of the bath, level with the top edges, as shown in Figs. 96, 99, and 102. The end boards are cut off level with the handles as shown in Fig. 96.

The finished bath could be left as it is, and the bottom would rest on the floor, but the better way is to provide it with two feet shaped as Fig. 103, and screwed on underneath from the outside.

following are suitable methods that may be used; but the plain joints have stood the test satisfactorily in every way. One method of making joints water-tight is to paint them before putting together with thick white-lead paint; if this is done the paint must be spread very evenly and smoothly, otherwise the remedy will be far from satisfactory, and instead of preventing the paint will cause leakage. Another method is to batter the edges of the boards before making the joints, hammering a groove as it were along them, afterwards planing the wood away until the surface is level again. The theory of this method is that the battering compresses the wood, which afterwards returns to its original position, thus tightening up the joint, especially under the influence of water. This sounds very probable in theory, but it does not always work out successfully in practice.

Yet another method of ensuring the joints against leakage is to batter along the edges as mentioned, and then to lay a dried rush (such as are used for chair bottoms) along the groove just formed. The idea is that not only will the wood swell out to its original size, but the rush will expand when it becomes wet, and effectively stop any leakage.

One thing which may be mentioned as being certain, no matter if the bath is made water-tight by means of good joints or by faking, if it is allowed to stand empty for any length of time it will leak. The remedy is to always keep a little water in the bath; or if it is necessary that this should be stowed away on end, then it should be damped occasionally to prevent shrinkage.

It is not advisable to fix a waste pipe for emptying purposes; this can always be done by the use of an indiarubber tube, used as a siphon.

Domestic Racks

STANDING PLATE-RACK

FOR the plate-rack illustrated by Figs. 1 to 3 good red deal should be used. The dimensions given are for one of a useful size, but these can be varied to meet requirements. For the rails and stiles of the framework, wood $1\frac{1}{4}$ in. thick and $1\frac{1}{4}$ in. or $1\frac{1}{2}$ in. wide will be suitable, except for the two top rails at the ends, which should be twice the breadth of the other rails, so as to allow the tenons to pass over each other, as shown in Fig. 4. The lengths of the various parts and the number of pieces required can be obtained from the illustrations.

First saw off the pieces about $\frac{1}{2}$ in.

Fig. 1.—Perspective View of Plate-rack

longer than the finished lengths, and plane the face side and face edges square. Then gauge them to thickness and breadth, and plane. Next set out and make the mortise-and-tenon joints, as shown in Fig. 4. Then set out the centres of the holes for the bars. The distance apart of the centres for the plate portion as preferred; the two middle rails should be bored right through. Care must be taken to ensure that these

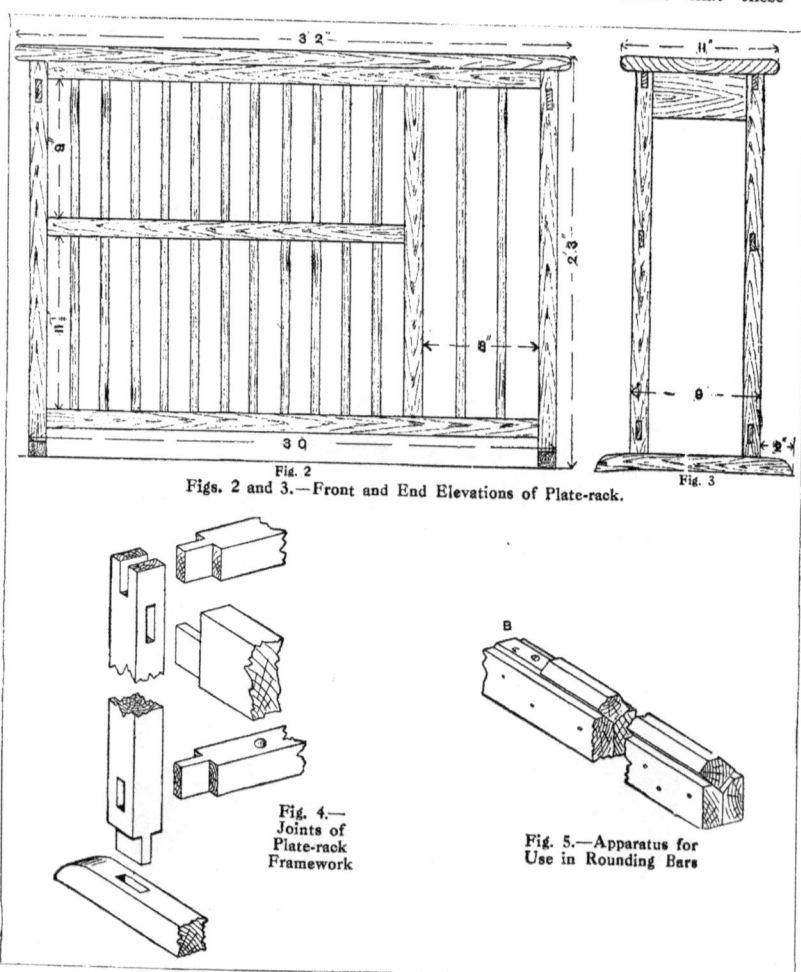

Figs. 2 and 3.—Front and End Elevations of Plate-rack.

Fig. 4.—Joints of Plate-rack Framework

Fig. 5.—Apparatus for Use in Rounding Bars

should be about 2 in., and for the dish part about 3 in. The holes can next be bored right through or partially, holes are bored as true as possible with a twist bit.

The bars should be about $\frac{9}{16}$ in. in

DOMESTIC RACKS

diameter, and can be prepared by hand as follows : Cut strips of wood about ¾ in. square, and of the full length required, and plane up to ⅝ in. square. Then plane off each corner so as to form an octagon in section, and next plane the resultant corners so as to form sixteen sides. The strips can then be made almost round with a hollow or bead plane. The bars can be finished with glass-paper. A simple apparatus for holding the bars whilst planing is shown by Fig. 5. It is made by chamfering one edge of two pieces of wood and nailing them together as shown. A piece of wood should be nailed at one end to form a stop as shown at B.

The plate-rack should now be fitted together and the tenons wedged into the mortises or fastened with hardwood pins. The joints should be painted with a little white-lead and red-lead mixed with a little oil before fastening together ; this preserves the joints and is better than glue. Any projecting parts of the joints should be smoothed off and the two parts connected to the feet pieces and top rails. The top is made of a 1-in. board, with the edges rounded as shown in Fig. 1 ; it should be secured to the top rails by means of a few nails or screws.

HANGING PLATE-RACK

The plate-rack or drainer shown by Fig. 6 is made almost entirely of ½-in. wood, and holds three dozen plates in three sizes. A special place has not been made for dishes, but the top is made full, so that if desired they can rest on it, leaning against the wall, and prevented from slipping by means of a small bead or fillet fixed along the front.

The two side pieces (Fig. 8) should be prepared first, the curved bottoms being cut out with a bow-saw, and finished with a spokeshave. To form the bars or uprights A (Figs. 7 and 10) which keep the plates in their places, rip two boards, 2 ft. 8½ in. by 11 in. by ¼ in., each into eleven equal strips, which must then be planed down to ¾ in. wide. The four thicker horizontal pieces are prepared about 1 in. thick and exactly 2 ft. 1 in. long ; three of them are 1¼ in. wide, as at B in Fig. 9, and the fourth is 2¼ in., as at

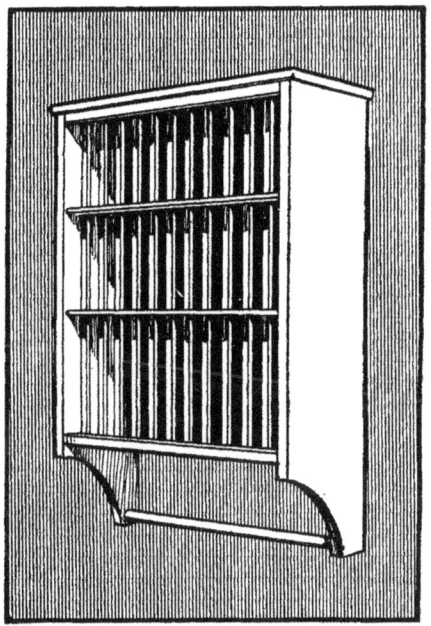

Fig. 6.—Hanging Plate-rack

c in the same figure. The two bottom pieces should each have the top inside corner slightly bevelled off. Take two of the narrower pieces, and, starting 1⅜ in. from one end, screw at even distances along them eleven of the ¾-in. strips, with their ends flush with the top piece, and lapped over the other slightly. Before screwing on the eleven other strips slightly bevel one edge of the horizontal pieces, and so compensate for the slight rake of the set of upright pieces nearer the wall.

Now get out the thinner horizontal strips, one D 3 in. wide, one E 2⅜ in., and two F 1 in. wide, all as in Fig. 9. Slightly bevel off the inside top corners, and fasten with brads and screws to the upright pieces. There are now two grids, which can be connected by attaching the four battens, ¾ in. thick, which support them in position, two at each end, as at G in which method the screw-heads are hidden, although this is rather awkward to do. A piece of broom-handle will serve for the dishcloth rod shown at the bottom.

IMPROVED PLATE-RACK

A rack of larger dimensions that will contain all the table crockery-ware is

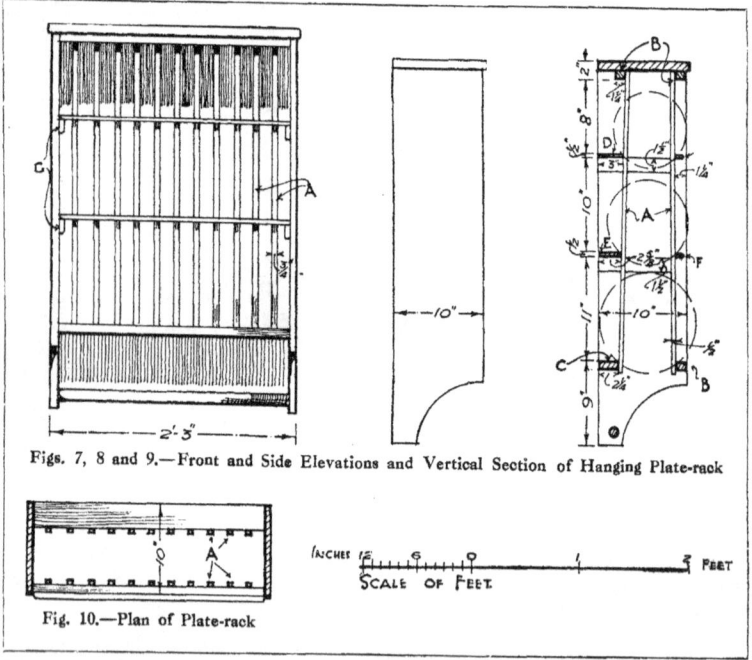

Figs. 7, 8 and 9.—Front and Side Elevations and Vertical Section of Hanging Plate-rack

Fig. 10.—Plan of Plate-rack

Fig. 7. Place the double grid on the floor, resting it on one end; lay one side piece carefully in its place on top, set off screw-holes accurately, and from the outside screw the battens in position; also put screws into the ends of the thick horizontal pieces. Turn it over, and, if all is square, screw on the other side in the same manner. It is quite possible to screw the battens on from the inside, by shown in Fig. 11. It is constructed to receive the usual plates and dishes in the upper part of the rack, and to receive all cups, saucers, basins, and jugs in the lower rack. The complete rack is a full average size, and in most cases will prove sufficiently large enough for family use.

The most suitable material to use is yellow deal; but white deal can be used if free from knots. The outside dimensions are 2 ft. 8 in. high, 2 ft. 10 in. wide, and the space between the front and back frames is 5½ in. It will be seen that the lower rack is much wider than 5½ in., because the space behind the frames is small plates if required. This bar also has small grooves cut in its corner to prevent the smaller plates slipping sidewise. The lower rack is a crate-like arrangement. The fillets are nailed on

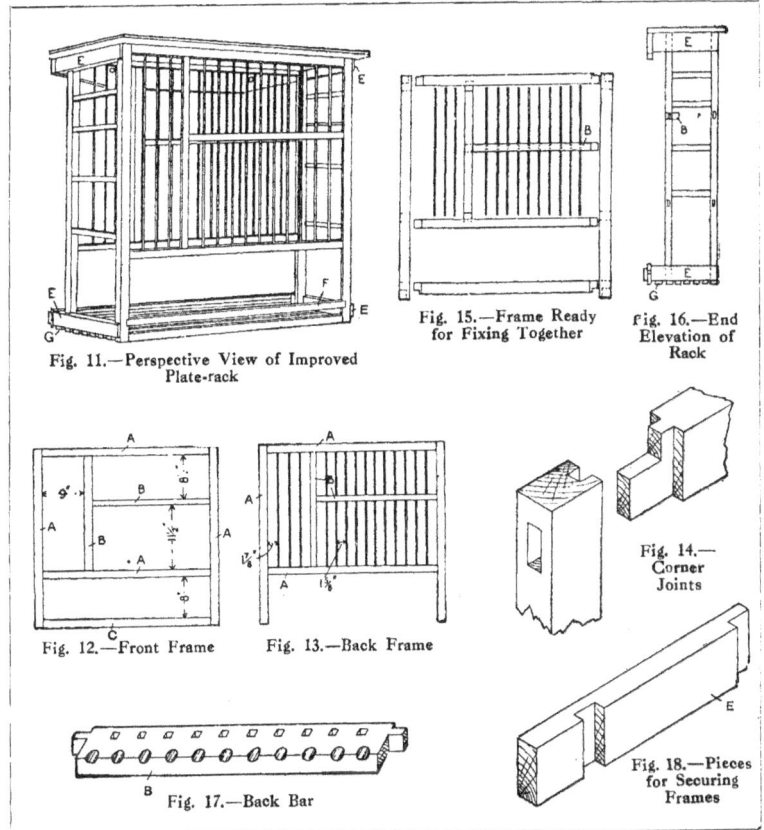

Fig. 11.—Perspective View of Improved Plate-rack

Fig. 12.—Front Frame

Fig. 13.—Back Frame

Fig. 14.—Corner Joints

Fig. 15.—Frame Ready for Fixing Together

Fig. 16.—End Elevation of Rack

Fig. 17.—Back Bar

Fig. 18.—Pieces for Securing Frames

utilised, which gives a width of 8 in. or more. The length of the lower part is 2 ft. 10 in., being the same as the width of the rack. A wide bar is arranged on the back frame, on the part that receives the small plates, so as to hold the very with ½-in. spaces, which are sufficient to allow the saucers to be placed in vertically. Such articles as cups, basins, and jugs should be racked in a tilted position for better drainage, so the spaces between the fillets enable one to place them in at random without danger of breakage through slipping.

Figs. 12 and 13 show the front and back frames respectively. The bars and posts A are finished 1¼ in. wide, B is 1 in. wide, and the front bottom bar C is 1½ in. wide. All these bars are made of 1-in. material, so that when the frames are finished they are ⅞ in. thick. The bar B on the back frame is finished 2 in. wide and 1 in. thick for the smaller plates. It will be noticed there is not a lower bar on the back frame, like C on the front one. All the joints are wedged mortise-and-tenon, with tenons ⅜ in. thick. The corner joints are haunched, as shown in Fig. 14. Round rods ½ in. in diameter can be obtained for the plate bars; or ½ in. square bars can be made and fixed with a little extra trouble.

When ready for gluing together, the plate bars should first be driven into the horizontal bars B. The middle vertical posts are then glued and wedged on square and the ends of the tenons smoothed off before the top and bottom rails are fixed. Finally the outer posts complete the framing. Fig. 15 shows this method of fixing. The end view of the rack is shown in Fig. 16. The back bar B is shown to project; the notches are cut as in Fig. 17. The four pieces E are grooved to fit over the outside posts and to project 2 in. at the back to give clearance for the plates. These are of 2¼-in. by 1-in. material, and grooved ½ in. deep, as in Fig. 18. They are then secured with nails, so as to be flush with the top and bottom of the frames. The back board, with two holes for supporting the rack, is 3 in. by ¾ in. and nailed on the back ends of the top pieces. Two fillets for the lower rack, 1¼ in. by ⅝ in., are nailed on to the back ends of the lower pieces, and fillets of the same material on the bottom. The front fillet F (Fig. 11) should be neatly let in flush and bradded. The fillets should be arranged so as not to have any corroding corners. The fillets G (Figs. 11 and 16) are fixed away from the side pieces with this object. Two small pieces ⅜ in. thick are nailed at the back of the lower rack so that the fillets shall clear the wall.

Fig. 19.—Simple Boot and Shoe Rack

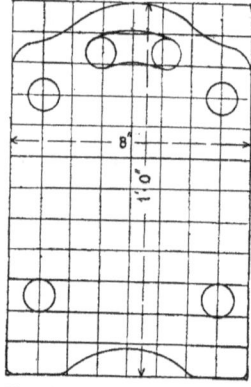

Fig. 20.—Method of Setting-out Rack Ends

The covering board for the top is made of ½-in. material, and overhangs the rack a trifle at the ends and front.

BOOT AND SHOE RACKS

Fig. 19 shows a rack of very simple construction. It is made in oak of 1-in. thickness. For the two end pieces a pattern may be drawn on stiff paper, ruling it into 1 in. squares, as in Fig. 20. It can then be cut out to the shape to mark on to the wood. The hand-holes are made by boring two holes with a 1-in. centre-bit and cutting through with a bow-saw. The rail-holes are ⅜ in. deep.

The rails may be any length required; in the present case they are 2 ft. 9 in. with the hand-planes and smoothed up with glasspaper. In smoothing up the

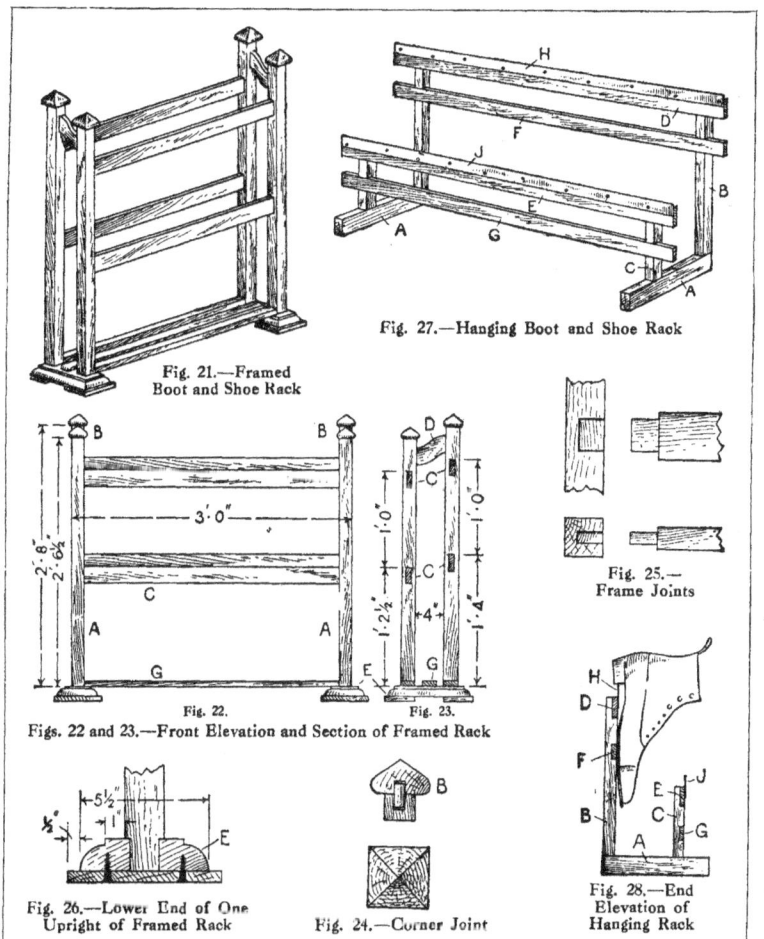

Fig. 21.—Framed Boot and Shoe Rack

Fig. 27.—Hanging Boot and Shoe Rack

Figs. 22 and 23.—Front Elevation and Section of Framed Rack

Fig. 25.—Frame Joints

Fig. 26.—Lower End of One Upright of Framed Rack

Fig. 24.—Corner Joint

Fig. 28.—End Elevation of Hanging Rack

They are first cut 1 in. square, and marked on each end with the compasses to 1 in. diameter; then they are rounded end boards all the square corners are rounded off. The rail ends are tight-fitting in the holes and well glued in.

378 THE PRACTICAL WOODWORKER

Care should be taken to see that the rack is square and level. When the glue is set, the oak may be stained with a solution of vandyke brown in soda and water. This raises the grain and makes it rough, so it requires another rub down with No. 1 glasspaper. Then it should be rubbed over with linseed oil and finished with french polish.

The boot and shoe rack shown by Fig. 21 should be made of oak, fumed or stained a golden brown colour, and wax-polished. If made of soft wood, such as pitchpine, it should be varnished. Figs. 22 and 23 are front elevation and section respectively, and if made to the dimensions shown it will be suitable for all ordinary requirements and be found compact and convenient.

The four posts A (Fig. 22) are 1½ in. square, and have on the top a square finial B secured by a dowel, as shown in Fig. 24. The rails C, to finish 2 in. wide by ¾ in. thick, are fixed to the posts A, as shown in Fig. 25. The curved end rails D (Fig. 23) are also 2 in. wide by ¾ in. thick, and are secured to the posts A with two small dowels in each end; or they could be secured by a joint similar to that shown in Fig. 25. The lower ends of the posts A are secured to the feet E, as shown in Fig. 26, the end of each being reduced to 1 in. square, and glued and wedged. The feet E 1¼ in. thick, and of the dimensions given, are moulded on all four edges, the pieces F being separate, and screwed to the underside as shown. The three bottom rails G are 1½ in. wide by ⅝ in. thick, the two outside ones being flush on both edges with the posts A, as shown in Fig. 23. The centre rail is 3 in. longer than the outside ones, and finishes level with the outside of the posts A, as shown in Fig. 21; the end of this rail should be rounded as shown. They are all secured to the feet E with screws driven from the underside.

Figs. 27 and 28 show a rack of entirely different design to those previously described.

Prepare two pieces of wood 9 in. by 2 in. by 1 in. for the feet A. At one end of each foot fasten an upright B of 1-in. stuff, 1 ft. 4 in. high. Then 5 in. nearer the front of each foot fasten two other uprights C 9 in. long. These four uprights may be screwed or nailed to the feet, or they may be halved on as shown. Connect the uprights of one foot to the uprights of the other foot by pieces D and E of ½-in. stuff, 2 in. wide and 2 ft. 6 in. long. Two inches below, and parallel to D and E, rails F and G must be fastened to the uprights, against which the sides of the boots rest when hanging in position. These rails should measure ½ in. by 1 in. by 2 ft. 6 in. Along the upper part of the face of each top rail screw or tack strips of zinc H and J 1½ in. wide. This zinc must project at least ¼ in. above the upper edge of the wood. A piece of old zinc from a roof answers admirably. The success or failure of the rack depends to a large extent on this strip of metal, the edge of which takes a grip of the leather in a manner far superior to any wooden edge.

The rack described will accommodate twelve pairs of boots or shoes.

Pigeon Cote and Rabbit Hutches

SMALL PIGEON COTE

THE photograph, Fig. 1, shows a simple design for an eight-pair pigeon cote, and the following description gives the method of its construction. Fig. 2 is an elevation. Vertical and horizontal sections with underneath plan are given in Figs. 3, 4 and 6 respectively.

The base A (Fig. 5) should be constructed first, of boarding 1¼ in. thick, each piece being 2 ft. 8 in. long and tongued and grooved together, as shown by Fig. 11, the whole of the base being worked to finish 2 ft. 8 in. square. In fitting these pieces together it will be advisable to consider how they are likely to warp afterwards, and arrange them in such a manner that the warp of one piece will counterbalance the warp of the other. On looking at the ends of the boarding the "annular rings" will be clearly seen as marked on Fig. 15. To minimise the warping, fit these together with the annular rings showing alternately alike as in Fig. 11. Having fitted the base piece together, mark on the position of groove B (Fig. 5), 1 in. wide, where the sides of the cote fit into the same. The outside line of the groove should finish 4 in. from the edge of the base all round, making a square of 2 ft. The boards may now be taken apart and each grooved separately ½ in. deep, using a chisel, and afterwards fitted together as before and nailed to the ledges C, which are 3 in. wide, 1 in. thick, and 2 ft. 5 in. long (see Fig. 12), with chamfered edges as shown on the enlarged section.

The sides of the cote are fitted with tongued-and-grooved boarding set slanting to finish 2 ft. square at the base and 1 ft. 8 in. square at the top. These may be butted together at the angles or rebated, as shown in Fig. 14. The latter joint is preferable to the former, which is liable to gape if the wood shrinks. The pigeon holes are cut out of the middle piece of each side, and should be not less than 3¾ in. wide. Fig. 19 shows a side complete, nailed to the battens D, 2 in. by ¾ in., and E, 1½ in. by ½ in. The angle jointing of these battens is shown externally by Fig. 20 and internally by Fig. 8. Fig. 18 shows the jointing of the partitions where they intersect. The ¾-in floor division is nailed to the battens D, and the ceiling piece to the top of the sides all round, projecting as shown 4 in. beyond the top edge.

The roofing ribs are shown by G and H (Figs. 16 and 17), and can be cut out of one piece 8½ in. by 2 in. by 3 ft. 1 in. Fig.10 shows these ribs fixed diagonally across the ceiling F with the tilting fillets J in position. These fillets should also be cut out of one piece of wood, the best method being as follows : Take a piece of wood 3½ in. by 2 in. and about 4 ft. 3 in. long, and halve it by cutting it along one of its diagonals, as in Fig. 21. This will give an angle of 30°, which is to be the pitch of the roof. Each piece should now be cut in half, and the ends cut across to mitre with the ribs. The fillets are now ready to be fixed to the ceiling F as indicated on the roof plan and the enlarged section, which show their edges finishing about ½ in. from the edge and parallel with the sides of the ceiling.

Fig. 1.—General View of Pigeon Cote

Having nailed up the ribs and tilting fillets to the ceiling F, plane off the top edges of the ribs and the ceiling F to the angle necessary to form a mitre joint with the splayed edges of the roof boarding.

The roof will now look as in Fig. 10, and is ready for the boarding, which may be cut out of a piece 14 ft. 3 in. long by 9 in. wide by ¾ in. thick into the finished shapes (see Fig. 13). The pieces M form the top of the roof and pieces K the lower part (see Fig. 7). In fitting these to the ribs G and H care should be taken to splay them so that they will mitre correctly with the splayed ribs as before mentioned, before nailing to the ribs, fillet, etc. The finial N is turned out of a 4-in. by 4-in. piece, the base being square and cut down to 3 in. by 3 in., and fixed on the apex of the roof over the felt. To do this it will be necessary to cut off the apex of the roof as shown on the enlarged section. Three stages of the construction of the roof are shown in Fig. 5.

The roofing felt is cut in four triangles, and is tacked on with the lower edges overlapping the sides of the cote to form a drip for the rainwater. The angles are covered with a strip 3 in. wide tacked down as shown on the roof plan.

Fig. 9 shows the pigeon rest O in perspective. This is 4 in. wide. It runs all round the cote, mitreing at the angles as shown, and is supported on eight brackets P and fillets Q. The ornamental brackets R (Fig. 21) are screwed on immediately over and central with the brackets P, and should be cut out of a 3-in. by 1¼-in. by 3-in. piece. This completes the construction of the pigeon cote, leaving to be considered the post and the method of fixing the cote to it.

The post is 4 in. by 4 in. on plan and about 10 ft. long. The corbel pieces S are each 3 ft. long and halved where they cross in the centre, and well secured to the base A and the top of the post. As will be seen on the enlarged section, grooves are cut at each end of the corbel piece where the ledges C fit into same when the core is in position. The struts T are 3 in. by 2 in.,

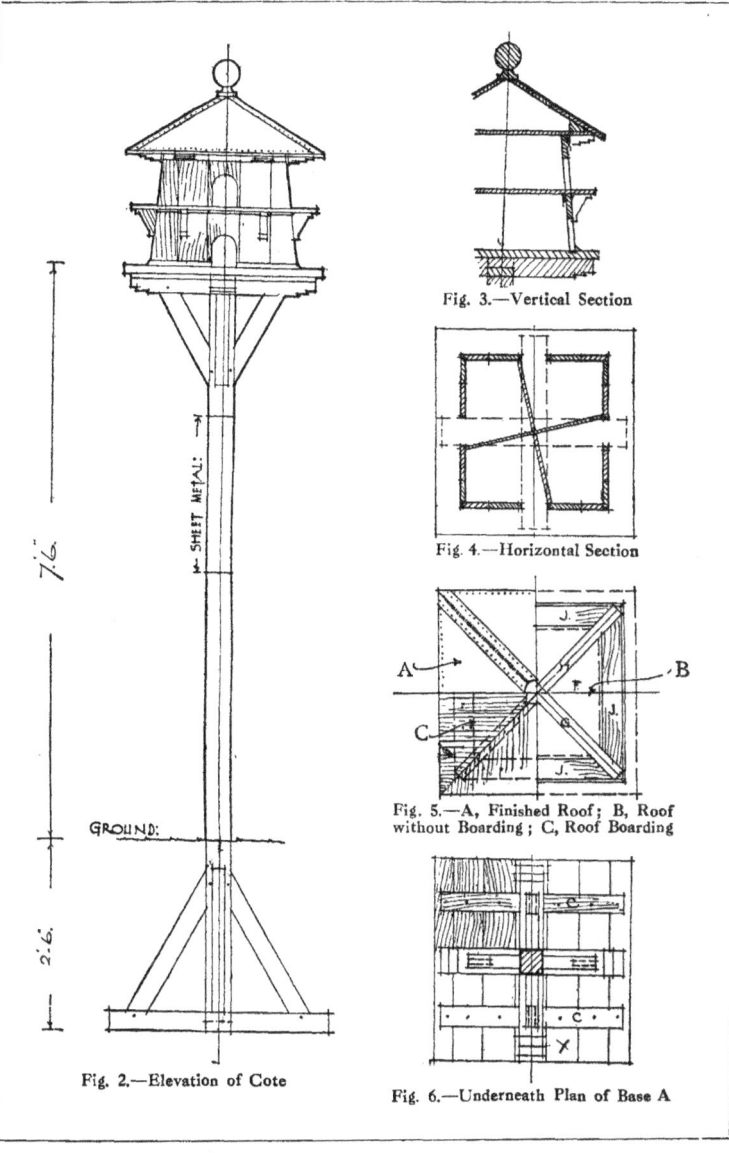

Fig. 2.—Elevation of Cote

Fig. 3.—Vertical Section

Fig. 4.—Horizontal Section

Fig. 5.—A, Finished Roof; B, Roof without Boarding; C, Roof Boarding

Fig. 6.—Underneath Plan of Base A

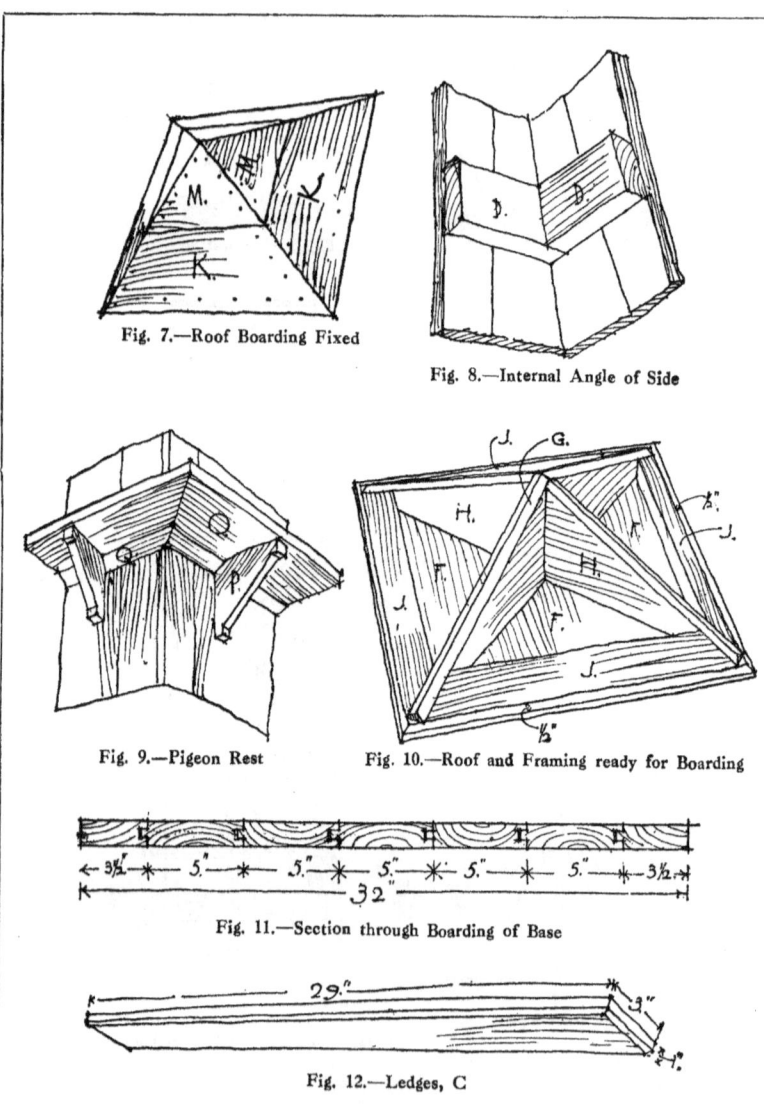

Fig. 7.—Roof Boarding Fixed

Fig. 8.—Internal Angle of Side

Fig. 9.—Pigeon Rest

Fig. 10.—Roof and Framing ready for Boarding

Fig. 11.—Section through Boarding of Base

Fig. 12.—Ledges, C

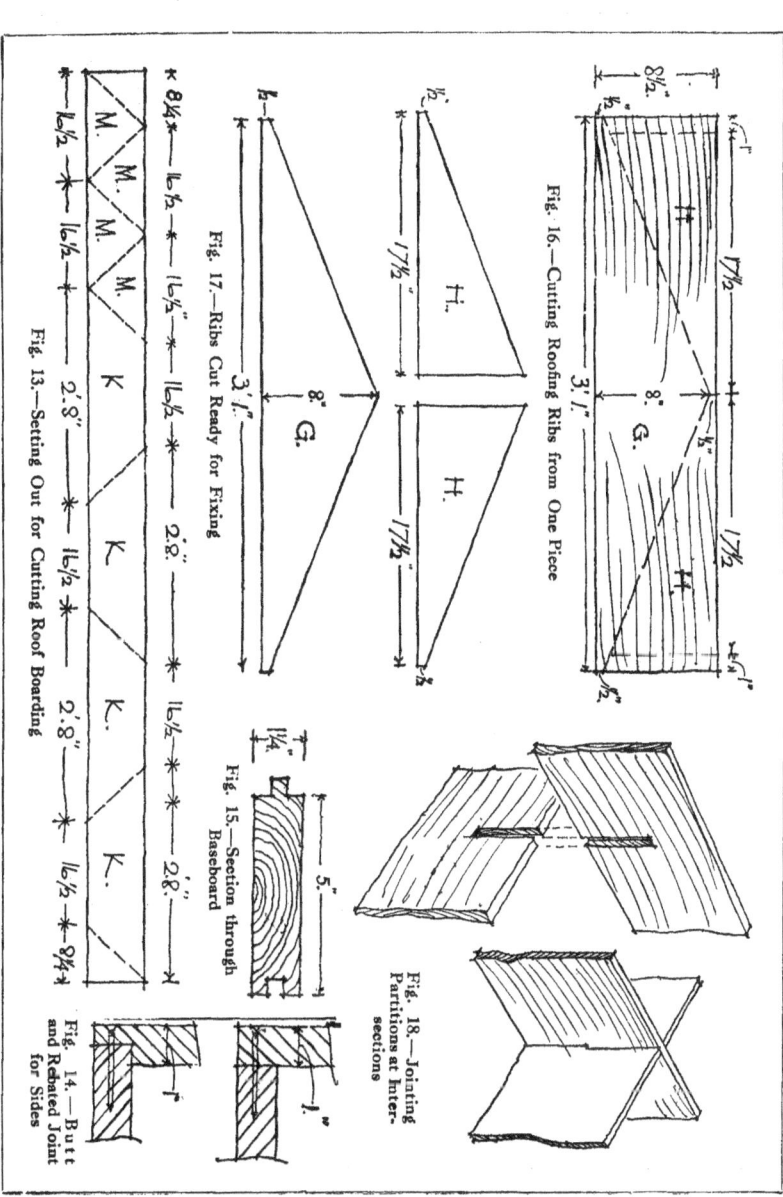

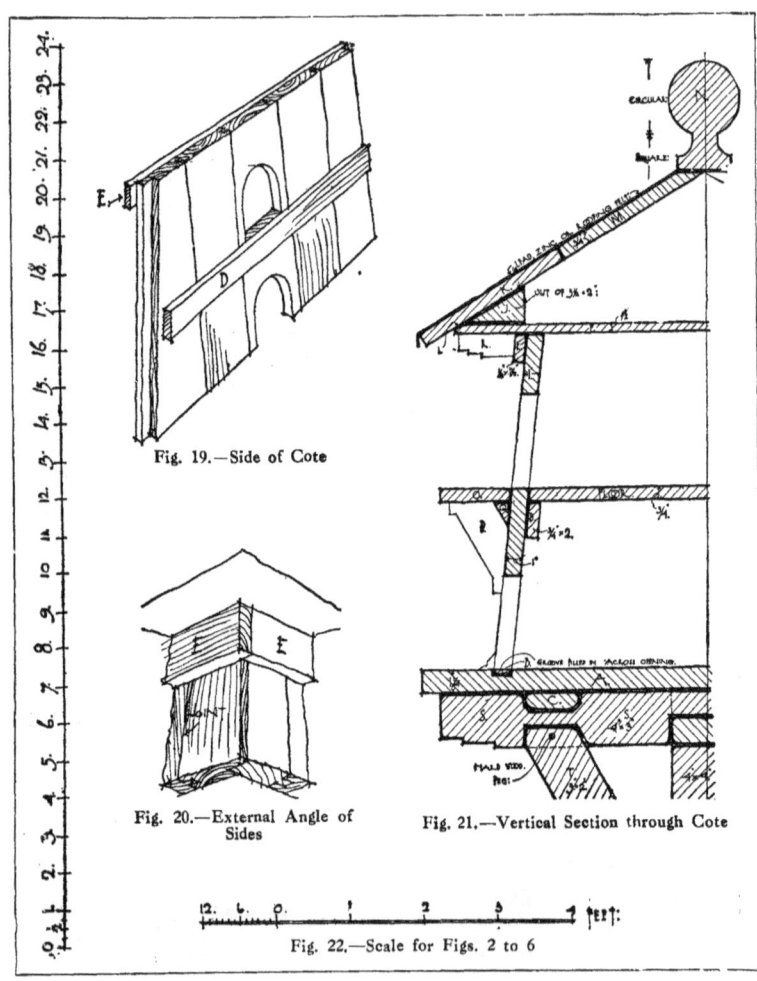

Fig. 19.—Side of Cote

Fig. 20.—External Angle of Sides

Fig. 21.—Vertical Section through Cote

Fig. 22.—Scale for Figs. 2 to 6

and fixed into the corbels s and the post with tenons and oak pegs. The bottom of the post has struts and sill piece as shown, and is taken 2 ft. 6 in. into the ground.

It is not unusual for a cat to climb the post. A good way of avoiding such an intrusion is to nail a strip of sheet metal about 2 ft. long round the post at a distance of 3 ft. 6 in. from the ground. It is suggested that the whole, with the exception of the roof and sides of the cote, should be

PIGEON COTE AND RABBIT HUTCHES

painted three coats of dark green colour, the roof being left the colour of the material with which it is covered, and the sides painted white. The part of the post, etc., below the ground level should be coated with tar, creosote, or some other preservative to prevent the wood rotting. When filling up the hole after inserting the end of the post, ram the earth well down after every few spadefuls.

EASILY-MADE RABBIT HUTCH

A rabbit hutch of very simple construction is shown by Fig. 23. Put together a butted or halved at the angles. This framework with wires should form half of the front, leaving a narrow door.

The outer door J covers both the opening K (Fig. 26) and the sleeping room, as shown on the plan in Fig. 27. On the partition fasten a stout strip, indicated by dotted lines L (Fig. 25), and hammer a staple to this. Opposite this cut a slit in the door to allow the staple to slip through, a bolt or padlock being used to secure it; or a simple wedge, as in Fig. 23, might be used. The dark or sleeping compartment should be hidden by an inner door hung as shown at M in Figs.

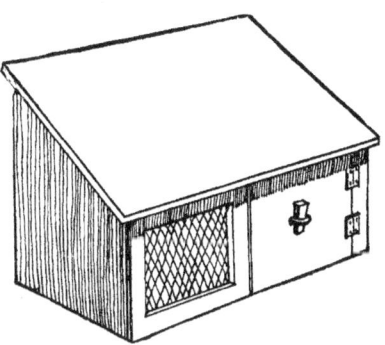

Fig. 23.—Simple Rabbit Hutch

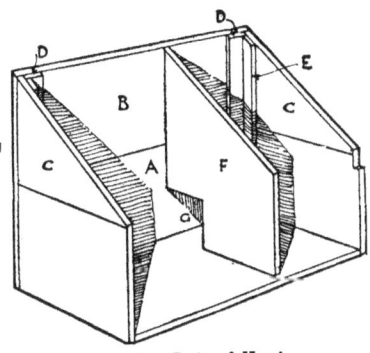

Fig. 24.—Body of Hutch

box of suitable size; or get a common packing-case and remove the lid and one of the long sides. Use this side to heighten the back A, as at B (Fig. 24), fastening it by wood strips D. Cut out two pieces C, and fasten them by strips E to form the body of the hutch. Cut out a piece to the shape of the sides C (one piece if possible) so as to form partition F. Measure one-third the length of the hutch from the end, and before inserting the partition, cut out a square of 4 in. or 5 in. from the corner to form the opening shown at G. Insert the partition, and place the lid on the three sloping pieces. Fasten down to form the sloping roof, and round the front of the day compartment nail strips as at H in Fig. 25,

26, 27 and 28, to secure a quiet place while breeding. The roof should be covered with tarred felt, and it will be advisable to project it a little all round, as shown in Fig. 23.

FRAMED RABBIT HUTCH

A comfortable hutch that would be suitable for breeding rabbits is shown by the half-tone reproduction, Fig. 29. It has two compartments, with doors panelled with wire netting, and a slanting roof so that the rain can run off freely behind. A loft is made of the upper part, opening at the front, for holding a supply of hay or straw for bedding. The hutch is also provided with outer doors or shutters to close at night or in severe weather, and at ordinary times to fold back to the sides, as indicated by the dotted cross in Fig. 36. Fig. 34 is a view of the front with the loft door and shutters closed. The timber required is as follows: 54 ft. of 2-in. square scantling; 20 ft. of 2-in. by

The framework (*see* Fig. 33) is first built up, with the 2-in. square scantling, to the dimensions given in Figs. 30 to 32. The two front uprights, 4 ft. long, and the two back uprights, 3 ft. 3 in., are cut first; then five rails 4 ft. long, and four 1 ft. 7½ in. The method of jointing is shown by

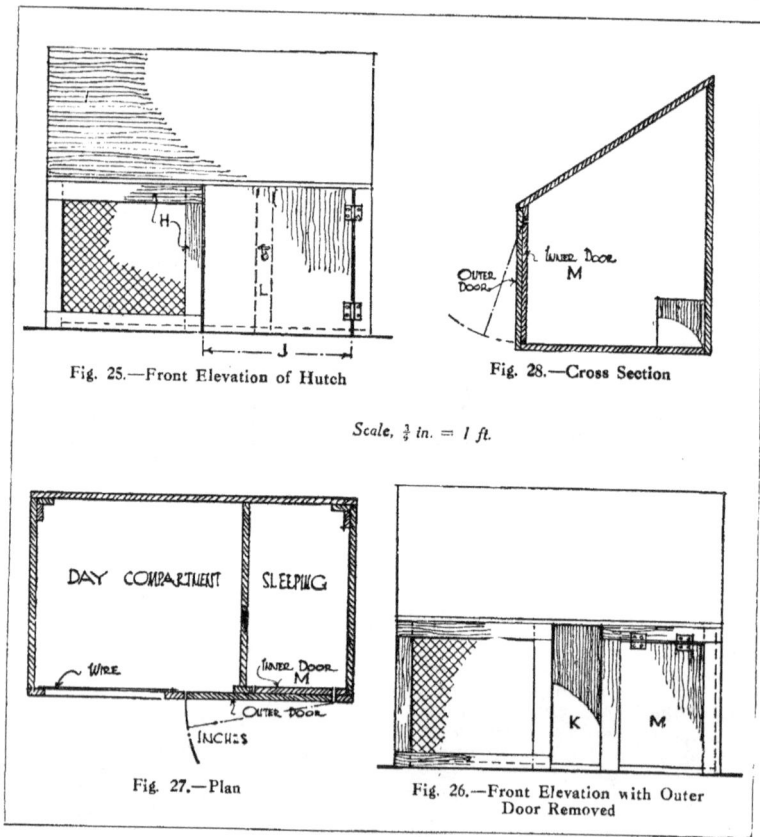

Fig. 25.—Front Elevation of Hutch

Fig. 28.—Cross Section

Scale, ¾ in. = 1 ft.

Fig. 27.—Plan

Fig. 26.—Front Elevation with Outer Door Removed

1-in. scantling; 20 ft. of ½-in. tongue-and-groove board (sometimes termed matchboard) 6 in. wide. It is as well to keep the timber for a week or two in a dry place before using, to allow it to shrink.

Fig. 37; A is the upper portion of the left-hand front upright, B the end of the second long rail, C the end of the short rail, D the top long rail, and E the top short rail. The front uprights are cut on the front side, 1 ft. 4 in. from the lower end, ½ in. deep, to the width of the rails, the waste being chiselled out; and the rail is then cut to fit. The other rail is fitted, 1 ft. 7 in. above it, in the same way. Two more are joined in a similar position to the back uprights. The long rails must not be fixed until the four side rails have been fitted; the ends of these are quite square, and are let into the uprights ⅛ in. deep as at C, corresponding in level with the long rails. When they are tightly fitted they must be nailed with 3-in. cut nails, two to each joint, first piercing with a suitable sprig bit to avoid splitting. The two ends of the framework may now be stood up 4 ft. apart, with the back uprights to the ground, and the two long front rails nailed in place; then turned over and the back rails fixed in the same way.

The frame may now be placed upright, and the two division pieces cut, 1 ft. 7½ in. long, and fitted midway by letting the ends into the rails, as shown in Fig. 38, where F is the division piece and G the lower back-rail. The cross-pieces H and J (Fig. 33) are simply cut to fit tight between the two lower rails, and then secured with long nails. The top ends of the uprights will require to be cut on the slant for the two sloping side rails, which are cut from the 2-in. by 1-in. stuff and nailed on as at A in Fig. 37. When this has been done, the top of the front upwards must be cut out to take the top long rail, as shown at D. A strip must be nailed along the top back rail as at K in Fig. 31, to bring it up flush for fixing on the roof. The frame is now ready for boarding, the sides being done first. The boards should be cut one at a time, and nailed to the three rails, and should be fitted together as tight as possible. The central partition is made by nailing the boards to the two inner rails vertically. Next the floors should be laid, the boards being fixed on the upper side of the lower rails, flush at the back, but 1 in. from the front, as in Fig. 31, and running from back to front. The ceiling is done in the same way on the underside of the upper rails,

Fig. 29.—General View of Rabbit Hutch

so as to give more space to the loft. The sloping boards of the roof are next put on, and should overhang 3 in. all round at the least. The back boards are put on vertically, like the sides.

For the doors, four pieces of the 2-in. by 1-in. stuff, 1 ft. 7 in. long, will be required, and four pieces 1 ft. 9 in. long;
over the frames inside with large-head tacks or small staples, thin laths of wood being nailed over to cover the ends of the wire. Now place the doors in with the hinges folded, mark the uprights, and hinge on. They are kept shut with a revolving wood button, the one marked L in Figs. 30 and 34.

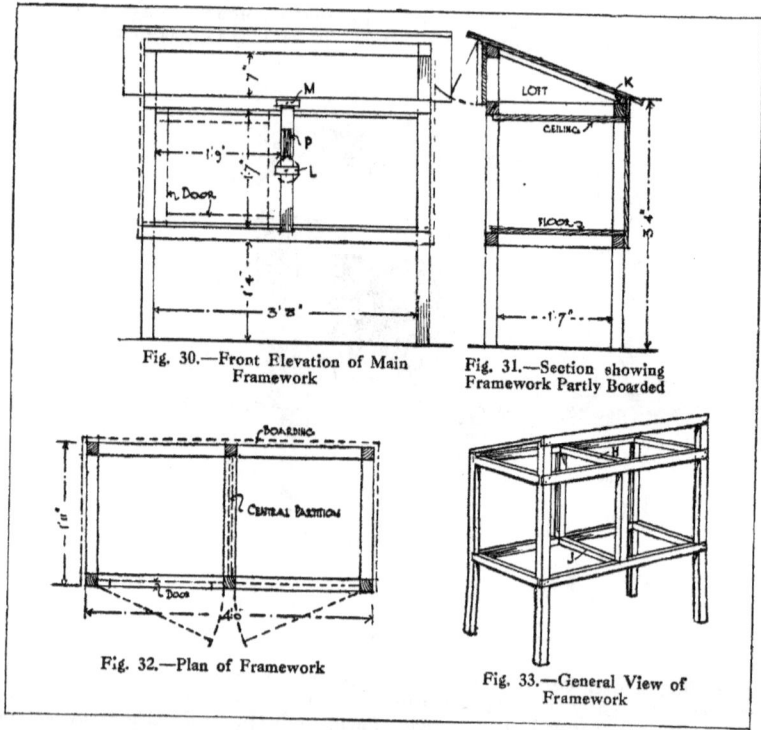

Fig. 30.—Front Elevation of Main Framework

Fig. 31.—Section showing Framework Partly Boarded

Fig. 32.—Plan of Framework

Fig. 33.—General View of Framework

these should be planed up and made into the frames, the joints being halved, glued, and screwed in the usual manner. They should be made to fit neatly but free, and hinged with 2-in. iron butt hinges, which must be let into the frames flush about 3 in. from the corners, with the round standing out. Some wire netting of about 1½-in. mesh must be obtained; this is fixed
To make the loft door, a board the full length of the hutch, and 9½ in. wide by ½ in. thick, must be got out, and two battens nailed on at the extreme ends, on the outside, as in Fig. 34. It is then hinged under the overhanging part of the roof with 5 in. T-hinges, and is kept closed by another wood button M, which will require a piece of ½-in. board fixed under it. A device

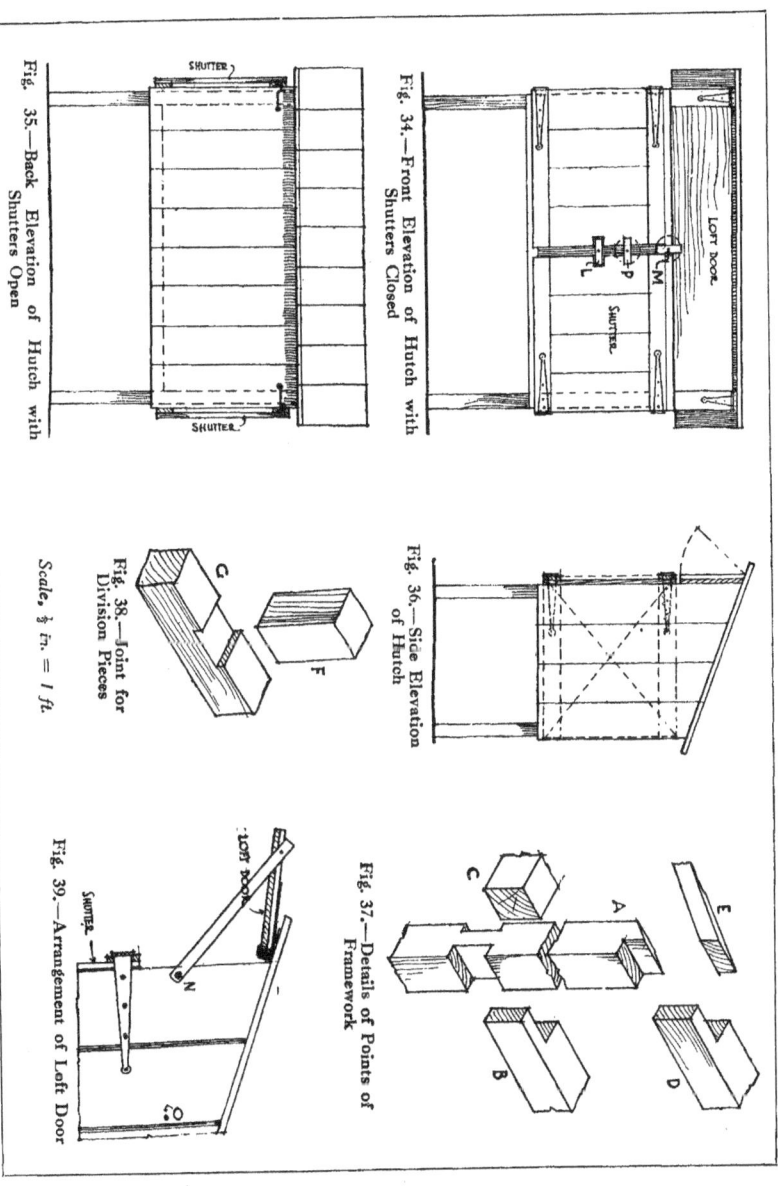

Fig. 34.—Front Elevation of Hutch with Shutters Closed.

Fig. 35.—Back Elevation of Hutch with Shutters Open.

Fig. 36.—Side Elevation of Hutch.

Fig. 37.—Details of Points of Framework.

Fig. 38.—Joint for Division Pieces.

Fig. 39.—Arrangement of Loft Door.

Scale, ½ in. = 1 ft.

390 THE PRACTICAL WOODWORKER

for propping it open is shown in Fig. 39. A strip of wood 1 ft. 2 in. by 1½ in. by 1 in., or a metal lath, has one end screwed tight to the batten 2½ in. from the corner; a screw is put in the side, as at N, and a hole made at the end of the prop large enough to pass over the screw-head. Another screw is put in farther back at O to take the prop when the loft is closed.

lap strap hinges. It will be necessary to cut pieces out of the end boards to clear the button of the inner doors when closed, as indicated at L in Fig. 34. They are kept shut by the middle button P, which requires a piece of ½-in. stuff behind it, and held open by hooks placed at the back of the hutch, as shown in Fig. 35, the eyes being fixed to the top battens of the

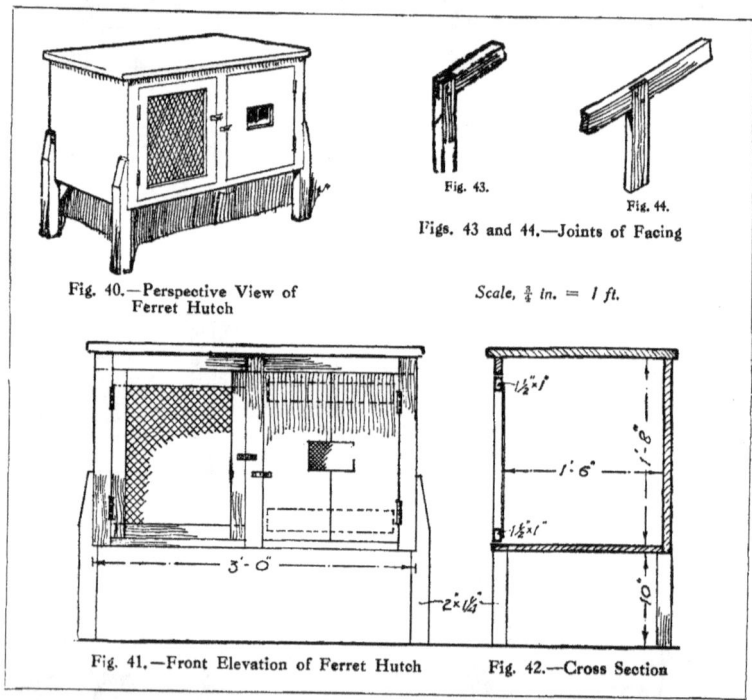

Fig. 40.—Perspective View of Ferret Hutch

Figs. 43 and 44.—Joints of Facing

Scale, ¾ in. = 1 ft.

Fig. 41.—Front Elevation of Ferret Hutch

Fig. 42.—Cross Section

It is a good plan to bore a number of small drainage holes in the bottom of the hutch, and air holes should be made at the back as high as possible, and at the tops of the sides, to air the loft.

The outer doors or shutters are made by cutting the required number of boards 1 ft. 9¼ in. long; these are held together by battens, and hinged on with 9-in. back- shutters. The inside of the hutch should be lime-washed, and the outside given two or three coats of paint, this being necessary to preserve the wood and iron.

FERRET HUTCH

A ferret hutch that is easily constructed is shown above by Figs. 40, 41 and 42.

Obviously the difference between this and a rabbit hutch need not be very pronounced. The ends, back, floor, and top may be of ¾-in. matchboarding, or a suitable size packing-case may be used instead.

The hutch is divided into two compartments by means of a partition with a small hole in it, to enable the inmates to be kept to one part whilst the other is being cleaned. The facing on the front may be halved together, as in Figs. 43 and 44. The door on the left-hand half of the hutch is made of 1½-in. by 1-in. rails, halved together and is filled in with fine wire netting and hinged as shown. The door on the right-hand half is made of boarding secured together with a couple of ledges, as dotted in Fig. 41, and a small hole is cut in the centre and covered with fine wire netting. These doors may be fastened with turnbuttons as shown, or with hooks and eyes. Four legs, which may be cut from 2-in. by 1¼-in. deal, are used to keep the hutch above the floor of the shed in which it may be placed.

It is an advantage to have the whole of the front to open as shown, and the door should be brought down to the floor of the hutch, as cleanliness is essential.

Dog Kennels

INDOOR DOG KENNELS

The illustrations (Figs. 1 to 7) show the construction of a dog-kennel provided with loose ends in order that it can easily be cleaned out. The ends are held in place by turn-buttons, and when removed a clean sweep can be made of the interior. The use of three-ply is a distinct advantage in the construction, as the smooth, level surface affords no lodgment for vermin.

First make three skeleton frames, each containing two uprights 2 ft. 6 in. long, 3 in. by $\frac{7}{8}$ in., planed, a bottom rail $22\frac{3}{4}$ in. long, 3 in. by $\frac{7}{8}$ in., and a top rail cut to the sweep of the roof out of a board 2 ft. 6 in. by $6\frac{1}{2}$ in. by $\frac{7}{8}$ in. Fig. 1 shows an upright trenched $\frac{1}{4}$ in. deep at the bottom to receive the bottom rail. The top edge of the trench is kept 3 in. from the floor. Half-way up shows where the side rail that holds the three frames in position is halved on (see Fig. 2). The slot in the top of the upright receives the top rail, and is cut down $4\frac{1}{4}$ in. by $\frac{3}{8}$ in. Fig. 3 shows how the top rail is marked for cutting from the board. First the three boards for the top rails are laid flat together on the bench, level at each end. Lay on the square, and mark a line 3 in. from each end. Lay the edge of an upright to these marks inside, and square through also; mark with a sharp point, not a pencil. The distance between the inside marks should be $22\frac{1}{4}$ in. Square the marks through the edges of each board, and return the marks along each side, so as to get them all equal; they are then ready for cutting to shape shown in Fig. 3.

Lay a piece of three-ply on the bench to form a drawing board. Then get a thin lath; a plasterer's lath is about the best thing to strike the radius. With a bradawl bore a hole 28 in. from one end, and another 32 in. Then lay a top rail on the drawing board, and with the bradawl stuck through the hole of the lath marked 28 in., strike the radius of the bottom edge of the top rail to just intersect at each shoulder. Then with the bradawl at 32 in. strike the radius from the same centre to mark the top line of the rail, which must be temporarily fastened down (see Fig. 4). The rails can then be sawn out to the lines and cleaned up, and the shoulders trenched $\frac{1}{8}$ in. deep each side shown at the dotted lines. This will allow the rails to slide into the $\frac{5}{8}$-in. slot cut in the uprights (see Fig. 5). The projecting lugs are gauged $\frac{7}{8}$ in. from the top edge, and cut to receive the top side rails, the remaining wood being cut to design.

Now, assuming that the uprights are all prepared like Fig. 1, the three skeleton frames can be nailed together; a $\frac{1}{4}$-in. bead run along the inside front edges would be an improvement, as the removable ends finish flush (see Fig. 6). The six side rails, 3 ft. long by 3 in. by $\frac{7}{8}$ in., are now required. Lay them all flat together level at the ends, mark 3-in. shoulder lines at each end, also in the centre, and square the marks through

DOG KENNELS

each piece. The two top rails only require the back edges bevelling to fit up to their places. The two middle rails are halved to fit over each upright. The ply is nailed to the sides. Four fillets 13½ in. long, ⅞ in. square, are nailed flush outside to the bottom rails (see Fig. 2) to receive the edge of three-ply that

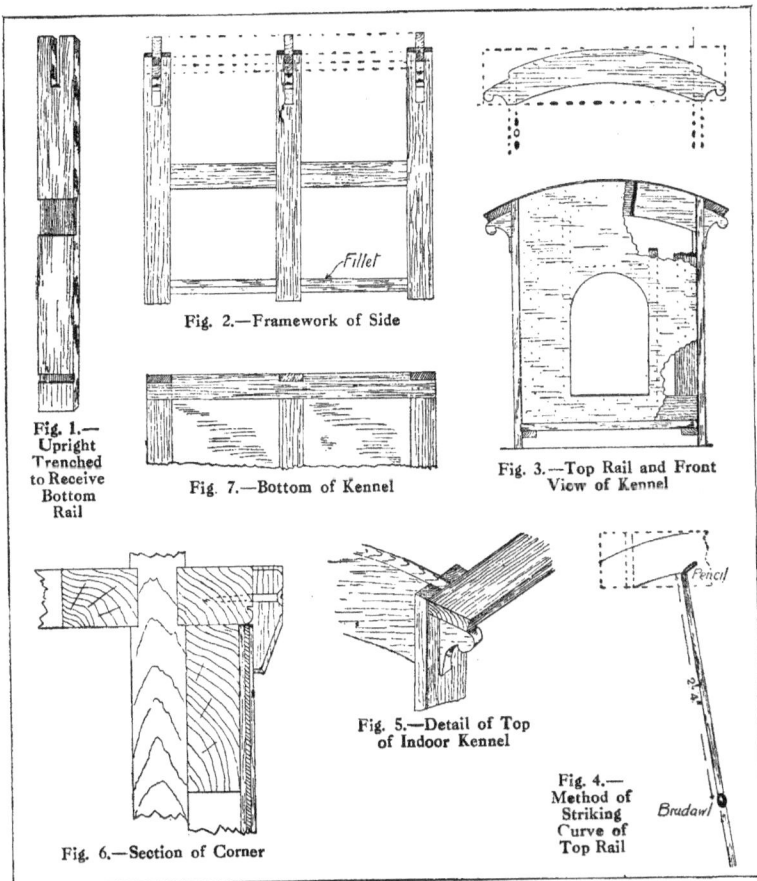

Fig. 1.—Upright Trenched to Receive Bottom Rail

Fig. 2.—Framework of Side

Fig. 7.—Bottom of Kennel

Fig. 3.—Top Rail and Front View of Kennel

Fig. 5.—Detail of Top of Indoor Kennel

Fig. 4.—Method of Striking Curve of Top Rail

Fig. 6.—Section of Corner

two bottom rails are notched out ⅞ in., and are nailed on the bottom to fit flush with the outside (see Fig. 7). Fasten the middle and bottom rails in position; the top rails are left off until the three- forms the floor of the kennel. Trim off any rough edges flush with the outside all round, then nail on the two sides. Do not go beyond the bottom rails, and see that the sides are kept high enough to nail to the back edges of the top rails, which can then be nailed into their position with 2-in. oval wire nails.

The top is next fastened on, bent to the sweep, and nailed well to the side rails with 1-in. flat-head wire nails. Trim off all the rough edges, and make and fit the two ends. Halve the frames together to fit in between the two uprights and the top and bottom. Nail a small fillet down each upright in line with the top rail, for fixing the two end frames. These end frames are covered with three-ply, one having to be cut as shown in Fig. 3 to allow the dog to enter. It must be noted

Fig. 8.—Portable Kennel

that ½-in. fillets should be nailed to strengthen the edges wherever cut. See that it is well painted; three coats at least.

PORTABLE DOG KENNEL

A kennel of good, sound construction, and at the same time possessing the merit of being easily taken to pieces for purposes of transit, etc., is shown by Figs. 8 to 12. Grooved and tongued boarding 6 in. wide and 1 in. thick is a suitable material to use. The boards of the sides should be nailed to a 1½-in. by 2-in. ledge at the top, and a 3-in. by 1½-in.

ledge at the bottom (see A and B, Fig. 9). The boards of the front and back should be nailed to similar ledges, as shown at C and D (Fig. 10). The boards forming each side of the roof should be nailed to the three bearers E (Fig. 9). The floor consists merely of several boards secured by means of a couple of ledges, as at F in Fig. 9. It will be seen that the kennel will be composed of seven main pieces. Fillets (to form angle pieces) about 1½ in. by 1½ in. should be nailed to each end of the sides, as shown at G in Figs. 9, 11 and 12. The latter is an enlarged section taken through H.

The front and back can be fixed to the sides by eight 2¼-in. by ¼-in. bolts and nuts, as shown by Figs. 8, 10 and 12. Each half of the roof can be fixed to the ends by eight bolts and nuts in a similar manner. The floor will rest on the ledges B (Fig. 9), round the bottom of the boarding.

The advantage of this bolted construction lies in the fact that the kennel can readily be packed flat if desired. Should such an arrangement not be desired the same general design will apply, using nails or screws in lieu of the small bolts. The roof should be covered with felt.

KENNEL WITH TWO COMPARTMENTS

Kennels are usually built with simply the one compartment, but that illustrated in Fig. 13 is of more elaborate construction, and is provided with day and night quarters. One end has a door which is useful in hot weather, and one side of the sleeping compartment is formed as a door. The dimensions given in Figs. 14 and 16 will be found suitable for an ordinary retriever, but, of course, the sizes can be increased or decreased as required. The most suitable wood for the kennel is sound red deal, and from the illustrations the lengths and sizes of the various pieces can be ascertained with very little trouble. First set out the four vertical posts for mortising, and the bottom rails for tenoning. The intermediate post A (Fig 15)

DOG KENNELS

and the bottom rail should be lap-halved together. The top rail may be simply a piece of stuff $1\frac{1}{4}$ in. by $4\frac{1}{2}$ in., which should be planed to the bevel of the roof, as shown at B (Figs. 14 and 17). Each end of these rails should be sub-tenoned into the angle posts. Then the intermediate post A (Fig. 17) can be notched out at the back c so as to nail on this rail. The posts and rails should be fitted together, and, when satisfactory, the joints should be painted, put together, and secured by a few stout screws or nails.

For the floor of the kennel grooved-

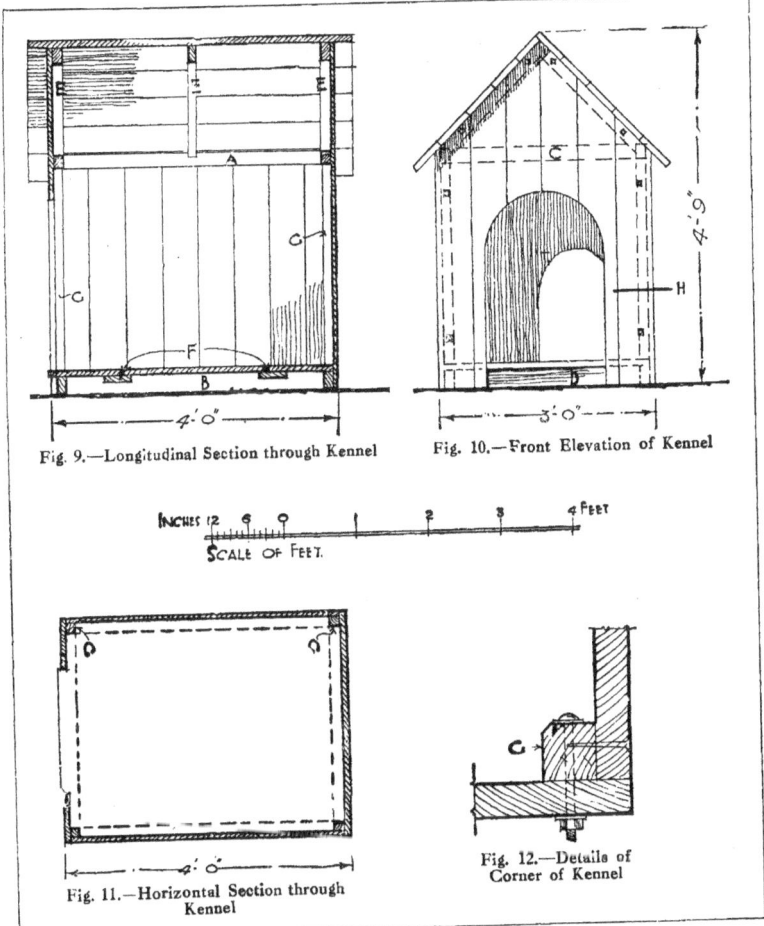

Fig. 9.—Longitudinal Section through Kennel

Fig. 10.—Front Elevation of Kennel

Fig. 11.—Horizontal Section through Kennel

Fig. 12.—Details of Corner of Kennel

and-tongued boards will be satisfactory, and will not require to be specially supported. Except the case of the opening of the board which is to form the sides. Therefore, obtain strips of breadth equal to the thickness of the boarding for the

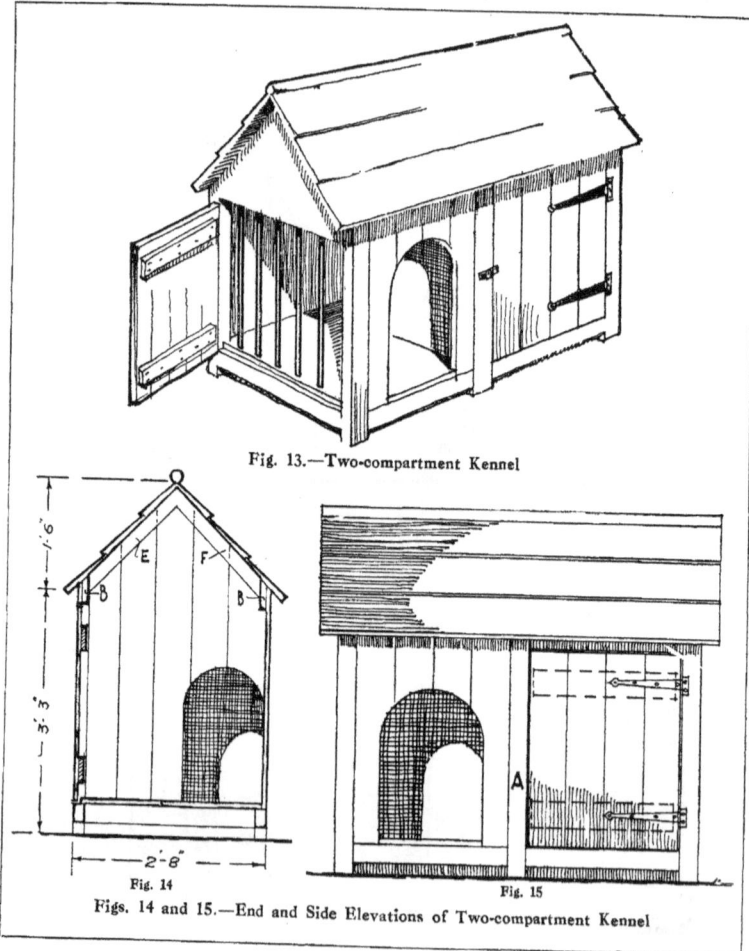

Fig. 13.—Two-compartment Kennel

Figs. 14 and 15.—End and Side Elevations of Two-compartment Kennel

at D (Fig. 16), the boards should be kept back from the outer face of the bottom rails by a distance equal to the thickness sides, and secure them with three or four small nails to the rails, just flush with the outside. Then the floorboards may be

DOG KENNELS

cut to fit between these strips and nailed in position; after which the strips may be taken off and the right space will be left for the boarding of the sides.

Narrow matchboarding, about ¾ in. or ⅞ in. thick, answers well for the sides, and must be cut to fit to the floorboards at the bottom and to the top rail. For the back it will be an advantage to cut the boards at a bevel; similarly cut those forming the opening in the front; then, after these boards are nailed in position, parts of the top ends projecting beyond the top rail may be planed flush. The boarding to form both the opening and closed ends should be cut to fit the bottom rail, and also the rake of the roof. The bottom ends, of course, will be secured to the floorboards and bottom rails. The upper ends of the two ledges E and F

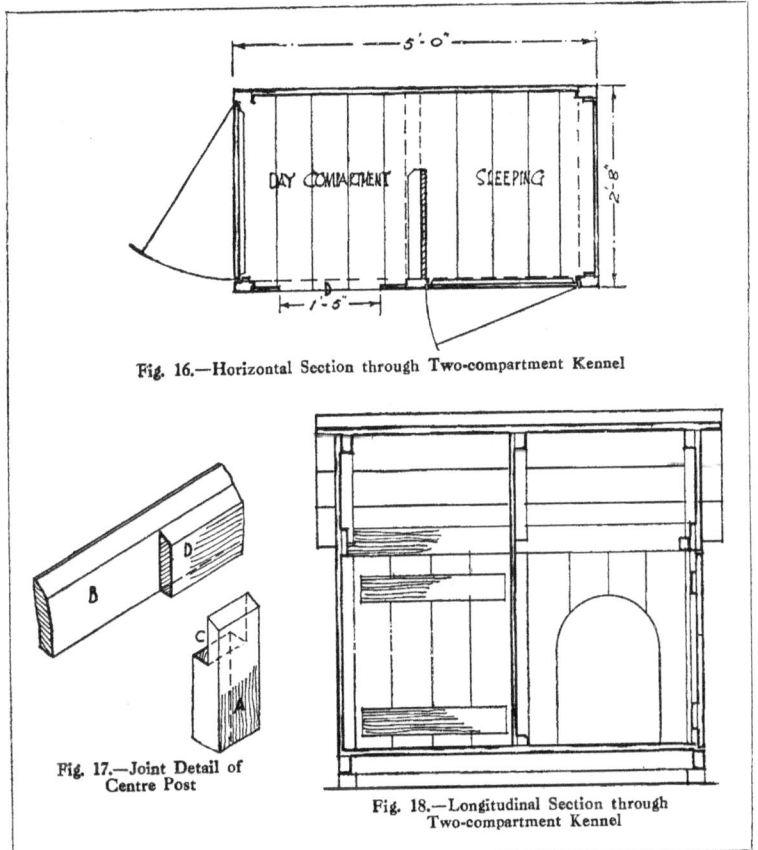

Fig. 16.—Horizontal Section through Two-compartment Kennel

Fig. 17.—Joint Detail of Centre Post

Fig. 18.—Longitudinal Section through Two-compartment Kennel

(Fig. 14) should be halved together and fixed to the top rails and angle posts. For the end that opens, the bottom end of the boards should be just tacked in position. Then, with a fine saw, cut along the line at G (Fig. 12), and the lower boards will form the door. This must have two ledges nailed on as dotted, and a ledge, also dotted, just above G should be nailed along the inside of the gable part, its lower edge projecting about $\frac{1}{2}$ in. below the ends of the boarding to answer as a stop. The partition, shown in Fig. 16, is simple, being fixed at the bottom to a fillet secured to the floor, and at the top to the central roof-bearers. The illustration makes the construction clear.

The door of the sleeping compartment is fully shown in Figs. 15 and 18. When this door is closed the top rail will not be flush with it, but this may be remedied by nailing on a piece of the same thickness as the door, as indicated at D (Fig. 17). The door should be hung with 12-in. cross garnets, and at the open end of the kennel five iron bars, about $\frac{5}{8}$ in. in diameter, are fitted in holes bored in a fillet at the bottom and in the ledge at the top. For the roof use 9-in. feather-edged boards, that is, $1\frac{1}{8}$ in. at the thick edge and $\frac{5}{8}$ in. at the thin edge, and rebate them together as indicated in Fig. 14. The top can be finished with a ridge roll prepared from $1\frac{3}{4}$-in. square stuff, rounded and **V**'d so as to fit over the top joint of the boards. To stand the weather well the kennel should have at least three coats of oil and white-lead paint.

Beehive and Fittings

The hive shown in the photograph (Fig. 1) is of the bar-frame variety and based upon the well-known "W. B. C." hives. Practically every dimension required for carrying out the work is given in the detailed illustrations of the various parts; it is necessary that these be strictly followed in order to accommodate the standard size of frames, and to ensure the proper fitting together of the whole. The construction employed may be of the most elementary character, but it will naturally prove a much more satisfactory job if the work is carefully executed, more particularly with regard to the tongueing and grooving together of boards for the flat surfaces and the use of dovetailing for the angles throughout.

The component parts are shown in their proper relationship but separated in Figs. 2 to 4, and working from the bottom are as follow :—

Floorboard and Stand.—This is explained by Fig. 6, and consists of a flat board and sloping alighting board, both ½ in. thick, nailed to shaped battens 2½ in. by 1½ in. (A Fig. 2), with shorter ones framed into them at front and back as shown in section in the same figure. Four stout legs sloped and notched, as in Fig. 7, should be firmly screwed on to complete this portion of the hive.

Outer Case.—(Fig. 8.) The inside measurements of this should be 1 ft. 5⅞ in. by 1 ft. 7¼ in., and a plinth dropping ¼ in., chamfered and slightly rebated, as in Fig. 9, should be mitred round. The construction of the porch will be apparent on

Fig. 1.—General View of Hive

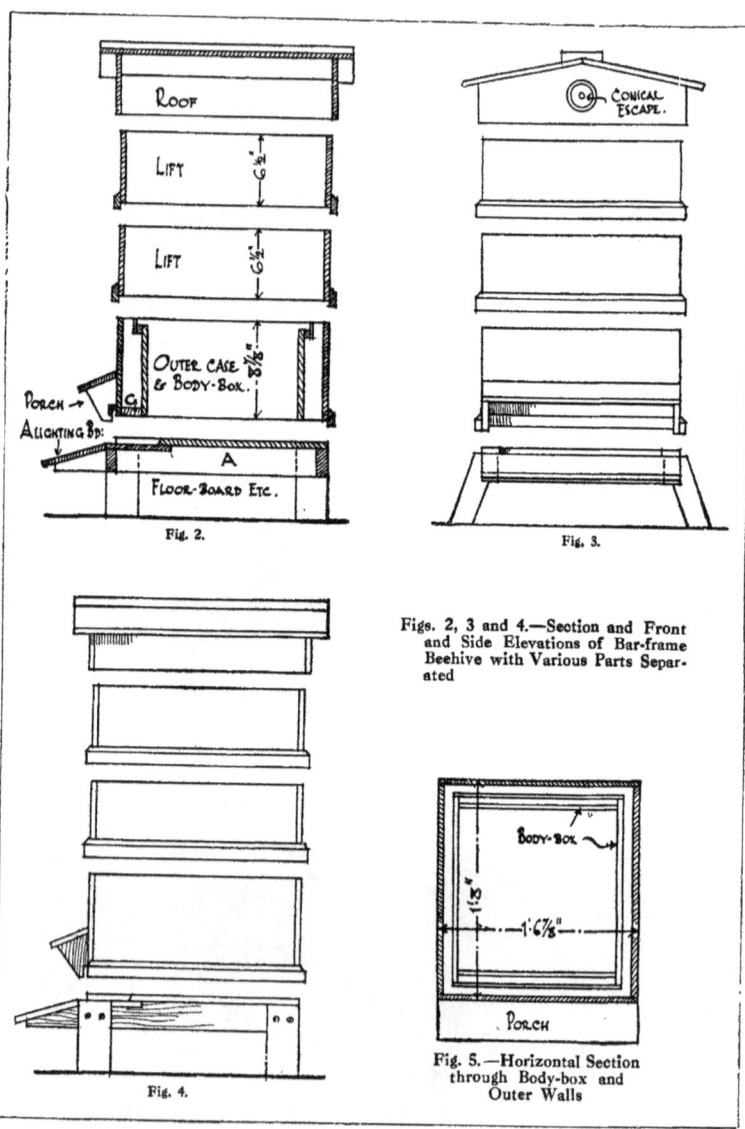

Figs. 2, 3 and 4.—Section and Front and Side Elevations of Bar-frame Beehive with Various Parts Separated

Fig. 5.—Horizontal Section through Body-box and Outer Walls

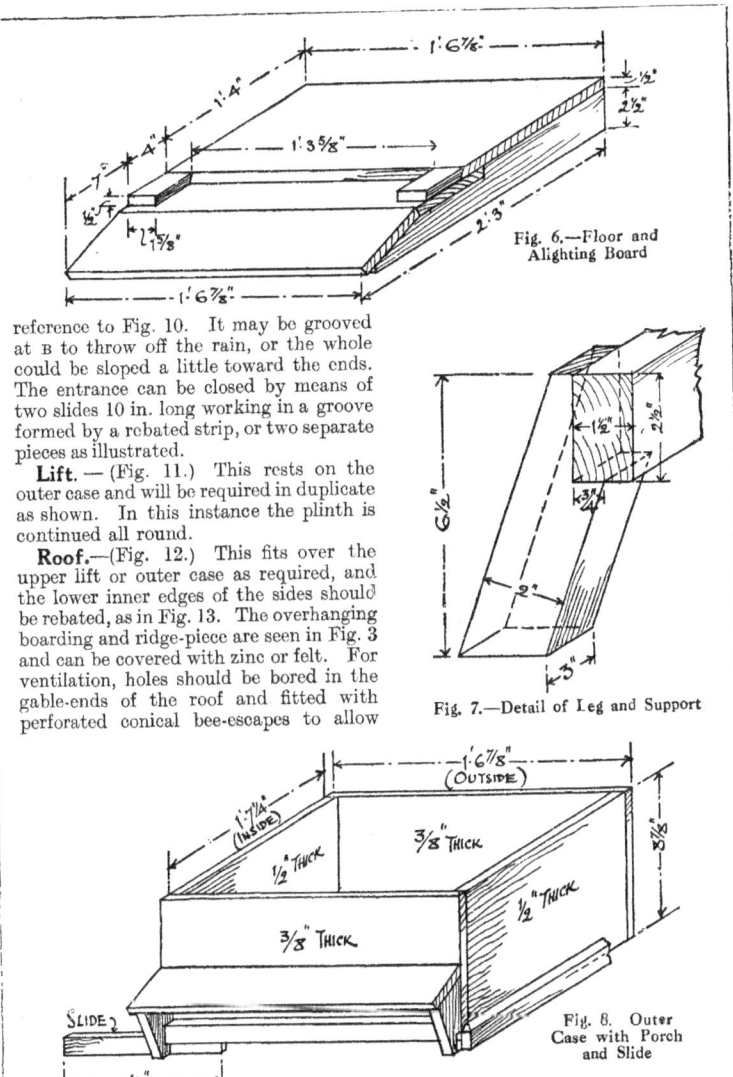

Fig. 6.—Floor and Alighting Board

Fig. 7.—Detail of Leg and Support

Fig. 8. Outer Case with Porch and Slide

reference to Fig. 10. It may be grooved at B to throw off the rain, or the whole could be sloped a little toward the ends. The entrance can be closed by means of two slides 10 in. long working in a groove formed by a rebated strip, or two separate pieces as illustrated.

Lift. — (Fig. 11.) This rests on the outer case and will be required in duplicate as shown. In this instance the plinth is continued all round.

Roof.—(Fig. 12.) This fits over the upper lift or outer case as required, and the lower inner edges of the sides should be rebated, as in Fig. 13. The overhanging boarding and ridge-piece are seen in Fig. 3 and can be covered with zinc or felt. For ventilation, holes should be bored in the gable-ends of the roof and fitted with perforated conical bee-escapes to allow the exit of any bees that happen to get above the quilt which is usually placed over the frames.

Body-box or Brood-chamber.—This is shown in Fig. 14 and a horizontal section is given by Fig. 5. It is constructed to hold ten standard frames and should in position, and a strip, as at E in Fig. 16, is nailed between them and the front and back pieces. A strip of zinc (F Fig. 16) is nailed on at the front and back: it is on this that the frames rest in the manner indicated by the dotted lines. A loose piece of wood, as at G in Fig. 2, should be fitted loosely in order to prevent any bees getting into the cavity between the inner and outer compartments.

Frame-Box or Super.—(Fig. 17). Except that it is only 6 in. deep this is exactly similar to the body-box over which it fits. The bar-frames to suit it are 5½ in. deep.

Eke.—(Fig. 18). This is intended for winter use only. Many bee-keepers find it possible entirely to dispense with this. It goes below the body-box and has four cleats, as shown, to keep it in position. It is used to raise the body-box to give bottom ventilation when wintering the bees; it can also be placed below the

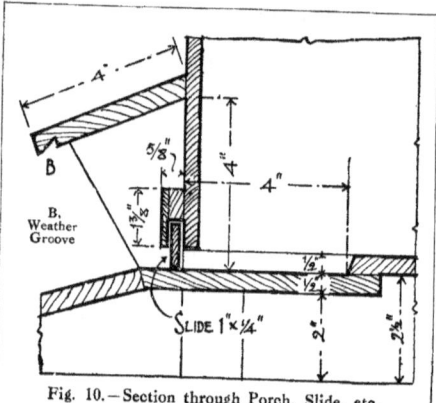

Fig. 10.—Section through Porch, Slide, etc.

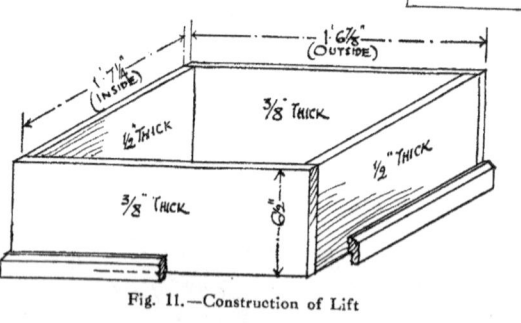

Fig. 11.—Construction of Lift

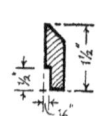

Fig. 9.—Section through Plinth to Outer Case and Lifts

be 1 ft. 2½ in. by 1 ft. 3 in. main inside measurements. The front and back pieces fit into grooves ⅞ in. from the ends of the side pieces, as in Fig. 15. From each top corner of the latter a piece is notched to receive strips of wood, as at D D in Figs. 14 and 16. These strips enclose the top of the bar-frame ends, keeping them frame-box in order to bring it to the size of the body-box.

Fittings.—In a bar-frame or movable-comb hive it is important that each comb be built straight in its frame, and that each frame be squarely in position and capable of being lifted from the hive without tearing any attachment to another

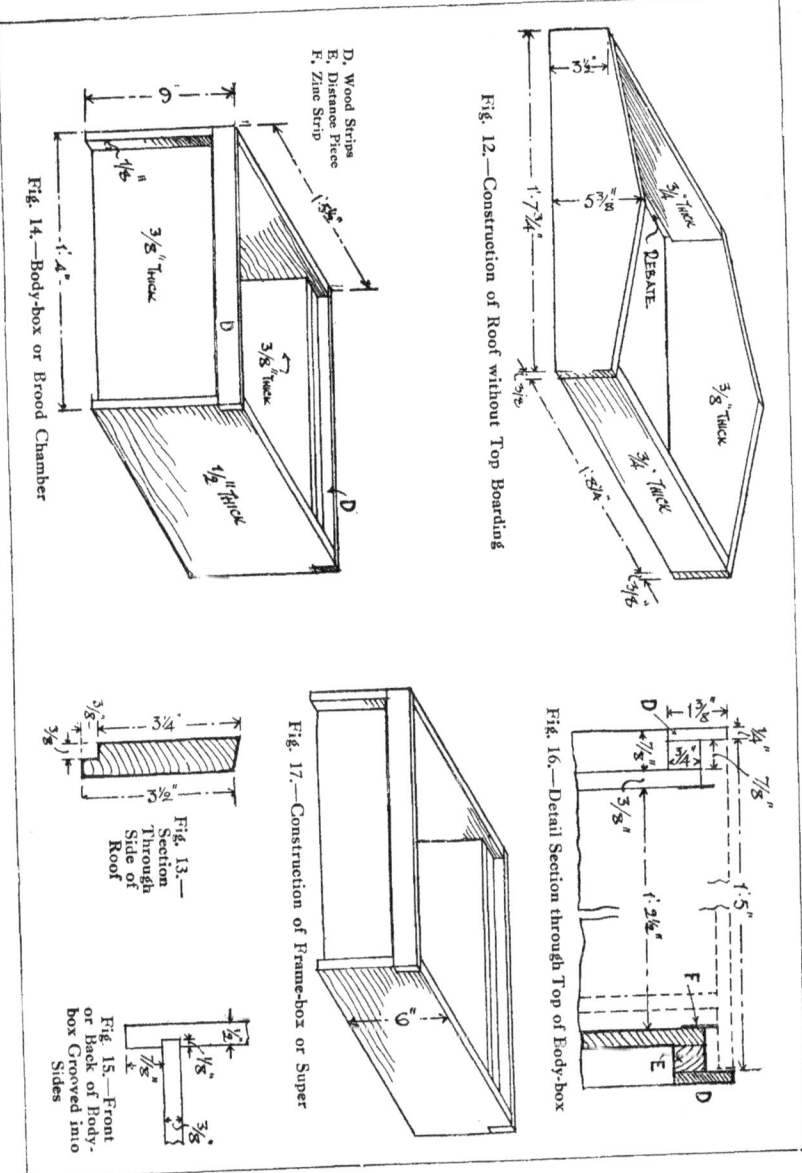

comb or the hive walls. The first requisite is a set of frames, each to eventually contain comb. The standard frame of the British Bee-keepers' Association is illustrated by Fig. 19, and provided that the measurements there given are adhered to the pattern of the frames does not much matter; it will vary according to the method of spacing employed. In a natural state bees build their combs from $1\frac{1}{4}$ in. to $1\frac{1}{2}$ in. apart centre to centre, and the spacing usually adopted in placing frames is $1\frac{9}{20}$ in. centre to centre, ten frames thus occupying $14\frac{1}{2}$ in. Frames are either "broad shouldered," which are self-spacing or shoulderless, these latter requiring some mechanical contrivance to ensure correct spacing. It is hardly

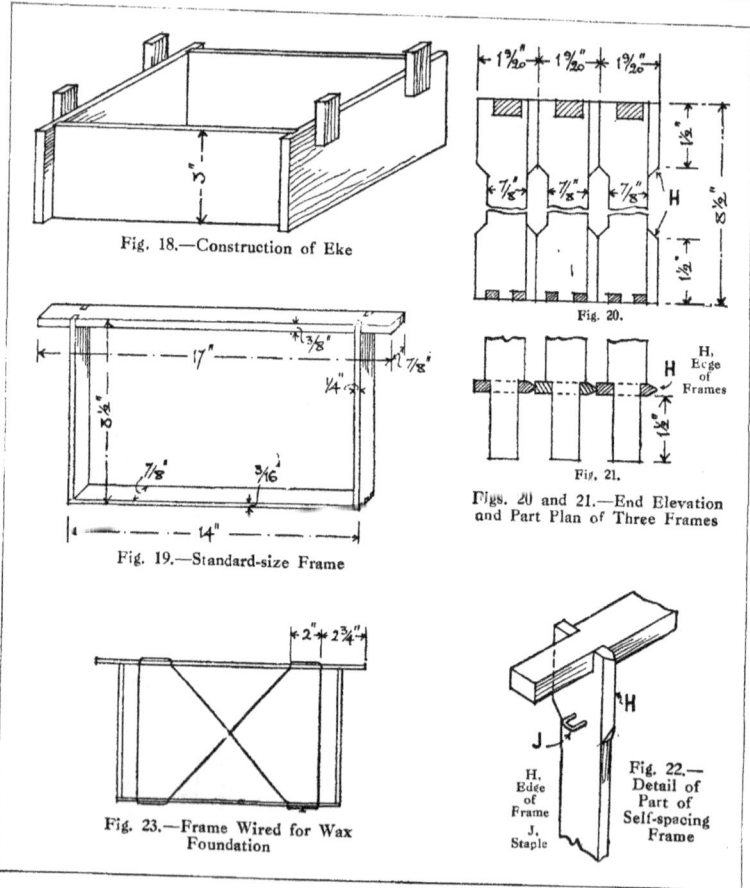

Fig. 18.—Construction of Eke

Fig. 19.—Standard-size Frame

Fig. 20.

Figs. 20 and 21.—End Elevation and Part Plan of Three Frames

Fig. 23.—Frame Wired for Wax Foundation

Fig. 22.—Detail of Part of Self-spacing Frame

worth while to make them when they can be purchased very readily, but if desired they can be made as in Fig. 19 and fitted with metal self-spacing ends attached to the top bar. There are several patterns the correct relationship. In order to prevent injury to any bees by squeezing between the hive-side and a frame, small staples, as at J in Fig. 22, should be driven in and left projecting ¼ in. near the top

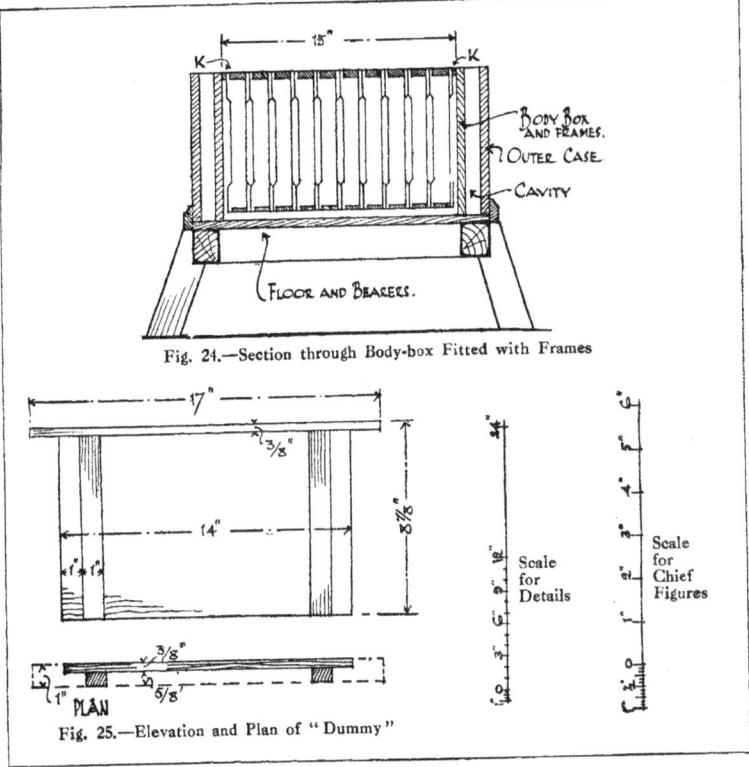

Fig. 24.—Section through Body-box Fitted with Frames

Fig. 25.—Elevation and Plan of "Dummy"

of such fittings which obviate any likelihood of the bees gluing the frames together, but an efficient all-wood self-spacing frame can be made as shown in Figs. 20 to 22. Here the uprights are shouldered top and bottom to the regulation width of 1⅜ in., and finished on one side to what is practically a knife-edge, as at H in all three figures. By this means they are kept strictly in and bottom of each side. To induce the bees to build in the bar-frames instead of across them, it is necessary to use sheets of foundation wax, impressed with the bases of the cells. This sheet of wax can be fixed by running molten wax along the junction with the wood, but a much more satisfactory plan is to wire them, as in Fig. 23, the wires being heated and bedded in the wax. No. 30 tinned iron wire should be used, threaded through holes in the centre of the frame and drawn tight and twisted round a small tack at the bottom, care being taken that the frame is not strained out of the square. For attaching the foundation the guide-board (Fig. 24) is necessary; it is $\frac{3}{8}$ in. thick and $\frac{1}{8}$ in. less each way than the inside of the frames, and to its underside are fixed two fillets projecting $\frac{1}{4}$ in. at least on either side. On this board a sheet of wax foundation is laid with a wired frame above it. Then a tool called an embedder or some substitute is heated just sufficiently and run along the wires; as the wax melts the wires are pressed into the sheet, in which they are firmly bedded when the wax cools.

Two plain strips of wood, $\frac{3}{8}$ in. by $\frac{1}{4}$ in., as at K K in Fig. 24, are necessary in order to increase the distance between each outer comb and the hive side of the "dummy" if one is in use. A dummy is a cleated or clamped board, fitting the inside of the hive, and having a top bar by means of which it can be suspended in the same way as a frame. Its purpose is to contract the brood nest when it is desired to give the bees a lesser number of frames. The usual form of dummy is explained by Fig. 25, and it should be an easy fit inside the hive.

To prevent the queen bee getting up into the sections, "excluder zinc" pierced with small slots through which only the workers can pass is used over the brood-nest. This can be obtained in sheets 16 in. square and is laid over the frames. Quilts are necessary for covering the frames, and for them nothing is better than thick american cloth laid on face down. Over this a number of thicknesses of carpet or sacking should be placed in order to keep the hive warm.

Steps and Ladders

HOUSEHOLD STEPS

HOUSEHOLD steps are of various kinds, but there is no doubt that for a serviceable article one cannot do better than make the solid variety.

Fig. 1.—Side View of Steps

Fig. 2.—Back View of Steps

Figs. 1 and 2 show a pair of steps of this kind. The steps as shown stand 6 ft. 9 in. high, but this is somewhat higher than usual, and may be reduced by one or more steps. The best material to use for the steps is good sound yellow deal. Approximately 1 in. (⅞ in. really) will be the right thickness, and 9 in. will be a convenient width to obtain. This will cut down the middle for the sides, and the framing for the back legs will come off the side of the treads. The correct angle may be taken from the side elevation (Fig. 3) both for the steps and for the back legs. The latter, as shown, should be shorter than the former, so that they will not project inconveniently backwards when in use.

The front and back elevations of the finished steps are given in Figs. 4 and 5, the latter being minus the back legs, which are shown separately by Fig. 6. As shown in Figs. 4 and 5, the actual steps are fixed in slots cut in the sides, and are held there with nails. Sometimes two or three of the steps are tenoned through the sides and wedged; but there is no advantage in doing this, the nails answering all purposes, and the sides are not weakened.

When the wood has been cut to size and planed up, the necessary setting out can be proceeded with. To do this, lay the two sides on the bench side by side, with the best edges facing each other, as in Fig. 7, make the mark for the bottom of the steps, as on the right, pairing them as shown. From these marks—measuring at right angles—set off 9 in., and continue marking off the same distance along the whole length of the sides. These marks represent the tops of the steps, and therefore in order to get the width of the trenches measure ⅞ in. from each of those numbered one to eight, towards the left. The extreme left-hand mark being the bottom of the steps is correct as it is, while that at the extreme right is the top of the steps, and thus requires cutting off ⅞ in. shorter to allow for the top board. This latter, however, will be stronger if the sides are housed into it. Therefore, instead of making the mark ⅞ in. to the left, make it ⅝ in. only.

The above marks must now be squared across the edges, and a gauge mark made for the depth of the trenches (¼ in.), when the sides will appear as Fig. 8. The ends of the sides can now be sawn off to the respective marks, the trenches sawn in, and the wood removed down to the gauge marks with a sharp chisel (see Fig. 9). To obtain the correct length of the treads (steps), take a piece of board, make eight marks along it at equal distances apart, as the numbered lines in Fig. 10, and one more the same distance. On the lower line set off the width of the finished steps at the bottom (18 in.), and on the extra line set off the width at the top (13 in.); connect these lines as shown, and measure off ⅝ in. inwards from each. On connecting these latter lines, the correct length of each step will be given.

The treads may be cut off at a right angle, both flatwise and edgewise, the very slight taper of the steps being negligible, and when tightly nailed the fit will be all that can be desired. The treads can now be driven into the trenches, keeping the bottom corner of each level with the front edge of the string, and inserting three nails in each, carefully driving them on the skew so that they will have the maximum holding power. After all the treads are nailed, the projecting front corner of each tread can be neatly chamfered out, as shown in Fig. 4, and the treads at the back must be planed off level with the edges of the strings.

The back legs must now be framed. The stiles (sides) are shown set out for mortising in Fig. 11; the mortises must be slightly on the bevel, as shown, and they must be made slightly wider on the outside (as on the right) to allow of the insertion of the fixing wedges. The top and bottom rails are shown in Figs. 12 and 13 respectively. The angle of the shoulders is the same as that formed by the treads and the sides in Fig. 5, and the length must be such as to bring the full width the same as that of the steps themselves.

The top board is shown by Fig. 14, trenched ready for fixing to the steps. The trenching is marked by laying the top on in its correct position, and marking round, cutting out to the marks to the depth of ¼ in. The top board should be rounded on all four edges, as shown in Figs. 3, 4, and 5. The backboard A (Fig. 5) is simply nailed on to the back of the sides in the position shown, and to

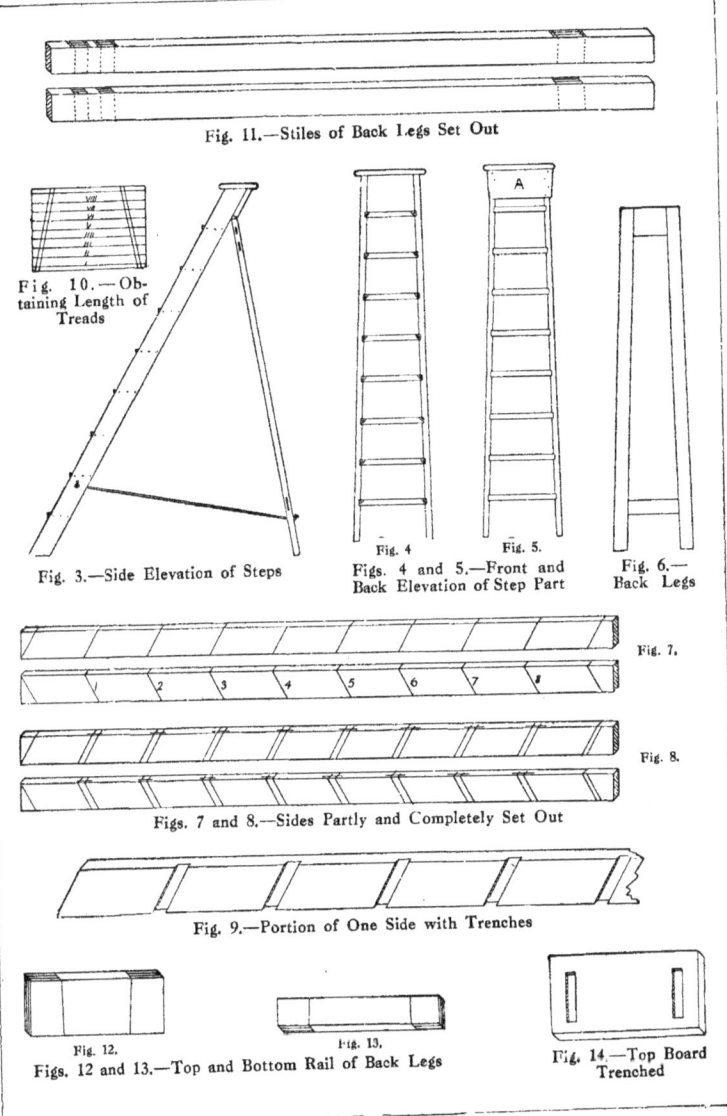

Fig. 11.—Stiles of Back Legs Set Out

Fig. 10.—Obtaining Length of Treads

Fig. 3.—Side Elevation of Steps

Figs. 4 and 5.—Front and Back Elevation of Step Part

Fig. 6.—Back Legs

Figs. 7 and 8.—Sides Partly and Completely Set Out

Fig. 9.—Portion of One Side with Trenches

Figs. 12 and 13.—Top and Bottom Rail of Back Legs

Fig. 14.—Top Board Trenched

it the back legs are hinged. This will practically finish the steps. The hinges used should be what are called back-flaps, and made from wrought-iron. The stretching cords should be fixed, as shown in Fig. 3, the reason for fixing the one end low in the back legs being to prevent the is a perspective view of the steps when in use, the height being 4 ft. 6 in. Fig. 16 shows them closed up. The steps can be made of deal or birch. The sizes given are for birch; but if deal is used the parts should be a trifle heavier. It is advisable in the larger steps to have the main

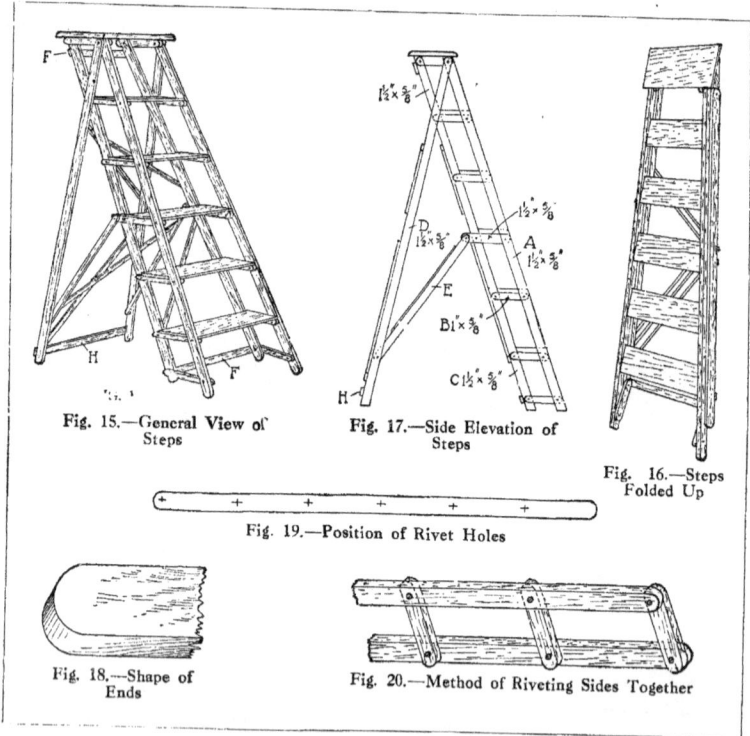

Fig. 15.—General View of Steps

Fig. 17.—Side Elevation of Steps

Fig. 16.—Steps Folded Up

Fig. 19.—Position of Rivet Holes

Fig. 18.—Shape of Ends

Fig. 20.—Method of Riveting Sides Together

latter from bending when the steps are in use. The cords should be regulated in length so that when they are tightly stretched the treads are level.

HOUSEHOLD FOLDING STEPS

Folding steps are lighter and more easily constructed than the solid kind. Fig. 15 rails of birch or hardwood, to ensure the strength necessary to the increased length. All the working joints are washered and riveted.

Fig. 17 is a side view of the steps, showing the angle of them when in use, and also the sizes of the various members. It should be noticed that when the steps fold up the back rails c and the tread

STEPS AND LADDERS

bearers B with the treads practically fit between the front rails A. When folded up the back rails C rise and swing forward. The main rails of the back frame D are the widest, and fold to the outside of A. The middle tread bearer is stronger, and has a projection 1½ in. longer than the others to receive the thrust of the back struts E.

First prepare the four rails A and C, 5 ft. 1 in. long, to the sizes shown. Round all ends to a semicircle, as shown by Fig. 18, to facilitate the folding arrangement.

sary, the rivets should be cut off close to the washers and lightly hammered over.

The two back pieces F (Fig. 15) are screwed on to secure the width of the steps, which should be 12 in. outside width at the top of the rails A and 18 in. at the bottom. Next prepare and screw on all treads excepting the top; they are of ⅜-in. birch boards 4¾ in. wide. Fig. 15 clearly shows how they are fitted between the front rails, and are made flush at the ends with the bearers. The top front

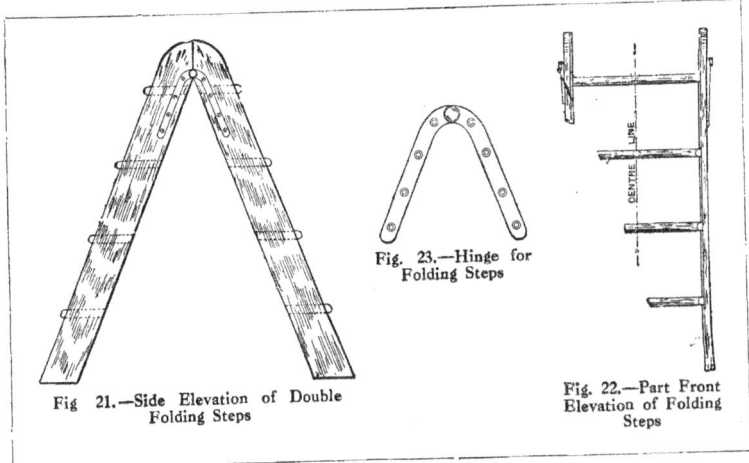

Fig. 21.—Side Elevation of Double Folding Steps

Fig. 23.—Hinge for Folding Steps

Fig. 22.—Part Front Elevation of Folding Steps

Then do the same to the tread bearers B, which, with the exception of the middle two, are 6 in. long, the two at the top being the same length but stronger. Now with a spoon-bit bore all holes for ₃⁄₁₆-in. rivets, measuring from the top ends of the rails A and C. The first hole is in the centre of the semicircle, and a 10 in. space will equally divide for six treads, as in Fig. 19. Then bore holes in bearers B 4¾ in. apart. Rivet the bearers to the rails to form sides, as shown in Fig. 20. The rivets should be cut from a ₃⁄₁₆-in. iron rod. Three washers are required for each joint, one between the joint and one each side. As only a small amount of riveting is neces-

edges of the treads should be chamfered or rounded off before fixing. The main rails for the back frame D are 4 ft. 7 in. long. The ends are rounded, and they are then riveted to the outside top of the front rails with the top tread bearers. Now folding these into position gives the width, therefore the bottom bar H can be fixed.

The struts E should next be fixed to projecting middle bearers, and the position ascertained for the lower rivet, which will be about 7 in. from the end of the back rails D. A good plan will be to close the steps and temporarily fasten the lower ends of the struts with screws. Then test by opening for correct position or inclination of the steps, and rivet accordingly. Braces are diagonally fixed with screws at the back to prevent distortion of the frames. These are five in number, and need only be of lighter material, $\frac{3}{4}$ in. by $\frac{5}{8}$ in. First fix one across the struts E, then close the steps and fasten two to the main steps and two to the back frame, allowing sufficient room for clearance. The top tread, 13 in. by $6\frac{1}{2}$ in. by $\frac{3}{8}$ in., can now be fastened on, and two extra bearers at the foot of the rails will strengthen same. These are riveted on the same as the others.

PAIR OF DOUBLE FOLDING STEPS

The double folding steps shown in side elevation by Fig. 21 and part front elevation by Fig. 22 can be made of $\frac{7}{8}$-in. deal. The two halves of the steps are made separately, and are joined together by two hinges at the top ; the portion of the steps projecting above the hinges act as stops when the steps are open.

The sides are $4\frac{1}{2}$ in. wide. There are four steps $5\frac{1}{2}$ in. wide, the distance between each step being 8 in., and the distance from the top of the top step to the top of the sides is $5\frac{1}{4}$ in. The top and bottom steps are grooved $\frac{1}{4}$ in. and tenoned into the sides, and the middle steps are grooved into the sides, the whole being fastened together with nails. The width of the steps over the sides is 1 ft. 6 in., and the length over the sides at the bottom when open is 3 ft. 3 in. The hinges (Fig. 23) are of $\frac{7}{8}$-in. half-round iron fixed to the sides with screws. Each half of the hinge is 9 in. long, and they are fastened together with a $\frac{3}{8}$-in. rivet in the centre on which they work.

MAKING A LADDER

Ladders are of two kinds. One is made from an ordinary batten sawn through the middle, and the other from a pole cut through in the same way. The latter is the better. In the former case, the batten is cut out of a tree, and the grain of the wood is certain to be cut asunder in places. In cutting it up to form the sides of a ladder it is cut again. In the case of a pole, the saw-cut runs up the pith, and thus follows the grain of the wood instead of crossing it. Thus a ladder made from a pole is much stronger than one twice as stout made from a batten ; and as lightness is a very necessary condition, the balance is in favour of pole sides in every way.

These poles are sold at all timber-yards for ladder making and scaffolding, and in choosing, pick one on which the bark is left, as those which have been peeled are very apt to be partly decayed. After choosing the pole, get it cut up the middle on the saw-bench, as it is not a nice job to do with the hand-saw, and it will be done at the yard much better. Having obtained the pole, the staves are next required. These can usually be obtained ready-made of oak, though spanish chestnut is good if cleft out of poles. As oak staves would be made in the same way, except that they would be cleft out of larger timber, it is supposed that chestnut staves are to be used. For a ladder 20 ft. long twenty-five staves will be required. Therefore, procure some chestnut poles from 4 in. to 5 in. in diameter, and cut off seven lengths, varying from 1 ft. 1 in. to 1 ft. 6 in. long, cutting the largest poles into the longest lengths ; then cleave them through, as shown by the lines A (Fig. 24). The ring B represents the sap, which should all be chopped away, as it soon rots. The four circles c show the four staves which can be made out of each length. When all are cleft out, they must be chopped up roughly, first square, then the corners taken off so as to make them eight-sided. They should vary in size from $1\frac{1}{4}$ in. in the middle and $\frac{7}{8}$ in. at the ends for the longest, to 1 in. in the middle and $\frac{5}{8}$ in. at the ends for the shortest. Some prefer to make them parallel throughout ; but it is better to have them stouter in the middle, where the wear and bending stress comes.

The staves can either be finished with the jack-plane, and left eight-sided, or they can be made round. A useful tool for rounding them (assuming a lathe is **not** available) is a plane as shown by Fig. 25. It is really a smoothing plane with a hollow face and iron. The best way to use it is to drive a peg into a post diagonally, about 3 ft. from the ground, as at D (Fig. 26), leaving it projecting about 9 in., and into the end drive a nail, leaving it about ½ in. out; this must be sharpened to a point. One end of the stave is pushed against this point, and the other held against the breast, while the stave is rounded, turning the latter round in the process, and reversing the ends when necessary. By this means the staves can be rounded very easily and quickly, and they look as well as the turned ones.

Both the sides and the staves being ready, begin on the ladder. Take a pair of trestles, and lay the two sides on them flatside uppermost. They should be fixed about 1 ft. apart, so as to leave room to get between them. Bore a hole close to the large end of each side, through trestle and all, and insert a pin so that the sides are held in position for later operation. The pins are shown at E (Fig. 27), and one of them at E (Fig. 28). Now make a centre line up each side, as shown in Fig. 27 (if the plane is just run over it will be all the better), and then cut a small strip of wood 9 in. long, and mark the places for the staves, starting just clear of the pins E. The sides must now be bored, using a ¾-in. twist-bit for the bottom twelve holes or so, and a ⅝-in. bit for the remainder. The best way to bore them so as to get the ladder out of twist, is to stride the side, and then bore one hole, and miss one for the whole length of the side; then, on getting to the other end, turn round, and bore at the marks which were missed, facing the opposite way. By this means, if there is a tendency to bore out of the upright, one hole will counteract the other.

Both sides being bored, the staves must be taken in hand. Lay them all side by side on a bench, or any flat surface, graduating them from the longest and stoutest to the smallest and shortest. Then mark 12 in. on the longest, leaving about an equal length at each end, and 8 in. on the shortest, and with a straight-edge make marks on the whole lot from one to the other; then, without moving them, number each stave as it lies, starting at the longest, or bottom stave, and finishing at the shortest, or top stave. Fig. 29 shows the bottom one, and Fig. 30 the top, the rest lying between them; the marks are shown at F in both figures.

A very useful tool now required is a bung-borer (Fig. 31), by means of which the holes are reamed out until each stave will fit in its proper place up to the marks F. If a taper auger is not available, an alternate method of fitting them is to bore a hole in a waste piece of wood with the same bits as were used for the sides; then cut away the wood of the staves from the marks F to the end, as shown by the dotted lines at G (Fig. 29), making a kind of shoulder until they fit into the hole the necessary distance. This is best done with a drawing-knife, although it can be done with a chisel; they must be made loose enough so that they can be pushed in with the hand, or the sides of the ladder will split when driving it together.

Having fitted all the staves, they can be driven into one of the sides, taking care to keep the numbers correct; the other side can be placed on the staves, entering them one by one into their holes. Then drive it on home, when most likely, if the staves are carefully fitted, both sides will be straight sidewise; and if the holes are bored correctly, the ladder will be out of winding. But if it is not so, do not attempt to alter it yet. The sides now require to be fastened on in some way, or the ladder will soon come to pieces. Some prefer to wedge each stave at both ends. If it is decided to do this the projecting ends of the staves must be split with a chisel at right angles to the side of the ladder, as at H (Fig. 32), and oak wedges driven in tightly. Do not split them in the same direction as the side runs or they will split when the wedges are inserted. But the better way to fix the ladder together is to bore a ¼-in. hole through the side and stave at intervals of about six staves, and insert a pin. There is no fear of the pins drawing out, and there is a great chance of the wedges doing so.

The ladder can now be taken off the pin E, turned flat on the trestles, and the end of the staves cut off level with the outside of the sides. The bark can also be taken off, and all knots and other projections trimmed off with the jack-plane, which tool can be also used to chamfer off the sharp edge, as shown in

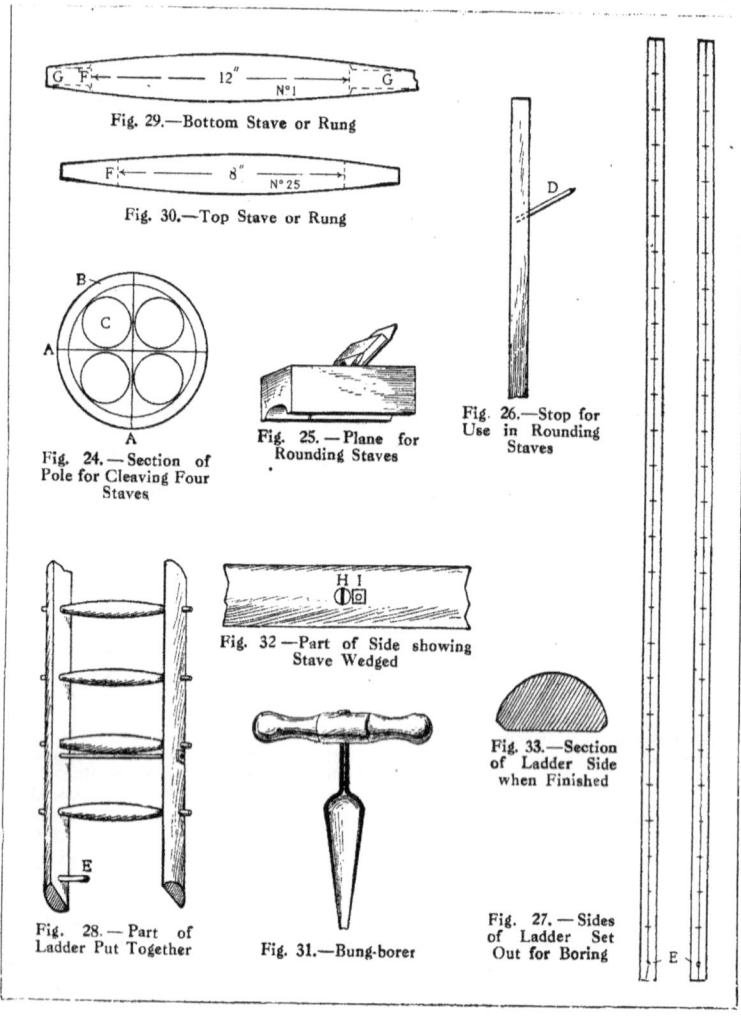

Fig. 29.—Bottom Stave or Rung
Fig. 30.—Top Stave or Rung
Fig. 24.—Section of Pole for Cleaving Four Staves
Fig. 25.—Plane for Rounding Staves
Fig. 26.—Stop for Use in Rounding Staves
Fig. 32.—Part of Side showing Stave Wedged
Fig. 33.—Section of Ladder Side when Finished
Fig. 28.—Part of Ladder Put Together
Fig. 31.—Bung-borer
Fig. 27.—Sides of Ladder Set Out for Boring

STEPS AND LADDERS

Fig. 33. The ends of the sides can also be cut off at both top and bottom, leaving them 9 in. from the centre of the top and bottom stave respectively. Three iron bolts must now be inserted as in Fig. 28, one under the next stave but one from the top and bottom, and one halfway between. Quarter-inch bolts are stout enough, and the nuts should be let into the sides so as not to catch the hand when the ladder is in use. The three bolts mentioned are for a 20-ft. ladder. Short ladders would only require two, and longer ones four or five or even six; but there should always be one just under the two staves next to the top and bottom, the others being placed between at equal distances, but always close under a stave.

If the ladder is winding or twisting it must be cramped down at each end so as to twist it forcibly the opposite way from that in which it twists itself, and after it has been left in this position for a night it will most likely be found all right in the morning. All that now remains is to paint the ladder, and this is what is too often neglected, thus causing a great many ladder accidents. It should have at least three coats of good lead paint, any other is useless. The usual way is to paint the staves about 2 in. from the side, finishing them neatly.

STRONG ADJUSTABLE LADDER

The ladder illustrated by Fig. 34 is one that can be conveniently taken apart and hung on the wall.

The timbers are slightly larger than the ladders used for window-cleaning purposes. The sides are made of the best-quality yellow deal, and are finished 3 in. wide and $1\frac{3}{8}$ in. thick. The staves are of English oak, and are planed up to $1\frac{1}{4}$ in. wide and $1\frac{1}{8}$ in. thick. The lower and wider ladder is about 16 ft. long, and the narrower one about 14 ft. The width inside the lower ladder is $12\frac{1}{4}$ in., and the width outside the upper ladder is 12 in. Both ladders are parallel, and can be used separately when desired.

Advantage is taken in the variation of the strength of yellow deal when placed in tension or compression. The upper or outer side of the ladder, when in use, being in compression and the underside in tension, the staves are mortised nearer the front or outer edge of the side pieces to give the maximum of strength to the ladder. Yellow deal is weaker in tension than compression, so this method of placing the staves out of the centre gives a larger portion to the underside which is in tension, and a smaller portion to the upper side in compression. As the upper ladder slides behind the lower ladder, this method of fixing the staves allows the ladders to fit more closely together, so bringing the staves more into line at the junction of the ladder than if arranged otherwise (see Fig. 34).

In setting out the mortises, any cast or sag that should be in the timbers should be allowed for, and arranged in pairs, with the convex edges uppermost; this will give the ladder a tendency to straighten when in use. Square pencil lines across the sides for the staves $1\frac{1}{4}$ in. apart, and arrange them so that the top of one stave is 11 in. from the top of the next. Then square these lines down both sides of the timbers, as in Fig. 35. The lines squared across on the outside for the wedges are a full $\frac{1}{8}$ in. away from the mortise lines. The mortise gauge should be set to the $\frac{3}{8}$-in. mortise chisel to be used, and the lines gauged so that the whole width of the mortise is above the centre line and $\frac{1}{8}$ in. away from it as shown. Mortise on the outer sides first, so as to give a better clearance for the waste when finishing from the inside. Then gauge for the $\frac{3}{8}$-in. haunch, and cut $\frac{3}{8}$ in. deep with a chisel. Fig. 36 shows the advantage of this kind of joint. The weakest part of a mortise-and-tenon joint is at the shoulder of the tenon. By making a double shoulder or haunch, this part is doubly strengthened. The tenon is reduced to the minimum thickness of $\frac{3}{8}$ in.; thereby the sides are strengthened by cutting away the minimum amount of material, and that, in the part of the timber in compression.

The staves for the larger ladder should be 15 in. long, and those for the smaller ladder 12 in. Make them ¼ in. longer at each end to allow for wedging and finishing off. Mark and cut the tenons, as shown, in the usual way. Plane off all sharp corners, and cut the wedges of oak about 1½ in. long in readiness for framing together. The ends of the tenons should waste ends, and finish with a smoothing plane.

The patterns for the irons should be accurately drawn on a board for the blacksmith. The two irons shown by Fig. 38 are made of 1½-in. by ¼-in. material, and are fixed about 3 in. from the top of the

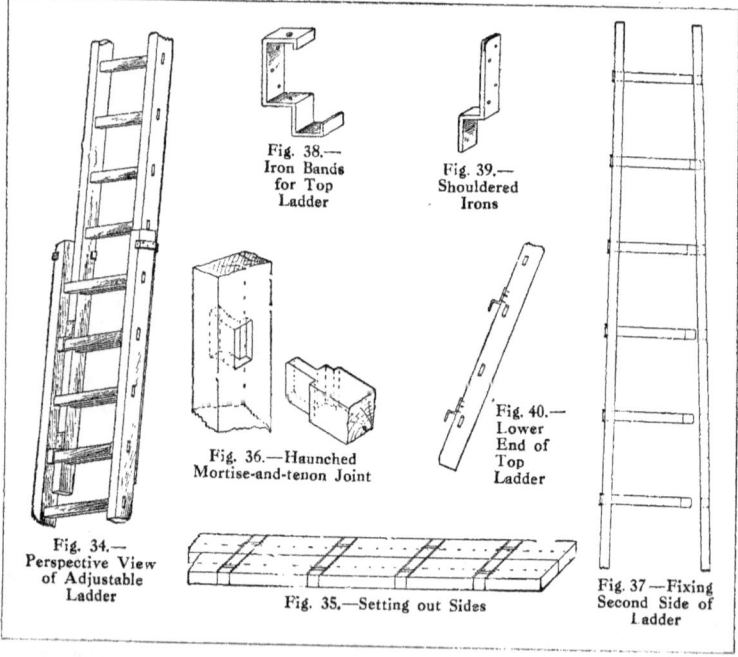

Fig. 38.—Iron Bands for Top Ladder

Fig. 39.—Shouldered Irons

Fig. 36.—Haunched Mortise-and-tenon Joint

Fig. 40.—Lower End of Top Ladder

Fig. 34.—Perspective View of Adjustable Ladder

Fig. 35.—Setting out Sides

Fig. 37.—Fixing Second Side of Ladder

be trimmed with a chisel. Glue well and drive in the staves and wedge one by one, testing each side of the stave with a try-square whilst wedging.

Fig. 37 shows the best method of fixing on the second side of the ladder. Proceed by entering the tenons one by one until all the tenons grip. Then quickly glue all the tenons, and cramp the side up to its shoulders. A good cramp should be used in preference to a hammer. Then glue and drive in all the wedges. Saw off lower ladder. The four irons shown by Fig. 39 are of 1¼-in. by ¼-in. material, and screwed securely on the front of the upper ladder. Each pair of irons is fixed on level with the first and third staves of the bottom end, as shown in Fig. 40. These irons should be fixed to grip the staves of the lower ladder, so as to make the double staves even to tread on. It is convenient to enter the upper ladder into the iron bands from the top end, and slide upwards to the height required.

PRINTED BY CASSELL & COMPANY, LIMITED, LA BELLE SAUVAGE, LONDON E.C.4.

www.ingramcontent.com/pod-product-compliance
Lightning Source LLC
Chambersburg PA
CBHW021139160426
43194CB00007B/629